DIMENSIONS OF THE WRITING PROCESS

CHOOSING
Purpose and Audience

COLLECTING

OBSERVING

Sensory details
Comparisons and images
Changes
What is not there

REMEMBERING

Specific scenes
Changes and conflict
Connections between
    past and present

READING

Active reading
Annotating
Summarizing
Responding

INVESTIGATING

Asking questions
Interviews
Questionnaires
Library research

SHAPING

Chronological order
Spatial order
Comparison/contrast
Definition
Example

Focusing and narrowing subject
Introductions
Body paragraphs
Conclusions

Causal analysis
Process analysis
Dialogue
Image
Voice and persona

DRAFTING

Planning
Re-reading
Talking

Reconsidering purpose and audience
Starting at the beginning
Starting at the middle

Writing nonstop
Stopping when you
    know what comes next

REVISING AND EDITING

MAJOR CHANGES

Changing purpose or audience
Collecting new information, ideas,
    evidence, examples
Reshaping paragraphs or reorganizing an essay
Choosing a new point of view

MINOR CHANGES

Revising sentences, transitions,
    word choice
Editing for grammar, punctuation,
    usage
Proofreading for spelling and mechanics

The Prentice Hall Guide For College Writers

6th Edition

The Prentice Hall Guide For College Writers

STEPHEN REID

COLORADO STATE UNIVERSITY

Prentice
Hall

UPPER SADDLE RIVER, NJ 07458

Library of Congress Cataloging-in Publication Data

Reid, Stephen
    The Prentice hall guide for college writers / Stephen Reid.-6th ed.
        p.cm.
    Includes bibliographical references and index.
    ISBN 0-13-044731-5
        1. English language—Rhetoric—Handbook, maunals, etc. 2. Report
    wriring—Handbook, manuals, etc. #. College readers.   I. Title

PE1408 .R424 2002
808′.042—de21

2002069984

VP, Editor-in-Chief: Leah Jewell
Senior Acquisitions Editor: Corey Good
Editorial Assistant: John Ragozzine
VP, Director of Production and Manufacturing: Barbara Kittle
Production Editor: Randy Pettit
Prepress and Manufacturing Manager: Nick Sklitsis
Prepress and Manufacturing Buyer: Mary Ann Gloriande
Director of Marketing: Beth Mejia
Senior Marketing Manager: Brandy Dawson
Marketing Assistant: Christine Moodie
Creative Design Director: Leslie Osher
Interior Design: Anne Bonanno Nieglos
Cover Design: Anne DeMarinis
Cover Art: Thomas F. McKnight, "Boston Public Gardens" G-20, 28″ × 30″ Casein on Canvas.
Director, Image Resource Center: Melinda Reo
Interior Image Specialist: Beth Boyd-Brenzel
Photo Researcher: Michelina Viscusi
Manager, Rights and Permissions: Zina Arabia

For permission to use copyrighted material, grateful
acknowledgment is made to the copyright holders listed on
page xxix–xxxi, which is considered an extension of this
copyright page.

This book was set in 10/12.5 Adobe Caslon by Clarinda
Corp. and was printed and bound by World Color, Inc.
The cover was printed by Phoenix Color Corp.

Prentice
Hall
© 2003, 2000, 1998, 1995, 1992, 1989 by Pearson Education, Inc.
Upper Saddle River, New Jersey 07458

Printed in the United States of America

10 9 8 7 6 5 4 3 2 1

ISBN: 0-13-044731-5

Pearson Education LTD., London
Pearson Education Australia PTY, Limited, Sydney
Pearson Education Singapore, Pte. Ltd
Pearson Education North Asia Ltd, Hong Kong
Pearson Education Canada, Ltd., Toronto
Pearson Educación de Mexico, S.A. de C.V.
Pearson Education - Japan, Tokyo
Pearson Education Malaysia, Pte. Ltd
Pearson Education, Upper Saddle River, New Jersey

Brief Contents

Contents

3 Observing   47

6   Investigating   213

11 Responding to Literature   513

12 Writing a Research Paper   557

Thematic Contents

The Prentice Hall Guide for College Writers, Sixth Edition, contains excerpts and selections from over fifty writers. Thematic clusters are indicated below. An asterisk (*) indicates a complete essay.

TECHNOLOGY AND THE INTERNET

ENVIRONMENTAL ISSUES

EDUCATION

LITERACY AND LANGUAGE

CULTURAL EXPLORATIONS

Preface

"A writer is a reader moved to emulation."
— Saul Bellow

A S WE DESIGN OUR WRITING COURSES, REASON TELLS US TO FOCUS ON TEACHING THE RHETORICAL SITUATION, CRITICAL READING AND THINKING, COMPUTER LITERACY, AND RESEARCH AND DOCUMENTATION. INTUITION, HOWEVER, TELLS us that writers learn to write simply by reading and rereading the writers they love. Three new authors in *The Prentice Hall Guide for College Writers* can teach our students nearly everything they need to know about the craft of writing. First, Adam Forest, a student writer, shows our own students how their voices can promote social awareness and effect change. In his essay, "Beauty and Violence," Forest models how to construct a public argument that opens discussion on the topic of media exploitation. In a second selection, "High Tide in Tucson," Barbara Kingsolver shows us how to observe and then vividly describe the natural world and its small wonders before making that writerly leap into reflection about both her own life and the human condition. If there were ever a model for "the personal essay" or a contemporary version of Montaigne's *essai,* "High Tide in Tucson" is it. Finally, Margaret Talbot's delightful send up of Martha Stewart in "Les Très Riches Heures de Martha Stewart" teaches us how to blend wit, research, and cultural analysis at the most sophisticated level. We could teach a semester's writing course using just these three authors. But who would want to stop there? In the sixth edition of *The Prentice Hall Guide for College Writers,* Barbara Ehrenreich, Neil Postman, and Deborah Tannen are still waiting to be read, as are Susan Estrich, Farley Mowat, Pico Iyer, Patricia Raybon, Wendell Berry, John Muir, Toni Cade Bambara, Jonathan Kozol, Helen Keller, Edward Abbey, and Mike Rose.

In its sixth edition, *The Prentice Hall Guide for College Writers* offers a host of new and continuing features that put writers in touch with other writers, with stimulating reading, and with advice about critical reading and writing that will place them in rhetorical situations and guide them as they move from idea to final draft.

New Features

New to the sixth edition of *The Prentice Hall Guide for College Writers* are the following features:

EIGHTEEN NEW PROFESSIONAL AND STUDENT ESSAYS   The sixth edition features new selections from professional writers such as Barbara Kingsolver, Margaret

Talbot, Deborah Tannen, David Ansen, Nicholas Lemann, Robin Morgan, Emily Prager, John O'Sullivan, and Jeremiah Creedon. In addition, new student selections by Adam Forest, Julie Bovard, La Mer Stepptoe, and Lauren Strain address topics such as media exploitation, rape and its consequences, multiracialness, and Native Americans in Hollywood films.

New Cluster of Essays in Arguing Chapter   The sixth edition also features a new group of three arguing essays representing three points of view (rather than just "pro" and "con") on the controversies surrounding the death penalty. Essays by Edward Koch, Robert Badinter, and John O'Sullivan create a conversation of argument and response that illustrates how a debate that seems to have only two possible sides can actually lead to multiple points of view.

Updated Emphasis on Writing with a Computer   Essays such as "How the Web Works," by Gene Cowan and "Plotting a Net Gain," by Connie Koenenn provide information about the Internet while new research sections on accessing Internet sources and updated MLA and APA citation formats give students timely information on accessing, evaluating, and documenting Internet texts.

Integration of Internet Sites in the Critical Reading Process   The sixth edition also includes one question following each professional essay that asks students to visit a website with additional background information, an e-forum where the conversation started in the essay continues on-line, or a site with another point of view about the topic of the essay. This feature encourages students to use their Internet access as an integral part of their critical response to each professional essay.

Increased Emphasis on Genres for Reading and Writing   *The Prentice Hall Guide* has always featured texts from a variety of genres that illustrate chapter assignments. In the sixth edition, the Evaluating chapter has an evaluation of the television show *ER,* by two British critics in the form of a letter debate, while the Observing and Explaining chapters include samples of an Internet posting and a transcript from a radio show. Other chapters feature genres such as letters, proposals, and journal entries as well as academic essays. Students are encouraged to consider a variety of genres as they assess their purpose, audience, and rhetorical situation.

Continuing Key Features

Continuing in the sixth edition of *The Prentice Hall Guide for College Writers* is a wide range of noteworthy features:

Annotated Instructor's Edition   The Annotated Instructor's Edition contains additional guidelines for teaching each chapter, teaching tips on critical reading, responding to assignments, and guiding peer group activities, and ESL teaching tips designed to alert teachers to possible problems and solutions for ESL writers.

ALTERNATE THEMATIC TABLE OF CONTENTS   The essays in the sixth edition combine to create thematic clusters of topics that reappear throughout the text: Race and Cultural Diversity, Gender Roles, Technology and the Internet, Environmental Issues, Education, Literacy and Language, Advertising and the Media, Social Issues, and a new section on Cultural Explorations.

EMPHASIS ON STUDENT WRITING   The sixth edition continues to showcase student writing, featuring the work of more than forty student writers from several colleges and universities. The sixth edition contains twenty-five full-length student essays and ten essays with sample prewriting materials, rough drafts, peer response sheets, and post-scripts.

LOGICAL SEQUENCE OF PURPOSE-BASED CHAPTERS   Aims and purposes, not rhetorical strategies, guide each writing assignment. Early chapters focus on invention strategies (observing, remembering, reading, and investigation), while later chapters emphasize exposition and argumentation (explaining, evaluating, problem solving, and arguing).

FOCUS ON WRITING PROCESSES   Every major chapter contains professional and student samples, rhetorical techniques, journal exercises, reading and writing activities, collaborative activities, peer-response guidelines, and revision suggestions designed to assist students with their work-in-progress.

JOURNAL WRITING   Throughout the text, write-to-learn activities help writers improve their critical reading skills, warm up for each assignment, and practice a variety of invention and shaping strategies.

MARGINAL QUOTATIONS   Nearly a hundred short quotations by composition teachers, researchers, essayists, novelists, and poets personalize for the inexperienced writer a larger community of writers still struggling with the same problems that each student faces.

AN INTRODUCTION TO MYTHS AND RITUALS FOR WRITING   Chapter One, "Writing Myths and Rituals," discounts some common myths about college writing courses, introduces the notion of writing rituals, and outlines the variety of journal writing used throughout the text. Rituals are crucial for all writers but especially so for novice writers. Effective rituals are simply those behavioral strategies that complement the cognitive and social strategies of the writing process. Illustrating a variety of possible writing rituals are quotations from a dozen professional writers on the nature of writing. These short quotations continue throughout the book, reminding students that writing is not some magical process, but rather a madness that has a method to it, a love that is built from labor, and a learning that is born of reading, thinking, observing, remembering, discussing, and writing.

AN ORIENTATION TO RHETORICAL SITUATION AND TO WRITING PROCESSES   Chapter Two, "Purposes and Processes for Writing," bases the writing process in the rhetorical situation (writer, subject, purpose, text, and audience). It restores the writer's intent or purpose (rather than a thesis sentence or a rhetorical strategy) as the driving force during the writing process. It demonstrates how meaning evolves from a variety of recursive, multidimensional, and hierarchical activities that we call the writing process. Finally, it reassures students that, because individual writing and learning styles differ, they will be encouraged to discover and articulate their own processes from a range of appropriate possibilities.

AIMS AND PURPOSES FOR WRITING   The text then turns to specific purposes and assignments for writing. Chapters Three through Six ("Observing," "Remembering," "Reading," and "Investigating") focus on invention strategies. These chapters illustrate how writing to learn is a natural part of learning to write. To promote reading, writing, discussing, revising, and learning, these chapters introduce four sources of invention—observing people, places, events, and objects; remembering people, places, and events; reading and responding to texts; and investigating information through interviews, surveys, and written sources. Although students write essays intended for a variety of audiences in each of these chapters, the emphasis is on invention strategies and on writer-based purposes for writing. Although this text includes expressive and transactional elements in every assignment, the direction of the overall sequence of assignments is from the more personal forms of discourse to the more public forms.

Chapters Seven through Ten ("Explaining," "Evaluating," "Problem Solving," and "Arguing") emphasize subject and audience-based purposes. The sequence in these chapters moves the student smoothly from exposition to argumentation (acknowledging the obvious overlapping), building on the skills and strategies of the previous chapters. The teacher may, in fact, use Chapters Seven through Ten as a minicourse in argument, teaching students how to develop and argue claims of fact, claims of cause and effect, claims about values, and claims about solutions or policies.

RESPONDING TO LITERATURE   Chapter Eleven guides students through the process of writing interpretive essays about short fiction, using many of the critical reading strategies, invention techniques, and shaping strategies practiced in the earlier chapters. This chapter contains three short fiction works and two student essays.

RESEARCH PAPER   Chapter Twelve ("Writing a Research Paper") draws on all the cognitive and social strategies presented in the first eleven chapters. Research papers are written for specific purposes and audiences, too, but the invention, composing, and revising processes are more extended. This chapter helps students select and plan their projects, use the library, find Internet sources, evaluate and document electronic and print sources, record their progress, and test ideas in research logs—learning all the while to integrate the information they gather with their own experiences and ideas.

HANDBOOK   A brief handbook includes a review of basic sentence elements, sentence structure and grammar, diction and style, and punctuation and mechanics.

Supplementary Material for Instructors and Students

ANNOTATED INSTRUCTOR'S EDITION (AIE)   In the margins of the Annotated Instructor's Edition are hundreds of teaching tips and suggestions for assignments and group activities. (0-13-099299-2)

Designed to accompany the Annotated Instructor's Edition, **Teaching Composition with the Prentice Hall Guide** contains sections on composition theory, policy statements, lesson plans, collaborative writing, writing in a computer classroom, teaching ESL writers, small-group learning, write-to-learn exercises, reading/writing exercises, prereading journal assignments, writing assignments, suggestions for student conferences, and ideas for responding to and evaluating writing. Also included are chapter commentaries and answers to discussion questions. (0-13-099294-1)

Available for a nominal fee, the **Critical Thinking Skills Journal** provides students with additional exercises and freewriting activities, as well as opportunities to consider and respond to opposing viewpoints. (0-13-099301-8)

FREE ONLINE STUDY RESOURCE . . . THE COMPANION WEBSITE[TM] www.prenhall.com/reid

Features of this site include:
- essay questions and writing exercises for every reading in the text
- Writing Workshop: step by step exercises on the writing process
- peer review exercises to enhance collaborative activities
- links to web images with analysis questions
- modules to help with research and documentation
- built-in routing that gives students the ability to forward essay responses and graded quizzes to their instructors
- *Blue Pencil* online—grammar and punctuation exercises in the context of a paragraph
- alliance with Turnitin.com—allows professors to check papers for plagiarism

COURSE COMPASS, WEB CT, AND BLACKBOARD COURSES FOR THE PRENTICE HALL GUIDE FOR COLLEGE WRITERS   These complete online courses include all of the functionality and content from the Companion Website[TM] along with additional material for students and instructors. Please visit our on-line course management website for more information (www.prenhall.com/cms).

FREE WHEN PACKAGED WITH ANY PRENTICE HALL ENGLISH TEXTBOOK. CONTACT YOUR LOCAL REPRESENTATIVE FOR DETAILS.

- THE NEW AMERICAN WEBSTER HANDY COLLEGE DICTIONARY
  An updated and expanded edition contains more than 115,000 definitions, covering current phrases, slang, and scientific terms, and including advice on usage and

grammar, notes on etymology, foreign words and phrases, and a world gazetteer. ISBN: 0-13-032870-7

- THE NEW AMERICAN ROGET'S COLLEGE THESAURUS This all-new edition of the classic reference work supplies at a glance the precise words and phrases needed to express your ideas most clearly and effectively. ISBN: 0-13-045258-0
- ENGLISH ON THE INTERNET 2002: EVALUATING ONLINE SOURCES WITH CONTENT SELECT Written by M. Neil Browne and Stuart Keeley. This completely revised guide helps students develop the critical thinking skills needed to evaluate online sources. In addition, an access code to Content Select, an online research database, is included free of charge. ISBN: 0-13-049620-0
- MODEL STUDENT ESSAYS BY MARK GALLAHER This anthology features 25 student essays collected from around the country which are organized into three broad categories: personal experience, explain and inform, and argue a position. ISBN: 0-13-645516-6
- THE WRITER'S GUIDE SERIES Provides students and instructors with in-depth coverage on contemporary topics, allowing instructors to cover relevant information based on their course structure and students' needs.

  A Writer's Guide to Research and Documentation ISBN: 0-13-081627-2
  A Writer's Guide to Document & Web Design ISBN 0-13-018929-4
  A Writer's Guide to WAC & Oral Presentations ISBN 0-13-018931-6
  A Writer's Guide to Public Writing ISBN 0-13-018932-4

AVAILABLE TO QUALIFIED ADOPTERS: PRENTICE HALL RESOURCES FOR COMPOSITION

- **WWW.TURNITIN.COM** turnitin This online service makes it easy for teachers to find out if students are copying their assignments from the Internet, and is now free to professors for those classes using *The Prentice Hall Guide for College Writers*. In addition to helping educators easily identify instances of Web-based student plagiarism, Turnitin.com also offers a digital archiving system and an online peer review service. Professors set up a "drop box" at the Turnitin.com. Website where their students submit papers. Turnitin.com then cross-references each submission with millions of possible online sources. Within 24 hours, teachers receive a customized, color-coded "Originality Report," complete with live links to suspect Internet locations, for each submitted paper.
- **COMPUTERS AND WRITING, Second Edition,** by Dawn Rodrigues— University of Texas at Brownsville ISBN: 0-13-084034-3
- **THE PRENTICE HALL/SIMON & SCHUSTER TRANSPARENCIES FOR WRITERS** ISBN: 0-13-703209-9
- **CLASSROOM STRATEGIES** by Wendy Bishop—Florida State University ISBN: 0-13-572355-8

- **PORTFOLIOS** by Pat Belanoff—SUNY Stonybrook
  ISBN: 0-13-572322-1
- **JOURNALS** by Chris Burnham – New Mexico State University
  ISBN: 0-13-572348-5
- **COLLABORATIVE LEARNING** by Harvey Kail—University of Maine
  & John Trimbur—Worcester Polytechnic Institute
  ISBN: 0-13-572371-X
- **ENGLISH AS A SECOND LANGUAGE** by Ruth Spack—Tufts University
  ISBN: 0-13-572389-2
- **DISTANCE EDUCATION** by W. Dees Stallings—University of Maryland,
  University College
  ISBN: 0-13-572314-0
- **TEACHING WRITING ACROSS THE CURRICULUM,** Second Edition by
  Art Young—Clemson University
  ISBN: 0-13-081650-7

The New York Times and Prentice Hall are sponsoring Themes of the Times, a program designed to enhance student access to current information of relevance in the classroom.

Through this program, the core subject matter provided in the text is supplemented by a collection of time-sensative articles from one of the world's most distinguished newspapers, *The New York Times*. These articles demonstrate the vital, ongoing connection between what is learned in the classroom and what is happening in the world around us.

To enjoy the wealth of information of *The New York Times* daily, a reduced subscription rate is available in deliverable areas. For information, call toll-free: 1-800-631-1222. Prentice Hall and *The New York Times* are proud to cosponsor Themes of the Times. We hope it will make the reading of both textbooks and newspapers a more dynamic, involving process.

Acknowledgments

Because teaching writing is always a situated enterprise, I would like to thank the members of the composition faculty and staff at Colorado State University whose teaching expertise and enthusiasm have improved every page of the text and the teacher's manual: Kate Kiefer, Mike Palmquist, Donna LeCourt, Sarah Sloane, Laura Thomas, Jamie Neufeld, Paul Barribeau, Kerri Eglin, Anne Gogela, Ted Rollins, Trish Taylor, and Stephanie Wardrop. Many of the innovative teaching strategies and resources developed by Colorado State University composition faculty members are available at <http://www.ColoState.edu/Depts/WritingCenter>.

In addition, the following teachers offered excellent advice about changes and additions for the sixth edition: Allison Fernley, Salt Lake Community College; Sara McLaughlin, Texas Tech University; M. Elizabeth Parker, Nashville State Tech; Susanmarie Harrington, Indiana University, Purdue University-Indianapolis; Cathryn Amdahl, Harrisburg Area Community College; Elizabeth Roeger, Shawnee Community College; Charley Boyd, Genesee Community College. I wish to thank them for their thorough, honest, and professional advice.

For the expert crew at Prentice Hall, I am especially grateful. Phil Miller, a fine editor and friend, has enthusiastically supported this text from the first edition. Leah Jewell and Corey Good provided ongoing revision and editorial support, and John Ragozzine handled the daily chores with care and courtesy. On the shortest of timelines, Randy Pettit did the expert and careful editing that made the book possible. To Brandy Dawson and Gina Sluss, I can only say thanks for being so professional—and for being such good friends.

Finally, I wish to thank my family for their continued patience and active support.

—*Stephen Reid*
Colorado State University

Credits

Edward Abbey, "The Damnation of a Canyon" (excerpts) from *Beyond the Wall.* Copyright 1971, 1976, 1977, 1979, 1984 by Edward Abbey. Reprinted with the permission of Henry Holt and Company, Inc. **Vicki Alexander and Grace Lyu-Volckhausen,** "Black/Asian Conflict: Where Do We Begin?" (excerpt) from *Ms. Magazine* (November/December 1991). Copyright 1991. Reprinted with the permission of *Ms. Magazine.* **David Ansen,** "Mr. Spielberg Strikes Again," from NEWSWEEK, June 25, 2001. © Newsweek, Inc. All rights reserved. Reprinted by permission. **Robert Badinter,** "Death Be Not Proud," © Time Inc. Reprinted by permission. **Russell Baker,** "Writing for Myself" (editor's title) from *Growing Up.* Copyright 1982 by Russell Baker. Reprinted with the permission of Congdon & Weed, Inc. and Contemporary Books. **Toni Cade Bambara,** "The Lesson" from *Gorilla, My Love.* Copyright 1972 by Toni Cade Bambara. Reprinted with the permission of Random House, Inc. **Joan Barthel,** "Here Comes Oprah," *MS. Magazine.* Used with permission. **Wendell Berry,** "Solving For Pattern" from *The Gift of Good Land: Further Essays Cultural and Agricultural.* Copyright 1981 by Wendell Berry. Reprinted with the permission of North Point Press, a division of Farrar, Straus & Giroux, Inc. **Geoffrey Canada,** "Peace in the Streets" (excerpt) from *Fist Stick Knife Gun.* Copyright 1995 by Geoffrey Canada. Reprinted with the permission of Beacon Press, Boston. **Terri Ciccarello,** journal entry. Reprinted with the permission of the author. **Cathleen A. Cleaver,** "The Internet: A Clear and Present Danger?" Reprinted with the permission of the author. **Gene Cowan,** "How the Web Works" from *Social Education* 60 (February 1996). Copyright 1996 by National Council for the Social Studies. Reprinted with the permission of the publishers. **Geoffrey Cowley,** "First Born, Later Born" from *Newsweek* (October 7, 1996). Copyright 1996 Newsweek, Inc. Reprinted with the permission of *Newsweek.* **Jeremiah Creedon,** "Life After Oil," from THE UTNE READER, March–April, 2001. Reprinted with special permission from Jeremiah Creedon. **Dudley Erskine Devlin,** "Teaching Tolerance in America." Reprinted with the permission of the author. **Danny Drennan,** "One Fan's Burden" from *Harper's* (July 1996). Copyright 1996. Reprinted by permission. **Barbara Ehrenreich,** "Teaching Diversity— With a Smile" from *Time* (April 8, 1991). Copyright 1991 by Time, Inc. Reprinted with the permission of *Time.* **Kathryn Hughes and Ben Rogers,** "Prime Time Art?" as published in THE UTNE READER, January–February, 2000. Reprinted by permission of Prospect Publishing Ltd. And THE UTNE READER. To subscribe, call 800-736-UTNE or visit our website at www.utne.com. **Roy Hoffman,** "On Keeping a Journal" from *Newsweek on Campus* (October 1983). Copyright 1983 by Roy Hoffman. Reprinted with the permission of the author. **Barbara Kingsolver,** excerpt [pages 1–10] from "High Tide in Tucson" from HIGH TIDE IN TUCSON: ESSAYS FROM NOW OR NEVER by Kingsolver.

The Prentice Hall Guide
For College Writers

Girl Writing, oil on canvas.
The Phillips Collection.

Chapter 1   Writing Myths and Rituals

One myth about writing I have believed my whole life is that "good writers are born, not made." My attitude when beginning this writing course was one of apprehension and dread. I wondered if I *could* improve my writing, or if I was destined to receive B's and C's on every essay for the rest of my life. This writing class has given me concrete examples and suggestions for improvement—not just grammar or essay maps. The freewriting is such a great help that whenever I'm stuck I immediately turn to my ten-minute freewriting to open up blocked passages. Once I get past my writer's block, I see that I can be a good writer.

For me, the most effective writing ritual is to gather up all of my stuff—legal pad and pencil, notes, dictionary, and thesaurus—and get on my bike, ride to campus, and set myself up in the art lounge in the student center. During the week, I'll do this in the evening after dinner. On a weekend, I go any time from 10 A.M. to midnight. I don't write effectively at home because there are always distractions. Some people will be moving around and I'll go see who they are and what they're doing, or I'll go get a cup of coffee or a piece of toast, or I'll snap on the TV, ignoring that tiny voice inside saying, "Get busy—you have to get this done!" So what makes the art lounge better? Simple—no distractions. I can lay out all of my stuff, get a cup of coffee, and go to work. All around me people are doing the same thing, and somehow all of those hardworking people are an encouragement. The art lounge is always quiet, too—quieter than the library—and it doesn't smell like the library.

A writer is someone who writes, that's all.
—GORE VIDAL, NOVELIST AND SOCIAL COMMENTATOR

I've always disliked words like inspiration. Writing is probably like a scientist thinking about some scientific problem or an engineer about an engineering problem.
—DORIS LESSING, AUTHOR OF ESSAYS AND FICTION, INCLUDING THE GOLDEN NOTEBOOK

I always worked until I had something done and I always stopped when I knew what was going to happen next. That way I could be sure of going on the next day.
—ERNEST HEMINGWAY, JOURNALIST AND NOVELIST, AUTHOR OF THE OLD MAN AND THE SEA

S YOU BEGIN A COLLEGE WRITING COURSE, YOU NEED TO GET RID OF SOME MYTHS ABOUT WRITING THAT YOU MAY HAVE BEEN PACKING AROUND FOR SOME TIME. DON'T ALLOW misconceptions to ruin a good experience. Here are a few common myths about writing, followed by some facts compiled from the experiences of working writers.

MYTH: "Good writers are born, not made. A writing course really won't help my writing."

FACT: *Writers acquire their skills the same way athletes do—through practice and hard work.* There are very few "born" writers. Most writers—even professional writers and journalists—are not continually inspired to write. In fact, they often experience "writer's block"-the stressful experience of staring helplessly at a piece of paper, unable to think or to put words down on paper. A writing course will teach you how to cope with your procrastination, anxiety, lack of "inspiration," and false starts by focusing directly on solving the problems that occur during the writing process.

MYTH: "Writing courses are just a review of boring grammar and punctuation. When teachers read your writing, the only thing they mark is that stuff, anyway."

FACT: *Learning and communicating—not grammar and punctuation—come first in college writing courses.* Knowledge of grammar, spelling, punctuation, and usage is essential to editing, but it is secondary to discovering ideas, thinking, learning, and communicating. In a writing course, students learn to revise and improve the content and organization of each other's writing. *Then* they help each other edit for grammar, punctuation, or spelling errors.

MYTH: "College writing courses are really 'creative writing,' which is not what my major requires. If I wanted to be another Shakespeare and write poetry, I'd change my major."

FACT: *Writing courses emphasize rhetoric, not poetry.* Rhetoric involves practicing the most effective means or strategies for informing or persuading an audience. All writing—even technical or business writing—is "creative." Deciding what to write, how to write it, how best to get your reader's attention, and how to inform or persuade your reader requires creativity and imagination. Every major requires the skills that writing courses teach: exploring new ideas, learning concepts and processes, communicating with others, and finding fresh or creative solutions to problems.

MYTH: "Writing courses are not important in college or the real world. I'll never have to write, anyway."

FACT: *Writing courses do have a significant effect on your success in college, on the job, and in life.* Even if you don't have frequent, formal writing assignments in other courses, writing improves your note-taking, reading comprehension, and thinking skills. When you do have other written tasks or assignments, a writing course teaches you to adapt your writing to a variety of different purposes and audiences—whether you are writing a lab report in biology, a letter to an editor, a complaint to the Better Business Bureau, or a memorandum to your boss. Taking a writing course helps you express yourself more clearly, confidently, and persuasively—a skill that comes in handy whether you're writing a philosophy essay, a job application, or a love letter.

The most important fact about writing is that you are already a writer. You have been writing for years. A writer is someone who writes, not someone who writes a nationally syndicated newspaper column, publishes a bestseller, or wins a Pulitzer Prize. To be an effective writer, you don't have to earn a million dollars; you just have to practice writing often enough to get acquainted with its personal benefits for you and its value for others.

■ WARM-UP EXERCISE: FREEWRITING Put this book aside—right now—and take out pencil or pen and a piece of paper. Use this free exercise (private, unjudged, ungraded) to remind yourself that you are already a writer. Time yourself for five minutes. Write on the first thing that comes to mind—*anything whatsoever.* Write nonstop. Keep writing even if you have to write, "I can't think of anything to say. This feels stupid!" When you get an idea, pursue it.

When five minutes are up, stop writing and reread what you have written. Whether you write about a genuinely interesting topic or about the weather, freewriting is an excellent way to warm up, to get into the habit of writing, and to establish a writing ritual.

My idea of a prewriting ritual is getting the kids on the bus and sitting down.

—BARBARA KINGSOLVER

AUTHOR OF

PRODIGAL SUMMER

Writing Fitness: Rituals and Practice

Writing is no more magic or inspiration than any other human activity that you admire: figure skating at the Olympics, rebuilding a car engine, cooking a gourmet meal, or acting in a play. Behind every human achievement are many unglamorous hours of practice—working and sweating, falling flat on your face, and picking yourself up again. You can't learn to write just by reading some chapters in a textbook or by memorizing other people's advice. You need help and advice, but you also need practice. Consider the following parable about a Chinese painter:

A rich patron once gave money to the painter Chu Ta, asking him to paint a picture of a fish. Three years later, when he still had not re-

Writing is [like] making a table. With both you are working with reality, a material just as hard as wood. Both are full of tricks and techniques. Basically very little magic and a lot of hard work are involved. . . . What is a privilege, however, is to do a job to your own satisfaction.

—GABRIEL GARCÍA MÁRQUEZ,

NOBEL PRIZE–WINNING AUTHOR OF ONE HUNDRED YEARS OF SOLITUDE

ceived the painting, the patron went to Chu Ta's house to ask why the picture was not done. Chu Ta did not answer but dipped a brush in ink and with a few strokes drew a splendid fish. "If it is so easy," asked the patron, "why didn't you give me the picture three years ago?" Again, Chu Ta did not answer. Instead, he opened the door of a large cabinet. Thousands of pictures of fish tumbled out.

Most writers develop little rituals that help them practice their writing. A ritual is a *repeated pattern of behavior* that provides structure, security, and a sense of progress to the one who practices it. Creating your own writing rituals and making them part of your regular routine will help reduce that dreaded initial panic and enable you to call upon your writing process with confidence when you need it.

PLACE, TIME, AND TOOLS

Some writers work best in pen and ink, sprawled on their beds in the afternoon while pets snooze on nearby blankets. Others start at 8 A.M. and rely on hard chairs, clean tables, and a handful of number 2 pencils sharpened to needle points. Still others are most comfortable with their keyboards and word processors at their desks or in the computer lab. Legal-sized pads help some writers produce, while others feel motivated by spiral notebooks with pictures of mountain streams on the covers. Only you can determine which place, time, and tools give you the best support as a writer.

The place where you write is also extremely important. If you are writing in a computer lab, you have to adapt to that place, but if you write a draft in longhand or on your own word processor, you can choose the place yourself. In selecting a place, keep the following tips in mind:

- **Keep distractions minimal.** Some people simply can't write in the kitchen, where the refrigerator is distractingly close, or in a room that has a TV in it. On the other hand, a public place—a library, an empty classroom, a cafeteria—can be fine as long as the surrounding activity does not disturb you.
- **Control interruptions.** If you can close the door to your room and work without interruptions, fine. But even then, other people often assume that you want to take a break when they do. Choose a place where you can decide when it's time to take a break.
- **Have access to notes, journal, textbooks, sources, and other materials.** If the place is totally quiet but you don't have room to work or access to important notes or sources, you still may not make much progress. Whatever you need—a desk to spread your work out on, ac-

cess to notes and sources, extra pens, or computer disks—make sure your place has it.

The time of day you write and the tools you write with can also affect your attitude and efficiency. Some people like to write early in the morning, before their busy days start; others like to write in the evening, after classes or work. Whatever time you choose, try to write regularly—at least three days a week-at about the same time. If you're trying to get in shape by jogging, swimming, or doing aerobics, you wouldn't exercise for five straight hours on Monday and then take four days off. Like exercise, writing requires regular practice and conditioning.

Your writing tools—pen, pencil, paper, legal pads, four-by-six-inch note-cards, notebooks, computer—should also be comfortable for you. Some writers like to make notes with pencil and paper and write drafts on computers; some like to do all composing on computers. As you try different combinations of tools, be aware of how you feel and whether your tools make you more effective. If you feel comfortable, it will be easier to establish rituals that lead to regular practice.

Rituals are important because they help you with the most difficult part of writing—getting started. So use your familiar place, time, and tools to trick yourself into getting some words down on paper. Your mind will devise clever schemes to avoid writing those first ten words—watching TV, balancing your checkbook, drinking some more coffee, or calling a friend and whining together about all the writing you have to do. But if your body has been through the ritual before, it will walk calmly to your favorite place, where all your tools are ready (perhaps bringing the mind kicking and screaming all the way). Then, after you get the first ten words down, the mind will say, "Hey, this isn't so bad— I've got something to say about that!" And off you'll go.

Each time you perform your writing ritual, the *next* time you write will be that much easier. Soon, your ritual will let you know: *"This is where you write. This is when you write. This is what you write with."* No fooling around. Just writing.

Writers are notorious for using any reason to keep from working: overresearching, retyping, going to meetings, waxing the floors—anything.
—GLORIA STEINEM,
FORMER EDITOR OF
MS. MAGAZINE

FRANK AND ERNEST ®by Bob Thaves

ENERGY AND ATTITUDE

Once you've tricked yourself into the first ten words, you need to keep your attitude positive and your energy high. When you see an intimidating wall starting to form in front of you, don't ram your head into it; figure out a way to sneak around it. Try these few tricks and techniques:

1. *Start anywhere, quickly.* No law says that when you sit down to write a draft, you have to "begin at the beginning." If the first sentence is hard to write, begin with the first thoughts that come to mind. Or begin with a good example from your experience. Use that to get you going; then come back and rewrite your beginning after you've figured out what you want to say.

2. *Write the easiest parts first.* Forcing yourself to start a piece of writing by working on the hardest part first is a sure way to make yourself hate writing. Take the path of least resistance. If you can't get your thesis to come out right, jot down more examples. If you can't think of examples, go back to brainstorming.

* *Keep moving.* Once you've plunged in, write as fast as you can—whether you are scribbling ideas out with a pencil or hitting the keys of a typewriter or a computer. Maintain your momentum. Reread if you need to, but then plunge ahead.

* *Quit when you know what comes next.* When you do have to quit for the day, stop at a place where you know what comes next. Don't drain the well dry; stop in the middle of something you know how to finish. Make a few notes about what you need to do next and circle them. Leave yourself an easy place to get started next time.

3. One of the most important strategies for every writer is to *give yourself a break from the past and begin with a fresh image.* In many fields—mathematics, athletics, art, engineering—some people are late bloomers. Don't let that C or D you got in English back in the tenth grade hold you back now like a ball and chain. Imagine yourself cutting the chain and watching the ball roll away for good. Now you are free to start fresh with a clean slate. Your writing rituals should include only positive images about the writer you are right now and realistic expectations about what you can accomplish.

4. *Visualize yourself writing.* Successful athletes know how to visualize a successful tennis swing, a basketball free throw, or a baseball swing. When you are planning your activities for the day, visualize yourself writing at your favorite place. Seeing yourself doing your writing will enable you to start writing more quickly and maintain a positive attitude.

- *Discover and emphasize the aspects of writing that are fun for you.* Emphasize whatever is enjoyable for you—discovering an idea, getting the organization of a paragraph to come out right, clearing the unnecessary words and junk out of your writing. Concentrating on the parts you enjoy will help you make it through the tougher parts.
- *Set modest goals for yourself.* Don't aim for the stars; just work on a sentence. Don't measure yourself against some great writer; be your own yardstick. Compare what you write to what *you* have written before.
- *Congratulate yourself for the writing you do.* Writing is hard work; you're using words to create ideas and meanings literally out of nothing. So pat yourself on the back occasionally. Keep in mind the immortal words of comedian and playwright Steve Martin: "I think I did pretty well, considering I started out with nothing but a bunch of blank paper."

KEEPING A JOURNAL

Many writers keep some kind of notebook in which they write down their thoughts for later use. Some writers call it a *journal,* a place for their day-to-day thoughts. Other writers call it a *daybook,* a place to record ideas, collected information, possible outlines, titles, questions—anything related to the process of writing, thinking, and learning. Scientists and social scientists keep daily logs in which they record data or describe behavior. The word *journal* is the general term referring to "a place for daily writing." Whatever you call it, it should become part of your writing ritual. In it should go all kinds of writing. Bits and pieces of experience or memory that might come in handy later. Summary/responses of essays you read. In-class write-to-learn entries. Plans for writing your essays. A log of your writing plans and the writing problems you face. Postscripts on your writing process. Your journal is a place to practice, a closet where all your "fish paintings" go.

As the following list indicates, there are many kinds of journal entries, but they fall into three categories: *Reading Entries, Write-to-Learn Entries,* and *Writing Entries.* Reading entries help you understand and actively respond to student or professional writing. Write-to-learn entries help you summarize, react to, or question ideas or essays discussed in class. Writing entries help you warm up, test ideas, make writing plans, practice rhetorical strategies, or solve specific writing problems. All three kinds of journal writing, however, take advantage of the unique relationship between thinking, writing, and learning. Simply put, writing helps you learn what you know (and don't know) by shaping your thoughts into language.

I carry a journal with me almost all the time . . .

—NTOZAKE SHANGE,

AUTHOR OF THE PLAY FOR COLORED GIRLS WHO HAVE CONSIDERED SUICIDE WHEN THE RAINBOW IS ENUF

The most valuable writing tool I have is my daybook. . . . I write in my lap, in the living room or on the porch, in the car or an airplane, in meetings at the university, in bed, or sitting down on a rock wall during a walk. . . . It is always a form of talking to myself, a way of thinking on paper.

—DONALD MURRAY, JOURNALIST, AUTHOR OF BOOKS AND ESSAYS ABOUT WRITING

Reading Entries

- *Prereading journal entries.* Before you read an essay, read the headnote and write for five minutes on the topic of the essay—what you know about the subject, what related experiences you have had, and what opinions you hold. After you write your entry, the class can discuss the topic before you read the essay. The result? Your reading will be more active, engaged, and responsive.
- *Double-entry logs.* Draw a line vertically down a sheet of paper. On the left-hand side, summarize key ideas as you reread an essay. On the right-hand side, write down your reactions, responses, and questions. Writing while you read helps you understand and respond more thoroughly.
- *Essay annotations.* Writing your comments in the margin as you read is sometimes more efficient than writing separate journal entries. Also, in a small group in class, you can share your annotations and collaboratively annotate a copy of the essay.
- *Vocabulary entries.* Looking up unfamiliar words in a dictionary and writing out definitions in your journal will make you a much more accurate reader. Often an essay's thesis, meaning, or tone will hinge on the meanings of a few key words.
- *Summary/response entries.* Double-entry logs help you understand while you reread, but a short one-paragraph summary and one-paragraph response after you finish your rereading helps you focus on both the main ideas of a passage and your own key responses.

Write-to-Learn Entries

- *Lecture/discussion entries.* At key points in a class lecture or discussion, your teacher may ask you to write for five minutes by responding to a few questions: What is the main idea of the discussion? What one question would you like to ask? How does the topic of discussion relate to the essay that you are currently writing?
- *Responses to essays.* Before discussing an essay, write for a few minutes to respond to the following questions: What is the main idea of this essay? What do you like best about the essay? What is confusing, misleading, or wrong in this essay? What strategies illustrated in this essay will help you with your own writing?
- *Time-out responses.* During a controversial discussion or argument about an essay, your teacher may stop the class, take time out, and ask you to write for five minutes to respond to several questions: What key issue is the class debating? What are the main points of disagreement? What is your opinion? What evidence, either in the essay or in your experience, supports your opinion?

Writing Entries

- *Warming up.* Writing, like any other kind of activity, improves when you loosen up, stretch, get the kinks out, practice a few lines. Any daybook or journal entry gives you a chance to warm up.
- *Collecting and shaping exercises.* Some journal entries will help you collect information by observing, remembering, or investigating people, places, events, or objects. You can also record quotations or startling statistics for future writing topics. Other journal entries suggested in each chapter of this book will help you practice organizing your information. Strategies of development, such as comparison/contrast, definition, classification, or process analysis will help you discover and shape ideas.
- Writing for a specific audience. In some journal entries, you need to play a role. Imagine that you are in a specific situation, writing for a defined audience. For example, you might write a letter of application for a job or letter to a friend explaining why you've chosen a certain major.
- Revision plans and postscripts. Your journal is also the place to keep a log-a running account of your writing plans, revision plans, problems, and solutions. Include your research notes, peer responses, and postscripts on your writing process in this log.
- Imitating styles of writers. Use your journal to copy passages from writers you like. Practice imitating their styles on different topics. Also, try simply transcribing a few paragraphs. Even copying effective writers' words will reveal some of their secrets for successful writing.
- Writing free journal entries. Use your journal to record ideas, reactions to people on campus, events in the news, reactions to controversial articles in the campus newspaper, conversations after class or work, or just your private thoughts.

■ WARM-UP: JOURNAL EXERCISES   Choose three of the exercises below and write for ten minutes on each. Date and number each entry.

1. Make an "authority" list of activities, subjects, ideas, places, people, or events that you already know something about. List as many topics as you can. If your reaction is "I'm not really an *authority* on anything," then imagine you've met someone from another school, state, country, or historical period. With that person as your audience, what are you an "authority" on?

2. Choose one activity, sport, or hobby that you do well and that others might admire you for. In the form of a letter to a friend, describe the steps or stages of the process through which you acquired that skill or ability.

3. In two or three sentences, complete the following thought: "I have trouble writing because . . ."

4. In a few sentences, complete the following thought: "In my previous classes and from my own writing experience, I've learned that the three most important rules about writing are . . ."

5. Describe your own writing rituals. *When, where,* and *how* do you write best?

6. Write an open journal entry. Describe events from your day, images, impressions, bits of conversation—anything that catches your interest. For possible ideas for open journal entries, read the following essay by Roy Hoffman.

P R O F E S S I O N A L   W R I T I N G

ON KEEPING A JOURNAL

Roy Hoffman

In a Newsweek On Campus *essay, Roy Hoffman describes his own experience, recording events and trying out ideas just as an artist doodles on a sketch pad. Your own journal entries about events, images, descriptions of people, and bits of conversation will not only improve your writing but also become your own personal time capsule, to dig up and reread in the year 2020.*

Wherever I go I carry a small notebook in my coat or back pocket for thoughts, observations and impressions. As a writer I use this notebook as an artist would a sketch pad, for stories and essays, and as a sporadic journal of my comings and goings. When I first started keeping notebooks, though, I was not yet a professional writer. I was still in college.

I made my first notebook entries . . . just after my freshman year,   *2*
in what was actually a travel log. A buddy and I were setting out to trek
from our Alabama hometown to the distant tundra of Alaska. With un-
bounded enthusiasm I began: "Wild, crazy ecstasy wants to wrench
my head from my body." The log, written in a university composition
book, goes on to chronicle our adventures in the land where the sun
never sets, the bars never close and the prepipeline employment
prospects were so bleak we ended up taking jobs as night janitors.

When I returned to college that fall I had a small revelation: the   *3*
world around me of libraries, quadrangles, Frisbees and professors was
as rich with material for my journals and notebooks as galumphing
moose and garrulous fishermen.

These college notebooks, which built to a pitch my senior year, are   *4*
gold mines to me now. Classrooms, girlfriends, cups of coffee and lines
of poetry—from mine to John Keats's—float by like clouds. As I lie beneath these clouds again, they take on familiar and distinctive shapes.

Though I can remember the campus's main quadrangle, I see it   *5*
more vividly when I read my description of school on a visit during
summer break: "the muggy, lassitudinal air . . . the bird noises that
can not be pointed to, the summer emptiness that grows emptier with
a few students squeaking by the library on poorly oiled bicycles." An
economics professor I fondly remember returns with less fondness in
my notebooks, "staring down at the class with his equine face." And
a girl I had a crush on senior year, whom I now recall mistily, reappears with far more vitality as "the ample, slightly-gawky, whole-
wheat, fractured object of my want gangling down the hall in spring
heat today."

When, in reading over my notebooks, I am not peering out at   *6*
quadrangles, midterm exams, professors or girlfriends, I see a portrait
of my parents and hometown during holidays and occasional weekend breaks. Like a wheel, home revolves, each turn regarded differently depending on the novel or political essay I'd been most influenced
by the previous semester.

Mostly, though, in wandering back through my notebooks, I meet   *7*
someone who could be my younger brother: the younger version of
myself. The younger me seems moodier, more inquisitive, more fun-
loving and surprisingly eager to stay up all night partying or figuring
out electron orbitals for a 9 a.m. exam. The younger me wanders
through a hall of mirrors of the self, writes of "seeing two or three of
myself on every corner," and pens long meditations on God and society before scribbling in the margin, "what a child I am." The younger

me also finds humor in trying to keep track of this hall of mirrors, commenting in ragged verse.

> *I hope that one day*
> *Some grandson or cousin*
> *Will read these books,*
> *And know that I was*
> *Once a youth*
> *Sitting in drugstores with*
> *Anguished looks.*
> *And poring over coffee,*
> *And should have poured*
> *The coffee*
> *Over these lines.*

I believe that every college student should attempt to keep some form of notebook, journal or diary. A notebook is a secret garden in which to dance, sing, muse, wander, perform handstands, even cry. In the privacy of this little book, you can make faces, curse, turn somersaults and ask yourself if you're really in love. A notebook or journal is one of the few places you can call just your own.   *8*

. . . Journal writing suffers when you let someone, in your mind, look over your shoulder. Honesty wilts when a parent, teacher or friend looms up in your imagination to discourage you from putting your true thoughts on the page. Journal writing also runs a related hazard: the dizzying suspicion that one day your private thoughts, like those of Samuel Pepys or Virginia Woolf, will be published in several volumes and land up required reading for English 401. How can you write comfortably when the eyes of all future readers are upon you? Keep your notebooks with the abandon of one who knows his words will go up in smoke. Then you might really strike fire a hundred years or so from now if anyone cares to pry.   *9*

By keeping notebooks, you improve your writing ability, increasing your capacity to communicate both with yourself and others. By keeping notebooks, you discover patterns in yourself, whether lazy ones that need to be broken or healthy ones that can use some nurturing. By keeping notebooks, you heighten some moments and give substance to others: even a journey to the washateria offers potential for some offbeat journal observations. And by keeping notebooks while still in college, you chart a terrain that, for many, is more dynamically charged with ideas and discussions than the practical, workaday world just beyond. Notebooks, I believe, not only help us remember this dynamic charge, but also help us sustain it.   *10*

Not long ago, while traveling with a friend in Yorktown, Va., I *11*
passed by a time capsule buried in the ground in 1976, intended to
be dug up in 2076. Keeping notebooks and journals is rather like
burying time capsules into one's own life. There's no telling what
old rock song, love note, philosophical complaint or rosy Saturday
morning you'll unearth when you dig up these personal time capsules.
You'll be able to piece together a remarkable picture of where you've
come from, and may well get some important glimmers about where
you're going.

Interior, 1981, by Heman Miranda.

Chapter  Purposes and Processes for Writing

As a Chinese-American woman growing up in America, you decide to write about the difficulty of living in two cultures. You recall how, during your childhood, you rebelled against your mother when she insisted that you learn about your Chinese heritage. You remember how much you hated your Chinese school and how embarrassed you were that your mother could not speak English properly. As you grew older, however, you realized the price you paid for your assimilation into American culture. After discussing this conflict with your friends, you decide to describe your experiences to others who share them or who may want to know what you learned. At that point, you write an autobiographical account of your experiences and send it to a metropolitan newspaper.

A veteran smoker, you have become increasingly irritated at the nonsmoking regulations that have appeared in restaurants, businesses, and other public places. And it's not just the laws that are irritating, but the holier-than-thou attitude of people who presume that what's good for them should be good for you. Nonsmoking laws seem to give people license to censure your behavior while totally ignoring their own offensive behavior: polluting the atmosphere with hydrocarbons, fouling the aquifers with fertilizers, and generally corrupting the social air with odors of false superiority. So after one particularly memorable experience, you write a letter to the editor of the local paper, intending not only to express your own frustration but also to satirize all those smug do-gooders.

*T*HE WRITING FOR THIS COURSE (AND THE STRUCTURE OF THIS TEXTBOOK) STARTS WITH THE PREMISE THAT EFFECTIVE COMMUNICATION BEGINS WITH LEARNING. IT ALSO assumes that learning results—at least in part—from your written efforts to make connections and see relationships between your own observations and experience and the written or collected knowledge of others. There are four important sources for learning, writing, and communication:

- observing and describing the world around you
- remembering and drawing on your experiences
- reading and responding to images, media, and textual material
- investigating knowledge through interviews, surveys, and library sources

Writing, as a means of learning and communicating, begins with what you see and have experienced. It then makes use of what you're reading in texts, hearing in lectures, finding out at work, or learning from friends and family.

■ FREEWRITING: INVENTORY OF YOUR WRITING

Before you read further in this chapter, take out a pen or pencil and a piece of paper and inventory what you have written in the last year or two. Brainstorm a list of everything you can think of: grocery lists, letters, wedding invitations, reports, school essays, notes to friends, applications for jobs, memos to your boss. Then for one of your longer writing projects, jot down several sentences describing the situation that called for that piece of writing—*when* you did it, *whom* you wrote it for, *what* its purpose was, *where* you wrote it, and *how* you went about writing it.

Most good writing has a personal dimension. It may be about the writer personally or it may address a subject or an idea the writer cares about. It begins with honesty, curiosity, inquiry, and even vulnerability. Good writers assert themselves, knowing that they are vulnerable to other people's criticism. They take risks—sometimes writing on subjects they don't completely understand—knowing that taking their thoughts to a public forum is one way to actively engage the information that threatens to overwhelm them. By continually probing and learning, being honest with themselves, and accepting risks, writers can use their writing to teach themselves as well as their readers.

WRITING FOR MYSELF

Russell Baker

For many years, Russell Baker wrote humorous essays for The New York Times. *Before that, however, he was just a writer—someone who wrote about his experiences, what he was learning or was curious about, or what he found amusing or absurd. In this selection from his autobiography,* Growing Up, *Baker describes how bored he was as a student required to write "compositions," until he found a topic that had a personal dimension for him. The essay he wrote for his composition class, on the art of eating spaghetti, taught Baker an important truth: Writers should write honestly about topics that are important—even fun—for them.*

The notion of becoming a writer had flickered off and on in my   *1*
head since the Belleville days, but it wasn't until my third year in high school that the possibility took hold. Until then I'd been bored by everything associated with English courses. I found English grammar dull and baffling. I hated the assignments to turn out leaden, lackluster paragraphs that were agonies for teachers to read and for me to write. The classics thrust on me to read seemed as deadening as chloroform.

When our class was assigned to Mr. Fleagle for third-year Eng-   *2*
lish I anticipated another grim year in that dreariest of subjects. Mr. Fleagle was notorious among City students for dullness and inability to inspire. He was said to be stuffy, dull, and hopelessly out of date. To me he looked to be sixty or seventy and prim to a fault. He wore primly severe eyeglasses, his wavy hair was primly cut and primly combed. He wore prim vested suits with neckties blocked primly against the collar buttons of his primly starched white shirts. He had a primly pointed jaw, a primly straight nose, and a prim manner of speaking that was so correct, so gentlemanly, that he seemed a comic antique.

I anticipated a listless, unfruitful year with Mr. Fleagle and for a   *3*
long time was not disappointed. Late in the year we tackled the informal essay. Mr. Fleagle distributed a homework sheet offering us a choice of topics. None was quite so simpleminded as "What I Did on My Summer Vacation," but most seemed to be almost as dull. I took the list home and dawdled until the night before the essay was due. Sprawled on the sofa, I finally faced up to the grim task, took the list out of my notebook, and scanned it. The topic on which my eye stopped was "The Art of Eating Spaghetti."

This title produced an extraordinary sequence of mental im-   *4*
ages. Surging up out of the depths of memory came a vivid rec-
ollection of a night in Belleville when all of us were seated around
the supper table—Uncle Allen, my mother, Uncle Charlie, Doris,
Uncle Hal—and Aunt Pat served spaghetti for supper. Spaghetti
was an exotic treat in those days. Neither Doris nor I had ever
eaten spaghetti, and none of the adults had enough experience to
be good at it. All the good humor of Uncle Allen's house reawoke
in my mind as I recalled the laughing arguments we had that night
about the socially respectable method for moving spaghetti from
plate to mouth.

Suddenly I wanted to write about that, about the warmth and   *5*
good feeling of it, but I wanted to put it down simply for my own joy,
not for Mr. Fleagle. It was a moment I wanted to recapture and hold
for myself. I wanted to relive the pleasure of an evening at New Street.
To write it as I wanted, however, would violate all the rules of formal
composition I'd learned in school, and Mr. Fleagle would surely give
it a failing grade. Never mind. I would write something else for Mr.
Fleagle after I had written this thing for myself.

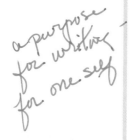

a purpose
for writing
for oneself

When I finished it the night was half gone and there was no time   *6*
left to compose a proper, respectable essay for Mr. Fleagle. There was
no choice next morning but to turn in my private reminiscence of
Belleville. Two days passed before Mr. Fleagle returned the graded
papers, and he returned everyone's but mine. I was bracing myself for
a command to report to Mr. Fleagle immediately after school for discipline when I saw him lift my paper from his desk and rap for the
class's attention.

"Now, boys," he said. "I want to read you an essay. This is titled,   *7*
'The Art of Eating Spaghetti.'"

And he started to read. My words! He was reading my words out   *8*
loud to the entire class. What's more, the entire class was listening.
Listening attentively. Then somebody laughed, then the entire class
was laughing, and not in contempt and ridicule, but with openheart-
ed enjoyment. Even Mr. Fleagle stopped two or three times to repress
a small prim smile.

I did my best to avoid showing pleasure, but what I was feeling was   *9*
pure ecstasy at this startling demonstration that my words had the
power to make people laugh. In the eleventh grade, at the eleventh
hour as it were, I had discovered a calling. It was the happiest moment
of my entire school career. When Mr. Fleagle finished he put the final
seal on my happiness by saying, "Now that, boys, is an essay, don't you
see. It's—don't you see—it's of the very essence of the essay, don't you
see. Congratulations, Mr. Baker."

Purposes for Writing

Getting a good grade, making a million dollars, or contributing to society may be among your motives for writing. However, as a writer, you also have more specific purposes for writing. These purposes help you make key decisions about content, structure, and style. When your main purpose is to *express* your feelings, you may write a private entry in your journal. When your main purpose is to *explain* how your sales promotion increased the number of your company's customers, you may write a factual report to your boss. When your main purpose is to *persuade* others to see a movie that you like, you may write a review for the local newspaper. In each case, the intended purpose—your desired effect on your audience—helps determine what you write and how you write it.

> *The writer may write to inform, to explain, to entertain, to persuade, but whatever the purpose there should be first of all, the satisfaction of the writer's own learning.*
>
> —**DONALD MURRAY,**
> TEACHER AND PULITZER PRIZE-WINNING JOURNALIST

WRITER-BASED PURPOSES

Because writing is, or should be, for yourself first of all, everything you write involves at least some purpose that benefits you. Of course, expressing yourself is a fundamental purpose of all writing. Without the satisfaction of expressing your thoughts, feelings, reactions, knowledge, or questions, you might not make the effort to write in the first place.

A closely related purpose is learning: Writing helps you discover what you think or feel, simply by using language to identify and compose your thoughts. Writing not only helps you form ideas but actually promotes observing and remembering. If you write down what you observe about people, places, or things, you can actually "see" them more clearly. Similarly, if you write down facts, ideas, experiences, or reactions to your readings, you will remember them longer. Writing and rewriting facts, dates, definitions, impressions, or personal experiences will improve your powers of recall on such important occasions as examinations and job interviews.

SUBJECT- AND AUDIENCE-BASED PURPOSES

Although some writing is intended only for yourself—such as entries in a diary, lists, class notes, reminders—much of your writing will be read by others, by those readers who constitute your "audience."

- You may write to *inform* others about a particular subject—to tell them about the key facts, data, feelings, people, places, or events.
- You may write to *explain* to your readers what something means, how it works, or why it happens.

I think writing is really a process of communication. . . . It's the sense of being in contact with people who are part of a particular audience that really makes a difference to me in writing.

—SHERLEY ANN WILLIAMS,

POET, CRITIC, AND NOVELIST

③ • You may write to *persuade* others to believe or do something—to convince others to agree with your judgment about a book, record, or restaurant, or to persuade them to take a certain class, vote for a certain candidate, or buy some product you are advertising.

④ • You may write to *explore* ideas and "truths," to examine how your ideas have changed, to ask questions that have no easy answers, and then to share your thoughts and reflections with others.

⑤ • You may write to *entertain*—as a primary purpose in itself or as a purpose combined with informing, explaining, persuading, or exploring. Whatever your purposes may be, good writing both teaches and pleases. Remember, too, that your readers will learn more, remember more, or be more convinced when your writing contains humor, wit, or imaginative language.

COMBINATIONS OF PURPOSES

In many cases, you write with more than one purpose in mind. Purposes may appear in combinations, connected in a sequence, or actually overlapping. Initially, you may take notes about a subject to learn and remember, but later you may want to inform others about what you have discovered. Similarly, you may begin by writing to express your feelings about a movie that you loved or that upset you; later, you may wish to persuade others to see it—or not to see it.

Purposes can also contain each other, like Chinese boxes, or overlap, blurring the distinctions. An explanation of how an automobile works will contain information about that vehicle. An attempt to persuade someone to buy an automobile may contain an explanation of how it handles and information about its body style or engine. Usually, writing to persuade others will contain explanations and basic information, but the reverse is not necessarily true; you can write simply to give information, without trying to persuade anyone to do anything.

Writing, as a rhetorical act, is carried out within a web of purpose.

—LINDA FLOWER,

TEACHER AND RESEARCHER IN COMPOSITION

T-A-P

SUBJECT, PURPOSE, AND THESIS

The *thesis*, *claim*, or *main idea* in a piece of writing is related to your purpose. As a writer, you usually have a purpose in mind that serves as a guide while you gather information about your subject and think about your audience. However, as you collect and record information, impressions, and ideas you gradually narrow your subject to a specific topic and thus clarify your purpose. You bring your purpose into sharper and sharper focus—as if progressing on a target from the outer circles to the bull's-eye—until you have narrowed your purpose down to a central thesis. The thesis is the dominant idea, explanation, evaluation, or recommendation that you want to impress upon your readers.

[handwritten marginalia: Audience — think about what magazine or paper — specific pop. an article reaches]

The following examples illustrate how a writer moves from a general subject, guided by purpose, to a specific thesis or claim.

SUBJECT	PURPOSE	THESIS, CLAIM, OR MAIN IDEA
Childhood experiences	To express your feelings and explain how one childhood experience was important.	The relentless competition between my sisters and me distorted my easygoing personality.
Heart disease	To inform readers about relationships between Type A personalities and heart attacks.	Type A personalities do not necessarily have an abnormally high risk of suffering heart attacks.
The death penalty	To persuade readers that the death penalty should be used.	Despite our belief that killing is wrong, a state-administered death penalty is fair, just, and humane.

Purpose and Audience

Writing for yourself is relatively easy; after all, you already know your audience and can make spontaneous judgments about what is essential and what is not. However, when your purpose is to communicate to other readers, you need to analyze your audience. Your writing will be more effective if you can anticipate what your readers know and need to know, what they are interested in, and what their beliefs or attitudes are. As you write for different readers, you will select different kinds of information, organize it in different ways, or write in a more formal or less formal style.

■ FREEWRITING: WRITING FOR DIFFERENT AUDIENCES   Before you read further, get a pen or pencil and several sheets of paper and do the following exercise:

1. For your eyes only, write about what you did at a recent party. Write for four minutes.
2. On a second sheet of paper, describe for the members of your writing class what you did at this party; you will read it aloud to the class. Stop after four minutes.
3. On a third sheet of paper, write a letter to one of your parents describing what you did at the party. Stop after four minutes.

good — use to illustrate different approaches due to audience

AUDIENCE ANALYSIS

If you are writing to communicate to other readers, analyzing your probable audience will help you answer some basic questions:

- How much information or evidence is enough? What should I assume my audience already knows? What should I not tell them? What do they believe? Will they readily agree with me or will they be antagonistic?
- How should I organize my writing? How can I get my readers' attention? Can I just describe my subject and tell a story or should I analyze everything in a logical order? Should I put my best examples or arguments first or last?
- Should I write informally, with simple sentences and easy vocabulary, or should I write in a more elaborate or specialized style, with technical vocabulary?

Analyze your audience by considering the following questions. As you learn more about your audience, the possibilities for your own role as a writer will become clearer.

1. **Audience profile**. How narrow or broad is your audience? Is it a narrow and defined audience—a single person, such as your Aunt Mary, or a group with clear common interests, such as the zoning board in your city or the readers of *Organic Gardening*? Is it a broad and diverse audience: educated readers who wish to be informed on current events, American voters as a whole, or residents of your state? Do your readers have identifiable roles? Can you determine their age, sex, economic status, ethnic background, or occupational category?

2. **Audience-subject relationship**. Consider what your readers know about your subject. If they know very little about it, you'll need to explain the basics; if they already know quite a bit, you can go straight to more difficult or complex issues. Also estimate their probable attitude toward this subject. Are they likely to be sympathetic or hostile? _WHY?_

3. **Audience-writer relationship**. What is your relationship with your readers? Do you know each other personally? Do you have anything in common? Will your audience be likely to trust what you say, or will they be skeptical about your judgments? Are you the expert on this particular subject and the readers the novices? Or are you the novice and your readers the experts?

4. **Writer's role**. To communicate effectively with your audience, you should also consider your own role or perspective. Of the many roles that you could play (friend, big sister or brother, student of psychology, music fan, employee of a fast-food restaurant, and so on), choose one that will be effective for your purpose and audience. If, for example, you are writing to

sixth-graders about nutrition, you could choose the perspective of a concerned older brother or sister. Your writing might be more effective, however, if you assume the role of a person who has worked in fast-food restaurants for three years and knows what goes into hamburgers, french fries, and milkshakes.

Writers may write to real audiences, or they may create audiences. Sometimes the relationship between writer and reader is real (sister writing to brother), so the writer starts with a known audience and writes accordingly. Sometimes, however, writers begin and gradually discover or create an audience in the process of writing. Knowing the audience guides the writing, but the writing may construct an audience as well.

Purpose, Audience, and Genre

In addition to considering your purpose and audience, think also about the possible forms or genres your writing might take. If you are writing to observe or remember something, you may want to write an informal essay, a letter, a memoir, or even an e-mail to reach your audience. If you are writing to inform your readers or explain some idea, you may write an article, essay, letter, report, or pamphlet to best achieve your purpose and address your audience. Argumentative writing—writing to evaluate, persuade, or recommend some position or course of action—takes place in many different genres, from e-mails and letters, to reviews and editorials, to proposals and researched documents. As you select a topic, consider which genre would most effectively accomplish your purpose for your intended audience.

THE WRITING SITUATION

Taken together, the writer's purpose or aim, the subject, and the probable audience (whether yourself or others) define the writing situation. Sometimes an instructor or employer assigns you a specific writing situation. At other times, you yourself construct a situation from scratch.

The components of the writing situation—writer, subject, purpose, thesis, and audience—are so interrelated that a change in one may affect the other three. As you write, therefore, you do not always follow a step-by-step order. You may begin, for example, with a specific audience on which you wish to make an impression; as you analyze the audience, you decide what subject and purpose would be most appropriate. Conversely, you may start with an interesting subject but no clear sense of purpose or audience. Or you may be asked to write for a certain audience, and then you discover that its needs and expectations have led you to discover or modify your purpose or subject. In short, subject, purpose, thesis, and audience are all modified, reconsidered, and revised as you write.

The following examples illustrate how subject, purpose, and audience combine to define a writing situation.

> In response to a request by an editor of a college recruiting pamphlet, a student decides to write an essay explaining the advantages of the social and academic life at his university. According to the editor, the account needs to be realistic but should also promote the university. It shouldn't be too academic and stuffy—the college catalog itself contains all the basic information—but it should give high school seniors a flavor of college life. The student decides to write a narrative account of his most interesting experiences during his first week at college.

> A student majoring in journalism reads about correspondents' accounts of restrictions during the Persian Gulf conflict. The military limited reporters to carefully controlled "pools," and during the ground offensive, television journalists' tapes were mysteriously delayed or lost until after the ground war was over. Following a class debate on the public's right to know versus the military's need to maintain secrecy in times of war, the student investigates specific incidents to see if the military exercised unnecessary or excessive censorship. The student researches these incidents and reports her findings in a letter to her congressional representative, asking for a further investigation of certain cases of alleged censorship.

Purpose and Audience in Two Essays

The two short essays that follow appeared as columns in newspapers. Both relate the writers' own experiences. They are similar in form but have different purposes and appeal to different kinds of readers. As you read each essay, decide which one you find more interesting—and explain why.

THE STRUGGLE TO BE AN ALL-AMERICAN GIRL

Elizabeth Wong

It's still there, the Chinese school on Yale Street where my brother 1 and I used to go. Despite the new coat of paint and the high wire fence, the school I knew 10 years ago remains remarkably, stoically the same.

Every day at 5 P.M., instead of playing with our fourth- and fifth- 2 grade friends or sneaking out to the empty lot to hunt ghosts and animal bones, my brother and I had to go to Chinese school. No amount of kicking, screaming, or pleading could dissuade my mother, who was solidly determined to have us learn the language of our heritage.

Forcibly, she walked us the seven long, hilly blocks from our home 3 to school, depositing our defiant tearful faces before the stern principal. My only memory of him is that he swayed on his heels like a palm tree, and he always clasped his impatient twitching hands behind his back. I recognized him as a repressed maniacal child killer, and knew that if we ever saw his hands we'd be in big trouble.

We all sat in little chairs in an empty auditorium. The room 4 smelled like Chinese medicine, and imported faraway mustiness. Like ancient mothballs or dirty closets. I hated that smell. I favored crisp new scents. Like the soft French perfume that my American teacher wore in public school.

Although the emphasis at the school was mainly language—speak- 5 ing, reading, writing—the lessons always began with an exercise in politeness. With the entrance of the teacher, the best student would tap a bell and everyone would get up, kowtow, and chant, "sing san ho," the phonetic for "How are you, teacher?"

Being ten years old, I had better things to learn than ideographs 6 copied painstakingly in lines that ran right to left from the tip of a *moc but*, a real ink pen that had to be held in an awkward way if blotches were to be avoided. After all, I could do the multiplication tables, name the satellites of Mars, and write reports on "Little Women" and "Black Beauty." Nancy Drew, my favorite book heroine, never spoke Chinese.

The language was a source of embarrassment. More times than 7 not, I had tried to disassociate myself from the nagging loud voice that followed me wherever I wandered in the nearby American supermarket outside Chinatown. The voice belonged to my grandmother, a fragile woman in her seventies who could outshout the best of the street vendors. Her humor was raunchy, her Chinese rhythmless, patternless. It was quick, it was loud, it was unbeautiful. It was not like the quiet, lilting romance of French or the gentle refinement of the American South. Chinese sounded pedestrian. Public.

In Chinatown, the comings and goings of hundreds of Chinese on their daily tasks sounded chaotic and frenzied. I did not want to be thought of as mad, as talking gibberish. When I spoke English, people nodded at me, smiled sweetly, said encouraging words. Even the people in my culture would cluck and say that I'd do well in life. "My, doesn't she move her lips fast," they would say, meaning that I'd be able to keep up with the world outside Chinatown. *8*

My brother was even more fanatical than I about speaking English. He was especially hard on my mother, criticizing her, often cruelly, for her pidgin speech—smatterings of Chinese scattered like chop suey in her conversation. "It's not 'What it is,' Mom," he'd say in exasperation. "It's 'What is it, what is it, what is it!'" Sometimes Mom might leave out an occasional "the" or "a," or perhaps a verb of being. He would stop her in mid-sentence: "Say it again, Mom. Say it right." When he tripped over his own tongue, he'd blame it on her: "See, Mom, it's all your fault. You set a bad example." *9*

After two years of writing with a *moc but* and reciting words with multiples of meanings, I finally was granted a cultural divorce. I was permitted to stop Chinese school. *10*

I thought of myself as multicultural. I preferred tacos to egg rolls; I enjoyed Cinco de Mayo more than Chinese New Year. *11*

At last, I was one of you; I wasn't one of them. *12*

Sadly, I still am. *13*

PROFESSIONAL   WRITING

I'm O.K., but You're Not

Robert Zoellner

The American novelist John Barth, in his early novel, *The Floating Opera*, remarks that ordinary, day-to-day life often presents us with embarrassingly obvious, totally unsubtle patterns of symbolism and meaning—life in the midst of death, innocence vindicated, youth versus age, etc. *1*

The truth of Barth's insight was brought home to me recently *2* while having breakfast in a lawn-bordered restaurant on College Avenue near the Colorado State University campus. I had asked to be seated in the smoking section of the restaurant—I have happily gone through three or four packs a day for the past 40 years.

As it happened, the hostess seated me—I was by myself—at a lit- *3* tle two-person table on the dividing line between the smoking and non-smoking sections. Presently, a well-dressed couple of advanced years, his hair a magisterial white and hers an electric blue, were seated in the non-smoking section five feet away from me.

It was apparent within a minute that my cigarette smoke was bug- *4* ging them badly, and soon the husband leaned over and asked me if I would please stop smoking. As a chronic smokestack, I normally comply, out of simple courtesy, with such requests. Even an addict such as myself can quit for as long as 20 minutes.

But his manner was so self-righteous and peremptory—he re- *5* minded me of Lee Iacocca boasting about Chrysler—that the promptings of original sin, always a problem with me, took over. I quietly pointed out that I was in the smoking section—if only by five feet—and that that fact meant that I had met my social obligation to non-smokers. Besides, the idea of morning coffee without a cigarette was simply inconceivable to me—might as well ask me to vote Republican.

The two of them ate their eggs-over-easy in hurried and sullen *6* silence, while I chain-smoked over my coffee. As well as be hung for a sheep as a lamb, I reasoned. Presently they got up, paid their bill, and stalked out in an ambiance of affronted righteousness and affluent propriety.

And this is where John Barth comes in. They had parked their *7* car—a diesel Mercedes—where it could be seen from my table. And in the car, waiting impatiently, was a splendidly matched pair of pedigreed poodles, male and female.

Both dogs were clearly in extremis, and when the back door of the *8* car was opened, they made for the restaurant lawn in considerable haste. Without ado (no pun intended), the male did a doo-doo that would have done credit to an animal twice his size, and finished off with a leisurely, ruminative wee-wee. The bitch of the pair, as might be expected of any well-brought-up female of Republican proclivities, confined herself to a modest wee-wee, fastidious, diffident, and quickly executed.

Having thus polluted the restaurant lawn, the four of them mar- *9* shalled their collective dignity and drove off in a dense cloud of blue smoke—that lovely white Mercedes was urgently in need of a valve-and-ring job, its emission sticker an obvious exercise in creative writing.

As I regretfully watched them go—after all, the four of them   *10*
had made my day—it seemed to me that they were in something of a hurry, and I uncharitably wondered if the husband was not anxious to get home in order to light the first Fall fire in his moss-rock fireplace, or apply the Fall ration of chemical fertilizer to his doubtlessly impeccable lawn, thus adding another half-pound of particulates to the local atmosphere and another 10 pounds of nitrates and other poisons to the regional aquifers. But that, of course, is pure and unkindly speculation.

In any case, the point of this real-life vignette, as John Barth would   *11*
insist, is obvious. The current controversy over public smoking in Fort Collins is a clear instance of selective virtue at work, coming under the rubric of, what I do is perfectly OK, but what you do is perfectly awful.

QUESTIONS FOR WRITING AND DISCUSSION

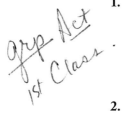

1. Choosing only one adjective to describe your main reaction to each essay, answer the following question: "When I finished the _____ [Wong, Zoellner] essay, I was _____ [intrigued, bored, amused, irritated, curious, confused, or _____] because _____. Explain your choice of adjectives in one or two sentences.

2. Referring to specific passages, explain the purpose and state the thesis or main point of each essay.

3. What personality or role does each writer project? Drawing from evidence in the essay, describe what you think both writers would be like if you met them.

4. Both of these essays appeared in newspapers. What kind of reader would find each essay interesting? What kind of reader would not enjoy each essay? For each essay, find examples of specific sentences, word choices, vocabulary, experiences, or references to culture or politics that would appeal to one reader but perhaps irritate another.

5. These two essays are similar in form—they are both informal essays narrating personal experiences and explaining what each writer discovered or learned. There are differences, however, in structure and style. What differences do you notice in the way each essay begins and concludes, in the order of the paragraphs, and in vocabulary or style of the sentences?

Dimensions of the Process

Processes for writing vary from one writer to the next and from one writing situation to the next. Most writers, however, can identify four basic stages, or dimensions, of their writing process: collecting, shaping, drafting, and revising. The writing situation may precede these stages—particularly if you are assigned a subject, purpose, audience, and form. Usually, however, you continue to narrow your subject, clarify your purpose, meet the needs of your audience, and modify your form as you work through the dimensions of your writing process.

COLLECTING

Mark Twain, author of *Huckleberry Finn*, once observed that if you attempt to carry a cat around the block by its tail, you'll gain a whole lot of information about cats that you'll never forget. You may collect such firsthand information, or you may rely on the data, experience, or expertise of others. In any case, writers constantly collect facts, impressions, opinions, and ideas that are relevant to their subjects, purposes, and audiences. Collecting involves observing, remembering, imagining, thinking, reading, listening, writing, investigating, talking, taking notes, and experimenting. Collecting also involves thinking about the relationships among the bits of information that you have collected.

SHAPING

Writers focus and organize the facts, examples, and ideas that they have collected into the recorded, linear form that is written language. When a hurricane hits the Gulf Coast, for example, residents of Texas, Louisiana, Mississippi, Alabama, and Florida are likely to collect an enormous amount of data in just a few hours. Rain, floods, tree limbs snapping in the wind, unboarded windows shattering, sirens blaring—all of these events occur nearly simultaneously. If you try to write about such devastation, you need to narrow your focus (you can't describe everything that happened) and organize your information (you can't describe all of your experiences at the same time).

A chronological order is just one of the shapes that a writer may choose to develop and organize experience. Such shaping strategies also help writers collect additional information and ideas. Reconstructing a chronological order, for example, may suggest some additional details—perhaps a wet, miserable-looking dog running through the heavy downpour—that you might not otherwise have remembered.

DRAFTING

At some point, writers actually write down a rough version of what will evolve into the finished piece of writing. Drafting processes vary widely from one writer to the next. Some writers prefer to reread their collecting and shaping notes, find a starting point, and launch themselves—figuring out what they want to say as they write it. Other writers start with a plan—a mental strategy, a short list, or an outline—of how they wish to proceed. Whatever approach you use in your draft, write down as much as possible: You want to see whether the information is clear, whether your overall shape expresses and clarifies your purpose, and whether your content and organization meet the needs and expectations of your audience.

REVISING

When writers revise rough drafts, they literally "resee" their subjects—and then modify drafts to fit new visions. Revision is more than just tinkering with a word here and there; revision leads to larger changes—new examples or details, a different organization, or a new perspective. You accomplish these changes by adding, deleting, substituting, or reordering words, sentences, and paragraphs. Although revision begins the moment you get your first idea, most revisions are based on the reactions—or anticipated reactions—of the audience to your draft. You often play the role of audience yourself by putting the draft aside and rereading it later when you have some distance from your writing. Wherever you feel readers might not get your point, you revise to make it clearer. You may also get feedback from readers in a class workshop, suggesting that you collect more or different information, alter the shape of your draft to improve the flow of ideas, or clarify your terminology. As a result of your rereading and your readers' suggestions, you may change your thesis or write for an entirely different audience.

Editing—in contrast to revising—focuses on the minor changes that you make to improve the accuracy and readability of your language. You usually edit your essay to improve word choice, grammar, usage, or punctuation. You also use a computer spell-check program and proofread to catch typos and other surface errors.

THE WHOLE PROCESS

In practice, a writer's process rarely follows the simple, consecutive order that these four stages or dimensions suggest. The writing process is actually recursive: It begins at one point, goes on to another, comes back to the first, jumps to the third, and so forth. A stage may last hours or only a second or two. While writing a letter to a friend, you may collect, shape, revise, and edit in one quick draft; a research paper may require repeated shaping over a two-week period. As writers draft, they may correct a few mistakes or typos, but they may not proofread until many days later. In the middle of reorganizing an essay, writers often reread drafts, go back and ask more questions, and collect more data. Even while editing, writers may throw out several paragraphs, collect some additional information, and draft new sections.

In addition to the recursive nature of the writing process, keep in mind that writing often occurs during every stage, not just during drafting and revising. During collecting, you will be recording information and jotting down ideas. During shaping, you will be writing out trial versions that you may use later when you draft or revise. Throughout the writing process, you use your writing to modify your subject, purpose, audience, and form.

The most important point to keep in mind is that the writing process is unique to each writer and to each writing situation. What works for one writer may be absolutely wrong for you. Some writers compose nearly everything in their heads. Others write only after discussing the subject with friends or drawing diagrams and pictures.

During the writing process, you need to experiment with several collecting, shaping, and drafting strategies to see what works best for you and for a particular piece of writing. As long as your process works, however, it's legitimate—no matter how many times you backtrack and repeat stages. When you are struggling with a piece of writing, remember that numerous revisions are a normal part of the writing process—even for most professionals.

Circling back over what you have already written—to sharpen your thesis, improve the organization, tighten up a paragraph, or add specific details to your examples—is likely to be the most time-consuming, yet worthwhile, part of your writing process. Most professional writers testify to the necessity and value of writing numerous drafts. When you are reworking a piece of writing, scrawling revisions over what you had hoped would be your finished product, remember what Nobel laureate Isaac Bashevis Singer once pointed out: "The wastepaper basket is the writer's best friend."

Writing with a Computer

Some students who are taking college writing courses have never used computers for writing essays or papers. If you are one of those students, don't panic. Most schools have computer laboratories with well-trained, knowledgeable staff who will help you learn how to write with a computer. Over the period of the

I don't see writing as communication of something already discovered, as "truths" already known. Rather, I see writing as a job of experiment. It's like any discovery job; you don't know what's going to happen until you try it.

—WILLIAM STAFFORD,
TEACHER, POET, AND ESSAYIST

The writing process is not linear, moving smoothly in one direction from start to finish. It is messy, recursive, convoluted, and uneven. Writers write, plan, revise, anticipate, and review throughout the writing process.

—MAXINE HAIRSTON,
TEACHER AND AUTHOR OF ARTICLES AND TEXTBOOKS ON WRITING

We must and do write each our own way.

—EUDORA WELTY,
NOVELIST AND ESSAYIST

semester, you'll become more comfortable at a keyboard and less worried when you press the wrong key or accidentally delete a sentence or paragraph. Gradually, you'll learn when you still want to use a pencil and paper and when you want to compose and revise on the computer. In the long run, the computer's revision capabilities and high-quality printing—not to mention its access to the Internet—will make your writing faster, easier, and more professional looking.

Many students, however, already have considerable experience with computers. They have written papers on personal computers. They have struggled through the frustration of learning to type, learning a word-processing program, and revising on a computer screen because they know the potential benefits are great. Now, they can create files for each of their courses or papers, and they know how to find information, draft, reorganize, revise, and edit their essays. If you are one of those students, you may learn how to make your writing even more efficient and productive by using your computer lab's updated equipment.

Usually, college computer writing laboratories or classrooms provide additional software programs to assist with the writing and revising processes. First, the lab computers may have some composing software—such as Blue Pencil, Writer's Helper, or Daedelus—that prompts writers to freewrite, brainstorm, dialogue, question, outline, organize, and revise. In addition, the lab computers have spelling checkers, thesauruses, and even style checkers to help with editing. Today, however, many college computer labs or classrooms have added two new capabilities that transform the computer from a writing machine into a high-tech communicating and information-gathering tool. These two technologies are *networks* and *hypertexts*.

For better or worse, less of me will remain unsaid because of the speed and ease and even intimacy of computer-assisted writing.

—PETER R. STILLMAN, TEACHER AND ESSAYIST

Networks are created when several computers are linked so that they can communicate with each other. Compared to a stand-alone computer, networked computers offer special advantages both within the writing classroom and outside the classroom. In the writing classroom or laboratory, writers can communicate with each other and with their teachers in a variety of ways. First, they can use electronic mail (e-mail) to send messages or even entire files to their peers or to teachers. Teachers and students can read drafts and offer suggestions while a student is revising. In addition, networked classrooms allow writers to send messages to or "chat" with each other on their computers, just as they might sit and talk across a table. Finally, most classrooms or labs have forums or electronic bulletin boards available for public comment and reaction. A writer can electronically send his or her essay draft to a bulletin board and have students in the class comment on his or her work-in-progress. If the class agrees, a writer's essay or his or her bulletin board comments can be anonymous or identified by a fictional name.

In addition to facilitating communication within a classroom, many computers can access the Internet and the World Wide Web in order to tap an incredible array of information sources across the campus and around the world. With immediate access to library on-line catalogs, writers don't have to make repeated trips

WRITING WITH COMPUTERS

The computer can assist you both as a writing tool and as a networking tool. Listed in the left-hand column are writing activities that a stand-alone computer provides. Listed in the right-hand column are the additional capabilities of computers tied into a network.

The Computer as a Writing Tool

- Freewriting
- Brainstorming
- Double-entry reading log
- Answers to "Wh" questions
- Insert/delete sentences
- Move paragraphs
- Style/usage checkers
- Thesaurus
- Spelling checker
- Print preview

The Computer as a Networking Tool

- Access to bulletin boards
- E-mail messages
- E-mail essays or files
- "Chat" dialogues
- Postings to Class Forum
- Access to on-line library catalogs
- Access to the Internet and the World Wide Web

across campus to the library to find information for their essays. In a few minutes, they can check the holdings of their library and—if they wish—the holdings of dozens of other libraries. In many cases, they can print out bibliographical information and even entire articles without leaving their computer. Overall, networked computers offer several key advantages for writers: They save time, paper, and printing costs; they give writers quick access to information; and they electronically reinforce the idea that a writing class is a supportive, interactive learning community.

■ **WARMING UP: JOURNAL EXERCISES**   The following exercises will help you review and practice the topics covered in this chapter. In addition, you may discover a subject for your own writing. Choose three of the following entries, and write for ten minutes on each.

1. Reread your "authority" list from Chapter 1. Choose one of those subjects and then explain your purpose and a possible audience for that subject.
2. Find a sample of writing from a magazine or newspaper article, an advertisement, a letter, or even graffiti on walls. What is the purpose of that writing? Who is the intended audience? Why is the writing effective or ineffective?
3. Read Neil Petrie's essay and postscript at the end of this chapter. Then find the best paper you've written during the past year or two and write a "postscript" for it. Describe (a) the writing situation, (b) your purpose, and (c) the process you used to write it.

4. If you have already been given a writing assignment in another course, explain the purpose and the intended audience for that assignment. What might be your process for writing that essay?
5. During the first week of the term, one of your friends, Mark Lindstrom, is in an accident and is hospitalized. While still under the effects of anesthesia, he scribbles the following note for you to mail to his parents.

> Dear Mom and Dad,
>
> I arrived here last week. The trip was terrible. Dr. Stevens says that my leg will be better soon. My roommate is very strange. The police say my money is gone forever.
>
> Please send $1,500 to my new address right away.
>
> Thanks!
>
> Your loving son
>
> Mark

Because you were at the accident and can fill in the details, Mark asks you to explain everything to his parents. Write a short letter to them. Next, write a paragraph to your best friend that describes what happened to Mark.

6. Explore the availability of computers on your campus. Where is the English Department computer lab? What services does it offer? What other computer facilities are available? Write up your report and post it on your class bulletin board or forum.

A Writing Process at Work: Collecting and Shaping

PROFESSIONAL WRITING

ATHLETES AND EDUCATION

Neil H. Petrie

In the following essay, which appeared in The Chronicle of Higher Education, *Neil H. Petrie argues that colleges have a hypocritical attitude toward student athletes. Although most universities claim that their athletes—both male and female—are in college to get a good education, in reality the pressures on athletes compromise their academic careers. The problem, Petrie argues, is not the old cliché that jocks are dumb, but the endless hours devoted to practice or spent on road trips, which drain even the good student-athlete's physical and mental energies. Colleges point with pride to a tiny number of athletes who become professionals, but much more frequently the collegiate system encourages athletes to settle for lower grades and incomplete programs. In far too many cases, athletes never graduate. These are the students whom, as Petrie says, "the system uses and then discards after the final buzzer."*

I have spent all my adult life in academe, first as a student and then as a professor. During that time I have seen many variations in the role of intercollegiate athletics in the university, and I've developed sharply split opinions on the subject. On one hand, I despise the system, clinging as it does to the academic body like a parasite. On the other hand, I feel sympathy and admiration for most of the young athletes struggling to balance the task of getting an education with the need to devote most of their energies to the excessive demands of the gym and the field. 1

My earliest experiences with the intrusion of athletics into the classroom came while I was still a freshman at the University of Colorado. While I was in my English professor's office one day, a colleague of hers came by for a chat. Their talk turned to the football coach's efforts to court the favor of the teachers responsible for his gladiators by treating them to dinner and a solicitous discussion of the academic progress of the players. I vividly recall my professor saying, "He can take me out to dinner if he wants, but if he thinks I'll pass his knuckleheads just because of that, he'd better think again." 2

Later, as a graduate teaching fellow, a lecturer, and then an assistant professor of English, I had ample opportunity to observe a Division I university's athletics program. I soon discovered that the prevailing stereotypes did not always apply. Athletes turned out to be as diverse as any other group of students in their habits, tastes, and abilities, and they showed a wide range of strategies for coping with the stress of their dual roles. 3

Some of them were poor students. An extreme example was the All-American football player (later a successful pro) who saw college only as a step to a six-figure contract and openly showed his disdain for the educational process. Others did such marginal work in my courses that I got the feeling they were daring me to give them D's or F's. One woman cross-country star, who almost never attended my composition class, used to push nearly illiterate essays under my office door at odd hours. 4

Yet many athletes were among the brightest students I had. Not so surprising, when you consider that, in addition to physical prowess, success in athletics requires intelligence, competitive drive, and dedication—all qualities that can translate into success in the classroom as well as on the field. The trouble is that the grinding hours of practice and road trips rob student athletes of precious study time and deplete their reserves of mental and physical energy. A few top athletes have earned A's; most are content to settle for B's or C's, even if they are capable of better.

The athletes' educational experience can't help being marred by their numerous absences and divided loyalties. In this respect, they are little different from the students who attempt to go to college while caring for a family or working long hours at an outside job. The athletes, however, get extra help in juggling their responsibilities. Although I have never been bribed or threatened and have never received a dinner invitation from a coach, I am expected to provide extra time and consideration for athletes, far beyond what I give other students.

Take the midterm grade reports, for example. At my university, the athletic department's academic counselor sends progress questionnaires to every teacher of varsity athletes. While the procedure shows admirable concern for the academic performance of athletes, it also amounts to preferential treatment. It requires teachers to take time from other teaching duties to fill out and return the forms for the athletes. (No other students get such progress reports.) If I were a cynic it would occur to me that the athletic department might actually be more concerned with athletes' eligibility than with their academic work.

Special attendance policies for athletes are another example of preferential treatment. Athletes miss a lot of classes. In fact, I think the road trip is one of the main reasons that athletes receive a deficient education. You simply can't learn as much away from the classroom and the library as on the campus. Nevertheless, professors continue to provide make-up tests, alternative assignments, and special tutoring sessions to accommodate athletes. Any other student would have to have been very sick or the victim of a serious accident to get such dispensations.

It is sad to see bright young athletes knowingly compromise their potential and settle for much less education than they deserve. It is infuriating, though, to see the ones less gifted academically exploited by a system that they do not comprehend and robbed of any possible chance to grow intellectually and to explore other opportunities.

One specific incident illustrates for me the worst aspects of college athletics. It wasn't unusual or extraordinary—just the all-too-ordinary case of an athlete not quite good enough to make a living from athletics and blind to the opportunity afforded by the classroom.

I was sitting in my office near the beginning of a term, talking to *11* a parade of new advisees. I glanced up to see my entire doorway filled with the bulk of a large young man, whom I recognized as one of our basketball stars from several seasons ago who had left for the pros and now apparently come back.

Over the next hour I got an intensive course on what it's like to *12* be a college athlete. In high school, John had never been interested in much outside of basketball, and, like many other indifferent students, he went on to junior college on an athletic scholarship. After graduating, he came to the university, where he played for two more years, finishing out his eligibility. He was picked in a late round of the N.B.A. draft and left college, but in the end he turned out to be a step too slow for the pros. By that time he had a family to support, and when he realized he could never make a career of basketball, he decided to return to college.

We both knew that his previous academic career hadn't been par- *13* ticularly focused, and that because of transferring and taking minimum course loads during the basketball season, he wouldn't be close to a degree. But I don't think either one of us was prepared for what actually emerged from our examination of his transcripts. It was almost as if he had never gone beyond high school. His junior-college transcript was filled with remedial and nonacademic courses.

Credit for those had not transferred to the university. Over the *14* next two years he had taken a hodgepodge of courses, mostly in physical education. He had never received any advice about putting together a coherent program leading to a degree. In short, the academic side of his college experience had been completely neglected by coaches, advisers, and, of course, John himself.

By the time we had evaluated his transcripts and worked out a ten- *15* tative course of study, John was in shock and I was angry. It was going to take him at least three years of full-time study to complete a degree. He thanked me politely for my time, picked up the planning sheets, and left. I was ashamed to be a part of the university that day. Why hadn't anyone in the athletic department ever told him what it would take to earn a degree? Or at least been honest enough to say, "Listen, we can keep you eligible and give you a chance to play ball, but don't kid yourself into thinking you'll be getting an education, too."

I saw John several more times during the year. He tried for a while. *16* He took classes, worked, supported his family, and then he left again. I lost track of him after that. I can only hope that he found a satisfying job or completed his education at some other institution. I know people say the situation has improved in the last few years, but when I read about the shockingly low percentages of athletes who graduate, I think of John.

Colleges give student athletes preferential treatment. We let them 17 cut classes. We let them slide through. We protect them from harsh realities. We applaud them for entertaining us and wink when they compromise themselves intellectually. We give them special dorms, special meals, special tutors, and a specially reprehensible form of hypocrisy.

I can live with the thought of the athletes who knowingly use the 18 college-athletics system to get their pro contracts or their devalued degrees. But I have trouble living with the thought of the ones whom the system uses and then discards after the final buzzer.

PROFESSIONAL WRITING

On Writing "Athletes and Education"

In the following postscript on his writing process, Neil Petrie describes why he wanted to write the paper, how he collected material to support his argument, and how he shaped and focused his ideas as he wrote. His comments illustrate how his purpose—to expose the hypocrisies of collegiate athletics—guided his writing of the essay. In addition, Petrie explains that other key questions affected the shape of his essay: how he should begin, where he should use his best example, and what words he should choose.

This essay has its origin, as all persuasive writing should, in a 1 strongly held opinion. I'm always more comfortable if I care deeply about my subject matter. As a teacher, I hold some powerful convictions about the uneasy marriage of big-time athletics and higher education, and so I wanted to write an essay that would expose what I think are the dangers and hypocrisies of that system.

At the beginning of my essay, I wanted to establish some author- 2 ity to lend credibility to my argument. Rather than gather statistics on drop-out rates of student athletes or collect the opinions of experts, I planned to rely on my own experiences as both a student and teacher. I hoped to convince my readers that my opinions were based on the authority of firsthand knowledge. In this introduction I was also aware of the need to avoid turning off readers who might dismiss me as a "jock hater." I had to project my negative feelings about the athletic system while maintaining my sympathy with the individual student ath-

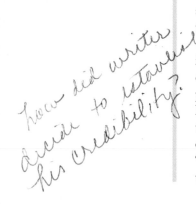
how did writer decide to establish his credibility?

letes involved in that system. The thesis, then, would emerge gradually as I accumulated the evidence; it would be more implied than explicitly stated.

Gathering the material was easy. I selected a series of examples 3 from my personal experiences as a college student and instructor, as well as anecdotes I'd heard from other instructors. Most of these stories were ones that I had shared before, either in private discussions with friends or in classrooms with students.

Shaping the material was a little tougher. As I began thinking 4 about my examples and how to order them, I saw that I really wanted to make two main points. The first was that most colleges give preferential treatment to athletes. The second point was that, despite the extra attention, the success of the athlete's academic career is often ignored by all parties involved. Many of my examples, I realized, illustrated the varieties of pressures put upon both athletes and instructors to make sure that the students at least get by in class and remain eligible. These examples seemed to cluster together because they showed the frustrations of teachers and the reactions of athletes trying to juggle sports and academics. This group would make a good introduction to my general exposé of the system. But I had one more example I wanted to use that seemed to go beyond the cynicism of some athletes or the hypocrisy of the educators. This was the case of John, an athlete who illustrated what I thought were the most exploitative aspects of varsity athletics. I originally planned on devoting the bulk of my essay to this story and decided to place it near the end where it would make my second point with maximum emotional effect.

A two-part structure for the essay now emerged. In the first seg- 5 ment following my introductory paragraph, I gave a series of shorter examples, choosing to order them in roughly chronological order (paragraphs 2–4). I then moved from these specific details to a more general discussion of the demands placed upon both students and teachers, such as lengthy practice time, grade reports, road trips, and special attendance policies. This concluded my description of the way the system operates (paragraphs 5–8).

Then it was time to shift gears, to provide a transition to the next 6 part of my essay, to what I thought was my strongest example. I wanted the story of John to show how the system destroyed human potential. To do this, I needed to increase the seriousness of the tone in order to persuade the reader that I was dealing in more than a little bureaucratic boondoggling. I tried to set the tone by my word choice: I moved from words such as "sad," "compromise," and "settle" to words with much stronger emotional connotations such as "infuriating,"

Saved strongest argument for last — most powerful position "exploited," and "robbed," all in a single short transitional paragraph (paragraph 9).

I then introduced my final extended example in equally strong language, identifying it as a worst-case illustration (paragraph 10). I elaborated on John's story, letting the details and my reactions to his situation carry the more intense outrage that I was trying to convey in this second part of the essay (paragraphs 10–16). The first version that I tried was a rambling narrative that had an overly long recounting of John's high school and college careers. So I tightened this section by eliminating such items as his progress through the ranks of professional basketball and his dreams of million-dollar contracts. I also cut down on a discussion of the various courses of study he was considering as options. The result was a sharper focus on the central issue of John's dilemma: the lack of adequate degree counseling for athletes.

7

After my extended example, all that was left was the conclusion. As I wrote, I was very conscious of using certain devices, such as the repetition of key words and sentence patterns in paragraph seventeen ("We let them . . . We let them . . . We protect them . . . We applaud them . . . We give them . . . ") to maintain the heightened emotional tone. I was also conscious of repeating the two-part structure of the essay in the last two paragraphs. I moved from general preferential treatment (paragraph 17) to the concluding and more disturbing idea of devastating exploitation (paragraph 18).

8

On the whole, I believe that this essay effectively conveys its point through the force of accumulated detail. My personal experience was the primary source of evidence, and that experience led naturally to the order of the paragraphs and to the argument I wished to make: that while some athletes knowingly use the system, others are used and exploited by it.

9

QUESTIONS FOR WRITING AND DISCUSSION

1. In your journal, describe how your extracurricular activities (athletics, jobs, clubs, or family obligations) have or have not interfered with your education. Recall one specific incident that illustrates how these activities affected your classwork—either positively or negatively.

2. Describe Petrie's audience and purpose for this essay. What sentences reveal his intended audience? What sentences reveal his purpose? What sentences contain his thesis, claim, or main idea? Do you agree with that thesis? Why or why not?

TAP'

3. Reread Petrie's postscript. Based on his comments and on your reading of the essay, how does Petrie describe or label each of the following sections of his essay:

paragraphs 1–4
paragraphs 5–8
paragraph 9
paragraphs 10–16
paragraphs 17–18.

4. Who do you think is most to blame for the situation that Petrie describes: The athletes themselves? The colleges for paying their scholarships and then ignoring them when they drop out? The students and alumni who pay to see their teams win?

5. Petrie does not explicitly suggest a solution to the problem that he describes. Assume, however, that he has been asked by the president of his university to propose a solution. Write the letter that you think Petrie would send to the president.

A Writing Process at Work: Drafting and Revising

While drafting and revising, writers frequently make crucial changes in their ideas and language. The first scribbled sentences, written primarily for ourselves, are often totally different from what we later present to other people in final, polished versions. Take, for example, the final version of Abraham Lincoln's Gettysburg Address. It begins with the famous lines "Four score and seven years ago our fathers brought forth on this continent a new nation . . . " But his first draft might well have begun, "Eighty-seven years ago, several politicians and other powerful men in the American Colonies got together and decided to start a new country . . . " It is difficult to imagine that language ingrained in our consciousness was once drafted, revised, drafted again, and edited, as the author or authors added, deleted, reordered, and otherwise altered words, sentences, and ideas. In fact, it usually was.

Carl Becker's study of the American Declaration of Independence assembles the early drafts of that famous document and compares them with the final version. Shown below is Thomas Jefferson's first draft, with revisions made by Benjamin Franklin, John Adams, and other members of the Committee of Five that was charged with developing the new document.

Thomas Jefferson's Rough Draft of the Opening Sentences of the Declaration of Independence

When in the course of human events it becomes necessary for ^*one* a people to dissolve the political bands which have connected them with another, and to ^~~advance from that subordination in which they have hitherto remained, & to~~ assume among the powers of the earth the ~~equal & independent~~ ^*separate and equal* station to which the laws of nature & of nature's god entitle them, a decent respect to the opinions of mankind requires that they should declare the causes which impel them to ^*the separation.* ~~the change.~~

We hold these truths ~~to be sacred & undeniable~~ ^*self-evident*; that all men are created equal ~~& independent~~; that ^*they are endowed by their creator with* ~~from that equal creation they derive in rights~~ inherent & inalienable ^*rights; that* among ~~which~~ ^*these* are ~~the preservation of~~ life, ~~&~~ liberty, & the pursuit of happiness. . . .

The Final Draft of the Opening Sentences of the Declaration of Independence, as Approved on July 4, 1776.

When in the Course of human events, it becomes necessary for one people to dissolve the political bands which have connected them with another, and to assume among the powers of the earth, the separate and equal station to which the Laws of Nature and of Nature's God entitle them, a decent respect to the opinions of mankind requires that they should declare the causes which impel them to the separation.

We hold these truths to be self-evident, that all men are created

equal, that they are endowed by their Creator with certain inalienable Rights,

that among these are Life, Liberty and the pursuit of Happiness.

QUESTIONS FOR WRITING AND DISCUSSION

1. Describe your reaction to the "rough draft" of the Declaration of Independence. Where did it seem strange or make you feel uncomfortable?

2. Select one change in a sentence that most improved the final version. Explain how the revised wording is more effective.

3. Find one change in a word or phrase that constitutes an alteration in meaning rather than just a choice of "smoother" or more appropriate language. How does this change affect the meaning?

4. Upon rereading this passage from the Declaration of Independence, one reader wrote, "I was really irritated by that 'all men are created equal' remark. The writers were white, free, well-to-do, Anglo-Saxon, mostly Protestant males discussing their own 'inalienable rights.' They sure weren't discussing the 'inalienable rights' of female Americans or of a million slaves or of nonwhite free Americans!" Revise the passage from the Declaration of Independence using this person as your audience.

5. On the Internet, visit the National Archives at www.nara.gov to see a photograph of the original Declaration of Independence and learn how the Dunlap Broadside of the Declaration was read aloud to troops. What does this historical context add to what you know about the Declaration of Independence? Do the revisions help make the document more revolutionary or propagandistic? In addition, this site has other treasures from the National Archives including the police blotter listing Abraham Lincoln's assassination, the first report of the *Titanic's* collision with an iceberg, and Rosa Parks's arrest records. Do you think these documents are as important to our history and culture as the Declaration itself? Explain.

Leonardo da Vinci. *Mona Lisa*. Louvre, Paris.

Chapter 3   Observing

In the far corner of a friend's living room is a lighted aquarium. Instead of water, the aquarium has a few inches of white sand, a dish of water, and a small piece of pottery. When you ask about the aquarium, your friend excitedly says, "You mean you haven't met Nino?" In a matter of seconds, you have a small, tannish-brown snake practically in your lap, and your friend is saying, "This is Nino. She—or he—is an African sand boa." You imagined that all boa constrictors were those huge snakes that suffocated and then swallowed babies. "Actually," replies your friend, "Nino is very shy. She prefers to burrow in the sand." The snake is fascinating. It is only fifteen inches long, with a strong, compact body and a stub tail. Before it burrows into your coat pocket, you observe it closely so you can describe it to your younger brother, who loves all kinds of snakes.

In the physics laboratory, you're doing an experiment on light refraction. You need to observe how light rays bend as they go through water, so you take notes describing the procedure and the results. During each phase of the experiment, you observe and record the angles of refraction. The data and your notes will help you write up the lab report that is due next Monday.

My task . . . is, by the power of the written word, to make you hear, to make you feel—it is, before all, to make you see.
—JOSEPH CONRAD,
AUTHOR OF HEART OF DARKNESS AND OTHER NOVELS

Seeing is of course very much a matter of verbalization. Unless I call my attention to what passes before my eyes, I simply won't see it.
—ANNIE DILLARD,
NATURALIST AND AUTHOR OF PILGRIM AT TINKER CREEK

BSERVING IS ESSENTIAL TO GOOD WRITING. WHETHER YOU ARE
WRITING IN A JOURNAL, DOING A LABORATORY REPORT FOR A
SCIENCE CLASS, OR WRITING A LETTER TO THE EDITOR OF A
newspaper, keen observation is essential. Writing or verbalizing
what you see helps you discover and learn more about your environment. Sometimes your purpose is limited to yourself: You observe and record to help you understand your world or yourself better. At other times, your purpose extends to
a wider audience: You want to share what you have learned with others to help
them learn as well. No matter who your audience is or what your subject may
be, however, your task is to see and to help your readers see.

Of course, observing involves more than just "seeing." Good writers draw
on all their senses: sight, smell, touch, taste, hearing. In addition, however, experienced writers also notice what is *not* there. The smell of food that should
be coming from the kitchen but isn't. A friend who usually is present but now
is absent. The absolute quiet in the air that precedes an impending storm.
Writers should also look for *changes* in their subjects—from light to dark, from
rough to smooth, from bitter to sweet, from noise to sudden silence. Good
writers learn to use their previous *experiences* and their *imaginations* to draw
comparisons and create images. Does a sea urchin look and feel like a pincush-
ion with the pins stuck in the wrong way? Does the room feel as cramped and
airless as the inside of a microwave oven? Finally, good writers write from a
specific point of view or role: a student describing basic laws of physics or an
experienced worker in a mental health clinic describing the clientele.

Depending on your purpose and audience, writing from observation can be relatively *objective*, as when you record what is actually, demonstrably there; or it can
be more *subjective*, as when you suggest how you feel, think, or react to a subject.
For example, you might describe a bicycle objectively as a "secondhand blue Bridge-
stone MB-3 mountain bike with a 25-inch Ritchey Logic frame, Shimano Deore
DX derailleurs, a Shimano crank, Dia Compe brakes, and an Avocet saddle." You
might need to communicate that kind of objective information to a prospective
buyer or to an employee in a cycle repair shop. On the other hand, you may wish
to communicate the bicycle's subjective feel—how easily it pedals; how it cranks up
steep, rocky trails; or how solid it feels on rough terrain. In most situations, however, good writers describe their subjects both objectively and subjectively. They
use some objectivity for accuracy and specific detail and some subjectivity to suggest the value or relevance of their subjects in a human environment.

The key to effective observing is to *show* your reader the person, place,
event, or object through *specific detail*. Good description allows the reader to
draw general conclusions based on specific detail. If your reader is going to learn

from your observations, you need to give the *exact details that you learned from*, not just your conclusions or generalizations. Even in writing, experience is the best teacher, so use specific details to communicate the feel, the data, the sights and sounds and smells. Whether you are a tourist describing the cliff dwellings at Mesa Verde, a salesperson analyzing consumer preferences for your boss, a physicist presenting data on a new superconducting material to other physicists, or a social worker putting together the details of a child abuse case, your first task is to describe your subject—to show your readers, to make them *see*.

Techniques for Writing About Observations

The short passages that follow all use specific techniques for observing people, places, objects, or events. Some emphasize objective detail; some recreate subjective reactions or feelings. In all the passages, however, the writer *narrows* or *limits* the scope of the observation and selects specific details. The result is some *dominant idea*. The dominant idea reflects the writer's purpose for that particular audience. As you read these excerpts, notice how the authors use the following six techniques for recording vivid observations:

- **Giving sensory details (sight, sound, smell, touch, taste).** Also include *actual dialogue* and *names of things* where appropriate. Good writers often "zoom in" on crucial details.
- **Using comparisons and images.** To help readers visualize the unfamiliar (or see the commonplace in a new light), writers often draw comparisons and use evocative images.
- **Describing what is *not* there.** Sometimes keen observation requires stepping back and noticing what is absent, what is not happening, or who is not present.
- **Noting changes in the subject's form or condition.** Even when the subject appears static—a landscape, a flower, a building—good writers look for evidence of changes, past or future: a tree being enveloped by tent worms, a six-inch purple-and-white iris that eight hours earlier was just a green bud, a sandstone exterior of a church being eroded by acid rain.
- **Writing from a distinct point of view.** Good writers assume distinct roles; in turn, perspective helps clarify what they observe. A lover and a botanist, for example, see entirely different things in the same red rose. *What* is seen depends on *who* is doing the seeing.
- **Focusing on a dominant idea.** Good writers focus on those details and images that clarify the main ideas or discoveries. Discovery often depends on the *contrast* between the reality and the writer's expectations.

The real voyage of discovery consists not in seeking new landscapes but in having new eyes.
—**MARCEL PROUST**
AUTHOR OF REMEMBRANCE OF THINGS PAST

. . . Not that it's raining, but the feel of being rained upon.
—**E. L. DOCTOROW,**
AUTHOR OF RAGTIME AND OTHER NOVELS

These six techniques are illustrated in the following two paragraphs by Karen Blixen, who wrote *Out of Africa* under the pen name Isak Dinesen. A Danish woman who moved to Kenya to start a coffee plantation, Blixen knew little about the animals in Kenya Reserve. In this excerpt from her journals, she describes a startling change that occurred when she shot a large iguana. (The annotations in the margin identify all six observing techniques.)

Role: a newcomer to the Reserve

Comparisons and images

Sensory details
Comparisons and images

In the Reserve I have sometimes come upon the Iguana, the big lizards, as they were sunning themselves upon a flat stone in a riverbed. They are not pretty in shape, but nothing can be imagined more beautiful than their coloring. They shine like a heap of precious stones or like a pane cut out of an old church window. When, as you approach, they swish away, there is a flash of azure, green and purple over the stones, the color seems to be standing behind them in the air, like a comet's luminous tail.

Changes in condition
Sensory detail

What is not there
Dominant idea: now colorless and dead

Once I shot an Iguana. I thought that I should be able to make some pretty things from his skin. A strange thing happened then, that I have never afterwards forgotten. As I went up to him, where he was lying dead upon his stone, and actually while I was walking the few steps, he faded and grew pale, all color died out of him as in one long sigh, and by the time that I touched him he was grey and dull like a lump of concrete. It was the live impetuous blood pulsating within the animal, which had radiated out all that glow and splendor. Now that the flame was put out, and the soul had flown, the Iguana was as dead as a sandbag.

OBSERVING PEOPLE

Observing people—their dress, facial features, body language, attitudes, behavior, skills, quirks, habits, and conversation—is a pastime that we all share. When writers describe people, however, they zero in on specific details that fit overall patterns or impressions. In an *Esquire* magazine article, for example, Joseph Nocera profiles Steven Jobs, the cocreator of the Apple and Macintosh computers and the ex-chairman of the board of Apple Computer. All of Nocera's details reinforce his dominant idea that Steven Jobs is a temperamental boy genius.

With personal computers so ubiquitous today, you tend to forget that . . . the Apple II, the machine that began it all, was unleashed upon an unsuspecting world in 1977. You forget, that is, until you sit in a room full of people who have built them and realize how young they are. Jobs himself is only thirty-one. If anything, he looks younger. He is lithe and wiry. He is wearing faded jeans (no belt), a white cotton shirt (perfectly pressed), and a pair of brown suede wing-tipped shoes. There is a bounce to his step that betrays a certain youthful cockiness; the quarterback of your high school football team used to walk that way. His thin, handsome face does not even appear to need a daily shave. And that impression of eternal youth is reinforced by some guileless, almost childlike traits: by the way, for instance, he can't resist showing off his brutal, withering intelligence whenever he's around someone he doesn't think measures up. Or by his almost willful lack of tact. Or by his inability to hide his boredom when he is forced to endure something that doesn't interest him, like a sixth grader who can't wait for class to end.

Role: writer as an outsider looks objectively at Jobs, is probably older
Dominant idea: youth
Sensory detail: visual description
Comparison and image
What is not there: facial hair
What is not there: tact
Comparison

OBSERVING PLACES

In the following passage, John Muir describes California and the Yosemite Valley as it looked over 130 years ago. John Muir, of course, was the founder of the Sierra Club, whose first mission was to preserve the vision of Yosemite that Muir paints in the following paragraphs. Notice how Muir uses all of the key techniques for observing as he vividly describes the California Sierra.

Arriving by the Panama steamer, I stopped one day in San Francisco and then inquired for the nearest way out of town. "But where do you want to go?" asked the man to whom I had applied for this important information. "To any place that is wild," I said. This reply startled him. He seemed to fear I might be crazy and therefore the sooner I was out of town the better, so he directed me to the Oakland ferry.

So on the first of April, 1868, I set out afoot for Yosemite. It was the bloom-time of the year over the lowlands and coast ranges; the landscapes of the Santa Clara Valley were fairly drenched with sunshine, all the air was quivering with the songs of the meadow-larks, and the hills were so covered with flowers that they seemed to be painted. Slow indeed was my progress through these glorious gardens, the first of the California flora I had seen. Cattle and cultivation were making few scars as yet, and I wandered enchanted in long wavering curves, knowing by my pocket map that Yosemite Valley lay to the east and that I should surely find it.

Looking eastward from the summit of the Pacheco Pass one shining morning, a landscape was displayed that after all my wanderings still appears as the most beautiful I have ever beheld. At my feet lay the Great Central Valley of California, level and flowery, like a lake of pure sunshine, forty or fifty miles wide, five hundred miles long, one rich furred garden of yellow *Compositae*. And from the eastern boundary of this vast golden flower-bed rose the mighty Sierra, miles in height, and so gloriously colored and so radiant, it seemed not clothed with light, but wholly composed of it, like the wall of some celestial city. Along the top and extending a good way down, was a rich pearl-gray belt of snow; below it a belt of blue and dark purple, marking the extension of the forests; and stretching along the base of the range a broad belt of rose-purple; all these colors, from the blue sky to the yellow valley smoothly blending as they do in a rainbow, making a wall of light ineffably fine. Then it seemed to me that the Sierra should be called, not the Nevada or Snowy Range, but the Range of Light.

In general views no mark of man is visible upon it, nor anything to suggest the wonderful depth and grandeur of its sculpture. None of its magnificent forest-crowned ridges seems to rise much above the general level to publish its wealth. No great valley or river is seen, or group of well-marked features of any kind standing out as distinct pictures. Even the summit peaks, marshaled in glorious array so high in the sky, seem comparatively regular in form. Nevertheless the whole range five hundred miles long is furrowed with canyons 2,000 to 5,000 feet deep, in which once flowed majestic glaciers, and in which now flow and sing the bright rejoicing rivers.

OBSERVING OBJECTS

In observing an inanimate object such as a cookie, Paul Goldberger—architecture critic for *The New York Times*—brings his special point of view to his description. He totally ignores the cookie's taste, ingredients, and calories, focusing instead on the architectural relationships of function and form. Goldberger's architectural perspective helps focus his observations, creating a dominant idea for each passage.

Sugar Wafer (Nabisco) There is no attempt to imitate the ancient forms of traditional, individually baked cookies here—this is a modern cookie through and through. Its simple rectangular form, clean and pure, just reeks of mass production and modern technological methods. The two wafers, held together by the sugar-cream filling, appear to float . . . this is a machine-age object.

Fig Newton (Nabisco) This, too, is a sandwich but different in every way from the Sugar Wafer. Here the imagery is more traditional, more sensual even; a rounded form of cookie dough arcs over the fig concoction inside, and the whole is soft and pliable. Like all good pieces of design, it has an appropriate form for its use, since the insides of Fig Newtons can ooze and would not be held in place by a more rigid form. The thing could have had a somewhat different shape, but the rounded tip is a comfortable, familiar image, and it's easy to hold. Not a revolutionary object but an intelligent one.

OBSERVING EVENTS

Observing events requires weaving specific details about people, places, and objects into some chronological order, as in the following account of a rhythm-and-blues performance by Bobby "Blue" Bland. The paragraph, taken from Peter Guralnick's *Lost Highway: Journeys & Arrivals of American Musicians,* demonstrates how vivid, specific details (names of singers, a description of barefoot dancing, titles of songs, the recording of actual dialogue and lyrics) create a dominant idea: a single night's performance blurs into an endless series of one-night stands.

Every night it is exactly the same. The band, a brass-heavy ten pieces with dilapidated reading stands that say "Mel Jackson/MFs Bobby Bland's Revue," does a desultory thirty-minute set. Then Burnett Williams, singer, valet, bus driver, and all-around good fellow, swings affably into a succession of Al Green numbers and current soul hits. The band plays dispiritedly behind him; even the bandleader, Mel Jackson, has disappeared from the stand; but Burnett always works up a sweat, finishing out his segment with shoes kicked off, doing the barefoot to the strains of "Love and Happiness." This invariably cracks up Mel Jackson, who reappears precisely at this point, dapper, diminutive, very much in charge. His eyes gleam and dart skittishly about the room as he laughs out loud, proclaims, "That boy doing some barefooting!" and gives Burnett a soul slap and quick little hug as the warm-up singer departs from the stage, his shoes held delicately aloft. Then it's Show Time, Ladies and Gentlemen, a Young Man Who Needs No Introduction, he'll Take Care of You, Further on Up the Road, won't let you Cry No More, cause when you Cry Cry Cry he just wants to Turn On Your Lovelights, well he's a Good-Time Charlie, and You're the One (That He Adores), but now The Feeling is Gone and he's

Two steps From the Blues. The string of hits becomes a litany, a numbing incantation. Audience talk becomes louder and more distracted, and then Bobby "Blue" Bland appears, big shambling, sleepy-eyed, a cigarette between his fingers, tongue licking at the edge of his lips. He plays aimlessly for a moment with the microphone, his eyes cast upwards as if for inspiration, the band kicks off, and that smooth, mellow, almost hornlike voice slides in among the three trumpets, trombone, and saxophone (guitar, bass, two drummers, and occasionally a piano round out the band). "I pity the fool/I pity the fool that falls in love with you. . . ." It is ten-thirty, and Bobby "Blue" Bland is just going to work.

■ WARMING UP: JOURNAL EXERCISES   The following topics will help you practice close, detailed observation and may possibly suggest a subject for your assignment on observing. Read the following exercises and then write on the two or three that interest you the most.

1. Go to a public place (library, bar, restaurant, hospital emergency room, gas station, laundromat, park, shopping mall, hotel lobby, police station, beach, skating rink, beauty salon, city dump, tennis court, church, etc.). Sit and observe everything around you. Use your pencil to help you see, both by drawing sketches and by recording sensory details in words. What do you see that you haven't noticed before? Then *narrow* your attention to a single person, *focus* on a restricted place, or *zoom* in on a single object. What do you see that you haven't noticed before?

2. Find a place where people (either friends or strangers) are talking (over lunch, at a bar, at a party). For ten or fifteen minutes, record the conversation word for word. To keep friends from being self-conscious, tell them that you're doing homework. If you're eavesdropping on strangers, be as inconspicuous as possible. Your purpose is to record as much of the dialogue as possible, with the pauses, interruptions, *uh*s and *er*s, unfinished sentences, slang—everything *exactly* as you hear it.

3. In one of your classes, use your repeated observations of the total learning environment (the room, the seating arrangements, the blackboards, the audiovisual or computer equipment, the teacher, the daily teaching or learning rituals, and the students) to speculate on who has authority, how knowledge is created or communicated, and what the learning goals are for this course.

4. *Obnoxious*, the dictionary says, means "highly disagreeable, offensive, irritating, odious." Describe the most obnoxious person you know by giving at least two detailed examples of his or her behavior. Or do just the reverse: Tell how the most obnoxious person you know would describe you.

5. Go to a gallery, studio, or museum where you can observe sculpture, paintings, or other works of art. Choose one work of art and draw it. Then describe it as fully as possible. Return to the gallery the next day, reread your first description, observe the work again, and add details that you didn't notice the first time.

6. Visit a local park. Pretend that you are a landscape architect, a photographer, a bird-watcher, an entomologist, an engineer building a road, a jogger, or a mother with two small children. Describe what you see. Now choose another role—you're a social worker, a woman alone in a park at night, a person without a home, a Secret Service agent assigned to protect the president of the United States, a Saint Bernard, or a sixth-grader just out of school for the day. Describe what you see. Then reread both descriptions. Compare them. Briefly, explain how and why they are similar or dissimilar.

7. Each of the chapters in this textbook begins with a piece of art. The "Observing" chapter, for example, reprints the famous painting by Leonardo da Vinci, *Mona Lisa*. Choose one of the paintings at the beginning of a chapter. Describe the picture in detail. Follow Scudder's advice about *repeated observation*. Based on specific details that you observe, what general conclusions can you draw about this painting?

8. After the September 11, 2001, attack on the World Trade Center, Robin Morgan wrote the following description of ground zero. The author of *Saturday's Child: A Memoir* (2001), Robin Morgan is a prolific writer of poetry, essays, and feminist tracts. Read the following excerpt from her posting to the Internet on September 18, 2001. What sensory details, statistics, and images help make her description so vivid and memorable? What memories of your own about September 11 does her description bring back?

I'll focus on New York—my firsthand experience—but this doesn't mean any less anguish for the victims of the Washington or Pennsylvania calamities. Today was Day 8. Incredibly, a week has passed. Abnormal normalcy has settled in. Our usually contentious mayor (previously bad news for New Yorkers of color and for artists) has risen to this moment with efficiency, compassion, real leadership. The city is alive and dynamic. Below 14th Street, traffic is flowing again, mail is being delivered, newspapers are back. But very early this morning I walked east, then south almost to the tip of Manhattan Island . The 16-acre site itself is closed off, of course, as is a perimeter surrounding it controlled by the National Guard, used as a command post and staging area for rescue workers. Still, one is able to approach nearer to the area than was possible last weekend, since the law-court district and parts of the financial district are now open and (shakily) working. The closer one gets the more one sees—and smells—what no TV report, and very few print reports, have communicated. I find myself giving way to tears again and again, even as I write this.

If the first sights of last Tuesday seemed bizarrely like a George Lucas special-effects movie, now the directorial eye has changed: it's the grim lens of Agnes Varda, juxtaposed with images so surreal they could have been framed by Buñuel or Kurosawa.

This was a bright, cloudless, early autumnal day. But as one draws near the site, the area looms out of a dense haze: one enters an atmosphere of dust, concrete powder, and plumes of smoke from fires still raging deep beneath the rubble (an estimated 2 million cubic yards of debris). Along lower 2nd Avenue, 10 refrigerator tractor-trailer trucks are parked, waiting; if you stand there a while, an NYC Medical Examiner van arrives—with a sagging body bag. Thick white ash, shards of broken glass, pebbles, and chunks of concrete cover street after street of parked cars for blocks outside the perimeter. Handprints on car windows and doors—handprints sliding downward—have been left like frantic graffiti. Sometimes there are messages finger-written in the ash: "U R Alive." You can look into closed shops, many with cracked or broken windows, and peer into another dimension: a wall-clock stopped at 9:10, restaurant tables meticulously set but now covered with two inches of ash, grocery shelves stacked with cans and produce bins piled high with apples and melons—all now powdered chalk-white. A moonscape of plenty. People walk unsteadily along these streets, wearing nosemasks against the still particle-full air, the stench of burning wire and plastic, erupted sewage; the smell of death, of decomposing flesh.

Probably your TV coverage shows the chain-link fences aflutter with yellow ribbons, the makeshift shrines of candles, flowers, scribbled notes of mourning or of praise for the rescue workers that have sprung up everywhere—especially in front of firehouses, police stations, hospitals. What TV doesn't show you is that near Ground Zero the streets for blocks around are still, a week later, adrift in bits of paper—singed, torn, sodden pages: stock reports, trading print-outs, shreds of appointment calendars, half of a "To-Do" list. What TV doesn't show you are scores of tiny charred corpses; now swept into the gutters. Sparrows. Finches. They fly higher than pigeons, so they would have exploded outward, caught midair in a rush of flame, wings on fire as they fell. Who could have imagined it: the birds were burning.

From a distance, you can see the lattices of one of the Towers, its skeletal bones the sole remains, eerily beautiful in asymmetry, as if a new work of abstract art had been erected in a public space. Elsewhere, you see the transformation of institutions: The New School and New York University are missing persons' centers. A movie house is now a rest shelter, a Burger King a first-aid center, a Brooks Brother's clothing store a body parts morgue, a record shop a haven for lost animals. Libraries are counseling centers. Ice rinks are morgues. A bank is now a supply depot: in the first four days, it distributed 11,000 respirators and 25,000 pairs of protective gloves and suits. Nearby, a mobile medical unit housed in a Macdonald's has administered 70,000 tetanus shots. The brain tries to process the numbers "only" 50,000 tons of debris had been cleared by yesterday, out of 1.2 million tons. The medical examiner's office has readied up to 20,000 DNA tests for unidentifiable cadaver parts. At all times, night and day, a minimum of 1000 people live and work on the site.

Such numbers daze the mind. It's the details—fragile, individual—that melt numbness into grief. An anklet with "Joyleen" engraved on it—found on an ankle. Just that: an ankle. A pair of hands—one brown, one white—clasped together. Just that. No wrists. A burly welder who drove from Ohio to help, saying softly, " We're working in a cemetery. I'm standing in—not on, in— a graveyard." Each lamppost, storefront, scaffolding, mailbox, is plastered with homemade photocopied posters, a racial/ethnic rainbow of faces and names: death the great leveler, not only of the financial CEOs—their images usually formal, white, male, older, with suit-and-tie—but the mailroom workers, receptionists, waiters. You pass enough of the MISSING posters and the faces, names, descriptions become familiar. The Albanian window-cleaner guy with the bushy eyebrows. The teenage Mexican dishwasher who had an American flag tattoo. The janitor's assistant who'd emigrated from Ethiopia. The Italian-American grandfather who was a doughnut-cart tender. The 23-year-old Chinese American junior pastry chef at the Windows on the World restaurant who'd gone in early that day so she could prep a business breakfast for 500. The firefighter who'd posed jauntily wearing his green shamrock necktie. The dapper African-American midlevel manager with a small gold ring in his ear who handled "minority affairs" for one of the companies. The middle-aged secretary laughing up at the camera from her wheelchair. The maintenance worker with a Polish name, holding his newborn baby. Most of the faces are smiling; most of the shots are family photos; many are recent wedding pictures. . . .

I have little national patriotism, but I do have a passion for New York, partly for our gritty, secular energy of endurance, and because the world does come here: 80 countries had offices in the Twin Towers; 62 countries lost citizens in the catastrophe; an estimated 300 of our British cousins died, either in the planes or the buildings. My personal comfort is found not in ceremonies or prayer services but in watching the plain, truly heroic (a word usually misused) work of ordinary New Yorkers we take for granted every day, who have risen to this moment unpretentiously, too busy to even notice they're expressing the splendor of the human spirit: fire fighters, medical aides, nurses, ER doctors, police officers, sanitation workers, construction-workers, ambulance drivers, structural engineers, crane operators, rescue worker "tunnel rats." . . .

PROFESSIONAL WRITING

Take This Fish and Look at It

Samuel H. Scudder

In this essay, Samuel H. Scudder (1837–1911), an American entomologist, narrates his early attempts at scientific observation. Scudder recalls how a famous Swiss naturalist, Louis Agassiz, taught him the skills of observation by having him examine a fish—a haemulon or snapper—closely, carefully, and repeatedly. Agassiz, a professor of natural history at Harvard, taught his students that both factual details and general laws are important. "Facts are stupid things," he said, "until brought into connection with some general law." Scudder, writing about his studies under Agassiz, suggests that repeated observation can help us connect facts or specific details with general laws. The essay shows us an important lesson that Scudder learned: To help us see, describe, and connect, "A pencil is one of the best of eyes."

It was more than fifteen years ago that I entered the laboratory of Professor Agassiz, and told him I had enrolled my name in the Scientific School as a student of natural history. He asked me a few

1

questions about my object in coming, my antecedents generally, the mode in which I afterwards proposed to use the knowledge I might acquire, and, finally, whether I wished to study any special branch. To the latter I replied that, while I wished to be well grounded in all departments of zoology, I purposed to devote myself specially to insects.

"When do you wish to begin?" he asked.   *2*

"Now," I replied.   *3*

This seemed to please him, and with an energetic "Very well!" he *4* reached from a shelf a huge jar of specimens in yellow alcohol. "Take this fish," he said, "and look at it; we call it a haemulon; by and by I will ask what you have seen."

With that he left me, but in a moment returned with explicit in- *5* structions as to the care of the object entrusted to me.

"No man is fit to be a naturalist," said he, "who does not know *6* how to take care of specimens."

I was to keep the fish before me in a tin tray, and occasionally *7* moisten the surface with alcohol from the jar, always taking care to replace the stopper tightly. Those were not the days of ground-glass stoppers and elegantly shaped exhibition jars; all the old students will recall the huge neckless glass bottles with their leaky, wax-besmeared corks, half eaten by insects, and begrimed with cellar dust. Entomology was a cleaner science than ichthyology, but the example of the Professor, who had unhesitatingly plunged to the bottom of the jar to produce the fish, was infectious; and though this alcohol had a "very ancient and fishlike smell," I really dared not show any aversion within these sacred precincts, and treated the alcohol as though it were pure water. Still I was conscious of a passing feeling of disappointment, for gazing at a fish did not commend itself to an ardent entomologist. My friends at home, too, were annoyed when they discovered that no amount of eau-de-Cologne would drown the perfume which haunted me like a shadow.

In ten minutes I had seen all that could be seen in that fish, and *8* started in search of the Professor—who had, however, left the Museum; and when I returned, after lingering over some of the odd animals stored in the upper apartment, my specimen was dry all over. I dashed the fluid over the fish as if to resuscitate the beast from a fainting fit, and looked with anxiety for a return of the normal sloppy appearance. This little excitement over, nothing was to be done but to return to a steadfast gaze at my mute companion. Half an hour passed—an hour—another hour; the fish began to look loathsome. I turned it over and around; looked it in the face—ghastly; from behind, beneath, above, sideways, at three-quarter's view—just as ghastly, I was in despair; at an early hour I concluded that lunch was necessary; so, with infinite relief, the fish was carefully replaced in the jar, and for an hour I was free.

On my return, I learned that Professor Agassiz had been at the Museum, but had gone, and would not return for several hours. My fellow-students were too busy to be disturbed by continued conversation. Slowly I drew forth that hideous fish, and with a feeling of desperation again looked at it. I might not use a magnifying-glass; instruments of all kinds were interdicted. My two hands, my two eyes, and the fish: it seemed a most limited field. I pushed my finger down its throat to feel how sharp the teeth were. I began to count the scales in the different rows, until I was convinced that was nonsense. At last a happy thought struck me—I would draw the fish; and now with surprise I began to discover new features in the creature. Just then the Professor returned. *9*

"That is right," said he; "a pencil is one of the best of eyes. I am glad to notice, too, that you keep your specimen wet, and your bottle corked." *10*

With these encouraging words, he added: "Well, what is it like?" *11*

He listened attentively to my brief rehearsal of the structure of parts whose names were still unknown to me: the fringed gill-arches and movable operculum; the pores of the head, fleshy lips and lidless eyes; the lateral line, the spinous fins and forked tail; the compressed and arched body. When I finished, he waited as if expecting more, and then, with an air of disappointment: *12*

"You have not looked very carefully; why," he continued more earnestly, "you haven't even seen one of the most conspicuous features of the animal, which is plainly before your eyes as the fish itself; look again, look again!" and he left me to my misery. *13*

I was piqued; I was mortified. Still more of that wretched fish! But now I set myself to my task with a will, and discovered one new thing after another, until I saw how just the Professor's criticism had been. The afternoon passed quickly; and when, towards its close, the Professor inquired: *14*

"Do you see it yet?" *15*

"No," I replied, "I am certain I do not, but I see how little I saw before." *16*

"That is next best," said he, earnestly, "but I won't hear you now; put away your fish and go home; perhaps you will be ready with a better answer in the morning. I will examine you before you look at the fish." *17*

This was disconcerting. Not only must I think of my fish all night, studying, without the object before me, what this unknown but most visible feature might be; but also, without reviewing my discoveries, I *18* must give an exact account of them the next day. I had a bad memory; so I walked home by Charles River in a distracted state, with my two perplexities.

The cordial greeting from the Professor the next morning was reassuring; here was a man who seemed to be quite as anxious as I that I should see for myself what he saw. *19*

"Do you perhaps mean," I asked, "that the fish has symmetrical sides with paired organs?" *20*

His thoroughly pleased "Of course! Of course!" repaid the wakeful hours of the previous night. After he had discoursed most happily and enthusiastically—as he always did—upon the importance of this point, I ventured to ask what I should do next. *21*

"Oh, look at your fish!" he said, and left me again to my own devices. In a little more than an hour he returned, and heard my new catalogue. *22*

"That is good, that is good!" he repeated; "but that is not all; go on"; and so for three long days he placed that fish before my eyes, forbidding me to look at anything else, or to use any artificial aid. "Look, look, look," was his repeated injunction. *23*

This was the best entomological lesson I ever had—a lesson whose influence has extended to the details of every subsequent study; a legacy the Professor had left to me, as he has left it to so many others, of inestimable value, which we could not buy, with which we cannot part. *24*

A year afterward, some of us were amusing ourselves with chalking outlandish beasts on the Museum blackboard. We drew prancing starfishes; frogs in mortal combat; hydra-headed worms, stately crawfishes with gaping mouths and staring eyes. The Professor came in shortly after, and was as amused as any at our experiments. He looked at the fishes. *25*

"Haemulons, every one of them," he said; "Mr. _____ drew them." *26*

True; and to this day, if I attempt a fish, I can draw nothing but haemulons. *27*

The fourth day, a second fish of the same group was placed beside the first, and I was bidden to point out the resemblances and differences between the two; another and another followed, until the entire family lay before me, and a whole legion of jars covered the table and surrounding shelves; the odor had become a pleasant perfume; and even now, the sight of an old, six-inch worm-eaten cork brings fragrant memories. *28*

The whole group of haemulons was thus brought in review; and whether engaged upon the dissection of the internal organs, the preparation and examination of the bony framework, or the description of *29* the various parts, Agassiz's training in the method of observing facts and their orderly arrangement was ever accompanied by the urgent exhortation not to be content with them.

"Facts are stupid things," he would say, "until brought into connection with some general law."   *30*

At the end of eight months, it was almost with reluctance that I left these friends and turned to insects; but what I had gained by this outside experience has been of greater value than years of later investigation in my favorite groups.   *31*

VOCABULARY

In your journal, write down the meanings of the following words:

- my *antecedents* generally **(1)**
- *Entomology* was a cleaner science than *ichthyology* **(7)**
- dared not show any *aversion* **(7)**
- to *resuscitate* the beast **(8)**
- instruments of all kinds were *interdicted* **(9)**
- movable *operculum* **(12)**
- I was *piqued* **(14)**
- with my two *perplexities* **(18)**
- his repeated *injunction* **(23)**
- *hydra-headed* worms **(25)**
- the urgent *exhortation* **(29)**

QUESTIONS FOR WRITING AND DISCUSSION

1. If you have taken any science classes with laboratory sections, describe any observing techniques you used while completing the lab assignments. What were you asked to observe? What were you asked to record? How were these sessions similar to or different from Scudder's experience? Explain.

2. Follow Professor Agassiz's advice about observing: Without looking again at the essay, record in writing what you found to be the most memorable parts of the essay. What parts seemed most vivid? Explain.

3. Apply Scudder's technique of *repeated observation* to his own essay. Read the essay a second time, carefully, looking for techniques for recording observations. Use a pencil to help you read, by underlining or making brief notes. What do you notice on the *second* reading that you did not see in the first?

4. What is the purpose of this essay? To inform us about fish? To explain how to learn about fish? To persuade us to follow Professor Agassiz's method? To entertain us with college stories? In your estimation what is the primary purpose?

5. Describe the intended audience for this essay. Which *sentences* most clearly address the intended audience?

6. "Facts are stupid things," Agassiz says, "until brought into connection with some general law." Reread paragraph 8. What is the "general law" about scientific observation—or, in this case, the *dominant idea*—created by the specific details describing Scudder's first session with his fish? Explain.

7. On the Internet, access a biography of Louis Agassiz at http://www.ucmp.berkeley.edu/history/agassiz.html. Does this biography explain why Agassiz was one of the scientists who paved the way for Darwin's discoveries but also attacked Darwin's theory of evolution? Should Agassiz's discoveries be discredited because he did not agree with Darwin?

8. Connect Scudder's techniques to those in the other essays you are reading in this chapter. Does Farley Mowat use repeated observation to make an important discovery? What does Barbara Kingsolver discover about her hermit crab by observing closely and attentively? In your own essay, how can you use Scudder's or Agassiz's advice to make your descriptions more vivid or insightful?

PROFESSIONAL WRITING

HIGH TIDE IN TUCSON
Barbara Kingsolver

Barbara Kingsolver was born in 1955 in Annapolis, Maryland, and received degrees in biology and science from DePauw University (B.A., 1977) and the University of Arizona (M.S., 1981). Her novels —many of which have won prestigious awards—include The Bean Trees *(1988),* Animal Dreams *(1990),* Pigs in Heaven *(1993),* The Poisonwood Bible *(1998), and*

Prodigal Summer *(2000); Her fiction and nonfiction have been published in numerous periodicals, including* Cosmopolitan, Redbook, Virginia Quarterly Review, Progressive, *and* Smithsonian. *One reviewer remarks that she draws her characters and themes from America's "shop owners, the unemployed, the displaced, the homeless, the mothers and children struggling to survive" and she depicts how, "by banding together, these seemingly forgotten people can thrive." Kingsolver herself says that she is "extremely interested in cultural difference, in social and political history, and the sparks that fly when people with different ways of looking at the world come together and reconcile or move through or celebrate those differences. All that precisely describes everything I've ever written." As you read the following selection from her 1996 collection entitled* High Tide in Tucson: Essays from Now or Never, *think about how Kingsolver makes the transitions from observing a hermit crab, to recalling her own displaced and wandering life, to reflecting on the cultural differences of all human beings.*

A hermit crab lives in my house. Here in the desert he's hiding out from local animal ordinances, at minimum, and maybe even the international laws of native-species transport. For sure, he's an outlaw against nature. So be it.

He arrived as a stowaway two Octobers ago. I had spent a week in the Bahamas, and while I was there, wishing my daughter could see those sparkling blue bays and sandy covers, I did exactly what she would have done: I collected shells. Spiky murexes, smooth purple moon shells, ancient-looking whelks sand-blasted by the tide—I tucked them in the pockets of any shirt and shorts until my lumpy, suspect hemlines gave me away, like a refugee smuggling the family fortune. When it was time to go home, I rinsed my loot in the sink and packed it carefully into a plastic carton, then nested it deep in my suitcase for the journey to Arizona.

I got home in the middle of the night, but couldn't wait till morning to show my hand. I set the carton on the coffee table for my daughter to open. In the dark living room her face glowed, in the way of antique stories about children and treasure. With perfect delicacy she laid the shells out on the table, counting, sorting, designating scientific categories like yellow-striped pinky, Barnacle Bill's pocketbook . . .Yeek! She let loose a sudden yelp, dropped her booty, and ran to the far end of the room. The largest, knottiest whelk had begun to move around. First, it extended one long red talon of a leg, tap-tap-tapping like a blind man's cane. Then came half a dozen more red legs, plus a pair of eyes on stalks, and a purple claw that snapped open and shut in a way that could not mean We come in Friendship.

Who could blame this creature? It had fallen asleep to the sound *4*
of the Caribbean tide and awakened on a coffee table in Tucson, Arizona, where the nearest standing water source of any real account was
the municipal sewage-treatment plant.

With red stiletto legs splayed in all directions, it lunged and *5*
jerked its huge shell this way and that, reminding me of the scene I
make whenever I'm moved to rearrange the living-room sofa by myself. Then, while we watched in stunned reverence, the strange beast
found its bearings and began to reveal a determined, crabby grace. It
felt its way to the edge of the table and eased itself over, not falling
bang to the floor but hanging suspended underneath within the long
grasp of its ice-tong legs, lifting any two or three at a time while
many others still held in place. In this remarkable fashion it scram-
bled around the underside of the table's rim, swift and sure and fear-
less like a rock climber's dream.

If you ask me, when something extraordinary shows up in your *6*
life in the middle of the night, you give it a name and make it the best
home you can.

The business of naming involved a grasp of hermit-crab gender *7*
that was way out of our league. But our household had a deficit of
males, so my daughter and I chose Buster, for balance. We gave him a
terrarium with clean gravel and a small cactus plant dug out of the
yard and a big cockleshell full of tap water. All this seemed to suit him
fine. To my astonishment our local pet store carried a product call Vi-
taminized Hermit Crab Cakes. Tempting enough (till you read the ingredients) but we passed, since our household leans more toward the
recycling ethic. We give him leftovers. Buster's rapture is the day I drag
the unidentifiable things in cottage cheese containers out of the back
of the fridge.

We've also learned to give him a continually changing assortment *8*
of seashells, which he tries on and casts off like Cinderella's stepsisters
preening for the ball. He'll sometimes try to squeeze into ludicrous
outfits too small to contain him (who can't relate?). In other moods he
will disappear into a conch the size of my two fists and sit for a day, immobilized by the weight of upward mobility. He is in every way the perfect housemate: quiet, entertaining, and willing to eat up the trash. He
went to school for first-grade show-and-tell, and was such a hit the
principal called up to congratulate me (I think) for being a broad-
minded mother.

It was a long time, though, before we began to understand the *9*
content of Buster's character. He required more patient observation
than we were in the habit of giving to a small, cold-blooded life. As

months went by, we would periodically notice with great disappointment that Buster seemed to be dead. Or not entirely dead, but ill, or maybe suffering the crab equivalent of the blues. He would burrow into a gravelly corner, shrink deep into his shell, and not move, for days and days. We'd take him out to play, dunk him in water, offer him a new frock—nothing. He wanted to be still.

Life being what it is, we'd eventually quit prodding our sick friend   10
to cheer up, and would move on to the next stage of a difficult friendship: neglect. We'd ignore him wholesale, only to realize at some point later on that he'd lapsed into hyperactivity. We'd find him ceaselessly patrolling the four corners of his world, turning over rocks, rooting out and dragging around truly disgusting pork-chop bones, digging up his cactus and replanting it on its head. At night when the household fell silent I would lie in bed listening to his methodical pebbly racket from the opposite end of the house. Buster was manic-depressive.

I wondered if he might be responding to the moon. I'm partial   11
to lunar cycles, ever since I learned as a teenager that human females in their natural state—which is to say, sleeping outdoors—arrive at menses in synchrony and ovulate with the full moon. My imagination remains captive to that primordial village: the comradely grumpiness of new-moon days, when the entire world at once would go on PMS alert. And the compensation that would turn up two weeks later on a wild wind, under that great round headlamp, driving both men and women to distraction with the overt prospect of conception. The surface of the land literally rises and falls—as much as fifty centimeters—as the moon passes over, and we clay-footed mortals fall like dominoes before the swell. It's no surprise at all if a full moon inspires lyricists to corny love songs, or inmates to slamming themselves against barred windows. A hermit crab hardly seems this impetuous, but animals are notoriously responsive to the full moon: wolves howl; roosters announce daybreak all night. Luna moths, Arctic loons, and lunatics have a sole inspiration in common. Buster's insomniac restlessness seemed likely to be a part of the worldwide full-moon fellowship.

But it wasn't, exactly. The full moon didn't shine on either end of   12
his cycle, the high or the low. We tried to keep track, but it soon became clear: Buster marched to his own drum. The cyclic force that moved him remained as mysterious to us as his true gender and the workings of his crustacean soul.

Buster's aquarium occupies a spot on our kitchen counter right   13
next to the coffeepot, and so it became my habit to begin mornings with chin in hands, pondering the oceanic mysteries while awaiting percolation. Finally, I remembered something. Years ago when I was

a graduate student of animal behavior, I passed my days reading about the likes of animals' internal clocks. Temperature, photoperiod, the rise and fall of hormones—all these influences have been teased apart like so many threads from the rope that pulls every creature to its regulated destiny. But one story takes the cake. F. A. Brown, a researcher who is more or less the grandfather of the biological clock, set about in 1954 to track the cycles of intertidal oysters. He scooped his subjects from the clammy coast of Connecticut and moved them into the basement of a laboratory in landlocked Illinois. For the first fifteen days in their new aquariums, the oysters kept right up with their normal intertidal behavior: they spent time shut away in their shells, and time with their mouths wide open, siphoning their briny bath for the plankton that sustained them, as the tides ebbed and flowed on the distant Connecticut shore. In the next two weeks, they made a mystifying shift. They still carried out their cycles in unison, and were regular as the tides, but their high-tide behavior didn't coincide with high tide in Connecticut, or for that matter California, or any other tidal charts known to science. It dawned on the researchers after some calculations that the oysters were responding to high tide in Chicago. Never mind that the gentle mollusks lived in glass boxes in the basement of a steel-and-cement building. Nor that Chicago has no ocean. In the circumstances, the oysters were doing their best.

When Buster is running around for all he's worth, I can only presume it's high tide in Tucson. With or without evidence, I'm romantic enough to believe it. This is the lesson of Buster, the poetry that camps outside the halls of science: Jump for joy, hallelujah. Even a desert has tides.   *14*

When I was twenty-two, I donned the shell of a tiny yellow Renault and drove with all I owned from Kentucky to Tucson. I was a typical young American, striking out. I had no earthly notion that I was bringing on myself a calamity of the magnitude of the one that befell poor Buster. I am the commonest kind of North American refugee: I believe I like it here, far-flung from my original home. I've come to love the desert that bristles and breathes and sleeps outside my windows. In the course of seventeen years I've embedded myself in a family here—neighbors, colleagues, friends I can't foresee living without, and a child who is native to this ground, with loves of her own. I'm here for good, it seems.   *15*

And yet I never cease to long in my bones for what I left behind. I open my eyes on every new day expecting that a creek will run through my backyard under broad-leafed maples, and that my mother will be whistling in the kitchen. Behind the howl of coyotes, I'm listening for   *16* meadowlarks, I sometimes ache to be rocked in the bosom of the blood relations and busybodies of my childhood. Particularly in my years as a mother without a mate, I have deeply missed the safety net of extended family.

In a city of half a million I still really look at every face, anticipating recognition, because I grew up in a town where every face meant something to me. I have trouble remembering to lock the doors. Wariness of strangers I learned the hard way. When I was new to the city, I let a man into my house one hot afternoon because he seemed in dire need of a drink of water; when I turned from the kitchen sink I found sharpened steel shoved against my belly. And so I know, I know. But I cultivate suspicion with as much difficulty as I force tomatoes to grow in the drought-stricken hardpan of my strange backyard. No creek runs here, but I'm still listening to secret tides, living as if I belonged to an earlier place: not Kentucky, necessarily, but a welcoming earth and a human family. A forest. A species. *17*

In my life I've had frightening losses and unfathomable gifts: A knife in my stomach. The death of an unborn child. Sunrise in a rain forest. A stupendous column of blue butterflies rising from a Greek monastery. A car that spontaneously caught fire while I was driving it. The end of a marriage, followed by a year in which I could barely understand how to keep living. The discovery, just weeks ago when I rose from my desk and walked into the kitchen, of three strangers industriously relieving my house of its contents. *18*

I persuaded the strangers to put down the things they were holding (what a bizarre tableau of anti-Magi they made, these three unwise men, bearing a camera, an electric guitar, and a Singer sewing machine), and to leave my home, pronto. My daughter asked excitedly when she got home from school, "Mom, did you say bad words?" (I told her this was the very occasion that bad words exist for.) The police said, variously, that I was lucky, foolhardy, and "a brave lady." But it's not good luck to be invaded, and neither foolish nor brave to stand your ground. It's only the way life goes, and I did it, just as years ago I fought off the knife; mourned the lost child; bore witness to the rain forest; claimed the blue butterflies as Holy Spirit in my private pantheon; got out of the burning car; survived the divorce by putting one foot in front of the other and taking good care of my child. On most important occasions, I cannot think how to respond, I simply do. What does it mean, anyway, to be an animal in human clothing? We carry around these big brains of ours like the crown jewels, but mostly I find that millions of years of evolution have prepared me for one thing only: to follow internal rhythms. To walk upright, to protect my loved ones, to cooperate with my family group—however broadly I care to define *19* it—to do whatever will help us thrive. Obviously, some habits that saw us through the millennia are proving hazardous in a modern context: for example, the yen to consume carbohydrates and fat whenever they cross our path, or the proclivity for unchecked reproduction. But it's surely worth forgiving ourselves these tendencies a little, in light of the fact that they are what got us here. Like Buster, we are creatures of inexplicable cravings. Thinking isn't everything. The way I stock my refrigerator would amuse a level-headed interplanetary observer, who would see I'm responding not to real necessity but to the dread of famine honed in the African savannah. I can laugh at my Rhodesian Ridgeback as she furtively sniffs the houseplants for a place to bury bones, and circles to beat down the grass before lying on my kitchen floor. But she and I are exactly the same kind of hairpin.

We humans have to grant the presence of some past adaptations, 20 even in their unforgivable extremes, if only to admit they are permanent rocks in the steam we're obliged to navigate. It's easy to speculate and hard to prove, ever, that genes control our behaviors. Yet we are persistently, excruciatingly adept at many things that seem no more useful to modern life than the tracking of tides in a desert. At recognizing insider/outsider status, for example, starting with white vs. black and grading straight into distinctions so fine as to baffle the bystander— Serb and Bosnian, Hutu and Tutsi, Crip and Blood. We hold that children learn discrimination from their parents, but they learn it fiercely and well, world without end. Recite it by rote like a multiplication table. Take it to heart, though it's neither helpful nor appropriate, any more than it is to hire the taller of two men applying for a position as bank clerk, though statistically we're likely to do that too. Deference to the physical superlative, a preference for the scent of our own clan: a thousand anachronisms dance down the strands of our DNA from a hidebound tribal past, guiding us toward the glories of survival, and some vainglories as well. If we resent being bound by these ropes, the best hope is to seize them out like snakes, by the throat, look them in the eye and own up to their venom.

But we rarely do, silly egghead of a species that we are. We in- 21 vent the most outlandish intellectual grounds to justify discrimination. We tap our toes to chaste love songs about the silvery moon without recognizing them as hymns to copulation. We can dress up our drives, put them in three-piece suits or ballet slippers, but still they drive us. The wonder of it is that our culture attaches almost unequivocal shame to our animal nature, believing brute urges must be hurtful, violent things. But it's no less an animal instinct that leads us to marry (species that benefit from monogamy tend to practicei it); to organize a neighborhood cleanup campaign (rare and doomed is the creature that fouls its nest); to improvise and enforce morality (many primates socialize their young to be cooperative and ostracize adults who won't share food).

It's starting to look as if the most shameful tradition of Western civilization is our need to deny we are animals. In just a few centuries of setting ourselves apart as landlords of the Garden of Eden, exempt from the natural order and entitled to hold dominion, we have managed to behave like so-called animals anyway, and on top of it to wreck most of what took three billion years to assemble. Air, water, earth, and fire—much of our own element so vastly contaminated, we endanger our own future. Apparently we never owned the place after all. Like every other animal, we're locked into our niche: the mercury in the ocean, the pesticides on the soybean fields, all comes home to our breastfed babies. In the silent spring we are learning it's easier to escape from a chain gang than a food chain. Possibly we will have the sense to begin a new century by renewing our membership in the Animal Kingdom. 22

Vocabulary

In your journal, write down the meanings of the following words:

- spikey *murexes* **(2)**
- ancient-looking *whelks* **(2)**
- red *stiletto* legs **(5)**
- *photoperiod* **(13)**
- a *bizarre tableau* **(19)**
- the *proclivity* for unchecked reproduction **(19)**
- a thousand *anachronisms* **(20)**
- almost *unequivocal* shame **(21)**
- *ostracize* adults **(21)**

Questions for Writing and Discussion

1. "The real voyage of discovery consists not in seeking new landscapes but in having new eyes." In this quotation, Proust suggests that bringing new knowledge to a subject helps us discover or "see" more. Explain how Kingsolver develops "new eyes" as she learns about hermit crabs and explains how crab behavior relates to her own life and to the lives of human beings. Cite specific sentences from the essay to illustrate what Kingsolver discovers with her "new eyes."

2. Annotate Kingsolver's essay for observing techniques. Note sensory details, images, descriptions of what is not there, and changes in her subject. Cite two specific examples (phrases or sentences) for each of these four observing techniques. Which techniques does she use most frequently? Which does she use most effectively?

3. Kingsolver connects with her readers through her personal and often humorous voice. In paragraph 7, for example, Kingsolver says, "Buster's rapture is the day I drag the unidentifiable things in cottage cheese containers out of the back of the fridge." In the next paragraph, she says that Buster "is in every way the perfect housemate: quiet, entertaining, and willing to eat up the trash." Cite at least two other places where you notice Kingsolver's personal, humorous voice. Is her humor appropriate in an essay that addresses serious questions such as racial discrimination and violence? Explain.

4. In the second half of her essay (beginning with paragraph 15) Kingsolver compares her earlier life with Buster's experiences in a new environment. List several parallels between Buster's life and Kingsolver's experiences.

5. In paragraph 19, Kingsolver asks, "What does it mean, anyway, to be an animal in human clothing?" How does she use Buster's experiences and events from her own life to answer this question? What is Kingsolver's answer to this question?

6. On the Internet, read William Olds's posting on hermit crabs at http://www.animalnetwork.com/critters/profiles/hermitcrab/ default.asp. Does his sketch suggest that Kingsolver has presented accurate information about hermit crabs? Does Olds suggest other information about hermit crabs that would be useful in this essay to reinforce the parallels that Kingsolver draws between hermit crab behavior and her own life?

PROFESSIONAL WRITING

OBSERVING WOLVES

Farley Mowat

Farley Mowat was born in Ontario in 1921 and received a B.A. from the University of Toronto. He has published over fifty books of fiction and nonfiction, including People of the Deer *(1952),* Never Cry Wolf *(1963), and* Woman in the Mists: The Story of Dian Fossey and the Mountain Gorillas of Africa *(1987). Never Cry Wolf (1963), from which "Observing Wolves" was taken, describes how the Canadian government sent Mowat to the Keewatin Barren Lands in the Northwest Territories to prove that the wolves were decimating the caribou herds—and thus should be exterminated. After observing wolves for a few short days, however, Mowat realized that "the centuries-old and universally accepted human concept of wolf character was a palpable lie. . . . I made my decision that, from this hour onward, I would go open-minded into the lupine world and learn to see and know the wolves, not for what they were supposed to be, but for what they actually were." In the first scene, Mowat learns how wolves establish territories; in the second, he discovers something about their diet. Mowat also gives names to each wolf that he observes: Angeline is a female wolf, George is her mate, and Uncle Albert is a male attached to the group.*

I

During the next several weeks I put my decision into effect with the thoroughness for which I have always been noted. I went completely to the wolves. To begin with I set up a den of my own as near to the wolves as I could conveniently get without disturbing the even tenor of their lives too much. After all, I *was* a stranger, and an unwolflike one, so I did not feel I should go too far too fast.

Abandoning Mike's cabin (with considerable relief, since as the days warmed up so did the smell) I took a tiny tent and set it up on the shore of the bay immediately opposite to the den esker. I kept my camping gear to the barest minimum—a small primus stove, a stew pot, a teakettle, and a sleeping bag were the essentials. I took no weapons of any kind, although there were times when I regretted this omission, even if only fleetingly. The big telescope was set up in the mouth of the tent in such a way that I could observe the den by day or night without even getting out of my sleeping bag.

During the first few days of my sojourn with the wolves I stayed inside the tent except for brief and necessary visits to the out-of-doors which I always undertook when the wolves were not in sight. The point of this personal concealment was to allow the animals to get used to the tent and to accept it as only another bump on a very bumpy piece of terrain. Later, when the mosquito population reached full flowering, I stayed in the tent practically all of the time unless there was a strong wind blowing, for the most bloodthirsty beasts in the Arctic are not wolves, but the insatiable mosquitoes.

My precautions against disturbing the wolves were superfluous. It had required a week for me to get their measure, but they must have taken mine at our first meeting; and, while there was nothing overtly disdainful in their evident assessment of me, they managed to ignore my presence, and indeed my very existence, with a thoroughness which was somehow disconcerting.

Quite by accident I had pitched my tent within ten yards of one 5 of the major paths used by the wolves when they were going to, or coming from, their hunting grounds to the westward; and only a few hours after I had taken up residence one of the wolves came back from a trip and discovered me and my tent. He was at the end of a hard night's work and was clearly tired and anxious to go home to bed. He came over a small rise fifty yards from me with his head down, his eyes half-closed, and a preoccupied air about him. Far from being the preternaturally alert and suspicious beast of fiction, this wolf was so self-engrossed that he came straight on to within fifteen yards of me, and might have gone right past the tent without seeing it at all, had I not banged my elbow against the teakettle, making a resounding clank. The wolf's head came up and his eyes opened wide, but he did not stop or falter in his pace. One brief, sidelong glance was all he vouchsafed to me as he continued on his way.

It was true that I wanted to be inconspicuous, but I felt uncom- 6 fortable at being so totally ignored. Nevertheless, during the two weeks which followed, one or more wolves used the track past my tent almost every night—and never, except on one memorable occasion, did they evince the slightest interest in me.

By the time this happened I had learned a good deal about my 7 wolfish neighbors, and one of the facts which had emerged was that they were not nomadic roamers, as is almost universally believed, but were settled beasts and the possessors of a large permanent estate with very definite boundaries.

The territory owned by my wolf family comprised more than a 8 hundred square miles, bounded on one side by a river but otherwise not delimited by geographical features. Nevertheless there *were* boundaries, clearly indicated in wolfish fashion.

Anyone who has observed a dog doing his neighborhood rounds 9 and leaving his personal mark on each convenient post will have already guessed how the wolves marked out *their* property. Once a week, more or less, the clan made the rounds of the family lands and freshened up the boundary markers—a sort of lupine beating of the bounds. This careful attention to property rights was perhaps made necessary by the presence of two other wolf families whose lands abutted on ours, although I never discovered any evidence of bickering or disagreements between the owners of the various adjoining estates. I suspect, therefore, that it was more of a ritual activity.

In any event, once I had become aware of the strong feeling of property rights which existed amongst the wolves, I decided to use this knowledge to make them at least recognize my existence. One evening, after they had gone off for their regular nightly hunt, I staked out a property claim of my own, embracing perhaps three acres, with the tent at the middle, and *including a hundred-yard long section of the wolves' path.* *10*

Staking the land turned out to be rather more difficult than I had anticipated. In order to ensure that my claim would not be overlooked, I felt obliged to make a property mark on stones, clumps of moss, and patches of vegetation at intervals of not more than fifteen feet around the circumference of my claim. This took most of the night and re- quired frequent returns to the tent to consume copious quantities of tea; but before dawn brought the hunters home the task was done, and I retired, somewhat exhausted, to observe results. *11*

I had not long to wait. At 0814 hours, according to my wolf log, the leading male of the clan appeared over the ridge behind me, padding homeward with his usual air of preoccupation. As usual he did not deign to glance at the tent; but when he reached the point where my property line intersected the trail, he stopped as abruptly as if he had run into an invisible wall. He was only fifty yards from me and with my binoculars I could see his expression very clearly. *12*

His attitude of fatigue vanished and was replaced by a look of bewilderment. Cautiously he extended his nose and sniffed at one of my marked bushes. He did not seem to know what to make of it or what to do about it. After a minute of complete indecision he backed away a few yards and sat down. And then, finally, he looked direct- ly at the tent and at me. It was a long, thoughtful, considering sort of look. *13*

Having achieved my object—that of forcing at least one of the wolves to take cognizance of my existence—I now began to wonder if, in my ignorance, I had transgressed some unknown wolf law of major importance and would have to pay for my temerity. I found myself re- gretting the absence of a weapon as the look I was getting became longer, yet more thoughtful, and still more intent. *14*

I began to grow decidedly fidgety, for I dislike staring matches, and in this particular case I was up against a master, whose yellow glare seemed to become more baleful as I attempted to stare him down. *15*

The situation was becoming intolerable. In an effort to break the impasse I loudly cleared my throat and turned my back on the wolf (for a tenth of a second) to indicate as clearly as possible that I found his continued scrutiny impolite, if not actually offensive. *16*

He appeared to take the hint. Getting to his feet he had another 17 sniff at my marker, and then he seemed to make up his mind. Briskly, and with an air of decision, he turned his attention away from me and began a systematic tour of the area I had staked out as my own. As he came to each boundary marker he sniffed it once or twice, then carefully placed his mark on the outside of each clump of grass or stone. As I watched I saw where I, in my ignorance, had erred. He made *his* mark with such economy that he was able to complete the entire circuit without having to reload once, or, to change the simile slightly, he did it all on one tank of fuel.

The task completed—and it had taken him no longer than fifteen 18 minutes—he rejoined the path at the point where it left my property and trotted off towards his home—leaving me with a good deal to occupy my thoughts.

II

After some weeks of study I still seemed to be as far as ever from 19 solving the salient problem of how the wolves made a living. This was a vital problem, since solving it in a way satisfactory to my employers was the reason for my expedition.

Caribou are the only large herbivores to be found in any numbers 20 in the arctic Barren Lands. Although once as numerous as the plains buffalo, they had shown a catastrophic decrease during the three or four decades preceding my trip to the Barrens. Evidence obtained by various Government agencies from hunters, trappers and traders seemed to prove that the plunge of the caribou toward extinction was primarily due to the depredations of the wolf. It therefore must have seemed a safe bet, to the politicians-cum-scientists who had employed me, that a research study of wolf–caribou relationships in the Barrens would uncover incontrovertible proof with which to damn the wolf wherever he might be found, and provide a more than sufficient excuse for the adoption of a general campaign for his extirpation.

I did my duty, but although I had searched diligently for evidence 21 which would please my superiors, I had so far found none. Nor did it appear I was likely to.

Toward the end of June, the last of the migrating caribou herds had 22 passed Wolf House Bay heading for the high Barrens some two or three hundred miles to the north, where they would spend the summer.

Whatever my wolves were going to eat during those long months, 23 and whatever they were going to feed their hungry pups, it would not be caribou, for the caribou were gone. But if not caribou, what *was* it to be?

I canvassed all the other possibilities I could think of, but there   *24*
seemed to be no source of food available which would be adequate to
satisfy the appetites of three adult and four young wolves. Apart from
myself (and the thought recurred several times) there was hardly an
animal left in the country which could be considered suitable prey for
a wolf. Arctic hares were present; but they were very scarce and so fleet
of foot that a wolf could not hope to catch one unless he was extremely
lucky. Ptarmigan and other birds were numerous; but they could fly, and
the wolves could not. Lake trout, arctic grayling and whitefish filled the
lakes and rivers; but wolves are not otters.

About this time I began having trouble with mice. The vast ex-   *25*
panses of spongy sphagnum bog provided an ideal milieu for several
species of small rodents who could burrow and nest-build to their
hearts'content in the ready-made mattress of moss.

They did other things too, and they must have done them with   *26*
great frequency, for as June waned into July the country seemed to become alive with little rodents. The most numerous species were the
lemmings, which are famed in literature for their reputedly suicidal
instincts, but which, instead, *ought* to be hymned for their unbelievable
reproductive capabilities. Red-backed mice and meadow mice began in-
vading Mike's cabin in such numbers that it looked as if *I* would soon
be starving unless I could thwart their appetites for my supplies. *They*
did not scorn my bread. They did not scorn my bed, either; and when
I awoke one morning to find that a meadow mouse had given birth to
eleven naked offspring inside the pillow of my sleeping bag, I began to
know how Pharaoh must have felt when he antagonized the God of the
Israelites.

I suppose it was only because my own wolf indoctrination had   *27*
been so complete, and of such a staggeringly inaccurate nature, that it
took me so long to account for the healthy state of the wolves in the
apparent absence of any game worthy of their reputation and physical
abilities. The idea of wolves not only eating, but actually thriving and
raising their families on a diet of mice was so at odds with the character of the mythical wolf that it was really too ludicrous to consider.
And yet, it was the answer to the problem of how my wolves were
keeping the larder full.

Angeline tipped me off.   *28*

Late one afternoon, while the male wolves were still resting in   *29*
preparation for the night's labors, she emerged from the den and nuz-
zled Uncle Albert until he yawned, stretched and got laboriously to
his feet. Then she left the den site at a trot, heading directly for me
across a broad expanse of grassy muskeg, and leaving Albert to entertain the pups as best he could.

There was nothing particularly new in this. I had several times *30* seen her conscript Albert (and on rare occasions even George) to do duty as a babysitter while she went down to the bay for a drink or, as I mistakenly thought, simply went for a walk to stretch her legs. Usually her peregrinations took her to the point of the bay farthest from my tent where she was hidden from sight by a low gravel ridge; but this time she came my way in full view and so I swung my telescope to keep an eye on her.

She went directly to the rocky foreshore, waded out until the icy *31* water was up to her shoulders, and had a long drink. As she was doing so, a small flock of Old Squaw ducks flew around the point of the Bay and pitched only a hundred yards or so away from her. She raised her head and eyed them speculatively for a moment, then waded back to shore, where she proceeded to act as if she had suddenly become demented.

Yipping like a puppy, she began to chase her tail; to roll over and *32* over among the rocks; to lie on her back; to wave all four feet furiously in the air; and in general to behave as if she were clean out of her mind.

I swung the glasses back to where Albert was sitting amidst a gag- *33* gle of pups to see if he, too, had observed this mad display, and, if so, what his reaction to it was. He had seen it all right, in fact he was watching Angeline with keen interest but without the slightest indication of alarm.

By this time Angeline appeared to be in the throes of a manic *34* paroxysm, leaping wildly into the air and snapping at nothing, the while uttering shrill squeals. It was an awe-inspiring sight, and I realized that Albert and I were not the only ones who were watching it with fascination. The ducks seemed hypnotized by curiosity. So interested were they that they swam in for a closer view of this apparition on the shore. Closer and closer they came, necks outstretched, and gabbling incredulously among themselves. And the closer they came, the crazier grew Angeline's behavior.

When the leading duck was not more than fifteen feet from shore, *35* Angeline gave one gigantic leap towards it. There was a vast splash, a panic-stricken whacking of wings, and then all the ducks were up and away. Angeline had missed a dinner by no more than inches.

This incident was an eye-opener since it suggested a versatility at *36* food-getting which I would hardly have credited to a human being, let alone to a mere wolf. However, Angeline soon demonstrated that the charming of ducks was a mere side line.

Having dried herself with a series of energetic shakes which mo- *37* mentarily hid her in a blue mist of water droplets, she padded back across the grassy swale. But now her movements were quite different from what they had been when she passed through the swale on the way to the bay.

Angeline was of a rangy build, anyway, but by stretching herself so *38* that she literally seemed to be walking on tiptoe, and by elevating her neck like a camel, she seemed to gain several inches in height. She began to move infinitely slowly upwind across the swale, and I had the impression that both ears were cocked for the faintest sound, while I could see her nose wrinkling as she sifted the breeze for the most ephemeral scents.

Suddenly she pounced. Flinging herself up on her hind legs like *39* a horse trying to throw its rider, she came down again with driving force, both forelegs held stiffly out in front of her. Instantly her head dropped; she snapped once, swallowed, and returned to her peculiar mincing ballet across the swale. Six times in ten minutes she repeated the straight-armed pounce, and six times she swallowed—without my having caught a glimpse of what it was that she had eaten. The seventh time she missed her aim, spun around, and began snapping frenziedly in a tangle of cotton grasses. This time when she raised her head I saw, quite unmistakably, the tail and hind quarters of a mouse quivering in her jaws. One gulp, and it too was gone.

Although I was much entertained by the spectacle of one of this *40* continent's most powerful carnivores hunting mice, I did not really take it seriously. I thought Angeline was only having fun; snacking, as it were. But when she had eaten some twenty-three mice I began to wonder. Mice are small, but twenty-three of them adds up to a fair-sized meal, even for a wolf.

It was only later, by putting two and two together, that I was able *41* to bring myself to an acceptance of the obvious. The wolves of Wolf House Bay, and, by inference at least, all the Barren Land wolves who were raising families outside the summer caribou range, were living largely, if not almost entirely, on mice.

Vocabulary

In your journal, write down the meanings of the following words:
- the den *esker* (2)
- *superfluous* (4)
- somehow *disconcerting* (4)
- *preternaturally* (5)
- *evince* the slightest interest (6)

- *lupine* **(9)**
- *extirpation* **(20)**
- her *peregrinations* **(30)**

QUESTIONS FOR WRITING AND DISCUSSION

1. Describe what you knew about wolves before you read Mowat's description. Which parts of Mowat's description agreed with your preconceptions? Which parts gave you new information or a different opinion?

2. What equipment and habits of observation does the narrator employ in his study of wolves?

3. *What* is observed depends on *who* is doing the observing. Describe the narrator's behavior and personality. How do his preconceptions affect what he observes? Should a scientific observer interfere with the lives of the wolves, as the narrator does? What does the narrator learn?

4. Four keys to effective description are repeated observation, attention to sensory details, noticing changes in the subject or the subject's behavior, and noticing what is not present. Find examples of each of these four strategies in this essay.

5. On the Internet, log on to one of the wolf organization sites such as the International Wolf Center at http://www.wolf.org, the North American Wolf Association at http://www.nawa.org, or Wolfcountry at http://www.wolfcountry.net to check the accuracy of Mowat's essay. For example, the Wolfcountry site explains that wolves are, as Mowat suggests, very opportunistic in their feeding. Although they will prey on deer, moose, bison, elk, and caribou, they also eat beavers, rabbits, rodents, and wild berries. They are also able to catch fish to supplement their diet. Check the information about wolves on these sites— are Mowat's conclusions about wolf behavior scientifically accurate? Explain.

6. Naturalists have reintroduced wolves into Yellowstone National Park. Nearby ranchers, however, are still fearful that wolves will continue to leave the park and kill their livestock. How would Mowat respond to this debate? Imagine that Mowat has logged on to one of the wolf sites and is going to post a response to one of the ranchers. Write the response that Mowat might post.

Observing: The Writing Process ●●●

■ ASSIGNMENT FOR OBSERVING   Do a piece of writing in which you observe a specific person, place, object, or event. Your goal is to show how specific, observed details create dominant ideas about the person, place, object, or event. Your initial purpose is to use your writing to help you observe, discover, and learn about your subject; your final purpose will be to show your reader what you have seen and learned.

While your main purpose is to observe, you also need to think about a possible audience and genre. Are you writing primarily for yourself, to observe and learn? Are you writing for a specific audience? What genre or form would best suit your purpose and audience: a journal entry, a letter to a friend, a personal essay, an editorial, an article to be published in a particular magazine, or a posting to an Internet forum?

Important: Repeated observation is essential. Choose some *limited* subject—a person or small group of people, a specific place, a single object or animal, or a recurring event—that *you can reobserve over a period of several days during the writing process.*

CHOOSING A SUBJECT

If one of your journal entries suggested an interesting subject, try the collecting and shaping strategies. If none of those exercises caught your interest, consider the following ideas:

- Think about your current classes. Do you have a class with a laboratory—chemistry, physics, biology, engineering, animal science, horticulture, industrial sciences, physical education, social work, drawing, pottery—in which you have to make detailed observations? Use this assignment to help you in one of those classes: Write about what you observe and learn during one of your lab sessions.
- Seek out a new place on campus that is off your usual track. Check the college catalog for ideas about places you haven't yet seen: a theater where actors are rehearsing, a greenhouse, a physical education class in the martial arts, a studio where artists are working, a computer laboratory, or an animal research center. Or visit a class you wouldn't take for credit. Observe, write, and learn about what's there and what's happening.
- Get a copy of the Yellow Pages for your town or city. Open to a page at random and place your finger on the page. If it lands on an advertisement for a nearby store, take your notebook there for a visit. Describe the chocolate mousse at a restaurant, an expensive wine at a

"Write about dogs!"

liquor store, a new car at a dealership, a headstone at a burial-monument company, a twelve-string guitar at a music shop—whatever you would like to learn about through careful observation.

As you write on your subject, consider a tentative audience and purpose. Who might want to know what you learn from your observations? What do you need to explain? What will readers already know? Jot down tentative ideas about your subject, audience, and purpose. Remember, however, that these are not cast in concrete: You may discover some new idea, focus, or angle as you write.

COLLECTING

Once you have chosen a subject from your journal or elsewhere, begin collecting information. Depending on your purpose, your topic, or even your personal learning preferences, some activities will work better than others. However,

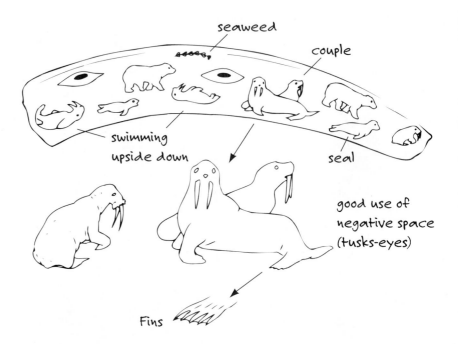

We don't take in the
world like a camera or a
set of recording devices.
The mind is an agent,
not a passive receiver. . . .
The active mind is a
composer and everything
we respond to, we
compose.
—ANN BERTHOFF,
AUTHOR AND TEACHER

you should *practice* all of these activities to determine which is most successful for you and most appropriate to your topic. During these collecting activities, go back and *reobserve your subject.* The second or third time you go back, you may see additional details or more actively understand what you're seeing.

Sketching   Begin by *drawing* what you see. The essayist Samuel Scudder says that pen or pencil can be "the best of eyes." Your drawing doesn't have to be great art to suggest other details, questions, or relationships that may be important. Instead of trying to cover a wide range of objects, try to focus on one limited subject and draw it in detail.

Here's an example. Writing student Brad Parks decided to visit an Eskimo art display at a local gallery. As part of his observing notes, he drew these sketches of Eskimo paintings. As he drew, he made notes in the margins of his sketches and zoomed in for more detail on one pair of walruses.

Taking Double-Entry Notes   Taking notes in a double-entry format is a simple but effective system for recording observed details. Draw a vertical line down the middle of a page in your journal. On the left-hand side, record bits of description and sensory details. On the right-hand side, jot down your reactions, thoughts, or ideas. On the left-hand side, make your observed details as *objective* as possible. Comments on the right-hand side will be more *subjective,* noting your impressions, reactions, comparisons, and images, as well as additional questions and ideas.

SENSORY DETAILS, FACTS, DATA	IMPRESSIONS, REACTIONS, IDEAS, QUESTIONS
size, color, shape, sounds, smell, touch, taste, actions, behavior	impressions, associations, feelings, reactions, ideas, images, comparisons, related thoughts, questions

Answering Questions   To help you describe the person, place, object, or event, write a short response in your journal to each of the following questions:

- What exactly is it? Can you *define* this person, place, object, or event? If it's an object, are its parts related? Who needs it, uses it, or produces it?
- How much could it change and still be recognizable?
- Compare and contrast it. How is it similar to or different from other comparable people, places, things, or events?
- From what points of view is it usually seen? From what point of view is it rarely seen?

Freewriting   Freewriting means exactly what it says. Write about your subject, nonstop, for five to ten minutes. Sometimes you may have to write, "I can't think of anything" or "This is really stupid," but keep on writing. Let your words and ideas suggest other thoughts and ideas. For observing, the purpose of freewriting is to let your *imagination* work on the subject, usually *after* you have observed and recorded specific details. Freewriting on your subject will also develop more *associations* or *comparisons* for the right-hand side of your double-entry log. It should also help you to identify a dominant idea for your details.

SHAPING

To focus once again on the shaping process, consider your subject, purpose, and audience. Has your purpose changed? Can you narrow your subject to a specific topic? You may know the answers to some questions immediately; others you may not know until after you complete your first draft. Jot down your current responses to the following questions:

- *Subject:* What is your general subject?
- *Specific topic:* What aspect of your subject are you interested in? Try to *narrow* your field or limit your focus.
- *Purpose:* Why is this topic interesting or important to you or to others? From what point of view will you be writing? What is the *dominant idea* you are trying to convey?

- *Audience:* Who are your readers? What are these readers like, and why might they be interested in this topic? How can you direct your description of your subject to your particular audience?

With answers to these questions in mind, you should experiment with several of the following shaping strategies. These strategies will not only organize your specific examples but may also suggest related ideas to improve your description.

As you practice these strategies, try to *focus* on your subject. In a profile of a person, for example, focus on key facial features or revealing habits or mannerisms. If you're writing about a place or an event, narrow the subject. Describe, for instance, the street at night, a spider spinning a web in a windowsill, a man in a laundromat banging on a change machine, a bird hovering in midair, a photograph, a fish. Write in depth and detail about a *limited* subject.

With a limited subject, a shaping strategy such as spatial order, classification, or comparison/contrast will organize all the specific details for your audience. Shaping strategies give you ways of seeing relationships among the many bits of your description and of presenting them in an organized manner for your reader. Seeing these relationships will also help you discover and communicate the *dominant idea* to your reader.

Spatial Order   Spatial order is a simple way to organize your descriptive details. Choose some sequence—left to right, right to left, bottom to top—and describe your observed details in that sequence. In the following description of his "trashed" dorm room, Dale Furnish, a student who was the victim of a prank, uses spatial order. The italicized words illustrate the spatial order.

As I walked in the door, I could hardly believe that this scene of destruction used to be my room. *Along the left-hand wall,* nearly hiding my desk and mirror, was a pile of beer cans and bottles, paper cups, and old crumpled newspapers. The small window *on the far wall* was now covered with the mattress of the bed, and the frame of the bunk bed stood on end. The clothes closet, *to the right of the window,* looked as though it were a giant washing machine which had just gone through spin cycle—clothes were plastered all over, and only four hangers remained, dangling uselessly on the pole. *On the right wall,* where the bed had been, was the real surprise. Tied to the heating pipe was a mangy looking sheep. I swear. It was a real sheep. As I looked at it, it turned to face me and loudly and plaintively said, "Baaaa." *Behind me,* in the hall, everyone began laughing. I didn't know whether to laugh or cry.

Chronological Order   Chronological order is simply the time sequence of your observation. In the following passage, Gregory Allen, writing from his point of view as a five-foot-six-inch guard on a basketball team, describes sights, sounds, and his feelings during a pickup game. The italicized words emphasize the chronological order.

> The game *begins*. The guy checking me is about 6′1″, red hair, freckles, and has no business on the court. He looks slow, so I decide to run him to tire him. I dribble twice, pump fake, and the guy goes for it, thinking that he's going to block this much smaller guy's shot. *Then* I leap, flick my wrist, and the ball glides through the air and flows through the net with a swish as the net turns upside down. I come down and realize that I have been scratched. *Suddenly*, I feel a sharp pain as sweat runs into the small red cut. I wipe the blood on my shorts and *continue playing* the game. *After* that first play, I begin to hear the common song of the game. There's the squeak of the high-top Nike sneakers, the bouncing ball, the shuffle of feet. *Occasionally*, I hear "I'm open!" "Pass the ball!" "Aughhh!" And *then*, "Nice play, man!"

Comparison/Contrast   If what you've observed and written about your subject so far involves seeing similarities or differences, you may be able to use comparison/contrast as a shaping strategy—either for a single paragraph or for a series of paragraphs. The following two paragraphs, for example, are taken from Albert Goldman's biography of Elvis Presley, entitled *Elvis*. In these paragraphs, Goldman's dominant idea depends on the striking contrast between what he finds on the front lawn of Graceland, the rock star's mansion in Memphis, and what he notices when he steps through the front door.

> Prominently displayed on the front lawn is an elaborate creche. The stable is a full-scale adobe house strewn with straw. Life-sized are the figures of Joseph and Mary, the kneeling shepherds and Magi, the lambs and ewes, as well as the winged annunciatory angel hovering over the roof beam. Real, too, is the cradle in which the infant Jesus sleeps.

> When you step through the ten-foot oak door and enter the house, you stop and stare in amazement. Having just come from the contemplation of the tenderest scene in the Holy Bible, imagine the shock of finding yourself in a *whorehouse!* Yet there is no other way to describe the drawing room of Graceland except to say that it appears to have been lifted from some turn-of-the-century bordello down in the French Quarter of New Orleans. . . . The room is a

gaudy melange of red velour and gilded tassels, Louis XV furniture and porcelain bric-a-brac, all informed by the kind of taste that delights in a ceramic temple d'amour housing a miniature Venus de Milo with an electrically simulated waterfall cascading over her naked shoulders.

Examine once again your collecting notes about your subject. If there are striking similarities or differences between the two parts or between various aspects of your subject, perhaps a comparison or contrast structure will organize your details.

Classification   Classifying people, events, or things by *types* may provide a shape that you can use for either a paragraph or a whole essay. In the following paragraph from "Speedway," an essay on racing at the Indianapolis 500, cultural critic Paul Fussell categorizes spectators into three social classes: the middle classes, or "middles"; the high proletarians, or "high proles"; and the "uglies."

> I'd say the people can be divided into three social classes: the middles, who on race day tend, in homage to the checkered flag, to dress all in black and white and who sit in reserved seats; the high proles, who watch standing or lolling in the infield, especially at the turns, "where the action is"; and the uglies, the overadvertised, black-leathered, beer-sodden, pot-headed occupiers of that muddy stretch of ground in the infield at the first turn, known as the Snake Pit. These are the ones who, when girls pass, spiritlessly hold up signs reading "Show Us Your T__s." The uglies are sometimes taken to be the essence of Indy, and they are the people who, I think, Frank Deford has in mind when he speaks of "barbarians." But they are not the significant Indy audience. The middle class is all those people arriving at the Speedway in cars bearing Purdue and Indiana State stickers.

Classification is often a useful method of shaping description. To see if it is appropriate for your subject, ask, "What types do you observe?" The answer may lead to categories or types that you had failed to observe, and the categories may provide a shape you can adopt.

Definition   Definition is the essence of observation. Defining a person, place, or object requires stating its exact meaning and describing its basic qualities. Literally, a definition sets the boundaries, indicating, for example, how an apple is distinct from an orange or how a canary is different from a sparrow. *Definition*, however, is a catchall term for a variety of strategies. It uses classification and comparison as well as description. It often describes a thing by negation—by saying what it is not. For example, Sidney Harris, a columnist for many years for the *Chicago Daily News*, once defined a "jerk" by referring to several types of people ("boob," "fool," "dope," "bore," "egotist," "nice person," "clever person") and then compared or contrasted these terms to show where "jerk" leaves off and "egotist" begins. In the following excerpt, Harris also defines by negation, saying that a jerk has no grace and is tactless. The result, when combined with a description of qualities he has observed in jerks, is definition.

> Thinking it over, I decided that a jerk is basically a person without insight. He is not necessarily a fool or a dope, because some extremely clever persons can be jerks. In fact, it has little to do with intelligence as we commonly think of it; it is, rather, a kind of subtle but persuasive aroma emanating from the inner part of the personality.

> I know a college president who can be described only as a jerk. He is not an unintelligent man, or unlearned, nor even unschooled in the social amenities. Yet he is a jerk *cum laude*, because of a fatal flaw in his nature—he is totally incapable of looking into the mirror of his soul and shuddering at what he sees there.

> A jerk, then, is a man (or woman) who is utterly unable to see himself as he appears to others. He has no grace, he is tactless without meaning to be, he is a bore even to his best friends, he is an egotist without charm. All of us are egotists to some extent, but most of us—unlike the jerk—are perfectly and horribly aware of it when we make asses of ourselves. The jerk never knows.

At this stage in the writing process, you have already been defining your subject simply by describing it. But you may want to use a deliberately structured definition, as Harris does, to shape your observations.

Simile, Metaphor, and Analogy   Simile, metaphor, and analogy create vivid word pictures or *images* by making *comparisons*. These images may take up only a sentence or two, or they may shape several paragraphs.

- A *simile* is a comparison using *like* or *as*: A is like B. "George eats his food like a vacuum cleaner."
- A *metaphor* is a direct or implied comparison suggesting that A is B: "At the dinner table, George is a vacuum cleaner."
- An *analogy* is an extended simile or metaphor that builds a point-by-point comparison into several sentences, a whole paragraph, or even a series of paragraphs. Writers use analogy to explain a difficult concept, idea, or process by comparing it with something more familiar or easier to understand.

If the audience, for example, knows about engines but has never seen a human heart, a writer might use an analogy to explain that a heart is like a simple engine, complete with chambers or cylinders, intake and exhaust valves, and hoses to carry fuel and exhaust.

As an illustration of simile and metaphor, notice how Joseph Conrad, in the following brief passage from *Heart of Darkness*, begins with a simile and then continues to build on his images throughout the paragraph. Rather than creating a rigid structural shape for his details (as classification or comparison/contrast would do), the images combine and flow like the river he is describing.

Going up that river was like travelling back to the earliest beginnings of the world, when vegetation rioted on the earth and the big trees were kings. An empty stream, a great silence, an impenetrable forest. The air was warm, thick, heavy, sluggish. There was no joy in the brilliance of sunshine. The long stretches of the waterway ran on, deserted, into the gloom of overshadowed distances. On silvery sandbanks hippos and alligators sunned themselves side by side. The broadening waters flowed through a mob of wooded islands; you lost your way on that river as you would in a desert, and butted all day long against shoals, trying to find the channel, till you thought yourself bewitched and cut off forever from everything you had known once—somewhere—far away—in another existence perhaps.

An analogy helps shape the following paragraph by Carl Sagan, author of *The Dragons of Eden* and *Cosmos*. To help us understand a difficult concept, the immense age of the Earth (and, by comparison, the relatively tiny span of human history), Sagan compares the lifetime of the universe to something simple and familiar: the calendar of a single year.

The most instructive way I know to express this cosmic chronology is to imagine the fifteen-billion year lifetime of the universe . . . compressed into the span of a single year. . . . It is disconcerting to find that in such a cosmic year the Earth does not condense out of interstellar matter until early September; dinosaurs emerge on Christmas Eve; flowers arise on December 28th; and men and women originate at 10:30 P.M. on New Year's Eve. All of recorded history occupies the last ten seconds of December 31; and the time from the waning of the Middle Ages to the present occupies little more than one second.

Consider whether a good analogy would help you shape one or more paragraphs in your essay. Ask yourself, "What is the most difficult concept or idea I'm trying to describe?" Is there an extended point-by-point comparison—an analogy—that would clarify it?

Title, Introduction, and Conclusion   Depending on your purpose and audience, you may want a title for what you're writing. At the minimum, titles—like labels—should accurately indicate the contents in the package. In addition, however, good titles capture the reader's interest with some catchy phrasing or imaginative language—something to make the reader want to "buy" the package. Barbara Kingsolver uses the title "High Tide in Tucson" to catch our interest: What are tides doing in landlocked Tucson, Arizona? Samuel H. Scudder's title is a good label (the essay is about looking at fish) and uses catchy phrasing: "Take This Fish and Look at It." If a title is appropriate for your observation, write out several possibilities in your journal.

The introduction should set up the context for the reader—*who, what, when, where,* and *why*—so that readers can orient themselves. Depending on your audience and purpose, introductions can be very brief, pushing the reader quickly into the scene, or they can take more time, easing readers into the setting. Stephen White, in his essay about Mesa Verde at the end of this chapter, begins mysteriously: "It is difficult for me to say exactly what it was that drew me to this solitary place." White doesn't tell his reader that he's talking about Mesa Verde until the second paragraph.

Conclusions should wrap up the observation, providing a sense of completeness. Conclusions vary, depending upon a writer's purpose and audience, but they tend to be of two types or have two components: a *summary* and a *reference* to the introduction. Mowat uses both components when he concludes his essay. Part II of his essay ends by referring to and then answering the central question of his expedition, that is: How do wolves survive? "The wolves of Wolf House Bay," Mowat tells us, "were living largely, if not almost entirely, on mice."

As you work on shaping strategies and drafting, make notes about possible titles, appropriate introductions, or effective conclusions for your written observations.

DRAFTING

The idea is to get the pencil moving quickly.
—BERNARD MALAMUD, NOVELIST

Reread Journal Entries and Notes from Collecting and Shaping Before you start drafting, review your material so you aren't writing cold. Stop and reread everything you've written on your subject. You're not trying to memorize particular sentences or phrases; you're just getting it all fresh in your mind, seeing what you still like and discarding details that are no longer relevant.

Reobserve Your Subject If necessary, go back and observe your subject again. One more session may suggest an important detail or idea that will help you get started writing.

Reexamine Purpose, Audience, Dominant Idea, and Shape After all your writing and rereading, you may have some new ideas about your purpose, audience, or dominant idea. Take a minute to jot these down in your journal. Remember that your specific details should show the main point or dominant idea, whether you state it explicitly or not.

Next, if the shaping strategies suggested an order for your essay, use it to guide your draft. You may, however, have only your specific details or a general notion of the dominant idea you're trying to communicate to your reader. In that case, you may want to begin writing and work out a shape or outline as you write.

Create a Draft   With the above notes as a guide, you are ready to start drafting. Work on establishing your ritual: Choose a comfortable, familiar place with the writing tools you like. Make sure you'll have no interruptions. Try to write nonstop. If you can't think of a word, substitute a dash. If you can't remember how to spell a word, don't stop to look it up now—keep writing. Write until you reach what feels like the end. If you do get stuck, *reread* your last few lines or some of your writing process materials. Then go back and pick up the thread. Don't stop to count words or pages. You should shoot for more material than you need because it's usually easier to cut material later, when you're revising, than to add more if you're short.

REVISING

All the stuff you see back there on the floor is writing I did last week that I have to rewrite this week.

—ERNEST J. GAINES,

AUTHOR OF THE AUTOBIOGRAPHY OF MISS JANE PITTMAN

Gaining Distance and Objectivity   Revising, of course, has been going on since you put your first sentence down on paper. You've changed ideas, thought through your subject again, and observed your person, place, object, or event. After your rough draft is finished, your next step is to revise again to resee the whole thing. But before you do, you need to let it sit at least twenty-four hours, to get away from it for a while, to gain some distance and perspective. Relax. Congratulate yourself.

About the time you try to relax, however, you may get a sudden temptation—even an overwhelming urge—to have someone else read it—immediately! Usually, it's better to resist that urge. Chances are, you want to have someone else read it either because you're bubbling with enthusiasm and you want to share it or because you're certain that it's all garbage and you want to hear the bad news right away. Most readers will not find it either as great as you hope *or* as awful as you fear. As a result, their offhand remarks may seem terribly insensitive or condescending. In a day or so, however, you'll be able to see your writing more objectively: Perhaps it's not great yet, but it's not hopeless, either. At that point, you're ready to get some feedback and start your revisions.

Rereading and Responding to Your Readers   When you've been away from the draft for a while, you are better able to see the whole piece of writing. Start by rereading your own draft and making marginal notes. Don't be distracted by spelling errors or typos; concentrate on the quality of the details and the flow of the sentences. Focus on the overall effect you're creating, see if your organi-

PEER RESPONSE

The instructions below will help you give and receive constructive advice about the rough draft of your observing essay. You may use these guidelines for an in-class workshop, a take-home review, or a computer e-mail response.

Writer: Before you exchange drafts with another reader, write out the following information about your rough draft:

1. What is the dominant impression that you want your description to make? What overall idea or impression do you want your reader to have?

2. What paragraph(s) contains your best and most vivid description? What paragraph(s) still needs some revision?

3. Explain one or two things you would like your reader to comment on as he or she responds to your draft.

Reader: First, without making any marks, read the entire draft from start to finish. As you *reread* the draft, answer the following questions.

1. What *dominant impression* does the draft create? Does the dominant impression you received agree with the writer's own idea? If not, how might the writer better achieve that overall impression?

2. Look at the writer's responses to Question 2. Does the writer, in fact, use vivid description in his or her best paragraph(s)? How might the paragraphs that the writer says need revision be improved? Review the six techniques for descriptive writing at the beginning of this chapter. Where or how might the writer improve the *sensory details*, *images*, descriptions of what is *not there*, *changes* in the subject, or *point of view?* Offer specific suggestions.

3. Reread the assignment for this essay. Explain how this essay should be revised to more clearly *meet the assignment.*

4. List the *two most important things* this writer should work on as he or she revises this draft. Explain why these are important.

zation still makes sense, and check to make sure that all the details support the dominant idea. Now you're ready to get some peer feedback. Depending on the reactions of your readers, you may need to change the point of view, add a few specific examples or some comparisons or images, fix the organization of a paragraph, reorder some details, delete some sentences, or do several of the above. Be prepared, however, to rewrite several paragraphs to help your readers really see what you are describing.

Guidelines for Revision

As you revise your essay, keep the following tips and checklist questions in mind:

- **Reexamine your purpose and audience**. Are you doing what you intended? If your purpose or audience has changed, what other changes do you need to make as you revise?
- **Pay attention to the advice your readers give you, but don't necessarily make all the changes they suggest.** Ask them *why* something should be changed. Ask them specifically *where* something should be changed.
- **Consider your point of view.** Would changing to another point of view clarify what you are describing?
- **Consider your vantage point.** Do you have a bird's-eye view, or are you observing from a low angle? Do you zoom in for a close-up of a person or object? Would a different vantage point fit your purpose and audience?
- **Make sure you are using sensory details where appropriate.** Remember, you must *show* your reader the details you observe. If necessary, *reobserve* your subject.
- **Do all your details and examples support your dominant idea?** Reread your draft and omit any irrelevant details.
- **What is *not* present in your subject that might be important to mention?**
- **What changes occur in the form or function of your subject?** Where can you describe those changes more vividly?
- **Make comparisons if they will help you or your reader understand your subject better.** Similes, metaphors, or analogies may describe your subject more vividly.
- **Does what you are observing belong to a class of similar objects?** Would classification organize your writing?
- **Be sure to cue or signal your reader with appropriate transition words.** Transitions will improve the coherence or flow of your writing.
  - *Spatial order:* on the left, on the right, next, above, below, higher, lower, farther, next, beyond
  - *Chronological order:* before, earlier, after, afterward, thereafter, then, from then on, the next day, shortly, by that time, immediately, slowly, while, meanwhile, until, now, soon, within an hour, first, later, finally, at last
  - *Comparison/contrast:* on one hand, on the other hand, also, similarly, in addition, likewise, however, but, yet, still, although, even so, nonetheless, in contrast.
- **Revise sentences for clarity, conciseness, emphasis, and variety**.

I went for years not finishing anything. Because, of course, when you finish something you can be judged.

—**ERICA JONG,**

AUTHOR OF FEAR OF FLYING

- **When you have revised your essay, edit your writing for correct spelling and appropriate word choice, punctuation, usage, and grammar**.

■ POSTSCRIPT ON THE WRITING PROCESS   When you've finished writing this assignment, do one final journal entry. Briefly, answer the following questions:

1. What was the hardest part of this writing assignment for you?
2. Put brackets ([ ]) around the paragraph containing your most vivid sensory details. Explain what makes this paragraph so vivid.
3. What exercise, practice, strategy, or workshop was the "breakthrough" for you? What led you to your discovery or dominant idea?
4. State in one sentence your discovery or the dominant idea of your essay.
5. What did you learn about your writing ritual and process? What did you learn about observing?

STUDENT   WRITING

PERMANENT TRACINGS

Jennifer Macke

Jennifer Macke, a student in Professor Rachel Henne-Wu's class at Owens Community College in Findlay, Ohio, decided to write her observing essay about a tattoo parlor. She visited the Living Color Tattoo Parlor and took notes on the office, the clientele, the conversations, the artwork of the tattoos, and the owner of the establishment. Ms. Macke wrote that her preconceptions about tattoo parlors were that they were "smoke-filled, dimly lit places" where "undesirables gathered." Gradually, her impressions changed as she saw firsthand the high quality and the remarkable artistry of the tattoos. Reprinted below are some of her original notes, questions and answers, an outline, and the final version of her essay.

Notes on a Visit

—A couple with a young school-aged daughter looks at the artwork on the walls for about 15 minutes before saying anything to the owner. They are looking for a design for the wife for her birthday. They appear to be a typical young couple with a limited amount of money. They ask how much a particular design will be and say they will have to save for it. "How much for this ankle bracelet?" he says. "It'll run you between $45 and $60, depending on how thick you want the rose vine," Gasket says.

—Two Latino men enter the waiting room. One peeks his head into the office and says, "I'm here early for my appointment because I'm not sure exactly what I want. Do you have any books or more pictures I can look through?" Gasket gives him six photo albums full of ideas (designs).

—Five young adult black men enter. They begin browsing through the photos on the wall. There are designs with prices below them so you know what it costs without asking. They too look through the photo albums the Latinos left on the floor. One of the black guys announces, "I'll go first 'cause I want to get it over with." One says, "I'm not going to do this. I can't stand the sound of that needle!" Gasket looks at me and says, "It's amazing how many people just think all you have to do is walk through the door like a walk-in barber shop. They don't know I'm booked for at least a week. During the summer, it's three weeks."

—The phone rings and since his daughter, who normally works there, is gone to visit her mother, he tells me to pick it up. The guy on the other end says, "My uncle wants to know if Jeff's cousin works here?" I relay the message to the owner and he replies, "Yes, that's me." Back on the phone, "He says he's the best in the business. Does he have any time today?" Gasket says, "Here we go again." I tell the guy it will be a week. He says, "OK, I'll call back then." I tell Gasket what he said and he comments, "He'll call back next week, and I'll have to tell him it'll be another week. You would not believe the intelligence level of some people."

—The next girl is going to have lips tattooed on her right hip. She is a petite nurse whom you would never guess would even consider such a thing. Her husband put lipstick on and kissed a napkin which she brought to use for the pattern. Gasket took a photocopy of this and made a transfer from it to use as the template. She dropped her shorts to expose where the art would be placed. She lay down on the table which Gasket explained he had gotten in trade for a tattoo. He also said the stirrups were still in the drawer. The girl smiled and talked the whole time he worked. At one point, he asked her, "Does it hurt?" She said, "No." He said, "I can go deeper!" She said, "Are you supposed to?" He said, laughing, "It's just a joke. If I see someone who's comfortable, I'll ask them this." It only took about 30 minutes to complete this one. You would swear someone just kissed her with bright red lipstick. It's amazing how realistic his work looks.

Questions and Answers

1. "Why do people get tattoos?"
   "A tattoo is a very personal thing. It's an expression of one's self."
2. "Does it hurt to get a tattoo?"

"It all depends on the placement and the person. Guys tend to be bigger wimps. I'd rather do women any day. The most painful areas are the ankle and higher up on the belly. I've had the pain described as something annoying but not necessarily painful to such a point that they cannot stand it. I've never had anyone pass out, though."

3. "What kind of person gets a tattoo?"
"There's not one particular type of person who gets a tattoo. I once had a call from some lawyers from Findlay. They wanted to know if they had five or so people who wanted a tattoo, would I come over? I said, yes, and I tattooed six lawyers at a party."

4. "What is the process of getting a tattoo?"
"Depending if it will be freehand or something the people bring in, it starts with drawing the art. It is drawn either on the person or on carbon paper backwards. The carbon design is transferred to the skin with Speed Stick deodorant. The outline is applied first. As the single needle picks up and sews into the skin, excess ink covers the work area."

As Gasket works, it's hard to see the actual area he's working on because of the excess ink. When asked how he can work with the excess ink obstructing the guidelines, he says he just knows where the line goes. (I wouldn't.) Once the outline is complete he changes to use a 3 or 4 needle set, depending on the coverage necessary. He colorizes the art, which brings it to life. After it's complete, he puts a thick coat of Bacitracin on and covers it with a gauze bandage. The gauze must remain on for one and a half to two hours.

5. "What is the most common place for a tattoo?"
"Placement runs in cycles, sometimes the upper arm, sometimes the ankle." While we were talking, a man came in with one on the back of his neck.

6. "How expensive are tattoos?"
The minimum is $30. Depending on how detailed and how big. Gasket has bartered for the tattoos, too.

7. "Do most people get more than one tattoo?"
"I've seen people go through life with only one or maybe two, but it's said when you get your third, you're hooked. You'll be back for more."

8. "Are there health department requirements?"
"At the beginning, the requirements (laws) weren't very strict. I knew I wanted to be supersterile, so I put my needles and equipment through a much stricter procedure. Since then, the health department has taken on my policy and requires everyone to process their stuff like me. They drop in to make sure the laws are being followed."

9. "How many times do you use your needles?"

"They are single-application needles, but they still need to be sterilized. People ask me if they can watch their needles being sterilized so they can make sure. I say fine, but it will be two and a half hours until I can work on you."

Outline

Working Thesis: "Gasket's creative artistic ability and perfectionist work ethic make his designs worth sewing into your body for a lifetime."

I. Describe the Tattoo Parlor

A. Outer area (waiting room)

B. Inner office

II. Describe the owner

A. The way he looks

B. The way he feels about his work

III. Describe the people

A. People getting a tattoo

B. People not getting a tattoo

Final Version

PERMANENT TRACINGS

At first glance, the Living Color Tattoo Parlor appears to be just   *1*
another typical tattoo establishment. You enter through a glass door
only to find a waiting room with the decor reminiscent of the 1970s.
The dark paneled walls display numerous types of artwork that range
from pencil sketching to color Polaroid snapshots of newly completed tattoos. The gold and green davenport looks as if it came from a
Saturday morning garage sale. The inner office is celery green with a
dental chair and an obstetrics table that the owner bartered for a tattoo (the stirrups are still in the drawer). A filing cabinet, desk, and
copy machine make you feel as if you're in a professional office. The
sterilizer is in plain sight and is in operation. Bottle after bottle of
brightly colored inks are neatly arranged on a tiered wooden stand.
The sound of the oscillating fan that cools the client interrupts the
buzz of the needle sewing the paint into the client's skin. A freeze-
dried turtle is displayed on a table in the office.

I still wondered, though. Could tattoos actually be a form of art?   *2*

As soon as I could, I asked the owner, a man called Gasket, about   *3*
his occupation. "I was a suit for fifteen years and now I can work as

much as I want. There's always somebody wanting a tattoo or something pierced," Gasket said. He's often asked if he'll scratch out the
name of a previous girlfriend, and he always replies that he would never
even consider it. "That would be defacement," he said. "When I'm
done, the design should look better than when I started." Gasket is
not his given name but one he acquired because of his expert repair
work on Harley Davidson motorcycles. Gasket is the owner of this establishment, and to look at him, you would never guess he is a college-
educated engineer. His long curly, graying hair flows from under his
Harley hat, and examples of his handiwork are visible under the rolled
up sleeves of his black Harley T-shirt. The harshness of his heavily
bearded face is softened by his slate-blue eyes, which mirror his gentle demeanor. If you look past his casual exterior, you will find a
code of steel. "At the beginning, the laws weren't very strict. I knew I
wanted to be supersterile, so I put my single-use needles and equipment
through a much stricter procedure. Since then, the health department
has taken on my policy and requires everyone to process their stuff like
me," he said.

The appearance of the Living Color Tattoo Parlor may be typ- *4*
ical, but two things are distinctly different: the quality and the creativity of the tattoo designs. A young college couple from Toledo
was asked why they would drive to Fremont for an appointment.
They answered, "Gasket's the best! We wouldn't trust something
that's going to be on our body for the rest of our lives to someone
other than him."

"I already have two tattoos from you, and I love your work," a mid- *5*
dle-aged woman said. Displaying two greeting cards, she asked, "Is it
possible to get a combination of these two designs?"

"I can create anything you want," Gasket said. *6*

"I'll have to wait a couple of weeks because I'm not working much *7*
and my other bills come first," she said.

"Yes, you have to get your priorities straight. When you're ready, *8*
I'm here," he said.

Gasket is performing his tattoo magic on a young college female. *9*
He's creating a rose with a heart stem wrapping around her belly button, which is pierced. The girl is nervously seated in the green dental chair, which is tilted back to flatten the skin surface. First, Gasket
draws the sketch on her belly. He covers his hands with a thin layer
of latex once the exact position and specific details are decided upon.
A small device resembling a fountain pen with a brightly colored
motor and a single needle moving at 1,000 rpm is used to apply the
black outline first. As the needle moves up and down, it picks up a
small amount of ink and deposits it just under the surface of the skin.

When asked how he can work with the excess ink obstructing the guidelines, he simply said he just knows where the line goes. This is a difficult task because unlike a paint-by-number design, the image not only has to be in his mind but he also has to have the artistic ability to convert the image to the skin. The girl asks a pain-filled question, "How much longer?"

"I can stop and let you take a break at any time," Gasket says. His   10
soft tone and slow-paced voice help soothe the girl. "The higher up on the belly, the more painful," he says. The process of colorizing the tattoo begins once the outline is complete. This is accomplished with a three- or four-needle set, depending on the amount of coverage desired. It takes about forty-five minutes to complete the multicolored masterpiece, which is literally sewn into her skin. Some of Gasket's designs can be compared to Picasso's brilliantly colored, dreamlike images. Upon completion, the girl is directed to a full-length mirror to inspect her permanently altered abs.

"It looks fantastic!" she exclaims. "I was a little vague on how I   11
pictured it would look, but it looks even better than I had imagined. I'm thrilled."

Once thought of as green-toned disfigurements that only drunk-   12
en sailors and lowlife people would don, tattoos are now high fashion. Now it is possible to see skin art on TV stars, sports superstars, and a multitude of individuals you might not suspect. The future of this trendy fashion has its roots firmly planted in today's society. Young people seem to be one of its biggest supporters.

"I'll go first 'cause I want to get it over with," one young black   13
man states to his four companions.

"I'm not going to do this. I can't stand the sound of that needle!"   14
another man proclaims.

"It's amazing how many people think all you have to do is just   15
walk through the door like a walk-in barber shop. They don't know I'm booked for at least a week. During the summer, it's three weeks," Gasket claims. He explains this to the young men, who make appointments. They leave, disappointed.

Gasket's tattoo designs can be compared to the famous fashion   16
designs by Bob Mackie. Like Mackie's one-of-a-kind designs, they are not mass-produced, but are hand-sewn for a specific individual. As I left, my first impression of the Living Color Tattoo Parlor was changed by the incredibly beautiful skin art and the comments of the satisfied clients. For many, Gasket's artistic ability and perfectionism make his designs worth sewing into your body for a lifetime.

QUESTIONS FOR WRITING AND DISCUSSION

1. Review the techniques for writing observing papers at the beginning of the chapter. Which paragraph(s) in Macke's essay have the best sensory detail, images, comparisons, and other effective bits of description? Which paragraphs might use more descriptive detail?

2. Macke describes the office, the owner, the customers, the process of tattooing, and the prices of a tattoo. Should she also describe several of the tattoos? Should she describe the colors in a typical tattoo? If she did these descriptions, where might she put them in her essay?

3. Reread Macke's notes of her visit, including her questions and answers. What interesting ideas and descriptions in her notes might be included in her final draft? Why might Macke have left these details out? Assume that you are a peer reader for Macke's essay. Fill out the peer response questions printed earlier in this chapter so you can help her with a revision of her essay.

4. List the three things that you like best about Macke's essay. Which of her strategies might work for a revision of your own essay? Make a revision plan for your own essay, based on what you learned from reading "Permanent Tracings."

STUDENT WRITING

EMPTY WINDOWS

Stephen White

In this essay written for Professor John Boni at Colorado State University, Stephen White describes both what his senses tell him and what he can only imagine about the Anasazi, the ancient Native Americans who more than a thousand years ago built the cliff dwellings at Mesa Verde in southwestern Colorado. Writing about those empty dwellings with their darkened windows, White says, "Perhaps there lurks, behind every blackened window, a certain unexplainable something we can never understand."

It is difficult for me to say exactly what it was that drew me to this *1* solitary place and held me here, virtually entranced, the entire day. It's the silence, maybe, or the empty houses perched precariously on the canyon wall below me. Or could it be the knowledge that something seemingly nonexistent does indeed exist?

I awoke this morning with a sense of unexplainable anticipation   *2*
gnawing away at the back of my mind, that this chilly, leaden day at
Mesa Verde would bring something new and totally foreign to any of
my past experiences. It was a sensation that began to permeate my entire being as I sat crouched before my inadequate campfire, chills running up my spine. Chills which, I am certain, were due not entirely to
the dreary gray of a winter "sunrise."

It had been my plan to travel the so-called Ruins Road early today   *3*
and then complete my visit here, but as I stopped along the road and
stood scanning the opposite wall of the canyon for ruins, I felt as if
some force had seized control of my will. I was compelled to make my
way along the rim.

Starting out upon the rock, I weaved in and out repeatedly as the   *4*
gaping emptiness of the canyon and the weathered standstone of the
rim battled one another for territory. At last arriving here, where a narrow peninsula of canyon juts far into the stone, I was able to peer back
into the darkness of a cave carved midway in the vertical wall opposite,
within whose smoke-blackened walls huddle, nearly unnoticeable, the
rooms of a small, crumbled ruin.

They are a haunting sight, these broken houses, clustered to-   *5*
gether down in the gloom of the canyon. It presents a complete
contrast to the tidy, excavated ruins I explored yesterday, lost within a cluster of tourists and guided by a park ranger who expounded constantly upon his wealth of knowledge of excavation techniques
and archaeological dating methods. The excavated ruins seemed, in
comparison, a noisy, almost modern city, punctuated with the click-
ing of camera shutters and the bickering of children. Here it is quiet.
The silence is broken only by the rush of the wind in the trees and
the trickling of a tiny stream of melting snow springing from ledge
to ledge as it makes its way down over the rock to the bottom of the
canyon. And this small, abandoned village of tiny houses seems almost as the Indians left it, reduced by the passage of nearly a thousand years to piles of rubble through which protrude broken red
adobe walls surrounding ghostly jet-black openings, undisturbed by
modern man.

Those windows seem to stare back at me as my eyes are drawn to   *6*
them. They're so horribly empty, yet my gaze is fixed, searching for
some sign of the vitality they must surely have known. I yearn for
sounds amidst the silence, for images of life as it once was in the
bustling and prosperous community of cliff dwellers who lived here so
long ago. It must have been a sunny home when the peaceful, agrari-
an Anasazi, or ancient ones, as the Navajo call them, lived and dreamed
their lives here, wanting little more than to continue in their ways and

be left alone, only to be driven away in the end by warring people with whom they could not contend.

I long to hear, to see, and to understand, and though I strain all my 7 senses to their limits, my wishes are in vain. I remain alone, confronted only by the void below and the cold stare of those utterly desolate windows. I know only an uneasy sensation that I am not entirely alone, and a quick, chill gust gives birth once again to that restless shiver tracing its path along the length of my spine.

As a gray afternoon fades into a gray evening, I can find neither 8 a true feeling of fear nor one of the quiet serenity one would expect to experience here. It is comforting for me to believe that it was the explorer in me which brought me here, to feel that I was lured to stand above this lonely house by that same drive to find and explore the unknown which motivated the countless others who have come here since seeking knowledge and understanding of the ancient people of the "Green Table." Yet as I begin the journey back to my car and the security of an evening fire, I remain uncomfortably unconvinced.

Perhaps the dreariness of a cloudy day united with my solitude to 9 pave a mental pathway for illusion and mystery. Or perhaps all homes are never truly empty, having known the multitude of experience which is human life. Perhaps there lurks, behind every blackened window, a certain unexplainable something we can never understand. I know only that the Indian has long respected these places and given them wide berth, leaving their sanctity inviolate.

QUESTIONS FOR WRITING AND DISCUSSION

1. Describe a similar experience you have had with an empty room or a vacant house. White says that "perhaps all homes are never truly empty, having known the multitude of experience which is human life." Based on your experience, do you agree with him?

2. Through his description, what did White help you "see" about the Anasazi and their cliff dwellings? What did you learn?

3. Consider once again the basic techniques for observing—using sensory detail, comparisons, and images; describing what is not there; noting changes; and writing from a clear point of view. Which ones does White use most effectively? Cite an example of each technique from his essay.

4. In which paragraphs does White use each of the following shaping strategies: spatial order, chronological order, comparisons or contrasts, and simile, metaphor, or analogy? Which strategies did you find most effective in organizing the experience for you as a reader?

"Unlocked Memory Box" by artist Patricia S. Brown

Chapter 4   Remembering

This morning you accidentally ran into a certain person whom you knew several years ago, and for several hours you've been in a bad mood. You called your best friend, but no one answered the phone. You went to class and then for your usual jog, but you pooped out after only half a mile. You even watched a game show on television in the middle of the afternoon and ate half a bag of potato chips, but you still felt lousy. You yell at the television: "Why do I always react this way when I see that person?" But the television has no reply. So you grab some paper and begin scrawling out every memory you have of your experiences with the person you ran into this morning, hoping to understand your feelings.

You and several coworkers have formed a committee to draft a report for your company's vice president in charge of personnel. You have grievances about workload, pay scale, daily procedures, and the attitudes of supervisors. Your report needs to recommend changes in current policies. The committee decides that each person will contribute part of the report by describing actual incidents that have had negative effects on efficiency and human relations. You decide to describe a day last June when your immediate supervisor expected you to learn a new word-processing system and at the same time meet a 3:00 P.M. deadline for a thirty-seven-page budget analysis.

For me the initial delight is in the surprise of remembering something I didn't know I knew.
—ROBERT FROST, POET

The fact is that there's no understanding the future without the present, and no understanding where we are now without a glance, at least, to where we have been.
—JOYCE MAYNARD, COLUMNIST AND AUTHOR OF LOOKING BACKWARD: A CHRONICLE OF GROWING UP OLD IN THE SIXTIES

*T*HE HUMAN BRAIN IS A PACK RAT: NOTHING IS TOO SMALL, OBSCURE, OR MUNDANE FOR THE BRAIN'S COLLECTION. OFTEN THE BRAIN COLLECTS AND DISCARDS INFORMATION WITHOUT regard to our wishes. Out of the collection may arise, with no warning, the image of windblown whitecaps on a lake you visited more than five years ago, the recipe for Uncle Joe's incomparable chili, or even the right answer to an exam question that you've been staring at for the past fifteen minutes.

Remembering is sometimes easy, sometimes difficult. Often careful concentration yields nothing, while the most trivial occurrence—an old song on a car radio, the acrid smell of diesel exhaust, the face of a stranger—will trigger a flood of recollections. Someone tells a story and you immediately recall incidents, funny or traumatic, from your own life. Some memories, however, are nagging and troublesome, keeping you awake at night, daring you to deal with them. You pick at these memories. Why are they so important? You write about them, usually to probe that mystery of yesterday and today. Sights, sounds, or feelings from the present may draw you to the past, but the past leads, just as surely, back to the present.

Direct observations are important to learning and writing, but so are your memories, experiences, and stories. You may write an autobiographical account of part of your life, or you may recall a brief event, a person, or a place just as an example to illustrate a point. Whatever form your writing from memory takes, however, your initial purpose is to remember experiences so that you can understand yourself and your world. The point is not to write fiction, but to practice drawing on your memories and to write vividly enough about them so that you and others can discover and learn.

The value of remembering lies exactly here: Written memories have the power to teach you and, through the *empathy* of your readers, to inform or convince them as well. At first, you may be self-conscious about sharing your personal memories. But as you reveal these experiences, you realize that your story is worth telling—not because you're such an egotist, but because sharing experiences helps everyone learn.

Time passes and the past becomes the present. . . . These presences of the past are there in the center of your life today. You thought . . . they had died, but they have just been waiting their chance.

—CARLOS FUENTES,

MEXICAN ESSAYIST AND NOVELIST, AUTHOR OF THE CRYSTAL FRONTIER.

Techniques for Writing About Memories

Writing vividly about memories includes all the skills of careful observing, but it adds several additional narrative strategies. Listed below are five techniques that writers use to compose effective remembering essays. As you read the essays that follow in this chapter, notice how each writer uses these techniques. Then, when you write your own remembering essay, use these techniques in your own essay. Remember: Not all writing about memories uses all five techniques, but one or two of them may transform a lifeless or boring account into an effective narrative.

- **Using** *detailed observation* **of people, places, and events.** Writing vividly about memories requires many of the skills of careful observation. Give actual dialogue where appropriate.
- **Creating** *specific scenes* **set in time and space.** Show your reader the actual events; don't just tell about events; Narrate specific incidents as they actually happened. Avoid monotonously summarizing events or presenting just the conclusions (for instance, "those experiences really changed my life").
- **Noting** *changes, contrasts,* **or** *conflicts.* Changes in people or places, contrasts between two different memories or between memories of expectations and realities, and conflicts between people or ideas—any of these may lead to the meaning or importance of a remembered person, place, or event.
- **Making** *connections* **between past events, people, or places and the present.** The main idea of a narrative often grows out of changes and conflicts or arises from the connections you make between past and present.
- **Discovering and focusing on a** *main idea.* A remembering essay is not a random narrative of the writer's favorite memories. A narrative should have a clear main point, focus on a main idea, or make a discovery. The essay should clearly show why the memories are important.

All of these techniques are important, but you should also keep several other points in mind. Normally, you should write in the *first person*, using *I* or *we* throughout the narrative. Although you will usually write in *past tense*, sometimes you may wish to lend immediacy to the events by retelling them in the *present tense*, as if they are happening now. Finally, you may choose straightforward *chronological order*, or you may begin near the end and use a *flashback* to tell the beginning of the story.

The key to effective remembering, however, is to get beyond *generalities and conclusions* about your experiences ("I had a lot of fun—those days really changed my life"). Your goal is to recall *specific incidents set in time and place* that *show* how and why those days changed your life. The specific incidents should show your *main point* or *dominant idea.*

The following passage by Andrea Lee began as a journal entry during a year she spent in Moscow and Leningrad following her graduation from college. She then combined these firsthand observations with her memories and published them in a collection called *Russian Journal.* She uses first person and, frequently, present tense as she describes her reactions to the sights of Moscow. In these paragraphs, she weaves observations and memories together to show her main idea: The contrast between American and Russian advertising helped her understand both the virtues and the faults of American commercialism.

(The annotations in the margin illustrate how Lee uses all five remembering techniques.)

Specific scene

In Mayakovsky Square, not far from the Tchaikovsky Concert Hall, a big computerized electric sign sends various messages flashing out into the night. An outline of a taxi in green dots is accompanied by the words: "Take Taxis—All Streets Are Near." This is replaced by multicolored human figures and a sentence urging Soviet citizens to save in State banks. The bright patterns and messages come and go, making this one of the most sophisticated examples of advertising in Moscow. Even on chilly nights when I pass through the square, there is often a little group of Russians standing in front of the sign, watching in fascination for five and ten minutes as the colored dots go through their magical changes. The first few times I saw this, I chuckled and recalled an old joke about an American town so boring that people went out on weekends to watch the Esso sign.

Detailed observation

Connections past and present

Advertising, of course, is the glamorous offspring of capitalism and art: why advertise in a country where there is only one brand, the State brand, of anything, and often not enough even of that? There is nothing here comparable to the glittering overlay of commercialism that Americans, at least, take for granted as part of our cities; nothing like the myriad small seductions of the marketplace, which have led us to expect to be enticed. The Soviet political propaganda posters that fill up a small part of the Moscow landscape with their uniformly cold red color schemes and monumental robot-faced figures are so unappealing that they are dismissable.

Contrast

Main idea

Detailed observation

I realize now, looking back, that for at least my first month in Moscow, I was filled with an unconscious and devastating disappointment. Hardly realizing it, as I walked around the city, I was looking for the constant sensory distractions I was accustomed to in America. Like many others my age, I grew up reading billboards and singing advertising jingles; my idea of beauty was shaped—perniciously, I think— by the models with the painted eyes and pounds of shining hair whose beauty was accessible on every television set and street corner.

Connections past and present

Contrast and change

Main idea

REMEMBERING PEOPLE

In the following passage from the introduction to *The Way to Rainy Mountain*, N. Scott Momaday remembers his grandmother. While details of place and event are also recreated, the primary focus is on the character of his grandmother as revealed in several *specific*, recurring actions. Momaday does not give us generalities about his feelings (for instance, "I miss my grandmother a lot, especially now that she's gone"); instead, he begins with specific memories of scenes that *show* how he felt.

A writer is a reader moved to emulation.
—SAUL BELLOW,
AUTHOR OF HENDERSON
THE RAIN KING

> Now that I can have her only in memory, I see my grandmother in the several postures that were peculiar to her: standing at the wood stove on a winter morning and turning meat in a great iron skillet; sitting at the south window, bent above her beadwork, and afterwards, when her vision failed, looking down for a long time into the fold of her hands; going out upon a cane, very slowly as she did when the weight of age came upon her; praying. I remember her most often at prayer. She made long, rambling prayers out of suffering and hope, having seen many things. I was never sure that I had the right to hear, so exclusive were they of all mere custom and company. The last time I saw her she prayed standing by the side of her bed at night, naked to the waist, the light of a kerosene lamp moving upon her dark skin. Her long, black hair, always drawn and braided in the day, lay upon her shoulders and against her breasts like a shawl. I do not speak Kiowa, and I never understood her prayers, but there was something inherently sad in the sound, some merest hesitation upon the syllables of sorrow. She began in a high and descending pitch, exhausting her breath to silence; then again and again—and always the same intensity of effort, of something that is, and is not, like urgency in the human voice. Transported so in the dancing light among the shadows of her room, she seemed beyond the reach of time. But that was illusion; I think I knew then that I should not see her again.

REMEMBERING PLACES

In the following passage from *Farewell to Manzanar*, Jeanne Wakatsuke Houston remembers the place in California where, as Japanese-Americans, her family were imprisoned during World War II. As you read, look for specific details and bits of description that convey her main idea.

> In Spanish, Manzanar means "apple orchard." Great stretches of Owens Valley were once green with orchards and alfalfa fields. It has been a desert ever since its water started flowing south into Los Angeles, sometime during the twenties. But a few rows of untended pear and apple trees were still growing there when the camp opened, where a shallow water table had kept them alive. In the spring of 1943 we

moved to block 28, right up next to one of the old pear orchards. That's where we stayed until the end of the war, and those trees stand in my memory for the turning of our life in camp, from the outrageous to the tolerable.

Papa pruned and cared for the nearest trees. Late that summer we picked the fruit green and stored it in a root cellar he had dug under our new barracks. At night the wind through the leaves would sound like the surf had sounded in Ocean Park, and while drifting off to sleep, I could almost imagine we were still living by the beach.

REMEMBERING EVENTS

In the following essay, called "The Boy's Desire," Richard Rodriguez recalls a particular event from his childhood that comes to mind when he remembers Christmas. In his memory, he sorts through the rooms in his house on Thirty-ninth Street in Sacramento, recalling old toys: a secondhand bike, games with dice and spinning dials, a jigsaw puzzle, and a bride doll. In this passage, Rodriguez describes both the effort to remember and the memory itself—the one memory that still "holds color and size and shape." Was it all right, he wonders, that a boy should have wanted a doll for Christmas?

The fog comes to mind. It never rained on Christmas. It was never sharp blue and windy. When I remember Christmas in Sacramento, it is in gray: The valley fog would lift by late morning, the sun boiled haze for a few hours, then the tule fog would rise again when it was time to go into the house.

The haze through which memory must wander is thickened by that fog. The rooms of the house on 39th Street are still and dark in late afternoon, and I open the closet to search for old toys. One year there was a secondhand bike. I do not remember a color. Perhaps it had no color even then. Another year there were boxes of games that rattled their parts—dice and pegs and spinning dials. Or perhaps the rattle is of a jigsaw puzzle that compressed into an image . . . of what? of Paris? a litter of kittens? I cannot remember. Only one memory holds color and size and shape: brown hair, blue eyes, the sweet smell of styrene.

That Christmas I announced I wanted a bride doll. I must have been seven or eight—wise enough to know not to tell anyone at school, but young enough to whine out my petition from early November.

My father's reaction was unhampered by psychology. A shrug—"Una muñeca?"—a doll, why not? Because I knew it was my mother who would choose all the presents, it was she I badgered. I wanted a bride doll! "Is there something else you want?" she wondered. No! I'd make clear with my voice that nothing else would appease me. "We'll see," she'd say, and she never wrote it down on her list.

By early December, wrapped boxes started piling up in my parents' bedroom closet, above my father's important papers and the family album. When no one else was home, I'd drag a chair over and climb up to see . . . Looking for the one. About a week before Christmas, it was there. I was so certain it was mine that I punched my thumb through the wrapping paper and the cellophane window on the box and felt inside—lace, two tiny, thin legs. I got other presents that year, but it was the doll I kept by me. I remember my mother saying I'd have "to share her" with my younger sister—but Helen was four years old, oblivious. The doll was mine. My arms would hold her. She would sleep on my pillow.

And the sky did not fall. The order of the universe did not tremble. In fact, it was right for a change. My family accommodated itself to my request. My brother and sisters played round me with their own toys. I paraded my doll by the hands across the floor.

The other day, when I asked my brother and sisters about the doll, no one remembered. My mother remembers. "Yes," she smiled. "One year there was a doll."

The closet door closes. (The house on 39th Street has been razed for a hospital parking lot.) The fog rises. Distance tempts me to mock the boy and his desire. The fact remains: One Christmas in Sacramento I wanted a bride doll, and I got one.

Some very small incident that takes place today may be the most important event that happens to you this year, but you don't know that when it happens. You don't know it until much later.

—TONI MORRISON,
NOBEL PRIZE-WINNING
AUTHOR OF BELOVED AND
SONG OF SOLOMON

■ WARMING UP: JOURNAL EXERCISES   The following topics will help you practice writing about your memories. Read all of the following exercises, and then write on three that interest you the most. If another idea occurs to you, write a free entry about it.

1. Select one moment in your past that either changed your life or showed you how your life had already changed. What was the event? What were you like before—and afterward?
2. Go through old family photographs and find one of yourself, taken at least five years ago. Describe the person in the photograph—what he or

she did, thought, said, or hoped. How is that person like or unlike the person you are now?

3. Remember the first job you had. How did you get it, and what did you do? What mistakes did you make? What did you learn? Were there any humorous or serious misunderstandings between you and others?

4. Pick a favorite record from your collection—one that you've owned for a few years—and play one track. As you listen, write down the associations or memories that come to mind. What were you doing when you first heard the song? What other people, places, or events does it remind you of?

5. What are your earliest memories? Choose one particular event. How old were you? What was the place? Who were the people around you? What happened? After you write down your earliest memories, call members of your family, if possible, and interview them for their memories of this incident. How does what you actually remember differ from what your family tells you? Revise your first memory to incorporate additional details provided by your family.

6. At some point in the past, you may have faced a conflict between what was expected of you—by parents, friends, family, coach, or employer—and your own personality or abilities. Describe one occasion when these expectations seemed unrealistic or unfair. Was the experience entirely negative or was it, in the long run, positive?

7. At at least one point in our lives, we have felt like an outsider. In a selection earlier in this chapter, for instance, Richard Rodriguez recalls feelings of being different, rejected, or outcast. Write about an incident when you felt alienated from your family, peers, or social group. Focus on a key scene or scenes that show what happened, why it was important, and how it affects you now.

8. Read Helen Keller's or Mike Rose's essay later in this chapter and write your own literacy narrative. What are your early memories about learning to read and write? At what points did you struggle or fail? When did you most enjoy reading or writing?

PROFESSIONAL WRITING

THE DAY LANGUAGE CAME INTO MY LIFE

Helen Keller

At the age of eighteen months, Helen Keller (1880–1968) lost her sight and hearing as a result of illness. During the next five years of her childhood, Keller became increasingly wild and unruly as she struggled against

*her dark and silent world. In "The Day Language Came into My Life,"
Keller remembers how, at age seven, her teacher, Anne Sullivan, arrived and
taught her the miracle of language. After learning sign language and braille,
Keller began her formal schooling and—with continued help from Sullivan—eventually graduated with honors from Radcliffe College. In her
adult years, Keller became America's best-loved ambassador for the blind
and disabled. She met nearly every American president, traveled to dozens
of countries to speak on behalf of blind and deaf people, and wrote several
books, including* The Story of My Life *(1903),* The World I Live In
(1908), and Midstream: My Later Life *(1930). The story of Anne Sullivan's teaching is told in William Gibson's Pulitzer Prize-winning play,*
The Miracle Worker.

The most important day I remember in all my life is the one on which   *1*
my teacher, Anne Mansfield Sullivan, came to me. I am filled with
wonder when I consider the immeasurable contrast between the two
lives which it connects. It was the third of March 1887, three months
before I was seven years old.

On the afternoon of that eventful day, I stood on the porch, dumb,   *2*
expectant. I guessed vaguely from my mother's signs and from the
hurrying to and fro in the house that something unusual was about to
happen, so I went to the door and waited on the steps. The afternoon
sun penetrated the mass of honeysuckle that covered the porch and fell
on my upturned face. My fingers lingered almost unconsciously on
the familiar leaves and blossoms which had just come forth to greet
the sweet southern spring. I did not know what the future held of
marvel or surprise for me. Anger and bitterness had preyed upon me
continually for weeks and a deep languor had succeeded this passionate struggle.

Have you ever been at sea in a dense fog, when it seemed as if a   *3*
tangible white darkness shut you in, and the great ship, tense and anxious, groped her way toward the shore with plummet and sounding-
line, and you waited with beating heart for something to happen? I
was like that ship before my education began, only I was without compass or sounding-line and had no way of knowing how near the harbor was. "Light! give me light!" was the wordless cry of my soul, and
the light of love shone on me in that very hour.

I felt approaching footsteps. I stretched out my hand as I sup-   *4*
posed to my mother. Someone took it, and I was caught up and held
close in the arms of her who had come to reveal all things to me, and,
more than all things else, to love me.

The morning after my teacher came she led me into her   *5*
room and gave me a doll. The little blind children at the Perkins

Institution had sent it and Laura Bridgman had dressed it; but I did not know this until afterward. When I had played with it a little while, Miss Sullivan slowly spelled into my hand the word "d-o-l-l." I was at once interested in this finger play and tried to imitate it. When I finally succeeded in making the letters correctly I was flushed with childish pleasure and pride. Running downstairs to my mother I held up my hand and made the letters for doll. I did not know that I was spelling a word or even that words existed; I was simply making my fingers go in monkeylike imitation. In the days that followed I learned to spell in this uncomprehending way a great many words, among them *pin, hat, cup* and a few verbs like *sit, stand* and *walk.* But my teacher had been with me several weeks before I understood that everything has a name.

One day, while I was playing with my new doll, Miss Sullivan put 6 my big rag doll into my lap also, spelled "d-o-l-l" and tried to make me understand that "d-o-l-l" applied to both. Earlier in the day we had had a tussle over the words "m-u-g" and "w-a-t-e-r." Miss Sullivan had tried to impress it upon me that "m-u-g" is *mug* and that "w-a-t-e-r" is *water,* but I persisted in confounding the two. In despair she had dropped the subject for the time, only to renew it at the first opportunity. I became impatient at her repeated attempts and, seizing the new doll, I dashed it upon the floor. I was keenly delighted when I felt the fragments of the broken doll at my feet. Neither sorrow nor regret followed my passionate outburst. I had not loved the doll. In the still, dark world in which I lived there was no strong sentiment or tenderness. I felt my teacher sweep the fragments to one side of the hearth, and I had a sense of satisfaction that the cause of my discomfort was removed. She brought me my hat, and I knew I was going out into the warm sunshine. This thought, if a wordless sensation may be called a thought, made me hop and skip with pleasure.

We walked down the path to the well-house, attracted by the fra- 7 grance of the honeysuckle with which it was covered. Someone was drawing water and my teacher placed my hand under the spout. As the cool stream gushed over one hand she spelled into the other the word *water,* first slowly, then rapidly. I stood still, my whole attention fixed upon the motions of her fingers. Suddenly I felt a misty consciousness as of something forgotten—a thrill of returning thought; and somehow the mystery of language was revealed to me. I knew then that "w-a-t-e-r" meant the wonderful cool something that was flowing over my hand. The living word awakened my soul, gave it light, hope, joy, set it free! There were barriers still, it is true, but barriers that could in time be swept away.

I left the well-house eager to learn. Everything had a name, and *8* each name gave birth to a new thought. As we returned to the house every object which I touched seemed to quiver with life. That was because I saw everything with the strange, new sight that had come to me. On entering the door I remembered the doll I had broken. I felt my way to the hearth and picked up the pieces. I tried vainly to put them together. Then my eyes filled with tears; for I realized what I had done, and for the first time I felt repentance and sorrow.

I learned a great many new words that day. I do not remember what *9* they all were; but I do know that *mother, father, sister, teacher* were among them—words that were to make the world blossom for me, "like Aaron's rod, with flowers." It would have been difficult to find a happier child than I was as I lay in my crib at the close of that eventful day and lived over the joys it had brought me, and for the first time longed for a new day to come.

Vocabulary

In your journal, write the meanings of the following words:

- I stood on the porch, *dumb* (**2**)
- a deep *languor* (**2**)
- with *plummet* and *sounding-line* (**3**)
- no strong *sentiment* (**6**)
- like *Aaron's rod* (**9**)

Questions for Writing and Discussion

1. Write for five minutes, recalling your earliest memories of reading, speaking, or writing. Focus on one specific incident. How old were you? Where were you? What were you reading or writing?

2. Helen Keller's books have been translated into more than fifty languages. Explain why you believe her story, as illustrated in this essay, has such universal appeal.

3. In paragraph 3, Keller uses an analogy to explain her feelings and her state of mind before language opened her life. Identify the extended comparison. What "difficult concept" does Keller explain through her analogy?

4. In paragraph 8, Keller says, "Everything had a name, and each name gave birth to a new thought." Explain what Keller means by using examples of the names of things from your own life.

5. Contrast Keller's actions and feelings before she discovers language to her actions and feeling afterward. In addition to learning words, how do her feelings and personality change?

6. A century ago, when Helen Keller was learning to read and speak, people who were blind and deaf were classified by the law as "idiots." Describe one experience you have had with a disabled person. Based on that experience, explain how Americans' attitudes toward people with some disability have (or have not) improved.

7. On the Internet, use a search engine to gather articles on the education of deaf and/or blind children. What technologies are available to help teachers and students? One recent program on ABC's 20/20 featured a computer animation character named Baldi who helps children learn to read lips. Kids wear headphones over an acoustic nerve implant that converts sound into electrical signals that are relayed to the brain. Check out the article entitled "Look Who's Talking" from ABCNEWS.com: PrimeTime: Teaching Deaf Kids to Speak.

PROFESSIONAL WRITING

LIVES ON THE BOUNDARY
Mike Rose

Mike Rose was born to Italian immigrant parents in 1944, and his family moved to Los Angeles, where he attended Our Lady of Mercy, a private Catholic school. He continued his education at Loyola University, graduating in 1966, and went on to earn his Ph.D. from UCLA in 1981. Rose currently teaches at UCLA and is the author of numerous articles and books, including When a Writer Can't Write: Studies in Writer's Block and Other Composing Problems *(1985),* Lives on the Boundary *(1989), and* Possible Lives: The Promise of Public Education in America *(1995). In the following selection, taken from the second chapter of* Lives on the Boundary, *Rose recalls how he was originally misplaced in a high school vocational track and then was shifted to college prep courses. Rose focuses his memories on his fellow students in the voc. ed. track and on one English teacher, Jack MacFarland, who opened his mind to the world of books and*

*ideas and who helped him get to college and live "beyond the limiting bound-
aries" of his South Los Angeles neighborhood.*

My parents used to say that their son would have the best education   *1*
they could afford. Maybe I would be a doctor. There was a public school
in our neighborhood and several Catholic schools to the west. They had
heard that quality schooling meant private, Catholic schooling, so they
somehow got the money together to send me to Our Lady of Mercy,
fifteen or so miles southwest of Ninety-first and Vermont.

It took two buses to get to Our Lady of Mercy. The first started   *2*
deep in South Los Angeles and caught me at midpoint. The second
drifted through neighborhoods with trees, parks, big lawns, and lots of
flowers. The rides were long but were livened up by a group of South
L.A. veterans whose parents also thought that Hope had set up shop
in the west end of the county. There was Christy Biggars, who, at sixteen, was dealing and was, according to rumor, a pimp as well. There
were Bill Cobb and Johnny Gonzales, grease-pencil artists extraordi-
naire, who left Nembutal-enhanced swirls of "Cobb" and "Johnny" on
the corrugated walls of the bus. And then there was Tyrrell Wilson.
Tyrrell was the coolest kid I knew. He ran the dozens like a metric halfback, laid down a rap that outrhymed and outpointed Cobb, whose rap
was good but not great—the curse of a moderately soulful kid trapped
in white skin. But it was Cobb who would sneak a radio onto the bus,
and thus underwrote his patter with Little Richard, Fats Domino,
Chuck Berry, the Coasters, and Ernie K. Doe's mother-in-law, an awful
woman who was "sent from down below." And so it was that Christy
and Cobb and Johnny G. and Tyrrell and I and assorted others picked
up along the way passed our days in the back of the bus, a funny mix
brought together by geography and parental desire.

Entrance to school brings with it forms and releases and assess-   *3*
ments. Mercy relied on a series of tests, mostly the Stanford-Binet, for
placement, and somehow the results of my tests got confused with
those of another student named Rose. The other Rose apparently did-
n't do very well, for I was placed in the vocational track, a euphemism
for the bottom level. Neither I nor my parents realized what this meant.
We had no sense that Business Math, Typing, and English-Level D
were dead ends. The current spate of reports on the schools criticizes
parents for not involving themselves in the education of their children.
But how would someone like Tommy Rose, with his two years of Italian schooling, know what to ask? And what sort of pressure could an
exhausted waitress apply? The error went undetected, and I remained
in the vocational track for two years. What a place.

Students will float to the mark you set. I and the others in the vocational classes were bobbing in pretty shallow water. Vocational education has aimed at increasing the economic opportunities of students who do not do well in our schools. Some serious programs succeed in doing that, and through exceptional teachers—like Mr. Gross in *Horace's Compromise*—students learn to develop hypotheses and troubleshoot, reason through a problem, and communicate effectively—the true job skills. The vocational track, however, is most often a place for those who are just not making it, a dumping ground for the disaffected. There were a few teachers who worked hard at education; young Brother Slattery, for example, combined a stern voice with weekly quizzes to try to pass along to us a skeletal outline of world history. But mostly the teachers had no idea of how to engage the imaginations of us kids who were scuttling along at the bottom of the pond.

4

But I did learn things about people and eventually came into my own socially. I liked the guys in Voc. Ed. Growing up where I did, I understood and admired physical prowess, and there was an abundance of muscle here. There was Dave Snyder, a sprinter and a halfback of true quality. Dave's ability and his quick wit gave him a natural appeal, and he was welcome in any clique, though he always kept a little independent. It was a testament to his independence that he included me among his friends—I eventually went out for track, but I was no jock. Owing to the Latin alphabet and a dearth of Rs and Ss, Snyder sat behind Rose, and we started exchanging one-liners and became friends.

5

There was Ted Richard, a much-touted Little League pitcher. He was chunky and had a baby face and came to Our Lady of Mercy as a seasoned street fighter. Ted was quick to laugh and he had a loud, jolly laugh, but when he got angry he'd smile a little smile, the kind that simply raises the corner of the mouth a quarter of an inch. For those who knew, it was an eerie signal. Those who didn't found themselves in big trouble, for Ted was very quick. He loved to carry on what we would come to call philosophical discussions: What is courage? Does God exist? He also loved words, enjoyed picking up big ones like *salubrious* and *equivocal* and using them in our conversations—laughing at himself as the word hit a chuckhole rolling off his tongue. Ted didn't do all that well in school—baseball and parties and testing the courage he'd speculated about took up his time. His textbooks were *Argosy* and *Field and Stream*, whatever newspapers he'd find on the bus stop—from the *Daily Worker* to pornography— conversations with uncles or hobos or businessmen he'd meet in a coffee shop, *The Old Man and the Sea*. With hindsight, I can see that

6

Ted was developing into one of those rough-hewn intellectuals whose sources are a mix of the learned and the apocryphal, whose discussions are both assured and sad.

And then there was Ken Harvey. Ken was good-looking in a puffy way and had a full and oily ducktail and was a car enthusiast . . . a hodad. One day in religion class, he said the sentence that turned out to be one of the most memorable of the hundreds of thousands I heard in those Voc. Ed. years. We were talking about the parable of the talents, about achievement, working hard, doing the best you can do, blah-blah-blah, when the teacher called on the restive Ken Harvey for an opinion. Ken thought about it, but just for a second, and said (with studied, minimal affect), "I just wanna be average." That woke me up. Average?! Who wants to be average? Then the athletes chimed in with the clichés that make you want to laryngectomize them, and the exchange became a platitudinous melee. At the time, I thought Ken's assertion was stupid, and I wrote him off. But his sentence has stayed with me all these years, and I think I am finally coming to understand it. . . .

My own deliverance from the Voc. Ed. world began with sophomore biology. Every student, college prep to vocational, had to take biology, and unlike the other courses, the same person taught all sections. When teaching the vocational group, Brother Clint probably slowed down a bit or omitted a little of the fundamental biochemistry, but he used the same book and more or less the same syllabus across the board. If one class got tough, he could get tougher. He was young and powerful and very handsome, and looks and physical strength were high currency. No one gave him any trouble.

I was pretty bad at the dissecting table, but the lectures and the textbook were interesting: plastic overlays that, with each turned page, peeled away skin, then veins and muscle, then organs, down to the very bones that Brother Clint, pointer in hand, would tap out on our hanging skeleton. Dave Snyder was in big trouble, for the study of life—versus the living of it—was sticking in his craw. We worked out a code for our multiple-choice exams. He'd poke me in the back: once for the answer under A, twice for B, and so on; and when he'd hit the right one, I'd look up to the ceiling as though I were lost in thought. Poke: cytoplasm. Poke, poke: methane. Poke, poke, poke: William Harvey. Poke, poke, poke, poke: islets of Langerhans. This didn't work out perfectly, but Dave passed the course, and I mastered the dreamy look of a guy on a record jacket. And something else happened. Brother Clint puzzled over this Voc. Ed. kid who was racking up 98s and 99s on his tests. He checked the school's records and discovered the error. He recommended that I begin my junior year in the College Prep program. According to all I've read since, such a shift, as one report puts it, is virtually impossible. Kids at that level rarely cross tracks. The telling thing is how chancy both my placement into and exit from Voc. Ed. was; neither I nor my parents had anything to do with it. I lived in one world during spring semester, and when I came back to school in the fall, I was living in another.

Switching to College Prep was a mixed blessing. I was an errat-   *10* ic student. I was undisciplined. And I hadn't caught onto the rules of the game: Why work hard in a class that didn't grab my fancy? I was also hopelessly behind in math. Chemistry was hard; toying with my chemistry set years before hadn't prepared me for the chemist's equations. Fortunately, the priest who taught both chemistry and second year algebra was also the school's athletic director. Membership on the track team covered me; I knew I wouldn't get lower than a C. U.S. history was taught pretty well, and I did okay. But civics was taken over by a football coach who had trouble reading the textbook aloud—and reading aloud was the centerpiece of his pedagogy. College Prep at Mercy was certainly an improvement over the vocational program—at least it carried some status—but the social science curriculum was weak, and the mathematics and physical sciences were simply beyond me. . . .

Jack MacFarland couldn't have come into my life at a better time.   *11* Mr. MacFarland had a master's degree from Columbia and decided, at twenty-six, to find a little school and teach his heart out. He never took any credentialing courses, couldn't bear to, he said, so he had to find employment in a private system. He ended up at Our Lady of Mercy teaching five sections of senior English. He was a beatnik who was born too late. His teeth were stained, he tucked his sorry tie in between the third and fourth buttons of his shirt, and his pants were chronically wrinkled. At first, we couldn't believe this guy, thought he slept in his car. But within no time, he had us so startled with work that we didn't much worry about where he slept or if he slept at all. We wrote three or four essays a month. We read a book every two to three weeks, starting with the *Iliad* and ending up with Hemingway. He gave us a quiz on the reading every other day. He brought a prep school curriculum to Mercy High.

MacFarland's lectures were crafted, and as he delivered them he   *12* would pace the room jiggling a piece of chalk in his cupped hand, using it to scribble on the board the names of all the writers and philosophers and plays and novels he was weaving into his discussion. He asked questions often; raised everything from Zeno's paradox to the repeated last line of Frost's "Stopping by Woods on a Snowy Evening." He slowly and carefully built up our knowledge of Western intellectual history—with facts, with connections, with speculations. We learned about Greek philosophy, about Dante, the Elizabethan world view, the Age of Reason, existentialism. He analyzed poems with us, had us reading sections from John Ciardi's *How Does a Poem Mean?*, making a potentially difficult book accessible with his own explanations. We gave oral reports on poems Ciardi didn't cover. We imitated the styles of Conrad, Hemingway, and *Time* magazine. We wrote and talked, wrote and talked. The man immersed us in language.

Even MacFarland's barbs were literary. If Jim Fitzsimmons, hung *13* over and irritable, tried to smart-ass him, he'd rejoin with a flourish that would spark the indomitable Skip Madison—who'd lost his front teeth in a hapless tackle—to flick his tongue through the gap and opine, "good chop," drawing out the single "o" in stinging indictment. Jack MacFarland, this tobacco-stained intellectual, brandished linguistic weapons of a kind I hadn't encountered before. Here was this *egghead*, for God's sake, keeping some pretty difficult people in line. And from what I heard, Mike Dweetz and Steve Fusco and all the notorious Voc. Ed. crowd settled down as well when MacFarland took the podium. Though a lot of guys groused in the schoolyard, it just seemed that giving trouble to this particular teacher was a silly thing to do. Tomfoolery, not to mention assault, had no place in the world he was trying to create for us, and instinctively everyone knew that. If nothing else, we all recognized MacFarland's considerable intelligence and respected the hours he put into his work. It came to this: The troublemaker would look foolish rather than daring. Even Jim Fitzsimmons was reading *On the Road* and turning his incipient alcoholism to literary ends.

There were some lives that were already beyond Jack MacFar- *14* land's ministrations, but mine was not. I started reading again as I hadn't since elementary school. I would go into our gloomy little bedroom or sit at the dinner table while, on the television, Danny McShane was paralyzing Mr. Moto with the atomic drop, and work slowly back through *Heart of Darkness*, trying to catch the words in Conrad's sentences. I certainly was not MacFarland's best student; most of the other guys in College Prep, even my fellow slackers, had better backgrounds than I did. But I worked very hard, for MacFarland had hooked me. He tapped my old interest in reading and creating stories. He gave me a way to feel special by using my mind. And he provided a role model that wasn't shaped on physical prowess alone, and something inside me that I wasn't quite aware of responded to that. Jack MacFarland established a literacy club, to borrow a phrase of Frank Smith's, and invited me—invited all of us—to join.

In my last semester of high school, I elected a special English   *15*
course fashioned by Mr. MacFarland, and it was through this elective that there arose at Mercy a fledgling literati. Art Mitz, the editor of the school newspaper and a very smart guy, was the kingpin. He was joined by me and Mark Dever, a quiet boy who wrote beautifully and who would die before he was forty. MacFarland occasionally invited us to his apartment, and those visits became the high point of our apprenticeship: We'd clamp on our training wheels and drive to his salon.

He lived in a cramped and cluttered place near the airport, tucked   *16*
away in the kind of building that architectural critic Reyner Banham calls a *dingbat*. Books were all over: stacked, piled, tossed, and crated, underlined and dog eared, well worn and new. Cigarette ashes crusted with coffee in saucers or spilled over the sides of motel ashtrays. The little bedroom had, along two of its walls, bricks and boards loaded with notes, magazines, and oversized books. The kitchen joined the living room, and there was a stack of German newspapers under the sink. I had never seen anything like it: a great flophouse of language furnished by City Lights and Café le Metro. I read every title. I flipped through paperbacks and scanned jackets and memorized names: Gogol, *Finnegan's Wake*, Djuna Barnes, Jackson Pollock, *A Coney Island of the Mind*, F. O. Matthiessen's *American Renaissance*, all sorts of Freud, *Troubled Sleep*, Man Ray, the *Education of Henry Adams*, Richard Wright, *Film as Art*, William Butler Yeats, Marguerite Duras, *Redburn, a Season in Hell, Kapital*. On the cover of Alain-Fournier's *The Wanderer* was an Edward Gorey drawing of a young man on a road winding into dark trees. By the hotplate sat a strange Kafka novel called *Amerika*, in which an adolescent hero crosses the Atlantic to find the Nature Theater of Oklahoma. Art and Mark would be talking about a movie or the school newspaper, and I would be consuming my English teacher's library. It was heady stuff. I felt like a Pop Warner athlete on steroids.

Let me be the first to admit that there was a good deal of ado-   *17*
lescent passion in this embrace of the avant-garde: self-absorption, sexually charged pedantry, an elevation of the odd and abandoned. Still it was a time during which I absorbed an awful lot of information: long lists of titles, images from expressionist paintings, new wave shibboleths, snippets of philosophy, and names that read like Steve Fusco's misspellings—Goethe, Nietzsche, Kierkegaard. Now this is hardly the stuff of deep understanding. But it was an introduction, a phrase book, a Baedeker to a vocabulary of ideas, and it

felt good at the time to know all these words. With hindsight I realize how layered and important that knowledge was.

It enabled me to do things in the world. I could browse bohemi- *18* an bookstores in far-off, mysterious Hollywood; I could go to the Cinema and see events through the lenses of European directors; and, most of all, I could share an evening, talk that talk, with Jack MacFarland, the man I most admired at the time. Knowledge was becoming a bonding agent. Within a year or two, the persona of the disaffected hipster would prove too cynical, too alienated to last. But for a time it was new and exciting: It provided a critical perspective on society, and it allowed me to act as though I were living beyond the limiting boundaries of South Vermont.

VOCABULARY

In your journal, write the meanings of the following words:

- a *euphemism* for the bottom level **(3)**
- picking up big ones like *salubrious* and *equivocal* **(6)**
- a mix of the learned and the *apocryphal* **(6)**
- centerpiece of his *pedagogy* **(10)**
- turning his *incipient* alcoholism to literary ends **(13)**
- beyond Jack MacFarland's *ministrations* **(14)**
- this embrace of the *avant-garde* **(17)**
- new wave *shibboleths* **(17)**
- a *Baedeker* to a vocabulary of ideas **(17)**

QUESTIONS FOR WRITING AND DISCUSSION

1. The title of Mike Rose's book is *Lives on the Boundary*. In this selection, what "boundaries" do the voc. ed. students face? What boundaries does Rose face? Which of these boundaries is Rose able to cross? (How are these boundaries similar to or different from the boundaries you faced growing up?)

2. Effective remembering essays build on detailed descriptions. Review the *observing* techniques from Chapter 3. Of the techniques discussed there (using sensory details and images, describing what is not present, noting changes, writing from a point of view, and focusing on a dominant idea), which does Rose use most effectively? To support your choice(s), find examples from Rose's essay.

3. Review the remembering techniques listed early in this chapter. Which does Rose use most effectively in his essay? Cite examples to support your choice(s). Which techniques might he add to his essay? Where, for example, might Rose use dialogue to recreate a school scene more vividly?

4. In his essay, Rose creates two voices, which represent him as a high school student and as a forty-five-year-old man looking back on his early education. Find examples that illustrate each of these voices. (Should Rose interrupt the narration about his high school years with his older reflections? Why or why not?)

5. Write your own remembering essay describing a particular teacher from high school or college who impressed you or influenced the direction of your life. Recall scenes from this time in your life that illustrate how this teacher changed your life.

6. Although Rose overcame his misplacement in the voc. ed. track, the consequences of standardized tests can be disastrous. What is your experience with state tests, high stakes tests, exit tests, and SAT tests? Have the results accurately indicated your abilities? Do these tests cause more harm than good? Read the essay by Eric Boese. Then check out two web sites, the Fordam Foundation at http://www.edexcellence.net/topics/standards.html and Assessment & Evaluation on the Internet at http://ericae.net/inbod.stm. Browse through some of the articles. Then write your own essay that draws on your experience with educational testing to recommend changes in testing procedures to the administrators of your high school.

PROFESSIONAL WRITING

BEAUTY: WHEN THE OTHER DANCER IS THE SELF

Alice Walker

The author of the Pulitzer Prize-winning novel The Color Purple *(1983), Alice Walker has written works of fiction and poetry, including* Love and Trouble: Stories of Black Women *(1973),* Meridian *(1976), and* By the Light of My Father's Smile: A Novel *(1998). "Beauty: When the Other Dancer Is the Self" originally appeared in* Ms. *magazine and was revised and published in Walker's collection of essays,* In Search of Our Mothers' Gardens *(1983). Walker, a former editor of* Ms., *refers in this essay to Gloria Steinem and an interview published in* Ms. *entitled "Do You Know This Woman? She Knows You—A Profile of Alice Walker." As you read the essay reprinted here, consider Walker's purpose: Why is she telling us—total strangers—about a highly personal and traumatic event that shaped her life?*

It is a bright summer day in 1947. My father, a fat, funny man with   *1* beautiful eyes and a subversive wit, is trying to decide which of his eight children he will take with him to the county fair. My mother, of course, will not go. She is knocked out from getting us ready: I hold my neck stiff against the pressure of her knuckles as she hastily completes the braiding and then beribboning of my hair.

My father is the driver for the rich old white lady up the road.   *2* Her name is Miss Mey. She owns all the land for miles around, as well as the house in which we live. All I remember about her is that she once offered to pay my mother thirty-five cents for cleaning her house, raking up piles of her magnolia leaves, and washing her family's clothes, and that my mother—she of no money, eight children, and a chronic earache—refused it. But I do not think of this in 1947. I am two-and-a-half years old. I want to go everywhere my daddy goes. I am excited at the prospect of riding in a car. Someone has told me fairs are fun. That there is room in the car for only three of us does-n't faze me at all. Whirling happily in my starchy frock, showing off my biscuit polished patent leather shoes and lavender socks, tossing my head in a way that makes my ribbons bounce, I stand, hands on hips, before my father. "Take me, Daddy," I say with assurance, "I'm the prettiest!"

Later, it does not surprise me to find myself in Miss Mey's shiny   *3* black car, sharing the backseat with the other lucky ones. Does not surprise me that I thoroughly enjoy the fair. At home that night I tell all the unlucky ones about the merry-go-round, the man who eats live chickens, and the abundance of Teddy bears, until they say: that's enough, baby Alice. Shut up now, and go to sleep.

It is Easter Sunday, 1950. I am dressed in a green, flocked   *4* scalloped-hem dress (handmade by my adoring sister Ruth) that has its own smooth satin petticoat and tiny hot-pink roses tucked into each scallop. My shoes, new T-strap patent leather, again highly biscuit pol-ished. I am six years old and have learned one of the longest Easter speeches to be heard in church that day, totally unlike the speech I said when I was two: "Easter lilies/pure and white/blossom in/the morning light." When I rise to give my speech I do so on a great wave of love and pride and expectation. People in the church stop rustling their new crinolines. They seem to hold their breath. I can tell they admire my dress, but it is my spirit, bordering on sassiness (womanishness), they secretly applaud.

"That girl's a little *mess*," they whisper to each other, pleased.   *5*

Naturally I say my speech without stammer or pause, unlike those   *6* who stutter, stammer, or, worst of all, forget. This is before the word "beautiful" exists in people's vocabulary, but "Oh, isn't she the *cutest thing!*" frequently floats my way. "And got so much sense!" they gratefully add . . . for which thoughtful addition I thank them to this day.

It was great fun being cute. But then, one day, it ended.   *7*

I am eight years old and a tomboy. I have a cowboy hat, cowboy   *8* boots, checkered shirt and pants, all red. My playmates are my brothers, two and four years older than I. Their colors are black and green, the only difference in the way we are dressed. On Saturday nights we all go to the picture show, even my mother: Westerns are her favorite kind of movie. Back home, "on the ranch," we pretend we are Tom Mix, Hopalong Cassidy, Lash LaRue (we've even named one of our dogs Lash LaRue); we chase each other for hours rustling cattle, being outlaws, delivering damsels from distress. Then my parents decide to buy my brothers guns. These are not "real" guns. They shoot "BBs," copper pellets my brothers say will kill birds. Because I am a girl, I do not get a gun. Instantly I am relegated to the position of Indian. Now there appears a great distance between us. They shoot and shoot at everything with their new guns. I try to keep up with my bow and arrows.

One day while I am standing on top of our makeshift "garage"—   *9* pieces of tin nailed across some poles—holding my bow and arrow and looking out toward the fields, I feel an incredible blow in my right eye. I look down just in time to see my brother lower his gun.

Both brothers rush to my side. My eye stings, and I cover it with   *10* my hand. "If you tell," they say, "we will get a whipping. You don't want that to happen, do you?" I do not. "Here is a piece of wire," says the older brother, picking it up from the roof; "say you stepped on one end of it and the other flew up and hit you." The pain is beginning to start. "Yes," I say. "Yes, I will say that is what happened." If I do not say this is what happened, I know my brothers will find ways to make me wish I had. But now I will say anything that gets me to my mother.

Confronted by our parents we stick to the lie agreed upon. They   *11* place me on a bench on the porch and I close my left eye while they examine the right. There is a tree growing from underneath the porch, that climbs past the railing to the roof. It is the last thing my right eye sees. I watch as its trunk, its branches, and then its leaves are blotted out by the rising blood.

I am in shock. First there is intense fever, which my father tries to *12* break using lily leaves bound around my head. Then there are chills: my mother tries to get me to eat soup. Eventually, I do not know how, my parents learn what has happened. A week after the "accident" they take me to see a doctor. "Why did you wait so long to come?" he asks, looking into my eye and shaking his head. "Eyes are sympathetic," he says. "If one is blind, the other will likely become blind too."

This comment of the doctor's terrifies me. But it is really how I *13* look that bothers me most. Where the BB pellet struck there is a glob of whitish scar tissue, a hideous cataract, on my eye. Now when I stare at people—a favorite pastime, up to now—they will stare back. Not at the "cute" little girl, but at her scar. For six years I do not stare at anyone because I do not raise my head.

Years later, in the throes of a mid-life crisis, I ask my mother and *14* sister whether I changed after the "accident." "No," they say, puzzled. "What do you mean?"

What do I mean?   *15*

I am eight, and for the first time, doing poorly in school, where I *16* have been something of a whiz since I was four. We have just moved to the place where the "accident" occurred. We do not know any of the people around us because this is a different county. The only time I see the friends I knew is when we go back to our old church. The new school is the former state penitentiary. It is a large stone building, cold and drafty, crammed to overflowing with boisterous, ill-disciplined children. On the third floor there is a huge circular imprint of some partition that has been torn out.

"What used to be here?" I ask a sullen girl next to me on our way *17* past it to lunch.

"The electric chair," says she.   *18*

At night I have nightmares about the electric chair, and about all *19* the people reputedly "fried" in it. I am afraid of the school, where all the students seem to be budding criminals.

"What's the matter with your eye?" they ask, critically.   *20*

When I don't answer (I cannot decide whether it was an "acci- *21* dent" or not), they shove me, insist on a fight.

My brother, the one who created the story about the wire, comes to *22* my rescue. But then brags so much about "protecting" me, I become sick.

After months of torture at the school, my parents decide to send *23* me back to our old community to my old school. I live with my grandparents and the teacher they board. But there is no room for Phoebe, my cat. By the time my grandparents decide there is room, and I ask for my cat, she cannot be found. Miss Yarborough, the boarding teacher, takes me under her wing, and begins to teach me to play the piano. But soon she marries an African—a "prince," she says—and is whisked away to his continent.

At my old school there is at least one teacher who loves me. She   *24*
is the teacher who "knew me before I was born" and bought my first baby clothes. It is she who makes my life bearable. It is her presence that finally helps me turn on the one child at the school who continually calls me "one-eyed bitch." One day I simply grab him by his coat and beat him until I am satisfied. It is my teacher who tells me my mother is ill.

My mother is lying in bed in the middle of the day, something I   *25*
have never seen. She is in too much pain to speak. She has an abscess in her ear. I stand looking down on her, knowing that if she dies, I cannot live. She is being treated with warm oils and hot bricks held against her cheek. Finally a doctor comes. But I must go back to my grandparents' house. The weeks pass, but I am hardly aware of it. All I know is that my mother might die, my father is not so jolly, my brothers still have their guns, and I am the one sent away from home.

"You did not change," they say.   *26*

Did I imagine the anguish of never looking up?   *27*

I am twelve. When relatives come to visit I hide in my room. My   *28*
cousin Brenda, just my age, whose father works in the post office and whose mother is a nurse, comes to find me. "Hello," she says. And then she asks, looking at my recent school picture which I did not want taken, and on which the "glob" as I think of it is clearly visible, "You still can't see out of that eye?"

"No," I say, and flop back on the bed over my book.   *29*

That night, as I do almost every night, I abuse my eye. I rant and   *30*
rave at it, in front of the mirror. I plead with it to clear up before morning. I tell it I hate and despise it. I do not pray for sight. I pray for beauty.

"You did not change," they say.   *31*

I am fourteen and baby-sitting for my brother Bill who lives in   *32*
Boston. He is my favorite brother and there is a strong bond between us. Understanding my feelings of shame and ugliness, he and his wife take me to a local hospital where the "glob" is removed by a doctor named O. Henry. There is still a small bluish crater where the scar tissue was, but the ugly white stuff is gone. Almost immediately I become a different person from the girl who does not raise her head. Or so I think. Now that I've raised my head, I win the boyfriend of my dreams. Now that I've raised my head, I have plenty of friends. Now that I've raised my head, classwork comes from my lips as faultlessly as

Easter speeches did, and I leave high school as valedictorian, most popular student and *queen*, hardly believing my luck. Ironically, the girl who was voted most beautiful in our class (and was) was later shot twice through the chest by a male companion, using a "real" gun, while she was pregnant. But that's another story in itself. Or, is it?

"You did not change," they say.   *33*

It is now thirty years since the "accident." A beautiful journalist *34* comes to visit and to interview me. She is going to write a cover story for her magazine that focuses on my last book. "Decide how you want to look on the cover," she says. "Glamorous, or whatever."

Never mind "glamorous," it is the "whatever" that I hear. Suddenly *35* all I can think of is whether I will get enough sleep the night before the photography session: if I don't, my eye will be tired and wander, as blind eyes will.

At night in bed with my lover I think up reasons why I should not *36* appear on the cover of a magazine. "My meanest critics will say I've sold out," I say. "My family will now realize I write scandalous books."

"But what's the real reason you don't want to do this?" he asks.   *37*

"Because in all probability," I say in a rush, "my eye won't be *38* straight."

"It will be straight enough," he says. Then, "Besides, I thought *39* you'd made your peace with that."

And I suddenly remember that I have.   *40*

I remember: *41*

I am talking to my brother Jimmy, asking if he remembers anything unusual about the day I was shot. He does not know I consider that day the last time my father, with his sweet home remedy of cool lily leaves, "chose" me, and that I suffered and raged inside because of this. "Well," he says, "all I remember is standing by the side of the highway with Daddy, trying to flag down a car. A white man stopped, but when Daddy said he needed somebody to take his little girl to the doctor, he drove off."

I remember: *42*

I am in the desert for the first time. I fall totally in love with it. I am so overwhelmed by its beauty, I confront for the first time, consciously, the meaning of the doctor's words years ago: "Eyes are sympathetic. If one is blind, the other will likely become blind too." I realize I have dashed about the world madly, looking at this, looking at that, storing up images against the fading of the light. But I might have missed seeing the desert! The shock of that possibility—and gratitude for over twenty-five years of sight—sends me literally to my knees. Poem after poem comes—which is perhaps how poets pray.

On Sight

I am so thankful I have seen
The Desert
And the creatures in the desert
And the desert Itself.
The desert has its own moon
Which I have seen
With my own eye
There is no flag on it.
Trees of the desert have arms
All of which are always up
That is because the moon is up
The sun is up
Also the sky
The stars
Clouds
None with flags.
If there were flags, I doubt
the trees would point.
Would you?

But mostly, I remember this: 43

I am twenty-seven, and my baby daughter is almost three. Since her birth I have worried over her discovery that her mother's eyes are different from other people's. Will she be embarrassed? I wonder. What will she say? Every day she watches a television program called "Big Blue Marble." It begins with a picture of the earth as it appears from the moon. It is bluish, a little battered-looking, but full of light, with whitish clouds swirling around it. Every time I see it I weep with love, as if it is a picture of Grandma's house. One day when I am putting Rebecca down for her nap, she suddenly focuses on my eye. Something inside me cringes, gets ready to try to protect myself. All children are cruel about physical differences, I know from experience, and that they don't always mean to be is another matter. I assume Rebecca will be the same.

But no-o-o-o. She studies my face intently as we stand, her inside   44
and me outside her crib. She even holds my face maternally between her dimpled little hands. Then, looking every bit as serious and lawyerlike as her father, she says, as if it may just possibly have slipped my attention: "Mommy, there's a *world* in your eye." (As in, "Don't be alarmed, or do anything crazy.") And then, gently, but with great interest: "Mommy, where did you *get* that world in your eye?"

For the most part, the pain left then. (So what if my brothers grew 45 up to buy even more powerful pellet guns for their sons and to carry real guns themselves. So what if a young "Morehouse man" once nearly fell off the steps of Trevor Arnett Library because he thought my eyes were blue.) Crying and laughing I ran to the bathroom, while Rebecca mumbled and sang herself off to sleep. Yes indeed, I realized, looking into the mirror. There *was* a world in my eye. And I saw that it was possible to love it; that in fact, for all it had taught me, of shame and anger and inner vision, I *did* love it. Even to see it drifting out of orbit in boredom, or rolling up out of fatigue, not to mention floating back at attention in excitement (bearing witness, a friend has called it), deeply suitable to my personality, and even characteristic of me.

That night I dream I am dancing to Stevie Wonder's song "Always" 46 (the name of the song is really "As," but I hear it as "Always"). As I dance, whirling and joyous, happier than I've ever been in my life, another bright-faced dancer joins me. We dance and kiss each other and hold each other through the night. The other dancer has obviously come through all right, as I have done. She is beautiful, whole and free. And she is also me.

VOCABULARY

In your journal, write the meanings of the following words:

- a *subversive* wit **(1)**
- rustling their new *crinolines* **(4)**
- Eyes are *sympathetic* **(12)**
- a hideous *cataract* **(13)**
- *boisterous*, ill-disciplined children **(16)**
- bearing *witness* **(45)**

QUESTIONS FOR WRITING AND DISCUSSION

1. Why does Alice Walker share this story with us? What memories from your own life did her story trigger? Write them down.

2. What does Walker discover or learn about herself? As a reader, what did you learn about your own experiences by reading this essay?

3. Reread the essay, looking for examples of the following techniques for writing about memories: (1) using detailed observations; (2) creating specific scenes; (3) noting changes, con-

trasts, or conflicts; and (4) seeing relationships between past and present. In your opinion, which of these techniques does she use most effectively?

4. What is Walker's main idea in this autobiographical account? State it in your own words. Where in the essay does she state it most explicitly?

5. How many scenes or episodes does Walker recount? List them according to her age at the time. Explain how each episode relates to her main idea.

6. Walker also uses images of sight and blindness to organize her essay. The story begins with a description of a father who has "beautiful eyes" and ends with her dancing in her dream to a song by Stevie Wonder. Catalog the images of sight and blindness from each scene or episode. Explain how, taken together, these images reinforce Walker's main idea.

7. Walker writes her essay in the present tense, and she uses italics not only to emphasize ideas but to indicate the difference between past thoughts and events and the present. List the places where she uses italics. Explain how the italicized passages reinforce her main point.

Remembering: The Writing Process

■ ASSIGNMENT FOR REMEMBERING   Write an essay about an important person, place, and/or event in your life. Your purpose is to recall and then use specific examples that *recreate* this memory and *show* why it is so important to you.

Memory is more indelible than ink.

—ANITA LOOS,

AUTHOR OF KISS
HOLLYWOOD GOODBYE

Think also about your possible audience and genre. Usually the audience for memoirs, autobiographical essays, and personal essays is fairly general. Since many people are interested in events from our lives, we may not want to restrict our audience too much. You may want to write just for your family or friends, however, or put your memories in the form of a letter you wish to send to a particular person. Also, you may want to think of a particular magazine that frequently publishes personal essays. Nearly every speciality magazine (sports, nature, outdoors, genealogy, cooking, clothing, style) occasionally publishes personal essays with memories that focus on the subject of the publication. Browsing through magazines may give you an idea for an audience and genre that would work for the event you wish to narrate.

CHOOSING A SUBJECT

If one of the journal entry exercises suggested a possible subject, try the collecting and shaping strategies below. If none of those exercises led to an interesting subject, consider the following ideas:

- Interview (in person or over the phone) your parents, a brother or sister, or a close friend. What events or experiences do they remember that were important to you?
- Get out a map of your town, city, state, or country and spend a few minutes doing an inventory of places you have been. Make a list of trips you have taken, with dates and years. Which of those places is the most memorable for you?
- Dig out a school yearbook and look through the pictures and the inscriptions that your classmates wrote. Whom do you remember most clearly? What events do you recall most vividly?
- Go to the library and look through news magazines or newspapers from five to ten years ago. What were the most important events of those years? What do you remember about them? Where were you and what were you doing when these events occurred? Which events had the largest impact on your life?
- Choose an important moment in your life, but write from the *point of view* of another person—a friend, family member, or stranger who was present. Let this person narrate the events that happened to you.

Note: Avoid choosing overly emotional topics such as the recent death of a close friend or family member. If you are too close to your subject, responding to your reader's revision suggestions may be difficult. Ask yourself if you can emotionally distance yourself from that subject. If you received a C for that essay, would you feel devastated?

COLLECTING

Once you have chosen a subject for your essay, try the following collecting strategies:

Brainstorming   Brainstorming is merely jotting down anything and everything that comes to mind that is remotely connected to your subject: words, phrases, images, or complete thoughts. You can brainstorm by yourself or in groups, with everyone contributing ideas and one person recording them.

Looping   Looping is a method of controlled freewriting that generates ideas and provides focus and direction. Begin by freewriting about your subject for eight to ten minutes. Then pause, reread what you have written, and *underline* the most interesting or important idea in what you've written so far. Then, using that sentence or idea as your starting point, write for eight to ten minutes more. Repeat this cycle, or "loop," one more time. Each loop should add ideas and details from some new angle or viewpoint, but overall you will be focusing on the most important ideas that you discover.

Clustering   Clustering is merely a visual scheme for brainstorming and free-associating about your topic. It can be especially effective for remembering because it helps you sketch relationships among your topics and subtopics. As you can see from the sample sketch, the sketch that you make of your ideas should help you see relationships between ideas or get a rough idea about an order or shape you may wish to use.

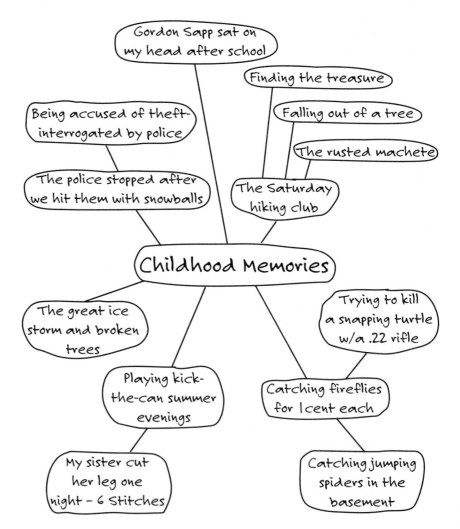

SHAPING

First, reconsider your purpose; perhaps it has become clearer or more definite since you recorded it in your journal entry. In your journal, jot down tentative answers for the following questions. If you don't have an answer, go on to the next question.

- *Subject*: What is your general subject?
- *Specific topic*: What aspect of your subject are you interested in?
- *Purpose*: Why is this topic interesting or important to you or your readers?
- *Main idea*: What might your main idea be?
- *Audience*: For whom are you writing this? What is your reader like, and why might he or she be interested in this topic?

Narrow and focus your subject. If you're going to write a three-page essay, don't try to cover everything in your life. Focus on one person, one episode, one turning point, one day, even one *part* of one day, and do that in depth and detail.

As you start your shaping activities, use the observing strategies discussed in Chapter 3. *Spatial order* may help you shape your description of a place you are remembering; *classification* or *definition* can shape your memories of people, places, or events. *Similes*, *metaphors*, and *analogies* will make your writing more vivid and may also suggest a shape or help you develop your subject.

In addition, use the following strategies for shaping written memories. Try each strategy to see if it works for your subject. Although some strategies may not be appropriate, others will work naturally, suggesting ways to shape and develop your writing.

Chronological Order   If you are writing about remembered events, you will probably use some form of chronological order. Try making a *chronological list of the major scenes or events*. Then go through the list, deciding what you will emphasize by telling about each item in detail and what you will pass over quickly. Normally, you will be using a straightforward chronological order, but you may wish to use a flashback, starting in the middle or near the end and then returning to tell the beginning. In his paragraph about a personal relationship, for example, student writer Gregory Hoffman begins the story at the most dramatic point, returns to tell how the relationship began, and then concludes the story.

> Her words hung in the air like iron ghosts. "I'm pregnant," she said as they walked through the park, the snow crackling beneath their feet. Carol was looking down at the ground when she told him, somewhat ashamed, embarrassed, and defiant all at once. Their relationship had only started in September, but both had felt the uneasiness surrounding them for the past months. She could remember the beginning so

well and in such favor, now that the future seemed so uncertain. The all-night conversations by the bay window, the rehearsals at the university theater—where he would make her laugh during her only soliloquy, and most of all the Christmas they had spent together in Vermont. No one else had existed for her during those months. Yet now, she felt duped by her affections—as if she had become an absurd representation of a tragic television character. As they approached the lake, he put his arm around her, "Just do what you think is best, babe. I mean, I think you know how I feel." At that moment, she knew it was over. It was no longer "their" decision. His hand touched her cheek in a benedictorial fashion. The rest would only be form now. Exchanging records and clothes with an aside of brief conversation. She would see him again, in the market or at a movie, and they would remember. But like his affection in September, her memory of him would fade until he was too distant to see.

Comparison/Contrast   Although you may be comparing or contrasting people, places, or events from the past, you will probably also be comparing or contrasting the past to the present. You may do that at the beginning, noting how something in the present reminds you of a past person, place, or event. You may do it at the end, as Andrea Lee does in *Russian Journal*. You may do it both at the beginning and at the end, as Richard Rodriguez does in "The Boy's Desire." You may even contrast past and present throughout, as Alice Walker does in "Beauty: When the Other Dancer Is the Self." Comparing or contrasting the past with the present will often clarify your dominant idea.

Image   Sometimes a single mental picture or recurring image will shape a paragraph or two in an essay. Consider how novelist George Orwell, in his essay "Shooting an Elephant," uses the image of a puppet or dummy to describe his feeling at a moment when he realized that, against his better judgment, he was going to have to shoot a marauding elephant in order to satisfy a crowd of two thousand Burmese who had gathered to watch him. The italicized words emphasize the recurring image.

> Suddenly I realized that I should have to shoot the elephant after all. The people expected it of me and I had got to do it; I could feel their *two thousand wills pressing me forward*, irresistibly. And it was at this moment, as I stood there with the rifle in my hands, that I first grasped the hollowness, the futility of the white man's dominion in the East. Here was I, the white man with his gun, standing in front of the unarmed native crowd—*seemingly the leading actor* of the piece; but in reality I was only an absurd *puppet pushed to and fro* by the will of those yellow faces behind. I perceived in this moment that when the white

man turns tyrant it is his own freedom that he destroys. He becomes a sort of *hollow, posing dummy*, the *conventionalized figure* of a sahib. For it is the condition of his rule that he shall spend his life in trying to impress the "natives" and so in every crisis he has got to do what the "natives" expect of him. He *wears a mask*, and his face grows to fit it. I had got to shoot the elephant. I had committed myself to doing it when I sent for the rifle. *A sahib has got to act like a sahib*; he has got to appear resolute, to know his own mind and do definite things.

Voice and Tone   When you have a personal conversation with someone, the way you look and sound—your body type, your voice, your facial expressions and gestures—communicates a sense of personality and attitude, which in turn affects how the other person reacts to what you say. In written language, although you don't have those gestures, expressions, or the actual sound of your voice, you can still create the sense that you are talking directly to your listener.

The term *voice* refers to a writer's personality as revealed through language. Writers may use emotional, colloquial, or conversational language to communicate a sense of personality. Or they may use abstract, impersonal language either to conceal their personalities or to create an air of scientific objectivity.

Tone is a writer's attitude toward the subject. The attitude may be positive or negative. It may be serious, humorous, honest, or ironic; it may be skeptical or accepting; it may be happy, frustrated, or angry. Often voice and tone overlap, and together they help us hear a writer talking to us. In the following passage, we hear student writer Kurt Weekly talking to us directly; we hear a clear, honest voice telling the story. His tone is not defensive or guilty: He openly admits he has a "problem."

Oh no, not another trash day. Every time I see all those trash containers, plastic garbage bags and junk lined up on the sidewalks, it drives me crazy. It all started when I was sixteen. I had just received my driver's license and the most beautiful Ford pickup. It was Wednesday as I remember and trash day. I don't know what happened. All of a sudden I was racing down the street swerving to the right, smashing into a large green Hefty trash bag filled with grass clippings. The bag exploded, and grass clippings and trash flew everywhere. It was beautiful and I was hooked. There was no stopping me.

At first I would smash one or two cans on the way to school. Then I just couldn't get enough. I would start going out the night before trash day. I would go down the full length of the street and wipe out

every garbage container in sight. I was the terror of the neighborhood. This was not a bad habit to be taken lightly. It was an obsession. I was in trouble. There was no way I could kick this on my own.
I needed help.

I received that help. One night after an evening of nonstop can smashing, the Arapahoe County Sheriff Department caught up with me.
Not just one or a few but the whole department. They were willing
to set me on the right path, and if that didn't work, they were going
to send me to jail. It was a long, tough road to rehabilitation, but I did
it. Not alone. I had the support of my family and the community.

Persona Related to voice and tone is the *persona*—the "mask" that a writer can
put on. Sometimes in telling a story about yourself, you may want to speak in
your own "natural" voice. At other times, however, you may change or exaggerate certain characteristics in order to project a character different from your
"real" self. Writers, for example, may project themselves as braver and more intelligent than they really are. Or to create a humorous effect, they may create per-
sonas who are more foolish or clumsy than they really are. This persona can
shape a whole passage. In the following excerpt, James Thurber, a master of autobiographical humor, uses a persona—along with chronological narrative—to
shape his account of a frustrating botany class.

I passed all the other courses that I took at my university, but I could
never pass botany. This was because all botany students had to spend
several hours a week in a laboratory looking through a microscope at
plant cells, and I could never see through a microscope. I never once
saw a cell through a microscope. This used to enrage my instructor.
He would wander around the laboratory pleased with the progress all
the students were making in drawing the involved and, so I am told,
interesting structure of flower cells, until he came to me. I would just
be standing there. "I can't see anything," I would say. He would begin
patiently enough, explaining how anybody can see through a microscope, but he would always end up in a fury claiming that I could too
see through a microscope but just pretended that I couldn't. "It takes
away from the beauty of flowers anyway," I used to tell him. "We are
not concerned with beauty in this course," he would say. "We are concerned solely with the mechanics of flowers." "Well," I'd say, "I can't see
anything." "Try it just once again," he'd say, and I would put my eye to
the microscope and see nothing at all, except now and again a nebu-
lous milky substance—a phenomenon of maladjustment. You were
supposed to see a vivid, restless clockwork of sharply defined plant
cells. "I see what looks like a lot of milk," I would tell him. This, he

claimed, was the result of my not having adjusted the microscope properly, so he would readjust it for me, or rather, for himself. And I would look again and see milk. I finally took a deferred pass, as they called it, and waited a year and tried again. (You had to pass one of the biological sciences or you couldn't graduate.) The professor had come back from vacation brown as a berry, bright-eyed, and eager to explain cell-structure again to his classes. "Well," he said to me, cheerily, when we met in the first laboratory hour of the semester, "we're going to see cells this time, aren't we?" "Yes, sir," I said. Students to the right of me and to the left of me and in front of me were seeing cells; what's more, they were quietly drawing pictures of them in their notebooks. Of course, I didn't see anything.

"We'll try it," the professor said to me, grimly, "with every adjustment of the microscope known to man. As God is my witness, I'll arrange this glass so that you see cells through it or I'll give up teaching. In twenty-two years of botany, I—" He cut off abruptly for he was beginning to quiver all over, like Lionel Barrymore, and he genuinely wished to hold onto his temper; his scenes with me had taken a great deal out of him.

So we tried it with every adjustment of the microscope known to man. With only one of them did I see anything but blackness or the familiar lacteal opacity, and that time I saw, to my pleasure and amazement, a variegated constellation of flecks, specks, and dots. These I hastily drew. The instructor, noting my activity, came back from an adjoining desk, a smile on his lips and his eyebrows high in hope. He looked at my cell drawing. "What's that?" he demanded, with a hint of a squeal in his voice. "That's what I saw," I said. "You didn't, you didn't, you didn't!" he screamed, losing control of his temper instantly, and he bent over and squinted into the microscope. His head snapped up. "That's your eye!" he shouted. "You've fixed the lens so that it reflects! You've drawn your eye!"

Dialogue   Dialogue, which helps to *recreate* people and events rather than just tell about them, can become a dominant form and thereby shape your writing. Recreating an actual conversation, you could possibly write a whole scene using nothing but dialogue. More often, however, writers use dialogue occasionally for dramatic effect. In the account of his battle with the microscope, for instance, Thurber uses dialogue in the last two paragraphs to dramatize his conclusion:

"We'll try it," the professor said to me, grimly, "with every adjustment of the microscope known to man. As God is my witness, I'll arrange this glass so that you see cells through it or I'll give up teaching. In twenty-two years of teaching botany, I—" . . . "What's that?" he demanded. . . . "That's what I saw," I said. "You didn't, you didn't, you didn't!" he screamed. . . . "You've fixed the lens so that it reflects! You've drawn your eye!"

Title, Introduction, and Conclusion   In your journal, sketch out several possible titles you might use. You may want a title that is merely an accurate label, such as *Russian Journal* or "The Boy's Desire," but you may prefer something less direct that gets your reader's attention. For example, for his essay about his hat that appears at the end of this chapter, student writer Todd Petry uses the title "The Wind Catcher." As a reader, what do you think about Alice Walker's title, "Beauty: When the Other Dancer Is the Self"?

Introductions or beginning paragraphs take several shapes. Some writers plunge the reader immediately into the action—as Gregory Hoffman does—and then later fill in the scene and context. Others are more like Kurt Weekly, announcing the subject—trash cans—and then taking the reader from the present to the past and the beginning of the story: "It all started when I was sixteen. . . ." At some point, however, readers do need to know the context—the *who*, *what*, *when*, and *where* of your account.

Conclusions are also of several types. In some, writers will return to the present and discuss what they have learned, as Andrea Lee does in *Russian Journal*. Some, like Alice Walker, end with an image or even a dream. Some writers conclude with dramatic moments, or an emotional scene, as student writer Juli Bovard does in the essay "The Red Chevy" that appears at the end of this chapter. But many writers will try to tie the conclusion back to the beginning, as Richard Rodriguez does at the end of "The Boy's Desire": "The closet door closes . . . the fog rises." In your journal, experiment with several possibilities until you find one that works for your subject.

I start at the beginning, go on to the end, then stop.

—GABRIEL GARCÍA MÁRQUEZ,

AUTHOR OF ONE HUNDRED YEARS OF SOLITUDE

I always know the ending; that's where I start.

—TONI MORRISON,

NOBEL PRIZE-WINNING NOVELIST

DRAFTING

When you have experimented with the above shaping strategies, reconsider your purpose, audience, and main idea. Have they changed? In your journal, re-examine the notes you made before trying the shaping activities. If necessary, revise your statements about purpose, audience, or main idea based on what you have actually written.

Working from your journal material and from your collecting and shaping activities, draft your essay. It is important *not* to splice different parts together or just recopy and connect segments, for they may not fit or flow together. Instead, reread what you have written, and then start with a clean sheet of paper. If you're working on a computer file, you can start with your list of events or one of your best shaping strategies and expand that file

PEER RESPONSE

The instructions below will help you give and receive constructive advice about the rough draft of your remembering essay. You may use these guidelines for an in-class workshop, a take-home review, or a computer e-mail response.

Writer: Before you exchange drafts with another reader, write out the following information about your own rough draft.

1. State the main idea that you hope your essay conveys.
2. Describe the best *one* or *two* key scenes that your narrative creates.
3. Explain one or two problems that you are having with this draft that you want your reader to focus on.

Reader: Without making any comments, read the *entire* draft from start to finish. As you *reread* the draft, answer the following questions.

1. Locate one or two of the *key scenes* in the narrative. Are they clearly set at an identified time and place? Does the writer use vivid description of the place or the people? Does the writer use dialogue? Does the writer include his or her reflections? Which of these areas need the most attention during the writer's revision? Explain.
2. Write out a *time line* for the key events in the narrative. What happened first, second, third, and so forth? Are there places in the narrative where the time line could be clearer? Explain.
3. When you finished reading the draft, *what characters or incidents were you still curious about*? Where did you want more information? What characters or incidents did you want to know more about?
4. What *overall idea* does the narrative convey to you? How does your notion of the main idea compare to the writer's answer to Question 1? Explain how the writer might revise the essay to make the main idea clearer.
5. Answer the *writer's questions* in Question 3.

After you have some feedback from other readers, you need to distance yourself and objectively reread what you have written. Review the advice you received from your peer readers. Remember, you will get both good

(continued)

(continued from previous page)

and bad advice, so *you* must decide what you think is important or not important. If you are uncertain about advice you received from one of your peers, ask for a third or fourth opinion. In addition, most writing centers will have tutors available who can help you sort through the advice you have received on your draft and figure out a revision plan. Especially for this remembering essay, make sure your memories are recreated on paper. Don't be satisfied with suggesting incidents that merely trigger your own memories: You must *show* people and events vividly for your reader.

as you draft. Concentrate on what you want to say and write as quickly as possible.

To avoid interruptions, choose a quiet place to work. Follow your own writing rituals. Try to write nonstop. If you cannot think of the right word, put a line or a dash, but keep on writing. When necessary, go back and reread what you have previously written.

The difference between the right word and the nearly right word is the same as that between lightning and the lightning bug.

—MARK TWAIN,
AUTHOR OF THE
ADVENTURES OF
HUCKLEBERRY FINN

REVISING

Revising begins, of course, when you get your first idea and start collecting and shaping. It continues as you redraft certain sections of your essay and rework your organization. In many classes, you will give and receive advice from the other writers in your class. Use the guidelines below to give constructive advice about a remembering essay draft.

Guidelines for Revision

- **Reexamine your purpose and audience.** Are you doing what you intended?
- **Revise to make the main idea of your account clearer.** You don't need a "moral" to the story or a bald statement saying, "This is why this person was important." Your reader, however, should know clearly why you wanted to write about the memory that you chose.
- **Revise to clarify the important relationships in your story.** Consider relationships between past and present, between you and the people in your story, between one place and another place, between one event and another event.
- **Close and detailed observation is crucial.** *Show*, don't just tell. Can you use any of the collecting and shaping strategies for observing discussed in Chapter 3?
- **Revise to show crucial changes, contrasts, or conflicts more clearly.** Keller's and Walker's essays, for instance, illustrate how *conflict* and

change are central to an effective remembering essay. See if their strategies will work in your essay.

- **Have you used a straight chronological order?** If it works, keep it. If not, would another order be better? Should you begin in the middle and do a flashback? Do you want to move back and forth from present to past or stay in the past until the end?

    If you are using a chronological order, cue your reader by occasionally using transitional words to signal changes: *then, when, first, next, last, before, after, while, as, sooner, later, initially, finally, yesterday, today.*

- **Be clear about point of view.** Are you looking back on the past from a viewpoint in the present? Are you using the point of view of yourself as a child or at some earlier point in your life? Are you using the point of view of another person or object in your story?

- **What are the key images in your account?** Should you add or delete an image to show the experience more vividly?

- **What voice are you using?** Does it support your purpose? If you are using a persona, is it appropriate for your audience and purpose?

- **Revise sentences to improve clarity, conciseness, emphasis, and variety.**

- **Check your dialogue for proper punctuation and indentation.** See the essay by Alice Walker in this chapter for a model.

- **When you are relatively satisfied with your draft, edit for correct spelling, appropriate word choice, punctuation, and grammar.**

POSTSCRIPT ON THE WRITING PROCESS

After you finish writing, revising, and editing your essay, you will want to breathe a sigh of relief and turn it in. But before you do, think about the problems that you solved as you wrote this essay. *Remember:* Your major goal for this course is to learn to write and revise more effectively. To do that, you need to discover and adapt your writing processes so you can anticipate and solve the problems you face as a writer. Take a few minutes to answer the following questions. Be sure to hand in this postscript with your essay.

1.   Review your writing process. Which collecting, shaping, and revising strategies helped you remember and describe incidents most quickly and clearly? What problems were you unable to solve?

2.   Reread your essay. With a small asterisk [*], identify in the margin of your essay sentences where you used sensory details, dialogue, or images to *show* or recreate the experience for your reader.

3.   If you received feedback from your peers, identify one piece of advice that you followed and one bit of advice that you ignored. Explain your decisions.

4.   Rereading your essay, what do you like best about it? What parts of your essay need work? What would you change if you had another day to work on this assignment?

THE WIND CATCHER
Todd Petry

Todd Petry decided to write about his cowboy hat, observing it in the present and thinking about some of the memories that it brought back. His notes, his first short draft paragraphs, and his revised version demonstrate how observing and remembering work together naturally: The details stimulate memories, and memories lead to more specific details.

NOTES AND DETAILS

DETAILS	MORE SPECIFIC DETAILS
Gray	Dirty, dust coated, rain stained cowdung color
Resistol	The name is stained and blurred
Size 7 3/8	
Diamond shape	Used to be diamond shape, now battered, looks abandoned
4" brim	Front tipped down, curled up in back
1" sweat band	blackish
5 yrs. old	still remember the day I bought it
4x beaver	
What it is not:	it is unlike a hat fresh out of the box
What it compares to:	point of crown like the north star like a pancake with wilted edges battered like General Custer's hat
What I remember:	the day I bought the hat a day at Pray Mesa

First Draft

THE WIND CATCHER

The other day while I was relaxing in my favorite chair and listening to Ian Tyson, I happened to notice my work cowboy hat hanging on the wall. Now I look at that old hat no less than a dozen times a day without too much thought, but on that particular day, my eyes remained fixed on it and my mind went to remembering.

I still remember I had $100 cash in my pocket the day I went hat shopping. The local tack, feed, and western wear CO-OP was my first and only stop. Finding a hat to meet my general specifications was no big deal. I wanted a gray Resistol, size 7 3/8, with a 4-inch brim and diamond-shaped crown. From there on, though, my wants became very particular. I took 30 minutes to find the one that had the right fit, and five times that long to come to terms with the hat shaper. Boy, but I was one proud young fellow the next day when I went to school sporting my new piece of head gear. I've had that wind catcher five years through rough times, but in a way, it really looks better now, without any shape, dirty, and covered with dust and cowdung.

Revised Version

THE WIND CATCHER

The other day, while I was relaxing in my favorite chair and listening to Ian Tyson, I happened to notice my work cowboy hat hanging on the wall. Now, I look at that old hat no less than a dozen times a day without too much thought, but on that particular day, my eyes remained fixed on it and my mind went to remembering.   *1*

I was fifteen years old and had $100 cash in my pocket the day I went hat shopping five years ago. The local tack, feed, and western wear CO-OP was my first and only stop. Finding a hat to meet my general specifications was no big deal. I wanted a gray 4X Resistol, size 7 3/8, with a four-inch brim and diamond-shaped crown. I wanted no flashy feathers or gaudy hatbands, which in my mind were only for pilgrims. From there on, though, my wants became very particular. I took thirty minutes to find the one that had the right fit, and five times that long to come to terms with the hat shaper. Boy, but I was one proud young fellow the next day when I went to school sporting my new piece of head gear.   *2*

About that time, Ian Tyson startled me out of my state of reminiscence by singing "Rose in the Rockies," with that voice of his sounding like ten cow elk cooing to their young in the springtime. As I sat there listening to the music and looking at that old hat, I   *3* had to chuckle to myself because that wind catcher had sure seen better days. I mean it looked rode hard and put up wet. The gray, which was once as sharp and crisp as a mountain lake, was now faded and dull where the sun had beat down. Where the crown and brim met, the paleness was suddenly transformed into a gritty black which ran the entire circumference of the hat. This black was unlike any paint or color commercially available, being made up of head sweat, dirt, alfalfa dust, and powdered cow manure. Water blemishes from too much rain and snow mottled the brim, adding to the colors' turbidity. Inside the crown and wherever the slope was less than ninety degrees, dust had collected to hide the natural color even more.

After a while, my attention lost interest in the various colors and began to work its way over the hat's shape, which I was once so critical of. General Custer's hat itself could not have looked worse. All signs of uniformity and definite shape had disappeared. The diamond-shaped crown, which was once round and smooth, now bowed out on the sides and had edges as blunt as an orange crate. The point, which once looked like the North Star indicating the direction, now was twisted off balance from excessive right hand use. Remembering last spring, how I threw that hat in the face of an irate mother cow during calving, I had to chuckle again. Throwing that hat kept my horse and me out of trouble but made the "off-balance look" rather permanent. As I looked at the brim, I was reminded of a three-day-old pancake with all its edges wilted. The back of that brim curled upward like a snake ready to strike, and the front had become so narrow and dipped, it looked like something a dentist would use on your teeth.

For probably half an hour, I sat looking at the wear and tear on that ancient hat. Awhile back, I remember, I decided to try to make my old hat socially presentable by having it cleaned and blocked, removing those curls and dips and other signs of use. However, when a hat shop refused to even attempt the task, I figured I'd just leave well enough alone. As I scanned my eyes over the hat, I noticed several other alterations from its original form, such as the absent hat band, which was torn off in the brush on Pray Mesa, and the black thread that drew together the edges of a hole in the crown. However, try as I might, I could not for the life of me see where any character had been lost in the brush, or any flair had been covered with cowdung.

QUESTIONS FOR WRITING AND DISCUSSION

1. Close observation often leads to specific memories. In the opening paragraph of his revised version, Todd Petry says that "on that particular day, my eyes remained fixed on it and my mind went to remembering." He then recalls the time when he was fifteen years old and bought his hat. Identify two other places where observation leads Petry to remember specific scenes from the past.

2. Petry chose "The Wind Catcher" as the title for his essay. Reread the essay and then brainstorm a list of five other titles that might be appropriate for this short essay. Which title do you like best?

3. Where does Petry most clearly express the main idea of his essay? Write out the main idea in your own words.

STUDENT WRITING

THE RED CHEVY

Juli Bovard

In the following essay, Juli Bovard recalls several of the most traumatic days of her life. She remembers not just the day she was raped by an unknown assailant, but the days she had to spend in the police station, the day she confronted her attacker in the courtroom, and the days she spent regaining control of her life. In the end, Bovard helps us understand how she overcame being a rape victim and reclaimed her life.

From the moment the man in the Chevy stopped to offer me a ride *1* on that blistering September afternoon, I knew I was in trouble. Before I could say, "No, but thanks anyway," the man in the passenger side of the car jumped at me, twisted my arm and held a shiny piece of steel to my side. I was pushed into the car and driven 30 miles over the county line. During the ride, I did everything every article or specialist on abduction had advised against: I cried, I babbled, and I lost control. In the end it was all futile. Two hours later—after they dumped me off near my home—I was another statistic. I had been raped, and was now a victim of the brutal, demeaning, sad violent crime of sexual assault. I was officially one of the 1,871 rapes that occur each day in the United States ("Sexual Assault Statistics").

Rape not only has physical repercussions, but has an enormous *2* psychological and emotional impact as well. During my "event" as I like to call it, I remembered an initial feeling of shock and numbness, and soon found myself babbling incoherently. I begged my attackers to let me go. I tried to talk my way out of the car. I even tried to beg or bargain my way out. However, the driver was very much in control of the situation, and my weak efforts failed. Eventually my babbling gave way to cold reason, and I became convinced that not only would I be raped, but that I would also die. My life did not pass before me—as is said to happen to dying people. In fact, I did not think of the past at all, but only the future and all the things I had not yet done. I had never ridden a horse other than the ponies at the fair. I had not learned to play golf—though I had intended to—or learned to snow ski down a mountain with my son. There were too many people I had not told how I really felt, too many people to whom I wanted to say good-bye. I seriously doubted I would ever be given another chance.

I did not die. In fact, other than a few bruises and scratches from the field grass (where I was forced to lie during my rape), and several cuts on my neck and cheek—left by the brass knuckle style knife, I was remarkably, physically unhurt. The greatest trauma was to my mind. The psychological and emotional wounds in the ensuing months were far worse than the actual sexual assault.   3

Within a week of my report, the man who raped me was arrested and held without bail (he had previously been convicted of attempted rape), his accomplice was not accused since he agreed to turn state's evidence—which means he made a deal to cover himself and agreed to testify against my assailant. What followed these events, I remember, was a long investigation that involved many tedious hours in the police station, and numbing revisits to the scene of the crime. Through it all I was alone, and I halfheartedly tried to comfort myself for enduring the stress so well. By late October, the month of the preliminary hearing, I had gone back to work, and was back in control of my life—or so I thought. The actual hearing proved me wrong.   4

Though I do not remember much about the actual courtroom or its proceedings, I will always remember the warmth of the day and the overwhelming odor of my perpetrator's cologne (to this day I become nauseous if I smell the cologne Obsession). Seeing my assailant again had an effect on me that I was not prepared for. I felt the same fear that I had experienced the day of my rape, and for the second time in my life I felt terror so deep it paralyzed me. The pressure from the entire incident finally overwhelmed me, and when I returned home that afternoon I climbed into bed and did not leave it for three days. I spent seventy-two hours staring at the ceiling and vomiting. When I finally emerged from my emotional coma, I could not eat or sleep. Everything seemed unreal and unclear to me. It was weeks before I could focus on everyday tasks, even something as simple as showering.   5

By the middle of November, I had lost close to fifteen pounds. I had constant diarrhea, my menstrual cycle had stopped, and I was constantly bombarded by anxiety attacks. I could no longer get up each day   6 and go to work and act like nothing had happened. Leaving the house left me with cold sweats, and sleeping through the night became impossible. I became paranoid and despondent. I knew I would have to seek professional help.

Fortunately, through counseling I learned that my reactions were 7 very common, and are shared by most rape victims. Through research, I found that all the feelings I was having were very normal. My fear that the rapist would return was natural, and my inability to face unfamiliar situations or people was a classic symptom. I also learned that the guilt that plagued me, which made me think that somehow I had provoked the rape or "wore" the wrong clothes to entice the rapist, was simply untrue. I was feeling a great amount of shame and embarrassment—a stigma I learned society often places on rape victims. My anger, which was the most natural response, was also the most helpful. When you are angry, you tend to want to fight back. My way of fighting back was to get on with living. Still I asked, "Why me?" I had followed all the rules set by society. I did not walk the streets at night, hang out in bars, or talk to strangers. I was an actively employed member of society. So why me? I found it wasn't just me or something I did. It could have been any woman walking the streets that day, and it went far beyond what I wore or how I walked, something noted author Susan Brownmiller eloquently affirms in her statement that, "any female may become a victim of rape. Factors such as youth, advanced age, physical homeliness and virginal lifestyle do not provide a foolproof deterrent to render a women impervious to sexual assault" (Brownmiller 348).

Through my experience and in talking with other victims I have 8 learned that rape has no typical "face." Certainly the man who raped me looked normal, (He was not obscene, ugly, or disfigured). He could have been my neighbor, my grocer, or even my boyfriend. Rape victims and its perpetrators are colorless and ageless. There is no stereotypical rapist *or* victim. We can be doctors, lawyers, mothers, or fathers. We are tall, short, fat, and skinny. And, as in most victims' cases, simply in the wrong place at the wrong time.

After the question of "why me?" I asked, "WHY, at all?" Why *does* 9 a man rape a woman? Initially I thought it was obvious—for sex. But I was wrong. The motivations of rape include anger, aggression, dominance, hostility, and power, but generally are not usually associated with just the actual act of sex. Quite simply it is violence. Men who rape do so because they are violent and psychotic. There is no other reason, and no valid excuse.

In the end, before I was to testify, the man who attacked me 10 changed his plea to guilty. I walked out of the district attorney's office and never asked how many years the rapist would serve in prison. It did not matter. He would be behind bars, but more importantly, I would be free to begin living again. Now, instead of dreading the month of September, I celebrate it. I celebrate the month, in which, instead of just existing, I started living. I was a victim of rape, but through years of counseling and support *I am not a victim any longer.*

Works Cited

Brownmiller, Susan. *Against Our Will*. New York: Simon and Schuster, 1975.

"Sexual Assault Statistics." Sexual Assault Site. *Abuse Counseling and Treatment.* 22 Oct. 2000 <http://actabuse.com/SAstatistics.html.>

VOCABULARY

In your journal, write down the meanings of the following words:

- babbling *incoherently* **(2)**
- the greatest *trauma* **(3)**
- a *stigma* **(7)**
- render a woman *impervious* **(7)**
- they are violent and *psychotic* **(9)**

QUESTIONS FOR WRITING AND DISCUSSION

1. Psychological research has shown that people remember traumatic events more vividly and with more detail than other events. Has that been true in your experience? Recall two experiences—one happy, one traumatic—and consider whether your experiences support or do not support the research.

2. Remembering essays should have a purpose—that is, they should focus on having a specific effect on their audience. Why is Juli Bovard writing about this experience? What effect does she want to have on her readers? Is she just giving information or does she want to convince us about something? Explain.

3. Review the techniques for writing a remembering essay listed at the beginning of this chapter? Which of these techniques does

Bovard use? Where does she use them? Which are, in your opinion, most effective? Why?

4. In addition to remembering specific scenes, Bovard uses some research and explains the causes and effects of the event. Should she have research and cite sources in a narrative essay? Do her explanations and her research help achieve her purpose or do they detract from the story? Support your response by citing specific sentences from her essay.

5. Bovard chose the title "The Red Chevy" for her essay. Brainstorm five other titles she might use for her essay. Compare your ideas with those of your classmates. Did you come up with titles that might be more effective for the purpose of her essay? Explain.

Philosophy class in Paris. Goya Museum.

Chapter 5   Reading

As an assignment in class, you are reading and critiquing an article by Deborah Tannen on how men and women respond differently during class conversations. As you read the article, you like the thought-provoking examples, but soon you find yourself becoming frustrated. First, you have trouble locating the main focus of the article, and then you are disturbed by some unsupported assertions that she makes about typical behavior of men and women. Do men really like to argue and dominate class discussions? Do women always benefit from smaller, more intimate group discussions? You reread the article and make notes in the margin. After discussing your reactions with other readers, you write the draft of your summary and response. You argue that readers should expect clearer organization and fewer unsupported assertions about the gender-based differences between men and women.

After discussing stereotyped and sexist images in advertising, you leaf through a copy of a popular magazine. A two-page advertisement for Fila jeans catches your attention. The first page shows a man in jeans and a jeans jacket in the foreground with football players pictured in the background. The caption at the bottom of the page says, "Some like their blues hard." On the facing page is a woman curled up in a chair and wearing her blue jeans. Her background photograph shows a woman clad in a bikini. The caption says, "Some like their blues soft." For your essay, you describe the features of the ad carefully and then offer your own analysis of the sexist features of the images and the language. The language and the imagery of the Fila jeans ad, you argue, stereotype and alienate the sexes by conveying the idea that men and women are not parallel in nature but are fundamentally separate and different.

If we think of it, all that a University, or final highest School can do for us, is still but what the first School began doing—teach us to read.

—THOMAS CARLYLE,

AUTHOR OF <u>ON HEROES AND HERO WORSHIP</u>

Reading involves a fair measure of push and shove. You make your mark on a book and it makes its mark on you. Reading is not simply a matter of hanging back and waiting for a piece, or its author, to tell you what the writing has to say.

—DAVID BARTHOLOMAE AND ANTHONY PETROSKY,

AUTHORS OF <u>WAYS OF READING</u>

A T FIRST GLANCE, A CHAPTER ON READING IN A TEXTBOOK ON WRITING MAY CATCH YOU BY SURPRISE. THIS CHAPTER, HOWEVER, IS NOT ABOUT LEARNING YOUR ABC'S OR ABOUT reading *The Cat in the Hat*. It is about learning to read texts actively and critically. It is about learning how to summarize and respond to what you read. It is about using reading—along with observing and remembering—as a source for your writing.

At the beginning of this chapter, we need to define two key terms: *texts* and *reading*. Normally, when you think about a text, you may think of a textbook. A text, however, can be any graphic matter—a textbook, an essay, a poem, a story, a newspaper editorial, a graph, a design, or an advertisement. Some people expand the definition of *texts* to include any thing or phenomenon in the world. In this widest sense, the layout of a restaurant, the behavior of children on a playground, or clouds in the sky could be "texts" that can be read.

Similarly, the term *reading* has both narrow and broad senses. In a narrow sense, reading is just understanding words on a page. But reading has a variety of wider meanings as well. Reading can mean analyzing, as when an architect "reads" blueprints and knows how to construct a roof. Reading can mean interpreting, as when a sailor "reads" the sky and knows that the day will bring winds and rough weather. Reading can also mean examining media or cultural patterns and perceiving textual messages of sexism or racism. All of these "readings" require close, repeated observation of the text and an ability to engage, analyze, respond to, and interpret the text.

In this chapter, you will practice a fairly specific kind of textual reading. Most of the texts are essays on academic topics, and your reading will be active, critical, and responsive. Implied in active, critical reading is writing. Reading and writing work together to make reading more active and writing more effective. Reading and writing are so inseparable that we sometimes use the phrase "reading/writing" to discuss any reading activity. In addition, there is an essential third dimension to critical reading: discussion. This third dimension can take a variety of forms—sharing ideas in small groups, engaging in a class conversation, posting e-mail responses, or taking sides in a debate. Reading, writing, and discussing are all "reading" activities. We may be able to read the words on a page and write out our reactions, but we must also engage other readers' reactions and points of view in order to fully grasp the possible meanings of a text.

This chapter will show you how to use reading/writing/discussing strategies for three important tasks. First, you will learn how to write short critiques or summary/response essays, which are frequent college writing assignments. Second, you will practice reading your peers' drafts and essays actively and critically. Third, you will use critical reading to find information and generate ideas for expository or argumentative essays. Just as observing gives you descriptive strategies and remembering helps you to practice drawing on your personal experience, reading will help you critically analyze ideas, facts, statistics, and arguments—a skill that you will need for many college writing assignments.

Techniques for Writing About Reading

As you approach your assignments in this chapter, remember that reading, writing, and discussing are all interrelated and interactive strategies. Writing assists reading, discussing, and rereading. Reading and rereading help you discuss and write. Conversations (written and oral) among readers and writers are integral to reading/writing. Focus on the techniques that follow as you write your summary/response or critique.

- **Using active and responsive reading/writing/discussing strategies.**
  Preview the author's background and the writing context. Prewrite about your own experiences with the subject. Read initially for information and enjoyment. As you reread, make annotations, write questions, or do a double-entry log. Discuss the text with other readers.
- **Summarizing the main ideas or features of the text.** A summary should *accurately* and *objectively* represent the key ideas. Summaries cite the author and title, accurately represent the main ideas, quote directly key phrases or sentences, and describe main features of the text.
- **Responding to or critiquing the ideas in the text.** A response should focus on your ideas and reactions. Types of responses include *analysis* of the argument, organization, or evidence in the text; *agreement* or *disagreement* with the author/text; or *interpretation* of the text.
- **Supporting the response with evidence.** As supporting evidence for the response, writers should analyze key features of the text, cite evidence from other relevant texts, and/or use examples from personal experience.
- **Combining summary and response into a coherent essay.** Usually, the summary appears first, followed by the reader's response, but be sure to *integrate* the two parts. Focus early on a main idea for your response. Use transitions between the summary and the response.

As you work on these techniques, don't simply read the text, discuss it in class, and then write out your critique. Instead, write notes as you read. Reread the text after class discussion. Reread and discuss the text after you have written your draft. Use the interactive powers of reading/writing/discussing to help you throughout your writing process.

Reading is not a passive process by which we soak up words and information from the page, but an active process by which we predict, sample, and confirm or correct our hypotheses about the written text.

—CONSTANCE WEAVER,

AUTHOR OF READING PROCESS AND PRACTICE

Reading . . . is a vital component of rhetorical invention, for it is an important way of participating in the conversation that gives us all of our meanings.

—DOUG BRENT,

AUTHOR OF READING AS RHETORICAL INVENTION

Reading depends upon prediction. . . . What I see is related to what I am looking for, not to all possible interpretations. . . . An important difference between a skilled driver and a learner is that the skilled driver is able to project the car into the future while the learner's mind is more closely anchored to where the car is now—when it is usually too late to avoid accidents.

—FRANK SMITH,
AUTHOR OF
UNDERSTANDING READING

As he engages with the text, the reader . . . entertains expectations as to what will follow, and uses these as guidelines for selecting out from alternative responses. As the text presents new elements, he may find it necessary to revise earlier syntheses or to develop new structuring principles.

—LOUISE ROSENBLATT,
AUTHOR OF THE READER, THE TEXT, THE POEM

HOW READERS READ

One of the purposes of this chapter is to show you how readers read. If you know how readers read and how they construct meaning from a text, you will become a more active reader and a more effective writer.

Reading, some theorists believe, involves a three-part process. First, readers bring their *prior experience* (about the subject, about language, and about culture) to their reading. Second, based on their prior experience, readers make *guesses* about how each passage relates to their prior experience and *predictions* about where the text is headed. Finally, as readers continue to read or reread, they *make meaning of* or *comprehend* the text by testing (confirming or rejecting) the guesses and predictions that they have made. If readers have limited experience with the subject or the language, making accurate predictions can be difficult. If readers have a good deal of prior experience, they are more likely to make accurate predictions.

If this theory of reading and comprehension is true, it has three important lessons for any reader/writer:

- **First, prior knowledge about a text and its subject is extremely important.** As a reader, you should activate your prior knowledge *before* reading the text. Doing a prereading journal exercise and discussing the subject with others are excellent strategies to access what you already know.
- **Second, making guesses and predictions enables readers to make meaning.** Making wrong guesses is just as important as making right guesses. Don't worry about making wrong guesses—they are a crucial part of the active reading process.
- **Third, learning to read actively will make you a better writer.** Good writers know the problems that readers have making meaning. Good writers activate their readers' prior knowledge by using examples from their own experience. Good writers preview their main ideas so that their readers can make better guesses. Good writers use transitions or signals to help readers make meaning.

DOUBLE-ENTRY LOG

One of the most effective strategies to promote active reading is a double-entry log. Draw a line down the middle of a page in your notebook. On the left-hand side, keep a running summary of the main ideas and features that you notice in the text. On the right-hand side, write your questions and reactions. A double-entry log, especially if used with the Rereading Guide that follows, can help you quickly organize your ideas for a summary/response essay.

Author and Title

| SUMMARY COMMENTS: MAIN IDEAS AND KEY FEATURES | RESPONSE: COMMENTS, REACTIONS, AND QUESTIONS |

REREADING GUIDE After you've read an essay once, let the following set of questions guide your *rereadings* of the text. The questions on the left-hand side will help you summarize and analyze the text; the questions on the right-hand side will help focus your response.

DESCRIPTION

I. Purpose
- Describe the author's overall *purpose* (to inform, explain, explore, evaluate, argue, negotiate, or other purpose).
- How does the author/text want to affect or change the reader?

II. Audience/Reader
- Who is the *intended* audience?
- What *assumptions* does the author make about the reader's knowledge or beliefs?
- From what *point of view* or *context* is the author writing?

III. Thesis and Main Ideas
- What key *question* or *problem* does the author/text address?
- What is the author's *thesis?*
- What *main ideas* support the thesis?
- What are the key passages or key moments in the text?

RESPONSE

- Is the overall purpose clear or muddled?
- Was the actual purpose different from the stated purpose?
- How did the text actually affect you?

- Are you part of the intended audience?
- Does the author misjudge the reader's knowledge or beliefs?
- Do you share the author's point of view on this subject?

- Where is the thesis stated?
- Are the main ideas related to the thesis?
- Where do you agree or disagree?
- Does the essay have contradictions or errors in logic?
- What ideas or arguments does the essay omit or ignore?
- What experience or prior knowledge do you have about the topic?
- What are the implications or consequences of the essay's ideas?

IV. Organization and Evidence

- Where does the author *preview* the essay's organization?
- How does the author *signal* new sections of the essay?
- What kinds of *evidence* does the author use (personal experience, descriptions, statistics, interviews, other authorities, analytical reasoning, or other)?

- At what point could you accurately predict the organization of the essay?
- At what points were you confused about the organization?
- What evidence was most or least effective?
- Where did the author rely on assertions rather than on evidence?
- Which of your own personal experiences did you recall as you read the essay?

V. Language and Style

- What is the author's *tone* (casual, humorous, ironic, angry, preachy, academic, or other)?
- Are *sentences* and *vocabulary* easy, average, or difficult?
- What key *words* or *images* recur throughout the text?

- Did the tone support or distract from the author's purpose or meaning?
- Did the sentences and vocabulary support or distract from the purpose or meaning?
- Did recurring words or images relate to or support the purpose or meaning?

Remember that not all these questions will be relevant to any given essay or text, but one or two of these questions may suggest a direction or give a *focus* to your overall response. When one of these questions suggests a focus for your response to the essay, *go back to the text, to other texts, and to your experience* to gather *evidence* and *examples* to support your response.

GUIDELINES FOR CLASS DISCUSSION

Class discussions are an important part of the reading/writing/discussing process. Often, however, class discussions are not productive because not everyone knows the purpose of the discussion or how to discuss openly and fairly. Following is a suggested list of goals for class discussion. Read them carefully. *Make notes about any suggestions, revisions, or additions for your class.* Your class will then review these goals and agree to adopt, modify, or revise them for your own class discussions for the remainder of the semester.

Discussion Goals

1. To understand and *accurately represent* the views of the author(s) of an essay. The first discussion goal should be to summarize the author's views fairly.

2. To understand how the views and arguments of individual authors *relate* to each other. Comparing and contrasting different authors' views help clarify each author's argument.

3. To encourage all members of the class to articulate their *understanding* of each essay and their *response* to the ideas in each essay. Class discussions should promote multiple responses rather than focus on a single "right" interpretation or response.

4. To hear class members' responses in an *open forum*. All points of view must be recognized. *Discussions in class should focus on ideas and arguments, not on individual class members.* Class members may attack ideas but not people.

5. To relate class discussions to the *assigned reading/writing task*. What effective writing strategies are illustrated in the essay the class is discussing? How can class members use any of these strategies in writing their own essays?

Summarizing and Responding to an Essay

Following is an essay by Barbara Ehrenreich, "Teach Diversity—with a Smile." First, write for five minutes on the suggested Prereading Journal Entry that precedes the essay. The purpose of the journal entry is to allow you to collect your thoughts about the subject *before* you read Ehrenreich's essay. You will be a much more responsive reader if you reflect on your experiences and articulate your opinions *before* you are influenced by the author and her text. If possible, discuss your experiences and opinions with your classmates after you write your entry but before you read the essay. Next, read the introductory note about Barbara Ehrenreich to understand her background and the context for the essay. Finally, practice active reading techniques as you read. Read first for information and enjoyment. Then, reread with a pen in your hand. Either write your comments and questions directly in the text or do a double-entry log, summarizing the main ideas on one side of a piece of paper and writing your questions and reactions on the other.

■ PREREADING JOURNAL ENTRY   Describe the ethnic groups of people who live in your neighborhood or who attended your previous school. List all the groups you can recall. Then choose one of the following terms and briefly explain what it means: *diversity*, *multiculturalism*, or *political correctness*. Finally, describe one personal experience that taught you something about diversity or political correctness. What was the experience and how did you react?

T E A C H   D I V E R S I T Y —
W I T H   A   S M I L E

Barbara Ehrenreich

Barbara Ehrenreich was born in Butte, Montana, in 1941 and received a B.A. degree from Reed College and a Ph.D. from Rockefeller University. She has been a health policy adviser and a professor of health sciences, but since 1974, she has spent most of her time writing books and articles about socialist and feminist issues. She has received a Ford Foundation award and a Guggenheim fellowship for her writings, which include The Worst Years of Our Lives: Irreverent Notes from a Decade of Greed *(1990),* The Snarling Citizen: Essays *(1995), and* Nickel and Dimed: On (Not) Getting by in America *(2001). Her articles and essays have appeared in* Esquire, Mother Jones, Ms., New Republic, The New York Times Magazine, *and* Time. *The following essay on cultural diversity appeared in* Time *magazine.*

Something had to replace the threat of communism, and at last a   *1*
workable substitute is at hand. "Multiculturalism," as the new menace
is known, has been denounced in the media recently as the new Mc-
Carthyism, the new fundamentalism, even the new totalitarianism—
take your choice. According to its critics, who include a flock of tenured
conservative scholars, multiculturalism aims to toss out what it sees as
the Eurocentric bias in education and replace Plato with Ntozake
Shange and traditional math with the Yoruba number system. And
that's just the beginning. The Jacobins of the multiculturalist movement, who are described derisively as P.C., or politically correct, are
said to have launched a campus reign of terror against those who slip
and innocently say "freshman" instead of "freshperson," "Indian" instead of "Native American" or, may the Goddess forgive them, "disabled" instead of "differently abled."

So you can see what is at stake here: freedom of speech, freedom   *2*
of thought, Western civilization and a great many professorial egos.
But before we get carried away by the mounting backlash against multiculturalism, we ought to reflect for a moment on the system that the
P.C. people aim to replace. I know all about it; in fact it's just about all

I *do* know, since I—along with so many educated white people of my generation—was a victim of monoculturalism.

American history, as it was taught to us, began with Columbus's "discovery" of an apparently unnamed, unpeopled America, and moved on to the Pilgrims serving pumpkin pie to a handful of grateful red-skinned folks. College expanded our horizons with courses called Humanities or sometimes Civ, which introduced us to a line of thought that started with Homer, worked its way through Rabelais and reached a poignant climax in the pensées of Matthew Arnold. Graduate students wrote dissertations on what long-dead men had thought of Chaucer's verse or Shakespeare's dramas; foreign languages meant French or German. If there had been high technology in ancient China, kingdoms in black Africa or women anywhere, at any time, doing anything worth noticing, we did not know it, nor did anyone think to tell us.

Our families and neighborhoods reinforced the dogma of monoculturalism. In our heads, most of us '50s teenagers carried around a social map that was about as useful as the chart that guided Columbus to the "Indies." There were "Negroes," "whites" and "Orientals," the latter meaning Chinese and "Japs." Of religions, only three were known—Protestant, Catholic and Jewish—and not much was known about the last two types. The only remaining human categories were husbands and wives, and that was all the diversity the monocultural world could handle. Gays, lesbians, Buddhists, Muslims, Malaysians, Mormons, etc. were simply off the map.

So I applaud—with one hand, anyway—the multiculturalist goal of preparing us all for a wider world. The other hand is tapping its fingers impatiently, because the critics are right about one thing: when advocates of multiculturalism adopt the haughty stance of political correctness, they quickly descend to silliness or worse. It's obnoxious, for example, to rely on university administrations to enforce P.C. standards of verbal inoffensiveness. Racist, sexist and homophobic thoughts cannot, alas, be abolished by fiat but only by the time-honored methods of persuasion, education and exposure to the other guy's—or, excuse me, woman's—point of view.

And it's silly to mistake verbal purification for genuine social reform. Even after all women are "Ms." and all people are "he or she," women will still earn only 65¢ for every dollar earned by men. Minorities by any other name, such as "people of color," will still bear a hugely disproportionate burden of poverty and discrimination. Disabilities are not just "different abilities" when there are not enough ramps for wheelchairs, signers for the deaf or special classes for the "specially" endowed. With all due respect for the new politesse, actions still speak louder than fashionable phrases.

But the worst thing about the P.C. people is that they are such   *7*
poor advocates for the multicultural cause. No one was ever won over
to a broader, more inclusive view of life by being bullied or relentless-
ly "corrected." Tell a 19-year-old white male that he can't say "girl"
when he means "teen-age woman," and he will most likely snicker.
This may be the reason why, despite the conservative alarms, P.C.-ness
remains a relatively tiny trend. Most campuses have more serious and
ancient problems: faculties still top-heavy with white males of the
monocultural persuasion; fraternities that harass minorities and women;
date rape; alcohol abuse; and tuition that excludes all but the upper
fringe of the middle class.

So both sides would be well advised to lighten up. The conserva-   *8*
tives ought to realize that criticisms of the great books approach to
learning do not amount to totalitarianism. And the advocates of multiculturalism need to regain the sense of humor that enabled their pre-
decessors in the struggle to coin the term P.C. years ago—not in
arrogance but in self-mockery.

Beyond that, both sides should realize that the beneficiaries of   *9*
multiculturalism are not only the "oppressed peoples" on the standard
P.C. list (minorities, gays, etc.). The "unenlightened"—the victims of
monoculturalism—are oppressed too, or at least deprived. Our educa-
tions, whether at Yale or at State U, were narrow and parochial and left
us ill-equipped to navigate a society that truly is multicultural and is
becoming more so every day. The culture that we studied was, in fact, *one*
culture and, from a world perspective, all too limited and ingrown.
Diversity is challenging, but those of us who have seen the alternative
know it is also richer, livelier and ultimately more fun.

*Inferences about the
writer's intentions
appear to be an essential
building block—one that
readers actively use to
construct a meaningful
text.*

—LINDA FLOWER,
AUTHOR OF "THE
CONSTRUCTION OF
PURPOSE"

SUMMARIZING

The purpose of a summary is to give a reader a condensed and objective account of the main ideas and features of a text. Usually, a summary has between
one and three paragraphs or one hundred to three hundred words, depending
on the length and complexity of the original essay and the intended audience
and purpose. Typically, a summary will do the following:

- **Cite the author and title of the text.** In some cases, the place of
  publication or the context for the essay may also be included.
- **Indicate the main ideas of the text.** Accurately representing the
  main ideas (while omitting the less important details) is the major
  goal of a summary.

- **Use direct quotation of key words, phrases, or sentences.** *Quote* the text directly for a few key ideas; *paraphrase* the other important ideas (that is, express the ideas in your own words).
- **Include author tags.** ("According to Ehrenreich" or "as Ehrenreich explains") to remind the reader that you are summarizing the author and the text, not giving your own ideas. *Note:* Instead of repeating "Ehrenreich says," choose verbs that more accurately represent the purpose or tone of the original passage: "Ehrenreich argues," "Ehrenreich explains," "Ehrenreich warns," "Ehrenreich asks," "Ehrenreich advises."
- **Avoid summarizing specific examples or data** unless they help illustrate the thesis or main idea of the text.
- **Report the main ideas as objectively as possible.** Represent the author and text as accurately and faithfully as possible. Do not include your reactions; save them for your response.

SUMMARY OF "TEACH DIVERSITY— WITH A SMILE"

Following is a summary of Ehrenreich's essay. Do *not* read this summary, however, until you have tried to write your own. After you have made notes and written a draft for your own summary, you will more clearly understand the key features of a summary. *Note:* There are many ways to write a good summary. If your summary conveys the main ideas and has the features described previously, it may be just as good as the following example. (Key features of a summary are annotated in the margin.)

In "Teach Diversity—with a Smile," journalist Barbara Ehrenreich explains the current conflict between people who would like to replace our Eurocentric bias in education with a multicultural approach and those critics and conservative scholars who are leading the backlash against multiculturalism and "political correctness." Writing for [readers of *Time* magazine,] Ehrenreich uses her own experience growing up in the 1950s to explain that her narrow education left her a "victim of monoculturalism," ill-equipped to cope with America's growing cultural diversity. Ehrenreich applauds multiculturalism's goal of preparing people for a culturally diverse world, but she is impatient at the "haughty stance" of the P.C. people because they mistake "verbal purification for genuine social reform" and they arrogantly bully people and "correct" their language. Since actions speak louder than words, Ehrenreich argues, the multiculturalists should focus more on genuine social reform—paying equal salaries to men and women, creating access for people with disabilities, and reducing date rape and alcohol abuse. The solution to the problem, according to Ehrenreich, is for both sides to "lighten up." The conservatives should recognize that criticizing the great books of Western civilization is not totalitarian, and the multiculturalists should be less arrogant and regain their sense of humor.

Title and author
Main idea
Paraphrase
Context for essay
Author tag

Direct quotations

Main idea

Paraphrase

Author tag
Main idea
Paraphrase

VIUTI
Buenos Aires
ARGENTINA

Cartoonists & Writers Syndicate

VIUTI

RESPONDING

Reading the world always precedes reading the word, and reading the word implies continually reading the world.

—PAULO FREIRE,

AUTHOR OF LITERACY: READING THE WORD AND THE WORLD

A response requires your reaction and interpretation. Your own perspective—your experiences, beliefs, and attitudes—will guide your particular response. Your response, as the Viuti cartoon illustrates, may be totally different from another reader's response, but that does not necessarily make yours better or worse. Good responses say what you think, but then they *show why* you think so. They show the relationships between your opinions and the text, between the text and your experience, and between this text and other texts.

Depending on its purpose and intended audience, a response to a text can take several directions. Responses may focus on one or more of the following strategies. Consider your purpose and audience or check your assignment to see which type(s) you should emphasize.

Types of Responses

- **Analyzing the effectiveness of the text.** In this case, the response analyzes key features such as the clarity of the main idea, the organization of the argument, the logical reasoning of an argument, the quality of the supporting evidence, and/or the effectiveness of the author's style, tone, and voice.
- **Agreeing and/or disagreeing with the ideas in the text.** Often responders react to the ideas or the argument of the essay. In this case, the responders show why they agree and/or disagree with what the author/text says.
- **Interpreting and reflecting on the text.** The responder explains key passages or examines the underlying assumptions or the implications of the ideas. Often, the responder reflects on how his or her own experiences, attitudes, and observations relate to the text.

Analyzing, agreeing/disagreeing, and interpreting are all slightly different directions that a response may take. But regardless of the direction, responses must be supported by evidence, examples, facts, and details. A responder cannot simply offer an opinion or agree or disagree. Good responses draw on several kinds of supporting evidence.

Kinds of Evidence

- **Personal experience.** Responders may use *examples* from their personal experiences to show why they interpreted the text as they did, why they agreed or disagreed, or why they reacted to the ideas as they did.
- **Evidence from the text.** Responders should cite *specific phrases* or sentences from the text to support their explanation of a section, their analysis of the effectiveness of a passage, or their agreement or disagreement with a key point.
- **Evidence from other texts.** If appropriate, responders may bring in ideas and information from other relevant essays, articles, books, or graphic material.

Not all responses use all three kinds of supporting evidence, but all responses *must* have sufficient examples to support the responder's ideas, reactions, and opinions. Responders should not merely state their opinions. They must give evidence to *show* how and why they read the text as they did.

One final—and crucial—point about responses: A response should make a coherent, overall main point. It should not be just a laundry list of reactions, likes, and dislikes. Sometimes the main point is that the text is not convincing because it lacks evidence. Sometimes the overall point is that the text makes an original statement even though it is difficult to read. Perhaps the basic point is that the author/text stimulates the reader to reflect on his or her experience. Every response should focus on a coherent main idea.

RESPONSE TO "TEACH DIVERSITY— WITH A SMILE"

Following is one possible response to Ehrenreich's essay. Before you read this response, however, write out your own reactions. You need to decide what you think before other responses influence your reading. There are, of course, many different but legitimate responses to any given essay. As you read this response, note the marginal annotations indicating the different types of responses and the different kinds of evidence this writer uses.

Analyzing effectiveness of text

Responder's main point

What I like best about Barbara Ehrenreich's article is her effective use of personal experience to clarify the issues on both sides of the multiculturalism debate. However, her conclusion, that we should "lighten up" and accept diversity because it's "more fun," weakens her argument by ignoring the social inequalities at the heart of the debate. The issue in this debate, I believe, is not just enjoying diversity, which is easy to do, but changing cultural conditions, which is much more difficult.

Evidence from text

Evidence from text

Ehrenreich effectively uses her own experiences—and her common sense—to let us see both the virtues and the excesses of multiculturalism. When she explains that her monocultural education gave her a social map that was "about as useful as the chart that guided Columbus to the 'Indies,'" she helps us understand how vital multicultural studies are in a society that is more like a glass mosaic than a melting pot. Interestingly, even her vocabulary reveals—perhaps unconsciously—her Western bias: *Jacobins, pensées, fiat,* and *politesse* are all words that reveal her Eurocentric education. When Ehrenreich shifts to discussing the P. C. movement, her commonsense approach to the silliness of excessive social correctness ("the other guy's—or, excuse me, woman's—point of view") makes us as readers more willing to accept her compromise position.

Reflecting on the text

Personal experience

My own experience with multiculturalism certainly parallels Ehrenreich's impatience with the "haughty stance" of the P.C. people. Of course, we should avoid racist and sexist terms and use our increased sensitivity to language to reduce discrimination. But my own backlash began several years ago when a friend said I shouldn't use the word *girl*. I said, "You mean, not ever? Not even for a ten-year-old female child?" She replied that the word had been so abused by people referring to a "woman" as a "girl" that the word *girl* now carried too many sexist connotations. Although I understood my friend's point, it seems that *girl* should still be a perfectly good word for a female child under the age of twelve. Which reminds me of a book I saw recently, *The Official Politically Correct Dictionary*. It is loaded with examples of political correctness out of control: Don't say *bald*, say *hair disadvantaged*. Don't use the word *pet*, say *nonhuman companion*. Don't call someone *old*, say that they are *chronologically gifted*.

Evidence from other texts

Ehrenreich does recommend keeping a sense of humor about the P.C. movement, but the conclusion to her essay weakens her argument. Instead of focusing on her earlier point that "it's silly to mistake verbal purification for genuine social reform," she advises both sides to lighten up and have fun with the diversity around us. Instead, I wanted her to conclude by reinforcing her point that "actions still speak louder than fashionable phrases." Changing the realities of illiteracy, poverty, alcohol abuse, and sexual harassment should be the focus of the multiculturalists. Of course, changing language is crucial to changing the world, but the language revolution has already happened—or at least begun. Ehrenreich's article would be more effective, I believe, if she concluded her essay with a call for both sides to help change cultural conditions rather than with a reference to the silly debate about what to call a teenage woman.

Analyzing effectiveness of text

Responder's main point

SUMMARIZING AND RESPONDING TO AN ADVERTISEMENT

Summarizing and responding to graphic material, such as advertisements, is an excellent way to practice responding to texts. In this case, a summary must observe and describe the key features of the advertisement (layout, color, proportion, images, and copy). The response then "reads" the advertisement for the message, selling tactics, cultural stereotypes, or other implications. The focus of the response may be to analyze and explain the persuasive tactics, to interpret cultural values or stereotypes, to judge the effectiveness of the ad, and/or to reflect on assumptions and implications.

The following two student essays read and respond to advertisements. The first, "Beauty and Violence," by Adam Forest responds to a TIGI Bed Head promotional video while the second, "Some Don't Like Their Blues at All," by Karyn M. Lewis responds to a magazine ad for Fila jeans. In both essays, the writers first summarize and describe the advertisement before they analyze and interpret the text for its key messages.

BEAUTY AND VIOLENCE

Adam Forest

"Real people, real life, real products." This catchy new motto from   1
the Bed Head 2000 line of TIGI hair and makeup products is missing only two words: "Real Violence."

The most dangerous social trends are those that subconsciously   2
shift the way society thinks about itself. A recent disturbing trend has
been the glorification of violence toward both men and women, pre-
dominately through the television and movie industry. Riding the societal surge of this trend comes an emerging, possibly more frightening
one—the beautification of violence. It is a trend aimed solely at unique-
ly susceptible, unassuming young women.

I recently had the opportunity to watch the TIGI Bed Head 2000   3
promotional video: it was gut-wrenching. It literally depicted or de-
capitated woman's head being bludgeoned by an invisible presence.
Her eyes jerking wildly about in fear, lips twitching, she shook her
head back and forth while her face was brutally beaten. Her lipstick was
smeared across her face to look like spilt blood, greenish-purple bruise-
like blotches appearing on her cheeks and eye sockets, her mouth letting go an occasional silent scream while still shaking her head "no."
This continued until her face was entirely covered by a multicolored
smear of makeup and her head dropped dead to the side, only to start
the process all over again. Amid the sickening array flashed hip tech-
no music and pictures of colorful beauty products accompanied by
words such as "Fat Lip," "Get-Whipped" and "Dominatrix," topped
off by the final catch phrase, "Makeup of the Future."

The scene presents an interesting metaphor: Women are indeed   4
being bludgeoned by the currently surfacing shock "fashion" trends in
American culture.

This video is obviously an extreme example of the trend, but less   5
blatant techniques grounded in the same principle are more prevalent
and difficult to spot, therefore making them more dangerous as well.
I recall having to stare at a poster of a model in a hair salon before ultimately realizing that her eyeliner had been applied to make her look
as though she had been socked in the face.

Media and fashion have a profound influence on how humans   6
think and behave through the creation of gradual shifts in societal
trends. While violent television advertisements and "beauty" products
such as "Fat-Lip" liplinear may not appear to directly affect the specific

actions of individuals, by gradually causing the abused and battered look among women to be socially accepted as sexy, they can have a substantial impact on how men and women think about themselves and each other, consequently causing violence to skyrocket. And the movement has no conceivable end. Sadly, one would not be hard-pressed to find a blatant example of media perpetuated violence toward women other than the TIGI video. The disconcerting part is that this has been going on for years.

Being able to consciously recognize the problem is only part of the solution. Many people do not understand the difference between being a non-exist and an anti-sexist individual. While someone who is nonsexist merely does nothing to further the problem, an anti-sexist takes an active stance against it. 7

A great example of anti-sexist individual in our community is Phyllis Thode, president of Headlines Salon of the Rockies. Having formerly supported TIGI products, she, too, saw their new promotional video. Afterward she wrote to the president of TIGI, announcing that Headlines would not sell many of its new line of products. She stated, "I am concerned that it is targeting a very narrow market with a strong emphasis on the youth" and "I feel that I need to evaluate my relationship with TIGI. I am not interested in 'Getting Whipped' this Christmas." Right on, Phyllis. 8

With a sexual assault occurring every 45 seconds in America and one in four Colorado women having been the victim of rape or attempted rape, sexual violence is a more serious problem than is often realized. With current media and fashion trends pointing American society in a dangerous direction, it will take a culture comprised of socially aware, anti-sexist men and women to counter the movement. I sincerely hope we can meet the challenge. 9

STUDENT WRITING

Some Don't Like Their Blues at All

Karyn M. Lewis

He strides toward us in navy and white, his body muscled and heavy-set, one arm holding his casually flung jeans jacket over his shoulder. A man in his prime, with just the right combination of macho and sartorial flair. 1

He is also black. *2*

She is curled and giggling upon a chair, her hair loose and flow- *3* ing around her shoulders, leaning forward innocently—the very picture of a blossoming, navy flower.

She is white. *4*

They are each pictured on a magazine page of their own, situated *5* opposite each other in a complementary two-page spread. They are stationed in front of a muted photograph which serves as a background for each one. They both merit their own captions: bold indigo letters presiding over them in the outer corners of each page.

His says: SOME LIKE THEIR BLUES HARD. *6*

Hers says: SOME LIKE THEIR BLUES SOFT. *7*

His background depicts a thrusting struggle between a quarterback *8* and a leaping defender, a scene of arrested violence and high tension.

Her background is a lounging, bikini-clad goddess, who looks at *9* the camera with intriguing, calm passion. She raises her hand to rest behind her head in a languid gesture as she tries to incite passion within the viewer.

At the bottom of the page blazes the proud emblem of the com- *10* pany that came up with this ad: FILA JEANS.

This advertisement blatantly uses stereotypes of men and women *11* to sell its product. It caters to our need to fit into the roles that society has deemed right for the individual sexes ever since patriarchal rule rose up and replaced the primitive worship of a mother goddess and the reverence for women. These stereotypes handed down to us throughout the centuries spell out to us that men are violence and power incarnate, and that the manly attitude has no room for weakness or softness of nature. And we find our role model of women in the compliant and eager female who obeys her man in all things, who must not say no to a male, and who is not very bright—someone who flutters her eyelashes, giggles a lot, and uses tears to get her way.

This ad tells us, by offering the image of a hard, masculine male, *12* who is deified in violence, that he is the role model men should aspire to, and that for women, their ideal is weak but sexual, innocent and at the same time old enough to have sex. In viewing this ad, we see our aspirations clothed in Fila jeans, and to be like them, we must buy the clothes pictured here. This ad also suggests that a man can become hard and powerful (or at least look it) dressed in these jeans; a woman can become sexually intense and desirable dressed in Fila's clothing

The words of the captions tantalize with their sexual innuendo. *13* The phrase "Some like their blues hard" hints at male sexual prowess. Most men and women in this country are obsessed with males' need to prove their virility, and Fila plays on this obsession. Females too have their own stereotype of what constitutes their sexuality. "Some like their blues soft" exemplifies this ideal: A woman should be soft and yielding. Her soft, sensuous body parts, which so excite her partners, have been transformed into her personal qualities. By using the term *soft*, Fila immediately links the girl with her sexuality and sexual organs.

We are shown by the models' postures that men and women are *14* (according to Fila) fundamentally different and total antonyms of one another. He is standing and walking with purpose; she sits, laughing trivially at the camera. Even the background hints at separation of the sexes.

The football players on the man's page are arranged in a diagonal *15* line which starts at the upper left-hand corner and runs to the opposite corner, which is the center of the ad. On her page, the enchanting nymph in the bathing suit runs on a diagonal, beginning where his ends, and traveling up to the upper right-hand corner of her page. These two photos in effect create a *V*, which both links the two models and suggests movement away from one another. Another good example of their autonomy from one another is their skin color. He is a black man, she's white. Black is the opposite color of white on an artist's color wheel and palette and symbolizes dynamically opposed forces: good and evil, night and day, man and woman. This ad hits us with the idea that men and women are not parallel in nature to one another but are fundamentally different in all things. It alienates the sexes from each other. Opposites may attract, but there is no room for understanding a nature completely alien to your own.

So in viewing this ad, and reading its captions, the consumer is left *16* with the view that a woman must be "soft" and sensual, a male's sexual dream, and must somehow still retain her innocence after having sex. She must be weak, the opposite of the violence which contrasts with her on the opposite page. The men looking at this ad read the message that they are supposed to be well-dressed and powerful and possess a strength that borders on violence. As we are told by the caption, men should be "hard." Furthermore, men and women are opposite creatures, as different as two sides of a coin.

This ad is supposed to cause us to want to meet these require- *17* ments, but it fills me with a deep-rooted disgust that we perpetuate the myth that men are unyielding creatures of iron and women are silly bits of fluff. The ad generates no good role models to aspire to, where men and women are equal beings, and both can show compassion and still be strong. Fila may like their blues hard and soft, but I don't like their blues at all.

■ WARMING UP: JOURNAL EXERCISES   The following topics will help you practice your reading and responding.

1. Find an advertisement in a magazine and do a summary/interpretation, following the model provided by Karyn Lewis. First, describe the advertisement carefully so your readers can visualize its graphic features. Quote directly any key parts of the ad copy or language. Then offer your response to this ad. You may wish to analyze the effectiveness of the ad and/or offer your interpretation of its cultural significance.

2. Because previewing material is an important part of active reading, most recent psychology and social science textbooks use previewing or pre-reading strategies at the beginning of each new chapter. Find one chapter in a textbook that uses these previewing techniques. How does the author preview the material? Does the preview help you understand the material in the chapter?

3. Reading the following paragraph illustrates how our prior experience can combine with our predictions to make meaning. The following passage describes a common procedure in our lives. Read the passage. Can you identify the procedure?

The procedure is actually quite simple. First, you arrange things into different groups. Of course, one pile may be sufficient depending on how much there is to do. If you have to go somewhere else because of lack of facilities, that is the next step; otherwise you are pretty well set. It is important not to overdo things. That is, it is better to do too few things at once than too many. In the short run this may not seem important, but complications can easily arise. A mistake can be expensive as well. At first, the whole procedure will seem complicated. Soon, however, it will become just another facet of life. It is difficult to foresee any end to the necessity for this task in the immediate future, but then one can never tell. After the procedure is completed, one arranges the materials into different groups again. Then they can be put into their appropriate places. Eventually, they will be used once more, and the whole cycle will then have to be repeated. However, that is part of life.

As you read, record your guesses. What words helped to orient you? Where did you make wrong guesses? Discuss your reactions in class.

4. Reading is a gradual process of making guesses and then confirming or rejecting those guesses. To dramatize how the process works, find an essay or a short story that you have not read before. (Either Edward Abbey's essay, "The Damnation of a Canyon," in Chapter 10 or Kate Chopin's short story, "The Story of an Hour," in Chapter 11 will work well.) Read two paragraphs and then stop. Write down what has happened and what you predict will happen next. Then read one more page and stop. Summarize in a sentence what has happened, and predict what is coming. A third time, read one more page. Now stop and write. Then read the essay

Day and Night by M. C. Escher. 1997 Cordon Art-Baam-Holland.

or the story through to the end. How accurately were you able to make predictions? Where did your guesses turn out to be wrong? If you read both the essay and the story, which was more predictable? Why?

5. Study the print by Maurits Escher reproduced here. How many different ways of perceiving this picture can you see? Describe each perspective. How is "reading" this picture similar to reading a printed text? How is it different?

6. The following short essay by Emily Prager is an excellent example of a critical reading of a cultural artifact—the Barbie doll. Prager's essay illustrates the third type of response: interpreting and reflecting. Prager draws on her own experiences to reflect on the implications of Barbie's creation and the effects the doll has had on images of women in America.

PROFESSIONAL WRITING

OUR BARBIES, OURSELVES
Emily Prager

Emily Prager was raised in Texas, the Far East, and Greenwich Village. She majored in anthropology at Barnard College and has been a contributing editor for The National Lampoon. *She is a short story writer, novelist, and journalist who has written for* The Village Voice, Viva, *and* Penthouse *and has published books of short stories and fiction including* A Visit from the Footbinder and Other Stories *(1982),* Clea and Zeus Divorce *(1987), and* Eve's Tattoo *(1991). "Our Barbies, Ourselves" was originally titled "Major Barbie" and appeared in the December 1991 issue of*

Interview *magazine. The occasion for the essay was Prager's discovery that Barbie was designed by a Mr. Jack Ryan, a former husband of Zsa Zsa Gabor and a weapons designer for a missile company.*

I read an astounding obituary in *The New York Times* not too long ago. It concerned the death of one Jack Ryan. A former husband of Zsa Zsa Gabor, it said, Mr. Ryan had been an inventor and designer during his lifetime. A man of eclectic creativity, he designed Sparrow and Hawk missiles when he worked for the Raytheon Company, and, the notice said, when he consulted for Mattel he designed Barbie. 1

If Barbie was designed by a man, suddenly a lot of things made sense to me, things I'd wondered about for years. I used to look at Barbie and wonder, What's wrong with this picture? What kind of woman designed this doll? Let's be honest: Barbie looks like someone who got her start at the Playboy Mansion. She could be a regular guest on *The Howard Stern Show.* It is a fact of Barbie's design that her breasts are so out of proportion to the rest of her body that if she were a human woman, she'd fall flat on her face. 2

If it's true that a woman didn't design Barbie, you don't know how much saner that makes me feel. Of course, that doesn't ameliorate the damage. There are millions of women who are subliminally sure that a thirty-nine-inch bust and a twenty-three-inch waist are the epitome of lovability. Could this account for the popularity of breast implant surgery? 3

I don't mean to step on anyone's toes here. I loved my Barbie. Secretly, I still believe that neon pink and turquoise blue are the only colors in which to decorate a duplex condo. And like many others of my generation, I've never married, simply because I cannot find a man who looks as good in clam diggers as Ken. 4

The question that comes to mind is, of course, Did Mr. Ryan design Barbie as a weapon? Because it *is* odd that Barbie appeared about the same time in my consciousness as the feminist movement—a time when women sought equality and small breasts were king. Or is Barbie the dream date of weapons designers? Or perhaps it's simpler than that: Perhaps Barbie is Zsa Zsa if she were eleven inches tall. No matter what, my discovery of Jack Ryan confirms what I have always felt: There is something indescribably masculine about Barbie—dare I say it, phallic. For all her giant breasts and high-heeled feet, she lacks a certain softness. If you asked a little girl what kind of doll she wanted for Christmas, I just don't think she'd reply, "Please, Santa, I want a hard-body." 5

On the other hand, you could say that Barbie, in feminist terms,   *6*
is definitely her own person. With her condos and fashion plazas and
pools and beauty salons, she is definitely a liberated woman, a gal on
the move. And she has always been sexual, even totemic. Before Barbie, American dolls were flatfooted and breastless, and ineffably dignified. They were created in the image of little girls or babies.
Madame Alexander was the queen of doll makers in the fifties, and
her dollies looked like Elizabeth Taylor in *National Velvet*. They represented the kind of girls who looked perfect in jodhpurs, whose hair
was never out of place, who grew up to be Jackie Kennedy—before
she married Onassis. Her dolls' boyfriends were figments of the imagination, figments with large portfolios and three-piece suits and presidential aspirations, figments who could keep dolly in the style to
which little girls of the fifties were programmed to become accustomed, a style that spasm-ed with the sixties and the appearance of
Barbie. And perhaps what accounts for Barbie's vast popularity is that
she was also a sixties woman into free love and fun colors, anticlass,
and possessed of real, molded boyfriend, Ken, with whom she could
chant a mantra.

But there were problems with Ken. I always felt weird about   *7*
him. He had no genitals, and, even at age ten, I found that ominous.
I mean, here was Barbie with these humongous breasts, and that was
OK with the toy company. And then, there was Ken with that trun-
cated, unidentifiable lump at his groin. I sensed injustice at work.
Why, I wondered, was Barbie designed with such obvious sexual
equipment and Ken not? Why was his treated as if it were more
mysterious than hers? Did the fact that it was treated as such indicate that somehow his equipment, his essential maleness, was considered more powerful than hers, more worthy of the dignity of
concealment? And if the issue in the mind of the toy company was
obscenity and its possible damage to children, I still object. How do
they think I felt, knowing that no matter how many water beds they
slept in, or hot tubs they romped in, or swimming pools they lounged
by under the stars, Barbie and Ken could never make love? No matter how much sexuality Barbie possessed, she would never turn Ken
on. He would be forever withholding, forever detached. There was a
loneliness about Barbie's situation that was always disturbing. And
twenty-five years later, movies and videos are still filled with topless
women and covered men. As if we're all trapped in Barbie's world and
can never escape.

God, it certainly has cheered me up to think that Barbie was de-   *8*
signed by Jack Ryan. . . .

ATLAS SHRUGS

Nicholas Lemann

A prolific and acclaimed journalist and national correspondent to the Atlantic Monthly, *Nicholas Lemann has written on social issues, culture, history, and contemporary politics in magazines such as* The New Republic, The Nation, The New Yorker, Washington Monthly, Time, *and* Newsweek. *His recent books include* The Promised Land: The Great Black Migration and How It Changed America *(1991) and* The Big Test: The Secret History of the American Meritocracy *(1999). In the following* New Yorker *essay, Lemann introduces the reader to the "new geography" or "critical geography" through several texts which he summarizes and then comments on. He focuses on two works of critical geography: J. B. Harley's* The New Nature of Maps *and Susan Schulten's* The Geographical Imagination in America, 1880–1950. *According to Lemann, these authors argue that maps are more than innocent directions indicating how to get from Point A to Point B; they are, in fact, "social constructions," "polemics," and "texts of power."*

After the Second World War, most of the Ivy League universities   *1*
abolished their departments of geography, and the subject inexorably began to slip, at least in the mind of the general public, into the realm of junior-high-school memorization of placenames and climatic zones. (The advent, whenever it was, of Geography, the annoying word game that children insist on playing during road trips, didn't elevate the image of the discipline, either.) But geography is back. In the past couple of decades, a group of mostly British, mostly left-wing scholars—David Harvey, David Woodward, J. B. Harley, and others—have created a field known, variously, as "critical geography" and "the new geography." They have taken up residence in the remaining university geography departments in this country, and have started turning out protégés and publications, promoting a new, more cunning way of looking at maps.

When you think about it, geography is a rich subject. Much of   *2*
the politics and economics of the world revolves around the question of who controls what space, and to what end. This was plainly true during the Age of Exploration that we all learned about—though we may have been so intent on remembering the difference between Vasco da Gama and Vasco Núñez de Balboa that we didn't notice — and it's still true today, in the age of the global economy and metropolitan sprawl. Here in the United States, the idea of the vanished

frontier, a pure geographical construct, has shaped our understanding of ourselves for a century.

One of the main subspecialties of critical geography is critical car- 3 tography, the study of maps and mapmaking. We're accustomed to thinking of maps as useful objects, whose purpose is to direct us from one location to another, or, in the case of old maps, as fanciful arrangements of bright-colored ink on paper, most evocative for what they get wrong. Clearly, though, maps have played an enormous part in shaping the nonphysical world. States, nations, empires, even continents are not natural geographic features, and their existence would be impossible without maps. The mapping of the world has been one of the monumental human endeavors.

Now playing at the New York Public Library is a charming exhi- 4 bition, assembled by Alice Hudson, the chief of the library's Map Division, called "Heading West: Mapping the Territory." The show, a cartographic record of the American West, is made up of selections from the library's collection of half a million maps: "This is the old geography," Hudson told me the other day, when she walked me through the show. She pointed to a Union Pacific Railway map from 1881, on which somebody had scribbled a couple of sentences, probably from a telegraphed message, and drawn fresh lines showing the latest extension of a rail line. What could be more straightforward and practical than that? The show has an aesthetic aspect, too. Hudson obviously loves the craftsmanship of cartography, and she has found some wonderful specimens. Geological and botanical maps from the period of initial Western exploration are composed and colored (usually by nameless government bureaucrats) with a startling intensity and grace. The star of the show—Hudson's big rediscovery—is the incredibly detailed, meticulously shaded engraving work of Frederick Von Egloffstein, a nineteenth-century Prussian émigré who produced both maps and views of the West. His drawing of the rim of the Grand Canyon, for example, makes it easy to strip away the many coats of tourist culture and imagine how forbidding and awful it must once have appeared.

At the same time, historical maps are necessarily suffused with 5 the agendas, beyond accuracy and elegance, of their makers: maps serve interests. The earliest maps exhibited in "Heading West," which date from before 1700, hopefully depict the Americas as an island or, at least, a raggedy blob that ships might cruise past on their way to trade in Asia. Almost immediately after the West was accurately mapped, the familiar ruler lines and colors of political division appear; very soon after that the property grids and rail lines of commerce are evident; and, finally, the maps acquire an exaggerated pictorial style associated with the promotion of tourism and residential real estate. Put into historical perspective, every map on display communicates a sense not just of a piece of land but also of the apportionment of money and power in the world at a particular moment.

The father of critical cartography, and therefore of the idea that a map should be understood as more than just a set of directions, was J. B. Harley, a map historian who died ten years ago. Harley spent most of his life in England and, in middle age, moved to the University of Wisconsin-Milwaukee, where he helped launch an ambitious publishing series called the History of Cartography. This spring, Johns Hopkins is bringing out a collection of his essays, "The New Nature of Maps." It is a curious book, which manages to make the case both for and (unwittingly) against critical cartography. Harley seems to have been one of those academics whose careers are spent reconnoitring the lower slopes of a magnum opus—in his case, a book to be called "The Map as Ideology"—without ever writing it. His oeuvre thus consists of essays that display great erudition but make quick, darting points rather than full, sustained arguments. Harley was a follower of Michel Foucault, who held that all knowledge is a form of power. Rummaging through the history of mapmaking, Harley has found enough material to bear out Foucault's idea, at least in the realm of cartography.

Before mass production, only the powerful had access to maps. Much early mapping was done by people who had job titles like Geographer to the King. (Even now, a large share of mapping, including American mapping, is done by governments.) Maps were a way of locating resources, so that the map-holding few could get their hands on them, and of establishing control over land. As Harley points out in one of his essays, old maps of England often demarcate the estates of noblemen as if they were natural features of the environment, and relegate the places where everybody else lives to (one of his favorite words) "silences." Cartouches, those small emblems drawn in the margins of old maps and now a godsend to critical cartographers, showed heraldic crests. "There are no map signs for poverty or squalor, and the bland washes of the map colorer denote a green and pleasant land," Harley notes, with characteristic grim satisfaction. The soil in the British Empire was not in fact colored pink, except on maps, but the uniform color there helped fix the empire in people's minds as an organic whole. ("The way things were going nothing was pink on the map any more," a character in Barbara Pym's declinist novel "Quartet in Autumn" reflects.)

As Harley's colleague J. H. Andrews puts it in his introduction to "The New Nature of Maps," Harley "gathered ideas from (to quote one of his own lists) "information-theory, linguistics, semi-

6

7

8

otics, structuralism, phenomenology, developmental theory, hermeneutics, iconology, Marxism, and ideology." Despite, or perhaps because of the capacious intellectual toolkit at his disposal, Harley is deeply unwilling to admit that most maps are used by most people for simple directional purposes. To him, a map is a "social construction," a "thick text," a "redescription of reality," a "silent arbiter of power," "a polemic," a "manifesto for a set of beliefs about the world," or a "text of power." Even the official state highway map of North Carolina, he insists, is "making other dialogical assertions behind its mask of innocence and transparence," by which he means that its emphasis on superhighways subjects other aspects of the Tarheel State to those dreaded "silences." As Jeremy Black, another critical cartographer, writes in his own, somewhat disjointed new collection of essays, "Maps and Politics" (Chicago), the work of Harley and his followers is flawed by an impulse to "search for conspiracy" and "a tendency to state the obvious."

The work of the Harley school, once encountered, makes it impossible to look at maps in a completely straightforward way ever again. Instead, the urge to decode arises every time you come across one (and, once you stop taking maps for granted, it's amazing how often you do). The question is whether the habit of reading maps as sociopolitical artifacts can generate something more complicated and coherent than mordantly ironic observations about the subtexts of specific maps—the scholarly equivalent of the running commentary that knowing college kids produce as they sprawl on couches and watch old television shows.   9

Another new book on maps, "The Geographical Imagination in America, 1880–1950" (Chicago), by Susan Schulten, steps up to the challenge of producing a full-length work about the political economy of mapmaking. Schulten, a historian at the University of Denver who has a basically Harleyan consciousness ("Maps are arguments that mediate our understanding of the world," she writes), has done an enormous amount of research and put together an ambitious history of the rise of popular cartography in the United States.   10

This country, Schulten says, was the birthplace of maps and geography for the masses. Published maps were traditionally made by the copper-engraving process, which yields fine but expensive work. The advent of the much cheaper, though less elegant, wax-engraving process, in the mid-nineteenth century, made it possible to publish maps for a popular audience. American map publishers—in particular, Rand McNally, of Chicago, whose archives Schulten has perused extensively—used wax engraving to develop a distinctively American   11 style of map, loud and commercial, crammed with as many place-names as possible, in thick type, and garishly colored state by state. Nineteenth-century American commercial mapmakers were pathologically particular in their treatment of the United States and pathologically general in their treatment of the rest of the world. "Most of the civilized people of the world belong to the white race, though in some countries the people of that race are half-civilized," reported Rand McNally's "Elementary Geography," a textbook published in 1894 for the booming public-school geography-class market. "The savages belong to the red, brown, and black races. Most people of the yellow race are half-civilized, but you will read some day of the yellow people of Japan."

With the Spanish-American War and the rise of American imperialism, Americans began to focus much more seriously on faraway places. Schulten is not exactly soft on imperialism, but she presents it as a developmental step in geography, objectionable on its own but less so if seen as a station on the way to true understanding: better to think of the world as an arena for commercial exploitation than not to think about it at all. Schulten explores this phase through the magazine *National Geographic,* which became prominent in the first two decades of the twentieth century. Like Rand McNally, *National Geographic* is a peculiarly American institution, part public agency (with its official expeditions and articles by government authorities), part academic journal (published by a society of experts), and part high-minded mass entertainment (naked photographs of dusky maidens). During and after the Spanish-American War, it published many articles about the new little siblings in the American family, Cuba and the Philippines, as a way not so much of justifying our foreign policy as of making people feel comfortable with the idea of being linked to such exotic locales. *National Geographic* reassured us by presenting them as charming and folkish, rather than as threatening; its central editorial goal, as the magazine's brilliant editor, Gilbert Grosvenor, put it later in a letter to one of his contributors, was to provide "mental relaxation without emotional stimulus." *12*

Unlike Harley, Schulten seems to have gone native in the course, of her research. To her, the leading mapmakers are more than just one-dimensional avatars of entrenched power, and she is sympathetic to them when, by her lights, they are trying to behave well. The last part of her book presents the mid-twentieth century as the dawn of a golden age of geographic understanding. The American map industry, having advanced from race-and-climate-are-destiny theories to an interest in faraway places as potential areas of economic exploitation, awoke to questions about the good of all people, not just Americans. Several *13* weeks after Pearl Harbor, Franklin Roosevelt gave a radio address urging people to go out and buy a world map, and an awful lot of them did. Sales of geographic material soared during the war years. *National Geographic* and then Rand McNally abandoned their habit of filling every available bit of map surface with place-names, and adopted a suaver, more European style of presentation. Commercial aviation led to maps that showed the world from a point above the North Pole, with the Arctic Ocean as the "new Mediterranean." Rand McNally replaced its old Imperial Atlas with an elaborately produced Cosmopolitan Atlas.

During the Second World War, Schulten reports, practically cheering, even the Mercator projection—which had dominated world mapping since it was devised, in 1569—finally fell out of favor. Mayor LaGuardia personally banned its use in New York City public schools in 1943, perhaps afraid that another generation of schoolchildren would grow up thinking that Greenland was the size of South America. *National Geographic* now uses the oval Robinson projection, and when you move out of the mass market in a leftward direction you encounter the Peters projection, developed in 1967, which makes the Third World look bigger than the First and the Second—and thus "embodies the map as redistributive polemic," according to Jeremy Black. At the end of Schulten's story, she finds a mapmaker she feels comfortable lionizing: Richard Edes Harrison, whose maps offered gorgeous, sweeping views of the globe from unfamiliar angles—they look like the photographs that astronauts take. Many of them were produced at the height of the war, and they implicitly communicate internationalist editorial messages (e.g., the United States is highly vulnerable to attack from all sides). Harrison, Schulten notes approvingly, understood "that all cartography was inherently argumentative, and all maps inherently suggestive." *14*

"The Geographical Imagination" is Schulten's first book. A more experienced author might have been able to produce out of all the institutional specifics a magisterial narrative that began at the beginning and ended at the end. Instead, each chapter is a mini-monograph, and the weight of detail about the different geographic institutions can become oppressive. Schulten has clearly demonstrated that mapping is a subject that can support sustained historical inquiry. What she hasn't demonstrated is that it can also support intellection richer and more interesting than the two or three fairly straightforward changes she manages to ring on the basic idea of critical cartography. *15*

Critical cartography is propelled by an odd mixture of cynicism and idealism. After having expertly seen through the bad faith of *16* mapmakers up to this point, writers in the field usually express the hope that future mapmakers, elevated by self-awareness and progressive principles, can produce maps that will be as benevolent as past maps have been baneful. They are reformers at heart. J. B. Harley, rather than wanting mapmaking to free itself of the indicia of power relations, merely wanted it to be more in line with his politics. His collection of essays winds up with a call for cartographers to endorse "principles of social justice" in order to produce "a socially responsible representation of the world." It is a hope that Susan Schulten seems to share.

Could this really happen? One of the critical cartographers' 17 strongest points is that maps, like every human endeavor, are saturated with temporal, social, political, and economic contexts that their makers can't transcend. Imagine if the Peters projection had been developed in 1569 and the Mercator four centuries later. Would history really have unfolded differently? And, if so, how, exactly? Critical cartography is persuasive in arguing that maps are more than straightforward collections of geographic data—"constitutive, not representative," as Jeremy Black puts it. What is not so persuasive is the idea that enlightened mapmakers could somehow break out of the perspectival prison in which we are all consigned to dwell, and direct us to a better world.

Vocabulary

In your journal, write the meaning of each of the following words:

- turning out *protégés* **(1)**
- a *cartographic* record **(4)**
- of a *magnum opus* **(6)**
- his *oeuvre* **(6)**
- display great *erudition* **(6)**
- often *demarcate* the estates **(7)**
- including . . . *semiotics* . . . *phenomenology* . . . *hermeneutics* **(8)**
- *mordantly* ironic observations **(9)**
- arguments that *mediate* our understanding **(10)**
- *avatars* of entrenched power **(13)**
- map as *redistributive polemic* **(14)**
- the *indicia* of power relations **(16)**
- *constitutive*, not representative **(17)**

Questions for Writing and Discussion

1. Take an inventory of the maps in your possession. Locate maps from your car, in magazines, or in an atlas that you have. What features do these maps highlight? What geographical or cultural features do they ignore? What power constructions can you find on these maps? Do they confirm or refute the arguments of the authors Lemann summarizes?

2. Lemann's essay was published in *The New Yorker*, whose readers are sophisticated but not necessarily experts in the "new geography." Where does Lemann give enough background information for his readers—and where might he give clearer explanations or a more accessible summary and response?

3. List the texts and authors that Lemann comments on. Does he spend more time summarizing each text or more time responding? Would less summary and more response make his essay more or less effective for you or for his audience? Explain.

4. In paragraph 17, Lemann quotes Jeremy Black as saying that maps are "more than straightforward collections of geographic data," that they are "constitutive, not representative." What does Black mean when he says that maps are "constitutive, not representative?" Is he right? Can't a map just be a set of directions showing how to get from Point A to Point B? Do all maps contain, as Lemann suggests, "social, political, and economic contexts that their makers can't transcend?"

5. On the Internet, find another review of J. B. Harley's book. Check Lexis-Nexis, for example, at http://web.lexis-nexis/universe and search in the news for a review of *The Nature of Maps* by Nick Saunders in the *New Scientist*, July 7, 2001. Does Saunders give a clear summary of Harley's argument? Is it more or less informative than Lemann's essay? Explain.

PROFESSIONAL WRITING

ANIMAL RIGHTS AND BEYOND
David Quammen

An award-winning writer of essays and fiction, David Quammen is best known for his regular column on nature in Outside *magazine. Essays originally published in his column appear in* Natural Acts: A Sidelong View of Science and Nature *(1985),* The Flight of the Iguana *(1988),* The

Song of the Dodo (1996), and Boilerplate Rhino: Nature in the Eye of the Beholder *(2001). Although Quammen often writes on the weird or offbeat curiosities of biology, such as the mating habits of the aphid, he can tackle subjects requiring philosophical depth as well as biological learning. "Animal Rights and Beyond," which appears in* Natural Acts, *shows Quammen's talent for understanding the difficult moral problems behind the animal rights movement and responding in a sensible but humorous manner. Do animals have moral rights? Should we cease all scientific experiments with animals? Should we all become vegetarians? Here is Quammen's summary of two books by animal rights philosophers—Peter Singer and Tom Regan—and his own responses to the difficult questions they raise.*

Do non-human animals have rights? Should we humans feel morally bound to exercise consideration for the lives and well-being of individual members of other animal species? If so, how much consideration, and by what logic? Is it permissible to torture and kill? Is it permissible to kill cleanly, without prolonged pain? To abuse or exploit without killing? For a moment, don't think about whales or wolves or the California condor; don't think about the cat or the golden retriever with whom you share your house. Think about chickens. Think about laboratory monkeys and then think about lab rats and then also think about lab frogs. Think about scallops. Think about mosquitoes.   *1*

It's a Gordian question, by my lights, but one not very well suited to Alexandrian answers. Some people would disagree, judging the matter simply enough settled, one way or the other. *Of course they have rights. Of course they don't.* I say beware any such snappy, steel-trap thinking. Some folk would even—this late in the evolution of human sensibility—call it a frivolous question, a time-filling diversion for emotional hemophiliacs and cranks. *Women's rights, gay rights, now for Christ sake they want ANIMAL rights.* Notwithstanding the ridicule, the strong biases toward each side, it is certainly a serious philosophical issue, important and tricky, with almost endless implications for the way we humans live and should live on this planet.   *2*

Philosophers of earlier ages, if they touched the subject at all, were likely to be dismissive. Thomas Aquinas announced emphatically that animals "are intended for man's use in the natural order. Hence it is not wrong for man to make use of them, either by killing or in any other way whatever." Descartes held that animals are merely machines. As late as 1901, a moral logician named Joseph Rickaby (who happened to be a Jesuit, but don't necessarily hold that against him) declared: "Brute beasts, not having understanding and therefore not being persons, cannot have any rights. The conclusion is clear."   *3*

Maybe not quite so clear. Recently, just during the past decade, professional academic philosophers have at last begun to address the matter more openmindedly.

Two thinkers in particular have been influential: an Australian *4* named Peter Singer, an American named Tom Regan. In 1975 Singer published a book titled *Animal Liberation*, which stirred up the debate among his colleagues and is still treated as a landmark. Eight years later Tom Regan published *The Case for Animal Rights*, a more thorough and ponderous opus that stands now as a sort of companion piece to the Singer book. In between there came a number of other discussions of animal rights—including a collection of essays edited jointly by Singer and Regan. Despite the one-time collaboration, Peter Singer and Tom Regan represent two distinct schools of thought: They reach similar conclusions about the obligations of humans to other animals, but the moral logic is very different, and possibly also the implications. Both men have produced some formidable work and both, to my simple mind, show some shocking limitations of vision.

I've spent the past week amid these books, Singer's and Regan's and *5* the rest. It has been an edifying experience, and now I'm more puzzled than ever. I keep thinking about monkeys and frogs and mosquitoes and—sorry, but I'm quite serious—carrots.

Peter Singer's view is grounded upon the work of Jeremy Ben- *6* tham, that eighteenth-century British philosopher generally known as the founder of utilitarianism. "The greatest good for the greatest number" is a familiar cartoon version of what, according to Bentham, should be achieved by the ethical ordering of society and behavior. A more precise summary is offered by Singer: "In other words, the interests of every being affected by an action are to be taken into account and given the same weight as the like interests of any other being." If this much is granted, the crucial next point is deciding what things constitute interests and who or what qualifies as a *being*. Evidently Bentham did not have just humans in mind. Back in 1789, optimistically and perhaps presciently, he wrote: "The day may come when the rest of the animal creation may acquire those rights which never could have been withholden from them but by the hand of tyranny." Most philosophers of his day were inclined (as most in our day are still inclined) to extend moral coverage only to humans, because only humans (supposedly) are rational and communicative. Jeremy Bentham took exception: "The question is not, 'Can they *reason?*' nor, 'Can they *talk?*' but, 'Can they *suffer?*'" On this crucial point, Peter Singer follows Bentham.

The capacity to suffer, says Singer, is what separates a being with *7* legitimate interests from an entity without interests. A stone has no interests that must be respected, because it cannot suffer. A mouse can suffer; therefore it has interests and those interests must be weighed in the moral balance. Fine, that much seems simple enough. Certain people of sophistic or Skinnerian bent would argue that there is no proof a mouse can in fact suffer, that it's merely an anthropomorphic assumption; but since each of us has no proof that *anyone* else actually suffers besides ourselves, we are willing, most of us, to grant the assumption. More problematic is that very large gray area between stones and mice.

Peter Singer declares: "If a being suffers, there can be no moral justification for disregarding that suffering, or for refusing to count it equally with the like suffering of any other being. But the converse of this is also true. If a being is not capable of suffering, or of enjoyment, there is nothing to take into account." Where is the boundary? Where falls the line between creatures who suffer and those that are incapable? Singer's cold philosophic eye travels across the pageant of living species—chickens suffer, mice suffer, fish suffer, um, lobsters most likely suffer, *look alive, you other creatures!*—and his damning stare lands on the oyster.   8

No, I'm not making this up. The oyster, by Singer's best guess, doesn't suffer. Its nervous system lacks the requisite complexity. Therefore, while lobsters and crawfish and shrimp possess inviolable moral status, the oyster has none. It is a difficult judgment, Singer admits, by no means an infallible one, but "somewhere between a shrimp and an oyster seems as good a place to draw the line as any, and better than most."   9

Moral philosophy, no one denies, is an imperfect science.   10

Tom Regan takes exception with Singer on two important points. First, he disavows the utilitarian framework, with its logic that abuse or killing of animals by humans is wrong because it yields a net *overall* decrease in welfare, among all beings who qualify for moral status. No, argues Regan, that logic is false and pernicious. The abuse or killing is wrong in its *essence*—however the balance comes out on overall welfare—because it violates the rights of those individual animals. Individual rights, in other words, take precedence over the maximizing of the common good. Second, in Regan's opinion the capacity to suffer is not what marks the elect. Mere suffering is not sufficient. Instead he posits the concept of *inherent value*, a complex and magical quality possessed by some living creatures but not others.   11

A large portion of Regan's book is devoted to arguing toward this concept. He is more uncompromisingly protective of certain creatures—those with rights—than Singer, but he is also more selective; the hull of his ark is sturdier, but the gangplank is narrower. According to Regan, individual beings possess inherent value (and therefore   12 inviolable rights) if they "are able to perceive and remember; if they have beliefs, desires, and preferences; if they are able to act intentionally in pursuit of their desires or goals; if they are sentient and have an emotional life; if they have a sense of the future, including a sense of their own future; if they have a psychophysical identity over time; and if they have an individual experiential welfare that is logically independent of their utility for, and the interests of, others." So Tom Regan is not handing rights around profligately, to every cute little beast that crawls over his foot. In fact we all probably know a few humans who, at least on a bad night, might have trouble meeting those standards. But how would Regan himself apply them? Where does he see the line falling? Who qualifies for inherent value, and what doesn't?

Like Singer, Regan has thought this point through. Based on his *13* grasp of biology and ethology, he is willing to grant rights to "mentally normal mammals of a year or more."

Also like Singer, he admits that the judgment is not infallible: *14* "Because we are uncertain where the boundaries of consciousness lie, it is not unreasonable to advocate a policy that bespeaks moral caution." So chickens and frogs should be given the benefit of the doubt, as should all other animals that bear a certain degree of anatomical and physiological resemblance to us mentally normal mammals.

But Regan does not specify just what degree. *15*

The books by Singer and Regan leave me with two very separate *16* reactions. The first combines admiration and gratitude. These men are applying the methods of systematic philosophy to an important and much-neglected question. Furthermore, they don't content themselves with just understanding and describing a pattern of gross injustice; they also emphatically say, "*Let's stop it!*" They are fighting a good fight. Peter Singer's book in particular has focused attention on the outrageous practices that are routine in American factory farms, in "psychological" experimentation, in research on the toxicity of cosmetics. Do you know how chickens are dealt with on the large poultry operations? How veal is produced? How the udders of dairy cows are kept flowing? Do you know the sorts of ingenious but pointless torment that thousands of monkeys and millions of rats endure, each year, to fill the time and the dissertations of uninspired graduate students? If you don't, by all means read Singer's *Animal Liberation*.

The second reaction is negative. Peter Singer and Tom Regan, *17* it seems to me, share a breathtaking smugness and myopia not too dissimilar to the brand they so forcefully condemn. Theirs is a righteous and vigorous smugness, not a passive and unreflective one. But still.

Singer inveighs against a sin he labels *speciesism*—discrimination   18
against certain creatures based solely upon the species to which they
belong. Regan uses a slightly less confused and less clumsy phrase,
human chauvinism, to indicate roughly the same thing. Both of them
arrive (supposedly by sheer logic) at the position that vegetarianism is
morally obligatory: To kill and eat a "higher" animal represents absolute violation of one being's rights; to kill and eat a plant evidently
violates nothing at all. Both Singer and Regan claim to disparage the
notion—pervasive in Western philosophy since Protagoras—that "Man
is the measure of all things." Both argue elaborately against anthro-
pocentrism, while creating new moral frameworks that are also decidedly anthropocentric. Make no mistake: Man is still the measure, for
Singer and Regan. The test for inherent value has changed only slightly. Instead of asking, "*Is the creature a human?*," they simply ask, "*How
similar to human is similar enough?*"

Peter Singer explains that shrimp deserve brotherly treatment but   19
oysters, so different from us, are fair game for the gumbo. In Tom
Regan's vocabulary, the redwood tree is an "inanimate natural object,"
sharing that category with clouds and rocks. But some simple minds
would say: Life is life.

VOCABULARY

In your journal, write the meaning of each of the following words:

- a *Gordian* question **(2)**
- *Alexandrian* answers **(2)**
- perhaps *presciently* **(6)**
- people of *sophistic* or *Skinnerian* bent **(7)**
- *anthropomorphic* assumption **(7)**
- *inviolable* moral status **(9)**
- biology and *ethology* **(13)**

QUESTIONS FOR WRITING AND DISCUSSION

1. Which of the following nonhuman species should or should not
   have rights protected by humans? Where would you draw the
   line, and on what basis? Use the following species—or make up
   your own list.

whales	snakes	fish	trees
wolves	scorpions	squid	orchids
cats and dogs	spiders	lobsters	cabbage
chickens	mosquitoes	clams	carrots
mice and rats	chiggers	oysters	lichen

2. A good summary should mention the author and title, use direct quotations for key ideas, include author tags, and describe the main ideas objectively and fairly. Examine Quammen's summary of either Singer's or Regan's texts. Is his summary effective?

3. Responses can focus on analyzing the effectiveness of the text, agreeing or disagreeing with the ideas in the text, or reflecting on the meaning of the text. Does Quammen use all three of these kinds of responses? Which one does he emphasize?

4. Quammen focuses on a difficult philosophical problem, but he makes the organization of his essay easy to follow. Below is the basic outline.

   I.   Introduction to the question of animal rights

   II.   Review of early philosophers' views on animal rights

   III. Summary and review of the books and philosophies of Singer and Regan

         A. Singer's philosophy

         B. Regan's philosophy

   IV.   Quammen's responses to Singer and Regan

         A. Positive reactions

         B. Negative reactions

   For the above outline, indicate by numbers which paragraphs belong with each section. Then underline or write down the transitions or key words or phrases near the beginning of each section that *signal* for the reader the focus for that section. Where are Quammen's signals clear? Where should he use a better transition or more clearly state the focus?

5. A writer's tone and sense of humor can make a passage appealing to readers. Find three sentences where Quammen's sense of humor is apparent. In each instance, did Quammen's humor make the passage more interesting for you? Explain.

6. Reread Quammen's essay and write out your own responses to his essay. Then read Paula Fisher's essay on Quammen later in this chapter. Discuss your responses to both articles with your classmates. Then write your own summary and response to the conversation created by your classmates about these authors.

7. On the Internet, visit one of the animal rights sites, such as Animal Concerns at http://animalconcerns.netforchange.com, People for the Ethical Treatment of Animals (PETA) at http://www.peta-online.org, or Animal Rights at http://animalrights.about.com. What are the latest topics of conversation? Are the issues that Singer and Quammen raise still being debated? PETA, for example, poses FAQs such as "Animals don't reason, don't understand rights, and don't always respect our rights, so why should we apply our ideas of morality to them?" What is PETA's answer to this question? How would Quammen answer this question?

Reading and Writing Processes

■ ASSIGNMENT FOR READING/WRITING   Write an essay that summarizes and then responds to one or more essays, articles, or advertisements. As you review your particular assignment, make sure you understand what text or texts you should respond to, how long your summary and response should be, and what type(s) of responses you should focus on.

Your purpose for this assignment is to represent the text(s) accurately and faithfully in your summary and to explain and support your response. Taken together, your summary and response should be a coherent essay, with a main idea and connections between summary and response. Assume that your audience is other members of the class, including the instructor, with whom you are sharing your reading.

Your instructor's assignment should indicate your audience and appropriate genres. You need to know your intended audience in order to decide and what kinds of evidence will make your analysis and response convincing and how detailed your summary should be. If your audience is not familiar with your text, for example, you'll need a more detailed summary. Typically, responses take the form of an essay, but a letter to the editor may be appropriate (see Adam Forest's "Beauty and Violence," which was originally published as an editorial in a daily newspaper).

CHOOSING A SUBJECT

Suggested processes, activities, and strategies for reading and writing will be illustrated in response to the following essay by Dudley Erskine Devlin.

Teaching Tolerance in America

Dudley Erskine Devlin

Dudley Erskine Devlin was born in Syracuse, New York, and attended the University of Kansas. Originally trained as a scientist, he currently teaches English at Colorado State University and writes columns and editorials on contemporary problems. The targets for his editorials are often the large and complicated issues of the day, such as education, violence, health care, and the media. "My first goal as a writer," Devlin said in a recent interview, "is to provoke response. If just one reader is angry enough to write me a letter of response, then my time is not wasted." As you read Devlin's essay, note places where you agree or disagree with his ideas. How would you respond to Devlin's argument?

In the past few years, American high schools have struggled with a variety of forces that have threatened to tear them apart: reduced funding, increased class sizes, fewer music and art classes, violence in schools, and racial and class divisions among students. Although educational reform in America tends to focus on curriculum issues, class sizes, and security issues, one lesson seems increasingly hard to teach— helping students appreciate and welcome differences in culture, racial heritage, and personal identity. Despite the emphasis on increasing respect and tolerance in schools, teenagers still bring the social and racial divisions found in society at large back into the halls of high schools across America. Social cliques based on race, gender, athletic prowess, income, social class, dress, and even body piercings still define the culture at most schools. 1

America, we fervently believe, is still the land of opportunity, the land where we can be judged on our merits and achievements, not on stereotypes or preconceptions or prejudices. Yet the social clique is based on the notion that one group imagines it is superior to another and thus can ridicule, taunt, or even bully another group. And nowhere does the social clique have more devastating and long-lasting effects than in our high schools. 2

High school cliques, which reproduce the class divisions found in society, originate from three distinct sources: racial differences, gender differences, and social differences. Racial problems in high schools need no explanation. Every high school in America has racial problems that have led to continuing conflicts. A reporter visiting one typical suburban high school found that each ethnic group—Hispanics, whites, blacks, Asians—had a place where they gathered between classes and 3 after school. Although individual members in an ethnic group gain security from being in the group, they make outsiders—people who do not belong to their racial group—feel insecure and often threatened. As one student put it, "The problem is that some people think they are better than others. So they make disparaging remarks about one another, creating tension and conflict in the school."

The ongoing gender problems in America's high schools are mentioned—if at all—on the back pages of newspapers, as if the sexist treatment of girls is a normal and inconsequential behavior. Nan Stein, author of *Classrooms and Courtrooms: Facing Sexual Harassment in K–12 Schools*, recounts numerous incidents where school administrations overlook student-on-student sexual harassment. In a recent interview with *Harvard Educational Letter*, Stein recalled a case in which "15 boys harassed this one girl verbally, mooing like cows whenever they saw her and talking about the size of her breasts. They did this outside of school, in school, on the way to school. Other kids heard it and saw it. Teachers and custodians told the administrator, who kept saying, 'It's not a big deal.'" When the case involves males of status, the chances are even more likely that school administrators will look the other way. Ignoring the flagrant behavior of the popular students happens at every school in America—despite a recent Supreme Court ruling that now holds schools liable in such cases of sexual harassment. 4

Finally, the differences in social classes among the various cliques—most notably between the jocks and the geeks, between the powerful and the weak—is a continuing source of conflict. As one student put it, "If you're not a jock in this school . . . you're not part of it." The outsiders, geeks, and gays are ridiculed by everyone and harassed, bullied, and picked on by the jocks and by other members of the elite social class. Bullying is sometimes connected to cliques and gangs, and it affects both boys and girls. Allan Beane, author of *The Bully Free Classroom*, writes that he has "heard from so many adults who are still very angry and hurt from when they were mistreated in school." Frequently school bullies are boys—and the ridicule and intimidation they inflict has played a role, Beane says, in "almost all of the school shootings that have outraged the nation in the past two years." Hara Marano, an editor for *Psychology Today*, points out that girls, too, engage in physical aggression even though they are "more apt to be masters of indirect bullying, spreading lies and rumors and destroying reputations." The result is that about one in seven schoolchildren is either a bully or a victim of bullying. 5

How do we solve these problems? First we need to eliminate those spineless liberal solutions that simply aren't working—thus releasing funds for more effective deterrents. Many schools, for example, have in- 6 troduced diversity issues into English and social studies classes, and some schools even have sensitivity training classes that seek to "instill respect for others and training students how to speak up when they hear insulting or intimidating comments." However, most students react negatively to such classes. In a recent report, one student said that he really didn't like having notions of tolerance and acceptance drilled into him: "It's like shoving something down our throats." Besides, we want students to be able to express their feelings—if more students were like John Rocker of the Atlanta Braves, then we would have more of these problems out in the open.

There are, however, some real and sensible solutions that could   7
solve the intolerance problem in our high schools. For years, parents and educators have recommended that schools adopt uniforms, so that every student wears the same clothing to school. Already, many schools ban specific colors or types of hats, shirts, or jewelry. We need uniforms not just to eliminate gangs, but to reduce the visual cues that enable one group to maintain social power. And we need to enforce those dress rules with a zero tolerance policy. Second, schools need to make single-sex classes a standard practice. Not only do boys and girls learn better in single-sex environments, but the segregated classes will reduce the differences and thus reduce conflicts. Finally, schools need to improve security—both to protect students from the outside and to protect students from each other. Schools need more video cameras, drug sniffing dogs, and spot checks of cars and lockers. Governor Jesse Ventura had an excellent idea when he suggested that every school needs to have teachers with paramilitary and anti-riot training. Last but not least, students need to wear picture ID tags hung on ribbons around their necks—so videotapes can easily identify any troublemakers.

The class system that is created and perpetuated by student cliques   8
is the most important problem in our high schools today. In any high school on any day, we see the strong picking on the weak, the bullies intimidating the outcasts, and the jocks and the social elite dominating everyone else. Only when we apply our zero tolerance policy to the dress code, the gender makeup of our classes, and the security of our schools will students learn how to treat all people and social classes with acceptance and tolerance.

COLLECTING

Once a text or texts have been selected or assigned for your summary and response, try the following reading/writing/discussing activities.

■ PREREADING JOURNAL ENTRY   In your journal, write what you already know about the subject of the essay. The following questions will help you to recall your prior experiences and think about your own opinions before you read the essay. The purpose of this entry is to think about your own experiences and opinions *before* you are influenced by the arguments of the essay.

- What classes or programs at your high school were designed to improve tolerance of social differences among students? Did they increase or decrease tolerance for social, sexual, or racial difference among students at your school?

- Were cliques a big problem at your school? Did your high school have bullies who picked on other students? Were the jocks or the upper-class students given preferential treatment?

- What measures to increase security, reduce potential violence, and increase tolerance had your high school taken in the last few years? Were these changes necessary? Did they improve the quality of your education? Did they make you feel more secure at school?

TEXT ANNOTATION   Most experts on reading and writing agree that you will learn more and remember more if you actually write out your comments, questions, and reactions in the margins of the text you are reading. Writing your responses helps you begin a conversation with the text. Reproduced below are one reader's marginal responses to paragraph 7 of Devlin's essay.

Second, schools need to make single-sex classes a standard practice.

Why not have them optional for some subjects?

Not only do boys and girls learn better in single-sex environments, but the segregated classes will reduce the differences and thus reduce conflicts.

In the real world men and women work together, so why not start now?

Finally, schools need to improve security—both to protect students from the outside and to protect students from each other. Schools need more video cameras, drug sniffing dogs, and spot checks of cars and lockers. Governor Jesse Ventura had an excellent idea when he suggested that every school needs to have teachers with paramilitary and anti-riot training. Last but not least, students need to wear picture ID tags hung on ribbons around their necks—so videotapes can easily identify any troublemakers.

A few cameras will provide security, but spot checks invade our privacy.

Students should not be treated like jail inmates!

What? Schools are not wrestling arenas and we don't have riots.

READING LOG A reading log, like text annotation, encourages you to interact with the author/text and write your comments and questions as you read. While text annotation helps you identify specific places in the text for commentary, a reading log encourages you to write out longer, more thoughtful responses. In a reading log, you can keep a record of your thoughts *while you read* and *reread* the text. Often, reading-log entries help you focus on a key idea to develop later in your response.

Below is one reader's response to Devlin's ideas about single-sex classes and bullying.

> I attended a private elementary school and junior high where a school uniform was required and some of the classes were single-sex. Personally, I can say that the uniform did not make a bit of difference where bullying was an issue. Kids still made fun of other kids no matter what they were wearing. The real reason that kids make fun of others is because of social differences and because they themselves do not want to be picked on, so they deflect the attention onto others.
>
> It is true that bullying is carried on with people throughout life, which is why there should be no tolerance at all for teasing. For example, I was talking with a very good friend of mine who told me that he is still haunted by memories of when children would call him a "fag" on the playground. This has affected him for a long time, and he is still fearful of admitting his homosexuality because he feels as if he is letting the bullies win and proving that they were right.

SHAPING

Summaries and responses have several possible shapes, depending on the writer's purpose and intended audience. Keep in mind, however, that in a summary/response essay or critique, *the summary and the response should be unified by the writer's overall response.* The summary and the response may be organized or drafted separately, but they are still parts of one essay, focused on the writer's most important or overall response.

SUMMARY SHAPING

Summaries should convey the main ideas, the essential argument, or the key features of a text. The purpose should be to represent the author's/text's ideas as accurately and as faithfully as possible. Summaries rely on description, paraphrase, and direct quotation. Below are definitions and examples for each of these terms.

DESCRIPTION The summary should *describe* the main features of an essay, including the author and title, the context or place of publication of the essay (if appropriate), the essay's thesis or main argument, and any key text features, such as sections, chapters, or important graphic material.

> In the article "Teaching Tolerance in America," Dudley Erskine Devlin reports some disturbing issues concerning America's high schools. Devlin states that intimidation, through dress, social cliques, gender, and race, is causing tension and danger in high schools today. According to Devlin, sexual harassment is allowed and condoned, and that in some cases jocks bully geeks and racial and social groups intimidate one another. As a solution, Devlin suggests that schools enforce strict, zero-tolerance dress codes, segregate the sexes in classes, increase security through surveillance cameras and drug-sniffing dogs, and require students to wear photo IDs.

PARAPHRASE A paraphrase restates a passage or text in different words. The purpose of a paraphrase is to recast the author's/text's words in your own language. A good paraphrase retains the original meaning without plagiarizing from the original text.

> **Original:** High school cliques, which reproduce the class divisions found in society, originate from three distinct sources: racial differences, gender differences, and social differences.

> **Paraphrase:** High school cliques mirror society's own class divisions and stem from racial, gender, and social differences.

DIRECT QUOTATION Often, summaries directly quote a few key phrases or sentences from the source. *Remember: Any words or phrases within the quotation marks must be accurate, word-for-word transcriptions of the original.* Guidelines for direct quotation and examples are as follows. Use direct quotations sparingly to convey the key points in the essay:

> Devlin focuses on what he believes is the school system's largest problem today, the issue of "helping students appreciate and welcome differences in culture, racial heritage, and personal identity."

Use direct quotations when the author's phrasing is more memorable, more concise, or more accurate than your paraphrase might be:

> Devlin claims that teenagers "still bring the social and racial divisions found in society at large back into the halls of high schools across America."

Use direct quotations for key words or phrases that indicate the author's attitude, tone, or stance:

According to Devlin, we should "eliminate those spineless liberal solutions that simply aren't working" in order to fund his solutions.

Don't quote long sentences. Condense the original sentence to the most important phrases. Use just a short phrase from a sentence or use an ellipsis (three spaced periods . . .) to indicate words that you have omitted.

Original: Although educational reform in America tends to focus on curriculum issues, class sizes, and security issues, one lesson seems increasingly hard to teach—helping students appreciate and welcome differences in culture, racial heritage, and personal identity.

Condensed Quotation: Educational reform, according to Devlin, should focus less on curriculum issues and class sizes and more on helping students "appreciate . . . differences in culture, racial heritage, and personal identity."

SAMPLE SUMMARIES Following are summaries of Devlin's essay written by two different readers. Notice that while both convey the main ideas of the essay by using description, paraphrase, and direct quotation, they are not identical. Check each summary to see how well it meets these guidelines:

- Cite the author and title of the text.
- Indicate the main ideas of the text.
- Use direct quotation of key words, phrases, or sentences.
- Include author tags.
- Do not summarize most examples or data.
- Be as accurate, fair, and objective as possible.

SUMMARY NO. 1

Dudley Erskine Devlin's essay "Teaching Tolerance in America" addresses several hot topics concerning the American public school system. Devlin focuses on what he believes is the school system's largest problem today, the issue of "helping students appreciate and welcome differences in culture, racial heritage, and personal identity." According to Devlin, the root of the problem lies within the social clique, particularly the social cliques found inside the halls of your local high school. According to Devlin, these cliques originate from three different sources: social, racial, and gender differences. Devlin suggests that we solve the problems these cliques create by eliminating "those spineless liberal solutions that simply aren't working—thus releasing funds for more effective deterrents." Devlin's solutions to eradicate the intolerance are to impose dress codes or uniforms, to create single-sex classrooms, and to markedly increase security at every high school.

SUMMARY NO. 2

The idea of social reform in education has been a pressing issue given the increase in youth violence in high schools across America. In Dudley Erskine Devlin's article "Teaching Tolerance in America," he outlines some of the problems in schools caused by members of cliques and bullies who feed on the "racial differences, gender differences, and social differences" found in society at large. Devlin's argument then moves on to attack the "spineless liberal solutions" (such as introducing diversity issues in classes) and proposes to replace them with "more effective deterrents" such as instituting single-sex classes, school uniforms, picture IDs, and heightened security measures. This zero-tolerance policy, Devlin believes, will teach students how to accept diversity and "appreciate and welcome differences in culture, racial heritage, and personal identity."

RESPONSE SHAPING

Strategies for organizing a response depend on the purpose of the response. Typically, responses include one or more of the following three purposes:

- Analyzing the effectiveness of the text.
- Agreeing and/or disagreeing with the ideas in the text.
- Interpreting and reflecting on the text.

As the following explanations illustrate, each of these types of responses requires supporting evidence from the text, from other texts, and/or from the writer's own experience.

ANALYZING Analysis requires dividing a whole into its parts in order to better understand the whole. In order to analyze a text for its effectiveness, start by examining key parts or features of the text, such as the purpose, the intended audience, the thesis and main ideas, the organization and evidence, and the language and style. Notice how the following paragraph analyzes Devlin's illogical argument.

> Devlin's essay has some clear problems with the logic of his argument. The title of his essay is "Teaching Tolerance in America," but his solutions contradict his stated purpose. Devlin's proposal to tighten security in our high schools is not going to teach tolerance in high schools across America. As a teenager in a post-Columbine era, I can tell you that ID card checks, patrolling security officers, and hall monitors do not create an atmosphere conducive to teaching tolerance. Students who are treated like prisoners in a maximum security ward do not feel increased warm wishes to faculty and administrators nor are they more likely to tolerate differences in their classmates. Being watched like a hawk by a hall monitor does nothing to make a person more socially outgoing or more tolerant of difference. These security measures will increase fear during the school hours and not encourage tolerance once students leave the school grounds. In short, Devlin's solutions do not, in fact, solve the problems with tolerance created by racial, gender, or social differences.

AGREEING/DISAGREEING   Often, a response to a text focuses on agreeing and/or disagreeing with its major ideas. Responses may agree completely, disagree completely, or agree with some points but disagree with others. Responses that agree with some ideas but disagree with others are often more effective because they show that the responder sees both strengths and weaknesses in an argument. In the following paragraphs, notice how the responder agrees and disagrees and then supports each judgment with evidence.

> About Devlin's recommendation that schools can "reduce conflicts" and teach tolerance by creating single-sex classrooms, I have mixed feelings. From my own personal experience, I agree that single-sex classes can have benefits. Perhaps I am biased, but attending an all-girls high school was very beneficial for me and many of my classmates. Although I have always been a very outgoing individual, I watched many of my friends grow from timid, shy freshmen to independent, strong women. Furthermore, I was never sexually harassed by a classmate, nor did I hear of any of the kinds of harassment Devlin mentions. On the other hand, however, I must disagree with Devlin that single-sex classes are a long-term solution. In the real world, women and men constantly interact, so they need to learn how to positively interact as girls and boys in school. Students need

to be comfortable and learn to work with the opposite sex in preparation for college and the workplace. Although my high school gave me academic confidence, it did not really prepare me for the diverse world I met once I went to college. Single-sex classrooms may just postpone learning about tolerance and difference rather than actually teaching it.

INTERPRETING AND REFLECTING Many responses contain interpretations of passages that might be read from different points of view or reflections on the assumptions or implications of an idea. An interpretation says, "Here is what the text says, but let me explain what it means, what assumptions the argument carries, or what the implications might be." Here is a paragraph from an interpretive response to Devlin's essay.

If we stop a moment and reflect on the purpose of schools, we realize that schools should be a place where learning and growth can take place. All of Devlin's solutions, however, are designed to increase security and control rather than actually teach tolerance. Perhaps Devlin has modeled his "final solution" on prisons, where students as inmates would have no rights, no privacy, no room to express either tolerance or hatred. Rather than place students in a maximum security prison, we should return to the more liberal approach of teaching tolerance and understanding—the very solution that Devlin initially rejects. While the simple method of teaching about cultural, social, and ethnic differences does not guarantee a conflict-free school environment, it does ensure that students have the opportunity to embrace rather than just accept differences. The forced tolerance that Devlin recommends through dress codes and maximum security measures ultimately discourages students from using their schools to actively examine and freely embrace the differences among their peers.

OUTLINES FOR SUMMARY/RESPONSE ESSAYS

Three common outlines for summary/response essays are as follows. Select or modify one of these outlines to fit your audience, purpose, and kind of response. Typically, a summary/response will take the following form:

I. Introduction to text(s)

II. Summary of text(s)

III. Response(s)

    A. Point 1

B. Point 2

C. Point 3, etc.

IV. Conclusion

A second kind of outline, illustrated by Quammen's essay in the chapter, focuses initially on key ideas or issues and then examines the text or texts for their contribution to these key ideas. This outline begins with the issues, then summarizes the text(s), and then moves to the reader's responses:

I. Introduction to key issues

II. Summary of relevant text(s)

III. Response(s)

    A. Point 1

    B. Point 2

    C. Point 3, etc.

IV. Conclusion

A third outline integrates the summary and the response. It begins by introducing the issue and/or the text, gives a brief overall idea of the text, but then summarizes and responds point-by-point.

I. Introduction to issues and/or text(s)

II. Summary of text's Point 1/response to Point 1

III. Summary of text's Point 2/response to Point 2

IV. Summary of text's Point 3/response to Point 3, etc.

V. Conclusion

DRAFTING

If you have been reading actively, you have been writing throughout the reading/writing/discussing process. At some point, however, you will gather your best ideas, have a rough direction or outline in mind, and begin writing a draft. Some writers like to have their examples and evidence ready when they begin drafting. Many writers have outlines in their heads or on paper. Perhaps you like to put your rough outline on the computer and then just expand each section as you write. Finally, most writers like to skim the text and *reread their notes* immediately before they start their drafts, just to make sure everything is fresh in their minds.

Once you start drafting, keep interruptions to a minimum. Because focus and concentration are important to good writing, try to keep writing as long as possible. If you come to a spot where you need an example that you don't have at your fingertips, just put in parentheses—(put the example about cosmetics and animal abuse here)—and keep on writing. Concentrate on making all your separate responses add up to a focused, overall response.

REVISING

Revision means, literally, *reseeing*. Revising requires rereading the text and rewriting your summary and response. While revision begins as you read and reread the text, it continues until—and sometimes after—you turn in a paper or send it to its intended audience.

A major step in your revision is receiving responses from peer readers and deciding on a revision plan, based on the feedback. Use the following guidelines as you read your peers' papers and respond to their advice.

Guidelines for Revision

- **Review the purpose and audience for your assignment**. Is your draft addressed to the appropriate audience? Does it fulfill its intended purpose?
- **Continue to use your active reading/writing/discussing activities as you revise your draft**. If you are uncertain about parts of your summary or response, reread the text, check your notes, or discuss your draft with a classmate.
- **Reread your summary for key features**. Make sure your summary indicates author and title, cites main ideas, uses an occasional direct quotation, and includes author tags. Check your summary for accuracy and objectivity.
- **Check paraphrases and direct quotations**. If you are paraphrasing (without quotation marks), you should put the author's ideas into your own language. If you are quoting directly, make sure the words within the quotation marks are accurate, word-for-word transcriptions.
- **Review the purpose of your response**. Are you analyzing, agreeing/disagreeing, interpreting, or some combination of all three? Do your types of responses fit the assignment or address your intended audience and satisfy your purpose?
- **Amplify your supporting evidence**. Summary/response drafts often need additional, relevant evidence. Be sure you use sufficient personal experience, evidence from the text, or examples from other texts to support your response.
- **Focus on a clear, overall response**. Your responses should all add up to a focused, overall reaction. Delete or revise any passages that do not maintain your focus.
- **Revise sentences to improve clarity, conciseness, emphasis, and variety**. (See Handbook.)

- **Edit your final version**. Use the spell check on your computer. Have a friend help proofread. Check the Handbook for suspected problems in usage, grammar, and punctuation.

PEER RESPONSE

The instructions below will help you give and receive constructive advice about the rough draft of your summary/response essay. You may use these guidelines for an in-class workshop, a take-home review, or a computer e-mail response.

Writer: Before you exchange drafts with another reader, write out the following information about your own rough draft:

1. On your draft, *label* the parts that are summary and the parts that are your own response.
2. *Underline* the sentence(s) that signal to the reader that you are shifting from objective summary to personal response.
3. Explain *one or two problems* that you are having with this draft that you want your reader to comment on.

Reader: Without making any comments, read the *entire* draft from start to finish. As you *reread* the draft, answer the following questions.

1. Review the guidelines for writing summaries. Has the writer remained *objective* in his or her summary? Does the summary *omit* any key ideas? Does the writer use *author tags* frequently and accurately? Can you clearly understand the main ideas of the article? Is the summary written in language appropriate for the intended audience?
2. Review the guidelines for writing responses. What type(s) of response is the writer using? In the margin, label the types. What kinds of evidence does the writer use in support of his or her response? In the margin, label the kinds of supporting evidence. Is this response addressed appropriately to the audience?
3. In your own words, state the main idea or the focus that organizes the writer's response.
4. Write out your own reactions to the writer's response. Where do you disagree with the writer's analysis or interpretation? Explain.
5. Answer the writer's questions in Number 3, above.

■ POSTSCRIPT ON THE WRITING PROCESS

1. As you finish your essay, what questions do you still have about how to summarize? What questions do you have about writing a good response?
2. Which paragraphs in your response contain your most effective supporting evidence? What kinds of evidence (analysis of the text, evidence from other texts, or personal experience) did you use?
3. What sentences in your response contain your overall reaction to the text?
4. If you had one more day to work on your essay, what would you change? Why?
5. What did you learn about active, critical reading that you applied to the writing of this essay? Where in your essay did you help your reader to make accurate predictions? Where did you use supporting evidence that might trigger your reader's prior knowledge?

STUDENT WRITING

DRAWING THE LINE
Paula Fisher

Paula Fisher, from Salt Lake City, Utah, wrote her essay while she was an occupational therapy major at Colorado State University. She chose to write a summary/response to David Quammen's essay "Animal Rights and Beyond" because she could draw on her own personal experiences, both in an animal rights course and in cattle ranching. While reading the essay and making notes for her double-entry log, which follows, Fisher says that she "specifically noticed that Quammen failed to present the anti-animal-rights issue, a perspective I am familiar with, since all of my mother's side of the family are involved with cattle farming." As you read her essay, see if she clearly summarizes Quammen's essay and then supports her response with examples from her experience.

Fisher's writing process was to read the essay carefully and make notes on her copy of the essay. Then, working on her computer, she used the "Rereading Guide" at the beginning of the chapter to make a double-entry log. Once she completed the double-entry log, she completely drafted her essay. Reprinted below are her double-entry log and her final version.

Double-Entry Log: Notes from Rereading Guide

DESCRIPTION	RESPONSES
I. Audience	
• Begins with questions for the reader. Audience is readers of *Outside* magazine, so they're probably pro-animal rights.	• Questions make beginning interesting.
II. Thesis and Main Ideas	
• Thesis: Animal rights are a complex issue with no easy answers.	• Difficult to pick out thesis—for me.
• Talks about history of animal rights. Talks about Singer's and Regan's views.	• Where is the boundary between those who suffer and those who don't—oysters? Quammen's references to issues in animal rights are vague or missing.
• Singer: Greatest good for greatest number.	
• Can animals suffer? Where is the boundary?	
• Regan—Abuse wrong in essence. Argues for "inherent value" "mentally normal animals of 1 year or more."	• My own experience—LD-50, humane society, cosmetics, animal testing, grad students, medical testing, farming
• Quammen's responses, positive and negative: Positive—they're fighting the good fight. Negative—they're too smug.	• What about the mentally retarded?
• They think everyone should be vegetarians.	• I had to read several times to grasp the references to "carrots," etc.
• They are still chauvanistic—"How similar to human is similar enough?" Where do we draw the line?	• I agree that issues are complex, but he ignores legitimate uses of farm animals and medical testing.
• Doesn't everything have value?	
• Quammen says man should not be the measure, since "Life is life."	• No rebuttal at end?
III. Organization and Evidence	
• No preview of ideas	• What about anti-animal rights—he has no fair mention.
• New sections signaled by extra space	

IV. Language and Style
* Tone is humorous, casual.
* Tad sarcastic, but well explained.

V.   Purpose
* Purpose to explain Singer's and Regan's ideas and give his responses. He wants to make us see animal rights as a complex issue.

* Gordian reference—didn't know Righteous gumbo— good metaphor

* Succeeded in purpose.

Final Version
D R A W I N G   T H E   L I N E

In David Quammen's essay "Animal Rights and Beyond," he dis-   *1*
cusses the issue of animal rights, taking the stance that it is a "serious philosophical issue" with no quick answers and with serious implications for the way humans should live. Quammen, a nature column writer for *Outside*, briefly presents the historical anti-animal-rights view but quickly dismisses it. He goes on to discuss the writings of Peter Singer, an important animal rights advocate. Singer is willing to grant rights to animals that suffer, concluding that anything below an oyster doesn't. Quammen next discusses Tom Regan's philosophy. Regan asserts that animals have rights because they have inherent value, but he is willing to grant this value only to mentally normal mammals. Quammen first commends these authors for their willingness to take a stance on this issue, but he also reprimands them for their lack of vision. According to Quammen, "man is still the measure" for these two authors. They simply changed the question from "Is the creature human?" to "How similar to human is enough?"

I think that Quammen makes an excellent point in his essay: An-   *2*
imal rights is not an issue that has black-and-white answers. Gray areas exist everywhere. Quammen asserts that animal rights are an "important and tricky" issue that needs to be thought out carefully. His purpose seems to be to make his readers think. This particular essay was published in an environmental magazine that probably has many readers who advocate animal rights. Quammen seems to be challenging them to consider why they believe in animal rights. Is it because of complicated philosophical arguments or simply because "life is life"? Either way, he asserts, and I agree, that it is a difficult issue.

When Quammen comments on Singer's and Regan's theories, he   *3*
compliments them for "fighting a good fight." He asserts that they are

focusing attention on "outrageous practices" that are commonplace throughout America. Not only are they writing about it, but they are also exclaiming, "Let's stop it!" I see this as an important distinction. Tests that blatantly mistreat animals, such as the LD-50 test, where a large number of animals are given a substance until 50 percent of them die, is cruel and wasteful. It often serves no other purpose than to be another figure in a scientist's logbook. Purposeless experiments by graduate students and brutal practices by some American farmers and cosmetic companies also need to be examined and controlled.

On the other hand, issues from the anti-animal-rights point of view also need to be carefully considered and weighed. This is an issue that Quammen fails to address fairly and realistically. One of the major issues involves the use of animals in medical research. Where does one draw the line between animal suffering and human suffering? The use of animals in medical research can and has helped scientists make breakthroughs that have saved human lives. I would have a hard time looking someone in the eye and saying, "You can't have a cure for cancer because some rats would have to die." It is not an issue that I can easily resolve for myself, and I contend it needs careful analysis and review. *4*

Another dilemma emerges when considering the rights of farmers versus the rights of farm animals. I come from a long line of cattle farmers, people whose livelihood revolves around raising animals. It's true, some practices are cruel and unnecessary and need to be regulated, but once again, we need to consider where the farmers' rights end and the animals' rights begin. *5*

All things considered, I believe that Quammen makes a good claim. The issue of animal rights is truly a complex and complicated issue with no easy answers; if we carry animal rights too far, we won't be able to walk for fear of stepping on an ant, but if we don't consider animal rights, we are blind and allowing cruel and inhumane practices to continue. *6*

QUESTIONS FOR WRITING AND DISCUSSION

1. Reread David Quammen's article and make your own double-entry log. On the left-hand side of a piece of paper, record Quammen's main points; on the right-hand side, write your own questions and reactions. Compare your notes to Fisher's summary/response. How would you advise Fisher to revise her summary to make it more complete and accurate? What suggestions would you make about revising her response?

2. Supporting evidence in a summary/response may take the form of analysis of passages from the text, references to ideas or facts from

outside texts, or specific examples from personal experience. Find examples of all three kinds of evidence in Fisher's essay. Which did she use most effectively?

3. Compare Fisher's notes in her double-entry log with her final essay. Which of those notes appear in her final version? Which do not? What ideas from her double-entry log would you suggest including or omitting in her final version? Explain your choices.

4. Using Quammen's article, Fisher's response, your class discussion, and your own ideas and experiences, write your own essay on the uses of animals in medical research. Should animals be used to develop cosmetics? To study neurotic behavior? To find a cure for cancer? Where would you draw the line—and why?

STUDENT WRITING

Two Responses to Deborah Tannen

Jennifer Koester and Sonja H. Browe

The two essays reprinted here were written in response to an essay by Deborah Tannen, "How Male and Female Students Use Language Differently," which appears in Chapter 7. Jennifer Koester and Sonja H. Browe have opposite responses to Tannen's essay. Jennifer Koester, a political science major at Colorado State University, argues that Tannen's essay is effective because she uses sufficient evidence and organizes her essay clearly. On the other hand, Sonja Browe, an English education major at the University of Wyoming, writes an essay that is critical of Deborah Tannen's focus and supporting evidence. Be sure to read Tannen's essay and decide for yourself before you read the following essays.

A Response to Deborah Tannen's Essay

Jennifer Koester

Deborah Tannen's "How Male and Female Students Use Language Differently" addresses how male and female conversational styles influence classroom discussions. Tannen asserts that women speak less than men in class because often the structure of discussion is more "congenial" to men's style of conversing.

1

Tannen looks at three differences between the sexes that shape *2* classroom interaction: classroom setting, debate format, and contrasting attitudes toward classroom discussion. First, Tannen says that during childhood, men "are expected to seize center stage: by exhibiting their skill, displaying their knowledge, and challenging and resisting challenge." Thus, as adults, men are more comfortable than women when speaking in front of a large group of strangers. On the other hand, women are more comfortable in small groups.

Second, men are more comfortable with the debate format. Tan- *3* nen asserts that many classrooms use the format of putting forth ideas followed by "argument and challenge." This too coincides with men's conversational experiences. However, Tannen asserts that women tend to "resist discussion they perceive as hostile."

Third, men feel it is their duty to think of things to say and to *4* voice them. On the other hand, women often regulate their participation and hold back to avoid dominating discussion.

Tannen concludes that educators can no longer use just one format *5* to facilitate classroom discussion. Tannen sees small groups as necessary for any "non-seminar" class along with discussion of differing styles of participation as solutions to the participation gap between the sexes.

Three things work together to make Deborah Tannen's essay *6* "How Male and Female Students Use Language Differently" effective: the qualifications of her argument, the evidence used, and the parallel format of comparison/contrast.

First, Tannen's efforts to qualify her argument prevent her from *7* committing logical errors. In the first paragraphs of her essay, she states, "This is not to say that all men talk in class, nor that no women do. It is simply that a greater percentage of discussion time is taken by men's voices." By acknowledging exceptions to her claim, Tannen avoids the mistake of oversimplification. She also strengthens her argument because this qualification tells the reader that she is aware of the complexity of this issue.

Later, Tannen uses another qualification. She says, "No one's con- *8* versational style is absolute; everyone's style changes in response to the context and others' styles." Not only does this qualification avoid a logical fallacy, but it also strengthens Tannen's argument that classroom discussion must have several formats. By acknowledging that patterns of participation can change with the setting, Tannen avoids oversimplifying the issue and adds to her argument for classroom variety.

Second, Tannen's evidence places a convincing argument before her *9* reader. In the beginning of her essay, Tannen states that a greater percentage of discussion time in class is taken by men and that those women who attend single-sex schools tend to do better later in life. These two pieces of evidence present the reader with Tannen's jumping-off point. These statistics are what Tannen wants to change.

In addition, Tannen effectively uses anecdotal evidence. She presents the reader with stories from her colleagues and her own research. These stories are taken from the classroom, a place which her audience, as educators, are familiar with. Her anecdotal evidence is persuasive because it appeals to the common sense and personal experiences of the audience. While some might question the lack of hard statistics throughout the essay, the anecdotal evidence serves Tannen best because it reminds her audience of educators of their own experiences. When she reminds the audience of their experiences, she is able to make them see her logic.   *10*

Third, the parallel format of comparison/contrast between the genders highlights for the reader Tannen's main points. Each time Tannen mentions the reactions of one gender, she follows with the reaction of the other gender. For example, Tannen states, "So one reason men speak in class more than women is that many of them find the 'public' classroom setting more conducive to speaking, whereas most women are more comfortable speaking in private to a small group of people they know well." Here, Tannen places the tendencies of men and of women together, thus preventing the reader from having to constantly refer back to another section of the essay.   *11*

In an earlier example, Tannen discusses men's comfort with the debate format in class discussion. The majority of that paragraph relates why men feel comfortable with that format. After explaining this idea, Tannen then tells the reader how women feel about the debate structure. Because how men and women feel about the debate format is placed within a paragraph, the readers easily see the difference between the genders. Tannen's use of the parallel format in the above examples and the rest of the essay provides a clear explanation of the differences in men's and women's interactions in the classroom.   *12*

Tannen writes her essay effectively. She makes the essay convincing by qualifying her claims about gender participation. This strengthens her argument that just as the classroom is diverse, so should the format be diverse. Her supporting evidence is convincing because it comes from Tannen's own experience, reminds the audience of its own experiences, and appeals to the audience's common sense. Finally, her parallel format for discussing the differences between men and women enhances the reader's understanding. Overall, Tannen's essay is effective because she qualifies her argument, uses convincing evidence, and makes clear how men and women use language differently through a parallel comparison/contrast format.   *13*

Is Deborah Tannen Convincing?

Sonja H. Browe

In her article entitled "How Male and Female Students Use Language Differently," Deborah Tannen explores the issue of gender as it affects the way we use language to communicate. Specifically, she discusses how differences in the way males and females are socialized to use language affect their classroom interactions. She explains that as females are growing up, they learn to use language to talk to friends, and to tell secrets. She states that for females, it is the "telling of secrets, the fact and the way they talk to each other, that makes them best friends." Boys, on the other hand, are "expected to use language to seize center stage: by exhibiting their skill, displaying their knowledge, and challenging and resisting challenge." [1]

According to Tannen, these differences make classroom language use more conducive to the way males were taught to use language. Tannen suggests that speaking in front of groups and the debatelike formats used in many classrooms are more easily handled by male students. [2]

Finally, Tannen describes an experiment she conducted in her own classroom which allowed students to evaluate their own conversation transcripts. From this experience, she deduced that small-group interaction is essential in the classroom because it gives students who don't participate in whole-class settings the opportunity for conversation and interaction. [3]

Though Tannen's research is a worthwhile consideration and provides information which could be of great interest to educators, this particular article lacks credibility and is unfocused. The points she is trying to make get lost in a world of unsupported assertions, and she strays from her main focus, leaving the reader hanging and confused. [4]

Tannen does take some time at the beginning of her article to establish her authority on linguistic analysis, but we may still hold her accountable for supporting her assertions with evidence. However, Tannen makes sweeping declarations throughout the essay, expecting the reader to simply accept them as fact. For example, when discussing the practice of the teacher playing devil's advocate and debating with the students, she states that "many, if not most women would shrink from such a challenge, experiencing it as public humiliation." Following such an assertion, we expect to see some evidence. Whom did Tannen talk to? What did they say? What percentage of women felt this way? This sort of evidence is completely lacking, so that what Tannen states as fact appears more like conjecture. [5]

Tannen makes another such unsupported pronouncement when   *6*
she discusses the debatelike formats used in many classrooms. She explains that this type of classroom interaction is in opposition to the
way that females, in contrast to males, approach learning. She states that
"it is not that females don't fight, but that they don't fight for fun. They
don't ritualize opposition." Again, where is Tannen's evidence to support such a claim?

When Tannen does bother to support her assertions, her evidence   *7*
is trite and unconvincing. For example, she reviews Walter Ong's work
on the pursuit of knowledge, in which he suggested that "ritual opposition . . . is fundamental to the way males approach almost any activity." Tannen supports this claim of Ong's in parentheses, saying,
"Consider, for example, the little boy who shows he likes a little girl by
pulling her braids and shoving her." This statement may serve as an example but is not enough to convince the reader that ritual opposition
is fundamental to the way males approach "almost any activity."

Other evidence which Tannen uses to support her declarations   *8*
comes in the form of conversations she has had with colleagues on
these issues. Again, though these may provide examples, they do not
represent a broad enough database to support her claims.

Finally, Tannen takes three pages of her article to describe in de-   *9*
tail an experiment she conducted in her classroom. Though the information she collected from this experiment was interesting, it strayed
from the main point of the essay. Originally, Tannen's article was directed specifically at gender differences in communication. In this classroom activity, she looked at language-use differences in general,
including cultural differences. She states that some people may be more
comfortable in classes where you are expected to raise your hand to
speak, while others prefer to be able to talk freely. She makes no mention of gender in regard to this issue.

Finally, at the close of her essay, where we can expect to get the   *10*
thrust of her argument or at least some sort of summary statement
which ties into her main thesis, Tannen states that her experience in her
classroom convinced her that "small-group interaction should be a part
of any classroom" and that "having students become observers of their
own interaction is a crucial part of their education." Again, these are
interesting points, but they stray quite a bit from the original intention
of the article.

In this article, Tannen discusses important issues of which those   *11*
of us who will be interacting with students in the classroom should be
aware. However, her article loses a great deal of its impact because she
does not stay focused on her original thesis and fails to support her
ideas with convincing evidence.

QUESTIONS FOR WRITING AND DISCUSSION

1. Do your own double-entry log for Tannen's essay (see Chapter 7). On the left-hand side of a piece of paper, record Tannen's main points. On the right-hand side, write your own questions and reactions. Compare your notes to Koester's and Browe's responses. Whose response most closely matches your own? Where or how does your response differ from each?

2. Koester and Browe use different strategies for writing their summaries of Tannen's essay. Describe how the two summaries are different. Which summary is more accurate? Why?

3. Responses to texts may analyze the effectiveness of the text, agree or disagree with the ideas in the text, and/or interpret or reflect on the text. What kinds of responses do Koester and Browe give? Would a different kind of response work better for either writer? Why or why not?

4. Koester focuses on three writing strategies that Tannen uses to make her essay more effective. What are they? What weaknesses of Tannen's essay does Koester ignore or downplay?

5. Browe's response focuses on two criticisms of Tannen's essay. What are they? In which paragraphs does Browe develop each criticism? What strengths of Tannen's essay does Browe ignore or downplay?

6. Neither Browe nor Koester uses personal experience as supporting evidence. Think of one experience that you have had in a specific class illustrating the conversational preferences of men and women. Write out that specific example. Could either Browe or Koester use such a specific example? Where might each writer use it in her response?

7. Reread the essays by Tannen, Koester, and Browe. Review your reactions with your classmates. Then write your own summary and response. In your response, mention both the strengths and the weaknesses of Tannen's article. Then indicate whether or not you found Tannen's essay, in general, thought-provoking or convincing.

Jan Vermeer van Delft, (1632–1675). *The Astronomer.* Oil on canvas, 1668, 31.5 × 45.5 cm. Louvre, Departement de Peintures, Paris.

Chapter 6   Investigating

Your boss at the local self-service gas station wants to expand the station's range of convenience items. Currently, you sell only snacks, such as soda pop, candy, and ice cream. Your boss asks you to find out what is sold at other gas station convenience stores. Next, she wants you to design a survey for your customers, asking which items they would like to have the station carry. After tabulating questionnaires from thirty-five customers, you write a short report for the boss outlining what the competition stocks, how you designed your questionnaire, and what the responses from your customers indicate.

While watching joggers running in the park one day, you notice their straining muscles, their labored breathing, and the grimaces etched on their faces. Why, you wonder, do people go through the pain of running? Does it have a physical or a psychological benefit? Or can it even become an addiction for those people who *have* to run every day? You decide to investigate this question in runners' magazines and professional journals and then interview a few serious runners to determine their motives and the effects that running has on them, both physically and psychologically. The results of your report, you hope, will prove interesting to those who run as well as to those who merely watch others run.

When you stop learning, stop listening, stop looking and asking questions, always new questions, then it is time to die.
—LILLIAN SMITH,
CIVIL RIGHTS ACTIVIST, JOURNALIST, AUTHOR OF KILLERS OF THE DREAM

As the free press develops, the paramount point is whether the journalist, like the scientist or scholar, puts truth in the first place or in the second.
—WALTER LIPPMANN,
JOURNALIST AND AUTHOR

I

NVESTIGATING BEGINS WITH QUESTIONS. WHAT CAUSES THE GREENHOUSE EFFECT? WHEN WILL THE WORLD BEGIN TO RUN OUT OF OIL? HOW DOES ILLITERACY AFFECT A PERSON'S LIFE? How was the World Wide Web created? How does rape affect the lives of women in America? How do colleges recruit applicants? What can you find out about a famous person's personality, background, and achievements? At what age do children first acquire simple mathematical abilities? Why are sunsets yellow, then orange, red, and finally purple?

Investigating also carries an assumption that probing for answers to such questions—by observing and remembering, researching sources, interviewing key people, or conducting surveys—will uncover truths not generally known or accepted. As you dig for information, you learn *who, what, where,* and *when.* You may even learn *how* and *why.*

The purpose of investigating is to uncover or discover facts, opinions, and reactions for yourself and then to *report* that information to other people who want to know. A report strives to be as objective and informative as possible. It may summarize other people's judgments, but it does not editorialize. It may represent opposing viewpoints or arguments, but it does not argue for one side or the other. A report is a window on the world, allowing readers to see the information for themselves.

Curiosity is my natural state and has led me headlong into every worthwhile experience . . . I have ever had.
—ALICE WALKER,
AUTHOR OF THE COLOR PURPLE

Techniques for Investigative Writing ●●●

Investigative writing begins with asking questions and finding informed sources: published material, knowledgeable people, or both. In most cases, collecting information in an investigation requires the ability to use a library and then to summarize, paraphrase, and quote key ideas accurately from other people's writing. In addition, personal interviews are often helpful or necessary. For an investigation, you might talk to an expert or an authority, an eyewitness or participant in an event, or even the subject of a personality profile. Finally, you may wish to survey the general public to determine opinions, trends, or reactions. Once you have collected your information, you must then present your findings in a written form suitable for your audience, with clear references in the text to your sources of information.

Investigative writing uses the following techniques:

- **Beginning with an interesting title and a catchy lead sentence or paragraph.** The first few sentences arouse your readers' *interest* and focus their attention on the subject.

- **Giving background information by answering relevant who, what, when, where, and why questions.** Answering the *reporter's "Wh" questions* ensures that readers have sufficient information to understand your report.
- **Stating the main idea, question, or focus of the investigation.** The purpose of a report is to convey information as *clearly* as possible. Readers shouldn't have to guess the main idea.
- **Summarizing or quoting information from written or oral sources; citing sources in the text.** Quote *accurately* any statistics, data, or sentences from your sources. Cite authors and titles.
- **Writing in a readable and interesting style appropriate for the intended audience.** Clear, direct, and readable language is essential in a report. Use graphs and charts as appropriate.

The following reports illustrate three common types of investigative writing: the *summary* of a single book or article, the *investigation* of a controversial issue (using multiple sources), and the *profile* of a person. The three types may overlap (the investigation of a controversial issue may contain a personality profile, for instance), and all three types may use summaries of written material, questionnaires, and interviews. While some investigative reports are brief, intended to be only short news items, others are full-length features.

The intended audience for each report is often determined by the publication in which the report appears: *Psychology Today* assumes that its readers are interested in personality and behavior; *Discover* magazine is for readers interested in popular science; readers of *Ms.* magazine expect coverage of contemporary issues concerning women.

SUMMARY OF A BOOK OR ARTICLE

The following report from *Psychology Today*, by journalist Jeff Meer, summarizes information taken from an article by Charlene L. Muehlenhard and Melaney A. Linton that appeared in the *Journal of Counseling Psychology*. Although the *Psychology Today* report summarizes only that one article, it demonstrates several key features of an investigative report.

PROFESSIONAL WRITING

DATE RAPE: FAMILIAR STRANGERS

By now, everyone knows the scenario. Boy meets girl, they go to a party, *1* get drunk, return to his apartment, and he forces her to have sex.

Attention-getting title
Lead-in paragraph

Focus of investigation or report

Most people assume that date rape occurs on a first or second date between relative strangers. But new research supports a different conclusion: The individuals involved generally know each other fairly well. *2*

Who, what, where questions answered

Psychologist Charlene L. Muehlenhard and undergraduate Melaney A. Linton asked more than 600 college men and women about their most recent dates, as well as their worst experience with "sexual aggression"—any time a woman was forced to participate in acts, ranging from kissing to intercourse, against her will. More than *3*

Summary of results

three quarters of the women and more than half of the men admitted to having an experience with sexual aggression on a date, either in high school or in college. And nearly 15 percent of the women and 7 percent of the men said they had intercourse against the woman's will.

Summary of results

The researchers found that when a man initiated the date, drove to and from and paid for the date, sexual aggression was more likely. They also found that if both people got drunk (at a party, for example) and "parked," or found themselves in the man's dorm room or apartment, the date was more likely to end with the woman being forced to perform against her wishes. Men and women who thought of themselves as having traditional values and those who were more accepting of violence were also more likely to have been involved in date rape. *4*

Summary of results

But contrary to what one might expect, date rape and sexual aggression were much more likely to happen between partners who knew each other. On average, students said they had known the partner almost a year before the incident. "If women were more aware of this, they might be less surprised and more prepared to deal with sexual aggression by someone they know well," Muehlenhard says. *5*

Quotation

Summary

She points out that communication is often a big problem on dates during which there is sexual aggression. Both men and women reported that the man had felt "led on" during such dates. Men said that women desired more sexual contact on these dates than had others on previous dates. Women said that they had desired less sexual contact than usual. *6*

Quotation

Muehlenhard believes that a direct approach, such as a woman saying "I don't want to do anything more than kiss," might clear up confusion better than simply saying "No." *7*

INVESTIGATION USING MULTIPLE SOURCES

Most investigative reports draw on multiple sources: books and articles, research studies, and interviews. The following article, which appeared in *Time* magazine has all the key features of an interesting investigative report. The author, Anastasia Toufexis, focuses on the popular psychiatric drug Prozac. She catches our interest with personal case histories. She asks probing questions about the medical and psychological effects of the drug. She focuses her report on a best-selling book by Peter Kramer, but she also weaves in several interviews with other authorities on Prozac. Despite the controversial nature of her topic, however, Toufexis remains as neutral as possible. She presents the background information and lets the experts debate the issues so that her readers can judge for themselves.

PROFESSIONAL WRITING

THE PERSONALITY PILL

Anastasia Toufexis

Susan Smith has everything going for her. A self-described workaholic, she runs a Cambridge, Massachusetts, real estate consulting company with her husband Charles and still finds time to cuddle and nurture their two young kids, David, 7, and Stacey, 6. What few people know is that Susan, 44, needs a little chemical help to be a supermom: she has been taking the antidepressant Prozac for five years.

Smith never had manic depression or any other severe form of mental illness. But before Prozac, she suffered from sharp mood swings, usually coinciding with her menstrual periods. "I would become highly emotional and sometimes very angry, and I really wasn't sure why I was angry," she recalls. Charles will never forget the time she threw her wedding band at him during a spat. Now, says Susan, "the lows aren't as low as they were. I'm more comfortable with myself." And she has no qualms about her long-term relationship with a psychoactive pill: "If there's a drug that makes you feel better, you use it."

Millions agree, making Prozac the hottest psychiatric drug in history. Since its introduction five years ago, 5 million Americans—and 10 million people worldwide—have used it. The drug is much more than a fad: it is a medical breakthrough that has brought unprecedented relief to many patients with severe depressions, phobias, obsessions and compulsions. But it is also increasingly used by people with milder problems, and its immense popularity is raising some unsettling questions. When should Prozac be prescribed? How does a doctor draw the line between illness and normal behavior? If you feel better after taking Prozac, were you ill before? When does drug therapy become drug abuse? Will Prozac become the medically approved feel-good drug, a cocaine substitute without the dangerous highs and lows?

At medical meetings or dinner parties, the talk turns more and more often to Prozac, and what frequently sets off the discussion is a provocative book about the drug—*Listening to Prozac: A Psychiatrist Explores Antidepressant Drugs and the Remaking of the Self* by Dr. Peter Kramer of Brown University. Having quickly become a must-read, the book has perched near the top of the best-seller lists for three months.

The author, who uses Prozac in his private practice, is both impressed by the drug and uneasy about what its widespread use may portend for human society. In case after case, he contends, Prozac does more than treat disease; it has the power to transform personality, instill self-confidence and enhance a person's performance at work and play. One of the patients profiled in the book, an architect named Sam, claims that the drug made him "better than well." His depression lifted, and he became more poised and thoughtful, with keener concentration and a more reliable memory than ever before. Prozac, writes Kramer, seems "to give social confidence to the habitually timid, to make the sensitive brash, to lend the introvert the social skills of a salesman."

The psychiatrist maintains that the power of Prozac challenges basic assumptions about the origins and uniqueness of individual personalities. They may be less the result of experiences and more a matter of brain chemistry. If temperament lies in a tablet, is there an essential, immutable Self? Ultimately, Kramer muses, society could enter a new era of "cosmetic psychopharmacology," in which changing personality traits may be as simple as shampooing in a new hair color. "Since you only live once, why not do it as a blond?" he asks, and "why not as a peppy blond?" Already, pharmaceutical houses are churning out a whole new class of similar drugs, including Paxil and Zoloft, that mimic the effects of Prozac.

So what makes Prozac any different from all the other popular mood-altering potions down through history, from alcohol, opium and marijuana to widely prescribed "mother's little helpers" such as Librium and Valium? Unlike the typical street drug, which sends people soaring and then crashing, Prozac has an effect that is even and sustained. And it seems safer and has fewer bothersome side effects than previous medicines prescribed to lift people out of depression. Prozac is what scientists call a "clean" drug. Instead of playing havoc with much of the brain's chemistry, the medication has a very specific effect: it regulates the level of serotonin, a crucial compound that carries messages between nerve cells. "Prozac makes people feel different without making them feel drugged," notes Kramer.

Patients don't all react the same way, of course; some don't feel a bit better. And many psychiatrists and patients don't agree with Kramer about the drug's transformative powers. "I have my ability to not snap at people back, my energy back," notes a rabbi who recently started taking Prozac for mild depression. But, he adds, "I don't feel like Superman, and I still can't stand parties."

"There's a lot less than meets the eye with Prozac," says Dr. Daniel Auerbach of the Veterans Health Administration in Sepulveda, California. "Nothing changes personality. What gets changed is symptoms of a disease." In other words, Prozac enables a person's true personality, often imprisoned by illness, to come out. Contends Dr. Hyla Cass, a psychiatrist in Santa Monica, California: "I don't think Prozac is manipulating people, turning them into feel-goods. It is correcting an imbalance, allowing people to be who they can be."

But, counters Kramer, doesn't that broaden the boundaries of mental illness to include any condition that responds to Prozac? If a person responds to an antidepressant, does that necessarily mean that he or she is suffering from depression? Kramer questions whether the "imbalances" cured by the drug are always bad; maybe they are just frowned upon by current society. Are the vivacity and blithe spirits often produced by Prozac superior to shyness and a touch of melancholy? Do decisiveness and vigor have more merit than reticence and calmness? Should a business executive who lacks aggressiveness feel compelled to take a pill?

Most psychiatrists argue that while Prozac may be abused, it is still a long way from being overused. A study by the National Institute of Mental Health shows that 40% to 50% of people with major depression are not receiving any kind of therapy.

With so many still going untreated, Kramer's book may do a service by alerting some of them to Prozac's potential benefits. But Kramer may also be raising expectations too high. Says Dr. Glen Gabbard, director of the Menninger Memorial Hospital in Topeka, Kansas: "We should not send patients rushing to their corner pharmacy in hopes of getting a magic chemical that will solve all their problems." For most people, happiness does not come packaged in a pill.

PROFILE OF A PERSON

The following passage is a *profile* of a person—a biographical sketch intended to give a sense of the person's appearance, behavior, character, and accomplishments. These paragraphs are part of a profile of Oprah Winfrey written by journalist Joan Barthel for *Ms.* magazine.

Here Comes Oprah!

A profile of Oprah Winfrey is not just the story of a survivor, though she obviously is one: besides that bottom-line day five years ago [when she wrote a suicide note], she's survived early adolescent years so troubled that she became a runaway and was nearly placed in a juvenile detention home.

Nor is it just a success story of a black woman who's made it in the white man's world of network television, though she's done that, too. At 19, she was anchoring the news in Nashville—the first woman, the first black. She worked for seven years in Baltimore, first paying her dues as a TV street reporter, "hating every minute of it," especially when she was required to ask a woman who'd just lost her children and her house in a fire how she felt. (When she didn't have the heart to do that piece, her boss told her to get it or lose her job. She came back to the studio with the story and, on the air live, apologized for it.) She did everything she was told, including trying to remake herself. "They told me my nose was too wide, my hair too thick and long, and they sent me to a place in New York to get my first perm. I felt the lotion burning my skull, and I kept saying, 'Excuse me, this is beginning to burn a little.' They kept saying, 'Oh, just a few more minutes.'" Within a week all her hair had fallen out. "You learn a lot about yourself when you're bald," she says now.

Nor is it even a rags-to-riches tale, though her dazzling condominium apartment (marble floors, four baths, including one with a gold swan as the tub faucet and another with adjoining sauna) is a glamorous world apart from the Milwaukee housing project where she spent part of her childhood. "I don't think of myself as a poor deprived ghetto girl who made good," she declares. "I think of myself as somebody who from an early age knew I was responsible for myself, and I *had* to make good."

Knowing did not always mean doing, though. Which is why a profile of Oprah Winfrey is, mostly, a look at a woman in process.

■ WARMING UP: JOURNAL EXERCISES   The following exercises will help you practice investigative writing. Read all of the following exercises and then, in your journal, write on the three that interest you most. One of these exercises may suggest an idea for your investigating essay.

1. Write an "authority" list of topics about which you have some expertise or information. Consider your hobbies, academic interests, occupational skills, social problems, community concerns, art, sports, travel, animals, films, TV shows, and so forth. Jot down a few words or phrases indicating what you know about each item on your list. Emphasize what or who it is, how it happens or how to do it, and when or where it happens. Because one of these topics may develop into an essay for this course, spend at least fifteen minutes on this exercise.

2. Page through the notebooks and texts from another course you are currently taking. What subjects mentioned in class or referred to in the text might you investigate? Make a list of topics for investigation that would help you in that course. During that class, jot down any other suggestions that occur to you. While the topics should not be assignments for essays already assigned in that course, they could relate to relevant background reading.

3. Next semester, you will be taking a course in your major field, but you aren't sure which professor you should pick. To investigate the differences among the teachers, interview several students who have taken this course from different professors. Prepare questions that encourage factual responses: How many papers or tests does the teacher require? What is the grade distribution? What textbook was required? What was the reading or homework load? What were typical lecture topics? Was the teacher available outside class?

4. As a member of the student governing board, your job is to solicit student opinions about some aspect of campus life that needs improving. Choose a subject such as dorms, classes, the library, parking, student clubs, the film or fine art series, or recreational opportunities. Then choose a question to focus your investigation and write a one-page questionnaire that you might distribute to students. (See the section on writing questionnaires in this chapter.)

5. Watch an investigative news show such as *60 Minutes or Nightline*, taking notes about the interviewer's techniques. Is there a sequence to the questions—say, from gentle and polite to critical or controversial? What information does the interviewer have *before* the interview? Can you tell which questions are planned or scripted and which are spontaneous? After taking notes on a show, explain what you think are the *three* most important tips for successful interviewing.

6. Interview a classmate for a 200- to 250-word "personality profile." Your object is to profile this person and one of his or her major interests. First, in your daybook, prepare questions you need to ask for biographical information. Then, in an eight- to ten-minute interview, ask questions

about the person and about several topics from that person's "authority" list. After the interview, take two or three minutes to review your notes. At home, write up the results of your interview, which will appear in your local or campus newspaper.

7. Start your own curiosity list by logging onto the World Wide Web and using your browser to locate sites for topics you are interested in. If you are not familiar with Internet research, read the following essay by Gene Cowan. If you have done web research, read the next essay by Elizabeth Larsen, "Surfin' the Louvre." Using her essay as a model, write your own short essay about web research on your topic. As Larsen does, take your reader on a "trip" through the websites you find.

If you are still unfamiliar with how the Internet and the Web work, check out the following brief article, "How the Web Works," by Gene Cowan.

PROFESSIONAL   WRITING

How the Web Works
Gene Cowan

1. When you enter a URL, or Universal Resource Locator, into your web browser, your computer sends that address to a computer called a name server which breaks it down into its parts, much like a mailing address. The Internet sees upper and lower case letters as being different, so it's important to enter a URL exactly as directed.

2. With the address decoded, the name server sends your request to the specific computer on the Internet you have asked for, using the best route possible. Because the Internet is actually over 7 million computers, all connected together, your request may be routed through a computer in China or Nigeria to make it to Washington, D.C.

3. When the destination computer receives your request, it first checks to see if you are allowed to have the file you asked for. If you are, it sends the file back over the Internet—but with a twist. In order to use the network with maximum efficiency, the computer splits the file up into small pieces called *packets*. These packets of information are sent back, often by completely different routes. One bit may be sent via Australia, and one bit via North Carolina. Each packet has a destination address attached, so it won't get lost.

4. Finally, after an excruciating wait of seconds, the requested data begins to arrive back at your computer, and is re-assembled from the

http://www.ncss.org/online/wwwhome.html

The *protocol*, or method the computer will use for transferring the data. HTTP is Hypertext Transfer Protocol. Other protocols include FTP and *gopher*.

The name of the computer containing the file you want. The address is always decoded in reverse. *org* means a non-profit organization in the United States. *ncss* is the name of the organization. *www* directs you to a specific area on the computer set aside for World Wide Web users.

Everything after the computer name is a directory path on that computer to the document you want. In this case, *online* is a folder called "online" in the *ncss.org* computer. "wwwhome.html" is a file in that folder. *html* stands for HyperText Markup Language, the format that web pages are written in.

packets to create a full file. Your web browser decodes the file and displays the information according to the instructions contained within the file. It continues to repeat the process as often as necessary for each graphic referenced in the web page.

Glossary

- **browser** A program that accesses the World Wide Web. A browser decodes and displays HTML documents.
- **domain** The last part of an Internet address, such as *.org* or *.com*, it tells where to begin looking for a specific computer.
- **FTP** File Transfer Protocol. A method of copying files from one computer to another.
- **gopher** A method of retrieving files from another computer—as in "go fer."
- **http** HyperText Transfer Protocol. A method of retrieving files that will be decoded by a web browser.
- **HTML** HyperText Markup Language. A method of writing text files with special codes that direct a web browser to format documents on the screen and create links to other documents.
- **name server** A computer that decodes addresses and sends messages on to the destination.
- **URL** Universal Resource Locator. The address of the file you are searching for. A URL tells the Internet the location of one specific file out of the billions available on the Internet.

SURFIN' THE LOUVRE

Elizabeth Larsen

I first studied art history the old-fashioned way: scribbling notes in a dark auditorium as a parade of yellowing slides whizzed past in an overwhelming progression from ancient Greece to Andy Warhol. Four years and tens of thousands of dollars later, I had traveled from the ruins of Tikal in Guatemala to a tiny Giotto-decorated chapel in Padua to Rodin's Paris atelier without ever leaving my college's urban campus.

Today it's possible to get a similar education—minus the sometimes inspired (and sometimes not-so-inspired) comments of a professor—on the Internet. In the past few years, virtually every museum of note has established a presence on the World Wide Web. While some sites still stick to the basics (cost of admission, hours, information about the permanent collection and current exhibits), more and more institutions are following the lead of the **Fine Arts Museums of San Francisco** (*www.thinker.org/index.shtml*) which is using the Web to promote its new commitment to "behave more like a resource and less like a repository." Currently the site houses over 65,000 images—from Mary Cassatt's *Woman Bathing* to more than 3,000 examples of Japanese ukiyo-e printmaking—with plans to double that number as the museum digitizes its entire collection.

That's a heck of a lot more reproductions than you'll find in that chiropractically unfriendly art history text, H. W. Janson's *History of Art*. Inspired by the sheer volume of images available on FAMSF's "Imagebase," I decided to try my hand at digitally designing my own art education.

My self-directed syllabus started in Spain at the new **Guggenheim Museum in Bilbao** (*www.bm30.es/guggenheim*), the recently opened critic's darling designed by maverick California architect Frank Gehry. As befits a museum where the architecture is as much a piece of art history as the works it houses, much of the site is devoted to Gehry's oddly gorgeous design, which looks like a cross between a medieval fortress and a bouquet of flowers sculpted in titanium. But there's a lot of other great stuff as well, including reproductions of the museum's most famous acquisitions—like Richard Serra's *Snake*, an appropriately jarring-yet-graceful panel of curving steel set smack dab in the middle of a gallery.

Eager to see more, I moved on to the Museums page of the **World Wide Web Virtual Library** (*www.comlab.ox.ac.uk/archive/other/museums.html*). A clearinghouse of links to museums, the site is most helpful for those who want to search according to the countries the museums are in. I started in Italy, which I soon discovered doesn't include that country-within-a-country, the **Vatican** (*www. christusrex. org/www1citta/O-Citta.html*). At the **Uffizi Gallery in Florence** (*www.italink.com/eng/egui/hogui.html*), I checked out a number of Renaissance heavy hitters, including Botticelli's *The Birth of Venus* and Paolo Ucello's *Battle of San Romano*. To get more of a feeling for Florentine art as it exists on the streets and in the churches of Florence, I used the Florence Art Guide to take me all over the city, from the Ponte Vecchio to the Piazzale Michelangelo.

My next stop was Paris, where my first visit was to—where else?— the **Louvre** (*www.mistral.culture.fr/Louvre/Louvrea.html*), where I lingered over a Watteau and a Poussin before getting absorbed in the history of the building. From there it was an easy trek to the countryside and the **Giverny home page** (*www.giverny.org/index.html*) to check out the gardens that inspired Monet.

From Giverny I hopped over to Greece and the **Hellenic Ministry of Culture's Guide to Athens** (*www.culture.gr/maps/sterea/attiki/athens. html*) where I gazed out over the Acropolis. Then I spent the rest of the afternoon in Japan at the **Kyoto National Museum** (*www.kyohaku. go.jp/*), where I studied up on the intricacies of Chinese and Japanese lacquerware.

I know I'm starting to sound pretty starry-eyed about my cyber-education, so I'll temper my enthusiasm with a few caveats. From the vantage point of my office chair, I obviously wasn't able to glean insights from the people standing next to me as I contemplated de Kooning's *Woman I*. But I don't require that every symphony I listen to be live, and I'm equally comfortable with the trade-offs inherent in a digital visual experience. Especially since I won't need to worry about those threatening form letters from the bursar's office.

PROFESSIONAL WRITING

PLOTTING A NET GAIN

Connie Koenenn

In this profile of sociologist and computer guru Sherry Turkle, Los Angeles Times *staff writer Connie Koenenn gives her readers information on Turkle's book,* Life on the Screen: Identity in the Age of the Internet, *as well as a perspectives on Turkle's private life. In writing this profile, notice how Koenenn interweaves material from interviews with Turkle, quo-*

tations and information from Turkle's book, information from a radio interview, and personal observations about Turkle's lifestyle.

Microsoft Chairman Bill Gates looks at the Internet and sees a transformation in the way we get information. MIT sociologist Sherry Turkle looks at the Internet and sees a transformation in the way we view ourselves.   *1*

Despite all the hype and babble about the information superhighway, Turkle says, most people actually have underestimated the coming knowledge revolution. When we log onto a bulletin board, chat room, forum or other cyberspace sites, she says, we are entering a world of possibility. There, we can change our name, our appearance, even our sex, and test ourselves in that different persona. "We can easily move through multiple identities," Turkle says, "and we can embrace—or be trapped by—cyberspace as a way of life."   *2*

This is the theme of her new book, *Life on the Screen: Identity in the Age of the Internet* (Simon & Schuster). It's based on her studies, which started 20 years ago when she noticed the way MIT students used computer language ("Let's debug this relationship") in everyday life.   *3*

And although Turkle has been tracking the emerging computer culture for two decades, the exploding popularity of the Internet world has turned a new spotlight on her. *Newsweek* magazine listed her among "50 for the Future" for 1995 and *Time* dubbed her the "Margaret Mead of Silicone."   *4*

"Sherry Turkle is an important thinker and very perspicacious—she was way ahead of the curve," says Constance Hale, associate managing editor of *Wired* magazine, which is excerpting Turkle's book in its January issue. "Her book is groundbreaking. Her theory—that the computer isn't a tool but that it is giving you access to parts of yourself that you didn't have before—is revolutionary."   *5*

Like Gates, Turkle says we are on the brink of a revolution, now that computers inhabit life at every turn. But while Gates' new book, *The Road Ahead* (Viking), focuses on the outward shapes of the computers and software (such as a wallet PC), Turkle is more concerned with the loosening of the boundaries between people and their computers. "If you want to call this an 'information revolution,' you can," she said on a recent visit to Los Angeles. "I think it is more than that."   *6*

Turkle, 47, who was wearing a trim black pantsuit and carrying an immense leather handbag, had just been a guest on Michael Jackson's CABC-AM (790) talk show. The discussion had turned to such new phenomena as "cyber-infidelity." Turkle had mentioned a wife who decided her husband's online affair was better than his looking around for real-life women.   *7*

That brought up the question of what constitutes infidelity in a *8* world where nothing is physical. "I think when you can connect via the computer, you can adopt a persona somewhat different than the one you ordinarily have," she told the radio audience. "People feel that the anonymity and distance allow them to experience different aspects of themselves."

Later, she elaborates. In person, Turkle is an engaging conversa- *9* tionalist, jumping from thought to thought with energy and humor. "People can experience other aspects of themselves online," she says. "I have seen it happen!"

She has seen how people, talking online in a low-risk setting, have *10* slowly developed social skills or been able to discuss physical problems, such as weight or disabilities, that they previously repressed. She has watched men and women gradually move from virtual online worlds into real relationships ("Rush Limbaugh met his wife on CompuServe," she says).

Turkle put six years into writing *Life on the Screen*. Despite its *11* catchy title and rich use of case studies, the heavily footnoted book, interweaving psychological and social analysis with an overview of intelligent machine development, is not light reading. "The meaning of the computer presence in people's lives is very different from what most expected in the late 1970s," Turkle writes. "One way to describe what has happened is to say we are moving from a modernist culture of calculation toward a postmodernist culture of simulation." In short, computers have moved from machines that do things for us (our tax returns or spreadsheets) to machines that do things to us, such as provide experiences that will affect our social and emotional life.

Describing e-mail as a "return to conversation over the backyard *12* fence," Turkle notes that in the Massachusetts Institute of Technology Media Lab, where she works, she can log on any morning and scroll through the staff messages. "Someone has died, someone has a baby, someone has won an award—it's like a small-town newspaper."

Now, her interest is turning to families. She recently interviewed a *13* woman whose son, just off to college, was studying for his first physics test. The woman had gotten America Online so they could keep in touch, and when she sent her first e-mail message, he replied, "Mom, you did it right!" She had insomnia and got up about 5 A.M. and, on an impulse, sent him another message. When he answered immediately, she realized he was very nervous about the test and had been studying all night. So she sent him a reassuring message that his parents will love him however he does on tests. "Here was a socially acceptable way to talk. She would never have called him at 5 in the morning, but this allows him to be in control, which is what kids that age need to be," Turkle says.

Computers were not on the agenda when Turkle graduated in *14* 1976 from Harvard with a double doctorate in sociology and personality psychology. She had spent a year in France analyzing how Freudian thought had been rejected and then accepted by the French; her first book, *Psychoanalytic Politics: Jacques Lacan & Freud's French Revolution*, has been reissued (Guilford Press, 1992).

"I thought I would have a career studying how complicated ideas *15* come into everyday life. I didn't anticipate the next set of ideas I would look at would be from computer science," Turkle says.

She was hired because MIT wanted somebody who studied the *16* cultural diffusion of scientific ideas. As technophobe Turkle began listening to the computer-savvy students, she realized they were using computer ideas (instead of "Freudian slip," they would say "information-processing error") to describe their lives. "It was like a 'Eureka!' experience to me," she says.

Beginning in her own backyard, Turkle organized pizza parties *17* for students playing MUDS (Multi-User Domains), the intricate online games in which participants can alter their real-life identities to improvise elaborate melodramas. She interviewed them at length about their experiences in the fantasies that grew out of the Dungeons and Dragons fantasy games of the early 1970s. She also studied children who were being introduced to computer toys. More recently, she began monitoring Internet chat and bulletin boards.

"I just kept studying people and machines," says Turkle, who has *18* steadily written articles for academic journals about the computer culture—about women and computers, physicists and computers, children and computers. Ten years ago she wrote *The Second Self: Computers and the Human Spirit* (Simon & Schuster).

Turkle estimates that she has interviewed more than 1,000 people. Mitchel Resnick, a colleague at the MIT Media Lab, admires *19* Turkle's ability to get people to open up in interviews. "She can make people feel comfortable sharing their deepest feelings," he says. "I think often they have been transformed by these [online] experiences and most people don't understand that world."

Although Turkle may meet her subjects online, she insists on interviewing them in person, usually in her MIT office. She doesn't even *20* have a computer there—it's reserved for seeing RL (real life) students and colleagues, she explains.

She is, however, surrounded by computers at home. Turkle is married to consultant Ralph Willard, and they have a daughter, 4. Her *21* routine in their Boston home is to wake up at 6 A.M. and devote two hours to e-mail, sitting at her Macintosh with a Powerbook nearby to receive faxes. "I have a little computer for my daughter and a palmtop I travel with. I don't watch TV and I write very few letters anymore— I spend a fair amount of time Internet-surfing."

And although she signs on daily to a huge amount of e-mail, she *22* says it is worth it. She recently heard from an old high school friend who had seen an article about her in a Boston paper. He had thought about contacting her previously, but with e-mail it was too easy to pass up, he said. She was delighted. "To me, making possible that kind of connection with your past, with people all over the world, is so precious. I am willing to bite the bullet and sort through all the e-mail." (22)

And although she acknowledges a darker side of cyberspace (peo- *23* ple can get stuck in the selves they have created on the screen, or hurt by an online relationship that turns out to be fraudulent, she says), Turkle has great hopes for the emerging computer culture.

"Here's the good news," she says briskly. "Being online can help *24* you develop parts of yourself that have been underdeveloped and it can help your personal growth. Here's the bad news: Some people find themselves just acting out the same problems they have in real life in virtual life. If they've been hostile, they become the 'flamers' on the Internet, using the anonymity to act out their hangups."

She doesn't like the question, "Is cyberspace good or bad?" The *25* point is, it is, she says. "It's going to demand ongoing conversations about the new definition of work, of marriage, of sexuality, of child care, of every aspect of our lives."

She thus welcomes the fuss over pornography on the Internet as *26* a signal that we are living in a very different time. "It's setting the stage for that longer-term reflection. It's important to keep in mind that we are not going to sort this out in the next two months or two years."

VOCABULARY

In your journal, write the meanings of the following words:

- *Margaret Mead* of Silicone **(4)**
- very *perspicacious* **(5)**
- *postmodernist* culture **(11)**
- cultural *diffusion* of scientific ideas **(16)**
- *technophobe* Turkle **(16)**
- *Freudian slip* **(16)**

QUESTIONS FOR WRITING AND DISCUSSION

1. Investigative essays focus on answering at least one key question. The question for Connie Koenenn's article might be "Who is Sherry Turkle and what does she think about the Internet?" Reread the article, focusing on Koenenn's answer to the second part of that question. Find at least three specific passages that reveal what Turkle finds important about the Internet.

2. Without looking back at the article, list any key bits of information about Sherry Turkle and her books that you can remember. Then reread the article, jotting down any important facts or pieces of information that you forgot. What additional questions about Turkle or her ideas are not answered? Explain why you think Connie Koenenn does or does not effectively meet her purpose of reporting to her readers interesting information about Turkle and her ideas.

3. Reread Koenenn's article, looking for evidences of the sources she used in writing this essay. Next to major paragraphs, indicate the probable source of the quotations, facts, or information. Does Koenenn rely most on quotations and information from a personal interview, on information from Turkle's books, on outside biographical information, on additional third-party interviews, on transcripts of a radio interview, or on other sources? Write a list of the kinds of sources Koenenn probably used.

4. Write your own investigative profile about a person from your school, an employee at your place of work, or a member of your family. Schedule an interview to find out about this person. Use your own observations. Interview other people about their acquaintance with this person. Read anything this person may have written. Assume that your profile will appear in a local or campus newspaper.

5. Sherry Turkle continues to be interviewed about her views on how computers and the Internet are changing and—especially—how they are changing us. Use Lexis-Nexis or Electric Library to find recent full-text articles on Sherry Turkle. In one interview published in *Fortune* magazine, Turkle had the following comments: "The Internet is a place of experimentation on your identity—in positive as well as negative ways." "The more complicated computer networks get, the more people use them as models for their own minds." "It's going to create a crisis about the simulated and the real. The notion of what it is to live in a culture of simulation . . . is going to become more and more [important]." What new information can you find about how computers are changing our identity, our culture, and our sense of what is real and what is only simulated?

LIFE AFTER OIL
Jeremiah Creedon

In the next decade, we will need to become more knowledgeable about alternative sources of energy and ways to make transportation more efficient because, according to Jeremiah Creedon, we are headed toward a global oil crisis. Jeremiah Creedon is senior editor at Utne *magazine and has written articles on a variety of subjects including brain research, religion, and abuses of the media. In "Life After Oil," Creedon uses an article by British writer David Fleming as a starting point to investigate the state of the world oil reserves and the economic, agricultural, and political scenarios we will face as oil supplies dwindle. The Big Rollover—the point where oil consumption exceeds supplies—is coming before the year 2020. "The crucial point," according to Creedon, is not when the Big Rollover arrives, "but how long after that we'll go on denying it."*

Long after the oil age has burned itself out, the future will assign a date   *1* to when the flame first wavered. It might have been 30 years ago when the world's great energy consumer, the United States, started using more oil than it produced. Or it might be tomorrow, if we end up drilling in Alaska's Arctic National Wildlife Refuge for what amounts to six months' worth of fuel. In any case, the crucial point will not be when the end begins, but how long after that we'll go on denying it. This lag will determine how well our country and the world move beyond the oil age; the longer we hesitate, the more brutal it will be.

We actually have a pretty good idea of when even car-loving   *2* Americans will have to face the truth. Certain energy experts have seen the moment coming for decades. They're waiting for what a recent report from the U.S. Geological Survey calls the Big Rollover—the point when the world starts needing more oil than it supplies. These forecasts began with a guy named M. King Hubbert, a geophysicist who in 1956 correctly predicted the initial American rollover in 1970. In 1974 he estimated that the global peak would occur in 1995—not a bad guess. Current forecasts range from 2003 to 2020.

In other words, we won't have to run completely out of oil to be   *3* rudely awakened. The panic starts once the world needs more oil than it gets. To understand why, you've got to fathom how totally addicted to oil we've become. We know that petroleum is drawn from deep wells and distilled into gasoline, jet fuel, and countless other products that form the lifeblood of industry and the adrenaline of military might. It's less well known that the world's food is now nourished by oil; petroleum and natural gas are crucial at every step of modern agriculture, from making fertilizer to shipping crops. The implications are grim. For millions, the difference between an energy famine and a biblical famine could well be academic.

With a global oil crisis looming like the Doomsday Rock, why do *4*
so few political leaders seem to care? As independent policy analyst David Fleming writes in the British magazine *Prospect* (Nov. 2000), many experts refuse to take the problem seriously because it "falls outside the mind-set of market economics." Thanks to the triumph of global capitalism, the free-market model now reigns almost everywhere. The trouble is, its principles "tend to break down when applied to natural resources like oil." The result is both potentially catastrophic and all too human. Our high priests—the market economists—are blind to a reality that in their cosmology cannot exist.

Fleming offers several examples of this broken logic at work. Many *5*
cling to a belief that higher oil prices will spur more oil discoveries, but they ignore what earth scientists have been saying for years: There aren't more big discoveries to make. Most of the oil reserves we tap today were actually identified by the mid-1960s. There's a lot of oil left in the ground—perhaps more than half of the total recoverable supply. Fleming says that's not the issue. The real concern is the point beyond which demand cannot be met. And with demand destined to grow by as much as 3 percent a year, the missing barrels will add up quickly. Once the pain becomes real, the Darwinian impulse kicks in and the orderly market gives way to chaos.

"The United States will fight hard and dirty," Fleming warns, be- *6*
cause we'll have the money to feed our addiction. Other countries won't. "The United States will export oil scarcity to the rest of the world," adds Fleming, and he's blunt about what happens after that: "There will be economic destabilization."

Some insist that industrial societies are growing less dependent on *7*
oil. Fleming says they're kidding themselves. They're talking about oil use as a percentage of total energy use, not the actual amount of oil burned. Measured by the barrel, we're burning more and more. In Britain, for instance, transportation needs have doubled in volume since 1973 and still rely almost entirely on oil. Transportation is the weak link in any modern economy; choke off the oil and a country quickly seizes.

This wouldn't matter much, Fleming laments, "if the world had *8*
spent the last 25 years urgently preparing alternative energies, conservation technologies, and patterns of land use with a much lower dependence on transport." (He figures 25 years to be the time it will take a country like Britain to break its habit.) Instead, "the long-expected shock finds us unprepared."

Insuring food is a major concern, he says. We need to localize food   *9*
production and return to using more human labor. Solar and wind
power must be developed. Fuel must be rationed, on both a domestic
and an international scale. We must resist the rising cry for more nuclear power, he says; it's too pricey, and radioactive waste gets even
more dangerous in times of political disarray. Fleming believes that
burning more coal may be the "lesser evil." Despite coal's negative impact on the climate, we'll have to burn something while we're working
on alternatives.

In any case, nothing will happen until political leaders and other   *10*
social engineers accept the problem and get the public involved in
solving it.

There are dissenting views. Some argue that the world's immedi-   *11*
ate problem is too much oil. They believe that low oil prices over the
next 20 years could trigger turmoil in Central Asia, the Middle East,
and other oil-rich hot spots. On a different front, the astronomer
Thomas Gold and others question whether we really know what oil is.
The usual rap is that oil began as tiny dead plants and animals filtering down through ancient seas. These stagnant beds were then buried
under sediments and pressure-cooked into the tarry goo that runs our
world. But according to Gold, oil may actually be an inorganic substance created deep in the earth's molten innards—not a fossil fuel at
all. And depleted fields might just fill again as more oil oozes upward.

Sounds hopeful, until you factor in global warming. The only thing   *12*
worse than running out of oil might be not running out of oil. The
carbon dioxide we create by burning oil continues to heat the planet,
yet the economy and the environment are still usually discussed as separate issues. Again, this reveals the need for better models than the
ones social engineers now rely on. We also need a better worldview
than the militant market optimism that so often underlies them. Without such a shift, the tension between reality and ideology could resolve
itself in tragic ways. Fleming implies that our governments should take
the lead, which is probably true, but can we wait?

There are several respected estimates as to when the Big Rollover   *13*
will occur. They all fall within the next 20 years. If you average them
out, it doesn't take much voodoo to end up on 2012. The winter sol-
stice that year is said to mark the end of a 5,125-year cycle in the Mayan
calendar. Decades ago, the late thinker Terence McKenna landed on the
same date when he plotted out his "Time Wave Zero" theory. He did
so before he knew of its significance among the Mayans, he claimed,
though he was just enough of a showman to make you wonder.

McKenna predicted modern society would descend at that mo-   *14*
ment into a "soft dark age," followed a few years later by a major mind

shift that will lift us out of the deadend thinking that shaped the angry, smoggy, smoldering 20th century. Some modern Mayans have interpreted it as a moment of cultural rebirth, stressing its positive aspects. Whatever led their star-gazing ancestors to pick that date, it is a good reminder that cultural patterns do change, and that other peoples have tried hard to anticipate why and when.

We should do the same—if for no other reason than to keep from being caught in traffic when it happens.   *15*

Vocabulary

In your journal, write the meaning of each of the following words:

- You've got to *fathom* (3)
- in their *cosmology* (4)
- a country quickly *seizes* (7)
- times of political *disarray* (9)

Questions for Writing and Discussion

1. In small groups in your class—or on your class computer forum—interview other members of your class about their attitudes toward oil and energy alternatives. Write out several questions to ask, such as "How many miles do you commute to school or work? What gas mileage does your automobile get? Do you use public transportation? Should the government permit more arctic or offshore oil drilling? What changes in your life would reduce your consumption of natural gas or oil? Should the federal government raise fuel taxes on gasoline to support alternative forms of public transportation?" Choose three or four questions, compile the responses, and be ready to report your findings to the class.

2. Investigating essays should begin with a lead paragraph or two that arouse the reader's interest and then give background information that answers relevant *who*, *what*, *when*, *where*, and *why* questions. Reread the opening paragraphs of Creedon's essay. Does he get your attention? Does he provide sufficient background information? Explain.

3. Investigating essays focus on answering one or two key questions. What investigating questions(s) does Jeremiah Creedon address? Indicate paragraph numbers where Creedon poses or answers these

questions. In your own words, write out the central investigating question for his article.

4. Creedon relies heavily on an article by David Fleming which appeared in the British magazine *Prospect* in November of 2000. Where does Creedon use "author tags," such as "according to Fleming," to indicate that he is quoting or summarizing ideas from Fleming's article? What other sources of information does Creedon use? Should he indicate those sources more explicitly?

5. The editors of *Utne* magazine accompanied Creedon's article with the following introduction. Read this paragraph and then analyze the audience that these editors are addressing. Based on this passage, create a brief profile of readers of *Utne*. Are they likely to be liberal or conservative? Are they likely to be sympathetic to environmental issues? Are they likely to favor or be hostile to Creedon's argument? Support your responses with reference to specific words or phrases.

"The last time Americans recognized that oil was a finite resource, we turned off lights, insulated houses, and reordered our transportation system. The results were remarkable: Energy use, especially gasoline, dropped markedly. But then Ronald Reagan barreled into the White House and convinced us there was nothing to worry about. Only now are we realizing, as a report in the British political magazine *Prospect* makes clear, how wrong he was. Oil supplies are dwindling—and much faster than most business, government, and even environmental leaders recognize. Problems are already appearing in the form of climbing gasoline prices, electricity shortages, and skyrocketing heating bills. But with two Texas oilmen in Washington's driver's seat, the government responses may be the wrong ones. Instead of loosening environmental regulations, resuscitating nuclear energy, and drilling in Alaska's wildlife refuges, we should once again learn to use less energy—starting with transportation. It can be done. Inspiring and practical solutions are all around, from the bikeways of Montreal to the boardrooms of Detroit."

6. On the Internet, log on to www.café.utne.com, register with the site, search for articles by Jeremiah Creedon, and read some of the hundreds of pages of responses from *Utne* readers that "Life After Oil" generated. What topics do these writers discuss? Are they energy-use amateurs or are they engineers and scientists? What political biases do they have? Print out two pages of response that caught your attention and write a response to one of those writers.

THE HOMELESS AND THEIR CHILDREN
Jonathan Kozol

In his most famous book, Illiterate America *(1985), Jonathan Kozol says that because more than one-third of America's adults are at least partially illiterate, we should organize a massive government and volunteer army to liberate people imprisoned by illiteracy. More recently, Kozol has written about children in underclass America in* Amazing Grace: The Lives of Children and the Conscience of a Nation *(1996) and* Ordinary Resurrections *(2000). In "The Homeless and Their Children," taken from* Rachel and Her Children *(1988), Kozol investigates individual cases of poverty in a New York City welfare hotel. Although welfare laws have changed and the Martinique Hotel has since been renovated, Kozol's investigative report accurately chronicles the effects of illiteracy on the lives of the poor. Kozol uses his own observations and interview transcripts to demonstrate vividly the connection between illiteracy and poverty. However, instead of arguing indignantly for literacy programs to save the lives of the poor and illiterate, Kozol simply reports the case of a single illiterate woman trying to raise her four children. The woman he calls Laura cannot decipher labels on products at the grocery store, cannot read notices from the welfare office, and cannot understand letters from the hospital warning of her children's lead poisoning.*

The Martinique Hotel, at Sixth Avenue and Thirty-second Street, is one of the largest hotels for homeless people in New York City. When I visited it, in December of 1985, nearly four hundred homeless families, including some twelve hundred children, were lodged in the hotel, by arrangement with the city's Human Resources Administration. One of the residents I spoke to at some length was an energetic, intelligent woman I'll call Kim. During one of our conversations, she mentioned a woman on the seventh floor who had seemingly begun to find her situation intolerable. Kim described this woman as "a broken stick," and offered to arrange for us to meet.

The woman—I will call her Laura, but her name, certain other names, and certain details have been changed—is so fragile that I find it hard to start a conversation when we are introduced, a few nights later. Before I begin, she asks if I will read her a letter from the hospital. The oldest of her four children, a seven-year-old boy named Matthew, has been sick for several weeks. He was tested for lead poisoning in November, and the letter she hands me, from Roosevelt Hospital, says that the child has a dangerous lead level. She is told to bring him back for treatment. She received the letter some weeks ago. It has been buried in a pile of other documents that she cannot read.

Although Laura cannot read, she knows enough about the dangers *3* of lead to grasp the darker implications of this information. The crumbling plaster in the Martinique Hotel is covered with sweet-tasting paint, and children eat or chew chips of the paint as it flakes off the walls. Some of the paint contains lead. Children with lead poisoning may suffer loss of coordination or undergo convulsions. The consequences of lead poisoning may be temporary or long lasting. They may appear at once or not for several years. This final point is what instills so much uneasiness; even months of observation cannot calm a parent's fear.

Lead poisoning, then, is Laura's first concern, but she has other *4* problems. The bathroom plumbing has overflowed and left a pool of sewage on the floor. A radiator valve is broken, and every now and then releases a spray of scalding steam at the eye level of a child. A crib provided by the hotel appears to be unstable. A screw that holds two of its sides together is missing. When I test the crib with my hand, it starts to sway. There are four beds in the room, and they are dangerous, too. They have metal frames with unprotected corners, and the mattresses do not fit the frames; at one corner or another, metal is exposed. If a child has the energy or the playfulness to jump or turn a somersault or wrestle with a friend, and if he falls and strikes his head against the metal corner, the consequences can be serious. The week before, a child on the fourteenth floor fell in just this way, cut his forehead, and required stitches. Most of these matters have been brought to the attention of the hotel management; in Laura's case, complaints have brought no visible results.

All of this would be enough to make life difficult for an illiterate *5* young woman in New York, but Laura has one other urgent matter on her hands. It appears that she has failed to answer a request for information from her welfare office, and, for reasons that she doesn't understand, she did not receive her benefits this week. The timing is bad; it's a weekend. The city operates a crisis center in the Martinique, where residents can go for food and other help, but today the crisis center is not open, so there's nobody around to tide her over with emergency supplies. Laura's children have been eating cheese and bread and peanut butter for two days. "Those on welfare," the Community Service Society of New York said in a report published in 1984, may be suddenly removed from welfare rolls "for reasons unrelated to their actual need," or even to eligibility standards. Welfare workers in New York City call this practice "churning." Laura and her children are being churned.

The room is lighted by fluorescent tubes in a ceiling fixture. They cast a stark light on four walls of greenish paint smeared over with sludge draining from someone's plumbing on the floor above. In the room are two boys with dark and hollowed eyes and an infant girl. A third boy is outside and joins us later. The children have the washed-out look of the children Walker Evans photographed for "Let Us Now Praise Famous Men." Besides the four beds and the crib, the room contains two chairs, a refrigerator, and a television set, which doesn't work. A metal hanger serves as an antenna, but there is no picture on the screen. Instead, there is a storm of falling flakes and unclear lines. I wonder why Laura keeps it on. There are no table lamps to soften the fluorescent glare, no books, no decorations. Laura tells me that her father is of Panamanian birth but that she went to school in New York City. Spanish is her first language. I don't speak Spanish well. We talk in English. *6*

"I cannot read," Laura says. "I buy the New York *Post* to read the pictures. In the grocery, I know what to buy because I see the pictures." *7*

What of no-name products—generic brands, whose labels have no pictures but which could save her a great deal of money? *8*

"If there are no pictures, I don't buy it," she says. "I want to buy pancakes, I ask the lady, 'Where's the pancakes?' So they tell me." *9*

She points to the boys and says, "He's two. He's five. Matthew's seven. My daughter is four months. She has this rash." She shows me ugly skin eruptions on the baby's neck and jaw. "The carpets, they was filthy from the stuff, the leaks that come down on the wall. All my kids have rashes, but the worst she has it. There was pus all over. Somewhere here I have a letter from the nurse." She shuffles around but cannot find the letter. "She got something underneath the skin. Something that bites. The only way you can get rid of it is with a cream." *10*

She finds the letter. The little girl has scabies. *11*

Laura continues, "I have been living here two years. Before I came here, I was in a house we had to leave. There was rats. Big ones, they crawl on us. The rats, they come at night. They come into our house, run over my son's legs. The windows were broken. It was winter. Snow, it used to come inside. My mother lived with us before. Now she's staying at my grandma's house. My grandma's dying in the bed. She's sixty-five. My mother comes here once a week to do the groceries. Tomorrow she comes. Then she goes back to help my grandma. *12*

"I know my name, and I can write my name, my children's names. To read, I cannot do it. Medicines, I don't know the instructions. I was living here when I was pregnant with Corinne. No, I didn't see no doctor. I was hungry. What I ate was rice and beans, potato chips and soda. Up to now this week we don't have food. People ask me, 'Can you *13* help? Do you got this? Do you got that?' I don't like to tell them no. If I have something, I give it. This week, I don't got. I can read baby books—like that, a little bit. If I could read, I would read newspapers. I would like to know what's going on. Matthew, he tells me I am stupid. 'You can't read.' You know, because he wants to read. He don't understand what something is. I tell him, 'I don't know it. I don't understand.' People laugh. You feel embarrassed. On the street. Or in the store." She weeps. "There's nothing here."

Laura sweeps one hand in a wide arc, but I can't tell whether she *14* means the gesture to take in the room or something more. Then she makes her meaning clear: "Everything I had, they put it on the sidewalk when I was evicted. I don't know if that's the law. Things like that—what is the law, what isn't? I can't read it, so I didn't understand. I lost everything I had. I sign papers. Somebody could come and take my children. They could come. 'Sign this. Sign that.' I don't know what it says. Adoption papers—I don't know. This here paper that I got I couldn't understand."

She hands me another letter. This one is from the management of *15* the hotel: "This notice is to inform you that your rent is due today. I would appreciate your cooperation in seeing to it that you go to your center today." Another form that she hands me asks her to fill out the names and the ages of her children.

"Papers, documents—people give it to me. I don't know it: I don't *16* understand." She pauses, and then says, "I'm a Catholic. Yes—I go two weeks ago to church. This lady say they have these little books that learn me how to spell. You see the letters. Put them together. I would like to read. I go to St. Francis' Church. Go inside and kneel—I pray. I don't talk to the priest. I done so many things—you know, bad things. I buy a bottle of wine. A bottle of beer. That costs a dollar. I don't want to say to God. I get a hundred and seventy-three dollars restaurant allowance. With that money I buy clothes. Food stamps, I get two hundred dollars. That's for groceries. Subway tokens I take out ten dollars. Washing machine, I do downstairs. Twenty-five dollars to dry and wash. Five dollars to buy soap. Thirty dollars twice a month."

Another woman at the Martinique calculates her laundry costs at *17* my request, and they come out to nearly the same figure. These may be the standard rates for a midtown site. The difficulty of getting out and traveling to find lower prices, whether for laundromats or for groceries, cannot be overstated. Families at the Martinique are trapped in a commercial district.

I ask Laura who stays with the children when she does her chores. *18*

"My mother keeps the children when I do the wash," she replies. *19* "If she can't, I ask somebody on the floor. 'Give me three dollars. I watch your kids.' For free? Nothing. Everything for money. Everybody's poor."

Extending a hand, she says, "This is the radiator. Something's wrong." She shows me where the steam sprays out. I test it with my hand. "Sometimes it stops. The children get too close. Then it starts—like that! Leak is coming from upstairs down." I see the dark muck on the wall. "The window is broke. Lights broke." She points to the fluorescent tubes. They flicker on and off. "I ask them, 'Please, why don't you give me ordinary lights?' They don't do nothing. So it been two weeks. I go downstairs. They say they coming up. They never come. So I complain again. Mr. Tuccelli—Salvatore Tuccelli, the manager of the Martinique—said to come here to his office. Desks and decorations and a lot of pictures. It's above the lobby. So the manager was there. Mr. Tuccelli sat back in his chair. He had a gun. He had it here under his waist. You know, under his belt. I said, 'Don't show it to me if you isn't going to use it.' I can't tell what kind of gun it was. He had it in his waist. 'You are showing me the gun so I will be afraid.' If he was only going to show it, I would not be scared. If he's going to use it, I get scared. 20

"So he says, 'You people bring us trouble.' I said, 'Why you give my son lead poison and you didn't care? My child is lead-poisoned.' He said, 'I don't want to hear of this again.' What I answer him is this: 'Listen. People like you live in nice apartments. You got a home. You got TV. You got a family. You got children in a school that learn them. They don't got lead poison.' 21

"I don't know the reason for the guards. They let the junkies into the hotel. When my mother comes, I have to sign. If it's a family living good, they make it hard. If it's the drug dealers, they come in. Why they let the junkies in but keep away your mother? The guards, you see them taking women in the corner. You go down twelve-thirty in the night, they're in the corner with the girls. This is true. I seen it." 22

She continues, "How I know about the lead is this: Matthew sits there and he reaches his fingers in the plaster and he put it in his mouth. So I ask him, 'Was you eating it?' He says, 'Don't hit me. Yes, I was.' So then I took him to the clinic and they took the blood. I don't know if something happen to him later on. I don't know if it affects him. When he's older . . . " 23

I ask Laura why she goes to church. 24

"I figure: Go to church. Pray God. Ask Him to help. I go on my knees. I ask Him from my heart. 'Jesus Christ, come help me, please. Why do you leave me here?' When I'm lying down at night, I ask, 'Why people got to live like this?' On the street, the people stare at you when you go out of the hotel. People look. They think, I wonder how they live in there. Sometimes I walk out this door. Garbage all 25 over in the stairs. When it's hot, a lot of bugs around the trash. Sometimes there are fires in the trash. I got no fire escape. You have to get out through the hall. I got no sprinkler. Smoke detector doesn't work. When I cook and food is burning, it don't ring. If I smoke, it starts to ring. I look up. I say, 'Why you don't work? When I need you, you don't work. I'm gonna knock you down.' I did!" She laughs.

There is a sprinkler system in the corridor. In 1987, the hotel man- 26 agement informed residents that the fire-alarm system was "inoperable."

I ask Laura if the older children are enrolled in school. Nodding 27 at Michael, her middle son, she says, "This one doesn't go to school. He's five. I need to call tomorrow. Get a quarter. Then you get some papers. Then you got to sign those papers. Then he can start school.

"For this room I pay fifteen hundred dollars for two weeks. I don't 28 pay. The welfare pays. I got to go and get it." The room, although it is undivided, was originally a two-room suite and is being rented at the two-room rate. "They send me this. I'm suppose to sign. I don't know what it is. Lots of things you suppose to sign. I sign it but I don't know what it is."

While we are talking, Matthew comes in and sits beside his moth- 29 er. He lowers his eyes when I shake his hand.

Laura goes on, "Looking for a house, I got to do it." She explains 30 that she's required to give evidence that she is searching for a place to live. "I can't read, so I can't use the paper. I get dressed. I put my make-up on. If I go like this, they look afraid. They say, 'They going to destroy the house!' You got to dress the children and look nice. Owners don't want homeless. Don't want welfare. Don't want kids. What I think? If they pay one thousand and five hundred dollars every two weeks, why not pay five hundred dollars for a good apartment?"

She hands me another paper. "Can you tell me what is this?"   31

It's a second letter from the hospital, telling her to bring her son 32 for treatment.

She says, "Every day, my son this week, last week was vomiting. 33 Every time he eat his food, he throw it right back out. I got to take him to the clinic.

"Christmas, they don't got. For my daughter I ask a Cabbage 34 Patch. For my boys I ask for toys. I got them stockings." She shows me four cotton stockings tacked to the wall with nothing in them. "They say, 'Mommy, there's no toys.' I say not to worry. 'You are going to get something.' But they don't. They don't get nothing. I could not afford. No, this isn't my TV. Somebody lended it to me. Christmas tree I can't afford. Christmas I don't spend it happy. I am thinking of the kids. What we do on Christmas is we spend it laying on the bed. If I go outside, I feel a little better. When I'm here, I see those walls, the bed, and I feel sad. If I had my own apartment, maybe there would be another room. Somewhere to walk. Walk back and forth."

I ask her, "How do you relax?"   *35*

"If I want to rest, relax, I turn out the light and lie down on the   *36*
bed," she says. "When I met his father, I was seventeen." She says she
knew him before she was homeless, when she lived in Brooklyn with
her mother. He was working at a pizza parlor near her mother's home.
"One night, he bought me liquor. I had never tasted. So he took me to
this hallway. Then my mother say that what I did is wrong. So I say that
I already did it. So you have to live with what you did. I had the baby.
No. I did not want to have abortion. The baby's father I still see. When
he has a job, he brings me food. In the summer, he worked in a flower
store. He would bring me flowers. Now he don't have any job. So he
don't bring me flowers."

She sweeps her hand in a broad arc and says again, "Nothing here.   *37*
I feel embarrassed for the room. Flowers, things like that, you don't
got. Pretty things you don't got. Nothing like that. No."

In the window is a spindly geranium plant. It has no flowers, but   *38*
some of the leaves are green. Before I go, we stand beside the window.
Blowing snow hits the panes and blurs the dirt.

"Some of the rooms high up, they got a view," Laura says. "You see   *39*
the Empire State."

I've noticed this—seen the building from a window. It towers high   *40*
above the Martinique.

"I talk to this plant. I tell him, 'Grow! Give me one flower!' He   *41*
don't do it." Then, in an afterthought, "No pets. No. You don't got.
Animals. They don't allow."

It occurs to me that this is one of the few places I have been ex-   *42*
cept a hospital or a reform school where there are hundreds of children
and virtually no pets. A few people keep cats illegally.

"I wish I had a dog," Laura says. "Brown dog. Something to   *43*
hug."

VOCABULARY

In your journal, write the meanings of the following words:

- the darker *implications* **(3)**
- call this practice "*churning*" **(5)**
- ugly skin *eruptions* **(10)**
- girl has *scabies* **(11)**

QUESTIONS FOR WRITING AND DISCUSSION

1. Describe your intellectual and emotional reaction to Kozol's article. What information about the lives of the poor and illiterate did you already know? What information surprised you? How did Kozol's essay make you feel about this problem?

2. The purpose of an investigative report is to give information without editorializing or arguing for or against a solution. In which paragraphs does Kozol remain most objective and unemotional? Which passages reveal Kozol's sympathy for Laura's situation? Does he avoid editorializing?

3. Reread the essay, marking those places where Laura's illiteracy causes her problems. Based on your notes, explain how her illiteracy (rather than her poverty) causes or magnifies her problems.

4. Describe the investigative techniques that Kozol probably used to write his essay. In addition to his interviews with Laura, what were his other probable sources of information?

5. According to the information provided by Kozol, what support does the welfare system provide Laura and her children? How does the welfare system encourage Laura to improve her life? List three changes that you believe the welfare system should make to solve Laura's problems and make her more self-sufficient.

6. On your next trip to the grocery store, see which products would appeal to an illiterate person. List the items (and their prices) that you might buy based on the pictures on the labels. Write a paragraph describing your findings. Is Kozol correct in assuming that Laura pays too much for her groceries?

7. Jonathan Kozol's latest investigate book, *Ordinary Resurrections* (2000), is a postscript to his earlier works such as *Savage Inequalities: Children in America's Schools* (1992) and *Amazing Grace: The Lives of Children and the Conscience of a Nation* (1995). Use the Internet to access full-text reviews of *Ordinary Resurrections.* On Amazon.com, you will find interesting but mostly positive comments—Amazon is, after all, in the business of selling books. A review in *Newsweek* by Ellis Cose is also positive, but check out Sol Stern's review, "America's Most Influential—And Wrongest—School Reformer," available in full text from Lexis-Nexis. Stern claims, for example, that "Kozol's mistaken but hugely influential diagnosis leads education advocates to keep proposing still more of the wrong cure [giving resources to these schools], while the real causes of school failure—the monopoly public education system, the teachers' unions, and the ed

schools—go on wreaking their damage unimpeded, and inner-city schools keep on failing." Read all of Stern's review. Do you agree or disagree with Stern's analysis? Explain.

Investigating: The Writing Process

■ ASSIGNMENT FOR INVESTIGATING   Choose a subject to investigate: one aspect of a current social or political policy, a scientific discovery or principle, a historical event, a profile of a controversial public figure, or perhaps just an ordinary event, person, process, or place that you find interesting. Your initial purpose should be to discover or learn about your subject. Then, with a specific audience in mind, report your findings. A report presents the information that you find; it should not argue for or against any idea or plan. With the final copy of your investigative report, you must turn in photocopies of any sources you have summarized or cited, notes from your interview(s), and/or copies of questionnaires that you used.

Selecting your audience and genre is especially important for your investigating piece. If an audience is not specified in your assignment, check out newspapers, magazines, websites for appropriate audiences and genres. You may want to do an investigating essay, but perhaps a pamphlet, website, or letter would be more effective. Limiting your audience and selecting a possible newspaper, journal, magazine, forum, or website will help you focus your information. Where possible, think globally but focus locally—what global topic has local implications that you can investigate, and what local publication might be interested in your essay?

CHOOSING A SUBJECT

If one of your journal topics does not suggest a subject for your investigation, consider the following ideas. If you have a subject, go on to the collecting and shaping strategies.

- Choose some idea, principle, process, or theory discussed in a class that you are currently taking. Begin by interviewing classmates, graduate students, or a professor about how to investigate the history, development, or personalities behind this idea. With information from the interview, continue your investigation in the library, looking in appropriate magazines, books, or journals. As you read, focus your question on one narrow or specific area.

- Investigate and report on a campus or community service organization. Choose any academic, minority, cultural, or community organization. Visit the office. Interview an official. Read the organization's literature. Talk to students or community members who have used the service. Check the library for background information. Find people who are dissatisfied with or critical of the organization. Select an audience who might use this service or who might be interested in volunteering for the organization, and report the relevant *who, what, when, where, why,* and/or *how* information.

- At your workplace, investigate how something does or does not work, research how the business (or your part of the business) is organized, do a profile of a coworker, or survey your customers to find out what they like best or least about your store or company.

- For practice, investigate one of the following questions on the Internet and/or in the library (be prepared to explain your answers to your class members): How can you minimize jet lag? Can aspirin prevent heart attacks? How expensive is television advertising? What is a wind tunnel used for? Why is the Antarctic ice shelf melting? How do endorphins work? What is a melanoma? What causes seasonal affective disorder? How does a "Zamboni" work? What effects does Megan's law have? Do Americans spend more money on cosmetics than on education? What are the newest ways to repair torn ACLs (anterior cruciate ligaments) in your knee? What is computer morphing, and how does it work?

- Investigate an academic major, a career, or a job you are interested in. List some of the *who, what, when, where,* and *why* questions you want to answer. Who is interested in this major? What background or courses are required? What is the pay scale or opportunities for advancement? What appeals to you about this major or job? What are the disadvantages of this major or career? Research your major or career on the Internet and in the library. Plan to interview an adviser, a friend who majors in the field, or a person who works at that job. Be prepared to report your findings to your classmates.

COLLECTING

The collecting strategies discussed in Chapters 3, 4, and 5 (brainstorming, clustering, looping, mapping, sketching, reading, summarizing, taking double-entry notes) may be useful as you collect ideas. Other strategies particularly useful for investigating are suggested here. Try each of the following collecting strategies for your subject.

ASKING QUESTIONS   Asking the *right questions* is crucial to investigative writing. Sets of questions (often called *heuristics*) will help you narrow and focus your subject and tailor your approach to the expectations or needs of your audience. You don't know what information you need to collect until you know what questions your investigation needs to answer.

Had I known the answer to any of these questions, I would never have needed to write.

—JOAN DIDION,
ESSAYIST AND NOVELIST

1. The "reporter's" or the familiar "Wh" questions are one basic heuristic: Who? What? When? Where? Why?

   Asking these questions of a topic ensures that you're not leaving out any crucial information. If, for example, you are investigating recreational opportunities in your city or on campus, you might ask the following questions to focus your investigation (remember to ask the *negative* version of each question, too):

   - *Whom* is the recreation for?
   - *Who* runs the programs?
   - *Who* is excluded from the programs?
   - *Who* pays for the programs?
   - *What* is the program?
   - *What* sports are included in the program?
   - *What* sports are not included?
   - *What* is the budget for these programs?
   - *When* are these opportunities available or not available?
   - *Where* do the activities take place?
   - *Where* are they restricted?
   - *Why* are these programs offered?
   - *Why* are certain activities not offered?
   - *Why* have activities been changed?

   These questions might lead you to focus your investigation on the scheduling, on why soccer has been excluded, or on why participants are charged a fee for one class or program but not for another.

2. The classical "topics" provide a second set of questions for an investigation.

Definition:	What is it?
Comparison:	What is it like or unlike?
Relationship:	What caused it? What are its consequences?
Testimony:	What has been said or written about it?

   These questions can be used in conjunction with the reporter's questions to focus an investigation. Applied to the topic on recreational opportunities, the questions might be as follows:

Definition:	What activities exist? How can the activities be described, classified, or analyzed?
Comparison:	What are similarities to or differences from other programs?
Relationship:	What caused these programs to be offered? What causes people to use or avoid these activities? What are the consequences of these programs?

Testimony: What do students think about these activities?
What do administrators think?
What have other schools done?
What does research show?
What proverbs or common sayings apply here?

These two sets of questions will *expand* your information, helping you collect facts, data, examples, and ideas—probably more than you can use in a short essay. Once you have all of this information, you can then *narrow* your topic.

USING THE LIBRARY   Knowing how to use a library is crucial for most investigations. For this essay, you will not need to do exhaustive research on your topic, but you will need some background information, statistics, or information about current research, public opinion trends, or recent discoveries. Chapter 12, "Writing a Research Paper," will answer your research questions in more depth, but you can get information quickly in a library by using a few key sources.

- **Ask librarians for assistance**. Every library has librarians stationed at information desks, checkout counters, or reference desks whose job is to answer your questions. Be sure to ask for their advice when you need it. Because frustration is the number-one enemy of research projects, ask for assistance early in your investigation. The best procedure is simply to explain your project—what you intend to do and have done so far—and ask for advice or help. *There are no stupid questions in a library.*

- **Acquaint yourself with the basic sources of information in the library**. Most libraries offer group tours that familiarize their users with the location and use of the following:
  The online catalog
  CD-ROM access
  Internet and Web access
  Microfilm and microfiche room
  Current periodical room
  Basic references such as encyclopedias, almanacs, and dictionaries

USING THE INTERNET AND THE WEB In the library, in a computer lab, or at home, access the Internet to get information about your possible topic. Use your favorite search engine to start with, but then be sure to try other sites you have not tried. Search engines can be hierarchical (Yahoo), standard search engines (Alta Vista, Excite, HotBot), alternative search engines (Northern Light, Ask Jeeves, Google), and meta search engines, which search other engines (Dogpile, MetaCrawler). For most informal research projects, however, if you use the big three—Yahoo, Google, and Alta Vista—you will probably cover your field.

In addition, check out the following sites:

- The Electric Library at http://ask.elibrary.com will give you access to articles on popular topics.
- The Internet Public Library at http://ipl.org will give you access to a library environment that looks like your public library.
- The WWW Virtual Library at http://vlib.org will access a variety of sources and articles

USING WRITTEN AND ELECTRONIC SOURCES

- **When printed copies are not available directly from your computer access, make photocopies of relevant articles.** The small amount of money you spend on copies will enable you to reread articles if necessary, quote or paraphrase from them accurately, and cite them accurately as references. (The money you spend is also excellent anti-frustration insurance, in case you return to the library stacks and discover that someone else has checked out your magazine or book.) On your photocopies, be sure to write *source information*: magazine or book title, author, publisher, date and place of publication, volume, and page numbers. For this investigative report, remember that you must turn in photocopies of any pages of articles or books you use.
- **Make notes and summaries from your photocopied sources**. As you collect information from photocopied sources, jot down key facts, ideas, and direct quotations. For every note you take, record the author, title, publishing information, and page numbers. You may *paraphrase*

another writer's ideas, examples, sentences, or short passages by writing them in your own words. Use *direct quotation* when words or phrases in a source are more striking than your paraphrase might be. You may edit a direct quotation by (1) deleting any irrelevant or unnecessary words or phrases by using ellipsis points (three spaced periods) to indicate the deleted words and by (2) inserting your own words in square brackets [] if you need to clarify a quoted passage. Otherwise, the words within the quotation marks must accurately reproduce the original: No altered spellings, changed words, or rephrasings are allowed.

- **Avoid plagiarism.** Use quotation marks whenever you quote more than a word or two from your source. Paraphrase in your own words rather than stringing together phrases and sentences written by someone else. Give credit for ideas, facts, and language by citing your sources. In informal investigative writing, you may simply mention the author and title of written sources, citing page numbers of direct quotations in parentheses. (All formal research papers and some investigative essays cite sources in full in a "Works Cited" section at the end. See Chapter 12, "Writing a Research Paper," for more details.)

SUMMARIZING   As explained in Chapter 5, a *summary* is a concise explanation of the main and supporting ideas in a passage, report, essay, book, or speech. It is usually written in the present tense. It identifies the author and title of the source; it may refer to the context or the actual place where the study took place; it contains the passage's main ideas; and it may quote directly a few forceful or concise sentences or phrases. It will not usually cite the author's examples. A *paraphrase* usually expresses all the information in the passage—including examples—in your own words. Summary, paraphrase, and direct quotation often occur together as you use sources. (See Chapter 5 for more details.)

CITING SOURCES IN YOUR TEXT   As you collect information, you should note authors, titles of books or magazines, dates of publication, publishers, and page numbers to give proper credit to your sources. For some journalistic writing, you may need to cite only the author, the title of your source, or both:

According to Constance Hale, associate managing editor of *Wired* magazine, "Sherry Turkle . . . was way ahead of the curve" **(2)**.

Newsweek magazine listed Sherry Turkle among their "50 for the Future" **(2)**.

For a more formal, academic context, the MLA (Modern Language Association) requires that the author and page numbers be given, in parentheses, at the end of the sentence—for example "(Turkle 24–25)":

A key point in *Life on the Screen: Identity in the Age of the Internet* is that we can "embrace—or be trapped by—cyberspace as a way of life" (Turkle 25).

If you refer to the author in the sentence that contains the citation, indicate just the page numbers in parentheses.

In her book, *Life on the Screen: Identity in the Age of the Internet,* Turkle argues that we can "embrace—or be trapped by—cyberspace as a way of life" (25).

For additional information on formal, in-text citation, consult Chapter 12, "Writing a Research Paper."

INTERVIEWING   After you have done some initial research, interviews are a logical next step. Remember that the more you know about the subject (and the person you're interviewing), the more productive the interview will be. In planning an interview, keep the following steps in mind:

1. Make an *appointment* with the person you wish to interview. Although you may feel hesitant or shy about calling or e-mailing someone for an interview, remember that most people are flattered that someone else is interested in them and wants to hear their opinions or learn about their areas of expertise.

2. Make a *list of questions*, in an appropriate *sequence*, that you can ask during the interview. The interview itself will generate additional topics, but your list will jog your memory if the interview gets off the track. Begin with relatively objective or factual questions and work your way, gradually, to the more subjective questions or controversial issues. Try to phrase your questions so that they require more than a yes or no answer.

3. Begin the interview by introducing yourself and describing *your* investigation. Keep your biases or opinions out of the questions. Be sure to *listen* carefully and ask follow-up questions: "What information do you have on that? What do the statistical studies suggest? In your opinion, do these data show any trends? What memorable experiences have you had relating to this topic?" Like a dog with a good bone, a reporter doesn't drop a topic until the meat's all gone.

4. During the interview, *take notes*, and, if appropriate, use a tape recorder to ensure accuracy. Don't hesitate to ask your interviewee to repeat or clarify a statement. Remember: People want you to get the facts right and quote them accurately. Especially if you're doing a personality profile, describe notable features of your interviewee: hair color, facial features, stature, dress, gestures, and nervous habits, as well as details about the room or surroundings. Finally, don't forget to ask your interviewee for

additional leads or sources. At the conclusion of the interview, express your thanks and ask if you can check with him or her later, perhaps by e-mail, for additional details or facts.

5.   Immediately after the interview, go over your notes. If you recorded the interview, listen to the tape and transcribe important responses. List other questions you may still have.

WRITING QUESTIONNAIRES Questionnaires are useful when you need to know the attitudes, preferences, or opinions of a large group of people. If you are surveying customers in your business, you may discover that 39 percent of those surveyed would prefer that your business stay open an additional hour, from 5 P.M. to 6 P.M. If you are surveying students to determine their knowledge of geography, you might discover that only 8 percent can correctly locate Beirut on a map of the Middle East. The accuracy and usefulness of a survey depend on the kinds of questions you ask, on the number of people you survey, and on the sample of people you select to respond to your questionnaire.

Open questions are easy to ask, but the answers can be difficult to interpret. For example, if you want to survey customers at a department store where you work, you might ask questions requiring a short written response:

- What is your opinion of the service provided by clerks at Macy's?
- What would make your shopping experience at Macy's more enjoyable?

While these questions may give you interesting—and often reliable—responses, the results may be difficult to tabulate. Open questions are often valuable in initial surveys because they can help you to determine specific areas or topics for further investigation.

Closed questions are more typical than open questions in surveys. They limit the responses so that you can focus on a particular topic and accurately tabulate the responses. Following are several types of closed questions:

- *Yes/no questions:* Have you shopped at Macy's in the last three months?
  - _____ Yes
  - _____ No
- *Multiple choice:* How far did you travel to come to Macy's?
  - _____ 0–5 miles
  - _____ 5–10 miles
  - _____ 10–15 miles
  - _____ Over 15 miles
- How would you characterize the salespeople at Macy's?
  - _____ Exceptionally helpful
  - _____ Helpful
  - _____ Indifferent

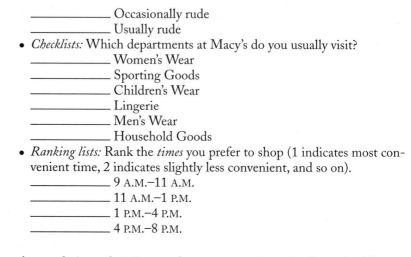

_____ Occasionally rude
_____ Usually rude

- *Checklists:* Which departments at Macy's do you usually visit?
  _____ Women's Wear
  _____ Sporting Goods
  _____ Children's Wear
  _____ Lingerie
  _____ Men's Wear
  _____ Household Goods
- *Ranking lists:* Rank the *times* you prefer to shop (1 indicates most convenient time, 2 indicates slightly less convenient, and so on).
  _____ 9 A.M.–11 A.M.
  _____ 11 A.M.–1 P.M.
  _____ 1 P.M.–4 P.M.
  _____ 4 P.M.–8 P.M.

As you design, administer, and use your questionnaire, keep the following tips in mind:

- Limit and focus your questions so that respondents can fill out the questionnaire quickly.
- Avoid loaded or biased questions. For example, don't ask, "How do you like the high-quality merchandise in Macy's sports department?"
- At the top of your questionnaire, write one or two sentences describing your study and thanking participants.
- Pretest your questionnaire by giving it to a few people. Based on their oral and written responses, focus and clarify your questions.
- Use a large sample group. Thirty responses will give you more accurate information about consumer attitudes than will three responses.
- Make your sample as *random* or as evenly representative as possible. Don't survey customers on only one floor, in only one department, or at only one time of day.
- Be sure to include a copy of your questionnaire with your article or essay.

But for whom have I tried so steadfastly to communicate? Who have I worried over in this writing? Who is my audience?

—CHERRIE MORAGA,

SOCIAL CRITIC AND POET

Note: If you intend to do a formal study using questionnaires, check your library for additional sources to help you design and administer statistically reliable surveys.

SHAPING

As you begin shaping your material, reconsider your purpose and audience. Limit your subject to create a *narrowed* and *focused* topic. Don't try to cover everything; focus on *the most interesting questions and information.* Take the time to write out a statement of your topic, key questions, purpose, and audience. Then try the following strategies.

INVERTED PYRAMID A common form for reports, especially in journalism, is the *inverted pyramid.* The writer begins with a succinct but arresting title, opens the story with a sentence or short paragraph that answers the reporter's "Wh" questions, and then fills in the background information and details in order of importance, from the *most important* to the *least important.*

Writers use the inverted pyramid when concrete information and the convenience of the reader are most important. The advantage of the inverted pyramid is that a hurried reader can quickly gather the most important information and determine whether the rest of the story is worth reading. The disadvantage is that some details or information may be scattered or presented out of clear sequence. In investigative writing, therefore, writers often supplement the inverted pyramid with other forms of development: chronological order, definition, classification, or comparison/contrast.

"Wh" question lead: Who, What, When, Where, Why
Most important information and details

Important information and details

Least important
information and
details

CHRONOLOGICAL ORDER Often, writers present their information in the order in which they discovered it, enabling the reader to follow the research as if it were a narrative or a story. In this format, the writer presents the steps of the investigation, from the earliest incidents, to the discoveries along the way, to the final pieces of information.

Elizabeth Larsen, for example, uses chronological order to make a story out of her report on websites in art history. The following sentences—most of them appearing at the beginning of paragraphs—illustrate how she uses time signals ("first," "today," "started," "my next stop," and "then") to create an interesting story about surfing the Web.

I first studied art history the old-fashioned way: scribbling notes in a dark auditorium . . .

Inspired by the sheer volume of images available . . . I decided to try my hand at digitally designing my own art education.

My self-directed syllabus started in Spain . . .

Eager to see more, I moved on to the Museums page of the **World Wide Web Virtual Library**.

I started in Italy, which I soon discovered doesn't include . . . the Vatican.

My next stop was Paris, where my first visit was to . . . the Louvre.

From Giverny I hopped over to Greece . . .

As these sentences illustrate, chronological order can transform a potentially boring list of websites into an interesting narrative journey through the information.

DEFINITION Definitions are central to investigating and reporting, whether they shape only a sentence or two or several paragraphs. In her article on Sherry Turkle, Connie Koenenn uses an informal definition of MUDS in order to shape one paragraph. Her definition helps us understand how the Internet can alter our real-life identity:

> Beginning in her own backyard, Turkle organized pizza parties for students playing MUDS (Multi-User-Domains), the intricate online games in which participants can alter their real-life identities to improvise elaborate melodramas.

COMPARISON AND CONTRAST Comparison and contrast are as essential to investigating and reporting as they are to observing and remembering. Consider how Lance Morrow uses comparison to shape the opening paragraphs of a *Time* magazine essay on AIDS. In this essay, entitled "The Start of a Plague Mentality," Morrow notes the similarities between attitudes created by a plague 200 years ago and contemporary attitudes toward AIDS.

> An epidemic of yellow fever struck Philadelphia in August 1793. Eyes glazed, flesh yellowed, minds went delirious. People died, not individ-

ually, here and there, but in clusters, in alarming patterns. A plague mentality set in. Friends recoiled from one another. If they met by chance, they did not shake hands but nodded distantly and hurried on. The very air felt diseased. People dodged to the windward of those they passed. They sealed themselves in their houses. The deaths went on, great ugly scythings. . . .

In the past four years, some 6,000 people have died of AIDS in the U.S. From a statistical point of view, AIDS is not a major plague. Still, one begins to detect a plague mentality regarding the disease and those who carry it.

ANALYSIS In the process of investigating any subject, writers frequently use analysis to organize or shape their writing. Analysis simply involves dividing a whole into its parts. In order to explain how the web works, Gene Cowan uses analysis to shape his brief article. The computer's server, he explains, breaks the URL down "into its parts, much like a mailing address." Those key parts, Cowan explains, are the protocol (http), the address name (as in www.yahoo.com), and the directory path (as in /headlines/pl/story.html).

ADDITIONAL SHAPING STRATEGIES Other shaping strategies, discussed in previous chapters, may be useful for your investigation, too. *Classifying people*, *places*, or *things* may help organize your investigation. *Simile, metaphor,* or *analogy* may develop and shape parts of your article. Even in investigative reporting, writers may create an identifiable *persona* or adopt a humorous tone. In the examples of reports given earlier in this chapter, Anastasia Toufexis, Jeff Meer, and Joan Barthel assume a reporter's objective persona and use a serious, straightforward tone. In contrast, Elizabeth Larsen, in "Surfin' the Louvre," establishes a friendly and humorous tone: "That's a heck of a lot more reproductions than you'll find in that chiropractically unfriendly art history text, H.W. Janson's *History of Art*." Larsen demonstrates that even journalistic writing can have a sense of fun.

TITLE, INTRODUCTION, AND CONCLUSION Especially in an investigative report, a catchy title is important to help get your readers' interest and attention. Jot down several ideas for titles now and add to that list *after* you've drafted your essay.

In your introductory paragraph(s), answering the "Wh" questions will help focus your investigation. Or you may wish to use a short *narrative*, as Larsen does in "Surfin' the Louvre." Joan Barthel begins her article with stories from Oprah Winfrey's life, pointing out that her profile "is not just the story of a survivor, though she obviously is one." Other types of lead-ins, such as a short *description*, a *question*, a *statement of a problem*, a *startling fact* or *statistic*, or an arresting *quotation*, may get the reader's interest and focus on the main idea you wish to investigate. (See Chapter 7 for additional examples of lead-ins.)

The conclusion should resolve the question or questions posed in the investigation, summarize the most important information (useful primarily for long or complicated reports), and give the reader a sense of completion, often by picking up an idea, fact, quotation, narrative, or bit of description used in the introduction.

Some writers like to have a title and know how they're going to start a piece of writing before they begin drafting. However, if you can't think of the perfect title or introduction, begin drafting, and continue working on the title, the introduction, and the conclusion after the first draft.

DRAFTING

Before you begin a first draft, reconsider your purpose in writing and further focus your questions, sense of audience, and shaping strategies.

All good writing is swimming under water and holding your breath.

—**F. SCOTT FITZGERALD,**

AUTHOR OF <u>THE GREAT GATSBY</u>

The actual drafting of an investigative essay requires that you have all your facts, statistics, quotations, summaries, notes from interviews, or results of surveys ready to use. Organize your notes, decide on an overall shaping strategy, or write a sketch outline. In investigative writing, a primary danger is postponing writing too long in the mistaken belief that if you read just one more article or interview just one more person, you'll get the information you need. At some point, usually *before* you feel ready, you must begin writing. (Professional writers rarely feel they know enough about their subject, but deadlines require them to begin.) Your main problem, you'll quickly discover, will be having too much to say rather than not enough. If you have too much, go back to your focusing questions and see whether you can narrow your topic further.

REVISING

After you have drafted your essay, you may wish to get some feedback from your peers about your work in progress. The peer response guidelines below will help you to review your goals for this investigative assignment and to construct a revision plan. When you read other students' drafts or ideas, be as constructively critical as possible. Think carefully about the assignment. Be honest about your own reactions as a reader. What would make the draft better?

PEER RESPONSE

The instructions that follow will help you give and receive constructive advice about the rough draft of your investigating essay. You may use these guidelines for an in-class workshop, a take-home review, or a computer e-mail response.

Writer: Before you exchange drafts with another reader, write out the following on your essay draft or in an e-mail message:

1. *Purpose.* Briefly, describe your purpose and intended audience. For your audience, write out the title of a newspaper or magazine that might print your investigative report.

2. *Revision plans.* Obviously, your draft is just a draft. What still needs work as you continue revising? Explain. (You don't want your reader to critique problems you are already intending to fix.)

3. *Questions.* Write out one or two questions that you still have about your draft. What questions would you like your reader to answer?

Reader: First, read the entire draft from start to finish. As you reread the draft, answer the following questions:

1. *Purpose.* Remember that the purpose of this essay is to accurately and objectively report information, not argue or editorialize. Does this writer go beyond reporting to editorializing or arguing? If so, point out specific sentences that need revision.

2. *Evidence.* List the kinds of evidence the writer uses. What additional kinds of sources might the writer use: an additional interview? a source on the Web? personal observation? other print sources? a survey? Make a specific suggestion about additional, appropriate sources.

3. *Key investigative question.* When you read the essay, the key question should become apparent. Write it out. If there are places in the essay that don't relate to that key question, should they be omitted? Explain. Are there other aspects of the key question that the writer should address? Explain.

4. *Reader's response.* An investigative essay should satisfy your curiosity about the topic. What did you want to learn about the topic that the essay did not answer? Write out any questions that you would like the writer to answer as he or she revises the essay.

5. *Answer the writer's questions in Number 3.*

Guidelines for Revision

As you add, delete, substitute, or rearrange materials, keep the following tips in mind:

- **Reexamine your purpose and audience:** Are you doing what you intended? You should be *reporting* your findings; you should *not* be arguing for or against any idea.
- **Is the form of your essay or report responsive to audience needs and expectations?** Use samples of other writing for your audience (from newspapers, magazines, or journals) as models.
- **Can you add any of your own observations or experiences to the investigation?** Remember that your own perceptions and experiences as a reporter are also relevant data.
- **Review the reporter's "Wh" questions.** Are you providing your readers with relevant information *early* in the report and also catching their interest with a key statistic, fact, quotation, example, question, description, or short narrative?
- **Recheck your summaries, paraphrases, or direct quotations.** Are they accurate, and have you cited these sources in your text?
- **Use signals, cues, and transitions to indicate your shaping strategies:**
  Chronological order: before, then, afterward, next, soon, later, finally, at last
  Comparison/contrast: likewise, similarly, however, yet, even so, in contrast
  Analysis: first, next, third, fourth, finally
- **Revise sentences for directness, clarity, and conciseness.** Avoid unnecessary passive voice.
- **Edit your report for appropriate word choice, usage, and grammar.** Check your writing for problems in spelling and punctuation.

■ POSTSCRIPT ON THE WRITING PROCESS   While the process of writing an investigative essay is still fresh in your mind, answer the following questions in your journal.

We are all apprentices at a craft where no one ever becomes a master.

—ERNEST HEMINGWAY, NOVELIST

1. What sources of information (articles, books, interviews, surveys) were most helpful in your investigation? Explain.
2. Most researchers discover that the more they learn, the more they still need to know about their subjects. If you had more time to work on this essay, which sources would you investigate further?
3. What was the most difficult problem you had to solve during your collecting, shaping, drafting, and revising? What helped you most as you tried to solve this problem (further reading, additional writing, advice from peers)? Explain.
4. What was the single most important thing you learned about investigating as you wrote this paper?
5. What do you like best about the final version of your investigative report?

THE HOLLYWOOD INDIAN

Lauren Strain

As the granddaughter of a Cherokee Indian, Lauren Strain decided to investigate how Native Americans have been portrayed in Hollywood films. How accurately have films such as Dances with Wolves, The Last of the Mohicans, *and Disney's* Pocahontas *portrayed American Indians? What stereotypes are presented in these films? Which Native American actors have helped change these stereotypes? In order to answer these questions, Stain watched old films, interviewed her grandfather, and researched several popular films about American Indians.*

Investigating Paper Proposal

Being a quarter Indian, I have grown up with only a few Indian images in my life. Those images come from my grandfather, a Cherokee, and from the Indians in movies and on television. I have always been curious about Hollywood's portrayal of Indians. My grandfather, being adopted, did not grow up with any traditional Indian beliefs or values, so I heard of none. So I wonder if my perceptions about Indian culture and value systems are correct. I would like to look into that more for my paper.

Using sources from movies, TV, photos and articles, I would like to go into the Native American resource center and speak to a full-blood Indian who has experienced some of the traditional ways and values. Using my grandfather as a resource will also be an option. I would like to ask him how he felt seeing the images of Indians on television, and if he thought that they truly reflected how he saw himself as an Indian.

I would start out my paper with the perception of Tonto in *The Lone Ranger*. Using Sherman Alexie's story, *The Lone Ranger and Tonto Fistfight in Heaven* as one view of Tonto, I would continue with written accounts of the actor who played Tonto in the TV show. Next, I would look at Hollywood's perceptions of Indians on reservations. I could use *Smoke Signals* and other movies for those images. I will also look for movie reviews in journals in the library's database for any articles on Indians in Hollywood. I will finish my paper with the perception of the traditional "soak" Indian in Hollywood—I mean when Indians had just been taken over by the white man. For this I will use old westerns and the written and visual accounts of the movies *Dances with Wolves* and *The Last of the Mohicans*.

I am looking forward to this assignment, although it will be challenging to collect all of the information. It will, however, give me the chance to talk with other Indians and perhaps I will be able to grow as a person as well as a Cherokee Indian. I will also have a reason to ask my grandfather all of the questions that I have had for him ever since I was a child. I would like to direct this paper to all white and red people to help them see that although many of us believe almost everything we see on television and in movies, some of that information might be false. It will be a journey to find out what is true and what is false about some of the first people to inhabit America.

Outline: The Hollywood Indian

I.   Introduce Topic
   A.   How are Indians portrayed in Hollywood?
   B.   Grandfather Cherokee and how I grew up with the TV and movie Indians as my models.
   C.   Introduce movies like *Dances with Wolves* and *The Last of the Mohicans.*

II.   Movie portrayal of Native Americans
   A.   The accurate portrayal and inaccurate portrayal of *Dances with Wolves.*
   B.   *The Last of the Mohicans*—are they really gone?
   C.   *Pocahontas*—an inaccurate portrayal of true women?
   D.   Jack Strain's account of Indians on the reservation in the movie theaters.
   E.   Tonto.

III.   Indian actors and their movies
   A.   *Outlaw Josey Wales* (Chief Dan George)
   B.   *Maverick* (Graham Green)
   C.   *Last of the Mohicans* (Russell Means)

IV.   Movies and ideals of Native Americans throughout history
   A.   The early movie portrayal of Native American.
   B.   President Ulysses S. Grant's quote and ideal.
   C.   John Ford's *Stagecoach* interprets Indians as enemies.

V.   Conclusions
   A.   My own beliefs of how Native Americans are portrayed in Hollywood
   B.   Interview with a Native American student at CSU and what his or her views are about Native Americans in movies

The Hollywood Indian

I am the granddaughter of an adopted Cherokee who grew up *1* knowing only the ways of the white man. Not knowing much about the traditional American Indian, my only perceptions of them were through movies and Hollywood. Now that I am older, I stop and ask myself: What is the perception of Indians in Hollywood movies? Some of the most popular movies portraying Indians came out in my younger years (late 1980's early 1990's). I remember sneaking in to watch *Dances with Wolves* with my parents in the movie theater, which is a source of my perceptions of Indians. I even watched *Last of the Mohicans* in my freshman history class. Not only do I wonder how accurate movies like these are, I am very curious about the actors who play the Indians. During this research I want to answer certain questions. Are recent movies historically correct and do they eliminate stereotypes that people have given to Native Americans? What Native American actors have helped to portray their people accurately? And lastly, how has history helped to portray Native Americans better?

Three films that, despite historical inaccuracies, helped to popu- *2* larize the life and culture of Native Americans were *Dances with Wolves*, *Last of the Mohicans*, and *Pocahontas*. *Dances with Wolves* has been the most critically acclaimed movie that portrays the "correct" Indian. When asking my grandfather about whether or not he thought this movie was a correct portrayal, he said, "Yes, except for one thing." He told me that at the end of the movie, you see a winter camp deep in the mountains. The Indians would never keep their camp that deep in the mountains during the winter; they would move on to a warmer place. This was a detail that I had never known about. In Armando J. Prats' essay about the comparison between the two cinematic versions of *Dances with Wolves*, he states that there was a normal film version shown in the theaters and the one released in a TV miniseries that added scenes. He brings up a very valid point: even though, in this movie, the Indians are portrayed in a valid way, the story's main character is a white man. This title is even the white man's given Indian name (3). Watching the movie myself, I noticed that the portrayal of the Sioux Indians was very human and realistic to tradition. The film showed strong bonds between family and tribesmen. I too—as well as many others I know—also have strong bonds with family and friends. The Indian characters even had a sense of humor, which also helped me connect to them easier.

The movie *Last of the Mohicans* is also a very realistic film but it *3* has some historical misrepresentations. It takes place during the French and Indian War in 1757. This movie was shown to me in my freshman history class to illustrate brutalities of the war itself. Those details of the movie were portrayed very clearly. In one scene, an Indian from the Mohawk tribe eats the heart of a British general. I am not quite sure whether or not this type of brutality actually happened but I do know that scalpings were regular occurrences during the French and Indian War. Just like humans today, people kill people in savage ways. And although there are many accurate historical details about the war itself, like the Mohegan tribe helping out the settlers in Canada, there are misrepresentations about the details concerning the Mohegan tribe.

One plot point that is incorrect is that the Mohegan tribe is extinct, as the movie suggests. Melissa Sayet, in her essay "The Lasting of the Mohegans," tells us "[I am] a Mohegan Indian, alive and well in 1993" (1). The Mohegan tribe still exists, although it is very small, in Uncasville, Connecticut. The small tribe has a church, museum and an all-Indian run institution that has existed for sixty-two years to help show their history. Sayet tells us that the media is responsible for putting the thought into people's heads that the tribe has been dead for a long time. The myth was actually created by Lydia Howard Sigourney. Sayet writes, "It seems that it was far easier for Lydia to romanticize dead Mohegan's than to deal with the realities of alcoholism and poverty among living ones" (2). A well-known poet that knew of the Mohegan tribe, Sigourney wrote of their extinction anyway.

An additional inaccuracy in *The Last of the Mohicans,* although it may be small, is that the spelling of the tribe's name is different in the movie compared to the spelling that the tribe uses (Mohican vs. Mohegan). According to Sayet, this was because of the miscommunication between the tribe and Europeans during first contact. The Mohegan tribe did not have an alphabet to help convey the correct spelling (2). Another reason for the misspelling is the fact that there are two tribes with the same name spelled differently. One tribe comes from Connecticut and the other from the Hudson Valley in New York. The author of *The Last of the Mohicans* just accidentally switched the names unknowingly, according to the First Nations Web Site (*First Nations*).

When I watched the movie, I saw the romantic reasons for saying that the tribe was extinct at the end. The Mohegan men were very stoic, smart, athletic and heroic. I have never met a Mohegan Indian, so I am not sure how they carry themselves. I do know that not all the Indians were known heroes. It was hard not to fall in love with these characters, though. The movie was designed to pull at your heart. In the end, when the character Changachook, the father of Uncas and the second-to-last Mohegan, tells us he is the only remaining Mohegan, it is very convincing and sad. This is how Hollywood wants us to feel. If movies did not leave people with any type of feeling, whether humor, sadness or happiness, then there would be no reason to watch.

In contrast to the more accurate portrayals of Native Americans in *Dances with Wolves* and *Last of the Mohicans,* a third poplar Native American film, *Pocahontas*, is very inaccurate historically speaking. Disney's version of *Pocahontas* focuses on a very historic American Indian. This movie is very factually inaccurate, however. The Indians were portrayed as very peaceful and loving in this film. Pocahontas is an Indian princess who falls in love with the handsome John Smith, an English soldier looking for land in the New World. She ends up saving his life, and he asks her to come with him back to England to be his wife. She declines his offer, saying she could never leave her family and her land.

The true story of Pocahontas is different in many ways. The age of the character in the Disney movie seems to be in her early twenties. The real Pocahontas was sixteen years old. She did save the life of John Smith, but she fell in love with his friend, John Rolfe. She also ended up leaving America and going to England to marry him. Shortly upon her arrival, she died of smallpox. Although the film is historically inaccurate, telling children the real story of Pocahontas would not have been a wise decision on the part of Disney. They like to show a happy story that promotes values. A sixteen-year-old girl marrying an older man is not a common thing these days. Plus, the main character never dies in Disney movies. I can see why Disney changed the story. They did, however, keep the happy and peaceful image of the Indians, thus promoting them; but they didn't tell the story in a historically correct manner.

The second question that I had was who were/are the Native American actors who have helped Hollywood portray a historically unstereotypical Indian? Three of the most recognized Indian actors in Hollywood who have portrayed historically accurate Indian characters are Graham Green, Russell Means, and Chief Dan George.

Graham Green is best known for his portrayal of Kicking Bird in *Dances with Wolves*. He received an Academy Award Nomination for best supporting actor for that role. Green is also a well-known draftsman, steel worker, civil technologist, and sound engineer. He graduated from a Native American theater school, where his comedy skills shined (*Graham Green*).

We see Green's comic acting shine through in the movie *Maverick.* In this movie, his character, Joseph, is earning money for his tribe by running around in war paint and having his tribe beat their drums for a European who wants to experience the "real west." When we see him encounter the European, he begins to speak the man's native language. When the European tells Joseph to speak as they do in the movies, Joseph says "How, white man," a stereotypical greeting. Joseph tells his friend Maverick how stupid he feels acting as if he is foolish and savage when in fact we see he is a very intellectual person (*Maverick*). I believe that Graham Green chose this role because he was able to show people how inaccurate and stupid the stereotypical Indian can be, when in reality Indians can be intellectual, caring people.

Russell Means is known more for his work outside Hollywood, but   12
he is still praised for the roles he has taken in movies. He has been involved in civil rights for Native Americans since the 1960s. He has also done work with the United Nations for over twelve years. His most recent spot in the public eye was not in a movie, but rather in the demonstration against Columbus Day celebrations. Means got involved in acting in 1991. His most recognizable role was in *Last of the Mohicans,* where he plays the eldest Mohegan, a wise and brave man. His character was the leader of the family of Mohegans in this movie and he never strayed and helped to keep the spirit of the tribe alive when it was "lost" with the passing of his son.

Chief Dan George (1899–1981) also helped to show film view-   13
ers that American Indians were intelligent and civilized and not the typical savages. George was the chief of the Salish Band in the Burrard Inlet, in British Columbia, Canada. He was a very gifted actor and the author of many books, such as *My Heart Soars* and *My Spirit Soars*. George was also nominated for an Academy Award for his role in *Little Big Man.* He was also in the TV miniseries "Centennial" (*Chief Dan George*).

In the movie *The Outlaw Josey Wales,* Chief Dan George's char-   14
acter, Lone Watie, explains to Josey Wales how he was part of the tribe the white man called "the civilized tribe," or the Cherokee. His character is wearing a top hat and a suit when we first see him in the film. He tells Wales that he dressed up as Abe Lincoln to impress Lincoln when he met him. Later we see Watie burning his clothes, wearing less casual traveling garments. He tells Wales how he forgot things and lost his way when he became "civilized" (*The Outlaw Josie Wales*). The clothes Chief Dan George wore in that movie were very symbolic in the story that he told. Although these were the words of a fictional character, I believe that they helped reflect the struggle of a Native American to be accepted as "civilized." Because of Hollywood, these struggles and lifestyles were able to get out to movie watchers.

The final question I was curious about was when and if historical   15
events helped to change the portrayal of Native Americans in Hollywood. The change from the savage enemy Indian came with World War II because the Nazis became the enemy rather then Native Americans. Angela Aleiss writes, "Previous images of menacing warriors who blocked Westward expansion gradually began to fade into one in

which Indians stood as allies, rather than enemies, alongside America's frontier heroes" (1). Most movies changed stereotypes, but there were still some that had inaccurate portrayals like *Geronimo* (1939) and *They Died With Their Boots On* (1941).

My grandfather grew up next to a reservation before World War 16 II, so I asked him in my interview how Native Americans reacted to the westerns depicting them as the enemy. He told me that most of them went to the movies for the cartoons before the movie itself. "They did not show any emotional reaction to it," he said. I found it interesting that they would even go to the movies at all. When telling my grandfather this, he told me that, "It was a way for the Indians to break into the western culture." That helped me to understand their reasons for going.

When conducting my survey of students in my class, three out of 17 ten thought that movies still portray Indians in a stereotypically savage manner. Two of them thought that Hollywood was doing a good job in the portrayal of the "correct" Native American. One person wrote, "Hollywood is more worried about offending anybody who is not white. Because people today are very sensitive, everyone, including Hollywood, watches what they say and do."

In addition to the change brought on by World War II, Aleiss 18 tells us that there were three other contributions. The first one was to keep the relations between America, the United Kingdom, and Canada on good terms. Puritanical leaders wanted a good portrayal of Americans with other races. The second contribution, Alesiss says, is "the pro-interventionist politics of Hollywood studios [that] helped to create a mindset that would reshape the Indians image at least two years before America's entry into the war" (2). Hollywood executives were trying to rid the movie industry of fascist ideals. The final element was that the image of the ally Indian was not a fad, but rather a gateway for other Western movie themes.

Throughout my research, I have found that Native Americans 19 are portrayed in a very positive light. The negative stereotypical Indian has slowly faded with images of "the true west." Although there are still few exceptions, one aspect that I see in movies with Native Americans is historical details being left out. For example, the Mohegan tribe still existing and the movie *Last of the Mohicans* portraying their extinction. Also, the Indians in the last scene of *Dances with Wolves*, who use an incorrect stopping ground during the winter. I believe that Hollywood is concerned about offending Native Americans, but historical context comes into play in what they write and put in movies. Hollywood has a duty to add accurate historical context to the films; movies are taken very seriously in today's culture. Children learn from what they see in movies and on TV. But should

Hollywood risk a good story just for entertainment value? I believe that the film industry can mix fact and fiction while still pulling off a good story. They should learn the correct history of America and all its people.

Work Cited

Aleiss, Angela. "Prelude to World War II: Racial Unity and the Hollywood Indian." *Journal of American Culture* 43403 (Summer 1995): 25–34.

Chief Dan George. Indigenous Peoples Literature. 14 December 1998. 7 May 2001 http//www.Indians.org/welker/dangeorge.html.

First Nations. Site Index. Unknown. 23 July 2001 http//www.dickshovel.com/www.html.

Graham Green. Home page. 16 January 2000. 7 May 2001 http//www.geocities.com/Hollywood/guild/9621/grahamgreen.html.

The Last of the Mohicans. Dir. Michael Mann. Perf. Russell Means and Daniel Day-Lewis. Twentieth Century Fox, 1992.

Maverick. Dir. Richard Donner. Perf. Graham Green and Mel Gibson. Warner Brothers, 1994.

Ostwalt, Conrad. "Dances with Wolves: An American Heart of Darkness." *Literature/Film Quarterly* 24.2 (1996): 209–16.

The Outlaw Josey Wales. Dir. Clint Eastwood. Perf. Clint Eastwood and Chief Dan George. Warner Brothers, 1976.

Prats, Armando J. "The Image of the Other and the Other Dances with Wolves: The Figured Indian and the Textual Supplement." *Journal of Film and Video* 50.1 (Spring 1998): 3–19.

The Outlaw Josey Wales. Dir. Clint Eastwood. Perf. Clint Eastwood and Chief Dan George. Warner Brothers, 1976.

Sayet, Melissa Fawcett. "The Lasting of the Mohegan." *Essence* 23.1 (March 1993): 55.

Strain, Jack. Phone interview. 11 April 2001.

Strain, Lauren. Personal survey. 3 May 2001.

VOCABULARY

In your journal, write down the meanings of the following words:

- some historical *misrepresentations* **(3)**
- the *romantic* reasons **(6)**

- *pro-interventionist* politics of Hollywood studios **(18)**
- rid the movie industry of *fascist* ideals **(18)**

QUESTIONS FOR WRITING AND DISCUSSION

1. Make a list of films you have seen that have Native Americans characters. Choose two of those films—one older, one more recent. Which characters in both films seemed most realistic and which most stereotypical? Describe the changes you notice between these two films' representations of Native American culture, language, politics, or heritage.

2. At the end of her essay, Strain says that Hollywood can "mix fact and fiction" while still creating a good story. Would you agree with that statement, or do you think historical accuracy should come first and entertainment values second? Choose a film about Native Americans—or any ethnic group—and explain what that film loses or gains by placing entertainment values over historical and cultural accuracy (or, conversely, by giving historical/cultural accuracy much more importance than entertainment values).

3. Strain conducts both a short survey and an interview which she reports on at the end of her paper. Assume you are in a peer-response group, giving her feedback on her essay. Would you advise her to integrate the information in paragraphs 16 and 17 earlier in her essay rather than tacking them on at the end? Where might that information fit? (How do you plan to integrate any interview or survey information in your own essay?)

4. Read the essay by Margaret Lazarus in Chapter 8, entitled "All's Not Well in Land of 'The Lion King.'" Rent *Pocahontas* from a video store and watch it. Are there racist or sexist scenes or images in Disney's version of *Pocahontas*? Does the film ultimately promote Native American cultural values or mainstream white American values? Explain.

STUDENT WRITING

MY FRIEND MICHELLE, AN ALCOHOLIC

Bridgid Stone

Bridgid Stone, a student at Southeast Missouri State University, decided to write her investigative essay on alcoholism. In the library, she was able to find quite a lot of information and statistics about alcohol. In her friend, Michelle, she had a living example of the consequences of alcohol abuse. The question, however, was how to combine the two. As you read her essay, notice how she interweaves description and dialogue with facts and statistics.

Attention

Five million teenagers are problem drinkers, according to *Group* magazine's article "Sex, Drugs, and Alcohol." One of these five million teenagers is my friend, Michelle. 1

"I can't wait to go out tonight and get drunk," Michelle announces as she walks into my dorm room. I just sigh and shake my head. Michelle has been drunk every night since Wednesday. In the last three days, she has been to more fraternity parties than classes. 2

We leave a few hours later for a Sig Tau party. Even though I have been attending these parties for weeks now, the amount of alcohol present still amazes me. Almost everyone is walking around with a twelve-pack of beer. Others are carrying fifths of vodka or Jack Daniels whiskey. As cited in *Fraternities and Sororities on Contemporary College Campuses*, 73 percent of fraternity advisers believe that alcohol is a problem in fraternities. I wish the other 27 percent could be here now. Fraternities are synonymous with drinking. 3

Michelle and I both have innocent-looking squeeze bottles, but inside are very stiff screwdrivers. They probably have more vodka than orange juice. Michelle finishes her drink before I am halfway through mine. So she finishes off mine, too, before disappearing into the throng of people at the party. The next time I see her, she is holding a beer in each hand. Her speech is slurred, and she can barely stand up on her own. 4

We head back to the dorm when Michelle starts vomiting. Once we are in her room, I help her undress and put her to bed. 5

"Bridgid, I am so sorry," Michelle cries, "I promise never to drink again." 6

"Okay, just get some sleep," I tell her as I leave. 7

It's Thursday night and Michelle is ready to party again. 8

"I haven't been to my Friday 8:00 class in a month. Do you think I should just stay up all night after the party and go to class drunk? Or should I just not go to class and sleep in?" Michelle asks. 9

"Don't go out and get drunk. Stay home tonight and get up and go to your classes tomorrow," I advise. 10

"I am just going to sleep in," Michelle informs me as she leaves for the party. 11

Topic

Like Michelle, an estimated 4.6 million adolescents experience negative consequences of alcohol abuse, such as poor school perfor- 12 mance. This was reported in a survey conducted by NIAAA for a United States Congressional report.

Early Friday morning, I get a phone call from the on-duty resident adviser. Michelle has passed out in the lobby of the Towers Complex. She couldn't remember her phone number or even what floor she lived on, but I had written my phone number on Michelle's hand, so she could call me if she got into any trouble. The R.A. had seen my number and decided to call, since Michelle was too drunk to dial the four digits. *13*

"Could you please escort your friend up to your room?" the R.A. asks. She doesn't sound very happy. *14*

"Sure, I will be down in a few minutes," I promise. It takes me and another girl from our floor to get Michelle onto the elevator. She keeps lying down or passing out. Thirty minutes later, we get Michelle into bed. She is mumbling incoherently, and she reeks of alcohol. Needless to say, Michelle doesn't make it to her 8:00 A.M. class, again. *15*

Saturday afternoon, I confront Michelle about the Thursday night incident. This is rather hard to do, since she doesn't remember any of it. *16*

"I just drink to loosen up. I'm much more fun if I've been drinking," Michelle tells me. *17*

"You are not much fun when you are puking or passing out," I reply. A desire to loosen up is one of the main reasons that teenagers drink, reports *Group* magazine. Other reasons include a need to escape and to rebel. *18*

"I have to release steam every once in a while," she argues. "School is really stressing me out." *19*

"Michelle, you don't even go to class," I tell her. *20*

"Everyone else drinks!" she says. "Why are you picking on me?" She stomps out of my room. *21*

Michelle was partially correct, though, when she stated, "Everyone else drinks." As reported in *Alcohol and Youth*, more than 80 percent of all college students surveyed had been drinking in the previous month. But this doesn't mean that what Michelle is doing is any less serious. In all probability, Michelle is an alcoholic. *22*

A test that is often used to determine if someone has a drinking problem can be found in *Getting Them Sober*, by Toby Rice Andrews. There are twenty questions on the test. A "yes" answer to two of the questions indicates a possible drinking problem. Questions include: "Do you miss time from school or work due to drinking?" "Do you drink to escape from worries or troubles?" "Do you drink because you are shy?" "Have you ever had a memory loss due to drinking?" Michelle would probably have answered "yes" to all of the above questions. *23*

I moved out of the dorm at the beginning of the second semester, *24* so I haven't seen much of Michelle. The last time I saw her was about three weeks ago. She had gotten arrested while in New Orleans for spring break. Apparently, Michelle had been out drinking and eventually had been arrested for public drunkenness.

"It wasn't that bad," she told me. "I don't even remember being in *25* the jail cell. I was pretty trashed."

Works Cited

Andrews, Toby Rice. *Getting Them Sober.* South Plainfield, N. J.: Bridge Publishing, 1980.

Barnes, Grace. *Alcohol and Youth.* Westport, Conn.: Greenwood Press, 1982.

Pruett, Harold, and Vivian Brown. *Crisis Intervention and Prevention.* San Francisco: Jossey-Bass Inc., 1987.

"Sex, Drugs, and Alcohol." *Group* February 1992: 17–20.

Van Pelt, Rich. *Intensive Care.* Grand Rapids, Mich.: Zondervan Publishing House, 1988.

Winston, Roger, William Nettles III, and John Opper, Jr. *Fraternities and Sororities on Contemporary College Campuses.* San Francisco: Jossey-Bass Inc., 1987.

QUESTIONS FOR WRITING AND DISCUSSION

1. Investigative reports should remain as objective as possible. Describe how Stone's essay affected you. Does Stone remain objective, or does she become emotionally involved? Where is she most objective? Where does her point of view color her report? How successfully does Stone maintain her reportorial stance?

2. Who is Stone's audience for her essay? Where would you recommend that Stone send her essay for possible publication? List two possible publication sources (magazines or newspapers), and explain your choices.

3. If Stone were revising her essay, what advice would you give her about balancing statistics and personal experience? Should she have more statistics? Should she have more narrative? Refer to specific paragraphs and examples in your response.

4. Stone's use of the present tense adds dramatic impact to her essay. Reread her essay, noticing where she uses the present tense and where she shifts to the past tense. Where was the use of the present tense

most effective? Did her tense shifting confuse you at any point? Where?

5. Compare Stone's essay with Kozol's essay earlier in this chapter. What reporting strategies does Stone adapt from Kozol? How are their reporting strategies different? Explain your response by referring to specific passages from each author.

The Happy Donor, René Magritte (1898–1967). Copyright 1966 ARS, NY. Musée d'Ixelles, Brussels, Belgium.

Chapter _7_ **Explaining**

You have decided to quit your present job, so you write a note to your boss giving thirty days' notice. During your last few weeks at work, your boss asks you to write a three-page job description to help orient the person who will replace you. The job description should include a list of your current duties as well as advice to your replacement on how to execute them most efficiently. To write the description, you record your daily activities, look back through your calendar, comb through your records, and brainstorm a list of everything you do. As you write up the description, you include specific examples and illustrations of your typical responsibilities.

As a gymnast and dancer, you gradually become obsessed with losing weight. You start skipping meals, purging the little food you do eat, and lying about your eating habits to your parents. Before long, you weigh less than seventy pounds, and your physician diagnoses your condition: anorexia nervosa. With advice from your physician and counseling from a psychologist, you gradually begin to control your disorder. To explain to others what anorexia is, how it is caused, and what its effects are, you write an essay in which you explain your ordeal, alerting other readers to the potential dangers of uncontrolled dieting.

> *Become aware of the two-sided nature of your mental make-up: one thinks in terms of the connectedness of things, the other thinks in terms of parts and sequences.*
>
> —GABRIELE LUSSER RICO,
> AUTHOR OF WRITING THE NATURAL WAY

> *What [a writer] knows is almost always a matter of the relationships he establishes, between example and generalization, between one part of a narrative and the next, between the idea and the counter idea that the writer sees is also relevant.*
>
> —ROGER SALE,
> AUTHOR OF ON WRITING

XPLAINING AND DEMONSTRATING RELATIONSHIPS IS A FREQUENT
PURPOSE FOR WRITING. EXPLAINING GOES BEYOND INVESTIGAT-
ING THE FACTS AND REPORTING INFORMATION; IT ANALYZES
the component parts of a subject and then shows how the parts
fit in relation to one another. Its goal is to clarify for a particular group of
readers *what* something is, *how* it happened or should happen, and/or *why*
it happens.

Explaining begins with *analysis:* You divide a thing or phenomenon (object,
person, place, feeling, belief, event, process, or cause) into its various parts. Explaining how to learn to play the piano, for example, begins with an analysis of
the parts of the learning process: playing scales, learning chords, getting instruction from a teacher, sight reading, and performing in recitals. Explaining
why two automobiles collided at an intersection begins with an analysis of the
contributing factors: the nature of the intersection, the number of cars involved,
the condition of the drivers, and the condition of each vehicle. Then you bring
the parts together and show their *relationships:* You show how practicing scales
on the piano fits into the process of learning to play the piano; you demonstrate
why one small factor—such as a faulty turn signal—combined with other factors to cause an automobile accident.

The emphasis you give to the *analysis* of the object or phenomenon and
the time you spend explaining *relationships* of the parts depends on your purpose,
subject, and audience. If you want to explain how a flower reproduces, for example, you may begin by identifying the important parts, such as the pistil and
stamen, that most readers need to know about before they can understand the
reproductive process. However, if you are explaining the process to a botany
major who already knows the parts of a flower, you might spend more time discussing the key operations in pollination or the reasons why some flowers cross-
pollinate and others do not. In any effective explanation, analyzing parts and
showing relationships must work together for that particular group of readers.

Because its purpose is to teach the reader, *expository writing*, or writing to
explain, should be as clear as possible. Explanations, however, are more than organized pieces of information. Expository writing contains information that is
focused by your point of view, by your experience, and by your reasoning powers. Thus, your explanation of a thing or phenomenon makes a point or has a
thesis: This is the *right* way to define *happiness*. This is how one *should* bake
lasagne or do a calculus problem. These are the *most important* reasons why the
senator from New York was elected. To make your explanation clear, you show
what you mean by using specific support: facts, data, examples, illustrations, statistics, comparisons, analogies, and images. Your thesis is a *general* assertion
about the relationships of the *specific* parts. The support helps your reader

identify the parts and see the relationships. Expository writing teaches the reader by alternating between generalizations and specific examples.

Techniques for Explaining ● ● ●

Explaining requires first that you assess your subject and your audience. Although you will need to draw on your own observations and memories about this subject, you may also need to do some reading or perhaps interview an expert. As you consider your subject, keep in mind that while an explanation (involving both analysis and showing relationships) focuses on what, how, or why, it may involve all three. Following are five important techniques for writing clear explanations.

- **Getting the reader's attention and stating the thesis.** Devise an accurate but interesting *title*. Use an attention-getting *lead-in*. State the *thesis* clearly.
- **Defining key terms and describing *what* something is.** Analyze and *define* by describing, comparing, classifying, and giving examples.
- **Identifying the steps in a process and showing *how* each step relates to the overall process.** Describe how something should be done or how something typically happens.
- **Describing causes and effects and showing *why* certain causes lead to specific effects.** Analyze how several causes lead to a single effect, or show how a single cause leads to multiple effects.
- **Supporting explanations with specific evidence.** Use descriptions, examples, comparisons, analogies, images, facts, data, or statistics to *show* what, how, or why.

In *Spirit of the Valley: Androgyny and Chinese Thought*, psychologist Sukie Colgrave illustrates many of these techniques as she explains an important concept from psychology: the phenomenon of *projection*. Colgrave explains how we "project" attributes missing in our own personality onto another person—especially someone we love:

> A one-sided development of either the masculine or feminine principles has [an] unfortunate consequence for our psychological and intellectual health: it encourages the phenomenon termed "projection." This is the process by which we project onto other people, things, or ideologies, those aspects of ourselves which we have not, for whatever reason, acknowledged or developed. The most familiar example of this is the obsession which usually accompanies being "in love." A person whose feminine side is unrealised will often "fall in love" with the

The main thing I try to do is write as clearly as I can.

—E. B. WHITE,
JOURNALIST AND COAUTHOR OF ELEMENTS OF STYLE

Explaining what: Definition example

Explaining why: Effects of projection

feminine which she or he "sees" in another person, and similarly with the masculine. The experience of being "in love" is one of powerful dependency. As long as the projection appears to fit its object nothing awakens the person to the reality of the projection. But sooner or later the lover usually becomes aware of certain discrepancies between her or his desires and the person chosen to satisfy them. Resentment, disappointment, anger and rejection rapidly follow, and often the relationship disintegrates. . . . But if we can explore our own psyches we may discover what it is we were demanding from our lover and start to develop it in ourselves. The moment this happens we begin to see other people a little more clearly. We are freed from some of our needs to make others what we want them to be, and can begin to love them more for what they are.

Explaining how: the process of freeing ourselves from dependency

EXPLAINING *WHAT*

Explaining *what* something is or means requires showing the relationship between it and the *class* of beings, objects, or concepts to which it belongs. *Formal definition*, which is often essential in explaining, has three parts: the thing or term to be defined, the class, and the distinguishing characteristics of the thing or term. The thing being defined can be concrete, such as a turkey, or abstract, such as democracy.

THING OR TERM	CLASS	DISTINGUISHING CHARACTERISTICS
A turkey is a	bird	that has brownish plumage and a bare, wattled head and neck; it is widely domesticated for food.
Democracy is	government	by the people, exercised directly or through elected representatives.

Frequently, writers use *extended definitions* when they need to give more than a mere formal definition. An extended definition may explain the word's etymology or historical roots, describe sensory characteristics of something (how it looks, feels, sounds, tastes, smells), identify its parts, indicate how something is used, explain what it is not, provide an example of it, and/or note similarities or differences between this term and other words or things. The following extended definition of *democracy* begins with the etymology and then explains—using analysis, comparison, example, and description—what democracy is and what it is not:

Formal definition

Since democracy is government of the people, by the people, and for the people, a democratic form of government is not fixed or static.

Democracy is dynamic; it adapts to the wishes and needs of the people. The term *democracy* derives from the Greek word *demos*, meaning "the common people," and *-kratia*, meaning "strength or power" used to govern or rule. Democracy is based on the notion that a majority of people creates laws and then everyone agrees to abide by those laws in the interest of the common good. In a democracy, people are not ruled by a king, a dictator, or a small group of powerful individuals. Instead, people elect officials who use the power temporarily granted to them to govern the society. For example, the people may agree that their government should raise money for defense, so the officials levy taxes to support an army. If enough people decide, however, that taxes for defense are too high, then they request that their elected officials change the laws or they elect new officials. The essence of democracy lies in its responsiveness: Democracy is a form of government in which laws and lawmakers change as the will of the majority changes.

Description: What democracy is
Etymology: Analysis of the word's roots

Comparison: What democracy is not

Example

Formal definition

Figurative expressions—vivid word pictures using similes, metaphors, or analogies—can also explain what something is. During World War II, for example, the Writer's War Board asked E. B. White (author of *Charlotte's Web* and many *New Yorker* magazine essays, as well as other work) to provide an explanation of democracy. Instead of giving a formal definition or etymology, White responded with a series of imaginative comparisons showing the *relationship* between various parts of American culture and the concept of democracy:

Surely the Board knows what democracy is. It is the line that forms on the right. It is the don't in Don't Shove. It is the hole in the stuffed shirt through which the sawdust slowly trickles; it is the dent in the high hat. Democracy is the recurrent suspicion that more than half of the people are right more than half of the time. It is the feeling of privacy in the voting booths, the feeling of communion in the libraries, the feeling of vitality everywhere. Democracy is the score at the beginning of the ninth. It is an idea which hasn't been disproved yet, a song the words of which have not gone bad. It's the mustard on the hot dog and the cream in the rationed coffee. Democracy is a request from a War Board, in the middle of a morning in the middle of a war, wanting to know what democracy is.

Sometimes we think that technical subjects are by nature objective and denotative, but some of these subjects also use definitions that contain images and metaphors. Consider the following definition of Web robots—so-called "bots"—by Andrew Leonard writing in *Wired* magazine:

Web robots—spiders, wanderers, and worms. Cancelbots, Lazarus, and Automoose. Chatterbots, soft bots, userbots, taskbots, knowbots, and mailbots. . . . In current online parlance, the word "bot" pops up everywhere, flung around carelessly to describe just about any kind of computer program—a logon script, a spellchecker—that performs a task on a network. Strictly speaking, all bots are "autonomous"—able to react to their environments and make decisions without prompting from their creators; while the master or mistress is brewing coffee, the bot is off retrieving Web documents, exploring a MUD, or combatting Usenet spam. . . . Even more important than function is behavior—bona fide bots are programs with personality. Real bots talk, make jokes, have feelings—even if those feelings are nothing more than cleverly conceived algorithms.

EXPLAINING *HOW*

Explaining *how* something should be done or how something happens is usually called *process analysis*. One kind of process analysis is the "how-to" explanation: how to cook a turkey, how to tune an engine, how to get a job. Such recipes or directions are *prescriptive*: You typically explain how something *should* be done. In a second kind of process analysis, you explain how something happens or is typically done—without being directive or prescriptive. In a *descriptive* process analysis, you explain how some natural or social process typically happens: how cells split during mitosis, how hailstones form in a cloud, how students react to the pressure of examinations, or how political candidates create their public images. In both prescriptive and descriptive explanations, however, you are analyzing a *process*—dividing the sequence into its parts or steps—and then showing how the parts contribute to the whole process.

Cookbooks, automobile-repair manuals, instructions for assembling toys or appliances, and self-improvement books are all examples of *prescriptive* process analysis. Writers of recipes, for example, begin with analyses of the ingredients and the steps in preparing the food. Then they carefully explain how the steps are related, how to avoid problems, and how to serve mouth-watering concoctions. Farley Mowat, naturalist and author of *Never Cry Wolf*, gives his readers the following detailed—and humorous—recipe for creamed mouse. Mowat became interested in this recipe when he decided to test the nutritional content of the wolf's diet. "In the event that any of my readers may be interested in personally exploiting this hitherto overlooked source of excellent animal protein," Mowat writes, "I give the recipe in full":

SOURIS À LA CRÈME

INGREDIENTS:

One dozen fat mice	Salt and pepper	One cup white flour
Cloves	One piece sowbelly	Ethyl alcohol

Skin and gut the mice, but do not remove the heads; wash, then place in a pot with enough alcohol to cover the carcasses. Allow to marinate for about two hours. Cut sowbelly into small cubes and fry slowly until most of the fat has been rendered. Now remove the carcasses from the alcohol and roll them in a mixture of salt, pepper and flour; then place in frying pan and sauté for about five minutes (being careful not to allow the pan to get too hot, or the delicate meat will dry out and become tough and stringy). Now add a cup of alcohol and six or eight cloves. Cover the pan and allow to simmer slowly for fifteen minutes. The cream sauce can be made according to any standard recipe. When the sauce is ready, drench the carcasses with it, cover and allow to rest in a warm place for ten minutes before serving.

Explaining *how* something happens or is typically done involves a *descriptive* process analysis. It requires showing the chronological relationship between one idea, event, or phenomenon and the next—and it depends on close observation. In *The Lives of a Cell*, biologist and physician Lewis Thomas explains that ants are like humans: While they are individuals, they can also act together to create a social organism. Although exactly how ants communicate remains a mystery, Thomas explains how they combine to form a thinking, working organism:

[Ants] seem to live two kinds of lives: they are individuals, going about the day's business without much evidence of thought for tomorrow, and they are at the same time component parts, cellular elements, in the huge, writhing, ruminating organism of the Hill, the nest, the hive. . . .

A solitary ant, afield, cannot be considered to have much of anything on his mind; indeed, with only a few neurons strung together by fibers, he can't be imagined to have a mind at all, much less a thought. He is more like a ganglion on legs. Four ants together, or ten, encircling a dead moth on a path, begin to look more like an idea. They fumble and shove, gradually moving the food toward the Hill, but as though by blind chance. It is only when you watch the dense mass of thousands of ants, crowded together around the Hill, blackening the ground, that you begin to see the whole beast, and now you observe it thinking, planning, calculating. It is an intelligence, a kind of live computer, with crawling bits for its wits.

At a stage in the construction, twigs of a certain size are needed, and all the members forage obsessively for twigs of just this size. Later, when outer walls are to be finished, thatched, the size must change, and as though given new orders by telephone, all the workers shift the search to the new twigs. If you disturb the arrangement of a part of the Hill, hundreds of ants will set it vibrating, shifting, until it is put right again. Distant sources of food are somehow sensed, and long lines, like tentacles, reach out over the ground, up over walls, behind boulders, to fetch it in.

EXPLAINING *WHY*

"Why?" may be the question most commonly asked by human beings. We are fascinated by the reasons for everything that we experience in life. We ask questions about natural phenomena: Why is the sky blue? Why does a teakettle whistle? Why do some materials act as superconductors? We also find human attitudes and behavior intriguing: Why is chocolate so popular? Why do some people hit small leather balls with big sticks and then run around a field stomping on little white pillows? Why are America's family farms economically depressed? Why did the United States go to war in Vietnam? Why is the Internet so popular?

Explaining *why* something occurs can be the most fascinating—and difficult—kind of expository writing. Answering the question "why" usually requires analyzing *cause-and-effect relationships*. The causes, however, may be too complex or intangible to identify precisely. We are on comparatively secure ground when we ask *why* about physical phenomena that can be weighed, measured, and replicated under laboratory conditions. Under those conditions, we can determine cause and effect with precision.

Fire, for example, has three *necessary* and *sufficient* causes: combustible material, oxygen, and ignition temperature. Without *each* of these causes, fire will not occur (each cause is "necessary"); taken together, these three causes are *enough* to cause fire (all three together are "sufficient"). In this case, the cause-and-effect relationship can be illustrated by an equation:

Cause 1	+	Cause 2	+	Cause 3	=	Effect
(combustible material)		(oxygen)		(ignition temperature)		(fire)

Analyzing both necessary and sufficient causes is essential to explaining an effect. You may say, for example, that wind shear (an abrupt downdraft in a storm) "caused" an airplane crash. In fact, wind shear may have *contributed* (been necessary) to the crash but was not by itself the total (sufficient) cause of the crash: An airplane with enough power may be able to overcome wind shear forces in certain circumstances. An explanation of the crash is not complete until you analyze the full range of necessary *and* sufficient causes, which may include wind shear, lack of power, mechanical failure, and even pilot error.

Sometimes, explanations for physical phenomena are beyond our analytical powers. Astrophysicists, for example, have good theoretical reasons for believing that black holes cause gigantic gravitational whirlpools in outer space, but they have difficulty explaining why black holes exist—or whether they exist at all.

In the realm of human cause and effect, determining causes and effects can be as tricky as explaining why black holes exist. Why, for example, do some children learn math easily while others fail? What effect does failing at math have on a child? What are necessary and sufficient causes for divorce? What are the effects of divorce on parents and children? Although you may not be able to explain all the causes or effects of something, you should not be satisfied until you have considered a wide range of possible causes and effects. Even then, you need to qualify or modify your statements, using such words as *might, usually, often, seldom, many,* or *most,* and then giving as much support and evidence as you can.

In the following paragraphs, Jonathan Kozol, a critic of America's educational system and author of *Illiterate America,* explains the multiple effects of a single cause: illiteracy. Kozol supports his explanation by citing specific ways that illiteracy affects the lives of people:

Illiterates cannot read the menu in a restaurant.

They cannot read the cost of items on the menu in the window of the restaurant before they enter.

Illiterates cannot read the letters that their children bring home from their teachers. They cannot study school department circulars that tell them of the courses that their children must be taking if they hope to pass the SAT exams. They cannot help with homework. They cannot write a letter to the teacher. They are afraid to visit in the classroom. They do not want to humiliate their child or themselves. . . .

Many illiterates cannot read the admonition on a pack of cigarettes. Neither the Surgeon General's warning nor its reproduction on the package can alert them to the risks. Although most people learn by word of mouth that smoking is related to a number of grave physical disorders, they do not get the chance to read the detailed stories which can document this danger with the vividness that turns concern into determination to resist. They can see the handsome cowboy or the slim Virginia lady lighting up a filter cigarette; they cannot heed the words that tell them that this product is (not "may be") dangerous to their health. Sixty million men and women are condemned to be the unalerted, high-risk candidates for cancer. . . .

Illiterates cannot travel freely. When they attempt to do so, they encounter risks that few of us can dream of. They cannot read traffic signs and, while they often learn to recognize and to decipher symbols, they cannot manage street names which they haven't seen before. The same is true for bus and subway stops. While ingenuity can sometimes help a man or woman to discern directions from familiar landmarks, buildings, cemeteries, churches, and the like, most illiterates are virtually immobilized. They seldom wander past the streets and neighborhoods they know. Geographical paralysis becomes a bitter metaphor for their entire existence. They are immobilized in almost every sense we can imagine. They can't move up. They can't move out. They cannot see beyond.

■ WARMING UP: JOURNAL EXERCISES   The following exercises will help you practice writing explanations. Read all of the following exercises and then write on the three that interest you most. If another idea occurs to you, write about it.

1. Write a one-paragraph explanation of an idea, term, or concept that you have discussed in a class that you are currently taking. From biology, for example, you might define *photosynthesis* or *gene splicing*. From psychology, you might define *psychosis* or *projection*. From computer studies, you might define *cyberspace* or *morphing*. First, identify someone who might need to know about this subject. Then give a definition and an illustration. Finally, describe how the term was discovered or invented, what its effects or applications are, and/or how it works.

2. Imitating E. B. White's short "definition" of democracy, use imaginative comparisons to write a short definition—serious or humorous—of one of the following words: *freedom, adolescence, mathematics, politicians, parents, misery, higher education, luck,* or a word of your own choice.

3. Novelist Ernest Hemingway once defined courage as "grace under pressure." Using this definition, explain how you or someone you know showed this kind of courage in a difficult situation.

4. When asked what jazz is, Louis Armstrong replied, "Man, if you gotta ask you'll never know." If you know quite a bit about jazz, explain what Armstrong meant. Or choose a familiar subject to which the same remark might apply. What can be "explained" about that subject, and what cannot?

5. Choose a skill that you've acquired (for example, playing a musical instrument, operating a machine, playing a sport, drawing, counseling others, driving in rush-hour traffic, dieting) and explain to a novice how he or she can acquire that skill. Reread what you've written. Then write another version addressed to an expert. What parts can you leave out? What must you add?

6. Three-year-old children are insatiably curious. They ask older people a never-ending series of "why" questions. Imagine you are going for a walk

in a familiar place with a three-year-old. What questions might the child ask you about either strange or commonplace things or occurrences? Select one "why" question. First, write out an explanation of that question for another adult. Then write your explanation for the three-year-old.

7. Sometimes writers use standard definitions to explain a key term, but sometimes they need to *resist* conventional definition in order to make a point. La Mer Stepptoe, an eleventh-grader in West Philadelphia, was faced with a form requiring her to check her racial identity. Like many Americans of multicultural heritage, she decided not to check one box. In the following paragraphs, reprinted from National Public Radio's *All Things Considered,* Ms. Stepptoe explains how she decided to (re)define herself. As you read her response, consider how you might need to resist a conventional definition in your own explaining essay.

Multiracialness

Caucasian, African-American, Latin American, Asian-American. Check one. I look black, so I'll pick that one. But, no, wait, if I pick that, I'll be denying the other sides of my family. So I'll pick white. But I'm not white or black, I'm both, and part Native American, too. It's confusing when you have to pick which race to identify with, especially when you have family who, on one side, ask, "Why do you talk like a white girl?" when, in the eyes of the other side of your family, your behind is black.

I never met my dad's mom, my grandmother, Maybelle Dawson Boyd Stepptoe(ph), and my father never knew his father. But my aunts or uncles or cousins all think of me as black or white. I mean, I'm not the lightest-skinned person, but my cousins down South swear I'm white. It bothers them, and that bothers me, how people could care so much about your skin color.

My mother's mother, Sylvia Gabriel, lives in Connecticut, near where my aunt, uncle and cousins on that side of the family live. Now, they're white, and where my grandma lives, there are very few black people or people of color. And when we visit, people look at us a lot, staring like, "What is that woman doing with those people?" It shocks the heck out of them when my brother and I call her Grandma.

My mother's side is Italian. I really didn't get any Italian culture except for the food. My father was raised much differently from my mother. My father is superstitious; he believes that a child should know his or her place and not speak unless spoken to. My father is very much into both his African-American and Native American heritage.

Multiracialness is a very tricky subject for my father. He'll tell people that I'm Native, African-American and Caucasian American, but at the same time he'll say things like, "Listen to jazz, listen to your cultural music." He says, "La Mer, look in the mirror. You're black. Ask any white person: they'll say you're black." He doesn't get it. I really would rather be colorless than to pick a race. I like other music, not just black music.

The term African-American bugs me. I'm not African. I'm American as a hot dog. We should have friends who are yellow, red, blue, black, purple, gay, religious, bisexual, trilingual, whatever, so you don't have a stereotypical view. I've met mean people and nice people of all different backgrounds. At my school, I grew up with all these kids, and I didn't look at them as white or Jewish or heterosexual; I looked at them as, "Oh, she's funny, he's sweet."

I know what box I'm going to choose. I pick D for none of the above, because my race is human.

Les Très Riches Heures DE MARTHA STEWART

Margaret Talbot

Currently a senior fellow at New America Foundation, Margaret Talbot has written columns and feature stories for The New Republic *on topics such as child abuse, computer programs, divorce, reproductive technology, and Hillary Clinton. The title of this essay, "Les Très Riches Heures" (The Very Rich Hours) refers to a series of illuminated manuscripts called Books of Hours done in 1413 for Jean, Duc de Berry, a wealthy nobleman from northern Europe. While Books of Hours were prayer books organized around the liturgical calendar, the paintings showed scenes from everyday life as well as from the lives of the nobility. Jean, Duc of Berry, collected art, jewels, and gold work, and led a life filled with the trappings of luxury: exquisite clothes, tapestries, silverware, and of course, sumptuous food. In her essay on Martha Stewart, Talbot wants to evoke the extravagant life of the privileged class because she intends to critique and parody the extremes to which Martha Stewart has taken the art of homemaking. (If you are not already acquainted with the world according to Martha Stewart, check out her website at marthastewart.com and spinoff websites devoted to Martha Stewart humor and parodies such as the Gothic Martha Stewart or the Ultimate Martha Stewart.) The central purpose of Talbot's essay, however, is to explain what the Martha Stewart cult is all about, why it appeals to women, and what the Martha phenomenon reveals about us and our culture.*

Every age gets the household goddess it deserves. The '60s had Julia Child, the sophisticated French chef who proved as permissive as Dr. Spock. She may have proselytized for a refined foreign cuisine from her perch at a Boston PBS station, but she was always an anti-snob, vowing to "take a lot of the la dee dah out of French cooking." With her madras shirts and her penumbra of curls, her 6'2" frame and her whinny of a voice, she exuded an air of Cambridge eccentricity—faintly bohemian and a little tatty, like a yellowing travel poster. She was messy and forgiving. When Julia dropped an egg or collapsed a soufflé, she shrugged and laughed. "You are alone in the kitchen, nobody can see you, and cooking is meant to be fun," she reminded her viewers. She wielded lethal-looking kitchen knives with campy abandon, dipped her fingers into crème anglaise and wiped her chocolate-smeared hands on an apron tied carelessly at her waist. For Child was also something of a sensualist, a celebrant of appetite as much as a pedant of cooking.

In the '90s, and probably well into the next century, we have Martha Stewart, corporate overachiever turned domestic superachiever, Mildred Pierce in earth-toned Armani. Martha is the anti-Julia. Consider the extent of their respective powers. At the height of her success, Child could boast a clutch of bestselling cookbooks and a *gemütlich* TV show shot on a single set. At what may or may not be the height of her success, here's what Stewart can claim: a 5-year-old magazine, *Martha Stewart Living*, with a circulation that has leapt to 1.5 million; a popular cable TV show, also called *Martha Stewart Living* and filmed at her luscious Connecticut and East Hampton estates; a dozen wildly successful gardening, cooking and lifestyle books; a mail-order business, Martha-by-Mail; a nationally syndicated newspaper column, "Ask Martha"; a regular Wednesday slot on the *Today* show; a line of $110-a-gallon paints in colors inspired by the eggs her Araucana hens lay; plans to invade cyberspace—in short, an empire.

Julia limited herself to cooking lessons, with the quiet implication that cooking was a kind of synecdoche for the rest of bourgeois existence; but Martha's parish is vaster, her field is all of life. Her expertise, as she recently explained to *Mediaweek* magazine, covers, quite simply, "Beautiful soups and how to make them, beautiful houses and how to build them, beautiful children and how to raise them." (From soups to little nuts.) She presides, in fact, over a phenomenon that, in other realms, is quite familiar in American society and culture: a cult, devoted to her name and image.

In the distance between these two cynosures of domestic life lies a question: *What does the cult of Martha mean?* Or, to put it another way, *what have we done, exactly, to deserve her?*   4

If you have read the paper or turned on the television in the last year or so, you have probably caught a glimpse of the WASPY good looks, the affectless demeanor, the nacreous perfection of her world. You may even know the outlines of her story. Middle-class girl from a Polish-American family in Nutley, New Jersey, works her way through Barnard in the early '60s, modeling on the side. She becomes a stock-broker, a self-described workaholic and insomniac who by the '70s is making six figures on Wall Street, and who then boldly trades it all in . . . for life as a workaholic, insomniac evangelist for domesticity whose business now generates some $200 million in profits a year. (She herself, according to the *Wall Street Journal*, makes a salary of $400,000 a year from Time Inc., which generously supplements this figure with a $40,000 a year clothing allowance and other candies.) You may even have admired her magazine, with its art-book production values and spare design, every kitchen utensil photographed like an Imogen Cunningham nude, every plum or pepper rendered with the loving detail of an eighteenth-century botanical drawing, every page a gentle exhalation of High Class.   5

What you may not quite realize, if you have not delved deeper into Stewart's oeuvre, is the ambition of her design for living—the absurd, self-parodic dream of it. To read Martha Stewart is to know that there is no corner of your domestic life that cannot be beautified or improved under careful tutelage, none that should not be colonized by the rhetoric and the discipline of quality control. Work full time though you may, care for your family though you must, convenience should never be your watchword in what Stewart likes to call, in her own twee coinage, "homekeeping." Convenience is the enemy of excellence. "We do not pretend that these are 'convenience' foods," she writes loftily of the bread and preserves recipes in a 1991 issue of the magazine. "Some take days to make. But they are recipes that will produce the very best results, and we know that is what you want." Martha is a kitchen-sink idealist. She scorns utility in the name of beauty. But her idealism, of course, extends no further than surface appearances, which makes it a very particular form of idealism indeed.   6

To spend any length of time in Martha-land is to realize that it   7
is not enough to serve your guests homemade pumpkin soup as a first
course. You must present it in hollowed-out, hand-gilded pumpkins as
well. It will not do to serve an Easter ham unless you have baked it in
a roasting pan lined with, of all things, "tender, young, organically-
grown grass that has not yet been cut." And, when serving a "casual"
lobster and corn dinner al fresco, you really ought to fashion dozens
of cunning little bamboo brushes tied with raffia and adorned with a
chive so that each of your guests may butter their corn with something pretty.

To be a Martha fan (or more precisely, a Martha adept) is to un-   8
derstand that a terracotta pot is just a terracotta pot until you have
"aged" it, painstakingly rubbing yogurt into its dampened sides, then
smearing it with plant food or "something you found in the woods"
and patiently standing by while the mold sprouts. It is to think that
maybe you could do this *kind* of thing, anyway—start a garden, say, in
your scruffy backyard—and then to be brought up short by Martha's
enumeration, in *Martha Stewart's Gardening,* of forty-nine "essential"
gardening tools. These range from a "polesaw" to a "corn fiber broom"
to three different kinds of pruning shears, one of which—the "lop-
pers"—Martha says she has in three different sizes. You have, perhaps,
a trowel. But then Martha's garden is a daunting thing to contemplate,
what with its topiary mazes and state-of-the-art chicken coop; its "antique" flowers and geometric herb garden. It's half USDA station, half
Sissinghurst.* And you cannot imagine making anything remotely like
it at your own house, not without legions of artisans and laborers and
graduate students in landscape design, and a pot of money that perhaps you'll unearth when you dig up the yard.

In *The Culture of Narcissism*, Christopher Lasch describes the ways   9
in which pleasure, in our age, has taken on "the qualities of work," allowing our leisure-time activities to be measured by the same standards of accomplishment that rule the workplace. It is a phenomenon
that he memorably characterizes as "the invasion of play by the rhetoric
of achievement." For Lasch, writing in the early '70s, the proliferation
of sex-advice manuals offered a particularly poignant example. Today,
though, you might just as easily point to the hundreds of products and
texts, from unctuous home-furnishings catalogs to upscale "shelter"
magazines to self-help books like *Meditations for Women Who Do Too
Much,* that tell us exactly how to "nest" and "cocoon" and "nurture,"
how to "center" and "retreat," and how to measure our success at these
eminently private pursuits. Just as late-nineteenth-century marketers

---

Sissinghurst: a 1930s English garden designed by Vita Sackville-West.

and experts promised to bring Americans back in touch with the nature from which modern industrial life had alienated them, so today's
"shelter" experts—the word is revealingly primal—promise to recon-
nect us with a similarly mystified home. The bourgeois home as lost
paradise, retrievable through careful instruction.

Martha Stewart is the apotheosis of this particular cult of exper-   *10*
tise, and its most resourceful entrepreneur. She imagines projects of
which we would never have thought—gathering dewy grass for our
Easter ham, say—and makes us feel the pressing need for training in
them. And she exploits, brilliantly, a certain estrangement from home
that many working women feel these days. For women who are working longer and longer hours at more and more demanding jobs, it's
easy to think of home as the place where chaos reigns and their own
competence is called into doubt: easy to regard the office, by comparison, as the bulwark of order. It is a reversal, of course, of the hoary
concept of home as a refuge from the tempests of the marketplace. But
these days, as the female executives in a recent study attested, the priority they most often let slide is housekeeping: they'll abide disorder
at home that they wouldn't or couldn't abide at the office. No working
couple's home is the oasis of tranquility and Italian marble countertops
that Marthaism seems to promise. But could it be? Should it be? Stewart plucks expertly at that chord of doubt.

In an era when it is not at all uncommon to be cut off from the tra-   *11*
ditional sources of motherwit and household lore—when many of us
live far from the families into which we were born and have started
our own families too late to benefit from the guidance of living parents
or grandparents—domestic pedants like Martha Stewart rightly sense
a big vacuum to fill. Stewart's books are saturated with nostalgia for lost
tradition and old moldings, for her childhood in Nutley and for her
mother's homemade preserves. In the magazine, her "Remembering"
column pines moralistically for a simpler era, when beach vacations
meant no television or video games, just digging for clams and napping
in hammocks. Yet Stewart's message is that such simplicity can only be
achieved now through strenuous effort and a flood of advice. We might
be able to put on a picnic or a dinner party without her help, she seems
to tell us, but we wouldn't do it properly, beautifully, in the spirit of
excellence that we expect of ourselves at work.

It may be that Stewart's special appeal is to women who wouldn't   *12*
want to take their mother's word anyway, to baby-boomer daughters
who figure that their sensibilities are just too different from their stay-
at-home moms', who can't throw themselves into housekeeping without thinking of their kitchen as a catering business and their backyards

as a garden show. In fact, relatively few of Martha's fans are house-wives—72 percent of the subscribers to *Martha Stewart Living* are employed outside the home as managers or professionals—and many of them profess to admire her precisely because she isn't one, either. As one such Martha acolyte, an account executive at a Christian radio station, effused on the Internet: "[Stewart] is my favorite independent woman and what an entrepreneur! She's got her own television show, magazine, books and even her own brand of latex paint. . . . Martha is a feisty woman who settles for nothing less than perfection."

For women such as these, the didactic faux-maternalism of Martha 13 Stewart seems the perfect answer. She may dispense the kind of home-keeping advice that a mother would, but she does so in tones too chill and exacting to sound "maternal," singling out, for example, those "who will always be too lazy" to do her projects. She makes housekeeping safe for the professional woman by professionalizing housekeeping. And you never forget that Stewart is herself a mogul, even when she's baking rhubarb crisp and telling you, in her Shakeresque mantra, that "It's a Good Thing."

It is tempting to see the Martha cult purely as a symptom of anti- 14 feminist backlash. Though she may not directly admonish women to abandon careers for hearth and home, Stewart certainly exalts a way of life that puts hearth and home at its center, one that would be virtual-ly impossible to achieve without *somebody's* full-time devotion. (Camille Paglia has praised her as "someone who has done a tremendous service for ordinary women—women who identify with the roles of wife, mother, and homemaker.") Besides, in those alarming moments when Stewart slips into the social critic's mode, she can sound a wee bit like Phyllis Schlafly[†]—less punitive and more patrician, maybe, but just as smug about the moral uplift of a well-ordered home. Her philosophy of cultivating your own walled garden while the world outside is con-demned to squalor bears the hallmarks of Reagan's America—it would not be overreading to call it a variety of conservatism. "Amid the hor-rors of genocidal war in Bosnia and Rwanda, the AIDS epidemic and increasing crime in many cities," Stewart writes in a recent column, "there are those of us who desire positive reinforcement of some very basic tenets of good living." And those would be? "Good food, gar-dening, crafts, entertaining and home improvement." (Hollow out the pumpkins, they're starving in Rwanda.)

Yet it would, in the end, be too simplistic to regard her as a tool 15 of the feminine mystique, or as some sort of spokesmodel for full-time

---

[†]*Phyllis Schlafly:* advocate for traditional family values.

mommies. For one thing, there is nothing especially June Cleaverish, or even motherly, about Stewart. She has taken a drubbing, in fact, for looking more convincing as a businesswoman than a dispenser of milk and cookies. (Remember the apocryphal tale that had Martha flattening a crate of baby chicks while backing out of a driveway in her Mercedes?) Her habitual prickliness and Scotchguard perfectionism are more like the badges of the striving good girl, still cut to the quick by her classmates' razzing when she asked for extra homework.

Despite the ritual obeisance that Martha pays to Family, more-   *16*
over, she is not remotely interested in the messy contingencies of family life. In the enchanted world of Turkey Hill, there are no husbands (Stewart was divorced from hers in 1990), only loyal craftsmen, who clip hedges and force dogwood with self-effacing dedication. Children she makes use of as accessories, much like Parisian women deploy little dogs. The books and especially the magazine are often graced with photographic spreads of parties and teas where children pale as waxen angels somberly disport themselves, their fair hair shaped into tasteful blunt cuts, their slight figures clad in storybook velvet or lace. "If I had to choose one essential element for the success of an Easter brunch," she writes rather menacingly in her 1994 *Menus for Entertaining*, "it would be children." The homemade Halloween costumes modeled by wee lads and lasses in an October 1991 issue of *Martha Stewart Living* do look gorgeous—the Caravaggio colors, the themes drawn from nature. But it's kind of hard to imagine a 5-year-old boy happily agreeing to go as an acorn this year, instead of say, Batman. And why should he? In Marthaland, his boyhood would almost certainly be overridden in the name of taste.

If Stewart is a throwback, it's not so much to the 1950s as to the   *17*
1850s, when the doctrine of separate spheres did allow married or widowed women of the upper classes a kind of power—unchallenged dominion over the day-to-day functioning of the home and its servants, in exchange for ceding the public realm to men. At Turkey Hill, Stewart is the undisputed chatelaine, micromanaging her estate in splendid isolation. (This hermetic pastoral is slightly marred, of course, by the presence of cameras.) Here the domestic arts have become ends in themselves, unmoored from family values and indeed from family.

Stewart's peculiar brand of didacticism has another nineteenth-   *18*
century precedent—in the domestic science or home economics movement. The domestic scientists' favorite recipes—"wholesome" concoctions of condensed milk and canned fruit, rivers of white sauce—would never have passed Martha's muster; but their commitment to painstakingly elegant presentation, their concern with the look of food even more than its taste, sound a lot like Stewart's. And, more impor-

tantly, so does their underlying philosophy. They emerged out of a tradition: the American preference for food writing of the prescriptive, not the descriptive, kind, for food books that told you, in M. F. K. Fisher's formulation, not about eating but about what to eat. But they took this spirit much further. Like Stewart, these brisk professional women of the 1880s and '90s believed that true culinary literacy could not be handed down or casually absorbed; it had to be carefully taught. (One of the movement's accomplishments, if it can be called that, was the home ec curriculum.)

Like Stewart, the domestic scientists were not bent on liberating *19* intelligent women from housework. Their objective was to raise housework to a level worthy of intelligent women. They wished to apply rational method to the chaos and the drudgery of housework and, in so doing, to earn it the respect accorded men's stuff like science and business. Neither instinct, nor intuition, nor mother's rough-hewn words of advice would have a place in the scientifically managed home of the future. As Laura Shapiro observes in *Perfection Salad*, her lively and perceptive history of domestic science, the ideal new housewife was supposed to project, above all, "self-sufficiency, self-control, and a perfectly bland façade." Sound familiar?

It is in their understanding of gender roles, however, that the *20* doyennes of home ec most closely prefigure Marthaism. Like Stewart, they cannot be classified either as feminists or traditionalists. Their model housewife was a pseudo-professional with little time for sublimating her ego to her husband's or tenderly ministering to his needs. She was more like a factory supervisor than either the Victorian angel of the home or what Shapiro calls the courtesan type, the postwar housewife who was supposed to zip through her chores so she could gussy herself up for her husband. In Martha's world, too, the managerial and aesthetic challenges of "homekeeping" always take priority, and their intricacy and ambition command a respect that mere wifely duties never could. Her husbandless hauteur is rich with the self-satisfaction of financial and emotional independence.

In the end, Stewart's fantasies have as much to do with class as *21* with gender. The professional women who read her books might find themselves longing for a breadwinner, but a lifestyle this beautiful is easier to come by if you've never needed a breadwinner in the first place. Stewart's books are a dreamy advertisement for independent wealth—or, more accurately, for its facsimile. You may not have a posh pedigree, but with a little effort (okay, a lot) you can adopt its trappings. After all, Martha wasn't born to wealth either, but now she attends the weddings of people with names like Charles Booth-Clibborn (she went to his in London, the magazine tells us) and caters them for couples named Sissy and Kelsey (see her *Wedding Planner*, in which their yacht is decorated with a "Just Married" sign).

She is not an American aristocrat, but she plays one on TV. And you can play one, too, at least in your own home. Insist on cultivating only those particular yellow plums you tasted in the Dordogne, buy your copper cleaner only at Delherin in Paris, host lawn parties where guests come "attired in the garden dress of the Victorian era," and you begin to simulate the luster of lineage. Some of Stewart's status-augmenting suggestions must strike even her most faithful fans as ridiculous. For showers held after the baby is born, Martha "likes presenting the infant with engraved calling cards that the child can then slip into thank you notes and such for years to come." What a great idea. Maybe your baby can gum them for a while first, thoughtfully imprinting them with his signature drool.

The book that best exemplifies her class-consciousness is *Martha Stewart's New Old House*, a step-by-step account of refurbishing a Federal-style farmhouse in Westport, Connecticut. Like all her books, it contains many, many pictures of Martha; here she's frequently shown supervising the work of plasterers, carpenters and other "seemingly taciturn men." *New Old House* establishes Stewart's ideal audience: a demographic niche occupied by the kind of people who, like her, can afford to do their kitchen countertops in "mottled, gray-green, hand-honed slate from New York state, especially cut" for them. The cost of all this (and believe me, countertops are only the beginning) goes unmentioned. If you have to ask, maybe you're not a Martha kind of person after all.

The fantasy of vaulting into the upper crust that Martha Stewart fulfilled, and now piques in her readers, is about more than just money, of course. Among other things, it's about time, and the luxurious plenitude of it. Living the Martha way would mean enjoying a surfeit of that scarce commodity, cooking and crafting at the artisanal pace her projects require. Trouble is, none of us overworked Americans has time to spare these days—and least of all the upscale professional women whom Stewart targets. Martha herself seemed to acknowledge this when she told *Inside Media* that she attracts at least two classes of true believers: the "Be-Marthas," who have enough money and manic devotion to follow many of her lifestyle techniques, and the "Do-Marthas," who "are a little bit envious" and "don't have as much money as the Be-Marthas."

To those fulsome categories, you could surely add the "watch Marthas" or the "read Marthas," people who might consider, say, making their own rabbit-shaped wire topiary forms, but only consider it,

22

23

24

25

who mostly just indulge in the fantasy of doing so, if only they had the time. There is something undeniably soothing about watching Martha at her absurdly time-consuming labors. A female "media executive" explained the appeal to Barbara Lippert in *New York* magazine: "I never liked Martha Stewart until I started watching her on Sunday mornings. I turn on the TV, and I'm in my pajamas, still in this place between sleep and reality. And she's showing you how to roll your tablecloths in parchment paper. She's like a character when she does her crafts. It reminds me of watching Mr. Green Jeans on Captain Kangaroo. I remember he had a shoebox he took out that was filled with craft things. There would be a close-up on his hands with his buffed nails. And then he would show you how to cut an oaktag with a scissor, or when he folded paper, he'd say: 'There you go, boys and girls,' and it was very quiet. It's like she brings out this great meditative focus and calm."

The show does seem strikingly unfrenetic. Unlike just about 26 everything else on TV, including the *Our Home* show, which follows it on Lifetime, it eschews Kathy Lee-type banter, perky music, swooping studio shots and jittery handheld cameras. Instead there's just Martha, alone in her garden or kitchen, her teacherly tones blending with birdsong, her recipes cued to the seasons. Whimsical recorder music pipes along over the credits. Martha's crisply ironed denim shirts, pearl earrings, and honey-toned highlights bespeak the fabulousness of Connecticut. Her hands move slowly, deliberately over her yellow roses or her Depression glasses. Martha is a Puritan who prepares "sinful" foods—few of her recipes are low-fat or especially health-conscious—that are redeemed by the prodigious labors, the molasses afternoons, involved in serving them. (She preys upon our guilt about overindulgence, then hints at how to assuage it.) Here at Turkey Hill, time is as logy as a honey-sated bumblebee. Here on Lifetime, the cable channel aimed at baby-boom women, Martha's stately show floats along in a sea of stalker movies, Thighmaster commercials and "Weddings of a Lifetime" segments, and by comparison, I have to say, she looks rather dignified. Would that we all had these *très riches heures*.

But if we had the hours, if we had the circumstances, wouldn't we 27 want to fill them with something of our own, with a domestic grace of our own devising? Well, maybe not anymore. For taste is no longer an expression of individuality. It is, more often, an instrument of conformism, a way to assure ourselves that we're living by the right codes, dictated or sanctioned by experts. Martha Stewart's "expertise" is really nothing but another name for the perplexity of her cowed consumers.

A lifestyle cult as all-encompassing as hers could thrive only at a time when large numbers of Americans have lost confidence in their own judgment about the most ordinary things. For this reason, *Martha Stewart Living* isn't really living at all.

VOCABULARY

In your journal, write down the meanings of the following words:

- She may have *proselytized* (**1**)
- a *gemütlich* TV show (**2**)
- cooking was a kind of *synecdoche* (**3**)
- between these two *cynosures* of domestic life (**4**)
- the *nacreous* perfection of her world (**5**)
- every page a gentle *exhalation* of High Class (**5**)
- deeper into Stewart's *oeuvre* (**6**)
- from *unctuous* home-furnishings (**9**)
- the *apotheosis* of this particular cult (**10**)
- despite the ritual *obeisance* (**16**)
- Stewart is the undisputed *chatelaine* (**17**)
- the *doyennes* of home ec (**20**)
- simulate the luster of *lineage* (**22**)
- seem strikingly *unfrenetic* (**26**)

QUESTIONS FOR WRITING AND DISCUSSION

1. In paragraph 10, Talbot says, "No working couple's home is the oasis of tranquility and Italian marble countertops that Marthaism seems to promise." Describe your own dream home. What would the kitchen, the garden, and the children's rooms be like? How would it be similar to or different from a house according to Martha?

2. Talbot begins her essay with an extended comparison of Julia Child and Martha Stewart. What are the similarities between their styles? What are the differences? Is this comparison an effective lead-in for Talbot's essay? Explain.

3. Following the introduction, the first part of Talbot's essay (paragraphs 5–9) explains what the cult of Martha means and what we have done to deserve her. What do we need to understand if we are to become Martha adept? What sentences or examples best clarify her explanation?

4. Talbot also explains, in paragraphs 10–13, why Martha Stewart has such special appeal for women—and especially for working women. What reasons does Talbot give? Which of these reasons make the most sense to you?

5. Beginning with paragraph 14, Talbot analyzes the cultural significance of the Martha cult. What does Talbot suggest about the relationship between feminism and Marthaism? What does Talbot suggest about the relationship between class status and Marthaism?

6. The opening sentence of Talbot's essay reads, "Every age gets the household goddess it deserves." In the final paragraph, Talbot says that the Martha Stewart cult makes matters of taste no longer an individual thing but an "instrument of conformism." What is Talbot saying about the relationship between Martha and her fans? Does that justify Talbot's conclusion that *Martha Stewart Living* isn't really living at all"? Explain.

7. Talbot makes fun of the more exaggerated and eccentric aspects of the Martha Stewart cult. In paragraph 22, for example, Martha Stewart recommends presenting an infant "with engraved calling cards" that the child can use in thank you notes. "What a great idea," Talbot says. "Maybe your baby can gum them for a while first, thoughtfully imprinting them with his signature drool." Find three other places where Talbot makes fun of Martha. Does Talbot's satire of Martha change your opinion of Martha Stewart? Is her satire fair? Explain.

8. On the Internet, use a search engine to find Martha Stewart's site as well as some of the sites that parody her. Which of the humorous sites are most entertaining? Print out several pages from these sites and take them to class for discussion.

PROFESSIONAL WRITING

THE GLOBAL VILLAGE FINALLY ARRIVES
Pico Iyer

Born in 1957 in Oxford, England, to Indian parents, Pico Iyer was educated at Eton, Oxford, and Harvard Universities. In addition to his regular features in Time *magazine, Iyer has published a novel and several travel books, including* The Lady and the Monk: Four Seasons in Kyoto *(1991),* Tropical Classical: Essays from Several Directions *(1997), and* The Global Soul: Jet Lag, Shopping Malls, and the Search for Home

(2000). Although Iyer is noted for his travel books, he is not a travel guide like Frommer or Fodor. Always his goal is to tell a story about cultural differences, in the narrative style of an "intimate letter to a stranger." In "The Global Village Finally Arrives," Iyer explains—relying on immediate details, striking contrasts, and metaphors—the new multicultural village we all inhabit.

This is the typical day of a relatively typical soul in today's diversified world. I wake up to the sound of my Japanese clock radio, put on a T-shirt sent me by an uncle in Nigeria and walk out into the street, past German cars, to my office. Around me are English-language students from Korea, Switzerland and Argentina—all on this Spanish-named road in this Mediterranean-style town. On TV, I find, the news is in Mandarin; today's baseball game is being broadcast in Korean. For lunch I can walk to a sushi bar, a tandoori palace, a Thai café or the newest burrito joint (run by an old Japanese lady). Who am I, I sometimes wonder, the son of Indian parents and a British citizen who spends much of his time in Japan (and is therefore—what else?—an American permanent resident)? And where am I?

I am, as it happens, in Southern California, in a quiet, relatively uninternational town, but I could as easily be in Vancouver or Sydney or London or Hong Kong. All the world's a rainbow coalition, more and more; the whole planet, you might say, is going global. When I fly to Toronto, or Paris, or Singapore, I disembark in a world as hyphenated as the one I left. More and more of the globe looks like America, but an America that is itself looking more and more like the rest of the globe. Los Angeles famously teaches 82 different languages in its schools. In this respect, the city seems only to bear out the old adage that what is in California today is in America tomorrow, and next week around the globe.

In ways that were hardly conceivable even a generation ago, the new world order is a version of the New World writ large: a wide-open frontier of polyglot terms and postnational trends. A common multiculturalism links us all—call it Planet Hollywood, Planet Reebok or the United Colors of Benetton. *Taxi* and *hotel* and *disco* are universal terms now, but so too are *karaoke* and *yoga* and *pizza*. For the gourmet alone, there is *tiramisù* at the Burger King in Kyoto, echt angel-hair pasta in Saigon and enchiladas on every menu in Nepal.

But deeper than mere goods, it is souls that are mingling. In Brussels, a center of the new "unified Europe," one new baby in every four is Arab. Whole parts of the Paraguayan capital of Asunción are largely Korean. And when the prostitutes of Melbourne distributed some

1

2

3

4

pro-condom pamphlets, one of the languages they used was Macedonian. Even Japan, which prides itself on its centuries-old socially engineered uniculture, swarms with Iranian illegals, Western executives, Pakistani laborers and Filipina hostesses.

The global village is defined, as we know, by an international youth 5
culture that takes its cues from American pop culture. Kids in Perth and Prague and New Delhi are all tuning in to *Santa Barbara* on TV, and wriggling into 501 jeans, while singing along to Madonna's latest in English. CNN (which has grown 70-fold in 13 years) now reaches more than 140 countries; an American football championship pits London against Barcelona. As fast as the world comes to America, America goes round the world—but it is an America that is itself multi-tongued and many hued, an America of Amy Tan and Janet Jackson and movies with dialogue in Lakota.

For far more than goods and artifacts, the one great influence 6
being broadcast around the world in greater numbers and at greater speed than ever before is people. What were once clear divisions are now tangles of crossed lines: there are 40,000 "Canadians" resident in Hong Kong, many of whose first language is Cantonese. And with people come customs: while new immigrants from Taiwan and Vietnam and India—some of the so-called Asian Calvinists—import all-American values of hard work and family closeness and entrepreneurial energy to America, America is sending its values of upward mobility and individualism and melting-pot hopefulness to Taipei and Saigon and Bombay.

Values, in fact, travel at the speed of fax; by now, almost half the 7
world's Mormons live outside the U.S. A diversity of one culture quickly becomes a diversity of many: the "typical American" who goes to Japan today may be a third-generation Japanese American, or the son of a Japanese woman married to a California serviceman, or the offspring of a Salvadoran father and an Italian mother from San Francisco. When he goes out with a Japanese woman, more than two cultures are brought into play.

None of this, of course, is new: Chinese silks were all the rage in 8
Rome centuries ago, and Alexandria before the time of Christ was a paradigm of the modern universal city. Not even American eclecticism is new: many a small town has long known Chinese restaurants, Indian doctors and Lebanese grocers. But now all these cultures are crossing at the speed of light. And the rising diversity of the planet is something more than mere cosmopolitanism: it is a fundamental re-coloring of the very complexion of societies. Cities like Paris, or Hong Kong, have always had a soigné, international air and served as magnets for exiles and émigrés, but now smaller places are multinational

too. Marseilles speaks French with a distinctly North African twang. Islamic fundamentalism has one of its strongholds in Bradford, England. It is the sleepy coastal towns of Queensland, Australia, that print their menus in Japanese.

The dangers this internationalism presents are evident: not for nothing did the Tower of Babel collapse. As national borders fall, tribal alliances, and new manmade divisions, rise up, and the world learns every day terrible new meanings of the word Balkanization. And while some places are wired for international transmission, others (think of Iran or North Korea or Burma) remain as isolated as ever, widening the gap between the haves and the have-nots, or what Alvin Toffler has called the "fast" and the "slow" worlds. Tokyo has more telephones than the whole continent of Africa.

Nonetheless, whether we like it or not, the "transnational" future is upon us: as Kenichi Ohmae, the international economist, suggests with his talk of a "borderless economy," capitalism's allegiances are to products, not places. "Capital is now global," Robert Reich, the Secretary of Labor, has said, pointing out that when an Iowan buys a Pontiac from General Motors, 60% of his money goes to South Korea, Japan, West Germany, Taiwan, Singapore, Britain and Barbados. Culturally we are being re-formed daily by the cadences of world music and world fiction: where the great Canadian writers of an older generation had names like Frye and Davies and Laurence, now they are called Ondaatje and Mistry and Skvorecky.

As space shrinks, moreover, time accelerates. This hip-hop mishmash is spreading overnight. When my parents were in college, there were all of seven foreigners living in Tibet, a country the size of Western Europe, and in its entire history the country had seen fewer than 2,000 Westerners. Now a Danish student in Lhasa is scarcely more surprising than a Tibetan in Copenhagen. Already a city like Miami is beyond the wildest dreams of 1968; how much more so will its face in 2018 defy our predictions of today?

It would be easy, seeing all this, to say that the world is moving toward the *Raza Cosmica* (Cosmic Race), predicted by the Mexican thinker Jose Vasconcelos in the '20s—a glorious blend of mongrels and mestizos. It may be more relevant to suppose that more and more of the world may come to resemble Hong Kong, a stateless special economic zone full of expats and exiles linked by the lingua franca of English and the global marketplace. Some urbanists already see the world as a grid of 30 or so highly advanced city-regions, or technopoles, all plugged into the same international circuit.

The world will not become America. Anyone who has been to a baseball game in Osaka, or a Pizza Hut in Moscow, knows instantly that she is not in Kansas. But America may still, if only symbolically, be a model for the world. *E Pluribus Unum*, after all, is on the dollar bill. As Federico Mayor Zaragoza, the director-general of UNESCO, has said, "America's main role in the new world order is not as a military superpower, but as a multicultural superpower."

The traditional metaphor for this is that of a mosaic. But Richard *14* Rodriguez, the Mexican-American essayist who is a psalmist for our new hybrid forms, points out that the interaction is more fluid than that, more human, subject to daily revision. "I am Chinese," he says, "because I live in San Francisco, a Chinese city. I became Irish in America. I became Portuguese in America." And even as he announces this new truth, Portuguese women are becoming American, and Irishmen are becoming Portuguese, and Sydney (or is it Toronto?) is thinking to compare itself with the "Chinese city" we know as San Francisco.

VOCABULARY

In your journal, write the meanings of the following words:

- a rainbow *coalition* (**2**)
- a world as *hyphenated* (**2**)
- frontier of *polyglot* terms (**3**)
- *postnational* trends (**3**)
- socially engineered *uniculture* (**4**)
- with dialogue in *Lakota* (**5**)
- *entrepreneurial* energy (**6**)
- Alexandria . . . was a *paradigm* (**8**)
- American *eclecticism* (**8**)
- a *soigné*, international air (**8**)
- new meanings of the word *Balkanization* (**9**)
- the *cadences* of world music (**10**)
- glorious blend of mongrels and *mestizos* (**12**)
- the *lingua franca* of English (**12**)

QUESTIONS FOR WRITING AND DISCUSSION

1. The purpose of Iyer's essay is to explain the multicultural dimensions of our new global village. But in explaining these dimensions, he actually *recreates* them by referring to over thirty countries, thirty cities, and ten languages. Make a list of these countries, cities, and languages. (Can you find these countries and cities on a map?) What effect does Iyer wish to create by including so many geographical and language references?

2. Unfamiliar vocabulary in Iyer's essay is a crucial part of the content, since Iyer's purpose is to explain and recreate the "wide open frontier of polyglot terms" that is "itself multi-tongued and many hued." Look up the words in the vocabulary list. Then reread the essay, looking for other words you do not know. Look them up in your dictionary. What effect does Iyer wish to create by using his polyglot or multicultural vocabulary?

3. In your own words, express the thesis of Iyer's essay. What is he trying to explain? Find at least three sentences from Iyer's essay that may suggest this thesis. How do these sentences each express a different aspect of the thesis? How are these sentences thematically related? Explain.

4. In paragraph 14, Iyer says that the traditional metaphor for the new transnational, multicultural world order is the mosaic. But taking his cue from Richard Rodriguez, Iyer suggests that the multicultural interaction is "more fluid than that, more human." In what other paragraphs does Iyer suggest the fluidity and humanity of the global village? Explain.

5. Iyer's essay celebrates the global village that technology has created, but he also points to potential dangers. What dangers does he cite? What other dangers exist? How might the technologies that have created the global village (television, fax, telephones, cell phones and pagers, airplanes, the Internet, and so forth) help solve these problems?

6. On the Internet, check out a site called Diversity and Multiculturalism at http://multiculturalism.aynrand.org. This site is sponsored by the Ayn Rand Institute. The opening paragraphs at this site claim that "multiculturalism is racism in a politically-correct guise." Read several pages or documents at this site. Then, assuming that you are Pico Iyer, write a response to the argument represented there. Or write your own response that finds some middle ground between what Iyer says and what the Rand site argues.

PROFESSIONAL WRITING

HOW MALE AND FEMALE STUDENTS USE LANGUAGE DIFFERENTLY

Deborah Tannen

Everyone knows that men and women communicate differently, but Deborah Tannen, a linguist at Georgetown University, has spent her career studying how and why their conversational styles are different. Tannen's books include Conversational Style: Analyzing Talk Among Friends *(1984), her best-selling* You Just Don't Understand: Women and Men in Conversation *(1990), and* I Only Say This Because I Love You *(2001). In the following article from* The Chronicle of Higher Education, *Tannen applies her knowledge of conversational styles to the classroom. How do men and women communicate differently in the classroom? What teaching styles best promote open communication and learning for both sexes? As you read her essay, think about your own classes. Do the men in your classes talk more than the women? Do men like to argue in large groups, while women prefer conversations in small groups? How clearly—and convincingly—does Tannen explain discussion preferences and their effects in the classroom?*

When I researched and wrote my latest book, *You Just Don't Understand: Women and Men in Conversation*, the furthest thing from my mind was reevaluating my teaching strategies. But that has been one of the direct benefits of having written the book. 1

The primary focus of my linguistic research always has been the 2 language of everyday conversation. One facet of this is conversational style: how different regional, ethnic, and class backgrounds, as well as age and gender, result in different ways of using language to communicate. *You Just Don't Understand* is about the conversational styles of women and men. As I gained more insight into typically male and female ways of using language, I began to suspect some of the causes of the troubling facts that women who go to single-sex schools do better in later life, and that when young women sit next to young men in classrooms, the males talk more. This is not to say that all men talk in class, nor that no women do. It is simply that a greater percentage of discussion time is taken by men's voices.

The research of sociologists and anthropologists such as Janet 3 Lever, Marjorie Harness Goodwin, and Donna Eder has shown that girls and boys learn to use language differently in their sex-separate peer groups. Typically, a girl has a best friend with whom she sits and talks, frequently telling secrets. It's the telling of secrets, the fact and the way that they talk to each other, that makes them best friends. For boys, activities are central: their best friends are the ones they do things with. Boys also tend to play in larger groups that are hierarchical. High-status boys give orders and push low-status boys around. So boys are expected to use language to seize center stage: by exhibiting their skill, displaying their knowledge, and challenging and resisting challenges.

These patterns have stunning implications for classroom interaction. Most faculty members assume that participating in class discussion is a necessary part of successful performance. Yet speaking in a classroom is more congenial to boys' language experience than to girls', since it entails putting oneself forward in front of a large group of people, many of whom are strangers and at least one of whom is sure to judge speakers' knowledge and intelligence by their verbal display.

Another aspect of many classrooms that makes them more hospitable to most men than to most women is the use of debate-like formats as a learning tool. Our educational system, as Walter Ong argues persuasively in his book *Fighting for Life* (Cornell University Press, 1981), is fundamentally male in that the pursuit of knowledge is believed to be achieved by ritual opposition: public display followed by argument and challenge. Father Ong demonstrates that ritual opposition—what he calls "adversativeness" or "agonism"—is fundamental to the way most males approach almost any activity. (Consider, for example, the little boy who shows he likes a little girl by pulling her braids and shoving her.) But ritual opposition is antithetical to the way most females learn and like to interact. It is not that females don't fight, but that they don't fight for fun. They don't *ritualize* opposition.

Anthropologists working in widely disparate parts of the world have found contrasting verbal rituals for women and men. Women in completely unrelated cultures (for example, Greece and Bali) engage in ritual laments: spontaneously produced rhyming couplets that express their pain, for example, over the loss of loved ones. Men do not take part in laments. They have their own, very different verbal ritual: a contest, a war of words in which they vie with each other to devise clever insults.

When discussing these phenomena with a colleague, I commented that I see these two styles in American conversation: many women bond by talking about troubles, and many men bond by exchanging playful insults and put-downs, and other sorts of verbal sparring. He exclaimed: "I never thought of this, but that's the way I teach: I have students read an article, and then I invite them to tear it apart. After we've torn it to shreds, we talk about how to build a better model."

This contrasts sharply with the way I teach: I open the discussion 8 of readings by asking, "What did you find useful in this? What can we use in our own theory building and our own methods?" I note what I see as weaknesses in the author's approach, but I also point out that the writer's discipline and purposes might be different from ours. Finally, I offer personal anecdotes illustrating the phenomena under discussion and praise students' anecdotes as well as their critical acumen.

These different teaching styles must make our classrooms wildly 9 different places and hospitable to different students. Male students are more likely to be comfortable attacking the readings and might find the inclusion of personal anecdotes irrelevant and "soft." Women are more likely to resist discussion they perceive as hostile, and, indeed, it is women in my classes who are most likely to offer personal anecdotes.

A colleague who read my book commented that he had always 10 taken for granted that the best way to deal with students' comments is to challenge them; this, he felt it was self-evident, sharpens their minds and helps them develop debating skills. But he had noticed that women were relatively silent in his classes, so he decided to try beginning discussion with relatively open-ended questions and letting comments go unchallenged. He found, to his amazement and satisfaction, that more women began to speak up.

Though some of the women in his class clearly liked this better, 11 perhaps some of the men liked it less. One young man in my class wrote in a questionnaire about a history professor who gave students questions to think about and called on people to answer them: "He would then play devil's advocate . . . *i.e.*, he debated us. . . . That class *really* sharpened me intellectually. . . . We as students do need to know how to defend ourselves." This young man valued the experience of being attacked and challenged publicly. Many, if not most, women would shrink from such "challenge," experiencing it as public humiliation.

A professor at Hamilton College told me of a young man who 12 was upset because he felt his class presentation had been a failure. The professor was puzzled because he had observed that class members had listened attentively and agreed with the student's observations. It turned out that it was this very agreement that the student interpreted as failure: since no one had engaged his ideas by arguing with him, he felt they had found them unworthy of attention.

So one reason men speak in class more than women is that many 13 of them find the "public" classroom setting more conducive to speaking, whereas most women are more comfortable speaking in private to a small group of people they know well. A second reason is that men are more likely to be comfortable with the debate-like form that discussion may take. Yet another reason is the different attitudes toward speaking in class that typify women and men.

Students who speak frequently in class, many of whom are men, *14* assume that it is their job to think of contributions and try to get the floor to express them. But many women monitor their participation not only to get the floor but to avoid getting it. Women students in my class tell me that if they have spoken up once or twice, they hold back for the rest of the class because they don't want to dominate. If they have spoken a lot one week, they will remain silent the next. These different ethics of participation are, of course, unstated, so those who speak freely assume that those who remain silent have nothing to say, and those who are reining themselves in assume that the big talkers are selfish and hoggish.

When I looked around my classes, I could see these differing ethics *15* and habits at work. For example, my graduate class in analyzing conversation had twenty students, eleven women and nine men. Of the men, four were foreign students: two Japanese, one Chinese, and one Syrian. With the exception of the three Asian men, all the men spoke in class at least occasionally. The biggest talker in the class was a woman, but there were also five women who never spoke at all, only one of whom was Japanese. I decided to try something different.

I broke the class into small groups to discuss the issues raised in *16* the readings and to analyze their own conversational transcripts. I devised three ways of dividing the students into groups: one by the degree program they were in, one by gender, and one by conversational style, as closely as I could guess it. This meant that when the class was grouped according to conversational style, I put Asian students together, fast talkers together, and quiet students together. The class split into groups six times during the semester, so they met in each grouping twice. I told students to regard the groups as examples of interactional data and to note the different ways they participated in the different groups. Toward the end of the term, I gave them a questionnaire asking about their class and group participation.

I could see plainly from my observation of the groups at work that *17* women who never opened their mouths in class were talking away in the small groups. In fact, the Japanese woman commented that she found it particularly hard to contribute to the all-woman group she was in because "I was overwhelmed by how talkative the female students were in the female-only group." This is particularly revealing because it highlights that the same person who can be "oppressed" into silence in one context can become the talkative "oppressor" in another. No one's conversational style is absolute; everyone's style changes in response to the context and others' styles.

Some of the students (seven) said they preferred the same-gender *18* groups; others preferred the same-style groups. In answer to the question "Would you have liked to speak in class more than you did?" six of the seven who said yes were women; the one man was Japanese. Most startlingly, this response did not come only from quiet women; it came from women who had indicated they had spoken in class never, rarely, sometimes, and often. Of the eleven students who said the amount they had spoken was fine, seven were men. Of the four women who checked "fine," two added qualifications indicating it wasn't completely fine: One wrote in "maybe more," and one wrote, "I have an urge to participate but often feel I should have something more interesting/relevant/wonderful/intelligent to say!!"

I counted my experiment a success. Everyone in the class found the *19* small groups interesting, and no one indicated he or she would have preferred that the class not break into groups. Perhaps most instructive, however, was the fact that the experience of breaking into groups, and of talking about participation in class, raised everyone's awareness about classroom participation. After we had talked about it, some of the quietest women in the class made a few voluntary contributions, though sometimes I had to ensure their participation by interrupting the students who were exuberantly speaking out.

Americans are often proud that they discount the significance of *20* cultural differences: "We are all individuals," many people boast. Ignoring such issues as gender and ethnicity becomes a source of pride: "I treat everyone the same." But treating people the same is not equal treatment if they are not the same.

The classroom is a different environment for those who feel com- *21* fortable putting themselves forward in a group than it is for those who find the prospect of doing so chastening, or even terrifying. When a professor asks, "Are there any questions?" students who can formulate statements the fastest have the greatest opportunity to respond. Those who need significant time to do so have not really been given a chance at all, since by the time they are ready to speak, someone else has the floor.

In a class where some students speak out without raising hands, *22* those who feel they must raise their hands and wait to be recognized do not have equal opportunity to speak. Telling them to feel free to jump in will not make them feel free; one's sense of timing, of one's rights and obligations in a classroom, are automatic, learned over years of interaction. They may be changed over time, with motivation and effort, but they cannot be changed on the spot. And everyone assumes his or her own way is best. When I asked my students how the class could be changed to make it easier for them to speak more, the most talkative woman said she would prefer it if no one had to raise hands, and a foreign student said he wished people would raise their hands and wait to be recognized.

My experience in this class has convinced me that small-group interaction should be part of any class that is not a small seminar. I also am convinced that having the students become observers of their own interaction is a crucial part of their education. Talking about ways of talking in class makes students aware that their ways of talking affect other students, that the motivations they impute to others may not truly reflect others' motives, and that the behaviors they assume to be self-evidently right are not universal norms. *23*

The goal of complete equal opportunity in class may not be attainable, but realizing that one monolithic classroom-participation structure is not equal opportunity is itself a powerful motivation to find more-diverse methods to serve diverse students—and every classroom is diverse. *24*

VOCABULARY

In your journal, write the meanings of the following words:

- ritual opposition is *antithetical* **(5)**
- personal *anecdotes* **(8)**
- *conducive* to speaking **(13)**
- *ethics* of participation **(14)**
- *monolithic* classroom-participation structure **(24)**

QUESTIONS FOR WRITING AND DISCUSSION

1. Reread Tannen's essay, noting places where your experiences as a student match or do not match her observations. In what contexts were your experiences similar to or different from Tannen's? Explain what might account for the different observations.

2. In her essay, Tannen states and then continues to restate her thesis. Reread her essay, underlining all the sentences that seem to state or rephrase her main idea. Do her restatements of the main idea make her essay clearer? Explain.

3. Explaining essays may explain *what* (describe and define), explain *how* (process analysis), and/or explain *why* (causal analysis). Find one example of each of these strategies in Tannen's essay. Which of these three is the dominant shaping strategy? Support your answer with references to specific sentences or paragraphs.

4. Effective explaining essays must have supporting evidence—specific examples, facts, quotations, testimony from experts, statistics, and so on.

Choose four consecutive paragraphs from Tannen's essay and list the kinds of supporting evidence she uses. Based on your inventory, rate her supporting evidence as weak, average, or strong. Explain your choice.

5. Does the style of Tannen's essay support her thesis that men and women have different ways of communicating? Does Tannen, in fact, use a "woman's style" of writing that is similar to women's conversational style? Examine Tannen's tone (her attitude toward her subject and audience), her voice (the projection of her personality in her language), and her supporting evidence (her use of facts and statistics or anecdotal, contextual evidence). Cite specific passages to support your analysis.

6. In another class where students discuss frequently, sit in the back row where you can observe the participation of men and women. First, record the number of men and the number of women in the class. Then, during one class period, record the following: (a) When the teacher calls on a student, record whether the student is male or female; (b) when a student talks without raising his or her hand, record whether the student is male or female; and (c) when students speak in class, record how long they talk and whether they are male or female. Once you have collected and analyzed your data, explain whether they seem to support or refute Tannen's claims.

7. On the Internet, visit Deborah Tannen's home page at http://www.georgetown.edu/faculty/tannend. Click on the link "Interviews with Deborah Tannen." How do her responses during these interviews shed light on the conversational styles of men and women? What points does she make that might apply to how men and women communicate and learn differently in the classroom?

Explaining: The Writing Process ●●●

■ ASSIGNMENT FOR EXPLAINING   Explain *what* something means or is, *how* it should be done or how it occurs, and/or *why* something occurs. Choose from your personal experiences, talents, or interests, or choose from ideas, concepts, theories, or strategies that you are learning in other courses. Your purpose is to explain something as clearly as possible for your audience by analyzing, showing relationships, and demonstrating with examples, facts, illustrations, data, or other information.

With a topic in mind, think about your audience and a possible genre. As in your investigating paper, the amount and kind of detail you need depend on how much your readers are likely to know about your topic. What do they already know? What have you discovered in your research that will help explain the topic for them? Is an essay the most appropriate genre, or would an article, editorial, Internet posting, pamphlet, or letter be more effective?

You can write about anything, and if you write well enough, even the reader with no intrinsic interest in the subject will become involved.

—TRACY KIDDER,
NOVELIST

CHOOSING A SUBJECT

If one of your journal entries suggested a possible subject, go on to the collecting and shaping strategies. If you still need an interesting subject, consider the following suggestions:

- Reread your authority list or the most interesting journal entries from previous chapters. Do they contain ideas that you might define or explain, processes suitable for how-to explanations, or causes or effects that you could analyze and explain for a certain audience?
- Brainstorm a list of the five most important things that you've done in the last three years. Focus on one thing, event, or idea. Now imagine that your audience is someone like you, only three years younger. Explain this topic.
- Reread your notes from another class in which you have an upcoming examination. Select some topic, idea, principle, process, famous person, or event from the text or your notes. Investigate other texts, popular magazines, or journals for information on that topic. If appropriate, interview someone or conduct a survey. Explain this principle or process to a member of your writing class.

COLLECTING

QUESTIONS   Once you have a tentative subject and audience in mind, consider which of the following will be your primary focus (all three may be relevant):

- *What* something means or is
- *How* something occurs or is done (or should be done)
- *Why* something occurs or what its effects are

To explain *what* something is, jot down answers to each of the following questions. The more you can write on each question, the more details you'll have for your topic.

- What are its class and distinguishing characteristics?
- What is its etymology?
- How can you describe it?
- What examples can you give?
- What are its parts or its functions?
- What is it similar to? What is it *not*?
- What figurative comparisons apply?
- How can it be classified?
- Which of the above is most useful to your audience?

To explain *how* something occurs or is done, answer the following questions:

- What are the component parts or steps in the whole process?
- What is the exact sequence of steps or events?
- Are several of the steps or events related?
- If steps or events were omitted, would the outcome change?
- Which steps or events are most crucial?
- Which steps or events does your audience most need to know?

To explain *why* something occurs or what its effects are, consider the following issues:

- Which are the necessary or sufficient causes?
- Which causes are remote in time, and which are immediate?
- What is the order or sequence of the causes? Do the causes occur simultaneously?
- What are the effects? Do they occur in a sequence or simultaneously?
- Do the causes and effects occur in a "chain reaction"?
- Is there an action or situation that would have prevented the effect?
- Are there comparable things or events that have similar causes or effects?
- Which causes or effects need special clarification for your audience?

BRANCHING   Often, *branching* can help you visually analyze your subject. Start with your topic and then subdivide each idea into its component parts. The resulting analysis will not only help generate ideas but may also suggest ways to shape an essay:

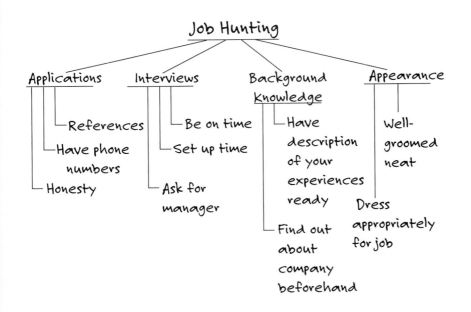

Branching can also take the form of a tree, with a main trunk for the subject and separate branches for each subtopic. For an essay on effective job hunting, information might be diagrammed this way:

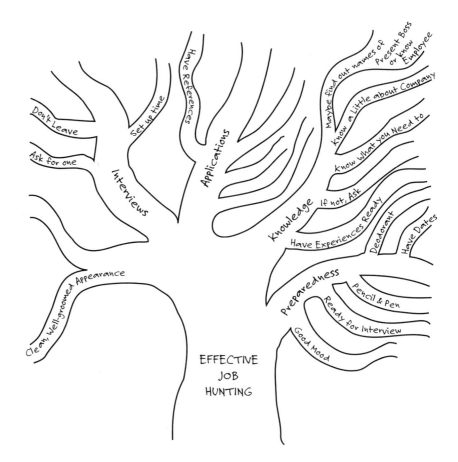

OBSERVING   If you can observe your subject, try drawing it, describing it, or taking careful notes. Which senses can you use to describe it—sight, sound, touch, smell, taste? If it is a scientific experiment that you can reproduce or a social situation you can reconstruct, go through it again and observe carefully. As you observe it, put yourself in your readers' shoes: What do you need to explain it to them?

REMEMBERING   Your own experience and memory are essential for explaining. *Freewriting, looping,* and *clustering* may all generate detailed information, good examples, and interesting perspectives that will make your explanation

RESEARCH TIPS

Review your topic for research possibilities. Four research strategies are direct *observation*, use of *memories* and personal experience, *field research* (including interviews and surveys), and *library/Internet research*. (See Chapter 6 for interview and survey techniques. See Chapter 12 on using and documenting sources.) Tips to remember: Make *photocopies* of all the sources that you plan to cite in your essay. When you make copies, be sure to *write all relevant information* on the photocopies, such as author, date, publisher, place of publication, journal title, and volume numbers. When you cite sources in the text, be sure to *introduce* your sources. Make sure your direct quotations are *accurate* word-for-word transcriptions.

clearer and more vivid. (See Chapter 4 for an explanation of looping and clustering.)

READING   When you find written texts about your subject, be sure to use your active reading strategies. You may need only a few sources if you reread them carefully. Write out a short summary for each source. Respond to each source by analyzing its effectiveness, agreeing or disagreeing with its ideas, or interpreting the text. The quality of your understanding is more important than the sheer number of sources you cite.

INVESTIGATING   Use sources available in the library, textbooks containing relevant information, or interviews with teachers, participants, or experts. Interview your classmates about their own subjects for this assignment: Someone else's subject may trigger an idea that you can write about or may suggest a fresh approach to the subject that you have already chosen.

SHAPING

As you collect information and generate ideas from your collecting activities, be sure to *narrow* and *focus* your subject into a topic suitable for a short essay. You will not be able to cover everything you've read, thought, or experienced about your subject. Choose the most interesting ideas—for you and for your audience—and shape, order, and clarify those ideas. In addition to *spatial order* and *comparison/contrast*, which are discussed in Chapters 3 and 4, one of the following shaping strategies may help you organize your essay.

Readers may be strangers who have no immediate reason to care about your writing. They want order, clarity, and stimulation.

—ELIZABETH COWAN NEELD,

TEACHER AND AUTHOR

DEFINITION AND CLASSIFICATION   An essay explaining *what* something means or is can be shaped by using a variety of definition strategies or by classifying the subject.

Definition itself is not a single organizing strategy; it supports a variety of strategies that may be useful in shaping your essay: description, analysis of parts or function, comparison/contrast, development by examples, or figures of speech such as simile, metaphor, and analogy.

Classification, on the other hand, is a single strategy that can organize a paragraph or even a whole essay quickly. Observers of human behavior, for example, love to use classification. Grocery shoppers might be classified by types: racers (the ones who seem to have just won forty-five seconds of free shopping and run down the aisles filling their carts as fast as possible), talkers (the ones whose phone must be out of order because they stand in the aisles gossiping forever), penny-pinchers (who always have their calculators out and read the unit price labels for everything), party shoppers (who camp out in the junk food aisles, filling their carts with potato chips, dip, candy, peanuts, and drink mixers), and dawdlers (who leave their carts crosswise in the aisles while they read twenty-nine different soup can labels). You can write a sentence or two about each type or devote a whole paragraph to explaining a single type.

EXAMPLE   Development by example can effectively illustrate what something is or means, but it can also help explain how or why something happens. Usually, an example describes a specific incident, located at a certain place and occurring at a particular time, that *shows* or *demonstrates* the main idea. In the following paragraph from *Mediaspeak*, Donna Woolfolk Cross explains what effects soap operas can have on addicted viewers. This paragraph is developed by several examples—some described in detail, others referred to briefly:

> Dedicated watchers of soap operas often confuse fact with fiction. . . . Stars of soap operas tell hair-raising stories of their encounters with fans suffering from this affliction. Susan Lucci, who plays the promiscuous Erica Kane on "All My Children," tells of a time she was riding in a parade: "We were in a crowd of about 250,000 traveling in an antique open car moving ver-r-ry slowly. At that time in the series I was involved with a character named Nick. Some man broke through, came right up to the car and said to me, 'Why don't you give me a little bit of what you've been giving Nick?'" The man hung onto the car, menacingly, until she was rescued by the police. Another time, when she was in church, the reverent silence was broken by a woman's astonished remark, "Oh, my god, Erica prays!" Margaret Mason, who plays the villainous Lisa Anderson in "Days of Our Lives," was accosted by a woman who poured a carton of milk all over her in the supermarket. And once a woman actually tried to force her car off the Ventura Freeway.

VOICE AND TONE   Writers also use voice and tone to shape and control whole passages, often in combination with other shaping strategies. In the following paragraph, Toni Bambara, author of *The Salt Eaters* and numerous short stories, explains *what* being a writer is all about. This paragraph is shaped both by a single extended example and by Bambara's voice talking directly to the reader:

> When I replay the tapes on file in my head, tapes of speeches I've given at writing conferences over the years, I invariably hear myself saying— "A writer, like any other cultural worker, like any other member of the community, ought to try to put her/his skills in the service of the community." Some years ago when I returned south, my picture in the paper prompted several neighbors to come visit. "You a writer? What all you write?" Before I could begin the catalogue, one old gent interrupted with—"Ya know Miz Mary down the block? She need a writer to help her send off a letter to her grandson overseas." So I began a career as the neighborhood scribe—letters to relatives, snarling letters to the traffic chief about the promised stop sign, nasty letters to the utilities, angry letters to the principal about that confederate flag hanging in front of the school, contracts to transfer a truck from seller to buyer, etc. While my efforts have been graciously appreciated in the form of sweet potato dumplings, herb teas, hair braiding, and the like, there is still much room for improvement—"For a writer, honey, you've got a mighty bad hand. Didn't they teach penmanship at that college?" Another example, I guess, of words setting things in motion. What goes around, comes around, as the elders say.

CHRONOLOGICAL ORDER AND PROCESS ANALYSIS   Writers use chronological order in expository writing to help explain how to do something or how something is typically done. In her essay "Anorexia Nervosa," student writer Nancie Brosseau uses transitional words to signal the various stages of anorexia. In the following sentences, taken from the third paragraph of her essay, the *italicized* words mark the chronological stages of her anorexia:

> Several serious health problems bombarded me, and it's a wonder I'm still alive. . . . *As my weight plummeted*, my circulation grew *increasingly worse*. . . . My hair *started* to fall out, and my whole body took on a very skeletal appearance. . . . I would force myself to vomit *as soon as possible* if I was forced to eat. The enamel on my teeth *started to be eaten away* by the acid in the vomit, and my lips cracked and bled regularly. I *stopped* menstruating completely because I was not producing enough estrogen. . . . *One time*, while executing a chain of back handsprings, I broke all five fingers on one hand and three on the other because my bones had become so brittle. . . . I chose to see a psychologist, and she helped me sort out the emotional aspects of anorexia, *which in turn* solved the physical problems.

CAUSAL ANALYSIS   In order to explain *why* something happens or what the effects of something are, writers often use one of the following three patterns of cause and effect to shape their material:

Cause 1 + Cause 2 + Cause 3 . . . + Cause n → Effect

In the case of fire, for example, we know that three causes lead to a single effect. These causes do not occur in any special sequence; they must all be present at the same time. For historical events, however, we usually list causes in chronological order.

Sometimes one cause has several effects. In that case, we reverse the pattern:

Cause → Effect 1 + Effect 2 + Effect 3 . . . + Effect n

For example, an explanation of the collapse of the economy following the stock market crash of 1929 might follow this pattern. The crash (itself a symptom of other causes) led to a depreciated economy, widespread unemployment, bankruptcy for thousands of businesses, foreclosures on farms, and so forth. An essay on the effects of the crash might devote one or two paragraphs to each effect.

In the third pattern, causes and effects form a pattern of chain reactions. One cause leads to an effect that then becomes the cause of another effect, and so on:

Cause 1 → Effect 1 (Cause 2) → Effect 2 (Cause 3) → Effect 3

We could analyze events in the Middle East prior to the Persian Gulf War as a series of actions and reactions in which each effect becomes the cause of the next effect in the chain of skirmishes, car bombings, air raids, terrorist hijackings, and kidnappings. An essay on the chain reaction of events in the Middle East might have a paragraph or two on each of the links in this chain.

INTRODUCTIONS AND LEAD-INS   Often, the first sentences of the introductory paragraph of an essay are the hardest to write. You want to get your reader's attention and focus on the main idea of your essay, but you don't want to begin, boringly, with your thesis statement. Below are several kinds of opening sentences designed to grab your reader's interest. Consider your topic—see if one of these strategies will work for you.

A personal example

I knew my dieting had gotten out of hand, but when I could actually see the movement of my heart beating beneath my clothes, I knew I was in trouble.

—"Anorexia Nervosa," Nancie Brosseau

A description of a person or place

He strides toward us in navy and white, his body muscled and heavyset, one arm holding his casually flung jeans jacket over his shoulder. A man in his prime, with just the right combination of macho and sartorial flair.

> —"Some Don't Like Their Blues at All," Karyn M. Lewis

It's still there, the Chinese school on Yale Street where my brother and I used to go. Despite the new coat of paint and the high wire fence, the school I knew ten years ago remains remarkably, stoically the same.

> —"The Struggle to Be an All-American Girl," Elizabeth Wong

An example from a case study

Susan Smith has everything going for her. A self-described workaholic, she runs a Cambridge, Massachusetts, real estate consulting company with her husband Charles and still finds time to cuddle and nurture their two young kids, David, 7, and Stacey, 6. What few people know is that Susan, 44, needs a little chemical help to be a supermom: she has been taking the antidepressant Prozac for five years.

> —"The Personality Pill," Anastasia Toufexis

A startling statement, fact, or statistic

Embalming is indeed a most extraordinary procedure, and one must wonder at the docility of Americans who each year pay hundreds of millions of dollars for its perpetuation, blissfully ignorant of what it is all about, what is done, how it is done.

> —"To Dispel Fears of Live Burial," Jessica Mitford

A statement from a book

The American novelist John Barth, in his early novel *The Floating Opera*, remarks that ordinary, day-to-day life often presents us with embarrassingly obvious, totally unsubtle patterns of symbolism and meaning— life in the midst of death, innocence vindicated, youth versus age, etc.

> —"I'm O.K., but You're Not," Robert Zoellner

A striking question or questions

Do non-human animals have rights? Should we humans feel morally bound to exercise consideration for the lives and well-being of individual members of other animal species? If so, how much consideration, and by what logic?

> —"Animal Rights and Beyond," David Quammen

A common error or mistaken judgment

There was a time when, in my search for essences, I concluded that the canyonland country has no heart. I was wrong. The canyonlands did have a heart, a living heart, and that heart was Glen Canyon and the golden, flowing Colorado River.

—"The Damnation of a Canyon," Edward Abbey

Combined strategies

Last December a man named Robert Lee Willie, who had been convicted of raping and murdering an 18-year-old woman, was executed in the Louisiana state prison. In a statement issued several minutes before his death, Mr. Willie said: "Killing people is wrong. . . . It makes no difference whether it's citizens, countries, or governments. Killing is wrong."

—"Death and Justice," Edward Koch

LEAD-IN, THESIS, AND ESSAY MAP   The introduction to an explaining essay—whether one paragraph or several—usually contains the following features:

- *Lead-In*: Some example, description, startling statement, statistic, short narrative, allusion, or quotation to get the reader's interest *and* focus on the topic you will explain.
- *Thesis*: Statement of the main idea; a "promise" to the reader that the essay fulfills.
- *Essay Map*: A sentence, or part of a sentence, that *lists* (in the order in which the essay discusses them) the main subtopics for the essay.

In her essay on anorexia nervosa at the end of this chapter, Nancie Brosseau's introductory paragraph has all three features:

Lead-in: Startling statement

Description

Statistics
Thesis
Essay map

I knew my dieting had gotten out of hand, but when I could actually see the movement of my heart beating beneath my clothes, I knew I was in trouble. At first, the family doctor reassured my parents that my rapid weight loss was a "temporary phase among teenage girls." However, when I, at fourteen years old and five feet tall, weighed in at sixty-three pounds, my doctor changed his diagnosis from "temporary phase" to "anorexia nervosa." Anorexia nervosa is the process of self-starvation that affects over 100,000 young girls each year. Almost 6,000 of these girls die every year. Anorexia nervosa is a self-mutilating disease that affects its victim both physically and emotionally.

The essay map is contained in the phrase "both physically and emotionally": The first half of the essay discusses the physical effects of anorexia nervosa; the second half explains the emotional effects. Like a road map, the essay map helps the reader anticipate what topics the writer will explain.

PARAGRAPH TRANSITIONS AND HOOKS   Transition words and paragraph hooks are audience cues that help the reader shift from one paragraph to the next. These connections between paragraphs help the reader see the relationships of the various parts. Transition words—*first, second, next, another, last, finally,* and so forth—signal your reader that a new idea or a new part of the idea is coming up. In addition to transition words, writers often tie paragraphs together by using a key word or idea from a previous paragraph in the first sentence of the following paragraph to "hook" the paragraphs together. The following paragraphs from Pico Iyer's essay, "The Global Village Finally Arrives," illustrate how transition words and paragraph hooks work together to create smooth connections between paragraphs.

The global village is defined, as we know, by an international youth culture that takes its cues from American pop culture. Kids in Perth and Prague and New Delhi are all tuning in to *Santa Barbara* on TV, and wriggling into 501 jeans, while singing along to Madonna's latest in English. . . . As fast as the world comes to America, America goes round the world—but it is an America that is itself multi-tongued and many hued, an America of Amy Tan and Janet Jackson and movies with dialogue in Lakota.

Far more than goods and artifacts, the one great influence being broadcast around the world in greater numbers and at greater speed than ever before is people. What were once clear divisions are now tangles of crossed lines: there are 40,000 "Canadians" resident in Hong Kong, many of whose first language is Cantonese. And with people come customs: while new immigrants from Taiwan and Vietnam and India— some of the so-called Asian Calvinists—import all-American values of hard work and family closeness and entrepreneurial energy to America, America is sending its values of upward mobility and individualism and melting-pot hopefulness to Taipei and Saigon and Bombay.

Values, in fact, travel at the speed of fax; by now, almost half the world's Mormons live outside the U.S. . . .

Transition: "FAR MORE . . . ."

Hooks: "goods" and "artifacts"

Hooks: "values" and "speed"

BODY PARAGRAPHS   Body paragraphs in expository writing are the main paragraphs in an essay, excluding any introductory, concluding, or transition paragraphs. They often contain the following features:

- *Topic sentence*: To promote clarity and precision, writers often use topic sentences to announce the main ideas of paragraphs. The main idea should be clearly related to the writer's thesis. A topic sentence usually occurs early in the paragraph (first or second sentence) or at the end of the paragraph.

- *Unity*: To avoid confusing readers, writers focus on a single idea for each paragraph. Writing unified paragraphs helps writers—and their readers—concentrate on one point at a time.
- *Coherence*: To make their writing flow smoothly from one sentence to the next, writers supplement their shaping strategies with coherence devices: repeated key words, pronouns referring to key nouns, and transition words.

The following body paragraph from Margaret Talbot's "*Les Très Riches Heures*" de Martha Stewart illustrates these features. The paragraph begins with a *topic sentence* that focuses on the idea of "class." It has *unity* because every sentence talks about class, about independent wealth, or about the trappings of wealth and status. It achieves coherence through the use of transitions, pronouns, and repeated key words and ideas.

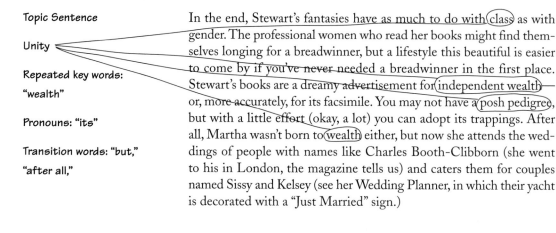

Topic Sentence

Unity

Repeated key words: "wealth"

Pronouns: "its"

Transition words: "but," "after all,"

In the end, Stewart's fantasies have as much to do with class as with gender. The professional women who read her books might find themselves longing for a breadwinner, but a lifestyle this beautiful is easier to come by if you've never needed a breadwinner in the first place. Stewart's books are a dreamy advertisement for independent wealth—or, more accurately, for its facsimile. You may not have a posh pedigree, but with a little effort (okay, a lot) you can adopt its trappings. After all, Martha wasn't born to wealth either, but now she attends the weddings of people with names like Charles Booth-Clibborn (she went to his in London, the magazine tells us) and caters them for couples named Sissy and Kelsey (see her Wedding Planner, in which their yacht is decorated with a "Just Married" sign.)

DRAFTING

Before you begin drafting, reconsider your purpose and audience. What you explain depends on what your audience needs to know or what would demonstrate or show your point most effectively.

As you work from an outline or from an organizing strategy, remember that all three questions—*what*, *how*, and *why*—are interrelated. If you are writing about causes, for example, an explanation of *what* the topic is and *how* the causes function may also be necessary to explain your subject clearly. As you write, balance your sense of plan and organization with a willingness to pursue ideas that you discover as you write. While you need to have a plan, you should be ready to change course if you discover a more interesting idea or angle.

PEER RESPONSE

The instructions that follow will help you give and receive constructive advice about the rough draft of your explaining essay. You may use these guidelines for an in-class workshop, a take-home review, or a computer e-mail response.

Writer: Before you exchange drafts with another reader, write out the following on your essay draft:

1. **Purpose** Briefly, describe your purpose and intended audience.
2. **Revision plans** What do you still intend to work on as you revise your draft?
3. **Questions** Write out one or two questions that you still have about your draft. What questions would you like your reader to answer?

Reader: First, read the entire draft from start to finish. As you reread the draft, answer the following questions:

1. **Clarity** What passages were clearest? Where were you most confused? Refer to specific sentences or passages to support your response. How and where could the writer make the draft clearer?
2. **Evidence** Where does the writer have good supporting evidence (specific examples, facts, analysis, statistics, interview results, or citations from sources)? Where does the writer need additional evidence? Refer to specific sentences or passages to support your response.
3. **Organization** Summarize or briefly outline the main ideas of the essay. Where was the organization most clear? Where were you confused? Refer to specific passages as you suggest ways to improve the draft.
4. **Purpose** Underline sentences that express the purpose or contain the thesis of the essay. Does your understanding of the essay's purpose match the writer's statement about purpose? Explain. How might the writer clarify the thesis?
5. **Reader's response** Overall, describe what you liked best about the draft. Then identify one major area that the writer should focus on during the revision. Does your suggestion match the writer's revision plans? Explain. Answer the writer's own question or questions about the draft.

REVISING

As you revise your explaining essay, concentrate on making yourself perfectly clear, on illustrating with examples where your reader might be confused, and on signaling the relationship of the parts of your essay to your reader.

I wish he would explain his explanation.

—LORD BYRON,

POET

Guidelines for Revision

- **Compare your thesis sentence with what you say in your conclusion**. You may have a clearer statement of your thesis near the end of your paper. Revise your original thesis sentence to make it clearer, more focused, or more in line with what your essay actually says.
- **Explaining means *showing* and *demonstrating* relationships**. Be sure to follow general statements with *specific examples*, *details*, *facts*, *statistics*, *memories*, *dialogues*, or other *illustrations*.
- **In a formal definition, be sure to include the class of objects or concepts to which the term belongs**. Avoid ungrammatical writing, such as "Photosynthesis is *when* plants absorb oxygen" or "The lymphatic system is *where* the body removes bacteria and transports fatty cells."
- **Avoid introducing definitions with "Webster says. . . . "** Instead, read definitions from several dictionaries and give the best or most appropriate definition.
- **Remember that you can modify the dictionary definition of a term or concept to fit your particular context**. For example, to you, *heroism* may mean having the courage to *say* what you believe, not just to endanger your life through selfless actions.
- **Don't mix categories when you are classifying objects or ideas**. If you are classifying houses *by floor design* (ranch, bilevel, split-level, two-story), don't bring in other categories, such as passive-solar, which could be incorporated into any of those designs.
- **In explaining *how* something occurs or should be done, be sure to indicate to your audience which steps are *most important*.**
- **In cause-and-effect explanations, avoid post hoc fallacies**. This term comes from the Latin phrase *post hoc, ergo propter hoc*: "After this, therefore because of this." For example, just because Event B occurred after Event A, it does not follow, necessarily, that A caused B. If, for example, statistics show that traffic fatalities in your state actually declined after the speed limit on interstate highways was increased, you should not conclude that higher speeds actually caused the reduction in fatalities. Other causes—increased radar patrols, stiffer drunk-driving penalties, or more rigorous vehicle-maintenance laws—may have been responsible for the reduction.
- **As you revise to sharpen your meaning or make your organization clearer, use appropriate transitional words and phrases to signal the *relationships among the various parts of your subject*.**

—*To signal relation in time*: before, meanwhile, later, soon, at last, earlier, thereafter, afterward, by that time, from then on, first, next, now, presently, shortly, immediately, finally
—*To signal similarity*: likewise, similarly, once again, once more
—*To signal difference*: but, yet, however, although, whereas, though, even so, nonetheless, still, on the other hand, on the contrary
—*To signal consequences*: as a result, consequently, therefore, hence, for this reason

■ POSTSCRIPT ON THE WRITING PROCESS   Before you hand in your essay, reflect on your writing and learning process. In your journal, spend a few minutes answering each of the following questions:

1. Describe the purpose and intended audience for your essay.
2. What was the best workshop advice that you received? What did you revise in your draft because of that advice? What piece of advice did you ignore? Why?
3. What caused you the most difficulty with this essay? How did you solve the problem—or attempt to solve it? With what parts are you still least satisfied?
4. What are the best parts of your paper? Refer to specific paragraphs—what do you like most about them?
5. What was the most important thing you learned about writing or your writing process as you wrote this paper?

STUDENT WRITING

ENGLISH ONLY
Christine Bishop

Christine Bishop decided to write on "English Only" as one of her semester portfolio topics. She had become interested in the topic in a previous year when she went to a speech tournament that debated the English-only issue. She wrote the following essay as the first step in her semester portfolio project. Following this explaining essay, she wrote a persuasive essay, arguing against English-only legislation. For this initial essay, however, she focused on reading key articles about English only, exploring the issues in each article, and explaining key arguments on both sides. Her goal was not to argue for one side or the other, but to explore the issues and explain the arguments on both sides of the English-only debate. As you read her essay, see if she explains the major arguments for both sides in a clear and balanced manner.

Prewriting for Topic Proposal

The English-only issue is a very controversial issue. Some say America should adopt an official language policy. Others think that this is a very racist idea. I have been reviewing reports of a recent vote on making Puerto Rico a state. Part of the legislation centered on making the people of Puerto Rico (which is predominantly Spanish-speaking) adopt English as their official language. Supporters of this bill claim that it is necessary that the Puerto Ricans learn English to become Americanized. Other people feel this will take away their language rights. Some people speculate that the English-only movement is a xenophobic reaction to the 1960 immigration amendments. These amendments made it illegal to restrict citizenship to America based on race. With this new amendment, there has been an influx in immigrants from diverse places. This influx of people could lead to xenophobia (fear of strangers or foreigners). I feel this speculation may be true. In 1912, when New Mexico became a state, it was allowed to keep Spanish as its official language provided that English was also an official language. Why such a radical change in policy when Puerto Rico applies to be a state? Is America afraid that it will lose its identity to non-English-speaking people? America started out as a conglomerate of immigrants who did not all speak the same language. What now?

I would like to explore this topic more. The two main positions on English-only legislation are as follows:

1. English needs to be the official language of the United States because we need one unifying language. Without English-only laws, immigrants will not learn English and will not contribute to society.

2. It is unfair to expect current citizens in the United States to learn English. Making English official will make people not learn other languages.

I know some about this subject, but I haven't done much research on my own. The questions I have are whether I could tie this into racism and whether I will be able to get enough information in the library and on the Internet.

First Draft

The issue has been raised that the United States needs to make English the official language of the nation. Currently, the Senate is reviewing a proposal to require Puerto Rico to adopt English as its official language before considering it for statehood. While everyone agrees that it is important for all Americans to speak English, there is disagreement as to whether the government should adopt an official language policy. Those who support an official language policy (such as Richard Rodriguez) believe that without a policy, immigrants to

America will not learn English. Those who do not support this policy believe that there is enough pressure on immigrants, and that they have enough desire to learn English quickly on their own. Some who oppose an official English policy believe that this policy will alienate immigrants and that Americans who support this policy are having a xenophobic reaction to recent immigrants from more diverse cultures initiated by 1960s immigration laws. I would like to explain exactly what these opposing positions are, using essays written by Richard Rodriguez, Samuel Hayakawa, James Crawford, and James Fallows.

As a champion of English-only legislation, Richard Rodriguez believes that without the government to push them into learning English, immigrants will not learn the language. In "Aria: A Memoir of a Bilingual Childhood," Mr. Rodriguez states, "What I did not believe was that I could speak a single public language. . . . It would have pleased me to hear my teachers address me in Spanish. . . . But I would have delayed—for how long postponed?—having to learn the language of public society [English]." Although Rodriguez was born in the United States, being the son of migrant workers, he had not been exposed to English until he had entered school. Without the church (he attended a Catholic school) to force him to learn English, he believes he would never have learned to speak English. Like all people on both sides of the issue, Rodriguez believes that it is necessary to speak English to succeed in the United States. Because Rodriguez was not motivated to speak English as a child, he feels that it is imperative for the government to push immigrants to learn English by making English the official language of the United States. People opposing English being the official language believe immigrants desire to learn English.

Both James Fallows, in "Viva Bilingualism," and James Crawford, author of *Hold Your Tongue: Bilingualism and the Politics of English Only*, oppose English-only legislation. Fallows, an English-speaking American who lived in Japan, feels that his experiences are contradictory to these beliefs. While living in Japan—a country that "makes many more accommodations to the English language than America does to Spanish"—Fallows found that most English-speaking people learned Japanese in order to participate in society. In America, Fallows thinks the incentives for immigrants to learn English are greater. The only way to get any kind of white-collar job or to attend college, according to Fallows, is through learning English. English is how communities in America are built.

Other English-only supporters, like former Senator Samuel Hayakawa, feel that a common language in the United States would better unite Americans. Hayakawa uses the example of Chinese- and Japanese-Americans, who didn't get along during World War II. Now they have begun to form Asian-American groups. Hayakawa believes this is the result of having learned English. Hayakawa states, "A common tongue encourages trust while reducing racial hostility and bigotry." Hayakawa believes that unless the United States implements an English-only policy, we will head the way of Quebec or India—"a chaotic mess which has led to countless problems in the government's efforts to manage the nation's business." According to Hayakawa, this problem is already apparent. He blames the 50 percent dropout rate among Hispanic students on the current bilingual policy.

People who do not support English-only, like James Crawford, do not believe that the differences in language will cause chaos. They further believe that an official English policy will separate Americans. In his book, James Crawford quotes Raul Yazquirre, President of the National Council of La Raza, as saying: "U.S. English is to Hispanics as the Ku Klux Klan is to blacks." Crawford says that this is the consensus among Latino leaders. Crawford goes on to say that Latino leaders believe English only "is a Xenophobic, intolerant act."

Because I believe that Rodriguez's experience might be unique and that there are many other people's experiences pointing the other way—including my own—I think Hayakawa's argument may be shaky. Possibly, Crawford and Fallows, because of their experience, may be correct. Crawford has spent ten years researching the issue, which gives his argument credibility. I think that although it is quite debatable, the new push for English as an official language may be due to a backlash against the recent influx of more diverse groups into the United States. But determining exactly how government laws might affect the motivation of immigrants to learn English is difficult. We seem to have different personal testimonies: Hayakawa and Rodriguez think an English-only policy will encourage immigrants to learn English; Fallows and Crawford think immigrants already have enough incentives to learn English.

Final Draft
ENGLISH ONLY

English-only laws have been in the news again, with a recent debate in   *1*
the Senate over a requirement that Puerto Rico adopt English as its official language before being allowed to become a state (Gugliotta 1). In the United States, English-only laws currently exist in twenty-three states—having passed recently in Alaska and Missouri—but they suffered a setback in Arizona, where the United States Supreme Court upheld a decision that struck down an Arizona law that passed originally in 1988 (Denniston 1). Basically, English-only laws such as Arizona's state that

"this state and all political subdivisions of this state shall act in English and no other language" (Denniston 2). While everyone agrees that it is important for all Americans to speak English, there is disagreement as to whether state governments should adopt an official language policy.

The debate over "English only" continues as groups such as U.S. English try to promote language laws in every state. Those who support an official language policy believe that without a policy, immigrants will not learn English. Those who oppose an official English policy believe that English-only laws alienate immigrants and that Americans who support these laws are having a xenophobic reaction to the flood of recent immigrants from more diverse cultures. In order to explain what this debate is about and what the major issues are on both sides, I will look primarily at four authors who have written about English-only laws. Two writers who support English only are the late Senator Samuel Hayakawa and Richard Rodriguez, author of *Hunger of Memory*. Two authors who oppose English only are James Fallows, Washington editor of *Atlantic* magazine, and James Crawford, author of *Hold Your Tongue: Bilingualism and the Politics of English Only*.

Those who support an English-only policy feel that it will encourage immigrants and non-English-speaking Americans to speak English. In his essay, "Bilingualism in America: English Should Be the *Only* Language," Hayakawa uses the example of Chinese- and Japanese-Americans, who didn't get along during World War II. Now they have begun to form Asian-American groups (252). Hayakawa believes this is the result of having learned English. Hayakawa states, "A common tongue encourages trust while reducing racial hostility and bigotry" (252). Hayakawa, one of the original founders of U.S. English, believes that unless the United States implements an English-only policy, we will head the way of Quebec or India: India's "ten official languages" have created a situation that is "a chaotic mess which has led to countless problems in the government's efforts to manage the nation's business" (253). According to Hayakawa, the problem in the United States is already apparent. He blames the 50 percent dropout rate among Hispanic students on the current bilingual policy (254). Writers such as Hayakawa forecast a Tower of Babel. They believe that unless we adopt an English-only policy, immigrants will not learn English and U.S. citizens will not be able to communicate with each other. Of course, Hayakawa's analogy with Quebec and India may be difficult to support, because immigrants to the United States have always learned English, whereas in Quebec and India, people have always spoken different languages.

As a champion of English-only legislation, Richard Rodriguez, like the late Senator Hayakawa, believes that without the government to push immigrants into learning English, they will not learn English. In "Aria: A

Memoir of a Bilingual Childhood," Rodriguez states, "What I needed to learn in school was that I had the right, and the obligation, to speak the public language. . . . It would have pleased me to hear my teachers address me in Spanish. . . . But I would have delayed—postponed for how long?—having to learn the language of public society" (270). Although Rodriguez was born in the United States, the son of migrant workers, he was not exposed to English until he entered school. Without his Catholic schoolteachers' forcing him to learn English, Rodriguez believes that he would never have learned to speak the public language (271). Like people on both sides of the English-only issue, Rodriguez believes that to succeed in the United States, it is necessary to be proficient in English. Because Rodriguez was not motivated to speak English as a child, he feels that it is imperative for the government to push immigrants to learn English by making English the official language of the United States.

In addition, the website for U.S. English agrees with Hayakawa   5
and Rodriguez that without English-only legislation, immigrants will "fail to learn English and separate into linguistic enclaves. This division of the United States into separate language groups contributes to racial and ethnic conflicts" (U.S. English 1). This is, of course, a controversial position because many other people believe that immigrants have plenty of incentive to learn English on their own, and those people have history to cite as evidence.

On the other side of the English-only debate, James Fallows, a   6
Washington editor of *Atlantic* magazine and author of "Viva Bilingualism," believes that there are enough incentives for immigrants to learn English without adding pressure to the situation. Fallows, an English-speaking American who lived in Japan, feels that his experiences show that English-only laws are unnecessary. When living in Japan, a country that "makes many more accommodations to the English language than America does to Spanish," Fallows found that he, as well as most English-speaking people, needed to learn Japanese to participate in society (262). In America, Fallows thinks the incentives for immigrants to learn English are greater. The only way to get a white-collar job or to attend college, according to Fallows, is to learn English. As Fallows puts it, in America, you can't take the SATs in Spanish or even watch *David Letterman* (262).

Writers such as James Fallows who do not support an English-only   7
policy do not believe that the differences in language will cause chaos. However, some believe that an official English-only policy will actually separate Americans. James Crawford, author of *Hold Your Tongue: Bilingualism and the Politics of English Only*, argues that English-only laws are racist and xenophobic. Crawford quotes Raul Yazguierre, President of the National Council of La Raza, as saying, "U.S. English is

to Hispanics as the Ku Klux Klan is to blacks" (1). Crawford says that this is the consensus among Latino leaders. Crawford goes on to say that Latino leaders believe English only is a xenophobic, intolerant act (1). When Spanish leaders are saying that English only is similar to something extreme like the KKK, something has to be wrong. That Latino leaders link English only to the KKK, coupled with the fact that immigrants have always learned English on their own, seems to be compelling evidence that many people think English-only laws are unnecessary and possibly destructive.

If there is any middle ground in this debate, I find it difficult to 8 explain. Often, arguments on both sides seem to come down to personal experiences. Rodriguez thinks his experiences show that there should be the pressure of English-only laws; Fallows's experiences in Japan persuade him that there are already sufficient pressures to encourage immigrants to learn English. Hayakawa does point to real problems in countries such as Canada and India, but his statistics may be shaky. Hayakawa quotes Hispanics as having a 50 percent dropout rate, saying that this could be due to the lack of English proficiency, and then later states that 90 percent of the Hispanics in the United States are fluent in English (254, 255). These two statements are contradictory and weaken Hayakawa's position. Crawford and Fallows, because of their experience, do have legitimate points. Crawford spent ten years of research on the issue, which adds to his credibility. In addition, Fallows has personal experience similar to my own. When I was living in a foreign country, I felt continual pressure to learn the language spoken in my host country, and because I did not have my family around, I couldn't hide from the new language and culture.

It is difficult to determine the long-term effects of English-only 9 legislation. I haven't found any evidence that the laws in twenty-three states have increased the number of immigrants who speak English, but I have found evidence that the debate about these laws can be heated and divisive. Although this issue is certainly debatable, I believe that the new push for English as an official language may be due to a backlash against the recent influx of more diverse groups into the United States. If state governments continue to support that backlash, it may further alienate our new citizens. On the other hand, many immigrants don't learn English very quickly, and they survive in linguistic enclaves, separated by language barriers from mainstream American culture. Possibly the economic pressures of earning a living will have a far greater effect on encouraging immigrants to learn English than any official English laws. If the momentum for English-only laws persists in state legislatures, we will continue to see arguments from both sides used in the debate.

Works Cited

Crawford, James. *Hold Your Tongue: Bilingualism and the Politics of English Only*. Reading, MA: Addison Wesley, 1992. 24 Sept. 1998. http://ourworld.compuserve.com/homepages/JWCRAWFORD/home.html.

Denniston, Lyle. "English-Only Measure Dealt Blow." *Baltimore Sun.* 12 Jan. 1998. 11 Jan. 1999. http://www.sunspot.net/cgibin/editorial.

Fallows, James. "Viva Bilingualism." *Exploring Language*. Ed. Gary Goshgarian. 8th ed. New York: Addison Wesley Longman, 1998. 259–63.

Gugliotta, Guy. "House Passes Puerto Rico Bill." *Washington Post On-line*. 5 March 1998. 24 Sept. 1998. http://ourworld.compuserve.com/homepages/JWCRAWFORD/WPOST4.html.

Hayakawa, S. I. "Bilingualism in America: English Should Be the *Only* Language." *Exploring Language*. Ed. Gary Goshgarian. 8th ed. New York: Addison Wesley Longman, 1998. 251–56.

Rodriguez, Richard. "Aria: A Memoir of a Bilingual Childhood." *Exploring Language*. Ed. Gary Goshgarian. 8th ed. New York: Addison Wesley Longman, 1998. 266–75.

U.S. English Page. 13 Jan. 1999. http://www.us-english.org/why.htm.

QUESTIONS FOR WRITING AND DISCUSSION

1. Compare Bishop's first and revised drafts. What information and explanations did she add in the revised version? How did she reorganize her essay for the revised version? Explain.

2. Bishop's purpose in this first essay for her portfolio was to explore the arguments on each side of the English-only debate and then explain these arguments to her reader. She did *not* want to argue for or against English only until the final essay in her portfolio. What paragraphs does she devote to the advocates of the English-only movement? What paragraphs explain the arguments of those who oppose English only? Does she balance the arguments without taking sides herself? Explain.

3. Explaining essays should define key terms, concepts, or ideas. What terms or ideas does Bishop explain or define? Are there other terms or ideas that she needed to define? Explain.

4. Assume that Bishop wants your advice before writing another revised draft of her essay. Review the peer response guidelines earlier in this chapter. Using those questions, decide what advice you would give her to make her essay more effective.

5. In this chapter, read Pico Iyer's essay, "The Global Village Finally Arrives." What side might Iyer take in this English-only debate?

Assume you are Pico Iyer, and write a response—to Bishop or any of the authors she cites—explaining how you react to these English-only issues. In a postscript, indicate how your own personal views might differ from the views of Pico Iyer.

ANOREXIA NERVOSA

Nancie Brosseau

In her essay on anorexia nervosa, Nancie Brosseau writes from her own experience, explaining what anorexia nervosa is and what its effects are. Her essay succeeds not only because it is organized clearly, but also because it is so vivid and memorable. Relying on specific details, her explanation shows the effects of anorexia on her life.

I knew my dieting had gotten out of hand, but when I could actually   *1*
see the movement of my heart beating beneath my clothes, I knew I was in trouble. At first, the family doctor reassured my parents that my rapid weight loss was a "temporary phase among teenage girls." However, when I, at fourteen years old and five feet tall, weighed in at sixty-three pounds, my doctor changed his diagnosis from "temporary phase" to "anorexia nervosa." Anorexia nervosa is the process of self-starvation that affects over 100,000 young girls each year. Almost 6,000 of these girls die every year. Anorexia nervosa is a self-mutilating disease that affects its victim both physically and emotionally.

As both a gymnast and a dancer, I was constantly surrounded by   *2*
lithe, muscular people, all of them extremely conscious about their weight. Although I wasn't overweight to begin with, I thought that if I lost five to ten pounds I would look, feel, dance, and tumble better. I figured the quickest way to accomplish this was by drastically limiting my intake of food. By doing this, I lost ten pounds in one week and gained the approval of my peers. Soon, I could no longer control myself, and ten pounds turned into twenty, twenty into forty, and so on, until I finally ended up weighing fifty-eight pounds.

Several serious health problems bombarded me, and it's a wonder I'm   *3*
still alive. Because my body was receiving no nourishment at all, my muscles and essential organs, including my heart, liver, kidneys, and intestines, started to compensate by slowly disintegrating. My body was feeding on itself! As my weight plummeted, my circulation grew increasingly worse. My hands, feet, lips, and ears took on a bluish-purple tint, and I was constantly freezing cold. My hair started to fall out and my whole body

took on a very skeletal appearance. My eyes appeared to have sunken into my face, and my forehead, cheekbones, and chin protruded sharply. My wrists were the largest part of my entire arm, as were my knees the widest part of my legs. My pants rubbed my hips raw because I had to wear my belts at their tightest notch to keep them up. I would force myself to vomit as soon as possible if I was forced to eat. The enamel on my teeth started to be eaten away by the acid in the vomit, and my lips cracked and bled regularly. I stopped menstruating completely because I was not producing enough estrogen. Instead of improving my skills as a dancer and a gymnast, I drastically reduced them because I was so weak. One time, while executing a chain of back handsprings, I broke all five fingers on one hand and three on the other because my bones had become so brittle. My doctor realized the serious danger I was in and told me I either had to see a psychologist or be put in the hospital. I chose to see a psychologist, and she helped me sort out the emotional aspects of anorexia, which in turn solved the physical problems.

The emotional problems associated with anorexia nervosa are equally disastrous to the victim's health. Self-deception, lying, and depression are three examples of the emotions and actions an anorexic often experiences. During my entire bout with anorexia, I deceived myself into thinking I had complete control over my body. Hunger pains became a pleasant feeling, and sore muscles from overexercising just proved to me that I still needed to lose more weight. When my psychologist showed me pictures of girls that were of normal weight for my age group, they honestly looked obese to me. I truly believed that even the smallest amount of food would make me extremely fat.   *4*

Another problem, lying, occurred most often when my parents tried to force me to eat. Because I was at the gym until around eight o'clock every night, I told my mother not to save me dinner. I would come home and make a sandwich and feed it to my dog. I lied to my parents every day about eating lunch at school. For example, I would bring a sack lunch and sell it to someone and use the money to buy diet pills. I always told my parents that I ate my own lunch. I lied to my doctor when he asked if I was taking an appetite suppressant. I had to cover one lie with another to keep from being found out, although it was obvious that I was not eating by looking at me.   *5*

Still another emotion I felt, as a result of my anorexia, was severe depression. It seemed that, no matter how hard I tried, I kept growing fatter. Of course, I was getting thinner all the time, but I couldn't see that. One time, I licked a postage stamp to put on a letter and immediately remembered that there was 1/4 of a calorie in the glue on the stamp. I punished myself by doing 100 extra situps every night for one week. I pinched my skin until it bruised as I lay awake at night be-   *6* cause I was so ashamed of the way I thought I looked. I doomed myself to a life of obesity. I would often slip into a mood my psychologist described as a "blue funk." That is, I would become so depressed, I seriously considered committing suicide. The emotional instabilities associated with anorexia nervosa can be fatal.

Through psychological and physical treatment, I was able to overcome anorexia nervosa. I still have a few complications today due to anorexia, such as dysmenorrhea (severe menstrual cramps) and the tendency to fast. However, these problems are minute compared to the problems I would have had if I hadn't received immediate help. Separately, the physical and emotional problems that anorexia nervosa creates can greatly harm its victim. However, when the two are teamed together, the results are deadly.

QUESTIONS FOR WRITING AND DISCUSSION

1. Without looking back at this essay, jot down the specific examples that you found most memorable. How would you describe these examples: tedious and commonplace, eye-opening, shocking, upsetting, persuasive? Explain.

2. Identify the thesis statement and essay map. Referring to paragraph numbers, show how the essay map sets up the organization of the essay.

3. Reread the opening sentences of each body paragraph. Identify one opening sentence that creates a smooth transition from the previous paragraph. Identify one opening sentence in which the transition could be smoother. Revise this sentence to improve the transition with a paragraph hook.

4. In this essay, Brosseau defines anorexia nervosa, explains its physical and emotional effects (and hints at its causes), and analyzes the process of the disorder, from its inception to its cure. Identify passages that illustrate each of these strategies: definition, cause-and-effect analysis, and process analysis.

5. A recent study by Judith Rabek-Wagener et al. has shown that the "mass marketing of body images through print media and television and advertising" has helped cause nearly 65 percent of young women and 35 percent of young men to "experience significant dissatisfaction with their body size, shape, condition, or appearance." For the complete article, see "The Effect of Media Analysis on . . . Body Image Among College Students" in the *Journal of American College Health*, August 1, 1998. Read the research on the connection between the media and eating disorders and then write your own essay explaining the causes of eating disorders or the effects that the media have on college students' self-images.

Portrait of *Ramon Gomez de la Serra, 1915* (oil on canvas)
by Diego Rivera (1886–1957), Private Collection,
Christie's Images.

Chapter 8   Evaluating

In a letter to your parents, you explain that you are considering transferring to a different school for the following year. You have some misgivings about your decision to change, but after listing your criteria and ranking them in order from most to least important, you are convinced that you're making the right choice. In the letter, you explain your decision, based on your criteria, and ask that your parents continue to support your education.

During your fall semester library-orientation tour, you discover a small office tucked away in the corner of the library building: the interlibrary loan office. Because you occasionally need to see articles and books that your library does not have, you decide to investigate the interlibrary loan service and evaluate the helpfulness of the staff as well as the convenience, speed, and cost of obtaining materials. As part of your evaluation, you interview the office coordinator as well as several teachers and students who have used the service. Their responses—combined with your own observations—indicate that although an interlibrary loan can sometimes take a couple of weeks, the loan office gets high marks for its service. The staff is always helpful and patient, the service is easily accessible through electronic mail, and the cost of books and articles is surprisingly low.

When we evaluate, we have in mind . . . an ideal of what a good thing—pianist, painting, or professor—should be and do, and we apply that ideal to the individual instance before us.

—JEANNE FAHNESTOCK AND MARIE SECOR, AUTHORS OF A RHETORIC OF ARGUMENT

Purpose and craftsmanship—ends and means—these are the keys to your judgment.

—MARYA MANNES, JOURNALIST AND SOCIAL COMMENTATOR

ARDLY A DAY PASSES WHEN WE DO NOT EXPRESS OUR LIKES OR DISLIKES. WE CONSTANTLY PASS JUDGMENT ON PEOPLE, PLACES, OBJECTS, EVENTS, IDEAS, AND POLICIES IN THE WORLD AROUND us: "Sue is a wonderful person." "The food in this cafeteria is horrible." "That movie we saw Saturday night ought to get an Oscar nomination for best picture." "The Vietnam War was a national tragedy." At the same time, we are constantly exposed to the opinions of our friends, family members, teachers, and business associates. And, of course, the media barrage us with claims about products, famous personalities, and candidates for public office.

A claim or opinion, however, is not an *evaluation*. Your reaction to a person, a sports event, a meal, a movie, or a public policy becomes an evaluation *only* when you support your value judgment with clear standards and specific evidence. Your goal in evaluating something is not only to express your viewpoint, but also to *persuade* others to accept your judgment. You convince your readers by indicating the standards for your judgment and then supporting it with evidence: "The food in this cafeteria is horrible [your claim]. I know that not all cafeteria food tastes great, but it should at least be sanitary [one standard of judgment]. Yesterday, I had to dig a piece of green mold out of the meat loaf, and just as I stuck my fork into the green salad, a large black roach ran out [evidence]."

Most people interested in a subject agree that certain standards are important, for example, that a cafeteria be clean and pest-free. The standards that you share with your audience are the *criteria* for your evaluation. You convince your readers that something is good or bad, ugly or beautiful, tasty or nauseating by analyzing your subject in terms of your criteria. For each separate criterion, you support your judgment with specific *evidence:* descriptions, statistics, testimony, or examples from your personal experience. If your readers agree that your standards or criteria are appropriate, and if you supply detailed evidence, your readers should be convinced. They will take your evaluation seriously—and think twice about eating at that roach-infested cafeteria.

It is as hard to find a neutral critic as it is a neutral country in a time of war.

—**KATHERINE ANNE PORTER,**
NOVELIST AND SHORT STORY WRITER

Techniques for Writing Evaluations

Any writing that requires a *value judgment* uses the techniques of evaluating—whether you're writing about consumer products or services, works of art, or performances by people. Effective evaluations use the following techniques:

- **Stating an *overall claim* about your subject.** This statement serves as the *thesis* for your evaluation.
- **Describing the person, place, object, text, event, service, or performance being evaluated.** Readers need basic information—*who, what, when,* and *where*—to form a clear judgment.
- **Clarifying the *criteria* for your evaluation.** A criterion is a standard of judgment that most people interested in your subject agree is important. A criterion serves as a yardstick against which you measure your subject.
- **Stating a *judgment* for each criterion.** The overall claim is based on your judgment of each separate criterion. Include both positive *and* negative judgments.
- **Supporting each judgment with *evidence*.** Support can include detailed description, facts, examples, testimony, or statistics.
- **Balancing your evaluation with both positive and negative judgments about your subject.** Evaluations that are all positive are merely advertisements; evaluations that are entirely negative may seem too harsh or mean-spirited.

In the following evaluation of a Chinese restaurant in Washington, D.C., journalist and critic Phyllis C. Richman illustrates the main features of an evaluation:

Hunan Dynasty

215 Pennsylvania Ave. SE. 546–6161

Open daily 11 A.M. to 3 P.M. for lunch, 3 P.M. to 10 P.M. for dinner, until 11 P.M. on Friday and Saturday.

Reservations suggested for large parties.

Prices for lunch: appetizers $2 to $4.50, entrees $4.75 to $6.50. For dinner: appetizers $1 to $13.95 (combination platter), entrees $6.75 to $18.

Complete dinner with wine or beer, tax, and tip about $20 a person.

Information and description

Chinese restaurants in America were once places one went just to eat. Now one goes to dine. There are now waiters in black tie, cloths on the tables and space between those tables, art on the walls and decoratively carved vegetables on the plate—elegance has become routine in Chinese restaurants. What's more, in Chinese restaurants the ingredients are fresh (have you ever found frozen broccoli in a Chinese kitchen?), and the cooking almost never sinks below decent. . . . And it is usually

Description

moderately priced. In other words, if you're among unfamiliar restaurants and looking for good value, Chinese restaurants now are routinely better than ever.

The Hunan Dynasty is an example of what makes Chinese restaurants such reliable choices. A great restaurant? It is not. A good value? Definitely. A restaurant to fit nearly any diner's need? Probably.

First, it is attractive. There are no silk tassels, blaring red lacquer or Formica tables; instead there are white tablecloths and subtle glass etchings. It is a dining room—or dining rooms, for the vastness has been carved into smaller spaces—of gracefulness and lavish space.

Second, service is a strong priority. The waiters look and act polished, and serve with flourishes from the carving of a Peking duck to the portioning of dishes among the diners. I have found some glitches—a forgotten appetizer, a recommendation of two dishes that turned out nearly identical—but most often the service has been expert. . . .

As for the main dishes, don't take the "hot and spicy" asterisks too seriously, for this kitchen is not out to offer you a test of fire. The peppers are there, but not in great number. And, like the appetizers, the main dishes are generally good but not often memorable. Fried dishes—and an inordinate number of them seem to be fried—are crunchy and not greasy. Vegetables are bright and crisp. Eggplant with hot garlic sauce is properly unctuous; Peking duck is as fat-free and crackly-skinned as you could hope (though pancakes were rubbery). And seafoods—shrimp, scallops, lobster—are tenderly cooked, though they are not the most full-flavored examples of those ingredients.

I have found only one dismal main dish in a fairly broad sampling: lemon chicken had no redeeming feature in its doughy, greasy, overcooked and underseasoned presentation. Otherwise, not much goes wrong. Crispy shrimp with walnuts might be preferable stir-fried rather than batter-fried, but the tomato-red sauce and crunchy walnuts made a good dish. Orange beef could use more seasoning but the coating was nicely crusty and the meat tender. . . .

So with the opening of the Hunan Dynasty, Washington did not add a stellar Chinese restaurant to its repertoire, but that is not necessarily what the city needed anyway. Hunan Dynasty is a top-flight neighborhood restaurant—with good food, caring service and very fair prices—that is attractive enough to set a mood for celebration and easygoing enough for an uncomplicated dinner with the family after work.

EVALUATING COMMERCIAL PRODUCTS OR SERVICES

Writers frequently evaluate commercial products or services. Consumer magazines test and rate every imaginable product or service—from cars and dishwashers to peanut butter and brokerage houses. Guidebooks evaluate tourist spots, restaurants, colleges, and hunting lodges. Specialty magazines, such as *Modern Photography*, *Road and Track*, *Skiing*, and *Wired*, often rate products and services of interest to their readers. To qualify as evaluation—and not just advertising—the authors and the publishers must maintain an independent status, uninfluenced by the manufacturers of the products or services they are judging.

Consider, first, the following "evaluation" of a wine, found on a bottle of Cabernet Sauvignon:

> This Cabernet Sauvignon is a dry, robust, and complex wine whose hearty character is balanced by an unusual softness.

This "evaluative" language is so vague and esoteric that it may mean very little to the average consumer who just wants some wine with dinner. *Dry*: How can a liquid be dry? *Robust*: Does this refer to physique? *Soft*: Wine is not a pillow, though it might put you to sleep. *Complex*: Are they describing a wine or conducting a psychological analysis? While an independent evaluator may legitimately use these terms for knowledgeable wine drinkers, this particular description suggests that the wine is absolutely everything the buyer would like it to be—dry yet robust, hearty but at the same time soft. Apparently, the writer's purpose here is not to evaluate a product but to flatter readers who imagine themselves connoisseurs of wine.

Now consider the following evaluation of the Honda S2000, a small, two-seat convertible sports car. In the following excerpt from *Consumer Reports*, we get an evaluation of three major categories: the driving experience, the inside of the car, and the safety and reliability of the car. Notice how the evaluation contains both positive and negative judgments, and how each judgment is accompanied by test data or direct observation.

Honda S2000

The Driving Experience   The S2000 delivered some of the best performance numbers we've ever recorded. Cornering is crisp and agile, thanks to quick-response steering and minimal body roll. The S2000 held on with astonishing tenacity through the fast, tight turns at our track and remained balanced and predictable when it did reach its cornering limits. In addition, it tackled our double-lane-change avoidance maneuver quickly and confidently.

As in the typical sports car, the ride is stiff; common road bumps and ruts jar the passengers. The ride is jittery even on smooth roads and on the highway. Engine and road noise are constant companions, befitting this kind of car.

Inside the Car   The cockpit fits an average-size adult like a glove. Tall people could feel cramped, though, and wish the seat would move farther back. With the top up, the view to the rear through the plastic window isn't good. The low seat makes it hard for a five-footer to see out well. Climbing in and out of the cockpit takes agility. The seats themselves are firm, comfortable, and supportive. . . .

The oddly shaped trunk won't accommodate even a single large rigid suitcase or a folded wheelchair, but it can hold a couple of duffels. The compact spare is intended to replace only a front tire. If you get a flat in the rear, you must replace it with a front tire and put the spare on the front.

Safety and Reliability   Safety gear included dual air bags, lap-and-shoulder belts, and belt pretensioners that take up slack in a crash. The shoulder-belt sections are anchored low and may pull down on some people's shoulders. The integrated head restraints are high enough to prevent whiplash in a rear-end collision. . . .

Driving with kids: You can't turn off the passenger air bag, so this is not a car for carrying young children. If you must mount a front-facing child seat, slide the passenger seat back all the way.

No reliability data are available. Other Hondas have been above average, and we expect the S2000 to be the same. Our car had two sample defects.

EVALUATING WORKS OF ART

Evaluations of commercial products and services tend to emphasize usefulness, practicality, convenience, and cost. Evaluations of works of art, on the other hand, focus on form, color, texture, design, balance, image, or theme. Even the phrase "appreciating a work of art" suggests that we are making a value judgment, though usually not one based on money. Through evaluation, writers teach us to appreciate all kinds of art: paintings, sculpture, photographs, buildings, antique cars or furniture, novels, short stories, essays, poems, and tapestries. A

Francisco de Goya y Lucientes, 1746–1828. *The Third of May*, 1808. Oil painting on canvas. Museo del prado, Madrid. Scala/Art Resource, NY.

Dior fashion, a quilt, a silverware pattern, even an old pair of jeans might be evaluated primarily on aesthetic rather than practical grounds.

In the following selection, art critic Mark Stevens evaluates Francisco Goya's painting *Tre Maggio* (The Third of May), which is reprinted here. This painting depicts the execution of Spanish hostages by Napoleon's forces, in retaliation for an attack by a mob on the previous day. As Stevens explains, Goya does not portray the doomed hostages as heroic martyrs; instead, he tries to show the horrors of war and death. In doing that, Stevens believes, Goya "told the truth: what happened on the third of May was a butchering."

The iconography, the color and light, the composition—all contribute to the power of this picture. Its most impressive aspect, in my view, is that Goya . . . transformed the conventions of hope into those of despair. This makes the horror all the greater, for we can see what we have lost, in addition to what we have. In the background, for example, the spire of the church is a dark, dim reminder, certainly not a cause for hope. The cruelty of the execution, which takes place in a melodramatic light, reminds us of acts of martyrdom—but without the traditional promise of heavenly reward.

(Detail) Francisco de Goya Lucientes, 1746–1828. *The Third of May*, 1808. Oil painting on canvas. Museo del Pardo, Madrid. Scala/Art Resources, NY.

Of course, the outstretched arms of the central figure also recall the Crucifixion, and the man's hands bear stigmata. However, the traditional religious gesture of acceptance—the outstretched arms of Christ—has here been turned into an expression of outrage, terror and meaninglessness. What is the victim saying? There is nothing he can say, for his situation is one in which neither faith nor reason matter. His outflung arms are mirrored by those of the corpse in the foreground: such is the promise of resurrection. The corpse itself is perhaps the most truthful ever painted, for it exhibits the unbearable banality, the crumpled emptiness of death.

The men around the central victim display a variety of other reactions to their fate, none noble. One looks heavenward, but his expression is groveling. The praying man cannot raise his eyes. A third hides his face, as do the victims who await execution. Goya's use of light enhances their horror. The light contains no spiritual overtone, but rather emanates from a common lantern; an intense glow is cast on the small, grisly scene, but it cannot pierce the dark reaches. This light—glaring, without delicacy, lurid, almost artificial—seems peculiarly modern. . . .

In addition to his brilliant use of light and shade, which isolates the central figure, Goya used several other formal devices to make his point. He employed sweeping diagonal lines to scissor the picture into sharp, claustrophobic spaces. He foreshortened the corpse, so that the body seems to draw toward the viewer. (It almost looks as though the dead man is bidding the viewer welcome.) Otherwise, Goya has positioned the figures so that the viewer, curiously, is placed on the side of the executioners. You and I, observing, are implicated in mankind's folly.

EVALUATING PERFORMANCES

Evaluating live, recorded, or filmed performances of people in sports, dance, drama, debate, public meetings or lectures, and music may involve practical criteria, such as the prices of tickets to sports events or rock concerts. However, there are also aesthetic criteria that apply to people and their performances. In film evaluations, for example, the usual criteria are good acting and directing, an entertaining or believable story or plot, memorable characters, dramatic special effects, and so forth.

PROFESSIONAL WRITING

MR. SPIELBERG STRIKES AGAIN

David Ansen

In the following review of Spielberg's A I.*, film critic David Ansen, writing in* Newsweek *magazine, evaluates the contributions by both Steven Spielberg and Stanley Kubrick, the plot of the film, the acting, and the overall theme of the film. Notice how Ansen's evaluation works through both positive and negative judgments before concluding that* A.I. *is "the most ambitious Hollywood movie in sight."*

How are we supposed to look at "A.I. Artificial Intelligence"? Is it a *1* Stanley Kubrick movie channeled through Steven Spielberg? Is it a Spielberg movie informed by the ghost of Kubrick? Is it a movie in which the sensibilities of two of the most powerful cinematic personalities of our times—who couldn't be more different—conduct a 140-minute duel for dominance?

Inspired by a Brian Aldiss short story, "A.I." tells the tale of a *2* boy robot who's programmed to love his adoptive mother. Kubrick had been developing the idea for years when he asked Spielberg to direct it. After Kubrick's death, Spielberg took up the challenge, writing the screenplay himself (his first since "Close Encounters of the Third Kind") and modeling much of the film's design on the storyboards and sketches Kubrick had commissioned from comic-book artist Chris Baker.

The result is fascinating—a rich, strange, problematical movie full of wild tonal shifts and bravura moviemaking. It's like nothing else Spielberg has done, though it calls to mind "E.T.," "Close Encounters" and "Empire of the Sun." You will also, along the way, think of "2001," "A Clockwork Orange," "The Wizard of Oz," "Mad Max Beyond Thunderdome," "The Abyss" and, above all, "Pinocchio," the tale of a puppet who, like the machine-made hero of "A.I.," wants to become a real boy.   3

Haley Joel Osment plays "David," the first of his robotic kind. He's created at a time in which many of the world's cities have been destroyed by polar melting, resources are low and everything is rationed—especially children. The experimental David is given as a test case to a couple (Sam Robards and Frances O'Connor) whose own real son, terminally ill, is in a state of cryogenic suspension. The mother, Monica, is first freaked out by this spookily human-looking toy, whose "emotional circuitry" has yet to be turned on. She has the choice whether or not to activate his love, but once she does, his devotion will be irreversibly embedded.   4

These early domestic scenes are deeply, wonderfully creepy. We're as unsettled as Monica by the mechanistic responses of David, who, in a ghastly mimicry of human spontaneity, breaks into wild, artificial laughter at the dinner table. In this first riveting hour, the Kubrick homages are everywhere: in the cool, bleached-out lighting; in the design of the sterile, modernistic house; in the choice of angles and camera moves. We haven't seen Spielberg working in this chilly, disorienting mode before, and he's damn good at it.   5

Monica does "imprint the protocol" on the robot, and before our eyes the uncanny Osment transforms himself from an automaton into a needy child. Like a fairy-tale figure dosed with a love potion, his adoration is sealed. But along with love comes vulnerability, pain and—when the couple's real son, recovered from his illness, rejoins the family—jealousy. David is now seen as a threatening presence, and must be discarded.   6

At this point—when David is abandoned in a forest with only his talking teddy bear for company—"A.I." radically shifts gears. The dark, delirious second hour is a neon-lit nightmare odyssey in which the boy and his new friend, Gigolo Joe (Jude Law)—a dapper robot programmed to pleasure women—must fight for survival in a world full of robot-hating humans. Obsessed with the Pinocchio fable, David is convinced that he can be magically transformed into a real boy, and that once he is, he'll regain the love of his lost mother.   7

But there's more to come—a third act (set many, many years later) *8* that's in yet another style: a kind of Oedipal combo of "2001" and "Close Encounters." And this is where Spielberg's screenplay loses its grip, the film goes limp, and you wonder whether the movie Kubrick envisioned and the one we're seeing have fatally parted ways.

The emotional thread that holds "A.I." together is in the gradual *9* unfolding of the robot boy's humanity. But how are we meant to feel about his obsessive, regressive quest for Mommy? In a way, David's monomaniacal devotion, his desire to be unique, becomes monstrous. He's been programmed for maternal love, but little else, and that makes him a one-note hero. Does his fixation on his mother make him more human, or more robotic? The movie could use more of Law's mischievous Gigolo Joe, a prancing fancy man the actor invests with great theatrical crackle.

"A.I." arouses more ambiguous feelings than we're used to in a *10* Spielberg movie, and there were times I wasn't sure if Spielberg was in control of his emotional effects. (That might be a first.) He seems to want "A.I." to break our hearts, but could that have been what Kubrick had in mind? This tug of war—between the darkness of the fable and Spielberg's need for warmth—is part of what makes "A.I." so mesmerizing and so open to interpretation. Some people may read it as a simple fable of a robot who learns to love, but what's on screen is not so cut and dried. It's a movie that makes us ponder the very nature of love—how it's hard-wired into us, how it blurs the line between the selfish and the selfless. Is love the ultimate affirmation of free will, or its negation? "A.I." exhilarates, frustrates and provokes: it's the most ambitious Hollywood movie in sight.

■ WARMING UP: JOURNAL EXERCISES   The following exercises will help you practice writing evaluations. Read all of the following exercises and then write on the three that interest you most. If another idea occurs to you, write about it:

1. Choose the best of the courses that you are currently taking. To persuade a friend to take it, evaluate the course, the teacher, or both. What criteria and evidence would you select to persuade your friend?

2. Evaluate an object related to one of your hobbies or special interests—stereo or video equipment, water or snow skis, a cooking appliance or utensil, diving or hiking equipment, photography or art equipment, ranching or farming apparatus, fishing rods or reels, some part of a car, or computers. Write an evaluation of that object following the format used by *Consumer Reports*.

3. Evaluate a TV show that you find particularly irritating, boring, or insipid, but that you find yourself watching occasionally anyway. Watch the show,

taking notes about scenes, characters, dialogue, and plot. Write a critique of the show for other students in this class.

4. To gather some information for yourself about a possible job or career, interview a person in your prospective field about his or her job or profession. Focus your questions on the person's opinions and judgments about this career. What criteria does this person use to judge it? What other jobs serve as a good basis for comparison? What details from this person's daily routine support his or her judgments?

5. At your place of work, evaluate one of your products or services. Write down the criteria and evidence that your business might use to determine whether it is a "good" product or service. Then list the criteria and evidence that your customers or patrons probably use. Are these two sets of criteria and evidence identical? Explain.

6. Choose a piece of modern art (painting, drawing, poster, sculpture, ceramics, and so forth). Describe and evaluate it for an audience that is indifferent or possibly even hostile to contemporary art. Explain why your readers should appreciate this particular art object.

7. Read the following review of Walt Disney's *The Lion King* by Margaret Lazarus. Notice how Lazarus quickly gives us a review of the plot and then launches into her cultural critique of this Disney classic. As you read, identify her judgments about the film. If you have seen *The Lion King*, do you think the evidence she gives to support her points is persuasive?

PROFESSIONAL WRITING

ALL'S NOT WELL IN LAND OF "THE LION KING"

Margaret Lazarus

It's official: Walt Disney's *The Lion King* is breaking box-office records. Unfortunately, it's not breaking any stereotypes.

My sons, along with millions of other kids around the world, joyously awaited *The Lion King*. I was intrigued because this time Disney appeared to be skipping the old folk-tales with their traditional and primal undercurrents.

I hoped Disney had grown weary of reinforcing women's subordinate status by screening fables about a beauty who tames an angry male beast or a mermaid who gives up her glorious voice and splits her body to be with a prince.

So off we went to the movies, figuring we would enjoy an original, well-animated story about animals on the African plain. Even before the title sequence, however, I started to shudder.

Picture this (and I apologize for spilling the plot): The golden-maned—that is, good—lion is presenting his first born male child to his subjects. All the animals in the kingdom, known as Pride Lands, are paying tribute to the infant son that will someday be their king. These royal subjects are basically lion food—zebras, monkeys, birds, etc.—and they all live together in supposed harmony in the "circle of life."

Outside the kingdom, in a dark, gloomy, and impoverished elephant graveyard, are the hyenas. They live dismally jammed together among bones and litter. The hyenas are dark—mostly black—and they are nasty, menacing the little lion prince when he wanders into their territory.

One of their voices is done by Whoopie Goldberg, in a clearly inner-city dialect. If this is not the ghetto, I don't know what is.

All is not perfect inside Pride Lands, however. The king's evil brother Scar has no lionesses or cubs. Scar has a black mane, and speaks in an effeminate, limp-pawed, British style done by Jeremy Irons—seemingly a gay caricature.

Scar conspires with the hyenas to kill the king and send the prince into exile. In exchange for their support, Scar allows the hyenas to live in Pride Lands. But property values soon crash: The hyenas overpopulate, kill all the game, and litter the once-green land with bones.

Already Disney has gays and blacks ruining the "natural order," and the stereotypes keep rolling. The lionesses never question whether they should be serving Scar and the hyenas—they just worry a lot. They are mistreated, but instead of fighting back these powerful hunters passively await salvation. (Even my 7-year-old wondered why the young, strong lioness didn't get rid of Scar.)

The circle of life is broken; disaster awaits everyone. But then the first-born male returns to reclaim power. The royal heir kills the gay usurper, and sends the hyenas back to the dark, gloomy, bone-filled ghetto. Order is restored and the message is clear: Only those born to privilege can bring about change.

This is not a story about animals—we know animals don't behave like this. This is a metaphor for society that originated in the minds of Disney's creators. These bigoted images and attitudes will lodge deeply in children's consciousness.

I'm not sure I always understand the law of the Hollywood jungle, but my boys definitely don't. Scared and frightened by *The Lion King*, they were also riveted, and deeply affected. But entranced by the "Disney magic," they and millions of other children were given hidden messages that can only do them—and us—harm.

P R O F E S S I O N A L   W R I T I N G

PRIME TIME ART?

Kathyrn Hughes and Ben Rogers

In the following exchange of letters, British critics Kathyrn Hughes and Ben Rogers debate the merits of the award-winning American television series ER. *Kathyrn Hughes is the author of* George Eliot: The Last Victorian *(1999) and Ben Rogers has published* A. J. Ayer: A Life *(1999). The following exchange appeared originally in* Prospect *magazine and was reprinted in* Utne. *Following the film debate format popularized by Siskel and Ebert, Hughes and Rogers debate, through letters, whether* ER *deserves to be called art. Both critics attempt to define "art" and then to show why* ER *does or does not meet this demanding criterion. As you follow their conversation, decide which—if either—critic is most persuasive. Are there other criteria you use to judge television programs that they don't consider?*

Dear Kathryn,

Wednesday nights (when *ER* is on) begin with skepticism and   1
end in rapture. I can't believe that the program is going to
meet my art-critical standards, but it does. The traumas and
dramas, the jokes and intimacies of County General Hospital emergency room—the ER in question—sweep me up. The
series knows its limitations, but it is art of a very high order
indeed.

I don't have to take sides in the elite versus popular culture   2
wars to champion *ER*. It is enough to draw attention to its
excellence. It has evolved a distinctive aesthetic, a distinctive
feel and vision. It moves through a wide array of moods—from
farce to romance, from pathos to high drama. Sometimes it is
clever—witness the allusions to *Reservoir Dogs* in the episode
directed by Quentin Tarantino. It flirts with kitsch, it dabbles
in parody, but it knows when to stop.

Characters like Romano or Jerry may come close to carica-   3
ture, but art has a place for this—and here they are brilliantly
done. And the central characters, with their all too human
foibles, their imperfect beauty and life-saving zeal, draw us in.
The minor characters, too, are invariably played by the strong
character actors so common in the United States. *ER* takes us
out of ourselves and, like the best fiction, gives us contact with
a heightened reality.

You have written about George Eliot, and I would hesitate to *4* compare *ER* to her infinitely subtle novels. Yet the series has some of the qualities of the 19th-century novel. Both have dramatic plots, comic minor characters, and keen social observation; and both are marked by moral seriousness. Didn't Dickens' novels first appear in serial form? If *ER* is sometimes sentimental, wasn't he?

America is a funny place. It can be the crass, corrupt, and un- *5* feeling country depicted by Tom Wolfe in *The Bonfire of the Vanities*, where rich and poor live in separate worlds. But it also remains in many respects the most democratic of countries. Status counts for little. This is the aspect of American life expressed in *ER*. It depicts men and women, black and white, working together; and it sets out quite consciously to drive home certain lessons—about health and violence, but also about fairness and respect. In the United States, where broadcasting has become ghettoized, it is almost the only show watched by blacks and whites. Blacks don't watch *Friends*, whites don't watch *Moesha*, but both tune in to *ER*.

The interesting question is not whether *ER* is art—obviously *6* it is—but how it comes to be such old-fashioned art. We are told that we live in postmodern times. The real has given way to the simulated, grand narrative to little stories. *ER*, though, does not fit this scheme. Its leading characters labor together united by an old-fashioned work ethic. In the emergency room all the divisions of American society are overcome. Doubtless Dr. Anspaugh takes home rather more than Nurse Hathaway, but we aren't reminded of that. Socialist artists—Charlie Chaplin, the painters Férnand Leger and Diego Rivera— would have understood *ER*.

Of course art does not have to serve progressive causes. But it *7* adds to its power when it does. George Eliot's novels condemn the subjection of women and Jews, they take aim at religious cant, moral hypocrisy, and commercial greed. In the end, *Middlemarch* and *ER* move us in much the same way.

Yours, Ben

Dear Ben,

I share your disbelieving rapture that television could ever get *8* this good, but is *ER* art? Well, no. It's a magnificent achievement, but it does not do the specific and important work of art.

Unlike George Eliot's novels, which you cite as a paradigm, *ER* neither extends nor explores the limits of its own genre. When Eliot put the "working day world" into her novels, she was doing something revolutionary. But when the producers of *ER* chose to set their drama in the workplace, they were staying firmly within the parameters set by Steven Bochco in the mid-1980s with *Hill Street Blues* and *L.A. Law*. With good reason: setting a series in an office or police station provides a central, socially stratified setting from which story lines can be compactly generated. And using an accident and emergency setting is hardly breaking new ground.

You say that *ER* is "old-fashioned art" and that its emphasis on shared endeavor and grand narrative represents a heroic rebuttal of postmodernism, with its small. whiny stories (were you thinking of *Ally McBeal?*). But *ER* places itself entirely in relation to other television narratives, and spends too much time playing postmodern games. Take that Tarantino episode. The allusions to *Reservoir Dogs* (itself generated from a web of references to other movies) undercut what little relationship *ER* had with social reality. The sight of Dr. Lewis and Nurse Hathaway in wraparound shades broke a trust in the storytelling process that took several episodes to repair.   9

I agree that if Dickens were around today he'd be writing TV drama. As you say, *ER* is stuffed with the kinds of caricatures he liked. Kerry Weaver's tics—the unexplained crutch, the management-speak—is a prime example. But Dickens, like the directors of *ER*, was not producing art. George Eliot, by contrast, was—and the proof lies in the absence of stereotypes in her work. Even her minor characters have lives that seem to have begun before the novels open and continue long after they have ended.   10

By contrast, when the characters in *ER* are taken out of context, they crumble into dust. Remember the episode when Peter Benton went to work in the Deep South? Or what about the two hours we were forced to watch Mark Greene return to his hometown and look after his ailing mother?   11

Another mark of Eliot's artistry is that she didn't create idealizations either. She demanded that people look like people, with potato heads, bad skin, and odd sniffs. You say that the main characters have an "imperfect beauty." But I can't see much that is imperfect about them. They look like a team of   12 gods and goddesses descended from the sky, who have decided for some reason to don surgical gloves. *ER* scarcely pushes back the boundaries of what television drama demands aesthetically of its main players.

Art is often ugly, usually difficult, sometimes boring. It doesn't 13 care whether it pleases, and indeed it would rather not. It refuses to give up its meaning without a fight, and insists that we work hard to make some sense of what is going on. *ER* is brilliant television, but it doesn't have the power to make up the world in a new way. I love it, but it isn't art.

Yours, Kathryn

Dear Kathryn,

You say that I offer George Eliot as a paradigm. Nothing could 14 be further from the case. You evidently see her as such, which is why you can't bring yourself to acknowledge *ER*'s claim to art. But to do so is to take a very narrow—even, I am afraid, stuffy—view of art.

Art comes in many forms. Sometimes it is a collective en- 15 deavor (the Gothic cathedrals), sometimes intensely individual (Gaudí's *Sagrada Familia*). It can appeal to a small group (Schoenberg) or to a whole people (Greek tragedy, Elizabethan drama). You say art is "usually difficult, sometimes boring." But it is, just as often, easy (Oscar Wilde's plays), and sometimes thrilling—*ER*. When you refer to "the specific and important work" art does, I hear echoes of all those guardians of high art, sure on *a priori* grounds that art cannot be too popular and cannot exist in a modern medium.

You are forcing "art" into a narrow mold, implying that it needs 16 to "break with tradition" or at least "explore and extend the limits of its own boundaries." But you underestimate the role tradition, convention, and genre play in art. You complain that the producers of *ER* set their drama in the workplace, like other shows, but was Shakespeare less of a poet because he "stayed firmly within the parameters" of the sonnet?

In any case, *ER* does "extend" and "explore" its own genre. 17 Look at its lead characters. They come in as types, as they tend to in any narrative: Elizabeth Corday the troubled English-woman; Benton the angry, driven African American; Carter the dissatisfied WASP. In time, however, these labels fall aside to reveal real people. And because it is a series, they are given time to breathe. You say that Eliot's characters have lives seemingly real enough to exist outside her novels. It seems to me that *ER*'s characters have just this "real" quality. Art has to meet certain standards—it has to be technically expert, relatively self-aware, enduring in its appeal. But it does not have to have all the qualities you think it requires.

Yours, Ben

P.S: The idea that Dickens was not a serious artist is absurd. you were joking. I presume?   *18*

Dear Ben,

You've got me wrong. I can't abide the sniffy attitude that just because something is popular or pleasurable it must be second-rate. As someone who started her working life on the fashion pages of a glossy magazine, I know what it feels like to be the casualty of other people's intellectual insecurity. Women, I recall, were the worst offenders.   *19*

So I was delighted when in the early 1980s the cultural studies revolution transformed the way in which we were allowed to think about, and admit to liking, popular culture.   *20*

But now, like most insurrectionaries, I wonder if the revolution hasn't gone too far. I gave up glossy magazines, retrained, and now teach university students. The 20-year-olds I meet in the seminar room have received their entire education in the postmodern age. I am shocked by how little discomfort they can bear in confronting a difficult text. I long ago gave up expecting all but the very keenest (often mature) students to get through *Middlemarch*. Mostly they watch it on video and hope for the best. I am besieged for advice about which courses involve the least reading.   *21*

So you see why I am edgy about elevating *ER* to art. It bothers me that a work as comfortable, regressive even, as *ER* should be given the status you claim for it. For if *ER* is allowed to bask in this central cultural space, then what place is there for the difficult, uncomfortable, or downright odd piece of work?   *22*

I do not, as you suggest, assume that anything that appears in a "modern medium" cannot be art. There is, in fact, an American import (now canceled in the U.S.) that might qualify as art. *Homicide: Life on the Street* is on the face of it a formulaic   *23* cop show. But it does things that *ER* only pretends to do—it makes the everyday and the real its subject matter. *Homicide* once did a whole episode on what happened when the station lavatory flooded. The main characters spent their time tiptoeing on planks, trying not to gag. That, it seems to me, is taking risks. That, indeed, is art.

Yours, Kathryn

VOCABULARY

In your journal, write the meaning of each of the following words:

- a distinctive *aesthetic* **(2)**
- it flirts with *kitsch*, it dabbles in *parody* **(2)**
- close to *caricature* **(3)**
- in *serial* form **(4)**
- serve *progressive* causes **(7)**
- cite as a *paradigm* **(8)**
- its own *genre* **(8)**
- the *allusions* **(9)**
- on *a priori* grounds **(15)**
- firmly within the *parameters* **(16)**

QUESTIONS FOR WRITING AND DISCUSSION

1. What is your favorite or least favorite television program? What criteria would you use to explain why it is or is not a great program—filming, acting, story line, relevant social themes, entertainment value, and so on? Using these criteria, explain why you would or would not recommend it to your friends.

2. In his letters to Kathyrn, Ben claims that *ER* is "art of a very high order." How does he define art? What are his main criteria? What evidence from *ER* does Ben cite to support his criteria?

3. In her responses to Ben, Kathyrn claims that *ER* is "a magnificent achievement," but it is not art. How is her definition of art different from Ben's? What are her main criteria? What evidence from *ER* does she give to support her claim?

4. Because Kathyrn and Ben carry out their discussion of *ER* through multiple letters, they are each able to respond to the other—creating

an argument in dialogue form. Where do you see each writer responding specifically to the other? Where do they make their argument clearer? Where do they give ground or negotiate their positions? Finally, is their dialogue format more interesting than reading a review of *ER* by a single author? Explain.

5. The authors are writing for the British magazine *Prospect*. Where is their English point of view expressed most clearly? Since the essay was reprinted in *Utne* magazine, do you think the authors' debate is just as interesting for American readers? Why or why not?

6. On the Internet, visit the alt.tv.er Web pages at http://www.digiserve. com/er. The editor, Mike Sugimoto, posts regular responses to episodes of *ER*. Originally a fan of *ER*, his later reviews complain about the degenerating quality of the show: "Recent episodes have been unraveling in front of my eyes faster than a cheap sweater. Asking me to believe that these formerly realistic people are now acting like . . . well, aliens . . . is a little much. It's very much like going to a circus, watching a puppet show, and being acutely aware of the presence of strings. You can see them bouncing around. Which is fine if you're watching Punch and Judy in the park. It's not very good when you're watching what is supposedly a realistic TV drama." Go to this site—or a similar one—and read responses to *ER* episodes. Then write your own evaluation of a particular episode of *ER*, responding to Ben, Kathyrn, and any of the on-line commentators you read.

P R O F E S S I O N A L   W R I T I N G

FIRST BORN, LATER BORN
Geoffrey Cowley

As a medical and health writer for Newsweek *magazine, Geoffrey Cowley has published dozens of articles on issues such as the Persian Gulf War syndrome, AIDS, abortion, gene tests, breast cancer, and Alzheimer's disease. His recent cover stories in* Newsweek *include "Herbal Warning," an article about dangerous herbal remedies; "Attention: Aging Men," an investigation of DHEA and hormonal treatments for men; and "Targeting a Deadly Scrap of Genetic Code," a report on current AIDS treatments. In "First Born, Later Born," Cowley turns to psychological issues to review Frank Sulloway's best-selling book* Born to Rebel *(Pantheon Books, 1996). Typically, book reviews have a dual purpose: to* inform *readers about the main ideas of the book and to* evaluate *the work's accuracy, interest level, and style. As you read Cowley's essay, think about your own relationship to your siblings. As a firstborn or later-born, do you—or your siblings—exhibit the personality traits Sulloway and Cowley describe?*

When 22-year-old Charles Darwin set out in 1831 to circle the globe   *1* on the HMS *Beagle*, his mind lay squarely in the mainstream. He assumed that life forms were fixed entities, each one hand-crafted by God for its special place in nature. But during his travels, Darwin started noticing things that didn't fit the paradigm. Why, he wondered, would finches and iguanas assume distinct but related forms on adjacent islands? And when Darwin proposed a revolutionary solution— that all nature's variety stems from a simple process that preserves useful variations and discards harmful ones—the authorities were appalled. "A scientific mistake," thundered Louis Agassiz, then the world's leading naturalist—"untrue in its facts . . . and mischievous in its tendency."

What drives people like Darwin to stick pins in conventional wis-   *2* dom? And why do radical innovations so enrage people like Agassiz? To Frank Sulloway, a science historian at MIT, it's no coincidence that Darwin was the fifth of six kids in his family, or that Agassiz was the firstborn in his. Sulloway has spent two decades gathering data on thousands of people involved in historic controversies—from the Copernican revolution to the Protestant Reformation—and running statistical tests to see what sets rebels apart from reactionaries. His findings, due out this month in a new book titled "Born to Rebel" (640 pages. *Pantheon Books*. $30), suggests that "the foremost engine of historical change" is not the church, state or economy but family structure. Sulloway makes a compelling case that firstborns, whatever their age, sex, class or nationality, specialize in defending the status quo while later-borns specialize in toppling it. Indeed, he says, people with the same birthranks have more in common with each other than they do with their own siblings.

It's an audacious claim (Sulloway himself is a later-born), and not   *3* one that social scientists will flock to embrace. Birth-order research, for all its intuitive appeal, has a reputation for flakiness. "Both lay people and experts tend to overinterpret the importance of birth order," says Joseph Rodgers, a psychologist at the University of Oklahoma. "There are very few birth-order effects." In a 1983 review of 2,000 studies dating to the 1940s, the Swiss psychologists Cecile Ernst and Jules Angst declared that since most had failed to control for variables like social class and family size, none could be taken seriously. Sulloway agrees that much of the past research has been marred by weak hypotheses and poor methods. But his own study tackles many of the issues left unresolved by earlier ones, and some experts are raving about it. "It's a monumental work of scholarship," says Sarah Blaffer Hrdy, an anthropologist at the University of California, Davis. "I think it will change the way all of us think about ourselves and our families."

Most of us already have a seat-of-the-pants sense of how birthrank   *4*
affects personality. Firstborns are by reputation the list makers and control freaks. "Show me a librarian who's not a first born," says pop psychologist Kevin Leman, author of "The Birth Order Book" and "Growing Up First Born." "They live by the Dewey Decimal System." Firstborns are supposedly at home in trades like accounting and architecture—and maybe airline piloting. Walter Cronkite, Peter Jennings and Ted Koppel are all firstborns or only children. Chevy Chase, Danny DeVito and Jay Leno are last-borns. Psychologists have theorized about sibling differences since the 1920s, when Freud's estranged disciple Alfred Adler alleged that firstborns spend their lives getting over their displacement by younger brothers and sisters. But the models have been vague enough to accommodate almost any real-world observation—or its opposite. Adler, for example, argued that last-borns are often spoiled and lazy because they don't have younger siblings challenging them. He also characterized them as go-getters, hardened by incessant competition with their elders. Take your pick.

Sulloway starts not by spinning random hypotheses but by think-   *5*
ing about the Darwinian pressures that foster sibling competition throughout the natural world. Parental support is often the key to a youngster's survival—and siblings are often the primary obstacle. When food is scarce, chicks in a nest may gang up to murder the youngest member of the brood, without a peep of parental protest. Humans harbor similar propensities. Many societies accord firstborns higher status than later-borns, and some still condone killing a newborn in times of scarcity, just to ensure an older child's survival. Sibling competition may take different forms in the New Jersey suburbs than it does among peasants facing starvation. But firstborns and later-borns still confront very different pressures and opportunities. And by Sulloway's reckoning, their experiences should foster very different qualities of character.

How, exactly, should they differ? Firstborns, who grow up know-   *6*
ing they're "bigger, stronger and smarter than their younger siblings," should be more assertive and dominant. They should also be more jealous and status-conscious, having seen their untrammeled turf invaded by newcomers. Their early experience as parents' lieutenants should make them more conscientious than later-borns. And the favoritism they enjoy should leave them more closely wedded to their parents' values and standards. Later-borns, since they can't get their way by force or bluster, should be more sociable and agreeable. And their

lesser state in the established family order should leave them more open to novelty and innovation.

Sulloway has found ingenious ways of testing these hypotheses. By sifting through the 2,000 studies that Ernst and Angst discarded in 1983, he found 196 in which researchers had factored out differences in social class and family size before looking for birth-order effects. And those studies, which included nearly 121,000 participants, supported his predictions about each of the five personality dimensions that psychological tests look for. Birth order was a lousy predictor of extroversion, a category so broad that it could encompass both a firstborn's assertiveness and a later-born's backslapping sociability. But most studies found that firstborns were more neurotic than were later-borns, and more conscientious (as in responsible, organized and achievement-oriented). Later-borns were consistently deemed more agreeable, and they were overwhelmingly more open to experience. People without siblings fell somewhere between firstborns and later-borns on most personality measures, but they were no more open to experience than were firstborns. [7]

So far, so good. But did these psychological tests say anything about how people would behave out in the world? That's where Sulloway's historical surveys come into play. To get at the roots of real-life radicalism, he compiled biographical data on 6,566 people who have played public roles in scientific or political controversies over the past five centuries. By having panels of historians rate these players on their resistance or receptivity to the innovations they confronted, he was able to plot their "openness to experience" in relation to everything from birth order to age, sex, race, temperament, social class, family size and even the tenor of their family relationships. [8]

In one case after another, the influence of birth order is remarkable. Later-borns were more likely than firstborns were to support each of the 61 liberal causes Sulloway surveyed, from the Protestant Reformation to the American civil-rights movement. Indeed birth order rivaled race as a predictor of who would support the abolition of slavery during the mid-1800s. Firstborns and later-borns differ more in their styles of thought than in their core beliefs—liberals can be rigidly doctrinaire and conservatives can be open to new ways of thinking. But the last-borns in Sulloway's survey were 18 times more likely to take up left-wing causes than to get involved in conservative ones, such as the temperance movement. Not surprisingly, Mahatma Gandhi and Martin Luther King Jr. were all later-borns, as were Leon Trotsky, Fidel Castro, Yasir Arafat and Ho Chi Minh. Rush Limbaugh, George Wallace and Newt Gingrich are all firstborns. [9]

The pattern was just as clear when Sulloway examined 28 scientific controversies. Later-borns were five times more likely than first-borns were to support the Copernican and Darwinian revolutions—and nine times more likely to embrace phrenology, a wacky 19th-century fad that involved divining character from the shape of a person's skull. By contrast, Sulloway found that "conservative innovations," such as the eugenics movement, have consistently been spearheaded by firstborns and opposed by later-borns.   *10*

This isn't to say that birth order is all that counts in life, or even in the contentious worlds of science and politics. "These are statistical patterns, not physical laws," says Harvard evolutionist Ernst Mayr. "There are always exceptions." Isaac Newton was a firstborn, for example, and Adolf Hitler wasn't. Sulloway is the first to admit that the effects of birth order can be offset, exaggerated or even overridden by other factors. Indeed, he devotes much of the new book to plotting the ways in which different influences interact. Gender has a huge and obvious impact on personality. But studies have found that firstborn girls are typically more confident, assertive and verbally aggressive than their younger brothers or sisters are. By the same token, age makes most people less open-minded, regardless of their birthrank. Within Sulloway's sample, young later-borns were more than twice as likely as elderly ones were to embrace the idea of evolution during the 19th century. But 80-year-old later-borns were still more receptive than 30-year-old firstborns.   *11*

Like age, certain features of a person's innate temperament can mask the effects of birth order. Congenital shyness, for example, tends to minimize birth-order differences. By placing a damper on other aspects of character, it makes firstborns less arch and later-borns less outwardly subversive. Likewise, extroversion tends to magnify the contrast. It might lead a firstborn to become a drill sergeant instead of a bank teller, and a last-born to do stand-up comedy instead of writing poems. Conflict with a parent can also offset a firstborn's conformist ways. Once estranged from the familial status quo and pushed into the underdog role, says Sulloway, anyone becomes more radical.   *12*

Sulloway's findings are sure to strike a chord with lay readers, but social scientists may not appreciate his chutzpah. In the years since Ernst and Angst declared birth order meaningless, few researchers have bothered to look at it, and many of those who have tried have been disappointed. In a recent book titled "Birth Order and Political Behavior," Alfred University political scientist Steven Peterson and two colleagues describe how they analyzed a huge list of eminent figures to see if it was dominated by firstborns. When they came up dry, they assumed there was nothing left to study. "There are always some   *13* people who are going to say, 'Gee, you just didn't look at enough variables,'" says Peterson's collaborator Alan Arwine. "It's like trying to kill a vampire." But Arwine and Peterson's findings don't contradict Sulloway's. They merely answer a less interesting question. "The question isn't whether firstborns are more eminent than later-borns," Sulloway insists. "Eminence isn't even a personality trait. It's an outcome. What's interesting is that firstborns and later-borns become eminent in different ways."

Other critics will dismiss Sulloway's whole approach. "From what *14* I read, it's not scientific," says Toni Falbo, a professor of educational psychology at the University of Texas at Austin. "He looks at special cases. If you're looking at special cases, particularly in history, you can find a case that fits almost any hypothesis you want." By her logic, history is just an endless series of special cases, not a lawful process that can be illuminated through hypothesis testing. Sulloway's real accomplishment is to show that's not the case. His "special cases" span five centuries and many countries, yet they repeatedly confirm his predictions. "Frank attacks questions that could not be more contingent," says John Tooby, an anthropologist at the University of California, Santa Barbara—"why some countries ended up Protestant, why France resisted Darwinism, who ended up in which faction in the French National Assembly—and shows that they fit into larger patterns."

Sulloway doesn't claim to have solved any ultimate questions. He *15* plans to expand his database, test new predictions and publish a revised edition of the book every five years or so. "The publisher put that in my contract," he says. "It was the only way I could make myself stop and publish this." Anyone who can stomach a revolution should be glad that he did.

VOCABULARY

In your journal, write the meanings of the following words:

- didn't fit the *paradigm* **(1)**
- defending the *status quo* **(2)**
- an *audacious* claim **(3)**
- spinning random *hypotheses* **(5)**
- humans harbor similar *propensities* **(5)**
- liberals can be rigidly *doctrinaire* **(9)**
- the *eugenics* movement **(10)**
- appreciate his *chutzpah* **(13)**

- firstborns are more *eminent* **(13)**
- could not be more *contingent* **(14)**

QUESTIONS FOR WRITING AND DISCUSSION

1. Reread Cowley's essay, underlining the major claim and the important ideas in Sulloway's book. Then write out Sulloway's major claim and the related key ideas (as summarized by Cowley). Which of those ideas do you personally agree or disagree with? Explain.

2. What does Cowley find to praise about Sulloway's book? What authorities does Cowley cite to support Sulloway's methods or claim? Where is Cowley skeptical about Sulloway's ideas or evidence? Why doesn't Cowley criticize Sulloway's lack of *female* firstborns or laterborns? What authorities does Cowley cite to question or refute Sulloway's ideas, evidence, or methods? Does Cowley offer an evaluation that sufficiently represents both the strengths and weaknesses of the book? Explain.

3. Do a sketch outline of Cowley's essay. Where is his introduction? Where are major divisions in the body of the essay? Where is his conclusion? Then, referring to the various types of lead-ins (see list in Chapter 7, pp. 314–316), identify the kind of lead-in Cowley uses. Did you find it effective? Choose three consecutive paragraphs in the body of Cowley's essay. What phrases or transitions does Cowley use to signal the connections between paragraphs? Are these transitions effective? Explain. Where is Cowley's conclusion? Explain why it is or is not effective.

4. Cowley's review article appeared in *Newsweek*. Find a recent copy of *Newsweek* and profile the kind of reader it targets. Assume that you are assigned to adapt and revise Cowley's essay for your campus or local newspaper. How might you revise the essay? Consider length, depth of treatment, paragraphing, and style. Write out your revision plan for this adaptation. Include several specific examples (actual revisions of sample sentences or paragraphs) of how and where you might revise content, organization, or style.

5. Write your own essay in response to Cowley and Sulloway explaining how birth order has affected your personality and the personalities of your siblings. First, write out your thoughts about how birth order has or has not affected the personalities of yourself and your siblings. Then call and interview your siblings about their opinions. (Be sure to ask them about their perceptions *before* you tell them about Sulloway's thesis or your own ideas.) Using your own perceptions (and supporting experiences), as well as the perceptions and experi-

ences of your siblings, evaluate Sulloway's thesis. How well do Sulloway's ideas account for personality differences in your family?

6. When Sulloway's book was published in 1996, it was reviewed in dozens of magazines. Locate three or four reviews (other than Cowley's) on Lexis-Nexis or Electric Library. Compare the reviews. Are the other reviews more positive or more critical than Cowley's? What ideas or reactions do they have that Cowley doesn't mention? Which of these reviews gives the best arguments and evidence to support its judgments? Explain.

PROFESSIONAL WRITING

WATCHING THE EYEWITLESS NEWS

Elayne Rapping

Culture critic Elayne Rapping is a professor of communications at Adelphi University and is the author of several books, including The Looking Glass World of Nonfiction TV *(1987),* Mediations: Forays into the Culture and Gender Wars *(1994), and* The Culture of Recovery: Making Sense of the Self-Help Movement in Women's Lives *(1996). She has also published dozens of articles about a variety of social, cultural, and media-related issues. "Watching the Eyewitless News," which originally appeared as a column in* The Progressive, *evaluates the local "Eyewitness" news programs featured daily in regional television markets.*

Jimmy Cagney, the ultimate street-smart wise guy, used to snap, "Whadya hear? Whadya know?" in the days of black-and-white movies and READ ALL ABOUT IT! headlines. But that was then and this is now. Today, when gangsta rap has replaced gangster movies, and television has replaced newsprint as the primary source of information (for two-thirds of us, the *only* source), Cagney's famous question is not only antiquated, it is beside the point. What we hear when we consume "the news" has only the most marginal relationship to what we *know* about anything.

I'm not referring here to CNN or the "evening news" on the national broadcast networks. I'm referring here to what passes for news in the homes and minds of the vast majority of Americans today: The Eyewitless, Happy Talk local newscasts that run in many cities for as much as an hour and a half to two hours a day, on as many as seven or eight different channels.

Topic

The rise of local news, the infotainment monster that ate the news 3
industry, is a long and painful story about a key battle-front in the endless media war between capitalism and democracy, between the drive
for profits and the constitutional responsibility of those licensed to use
the airwaves to serve the public interest. We know who's winning, of
course. The game was rigged from the start. . . .

Local news as we know it was invented in 1970, the brainchild of 4
a marketing research whiz hired by the industry to raise ratings by
finding out what audiences "wanted to see." The Jeffersonian notion
that public media should cover what citizens "need to know" was not
a big consideration. Nor was it a concern to respect the audience's intelligence or diversity.

The researchers offered a limited, embarrassingly vapid list of 5
choices of formats and subjects, while ignoring the possibility that different groups might want different kinds of information and analysis.
More annoying still, they ignored the possibility that individual viewers, of all kinds, might want and need different things at different times
for different reasons. Nope, said the marketing whizzes, this master
model of "The News" will buy us the most overall-ratings bang per
buck. Wrap it up and send it out.

And it worked. Their invention has conquered the TV world. The 6
set, the news lineups, the anchors, the weather maps, the sports features—all developed for a New York City market—quickly became a
universal formula, sent out to every network affiliate and independent
station in America, complete with fill-in-the-blanks guidelines for
adaptation to any community, no matter how large or small, urban or
rural. Local news today is the single most profitable form of nonfiction
television programming in the country and, for most stations, the only
thing they actually produce. Everything else comes from the networks.
As time went by, this tendency toward cookie-cutter formulas, exported
far and wide from a central media source, reached ever more depressing depths. The trend has led to ever more nationally produced, generic features exported to local stations to be passed off as "local."

So today we have a phenomenon euphemistically called "local 7
news," although it is anything but, filled with images of a pseudo-
community called "America," which is actually closer to Disney World
in its representation of American life. But why should that surprise us,
in a national landscape now filled, from coast to coast, with identical,
mass-produced shopping malls that pass for town marketplaces, and
hotels and airports that pass for village inns? In postmodern America,
after all, this kind of brand-name synthetic familiarity appears to be the
only thing that holds us—a nation of endlessly uprooted and mobile
strangers—together.

When you turn on the news, whether at home or in an airport or   *8*
Holiday Inn in some totally strange locale, you see a predictable, comforting spectacle. The town or city in question, whether Manhattan or
Moose Hill, Montana, is presided over by a group of attractive, charming, well-dressed performers—whose agents, salaries, and movements
up and down the ladder of media success, gauged by the size of the
"market" they infiltrate, are chronicled each week in *Variety*. They seem
to care endlessly for each other and us. "Tsk, tsk," they cluck at news
of yet another gang rampage or Congressional scandal. "Ooh," they
sigh, at news of earthquakes and plane crashes, far and near.

IF IT BLEEDS, IT LEADS is the motto of the commercial news in-   *9*
dustry and local news. Its endless series of fires, shootouts, collapsing
buildings, and babies beaten or abandoned or bitten by wild dogs is
the state-of-the-art showcase for the industry. As Don Henley once put
it, in a scathing song about the local news phenomenon, "It's interesting when people die." And it's especially interesting when they die in
bizarre or inhuman situations, when their loved ones are on camera to
moan and wail, when a lot of them die at once. And since so much of
our news is indeed personally terrifying and depressing, we need to
have it delivered as cleverly and carefully as possible. And so we have
the always smiling, always sympathetic, always confidently upbeat news
teams to sugarcoat the bad news.

Not that local news ignores the politically important stories. Well,   *10*
not entirely anyway. When wars are declared or covered, when elections
are won or lost, when federal budgets and plant closings do away with
jobs and services or threaten to put more and more of us in jail, for
less and less cause, the local news teams are there to calm our jagged
nerves and reassure us that we needn't worry.

This reassurance is sometimes subtle. National news items typically   *11*
take up less than two minutes of a half-hour segment. And what's said
and seen in that brief interlude is hardly enlightening. On the contrary,
the hole for "hard news" is generally filled with sound bites and head
shots, packaged and processed by the networks, from news conferences
with the handful of movers and shakers considered "newsworthy"—
the President and his key henchmen and adversaries, mostly.

But even local issues of serious import are given short shrift on   *12*
these newscasts. Hard news affecting local communities takes up only
a minute or two more airtime than national events. And local teams are
obsessed with "man-on-the-street" spot interviews. Neighbors on local
TV are forever gasping and wailing the most clichéd of reflex responses
to actual local horrors, whether personal or social.

"It's so horrible," they say over and over again, like wind-up dolls   *13*
with a limited repertoire of three-word phrases, when asked about a

local disaster. And when the crisis affects them directly—a school budget cut or neighborhood hospital closing, for example—their on-air responses are equally vapid. "I don't know what we're going to do without any teachers or books," they say with puzzled, frenzied expressions as they try desperately to articulate some coherent reply to a complex issue they've just heard about.

I am not suggesting that the news should not feature community residents' views and experiences. Of course it should. But the local news teams' way of presenting such community responses is deliberately demeaning and fatuous. No one could say much worth saying in such a format. And if someone managed to come up with something serious and intelligent, rest assured it would be cut in favor of a more sensational, emotional response.

But real news, even about cats in trees or babies in wells, is hardly what takes up the most airtime. "Don't bother too much about that stuff," say the guys and gals in the anchor chairs. Here's Goofy Gil with the weather, or Snappy Sam with the sports—the two features which, on every local newscast, are given the longest time slots and the most elaborate and expensive props. The number and ornateness of the weather maps on local news, and the endlessly amazing developments in special-effects technology to observe climate changes and movements of impending "fronts" is truly mind-boggling.

Who needs this stuff? But we're forgetting that this is not the question to ask. "Who wants it?" is the criterion for news producers, and it is, understandably, the weather and sports that most people, most of the time, are likely to sit still for. If local news is meant to be a facsimile of a sunny Disneyesque community of happy, cozy campers, in which the bothersome bad guys and events of the day are quickly dealt with so that community harmony may once more reign, at least for the moment—and that *is* the intended fantasy—then what better, safer, kind of information than weather reports. Historically, after all, the weather is the standard small-talk item for people wishing to be pleasant and make contact without getting into anything controversial or heavy. It is the only kind of news we can all share in—no matter what our race, class, gender, or political differences—as members of a common community.

The researchers are not entirely wrong, after all, about what people in this kind of society want. They do want comfort, reassurance, and a community where they belong and feel safe. And why shouldn't they? They find precious little of those things in the streets and buildings they traverse and inhabit in their daily lives. In my urban neighborhood, parents warn children never to make eye contact with anyone on the street or subway; never to speak to anyone, even in case of tragedy or emergency; never to look at or listen to the pathetic souls who regularly beg for money or ramble incoherently in the hope that someone, anyone, will take pity and respond.

Remember when California was God's country, the Promised *18* Land of Milk and Honey, to which people migrated for clean air, good jobs, and single-dwelling homes? Try to find these things in overpopulated, polluted, socially vexed and violent LA today. . . . But if we can't all dream of moving to sunny California anymore, there's always TV, where something resembling that innocent dream still exists. Eyewitness News and its various clones allow us to believe, just for a moment, that there really is a Santa Claus, a Mary Poppins, a Good Samaritan giving away fortunes to the needy, a spirit of Christmas Past to convert the most cold-hearted of corporate Scrooges. Indeed, this kind of "good news" is another staple of the genre. Charities, celebrations, instances of extraordinary good luck or good works by or for local residents are ever-present on local newscasts. Every day, in the midst of even the most dreadful and depressing news, there are legions of friends and neighbors to mourn and console each other, offering aid, bringing soup and casseroles to the victims of natural and manmade disasters, stringing lights and hanging balloons for festive neighborhood gatherings.

The news teams themselves often play this role for us. They march *19* at the head of holiday parades and shake hands and kiss babies at openings of malls and industrial parks. They are the neighbors—often thought of as friends by the loneliest among us—we wish we had in real life, there to do the right thing on every occasion. That is their primary function. They are not trained in journalism. They often cannot pronounce the local names and foreign words they read from teleprompters. But they sure can smile. . . .

Sociologist Joshua Gamson has suggested, in an insightful essay, *20* that there is a lesson to be learned from the enormous popularity of tabloid television—a category in which I would certainly include local news. The lesson is not that people are stupid, venal, "addicted," or otherwise blameworthy for their fascinated interest in junk TV. On the contrary, it is those responsible for the quality of our public life who are more deserving of such terms of contempt and opprobrium. For it is, says Gamson, "Only when people perceive public life as inconsequential, as not their own, [that] they readily accept the invitation to turn news into play." And people most certainly do perceive public life as inconsequential and worse these days, whether outside their doors or in Washington or on Wall Street.

Only I don't think it is primarily the desire to "play" that drives *21* people in droves to local newscasts, or even the trashier tabloid shows like *Hard Copy*. What people are getting from local newscasts—and here the researchers were right on the money, literally—is indeed what they want, in the most profound and sad sense of that phrase. They are getting what they always sought in fantasy and fiction, from *The Wizard of Oz* to *As the World Turns*. They are getting, for a brief moment, a utopian fantasy of a better, kinder, more decent and meaningful world than the one that entraps them.

It is not only that public life is inconsequential, after all. It is, far more tragically, that public and private life today are increasingly unjust, inhumane, painful, even hopeless, materially and spiritually, for many of us. And there is no relief in sight except, ironically, on the local newscasts that are a respite from reality. Only, unlike the utopian villages of soap opera and fairy tale, these "imagined communities" are supposed to be, pretend to be, real and true. And for that reason they are more troubling than the trashiest or silliest of pop-culture fictions.

22

VOCABULARY

In your journal, write down the meanings of the following words:

- is not only *antiquated* (1)
- *euphemistically* called "local news" (7)
- are given short *shrift* (12)
- a limited *repertoire* (13)
- equally *vapid* (13)
- demeaning and *fatuous* (14)
- be a *facsimile* (16)
- a *utopian* fantasy (21)

QUESTIONS FOR WRITING AND DISCUSSION

1. When you finish reading Elayne Rapping's essay, write out your personal responses. Did you agree or disagree with her analysis? Did you find her essay humorous or were you angry at her pronouncements? Were her judgments believable? Did her judgments fit with your own experiences watching your local news programs? Write out your reactions as fully as possible.

2. Reread Rapping's essay, identifying the criteria behind her judgments. In this case, criteria are statements describing what an ideal news program should be; for example, "Good news programs should

provide what the people need, not necessarily what they want." Find and list as many of these criteria as you can. Then make a three-column log for this essay, indicating the judgment that Rapping makes about each criterion and the supporting evidence that she provides.

3. Referring to the three-column log from Question 2, above, assess Rapping's use of supporting evidence—specific examples from local news shows illustrating her point. Which of Rapping's judgments have supporting evidence? Which are merely unsupported assertions? Based on your analysis, do you think Rapping has written an effective evaluative essay? Explain.

4. Observe a local news program. If possible, videotape the program. As you replay your videotape, list each segment of the news: local events, national news, weather, sports, business news, international news, medical and health issues, and so forth. Note any transitional sections (segues) that contain small talk among the anchors. Next to each segment, record the length of time. Next, indicate your opinion about quality or depth of coverage. Finally, record any evidence about the newscasters' personalities, on-camera style, or journalistic ability. Based on your observations and evidence, write an essay responding to Elayne Rapping. How accurately do her observations apply to the case you have observed? What other general conclusions about Rapping's article or about local news programs might you make?

5. Using Rapping's method of cultural analysis, observe and then analyze/evaluate a particular social, cultural, or media-related event. You might choose hall or club meetings at your university, lecture or lab classes, sports events, class registration rituals, TV sitcoms, Internet home pages—the list is bounded only by your imagination. (Be sure to focus on only one particular kind of cultural event or media program.) Your purpose is both to evaluate these cultural "events" and to explain why the cultural event itself is or is not constructed to avoid limited, stereotypical visions of reality or of people.

6. A study by the Kaiser Family Foundation and the Center for Media and Public Affairs found that "the five most common topics in local TV news coverage are crime (20 percent of news items), weather (11 percent), accidents and disasters (9 percent), human interest stories (7 percent), and health stories (7 percent), with all other topics ranking below the top five." "Local TV news wouldn't cover crime as much as it does if the public didn't reward such coverage with high ratings," according to Drew Altman, President of the Kaiser Family Foundation. "But," he continues, "does anyone seriously believe that crime is twice as important as any other issue that the public

needs to learn about from local television news?" On the Internet, access Electric Library and search for recent articles on "network news" and "local news." How do the findings described above or in the articles you locate compare with Rapping's argument? Write your own analysis of local or network TV news using the sources you find.

I love criticism so long as it's unqualified praise.

—NOEL COWARD,

PLAYWRIGHT, SONGWRITER, NOVELIST, DIRECTOR, AND PERFORMER

Evaluating: The Writing Process

■ ASSIGNMENT FOR EVALUATING   With a specific audience in mind, evaluate a product or service, a work of art, or a performance. Choose a subject that is *reobservable*—that you can revisit or re-view as you write your essay. Select criteria appropriate for your subject and audience. Collect evidence to support or determine a judgment for each criterion.

The review is the most common genre for evaluating pieces, but "reviews" cover a wide range of documents. Some film reviews are academic and critical while others merely indicate the major plot line without much evaluation. Similarly, some reviews of performances or products are short, informal, and intended mainly as information and entertainment for the reader. After you choose your topic, then be sure to consider the requirements or expectations of your audience. Are they expecting merely to be informed or entertained, or do they want the thorough and critical evaluation described in this chapter?

CHOOSING A SUBJECT

If you have already settled on a possible subject, try the following collecting and shaping strategies. If you have not found a subject, consider these ideas:

- Evaluating requires some expertise about a particular person, performance, place, object, or service. You generate expertise not only through experience but also through writing, reading, and rewriting. Review your authority list from Chapter 6. Which of those subjects could you evaluate? Reread your journal entries on observing and investigating. Did you observe or investigate some person, place, or thing that you could write about again, this time for the purpose of evaluating it?

- Comparing and contrasting lead naturally to evaluation. For example, compare two places you've lived, two friends, or two jobs. Compare two newspapers for their coverage of international news, local features, sports, or business. Compare two famous people from the same profession. Compare your expectations about a person, place, or event with the reality. The purpose of your comparison is to determine, for a specific audience, which is "better," based on the criteria you select and the evidence you find.

COLLECTING

Once you have a tentative subject and audience in mind, ask the following questions to focus your collecting activities:

- Can you narrow, restrict, or define your subject to focus your paper?
- What *criteria* will you use to evaluate your subject?
- What *evidence* might you gather? As you collect evidence, focus on three questions:
  What *comparisons* can you make between your subject and similar subjects?
  What are the *uses* or *consequences* of this subject?
  What *experiments* or *authorities* might you cite for support?
- What initial *judgments* are you going to make?

OBSERVING   Observation and description of your subject are crucial to a clear evaluation. In most cases, your audience will need to know *what* your subject is before they can understand your evaluation.

- Examine a place or object repeatedly, looking at it from different points of view. Take notes. Describe it. Draw it, if appropriate. Analyze its component parts. List its uses. To which senses does it appeal—sight, sound, touch, smell, taste? If you are comparing your subject to other similar subjects, observe them carefully. Remember: The second or third time you observe your subject, you will see even more key details.
- If you are evaluating a person, collect information about this person's life, interests, abilities, accomplishments, and plans for the future. If you are able to observe the person directly, describe his or her physical features, write down what he or she says, and describe the person's environment.
- If you are evaluating a performance or an event, a tape recording or videotape can be extremely useful. If possible, choose a concert, film, or play on tape so that you can stop and re-view it if and when necessary. If a tape recording or videotape is not available, attend the performance or event twice.

Making notes in a *three-column log* is an excellent collecting strategy for evaluations. Using the following example from Phyllis Richman's evaluation of the Hunan Dynasty restaurant, list the criteria, evidence, and judgments for your subject:

Subject: Hunan Dynasty Restaurant

CRITERIA	EVIDENCE	JUDGMENT
Attractive setting	No blaring red-lacquer tables	Graceful
	White tablecloths	
	Subtle glass etchings	
Good service	Waiters serve with flourishes	Often expert
	Some glitches, such as forgotten appetizer	

REMEMBERING   You are already an authority on many subjects, and your personal experiences may help you evaluate your subject. Try *freewriting, looping, branching,* or *clustering* your subject to help you remember relevant events, impressions, and information. In evaluating appliances for consumer magazines, for example, reporters often use products over a period of months, recording data, impressions, and experiences. Those experiences and memories are then used to support criteria and judgments. Evaluating a film often requires remembering similar films that you have liked or disliked. An evaluation of a great athlete may include your memories of previous performances. A vivid narrative of those memories can help convince an audience that a performance is good or bad.

READING   Some of the ideas and evidence for your evaluation may come from reading descriptions of your subject, other evaluations of your subject, or the testimony of experts. Be sure you read these texts critically: Who is the intended audience for the text? What evidence does the text give? What is the author's bias? What are other points of view? Read your potential sources critically.

INVESTIGATING   All evaluations involve some degree of formal or informal investigation as you probe the characteristics of your subject and seek evidence to support your judgments.

Using the Library or the Internet   Check the library and Internet resources for information on your subject, for ideas about how to design and conduct an evaluation of that subject, for possible criteria, for data in evaluations already performed, and for a sense of different possible audiences. In its evaluation of chocolate chip cookies, for example, *Consumer Reports* suggests criteria and outlines procedures. The magazine rated some two dozen popular store-bought brands, as well as four "boutique" or freshly baked varieties, on "strength of chocolate flavor and aroma, cookie and chip texture, and freedom from sensory defects." When the magazine's evaluators faced a problem sampling the fresh cookies in the lab, they decided to move the lab: "We ended up loading a station wagon with scoresheet, pencils, clipboards, water containers, cups, napkins . . . and setting off on a tasting safari to shopping malls."

Gathering Field Data   You may want to supplement your personal evaluation with a sample of other people's opinions by using *questionnaires* or *interviews*. (See Chapter 6.) If you are rating a film, for example, you might give people leaving the theater a very brief *questionnaire*, asking for their responses on key criteria relating to the movie that they just saw. If you are rating a class, you might want to *interview* several students in the class to support your claim that the class was either effective or ineffective. The interviews might also give you some specific examples: descriptions of experiences that you can then use as evidence to support your own judgments.

SHAPING

While the shaping strategies that you have used in previous essays may be helpful, the strategies that follow are particularly appropriate for shaping evaluations.

ANALYSIS BY CRITERIA   Often, evaluations are organized by criteria. You decide which criteria are appropriate for the subject and audience, and then you use those criteria to outline the essay. Your first few paragraphs of introduction establish your thesis or overall claim and then give background information: what the subject is, why you are evaluating it, what the competition is, and how you gathered your data. Then you order the criteria according to some plan: chronological order, spatial order, order of importance, or another logical sequence. Phyllis Richman's evaluation of the Hunan Dynasty restaurant follows the criteria pattern:

- Introductory paragraphs: *information* about the restaurant (location, hours, prices), general *description* of Chinese restaurants today, and *overall claim:* The Hunan Dynasty is reliable, a good value, and versatile.
- Criterion #1/judgment: Good restaurants should have an attractive setting and atmosphere/Hunan Dynasty is attractive.
- Criterion #2/judgment: Good restaurants should give strong priority to service/Hunan Dynasty has, despite an occasional glitch, expert service.
- Criterion #3/judgment: Restaurants that serve moderately priced food should have quality main dishes/Main dishes at Hunan Dynasty are generally good but not often memorable. (*Note:* The most important criterion—the quality of the main dishes—is saved for last.)
- Concluding paragraphs: Hunan Dynasty is a top-flight neighborhood restaurant.

COMPARISON AND CONTRAST   Many evaluations compare two subjects in order to demonstrate why one is preferable to another. Books, films, restaurants, courses, music, writers, scientists, historical events, sports—all can be evaluated by means of comparison and contrast. In evaluating two Asian restaurants, for example, student writer Chris Cameron uses a comparison-and-contrast structure to shape her essay. In the following body paragraph from her essay, Cameron compares two restaurants, the Unicorn and the Yakitori, on the basis of her first criterion—an atmosphere that seems authentically Asian:

> Of the two restaurants, we preferred the authentic atmosphere of the Unicorn to the cultural confusion at the Yakitori. On first impression, the Yakitori looked like a converted truck stop, sparsely decorated with a few bamboo slats and Japanese print fabric hanging in slices as Bruce Springsteen wailed loudly in the ears of the customers. The feeling at the Unicorn was quite the opposite as we entered a room that seemed transported from Chinatown. The whole room had a red tint from the light shining through the flowered curtains, and the place looked truly authentic, from the Chinese patterned rug on the wall to the elaborate dragon on the ceiling. Soft oriental music played as the customers sipped tea from small porcelain cups and ate fortune cookies.

Cameron used the following *alternating* comparison-and-contrast shape for her whole essay:

- Introductory paragraph(s)
- Thesis: Although several friends recommended the Yakitori, we preferred the Unicorn for its more authentic atmosphere, courteous service, and well-prepared food.
- Authentic atmosphere: Yakitori versus Unicorn
- Courteous service: Yakitori versus Unicorn
- Well-prepared food: Yakitori versus Unicorn
- Concluding paragraph(s)

On the other hand, Cameron might have used a *block* comparison-and-contrast structure. In this organizational pattern, the outline would be as follows:

- Introductory paragraph(s)
- Thesis: Although several friends recommended the Yakitori, we preferred the Unicorn for its more authentic atmosphere, courteous service, and well-prepared food.
- **The Yakitori:** atmosphere, service, and food
- **The Unicorn:** atmosphere, service, and food as compared to the Yakitori's
- Concluding paragraph(s)

CHRONOLOGICAL ORDER   Writers often use chronological order, especially in reviewing a book or a film, to shape parts of their evaluations. Film reviewers rely on chronological order to sketch the main outlines of the plot as they comment on the quality of the acting, directing, or cinematography. At the end of this chapter, for example, Kent Y'Blood's review of the film *The Big Chill* uses chronological order to organize the middle paragraphs of his essay.

CAUSAL ANALYSIS   Analyzing the *causes* or *effects* of a place, object, event, or policy can shape an entire evaluation. Evaluations of works of art or performances, for example, often measure the *effect* on the viewers or audience. Mark Stevens, for example, claims that Goya's painting has several definite effects on the viewer; those specific effects become the evidence that supports the claim:

- Criterion #1/judgment: The iconography, or use of symbols, contributes to the powerful effect of this picture on the viewer. *Evidence*: The church as a symbol of hopefulness contrasts with the cruelty of the execution. The spire on the church emphasizes for the viewer how powerless the Church is to save the victims.
- Criterion #2/judgment: The use of light contributes to the powerful effect of the picture on the viewer. *Evidence*: The light casts an intense glow on the scene, and its glaring, lurid, and artificial qualities create the same effect on the viewer that modern art sometimes does.
- Criterion #3/judgment: The composition or use of formal devices contributes to the powerful effect of the picture on the viewer. *Evidence*: The diagonal lines scissor the picture into spaces that give the viewer a claustrophobic feeling. The corpse is foreshortened, so that it looks as though the dead man is bidding the viewer welcome.

TITLE, INTRODUCTION, AND CONCLUSION   Titles of evaluative writing tend to be short and succinct, stating what product, service, work of art, or performance you are evaluating ("The Big Chill" or "Watching the Eyewitless News") or suggesting a key question or conclusion in the evaluation ("Borrowers Can Be Choosy").

Introductory paragraphs provide background information and description and usually give an overall claim or thesis. In some cases, however, the overall claim comes last, in a concluding "Recommendations" section or in a final summary paragraph. If the overall claim appears in the opening paragraphs, the concluding paragraph may simply review the strengths or weaknesses or may just advise the reader: This *is* or *is not* worth seeing, reading, watching, doing, or buying.

I have to stop being afraid of being wrong; I can't wait until everything is perfect before the work comes out. I don't have that kind of time.

—SHERLEY ANNE WILLIAMS,

NOVELIST AND CRITIC

RESEARCH TIP

Before you draft your evaluating essay, stop for a moment and *evaluate your sources* of information and opinion. If you are citing ideas or information from library articles—or especially from the Internet—be skeptical. How reliable is your source? What do you know about your source's reliability or editorial slant? Does the author have a particular bias? Be sure to *qualify* any biased or absolute statements you use from your sources. (See Chapter 12 for additional ideas on evaluating written sources.)

If you cite observations or field sources (interviews, surveys), evaluate the information you collected. Does it reflect only one point of view? How is it biased? Are your responses in surveys limited in number or point of view? Remember: You may use sources that reflect a limited perspective, but *be sure to alert your readers to those limitations*. For example, you might say, "Obviously, these reactions represent only four viewers who saw this film, but . . . " or "Of course, the administrator wanted to defend this student program when he said . . . "

DRAFTING

I have rewritten—often several times—every word I have ever published. My pencils outlast their erasers.

—VLADIMIR NABOKOV,

NOVELIST

With your criteria in front of you, your data or evidence at hand, and a general plan or sketch outline in mind, begin writing your draft. As you write, focus on your audience. If your evaluation needs to be short, you may have to use only those criteria that will appeal most effectively to your audience. As you write, check occasionally to be sure that you are including your key criteria. While some parts of the essay may seem forced or awkward as you write, other parts will grow and expand as you get your thoughts on paper. As in other papers, don't stop to check spelling or worry about an occasional awkward sentence. If you stop and can't get going, reread what you have written, look over your notes or sketch outline, and pick up the thread again.

REVISING

Remember that revision is not just changing a word here and there or correcting occasional spelling errors. Make your evaluation more effective for your reader by including more specific evidence, changing the order of your paragraphs to make them clearer, cutting out an unimportant point, or adding a point that one of your readers suggests.

PEER RESPONSE

These guidelines will help you give and receive constructive advice about the rough draft of your evaluating essay.

Reader: Before you answer the following questions, read the entire draft from start to finish. As you *reread* the draft, to the following:

1. Underline the sentence(s) that state the writer's *overall claim* about the subject.
2. In the margin, put large brackets [ ] around paragraphs that *describe* what the writer is evaluating.
3. On a separate piece of paper or at the end of the writer's essay, make a *three-column log* indicating the writer's criteria, evidence, and judgments. (Does the log include both positive and negative judgments?)
4. Identify with an asterisk (*) any passages in which the writer needs more *evidence* to support the judgments.
5. Write out one *criterion* that is missing or that is not appropriate ate for the given subject.
6. If possible, describe one of *your experiences*, with this subject that the writer might find interesting or relevant.

Writer: As you read your peer reviewer's notes and comments, do the following:

1. Consider your peer reviewer's comments and notes. Has your reviewer correctly identified your overall claim? Do you need to add more description of your subject? Does the reviewer's three-column log look like yours? Do you need to revise your criteria or add additional evidence? Do you balance positive and negative judgments?
2. Based on your review, draw up a *revision plan*. Write out the three most important things you need to do as you revise your essay.

Guidelines for Revision

During your revision, keep the following tips in mind:

- **Criteria are *standards of value*.** They contain categories and judgments, as in "good fuel economy," "good reliability," or "powerful use of light and shade in a painting." Some categories, such as "price," have clearly implied judgments ("low price"), but make sure that your criteria refer implicitly or explicitly to a standard of value.

- **Examine your criteria from your audience's point of view.** Which criteria are most important in evaluating your subject? Will your readers agree that the criteria you select are indeed the most important ones? Will changing the order in which you present your criteria make your evaluation more convincing?
- **Include both positive and negative evaluations of your subject.** If all of your judgments are positive, your evaluation will sound like an advertisement. If all of your judgments are negative, your readers may think you are too critical.
- **Be sure to include supporting evidence for each criterion.** Without any data or support, your evaluation will be just an opinion that will not persuade your reader.
- **Avoid overgeneralizing in your claims.** If you are evaluating only three software programs, you cannot say that Lotus 1-2-3 is the best business program around. You can say only that it is the best among the group or the best in the particular class that you measured.
- **Unless your goal is humor or irony, compare subjects that belong in the same class.** Comparing a Ford Focus to a BMW is absurd because they are not similar cars in terms of cost, design, or purpose.
- **If you need additional evidence to persuade your readers, review the questions at the beginning of the "Collecting" section of this chapter.** Have you addressed all the key questions listed there?
- **If you are citing other people's data or quoting sources, check to make sure your summaries and data are accurate.**
- *Signal* **the major divisions in your evaluation to your reader using clear transitions, key words, and paragraph hooks.** At the beginning of new paragraphs or sections in your essay, let your reader know where you are going.
- **Revise sentences for directness and clarity.**
- **Edit your evaluation for correct spelling, appropriate word choice, punctuation, usage, and grammar.**

■ POSTSCRIPT ON THE WRITING PROCESS   When you finish writing your essay, answer the following questions:

1. Who is the intended audience for your evaluation? Write out one sentence from your essay in which you appeal to or address this audience.
2. Describe the main problem that you had writing this essay, such as finding a topic, collecting evidence, or writing or revising the draft.
3. What parts or paragraphs of your essay do you like best? Indicate the words, phrases, or sentences that make it effective. What do you like about them?
4. Explain what helped you most with your revision: advice from your peers, conference with the teacher, advice from a writing center tutor, rereading your draft several times, or some other source.

5. Write out one question that you still have about the assignment or about your writing and revising process.

BORROWERS CAN BE CHOOSY
Linda Meininger

Linda Meininger wrote her evaluation essay on the Interlibrary Loan Office at her campus library. Her purpose was to advise her readers—other students—about the usefulness of the interlibrary loan service. In order to gather information for her essay, she visited the office, learned how to access an interlibrary loan with her computer, interviewed the coordinator of the office, and surveyed nine people who had used the library service. Overall, she discovered that the interlibrary loan office provided a surprisingly convenient, helpful, and inexpensive service. Included here are the following writing-process materials: a draft of her interview and survey questions, a three-column log, her first rough draft, questions for a conference with her instructor, and her final draft.

Draft of Interview and Survey Questions
Interview Questions for Interlibrary Loan Office (ILL) Coordinator

1. Have you surveyed your clients to get their impressions about the service? Results? Favorable—why? Unfavorable—why? Valid or not—why?
2. How do you and your employees rate your service?
3. Do you offer any special services for your clients?
4. Have you received any recognition for your work in the ILL?
5. What institutions lend documents to our library?
6. How convenient do you make it for clients to use your services?

Survey Questions

1. Were you satisfied with the interlibrary loan service you received? Why? Why not?
2. How often do you use the service?
3. How much lead time did you allow for your request?
4. What was your area of research?

5. What type of materials did you request? Periodicals? Books? Documents? Theses?

6. What was the cost of using the service?

Draft of Three-Column Log

Claim: The Interlibrary Loan Office runs a well-organized and efficient operation.

Audience: Students.

Purpose: To evaluate the service and encourage students to use it.

CRITERIA	EVIDENCE	JUDGMENT
1. Timely delivery of materials	Survey results	Mixed
2. Helpful service	Personal experience	Positive
3. Convenience for users	Survey	Positive
4. Scope of libraries available	Interview and brochure	Positive
5. Reasonable cost	Survey and interview	Positive

First Rough Draft

Are you someone who has searched endlessly through the library's *1*
computer database or the card catalog only to have that elusive title never appear? Go directly to Room 210, Morgan Library, and collect an Interlibrary Loan request card, or if that's too far to walk, place your order via e-mail from your PC.

How useful can this service be to you? Stay tuned and I'll show you *2*
everything you need to know about Morgan Library Interlibrary Loan (ILL). In evaluating this service, available to all who are affiliated with CSU as a student or employee, I will be looking at the following criteria: convenience and ease of use; timely arrival of materials requested; cooperation and assistance from the ILL staff; and reasonable fees for use of loaned materials.

Jane Smith of the ILL department informed me that request cards *3*
can be found in many locations in the library. These color-coded cards are used to request documents, periodicals, theses, or books. The color of the card corresponds to the type of material. Requests may be left at any of the reference desks, or you may drop off your request in person in Room 210 of the library, Monday through Friday.

Students and employees with a PC and a modem may request *4*
materials from their office or home. According to Jane Smith, elec-

tronic access was developed in-house by the ILL department. A new service has also been established, called the Library Retrieval and Delivery Service (LRDS). This is available to disabled students on campus. Requests may be made by the computer or manually.

Jane Smith of the ILL office informed me that normal turnaround 5 for requests is 24 hours. That translates to one day from the time the requests leave the ILL office for another lending institution. Unless . . . it's spring semester. Then, look out! Deadlines for theses and research are closing in and everyone is in need of the materials yesterday. Then the turnaround time is a week. Most likely materials will not arrive until the end of the school year. Requests in spring semester jump to 300–400 per day compared to a norm of approximately 200 daily.

I would say that being able to fill 300 requests for material is ef- 6 ficient by my standards. Jane was delighted to inform me that Morgan Library was chosen most efficient in the state by other ILLs in Colorado. I think that could be comparable to a Good Housekeeping Seal of Approval or a five-star rating by AAA.

When I visited the ILL office I discovered a staff willing to an- 7 swer my questions and with a sense of humor. They made me feel comfortable and at ease. One of the brochures I picked up was a pamphlet with their job descriptions: Queen of the World, Resident Geek, ILL's Mouthpiece, Double Agent, ILL's Movie Star and answer to Greta Garbo, and Leading (Lending) Lady. The pamphlet shows me that these people like what they do and can laugh at themselves and their idiosyncrasies. I believe this impression is relayed to their patrons.

Conference Questions

1. Are the criteria I have sufficient? Should I have chosen more of the criteria from my log? Or other criteria from my list?

2. My development needs improvement. I need more evidence to substantiate my criteria. What if I didn't secure the surveys necessary (ten) to be fairly objective?

3. Should I introduce my criteria in a subtle manner or just come right out and state them?

4. After class today, I felt that I needed to state judgments for each of my criteria, although they could change after the survey results.

5. Does it sound like I'm writing to a student audience?

Revised Version
Borrowers Can Be Choosy

Are you someone who has searched endlessly through the library's   *1*
computer listing, the card catalog, or even the stacks, only to have that
elusive title never appear? Don't give up. Go directly to Room 210,
Morgan Library, and collect an Interlibrary Loan request card. If that's
too far to walk, just place your order via e-mail with your PC, a modem,
and some communications software.

This service can be useful to you during your four-year educa-   *2*
tional experience at Colorado State University. So stay tuned, and I'll
review four characteristics of Morgan Library Interlibrary Loan (ILL).
In evaluating this service, which is available to all CSU students, faculty, or staff, I will be looking at the following criteria: convenience
and ease of use, timely arrival of materials requested, reasonable fees for
materials, and cooperation and assistance from the ILL staff. To gain
evidence about the performance of this department, I interviewed the
staff, observed their operation, and conducted a survey of CSU students, faculty, and employees (see Appendix for results of survey). Out
of nine survey respondents, the level of usage varied from four one-
time users to two weekly users.

The convenience and ease of using the interlibrary loan service   *3*
was definitely a high point. Jane Smith of the ILL department informed me that request cards have been placed in many locations in the
library for convenient access. These color-coded cards are used to request documents, periodicals, theses, or books. The color of the card
corresponds to the type of material requested. Cards may be left at any
of the reference desks, or you may drop off your request in person in
Room 210 of the library, just off to your left at the top of the stairs,
Monday through Friday, 8:00 A.M.–5:00 P.M.

The addition of computer access to interlibrary loans also adds to   *4*
the ease of requesting materials. At the present time, students, faculty, and employees with a PC and a modem may request materials from
their office or home. According to Ms. Smith, electronic access was
developed in-house by the ILL department, making their service available 24 hours per day. Julie Wessling, coordinator of the Interlibrary
Loan department, said, "About one third of our users request their specific information via our electronic service."

The ILL has also established another convenient new service, called   *5*
Library Retrieval and Delivery Service (LRDS). This is available to disabled students on campus and other off-campus users. Requests may be
made by computer or by using the request cards. Delivery or notice of

nonavailability of materials will be made within 48 hours to three sites on campus: Braiden Hall, the RDS Office in 116 Student Services Building, and the ILL office. There is also dial-up access to the library's computer listings. This service is especially valuable to off-campus users or students with mobility problems. The ILL staff retrieves requests, most of which—according to Ms. Wessling—are in the CSU stacks, and then delivers them to one of the collection sites for pickup by the patron.

Overall, I found the request forms and located the ILL office without any problem, and according to nine out of the nine people surveyed, the ILL service was "easy to use and locate." Judy Lira, a Rocky Mountain High School media specialist, faxes her requests and feels that the technology is a service to the staff and students at her school. Bonnie Mueller, a Morgan Library cataloguing employee, uses LAN to order materials, and she states, "It's wonderful!" While I was in the ILL office, a student was filling out request cards. I tried to enlist her aid for my survey, but she declined, saying that this was her first time using the Interlibrary Loan service. However, she did have one comment for me: "They [the ILL office] need to make us [students] more aware of this." It appears that the convenient access to the ILL system makes it an asset to CSU students and to the local schools. 6

I wished to experiment personally with the ILL to evaluate the timely arrival of requests, but Ms. Smith explained to me that it would be impossible to receive anything within the time frame I was allotted to finish this essay. Therefore, I will be relying on the experiences and testimony of others. 7

The normal processing turnaround time for requests, Ms. Smith informed me, is 24 hours. That means that it takes one day from the time the request is made by the borrower to the time it leaves the ILL office for another lending institution. Unless . . . it's spring semester. Then look out! Deadlines for theses and research papers are closing in, and students and faculty need their materials yesterday. Ms. Smith related the story of a student who recently came in on a Wednesday and wanted the item by Monday. She had to tell him, "Sorry, it's not possible, especially now." She said at this time of the year—spring semester—the processing time is approximately one week, and that's just until the request leaves the CSU ILL office. Most likely, materials will not arrive until April or the end of the school year. Normal arrival time seems to vary between ten days and two weeks, according to survey results. Requests at spring semester jump to 300–400 per day, and these requests include not only the CSU customers, but the borrowers from other institutions who are requesting materials from Morgan Library, reported Ms. Wessling. 8

The normal processing time can be speeded up, however, in some   *9*
cases. Ms. Wessling explained that "the use of e-mail allows us to locate and help process customers' requests faster. This allows the student or professor to receive the information more quickly. The only
thing holding the process back is the time it takes to get the specific request in the mail." Also, articles from periodicals or a document can be
sent electronically or by fax. When materials are needed in a hurry, a
RUSH may be affixed to the card and a last usable date recorded. This
will bring the request to the attention of the office, and they will give
it priority to try to locate a copy at a nearby library for pickup by the
client. Of the nine people I surveyed, six reported that their materials
arrived within 24 hours to two weeks, but one person reported that it
took eight weeks and didn't arrive in time to be of use. He allowed two
weeks of lead time, but he ordered the material in April. Another person stated that she had to wait over six weeks for materials to arrive. Her
materials were "very difficult to locate." My accounting professor, Dr.
Middlemist, usually allows a two-week lead time when ordering and
said that the "time taken to arrive depended on where the materials
were coming from." Dr. Middlemist stated that she uses the service
10–12 times per year, maybe more, depending on what her needs are.

By my standards, being able to fill 300 requests for materials is   *10*
efficient. In addition, Ms. Smith was delighted to inform me that Morgan Library was chosen most efficient by other ILLs in Colorado and
will be "looked over" by a team from the state so that their efficient and
innovative ideas may be used in other libraries. I think that could be
comparable to a Good Housekeeping Seal of Approval or a four-star
rating by AAA.

While the timely arrival of materials was a problem, especially in   *11*
the spring semester, the cost of materials received was very reasonable.
For most requests, there is no charge for the service. I found that only
on the journal request card was there a line item for maximum cost.
This is in the event that there could be photocopying charges. Eight
of my nine respondents said they received their materials (books, theses, and journals) free of charge, and the other paid a reasonable fee for
Xeroxing one time. It is through the lending and borrowing reciprocal agreement between libraries that the ILL service can be offered at
no cost or low cost to the user.

Perhaps the strongest feature of the ILL service was the willing-   *12*
ness of the staff to help patrons, answer questions, and keep their sense
of humor. They made me feel comfortable and at ease. One of the
brochures I picked up was a pamphlet with their job descriptions:
Queen of the World, Resident Geek, ILL's Mouthpiece, Double Agent,
ILL's Movie Star and Answer to Greta Garbo, and Leading (Lending)

Lady. This pamphlet shows that these people like what they do and can laugh at themselves and their idiosyncrasies. Something else Ms. Smith said really sticks in my mind. She said, "I think we're the only department in the whole library where everyone really likes what they do." I believe this impression is relayed to the patrons. My survey results concurred with this, as seven respondents felt that the staff was friendly and helpful. One dissenting student felt that the office could have presented the information she needed over the phone, saving her a trip to the library. The other person felt there wasn't any follow-up on a trace request to see if a book had been lost. Morgan Library has lost this patron to another library. Some of the positive comments received were as follows: "The ILL personnel went out of their way to help me." "What I needed was extremely obscure, and they got most of it." "They found a German book in Berlin, and they Xeroxed it and sent the whole thing FREE!"

As a result of my investigation and evaluation of the ILL office, I 13
hope I have occasion to use their service in the future. I know from my conversations with the staff and other users of ILL that the service and staff are reliable and willing to assist at any time (during office hours, of course). The cost is well within the reach of all patrons, and we have two methods of booking our requests: manually on cards and electronically by computer. So the next time you need an item that the CSU library doesn't own, remember that you do have another resource available at your fingertips: Morgan Library's Interlibrary Loan.

Works Cited

Interlibrary Loan. Fort Collins: Colorado State University, 1992.

It's Here! Fort Collins: Colorado State University, 1992.

Libraries Retrieval and Delivery Service. Fort Collins: Colorado State University, 1992.

Morgan Library Interlibrary Loan Survey. Personal Survey. 2 March 1992.

Self-Guided Tour of Morgan Library. Fort Collins: Colorado State University, 1992.

Smith, Jane. Personal Interview. 27 Feb. and 2 March 1992.

Wessling, Julie. Personal Interview. 2 March 1992.

APPENDIX

Morgan Library Interlibrary Loan Survey

The following survey was completed by nine students and faculty members. Responses follow each question.

1. What was the subject area of the materials requested?

    Accounting—1   Ben Jonson—17th C writer & critic—1
    Agriculture—1   Cognitive development—1
    Ancient Roman Art—1   Popular fiction—1
    Anthropology—1   Travelogues—1800s—1
    Archaeology—1   Various subjects—1

2. What type of material did you request?

    Book—7   Journal—6
    Thesis—1   Documents—0

3. How much lead time did you allow the Interlibrary Loan office to secure your materials?

    No deadline—5

    24 hours—1

    1 week—1

    2 weeks—2

4. At what time of the year did you request materials?

    Fall semester   Specify month   3 in Oct, Nov, and Dec
    Spring semester   Specify month   1—Jan, 4—Feb & Mar,
                                        2—April, 1—May

5. Did your materials arrive in a timely manner? How much time did it take?

    24 hours—1   Very quickly—1
    1 week—1   Not more than $1^1/_2$–2 months—1
    8 weeks—1   Over 3 weeks—1
    Typically timely—1   10 days—1

6. Were you satisfied with the service you received? Why? Why not?

    No, not friendly, no follow-up if lost—1

    Yes, friendly and helpful—1

    Yes—2

    Yes, very satisfied—1

    Very, needed extremely obscure stuff & got most of it—1

    Extremely satisfied, wonderful to have access to otherwise un-reachable materials—1

    No problem with service or individuals, satisfied—1

    Friendly—1

7. How often do you use the service?

1 time—3 Weekly—1
2 times/year—1 One semester a lot of times—1
10–12 times/year—1
Goes to Boulder-CU library—1
2–3 times/week ave., usually turns in requests in batches—1

8. Was there a charge for your requested materials? If so, did you feel the charge was reasonable or not? How much was it?

No charge—8

Xeroxing charge, reasonable—1

9. Was the staff of the Interlibrary Loan office helpful? Friendly? Did it give out-of-the-ordinary service?

Not friendly, not helpful, no out-of-ordinary service—1

Could have presented info over phone, save trip to library—1

Staff went out of their way to help—1

Worked hard on obscure stuff—1

Always do their best–1

Very friendly—3 Friendly & helpful—3
Regular service—1 Fax requests—1

10. Did you feel that the service was convenient to use (e.g., easy to order materials and pick them up, forms to be filled out, the open hours of the office)?

Easy to use—2 Very—2 Yes—2
Used LAN—1

Yes, feels guilty about amt. of paper involved in all of the re-quests—1

Fax technology availability real service to students & staff—1

11. From which institution did you receive your materials?

Northwestern—1

Dartmouth—1

Berlin—1

Denver Public Library—1

Oklahoma State University—1

CU-Boulder—1

Don't know—2

QUESTIONS FOR WRITING AND DISCUSSION

1. Evaluate Meininger's final draft, using the peer response guidelines in this chapter. What are the strengths and weaknesses of her essay? Now read Meininger's first rough draft. Which areas did she improve most in her revision?

2. Based on her final draft, make a revised version of Meininger's three-column log. Write out each criterion, the main supporting evidence for that criterion, and the judgment. Indicate the paragraphs (by number) that Meininger devotes to each of her criteria.

3. In her postscript, Meininger wrote, "I revised my criteria and rearranged them in a different order after we talked in class. I didn't want to have my weakest criteria last." Compare her criteria (see her three-column log) with her revised draft. Explain how her additions, deletions, and reordering improved her criteria—and her essay.

4. Reread the questionnaire in Meininger's Appendix. How might she improve that questionnaire? What questions might she add or delete? How might she rephrase the questions?

5. Brainstorm a list of other campus services or organizations that you could evaluate. Choose one of those services or organizations and write a three-column log, indicating the subject, the audience, the criteria, and the possible kinds of evidence that you might collect for your essay.

STUDENT   WRITING

THE BIG CHILL
Kent Y'Blood

In his review of The Big Chill, *Kent Y'Blood writes a compact evaluation of the film for a campus newspaper audience. Film review writers often need to walk a tightrope: They should give the basic information about key characters and plot—without revealing too much about the story; they should analyze and evaluate the film—without so much analysis that the reader is bored. As you read the essay, decide how successful Y'Blood is at both informing and entertaining the reader.*

The Big Chill is an actors' film in the very best sense. It's no easy   *1*
task to create eight major characters we can care about immediately
without resorting to some form of cinematic stereotyping, but director Lawrence Kasdan does it. We meet eight individuals whose stories
of fading youthful optimism are familiar in many ways. These characters are not mere representatives of those stories but living, breathing
people in a psychological comedy.

And what a dark comedy it is. Death pervades every scene, and not   *2*
just the death of The Movement, or the death of Revolutionary Ideals,
or the death of The Spirit of a Generation. Those generalizations have
little place here. *The Big Chill* is about a real, particular death: that of
Alex Marshall, permanent dropout, college friend of Sam, Sarah,
Michael, Nick, Harold, Meg, and Karen. He committed suicide in
Harold and Sarah's house, where he was staying with his young girlfriend, Chloe. The old friends, who haven't seen much of each other
in years, regroup for his funeral and all decide to spend a weekend at
Harold and Sarah's house in Georgia to try to sort out their confusion
over Alex's act.

At the beginning of the film, Kasdan packs plenty of character   *3*
information into a relatively short space so that we get to know the
people well. As they make their various ways to the funeral, spread out
across the country as they are, we begin to learn about them. Sam
(Tom Berenger) lines up four miniature vodka bottles on his airplane
tray and charms the stewardess out of just one more. Nick (William
Hurt) empties out a collection of pills on the seat of his Porsche,
downs a couple, and the car roars out ahead of the camera. We get
glimpses of the other characters intercut with shots of a man dressing in a pinstripe suit and white shirt, all to the tune of Marvin Gaye's
"I Heard It Through the Grapevine." Kasdan ends this scene with a
shocker. As a sewn-up wrist is slipped beneath a white cuff, we realize it was Alex's corpse we saw being dressed. This combination of expository information with emotionally powerful action is superb movie
making, and Kasdan does not let down after the promise of this opening sequence.

At the funeral itself, we learn more about the principals. Michael   *4*
(Jeff Goldblum) obviously wants more than comfort from Chloe
(Meg Tilly). Harold (Kevin Kline) intones a eulogy and breaks down
as he remembers, "There was something about Alex that was too
good for this world." His wife, Sarah (Glenn Close), weeps but holds
together admirably. Throughout the film, all the characters are true
to our first impressions of them but are not mechanically programmed to act predictably. They can still surprise us, and they all

do. Later, when the characters get assigned their bedrooms, we get a glimpse of their luggage. Knowing who brings the economy-size bottle of Maalox, who the TV script and a volume of Kafka, and who has many pairs of designer men's underwear just adds that much more to our sense of who each of these people is. It is a weekend of talk, but the talk is supplemented by what we've observed about these people, so the dialogue doesn't have to carry all the weight in the film.

When they do talk, the chat is brilliant. Their sentiment is con-   5
stantly undercut by jokes that don't weaken their emotions, just complicate them. When Beth rises to play Alex's favorite song on the organ at the funeral (Rolling Stones' "You Can't Always Get What You Want"), it is simultaneously funny and heartbreaking. The friends collectively try to work out how they failed Alex, how they failed their younger selves by becoming successful and rich, and how the people they were became the people they are.

The Big Chill is beautifully edited and masterfully acted and has a   6
script that has more depth than anything I've seen in a long time. The film directly confronts such tough themes as the endurance of friendship, the question of suicide, isolation, meaninglessness—and all to the '60s music of the Temptations, Smokey Robinson, and the Rascals. That's what I call a good movie.

Questions for Writing and Discussion

1. Profile yourself as a typical reader of this review: Give your age, note whether you frequently go to movies, describe the kinds of films you enjoy, describe your attitude toward music or events from the sixties, and indicate whether or not you have seen *The Big Chill*. With these notes, come to class prepared to discuss whether or not Y'Blood's review succeeded. Did it make you want to see the movie? If you've seen the film already, was his evaluation convincing? Was it entertaining?

2. Y'Blood's writing-process materials are not reproduced here, but how do you suppose that he collected all the information and supporting evidence for his review? Describe a plausible sequence for his collecting activities.

3. In his review, Y'Blood emphasizes Lawrence Kasdan's skills in directing this film. However, if he had chosen to focus on one particular actor's performance (for example, William Hurt's performance as Nick) or on the relationship of the songs to the story, how would that have changed the review? For practice, rewrite the opening paragraph of this review, focusing either on one principal actor or on the sixties songs.

Sonia Delaunay, "Electric Prism," 1914. Oil on canvas, 98⅜ × 98⅜ in. Musée National d'Art Moderne.

Chapter 9   Problem Solving

Trying to take notes in your Psych I lecture class—along with 250 other students—you realize that you are completely lost and confused. So you raise your hand to ask a question, but the professor keeps on talking, throwing out more new terms and examples. You look at your neighbor, who just shrugs and keeps on writing. After class, when you think about how hard you've worked to pay your tuition, you realize that you deserve better classes for your money. The problem, you decide, is in the large lecture format—there are just too many students for the teacher to answer questions and explain difficult concepts. So you decide to write a letter to the head of the psychology department (with a copy to the dean of arts and sciences) outlining your problems with this class and proposing that Psychology I be taught in classes no larger than fifty. Where the administrators get additional teachers, you decide, is their responsibility. You argue that, as administrators, it is their duty to give quality education the highest priority.

In your writing class, you read a conversation between two minority women about racial tensions in African-American and Asian-American communities. The problems, you realize, are continuing and widespread. Publicized instances include a boycott by blacks of Korean shops in New York City and the looting of Korean stores during the Los Angeles riots. As a member of the American-Korean community, you decide to propose three solutions to promote education and understanding. First, encourage the American-Korean media to educate Koreans about cultural differences. Next, ask Korean-American churches to cooperate with churches in African-American communities. Finally, appeal to Korean businesspeople to invest in the black communities where they work. Communities, you argue, cannot wait for local or federal governments to solve these problems. They must take the initiative and work cooperatively to solve their problems.

This country has more problems than it should tolerate and more solutions than it uses.
—RALPH NADER,
CONSUMER RIGHTS ADVOCATE

Whenever life doesn't seem to give an answer, we create one.
—LORRAINE HANSBERRY,
AUTHOR OF A RAISIN IN THE SUN

*W*E DON'T HAVE TO LOOK DILIGENTLY TO LOCATE PROBLEMS IN OUR LIVES. THEY HAVE A HABIT OF SEEKING US OUT. IT SEEMS THAT IF SOMETHING CAN GO WRONG, IT WILL. COUNTRIES ARE fighting each other, the environment is polluted, prejudice is still rampant, television shows are too violent, sports are corrupted by drugs and money, education is too impersonal, and people drive so recklessly that you take your life in your hands every time you go across town. Everywhere we look, someone else creates problems for us—from minor bureaucratic hassles to serious or life-threatening situations. (On rare occasions, of course, we're part of the problem ourselves.)

If you write in order to *propose a solution* to some problem, you have no lack of subjects. First, however, you may well ask whether your problem is one that can be solved. As journalist Charles Dudley Warner once observed, "Everybody talks about the weather, but nobody does anything about it." For the short term, the weather is not a problem that has a solution. Although we can predict the weather (sometimes), experiment with cloud seeding, or prepare for the effects of hurricanes or blizzards, wisdom dictates that we accept the weather that comes. For the long term, however, we know that ozone depletion and global warming are serious weather-related problems that need worldwide planning and cooperation.

If the problem can be solved, the difficult part is to propose a solution and then persuade others that your solution will in fact solve the problem—without creating new problems and without costing too much. Because your proposal may ask readers to take some action, vote in a certain way, or actually work to implement your proposal, you must make sure that your readers vividly perceive the problem and agree that your plan outlines the most logical and feasible solution.

Techniques for Problem Solving ●●●

You see things; and you say, "Why?" But I dream things that never were; and I say, "Why not?"

—GEORGE BERNARD SHAW,

DRAMATIST

Problem solving requires all your skills as a writer. You need to observe carefully to see if a problem exists. You may need to remember experiences that illustrate the seriousness of the problem. You need to read and investigate which solutions have worked or have not worked. You often have to explain what the problem is and why or how your proposal would remedy the situation. You may need to evaluate both the problem and alternative solutions. To help you identify the problem and convince your readers of the soundness of your proposal, keep the following techniques in mind:

- **Identifying and understanding your** *audience.* If you want something done, fixed, changed, improved, subsidized, banned, reorganized, or made legal or illegal, make sure that you are writing to the appropriate audience.
- **Demonstrating that a** *problem exists.* Some problems are so obvious that your readers will readily acknowledge them: high crime rates, conflicts in Africa and the Middle East, air pollution in industrialized nations, and drug and alcohol abuse. Often, however, you must first convince your audience that a problem exists: Are food preservatives really a serious problem, or would eliminating them cause even more problems?
- **Proposing a** *solution* **that will solve the problem.** After convincing your readers that a serious problem exists, you must then propose a remedy, plan, or course of action that will eliminate or reduce the problem.
- **Persuading your readers that your** *proposal will work,* **that it is** *feasible,* or that it is better than the *alternative solutions.* You convince your readers by supporting your proposal with *reasons* and *evidence.*

As you start your problem-solving paper, concentrate on ways to *narrow and focus* your topic. When you think about possible topics, follow the advice of environmentalists: "Think Globally, Act Locally." Rather than talk about education or drugs or crime or pollution on a national scale, find out how your community or campus is dealing with a problem. A local focus will help narrow your topic—and provide possibilities for using firsthand observations, personal experience, and interviews.

DEMONSTRATING THAT A PROBLEM EXISTS

A proposal begins with a description of a problem. Demonstrating that the problem exists (and is serious) will make your readers more receptive to your plan for a solution. The following selection from Frank Trippett's *Time* magazine essay "A Red Light for Scofflaws" identifies a problem and provides sufficient examples to demonstrate that scofflawry is pervasive and serious enough to warrant attention. Even if we haven't been personally attacked while driving the Houston or Miami or Los Angeles freeways, Trippett convinces us that *scofflawry*—deliberately disobeying ("scoffing at") laws—is serious. His vivid description makes us aware of the problem:

> Law and order is the longest-running and probably the best-loved political issue in U.S. history. Yet it is painfully apparent that millions of Americans who would never think of themselves as lawbreakers, let

Demonstrating that a problem exists

alone criminals, are taking increasing liberties with the legal codes that are designed to protect and nourish their society. Indeed, there are moments today—amid outlaw litter, tax cheating, illicit noise, and motorized anarchy—when it seems as though the scofflaw represents the wave of the future. Harvard sociologist David Riesman suspects that a majority of Americans have blithely taken to committing supposedly minor derelictions as a matter of course. Already, Riesman says, the ethic of U.S. society is in danger of becoming this: "You're a fool if you obey the rules."

Evidence: Authority

Evidence: Examples

The dangers of scofflawry vary wildly. The person who illegally spits on the sidewalk remains disgusting, but clearly poses less risk to others than the company that illegally buries hazardous chemical waste in an unauthorized location. The fare beater on the subway presents less threat to life than the landlord who ignores fire safety statutes. The most immediately and measurably dangerous scofflawry, however, also happens to be the most visible. The culprit is the American driver, whose lawless activities today add up to a colossal public nuisance. The hazards range from routine double parking that jams city streets to the drunk driving that kills some 25,000 people and injures at least 650,000 others yearly.

Evidence: Statistics

The most flagrant scofflaw of them all is the red-light runner. The flouting of stop signals has got so bad in Boston that residents tell an anecdote about a cabby who insists that red lights are "just for decoration." The power of the stoplight to control traffic seems to be waning everywhere. In Los Angeles, red-light running has become perhaps the city's most common traffic violation. In New York City, going through an intersection is like Russian roulette. Admits Police Commissioner Robert J. McGuire: "Today it's a 50–50 toss-up as to whether people will stop for a red light." Meanwhile, his own police largely ignore the lawbreaking.

Evidence: Authority

The prospect of the collapse of public manners is not merely a matter of etiquette. Society's first concern will remain major crime, but a foretaste of the seriousness of incivility is suggested by what has been happening in Houston. Drivers on Houston freeways have been showing an increasing tendency to replace the rules of the road with violent outbreaks. Items from the Houston police department's new statistical category—freeway traffic violence: (1) Driver flashes high-beam lights at car that cut in front of him, whose occupants then hurl a beer can at his windshield, kick out his tail lights, slug him eight stitches worth. (2) Dump-truck driver annoyed by delay batters trunk of stalled

Evidence: Examples

car ahead and its driver with steel bolt. (3) Hurrying driver of 18-wheel truck deliberately rear-ends car whose driver was trying to stay within 55 m.p.h. limit.

PROPOSING A SOLUTION AND CONVINCING YOUR READERS

Once you have vividly described the problem, you are ready to propose a solution and persuade your readers. In the following selection from his book *Fist Stick Knife Gun,* the essay "Peace in the Streets," as published in *The Utne Reader,* Geoffrey Canada proposes ways to create a safer world for our children. Geoffrey Canada is president and CEO of Harlem's Rheedlen Center for Children and Families, an organization that serves at-risk inner-city children. For his work with Harlem's children, Canada received the Heinze Award celebrating the power of the individual in American society. As you read Canada's proposal, notice how he narrows the problem to saving the lives of inner-city children. When he makes a recommendation, he talks about the advantages of his solution, but he talks about *feasibility problems* and real drawbacks. At several points, he gives *reasons* why we must change and supports his reasons with *evidence* from statistics and from his own personal experience.

If I could get the mayors, the governors, and the president to look into the eyes of the 5-year-olds of this nation, dressed in old raggedy clothes, whose jacket zippers are broken but whose dreams are still alive, they would know what I know—that children need people to fight for them. To stand with them on the most dangerous streets, in the dirtiest hallways, in their darkest hours. We as a country have been too willing to take from our weakest when times get hard. People who allow this to happen must be educated, must be challenged, must be turned around.

Personal experience

If we are to save our children we must become people they will look up to. We must stand up and be visible heroes. I want people to understand the crisis and I want people to act: Either we address the murder and mayhem in our country or we simply won't be able to continue to have the kind of democratic society that we as Americans cherish. Violence is not just a problem of the inner cities or of the minorities in this country. This is a national crisis and the nation must mobilize differently if we are to solve it.

Proposal

Part of what we must do is change the way we think about violence. Trying to catch and punish people after they have committed a violent act won't deter violence in the least. In life on the street, it's better to go to jail than be killed, better to act quickly and decisively even if you risk being caught.

Specific recommendations

There are, however, things that governments could and should do right away to begin to end the violence on our streets. They include the following:

Specific details

Create a peace officer corps. Peace officers would not be police; they would not carry guns and would not be charged with making arrests. Instead they would be local men and women hired to work with children in their own neighborhoods. They would try to settle "beefs" and mediate disputes. They would not be the eyes and ears of the regular police force. Their job would be to try to get these young people jobs, to get them back into school, and, most importantly, to be at the emergency rooms and funerals where young people come together to grieve and plot revenge, in order to keep them from killing one another.

Recommendation

Reduce the demand for drugs. Any real effort at diverting the next generation of kids from selling drugs must include plans to find employment for these children when they become teenagers. While that will require a significant expenditure of public funds, the savings from reduced hospitalization and reduced incarceration will more than offset the costs of employment. . . .

Recommendation

Reduce the amount of violence on television and in the movies. Violence in the media is ever more graphic, and the justification for acting violently is deeply implanted in young people's minds. The movie industry promotes the message that power is determined not merely by carrying a gun, but by carrying a big gun that is an automatic and has a big clip containing many bullets.

Reason + evidence

What about rap music, and especially "gangsta rap"? It is my opinion that people have concentrated too much attention on this one source of media violence. Many rap songs are positive, and some are neither positive nor negative—just kids telling their stories. But there are some rap singers who have decided that their niche in the music industry will be the most violent and vile. I would love to see the record industry show some restraint in limiting these rappers' access to fame and fortune.

Recommendation

Reduce and regulate the possession of handguns. I believe all handgun sales should be banned in this country. Recognizing, however, that other

Americans may not be ready to accept a ban on handguns, I believe there are still some things we must do.

Licensing. Every person who wants to buy a handgun should have to pass both a written test and a field test. The cost for these new procedures should be paid by those who make, sell, and buy handguns. . . .

Recommendation

Gun buy-backs. The federal government, which recently passed a $32 billion crime bill, needs to invest billions of dollars over the next ten years buying guns back from citizens. We now have more than 200 million guns in circulation in our country. A properly cared-for gun can last for decades. There is no way we can deal with handgun violence until we reduce the number of guns currently in circulation. We know that young people won't give up their guns readily, but we have to keep in mind that this is a long-term problem. We have to begin to plan now to get the guns currently in the hands of children out of circulation permanently.

Recommendation

Statistics

Response to feasibility problems

The truth of the matter is that reducing the escalating violence will be complicated and costly. If we were fighting an outside enemy that was killing our children at a rate of more than 5,000 a year, we would spare no expense. What happens when the enemy is us? What happens when those Americans' children are mostly black and brown? Do we still have the will to invest the time and resources in saving their lives? The answer must be yes, because the impact and fear of violence has overrun the boundaries of our ghettos and has both its hands firmly around the neck of our whole country. And while you may not yet have been visited by the spectre of death and fear of this new national cancer, just give it time. Sooner or later, unless we act, you will. We all will.

Evidence
Statistics

Call to action

■ WARMING UP: JOURNAL EXERCISES The following exercises will help you practice problem solving. Read all of the following exercises and then write on one or two that interest you most. If another idea occurs to you, write about it.

1. Wishful-thinking department: Assume that as a member of the student government, your organization has been given $10,000 to spend on a campus improvement project. Think of some campus problem that needs solving. Describe why it is a problem. Then outline your plan for a solution, indicating how you would spend the money to help solve the problem.
2. Reread Frank Trippett's analysis of the scofflaw problem. Write a letter to the city council recommending a solution to one of the problems that

A good solution solves more than one problem, and it does not make new problems. I am talking about health as opposed to almost any cure, coherence of pattern as opposed to almost any solution produced piecemeal or in isolation.

—WENDELL BERRY,
AUTHOR OF THE GIFT OF
THE GOOD LAND

Trippett identifies—a solution that the city council has the power to implement.

3. Eldridge Cleaver once said, "You're either part of the solution or part of the problem." Examine one of your activities or pastimes—sports, shopping, cruising, eating, drinking, or even studying. How does what you do possibly create a problem from someone else's point of view? Explain.

4. "Let the buyer beware" is a time-honored maxim for all consumers. Unless you are vigilant, you can easily be ripped off. Write a letter to the Better Business Bureau explaining some consumer problem or rip-off that you've recently experienced and suggest a solution that will prevent others from being exploited.

5. Changing the rules of some sports might make them more enjoyable, less violent, or fairer: moving the three-point line farther out, introducing the 30-second clock in NCAA basketball, using TV instant replays in professional and college football and basketball, imposing stiffer fines for brawls in hockey games, requiring boxers to wear padded helmets, giving equal pay and media coverage to women's sports. Choose a sport you enjoy as a participant or observer, identify and explain the problem you want to solve, and justify your solution in a letter to the editors of *Sports Illustrated.*

PROFESSIONAL WRITING

SOLVING FOR PATTERN

Wendell Berry

A native of Kentucky and professor of English at the University of Kentucky, Wendell Berry is a prolific writer of poetry, fiction, and nonfiction. He is most noted for his essays and books on agricultural and ecological topics, including The Unforeseen Wilderness: An Essay on Kentucky's Red River Gorge *(1971),* The Unsettling of America: Culture and Agriculture *(1977),* The Gift of Good Land *(1981),* Home Economics *(1987), and* What Are People For? *(1990). In this selection from "Solving for Pattern," which appears in* The Gift of Good Land, *while Berry talks about solving specific problems in farming and agriculture, he focuses on the nature of problem solving itself. Although too many farm "solutions" (larger tractors, feed lots, overuse of fertilizers and pesticides) solve one problem, they create a host of destructive side effects. Good solutions, Berry argues, do not address problems in isolation. Good solutions must promote the harmony, health, and quality of the whole system.*

Our dilemma in agriculture now is that the industrial methods that   *1*
have so spectacularly solved some of the problems of food production
have been accompanied by "side effects" so damaging as to threaten the
survival of farming. Perhaps the best clue to the nature and the gravity of this dilemma is that it is not limited to agriculture. My immediate concern here is with the irony of agricultural methods that
destroy, first, the health of the soil and, finally, the health of human
communities. But I could just as easily be talking about sanitation systems that pollute, school systems that graduate illiterate students, medical cures that cause disease, or nuclear armaments that explode in the
midst of the people they are meant to protect. This is a kind of surprise that is characteristic of our time: The cure proves incurable; security results in the evacuation of a neighborhood or a town. It is only
when it is understood that our agricultural dilemma is characteristic
not of our agriculture but of our time that we can begin to understand
why these surprises happen, and to work out standards of judgment
that may prevent them.

To the problems of farming, then, as to other problems of our   *2*
time, there appear to be three kinds of solutions:

There is, first, the solution that causes a ramifying series of new   *3*
problems, the only limiting criterion being, apparently, that the new
problems should arise beyond the purview of the expertise that produced the solution—as, in agriculture, industrial solutions to the problem of production have invariably caused problems of maintenance,
conservation, economics, community health, etc., etc.

If, for example, beef cattle are fed in large feed lots, within the   *4*
boundaries of the feeding operation itself a certain factorylike order
and efficiency can be achieved. But even within those boundaries that
mechanical order immediately produces biological disorder, for we
know that health problems and dependence on drugs will be greater
among cattle so confined than among cattle on pasture.

And beyond those boundaries, the problems multiply. Pen feed-   *5*
ing of cattle in large numbers involves, first, a manure-removal problem, which becomes at some point a health problem for the animals
themselves, for the local watershed, and for the adjoining ecosystems
and human communities. If the manure is disposed of without returning it to the soil that produced the feed, a serious problem of soil
fertility is involved. But we know too that large concentrations of animals in feed lots in one place tend to be associated with, and to promote, large cash-grain monocultures in other places. These
monocultures tend to be accompanied by a whole set of specifically
agricultural problems: soil erosion, soil compaction, epidemic infesta-
tions of pests, weeds, and disease. But they are also accompanied by a

set of agricultural-economic problems (dependence on purchased technology; dependence on purchased fuels, fertilizers, and poisons; dependence on credit)—and by a set of community problems, beginning with depopulation and the removal of sources, services, and markets to more and more distant towns. And these are, so to speak, only the first circle of the bad effects of a bad solution. With a little care, their branchings can be traced on into nature, into the life of the cities, and into the cultural and economic life of the nation.

6   The second kind of solution is that which immediately worsens the problem it is intended to solve, causing a hellish symbiosis in which problem and solution reciprocally enlarge one another in a sequence that, so far as its own logic is concerned, is limitless—as when the problem of soil compaction is "solved" by a bigger tractor, which further compacts the soil, which makes a need for a still bigger tractor, and so on and on. There is an identical symbiosis between coal-fired power plants and air conditioners. It is characteristic of such solutions that no one prospers by them but the suppliers of fuel and equipment.

7   These two kinds of solutions are obviously bad. They always serve one good at the expense of another or of several others, and I believe that if all their effects were ever to be accounted for they would be seen to involve, too frequently if not invariably, a net loss to nature, agriculture, and the human commonwealth.

8   Such solutions always involve a definition of the problem that is either false or so narrow as to be virtually false. To define an agricultural problem as if it were solely a problem of agriculture—or solely a problem of production or technology or economics—is simply to misunderstand the problem, either inadvertently or deliberately, either for profit or because of a prevalent fashion of thought. The whole problem must be solved, not just some handily identifiable and simplifiable aspect of it.

9   Both kinds of bad solutions leave their problems unsolved. Bigger tractors do not solve the problem of soil compaction any more than air conditioners solve the problem of air pollution. Nor does the large confinement-feeding operation solve the problem of food production; it is, rather, a way calculated to allow large-scale ambition and greed to profit from food production.

10   The real problem of food production occurs within a complex, mutually influential relationship of soil, plants, animals, and people. A real solution to that problem will therefore be ecologically, agriculturally, and culturally healthful.

11   Perhaps it is not until health is set down as the aim that we come in sight of the third kind of solution: that which causes a ramifying

series of solutions—as when meat animals are fed on the farm where the feed is raised, and where the feed is raised to be fed to the animals that are on the farm. Even so rudimentary a description implies a concern for pattern, for quality, which necessarily complicates the concern for production. The farmer has put plants and animals into a relationship of mutual dependence, and must perforce be concerned for balance or symmetry, a reciprocating connection in the pattern of the farm that is biological, not industrial, and that involves solutions to problems of fertility, soil husbandry, economics, sanitation—the whole complex of problems whose proper solutions add up to health: the health of the soil, of plants and animals, of farm and farmer, of farm family and farm community, all involved in the same internested, interlocking pattern— or pattern of patterns.

A bad solution is bad, then, because it acts destructively upon the *12* larger patterns in which it is contained. It acts destructively upon those patterns, most likely, because it is formed in ignorance or disregard of them. A bad solution solves for a single purpose or goal, such as increased production. And it is typical of such solutions that they achieve stupendous increases in production at exorbitant biological and social costs.

A good solution is good because it is in harmony with those larg- *13* er patterns—and this harmony will, I think, be found to have the nature of analogy. A bad solution acts within the larger pattern the way a disease or addiction acts within the body. A good solution acts within the larger pattern the way a healthy organ acts within the body. But it must at once be understood that a healthy organ does not—as the mechanistic or industrial mind would like to say—"give" health to the body, is not exploited for the body's health, but is a part of its health. The health of organ and organism is the same, just as the health of organism and ecosystem is the same. And these structures of organ, organism, and ecosystem belong to a series of analogical integrities that begins with the organelle and ends with the biosphere. ⬤-◖◗-⬤-

VOCABULARY

In your journal, write the meanings of the following words:

- *ramifying* series of new problems **(3)**
- *purview* of the expertise **(3)**
- hellish *symbiosis* **(6)**
- soil *husbandry* **(11)**

- *analogical* integrities **(13)**
- begins with the *organelle* **(13)**

QUESTIONS FOR WRITING AND DISCUSSION

1. Reread your response to the freewriting exercise at the beginning of this chapter. What campus problem did you describe, and what was your solution? Now, assume that you are Wendell Berry. Write one paragraph of Berry's response to your solution. Specifically, consider how well your solution meets Berry's goal of solving for the harmony, health, and quality of the whole college or university system.

2. Berry's essay explains three kinds of solutions. What are these three types of solutions, and what makes the third kind the best?

3. In paragraph 1, Berry says that he "could just as easily be talking about sanitation systems that pollute, school systems that graduate illiterate students, [or] medical cures that cause disease." Choose one of these problems (or another common problem) and explain how Berry would analyze the problem.

4. Berry clarifies his explanation for his reader by using audience cues (transitions, paragraph hooks, and topic sentences) at the beginning of paragraphs. Choose any three successive paragraphs (for example, paragraphs 3, 4, and 5) and identify any words or phrases that (a) make a transition from the previous paragraph or idea and (b) announce or preview the subject of the new paragraph. Make a sketch outline of Berry's essay.

5. An analogy is a comparison between two things or processes in which a simple or familiar thing helps to explain a complex or unfamiliar thing. Thus, we can explain how the human heart works by drawing an analogy with a simple mechanical pump. In paragraph 13, Berry says that a "bad solution acts within the larger pattern the way a disease or addiction acts within the body." Explain Berry's analogy. Then apply this analogy to one specific problem that you have discussed in class. Does Berry's organic analogy make sense in that particular case? Why or why not?

6. Apply Berry's ideas about "solving for pattern" to one of the following essays by Deborah Tannen and Neil Postman. How well do their arguments and solutions address the overall harmony, health, and quality of the system?

7. On the Internet, investigate what organic farming is and how food products get to be labeled "organic." Start with a site such as the Organic Farming Research Foundation at http://www.ofrf.org and

find out answers to your questions. Does eating organic foods help solve problems in farming? Does it create other problems—higher prices, shorter shelf life, less efficient production—that the organic farmer or the consumer needs to consider?

PROFESSIONAL WRITING

THE ARGUMENT CULTURE

Deborah Tannen

A professor of linguistics at Georgetown University, Deborah Tannen is also a best-selling author of many books on discourse and gender, including You Just Don't Understand: Women and Men in Conversation *(1990),* Talking from 9 to 5 *(1994),* The Argument Culture: Moving from Debate to Dialogue *(1998), and* I Only Say This Because I Love You *(2001). Throughout her career, Tannen has focused on how men and women have different conversational habits and assumptions, whether they talk on the job or at home. In the following essay, taken from* The Argument Culture, *Tannen tries to convince her readers that adversarial debates—which typically represent only two sides of an issue and thus promote antagonism—create problems in communication. As a culture, Tannen believes, we would be much more successful if we didn't always think of argument as a war or a fight but as a dialogue among a variety of different positions. As you read her essay, does Tannen persuade you that our "argument culture" really is a problem and that her solutions will help solve that problem?*

Balance. Debate. Listening to both sides. Who could question these noble American traditions? Yet today, these principles have been distorted. Without thinking, we have plunged headfirst into what I call the "argument culture." 1

The argument culture urges us to approach the world, and the people in it, in an adversarial frame of mind. It rests on the assumption that opposition is the best way to get anything done: The best way to discuss an idea is to set up a debate; the best way to cover news is to find spokespeople who express the most extreme, polarized views and present them as "both sides"; the best way to settle disputes is litigation that pits one party against the other; the best way to begin an essay is to attack someone; and the best way to show you're really thinking is to criticize. 2

More and more, our public interactions have become like arguing with a spouse. Conflict can't be avoided in our public lives any more 3 than we can avoid conflict with people we love. One of the great strengths of our society is that we can express these conflicts openly. But just as spouses have to learn ways of settling their differences without inflicting real damage, so we, as a society, have to find constructive ways of resolving disputes and differences.

The war on drugs, the war on cancer, the battle of the sexes, politicians' turf battles—in the argument culture, war metaphors pervade our talk and shape our thinking. The cover headlines of both *Time* and *Newsweek* one recent week are a case in point: "The Secret Sex Wars," proclaims *Newsweek*. "Starr at War," declares *Time*. Nearly everything is framed as a battle or game in which winning or losing is the main concern.   *4*

The argument culture pervades every aspect of our lives today. Issues from global warming to abortion are depicted as two-sided arguments, when in fact most Americans' views lie somewhere in the middle. Partisanship makes gridlock in Washington the norm. Even in our personal relationships, a "let it all hang out" philosophy emphasizes people expressing their anger without giving them constructive ways of settling differences.   *5*

Sometimes You Have to Fight

There are times when it is necessary and right to fight—to defend your country or yourself, to argue for your rights or against offensive or dangerous ideas or actions. What's wrong with the argument culture is the ubiquity, the knee-jerk nature of approaching any issue, problem or public person in an adversarial way.   *6*

Our determination to pursue truth by setting up a fight between two sides leads us to assume that every issue has two sides—no more, no less. But if you always assume there must be an "other side," you may end up scouring the margins of science or the fringes of lunacy to find it.   *7*

This accounts, in part, for the bizarre phenomenon of Holocaust denial. Deniers, as Emory University professor Deborah Lipstadt shows, have been successful in gaining TV air time and campus newspaper coverage by masquerading as "the other side" in a "debate." Continual reference to "the other side" results in a conviction that everything has another side—and people begin to doubt the existence of any facts at all.   *8*

The power of words to shape perception has been proved by researchers in controlled experiments. Psychologists Elizabeth Loftus and John Palmer, for example, found that the terms in which people are asked to recall something affect what they recall. The researchers showed subjects a film of two cars colliding, then asked how fast the   *9* cars were going; one week later they asked whether there had been any broken glass. Some subjects were asked, "How fast were the cars going when they bumped into each other?" Others were asked, "How fast were the cars going when they smashed into each other?"

Those who read the question with "smashed" tended to "remem- 10 ber" that the cars were going faster. They were also more likely to "re-member" having seen broken glass. (There wasn't any.) This is how language works. It invisibly molds our way of thinking about people, actions and the world around us.

In the argument culture, "critical" thinking is synonymous with 11 criticizing. In many classrooms, students are encouraged to read someone's life work, then rip it to shreds.

When debates and fighting predominate, those who enjoy verbal 12 sparring are likely to take part—by calling in to talk shows or writing letters to the editor. Those who aren't comfortable with oppositional discourse are likely to opt out.

How High-Tech Communication Pulls Us Apart

One of the most effective ways to defuse antagonism between two 13 groups is to provide a forum for individuals from those groups to get to know each other personally. What is happening in our lives, however, is just the opposite. More and more of our communication is not face to face, and not with people we know. The proliferation and increasing portability of technology isolates people in a bubble.

Along with the voices of family members and friends, phone lines 14 bring into our homes the annoying voices of solicitors who want to sell something—generally at dinnertime. (My father-in-law startles phone solicitors by saying, "We're eating dinner, but I'll call you back. What's your home phone number?" To the nonplused caller, he explains, "Well, you're calling me at home; I thought I'd call you at home, too.")

It is common for families to have more than one TV, so the adults 15 can watch what they like in one room and the kids can watch their choice in another—or maybe each child has a private TV.

E-mail, and now the Internet, are creating networks of human 16 connection unthinkable even a few years ago. Though e-mail has enhanced communication with family and friends, it also ratchets up the anonymity of both sender and receiver, resulting in stranger-to-stranger "flaming."

"Road rage" shows how dangerous the argument culture—and 17 especially today's technologically enhanced aggression—can be. Two men who engage in a shouting match may not come to blows, but if they express their anger while driving down a public highway, the risk to themselves and others soars.

The Argument Culture Shapes Who We Are

The argument culture has a defining impact on our lives and on our culture. *18*

- **It makes us distort facts,** as in the Nancy Kerrigan-Tonya Harding story. After the original attack on Kerrigan's knee, news stories focused on the rivalry between the two skaters instead of portraying Kerrigan as the victim of an attack. Just last month, *Time* magazine called the event a "contretemps" between Kerrigan and Harding. And a recent joint TV interview of the two skaters reinforced that skewed image by putting the two on equal footing, rather than as victim and accused.

- **It makes us waste valuable time,** as in the case of scientist Robert Gallo, who co-discovered the AIDS virus. Gallo was the object of a groundless four-year investigation into allegations he had stolen the virus from another scientist. He was ultimately exonerated, but the toll was enormous. Never mind that, in his words, "These were the most painful and horrible years of my life." Gallo spent four years fighting accusations instead of fighting AIDS.

- **It limits our thinking.** Headlines are intentionally devised to attract attention, but the language of extremes actually shapes, and misshapes, the way we think about things. Military metaphors train us to think about, and see, everything in terms of fighting, conflict and war. Adversarial rhetoric is a kind of verbal inflation—a rhetorical boy-who-cried-wolf.

- **It encourages us to lie.** If you fight to win, the temptation is great to deny facts that support your opponent's views and say only what supports your side. It encourages people to misrepresent and, in the extreme, to lie.

End the Argument Culture by Looking at All Sides

How can we overcome our classically American habit of seeing issues in absolutes? We must expand our notion of "debate" to include more dialogue. To do this, we can make special efforts not to think in twos. Mary Catherine Bateson, an anthropologist at Virginia's George Mason University, makes a point of having her class compare three cultures, not two. Then, students are more likely to think about each on its own terms, rather than as opposites. *19*

In the public arena, television and radio producers can try to avoid, whenever possible, structuring public discussions as debates. This means avoiding the format of having two guests discuss an issue. Invite three guests—or one. Perhaps it is time to re-examine the assumption that audiences always prefer a fight. *20*

Instead of asking, "What's the other side?" we might ask, "What *21* are the other sides?" Instead of insisting on hearing "both sides," let's insist on hearing "all sides."

We need to find metaphors other than sports and war. Smashing *22* heads does not open minds. We need to use our imaginations and ingenuity to find different ways to seek truth and gain knowledge through intellectual interchange, and add them to our arsenal—or, should I say, to the ingredients for our stew. It will take creativity for each of us to find ways to change the argument culture to a dialogue culture. It's an effort we have to make, because our public and private lives are at stake.

Vocabulary

In your journal, write down the meanings of the following words:

- in an *adversarial* frame of mind **(2)**
- the *ubiquity* **(6)**
- *synonymous* with criticizing **(11)**
- with *oppositional* discourse **(12)**
- the *proliferation* **(13)**
- a "*contretemps*" between Kerrigan and Harding **(18)**
- he was ultimately *exonerated* **(18)**
- imaginations and *ingenuity* **(22)**

Questions for Writing and Discussion

1. List three controversial topics currently in the news. Then choose one of those topics and explain the two "sides" of this argument. Now, imagine a third point of view. How is it different from the first two positions? Does coming up with a third position help you think creatively about how to resolve this dispute? Explain.

2. As she writes her essay, Tannen initially outlines the nature of the problem with the "argument culture" before she gives her solution. Which paragraphs most clearly demonstrate the problem? Which paragraphs explain her solution? Does she ignore any aspects of the problem? Would her solution really solve the problem she describes? Why or why not?

3. Read Tannen's advice in the final four paragraphs of her essay. Does she follow her own advice in writing this essay? Which pieces of

advice does she follow and which does she ignore? Cite examples from the essay to support your analysis. Would her essay be more effective if she followed her own advice? Explain.

4. As a professor of linguistics, Tannen can write in a formal, academic style, but she can also write in an informal style for general audiences. In this essay, is Tannen writing for academics or for anyone interested in culture and communication? Find examples of Tannen's "academic" style as well as her informal style. Does she successfully integrate the two or is she too informal or too academic? Explain.

5. According to Tannen, the language we choose and the metaphors we use affect our perceptions of the world. Where does Tannen discuss how words or metaphors shape our perceptions? What examples does she give? In her own argument, does Tannen herself avoid language or metaphors referring to war, violence, or conflict?

6. On the Internet, log on to the website of a national news magazine such as *Newsweek* or *Utne* magazine and read their e-mail letters in response to an essay on a controversial topic such as stem cell research, global warming, public transportation, educational testing, and so forth. Read several letters or responses. Can you find at least *three* positions on that issue—rather than just the standard "pro" and "con"? Explain the controversial topic and then write out at least three different positions or points of view which you discover in the responses.

PROFESSIONAL WRITING

VIRTUAL STUDENTS, DIGITAL CLASSROOM

Neil Postman

No doubt the last two decades of the twentieth century in America will be remembered for the explosive increase in numbers of computers and numbers of computer-literate Americans. In America's schools, students now use computers and do Internet and Web research in virtually every field of study. As we enter the twenty-first century, however, Neil Postman, professor of communications at New York University, questions whether computers have, in fact, arrived on earth to save our students. Will computers enable all students—rich or poor, black, brown, or white—to have equal access to the information so vital to their education? Will computers possibly make the school, as a place of learning, obsolete? In "Virtual Students, Digital Classrooms," Neil Postman critiques those computer-in-the-sky proposals and calls for a more conservative vision of the goals of education. Followers of Neil Postman's career as an educational reformist remind us that although Postman began his career with books such as Teaching as a Subversive Activity *(1969), which called for a radical reform of our nation's schools, his recent works advocate a more conservative vision of education. Since the late 1970s, Neil Postman's books include* Teaching as a Conserving Activity *(1979),* Amusing Ourselves to Death *(1985),* Technology: The Surrender of Culture to Technology *(1992), and* The End of Education: Redefining the Value of School *(1995). "Virtual Students, Digital Classroom," adapted from* The End of Education, *appeared in* The Nation.

If one has a trusting relationship with one's students, it is not alto- *1*
gether gauche to ask them if they believe in God (with a capital G). I have done this three or four times and most students say they do. Their answer is preliminary to the next question: If someone you love were desperately ill, and you had to choose between praying to God for his or her recovery or administering an antibiotic (as prescribed by a competent physician), which would you choose?

Most say the question is silly since the alternatives are not mutu- *2*
ally exclusive. Of course. But suppose they were—which would you choose? God helps those who help themselves, some say in choosing the antibiotic, therefore getting the best of two possible belief systems. But if pushed to the wall (e.g., God does not always help those who help themselves; God helps those who pray and who believe), most choose the antibiotic, after noting that the question is asinine and proves nothing. Of course, the question was not asked, in the first place, to prove anything but to begin a discussion of the nature of belief. And I do not fail to inform the students, by the way, that there has recently emerged evidence of a "scientific" nature that when sick people are prayed for they do better than those who aren't.

As the discussion proceeds, important distinctions are made *3*
among the different meanings of "belief," but at some point it becomes far from asinine to speak of the god of Technology—in the sense that people believe technology works, that they rely on it, that it makes promises, that they are bereft when denied access to it, that they are delighted when they are in its presence, that for most people it works in mysterious ways, that they condemn people who speak against it, that they stand in awe of it, and that, in the "born again" mode, they will alter their life-styles, their schedules, their habits, and their relationships to accommodate it. If this be not a form of religious belief, what is?

In all strands of American cultural life, you can find so many ex-   *4*
amples of technological adoration that it is possible to write a book
about it. And I would if it had not already been done so well. But
nowhere do you find more enthusiasm for the god of Technology than
among educators. In fact, there are those, like Lewis Perelman, who
argue (for example, in his book, *School's Out*) that modern information
technologies have rendered schools entirely irrelevant since there is
now much more information available outside the classroom than inside it. This is by no means considered an outlandish idea. Dr. Diane
Ravitch, former Assistant Secretary of Education, envisions, with considerable relish, the challenge that technology presents to the tradition that "children (and adults) should be educated in a specific place,
for a certain number of hours, and a certain number of days during the
week and year." In other words, that children should be educated in
school. Imagining the possibilities of an information superhighway offering perhaps a thousand channels, Dr. Ravitch assures us that:

> in this new world of pedagogical plenty, children and adults will be
> able to dial up a program on their home television to learn what-
> ever they want to know, at their own convenience. If little Eva can-
> not sleep, she can learn algebra instead. At her home-learning
> station, she will tune in to a series of interesting problems that are
> presented in an interactive medium, much like video games. . . .
>
> Young John may decide that he wants to learn the history of mod-
> ern Japan, which he can do by dialing up the greatest authorities
> and teachers on the subject, who will not only use dazzling graphs
> and illustrations, but will narrate a historical video that excites his
> curiosity and imagination.

In this vision there is, it seems to me, a confident and typical sense   *5*
of unreality. Little Eva can't sleep, so she decides to learn a little algebra? Where does Little Eva come from? Mars? If not, it is more likely she will tune in to a good movie. Young John decides that he wants
to learn the history of modern Japan? How did young John come to this
point? How is it that he never visited a library up to now? Or is it that
he, too, couldn't sleep and decided that a little modern Japanese history was just what he needed?

What Ravitch is talking about here is not a new technology but a   *6*
new species of child, one who, in any case, no one has seen up to now.
Of course, new technologies do make new kinds of people, which leads
to a second objection to Ravitch's conception of the future. There is a
kind of forthright determinism about the imagined world described

in it. The technology is here or will be; we must use it because it is there; we will become the kind of people the technology requires us to be, and whether we like it or not, we will remake our institutions to accommodate technology. All of this must happen because it is good for us, but in any case, we have no choice. This point of view is present in very nearly every statement about the future relationship of learning to technology. And, as in Ravitch's scenario, there is always a cheery, gee-whiz tone to the prophecies. Here is one produced by the National Academy of Sciences, written by Hugh McIntosh.

School for children of the Information Age will be vastly different than it was for Mom and Dad.

Interested in biology? Design your own life forms with computer simulation.

Having trouble with a science project? Teleconference about it with a research scientist.

Bored with the real world? Go into a virtual physics lab and rewrite the laws of gravity.

These are the kinds of hands-on learning experiences schools could be providing right now. The technologies that make them possible are already here, and today's youngsters, regardless of economic status, know how to use them. They spend hours with them every week—not in the classroom, but in their own homes and in video game centers at every shopping mall.

The role that new technology should play in schools or anywhere [7] else is something that needs to be discussed without the hyperactive fantasies of cheerleaders. In particular, the computer and its associated technologies are awesome additions to a culture, and are quite capable of altering the psychic, not to mention the sleeping, habits of our young. But like all important technologies of the past, they are Faustian bargains, giving and taking away, sometimes in equal measure, sometimes more in one way than the other. It is strange—indeed shocking—that with the twenty-first century so close, we can still talk of new technologies as if they were unmixed blessings—gifts, as it were, from the gods. Don't we all know what the combustion engine has done for us and against us? What television is doing for us and against us? At the very least, what we need to discuss about Little Eva, Young John, and McIntosh's trio is what they will lose, and what we will lose, if they enter a world in which computer technology is their chief source of motivation, authority, and, apparently, psychological sustenance. Will they become, as Joseph Weizenbaum warns, more impressed by calculation than human judgment? Will speed of response become, more than ever, a defining quality of intelligence? If, indeed, the idea of a school will be dramatically altered, what kinds of learning will be neglected, perhaps made impossible? Is virtual reality a new form of therapy? If it is, what are its dangers?

These are serious matters, and they need to be discussed by those who know something about children from the planet Earth, and whose vision of children's needs, and the needs of society, go beyond thinking of school mainly as a place for the convenient distribution of information. Schools are not now and have never been largely about getting information to children. That has been on the schools' agenda, of course, but has always been way down on the list. For technological utopians, the computer vaults information access to the top. This reshuffling of priorities comes at a most inopportune time. The goal of giving people greater access to more information faster, more conveniently, and in more diverse forms was the main technological thrust of the nineteenth century. Some folks haven't noticed it, but that problem was largely solved, so that for almost a hundred years there has been more information available to the young outside the school than inside. That fact did not make the schools obsolete, nor does it now make them obsolete.

Yes, it is true that Little Eva, the insomniac from Mars, could turn on an algebra lesson, thanks to the computer, in the wee hours of the morning. She could also, if she wished, read a book or magazine, watch television, turn on the radio or listen to music. All of this she could have done before the computer. The computer does not solve any problem she has but does exacerbate one. For Little Eva's problem is not how to get access to a well-structured algebra lesson but what to do with all the information available to her during the day, as well as during sleepless nights. Perhaps this is why she couldn't sleep in the first place. Little Eva, like the rest of us, is overwhelmed by information. She lives in a culture that has 260,000 billboards, 17,000 newspapers, 12,000 periodicals, 27,000 video outlets for renting tapes, 400 million television sets, and well over 500 million radios, not including those in automobiles. There are 40,000 new book titles published every year, and each day 41 million photographs are taken. And thanks to the computer, more than 60 billion pieces of advertising junk come into our mailboxes every year. Everything from telegraphy and photography in the nineteenth century to the silicon chip in the twentieth has amplified the din of information intruding on Little Eva's consciousness. . . . In the face of this we might ask, What can schools do for Little Eva besides making still more information available? If there is nothing, then new technologies will indeed make schools obsolete. But in fact, there is plenty.

One thing that comes to mind is that schools can provide her with a 10 serious form of technology education. Something quite different from instruction in using computers to process information, which, it strikes me, is a trivial thing to do, for two reasons. In the first place, approximately 35 million people have already learned how to use computers without the benefit of school instruction. In the second place, what we needed to know about cars—as we need to know about computers, television, and other important technologies—is not how to use them but how they use *us*. In the case of cars, what we needed to think about in the early twentieth century was not how to drive them but what they would do to our air, our landscape, our social relations, our family life, and our cities. Suppose in 1946 we had started to address similar questions about television: What will be its effects on our political institutions, our psychic habits, our children, our religious conceptions, our economy? Would we be better positioned today to control TV's massive assault on American culture? I am talking here about making technology itself an object of inquiry so that Little Eva and Young John are more interested in asking questions about the computer than getting answers from it.

I am not arguing against using computers in school. I am argu- 11 ing against our sleepwalking attitudes toward it, against allowing it to distract us from important things, against making a god of it. This is what Theodore Roszak warned against in *The Cult of Information:* "Like all cults," he wrote, "this one also has the intention of enlisting mindless allegiance and acquiescence. People who have no clear idea of what they mean by information or why they should want so much of it are nonetheless prepared to believe that we live in an Information Age, which makes every computer around us what the relics of the True Cross were in the Age of Faith: emblems of salvation." To this, I would add the sage observation of Alan Kay of Apple Computer. Kay is widely associated with the invention of the personal computer, and certainly has an interest in schools using them. Nonetheless, he has repeatedly said that any problems the schools cannot solve without computers, they cannot solve with them. What are some of those problems? There is, for example, the traditional task of teaching children how to behave in groups. One might even say that schools have never been essentially about individualized learning. It is true, of course, that groups do not learn, individuals do. But the idea of a school is that individuals must learn in a setting in which individual needs are subordinated to group interests. Unlike other media of mass communication, which celebrate individual response and are experienced in private, the classroom is intended to tame the ego, to connect the individual with others, to demonstrate the value and necessity of group cohesion. At present, most scenarios describing the uses of computers have children solving problems alone; Little Eva, Young John, and the others are doing just that. The presence of other children may, indeed, be an annoyance.

Like the printing press before it, the computer has a powerful   *12* bias toward amplifying personal autonomy and individual problemsolving. That is why educators must guard against computer technology's undermining some of the important reasons for having the young assemble (to quote Ravitch) "in a specific place, for a certain number of hours, and a certain number of days during the week and year."

Although Ravitch is not exactly against what she calls "state   *13* schools," she imagines them as something of a relic of a pretechnological age. She believes that the new technologies will offer all children equal access to information. Conjuring up a hypothetical Little Mary who is presumably from a poorer home than Little Eva, Ravitch imagines that Mary will have the same opportunities as Eva "to learn any subject, and to learn it from the same master teachers as children in the richest neighborhood." For all of its liberalizing spirit, this scenario makes some important omissions. One is that though new technologies may be a solution to the learning of "subjects," they work against the learning of what are called "social values," including an understanding of democratic processes. If one reads the first chapter of Robert Fulghum's *All I Really Need to Know I Learned in Kindergarten*, one will find an elegant summary of a few things Ravitch's scenario has left out. They include learning the following lessons: Share everything, play fair, don't hit people, put things back where you found them, clean up your own mess, wash your hands before you eat, and, of course, flush. The only thing wrong with Fulghum's book is that no one has learned all these things at kindergarten's end. We have ample evidence that it takes many years of teaching these values in school before they have been accepted and internalized. That is why it won't do for children to learn in "settings of their own choosing." That is also why schools require children to be in a certain place at a certain time and to follow certain rules, like raising their hands when they wish to speak, not talking when others are talking, not chewing gum, not leaving until the bell rings, exhibiting patience toward slower learners, etc. This process is called making civilized people. The god of Technology does not appear interested in this function of schools. At least, it does not come up much when technology's virtues are enumerated.

The god of Technology may also have a trick or two up its sleeve 14 about something else. It is often asserted that new technologies will equalize learning opportunities for the rich and poor. It is devoutly to be wished for, but I doubt it will happen. In the first place, it is generally understood by those who have studied the history of technology that technological change always produces winners and losers. There are many reasons for this, among them economic differences. Even in the case of the automobile, which is a commodity most people can buy (although not all), there are wide differences between the rich and poor in the quality of what is available to them. It would be quite astonishing if computer technology equalized all learning opportunities, irrespective of economic differences.

I do not say, of course, that schools can solve the problems of 15 poverty, alienation, and family disintegration, but schools can *respond* to them. And they can do this because there are people in them, because these people are concerned with more than algebra lessons or modern Japanese history, and because these people can identify not only one's level of competence in math but one's level of rage and confusion and depression. I am talking here about children as they really come to us, not children who are invented to show us how computers may enrich their lives.

I am a teacher myself and know how hard it is to contribute to the 16 making of a civilized person. Can we blame those who want to find an easy way, through the agency of technology? Perhaps not. After all, it is an old quest. As early as 1918, H. L. Mencken (although completely devoid of empathy) wrote, "There is no sure-cure so idiotic that some superintendent of schools will not swallow it. The aim seems to be to reduce the whole teaching process to a sort of automatic reaction, to discover some master formula that will not only take the place of competence and resourcefulness in the teacher but that will also create an artificial receptivity in the child."

Mencken was not necessarily speaking of technological panaceas 17 but he may well have been. In the early 1920s a teacher wrote the following poem:

> *Mr. Edison says*
> *That the radio will supplant the teacher.*
> *Already one may learn languages by means of Victrola records.*
> *The moving picture will visualize*
> *What the radio fails to get across.*
> *Teachers will be relegated to the backwoods,*
> *With fire-horses,*

> *And long-haired women;*
> *Or, perhaps shown in museums.*
> *Education will become a matter*
> *Of pressing the button.*
> *Perhaps I can get a position at the switchboard.*

I do not go as far back as the radio and Victrola, but I am old   *18*
enough to remember when 16-millimeter film was to be the sure-cure.
Then closed-circuit television. Then 8-millimeter film. Then teacher-
proof textbooks. Now computers.

I know a false god when I see one.   *19*

VOCABULARY

In your journal, write the meanings of the following words:

- it is not altogether *gauche* **(1)**
- alternatives are not *mutually* exclusive **(2)**
- they are *bereft* **(3)**
- an *outlandish* idea **(4)**
- they are *Faustian* bargains **(7)**
- a most *inopportune* time **(8)**
- but does *exacerbate* one **(9)**
- mindless *allegiance* and *acquiescence* **(11)**
- technological *panaceas* **(17)**
- be *relegated* to the backwoods **(17)**

QUESTIONS FOR WRITING AND DISCUSSION

1. Reflect on your own use of computer technology in your education. Have computers had a positive effect on your schooling? Have
   they had a negative effect? Has computer technology been a mixed
   blessing for you? Describe one memorable incident in your education which illustrates the actual educational benefit (or harm) of
   computer technology.

2. What, exactly, is Postman's thesis in this essay? First, find three sentences in the essay that express the main idea of the essay. Of these,
   which sentence comes closest to explaining the main point of the
   essay? Explain your choice.

3. Postman gives several reasons why we should be skeptical of the ability of the computer to bring about an educational utopia. Find at least three passages where Postman critiques the technological optimists. Which of his reasons most effectively refutes their position? Explain your choice.

4. In this essay, Postman critiques the utopian point of view of critics such as Diane Ravitch, and he also offers his own proposal for improving education. Identify at least three of Postman's own recommendations. Did you find his recommendations persuasive? Explain.

5. A "motif" is a recurring thematic element or image used to develop a literary work. In his essay, Postman uses the images of the "god of Technology" and the little children (Eva and John) "from Mars" to help develop his main themes. Trace each of these images through the essay. Where does each motif reappear? Explain how each motif contributes to the overall thesis of the essay.

6. Using the Internet and your own interviews, write an investigative essay on the effects of computer technology on education. Use your favorite search engine and enter the terms *education* and *technology*. Find an interesting topic and then narrow your focus. Print out the relevant articles you find. Then interview several of your classmates about the effects of technology on education. Where, specifically, has technology improved their education? Where has technology made education less personal or less interesting? Explain how the results of your investigation confirm or refute Postman's thesis.

Problem Solving: The Writing Process   ● ● ●

■   ASSIGNMENT FOR PROBLEM SOLVING   Select a problem that you believe needs a solution. Narrow and focus the problem and choose an appropriate audience. Describe the problem and, if necessary, demonstrate for your audience that it needs a solution. State your solution, and justify it with reasons and evidence. Where appropriate, weigh alternative solutions, examine the feasibility of your own solution, and answer objections to your solution.

The problem-solving assignment leads naturally to the genre of a proposal. Some proposals are long, formal documents addressed to knowledgeable readers, while others are short and informal, intended more for general audiences.

Review your assignment and your intended audience to help determine the amount of analysis and research you need for your essay.

CHOOSING A SUBJECT

If one of your journal entries suggests a possible subject, try the collecting and shaping strategies below. If none of these leads to a workable subject, consider the following suggestions:

- Evaluating leads naturally into problem solving. Reread your journal entries and topic ideas for "evaluating." If your evaluation of your subject was negative, consider what would make your evaluation more positive. Based on your evaluation, write a proposal, addressed to the proper audience, explaining the problem and offering your solution.
- Organized groups are already trying to solve a number of national and international problems: homelessness, illegal aliens, the slaughter of whales, acid rain, abuse of animals in scientific experiments, drug and alcohol abuse, toxic-waste disposal, and so forth. Read several current articles on one of these topics. Then narrow the problem to one aspect that students or residents of your town could help to resolve. Write an essay outlining the problem and proposing some *specific and limited* actions that citizens could take.

"I can't think of anything I have no problem with."

- Employers are always looking for workers with initiative and good ideas. At your place of work, take ten minutes during a break and observe what's going on around you. Take notes over a span of several days. Even though people may be getting the job done, would different procedures or policies improve efficiency, safety, quality, or personal relations? Write a letter to your boss identifying the problem that you've noticed and justifying your solution.

- Take an inventory of the personal problems that you regularly face, day to day. List the things that cost unnecessary amounts of time or money, that cause fear in your life, that increase your frustration level, or that simply make you less happy or productive than you could be. Then compare your inventory with a classmate's or friend's list. If there are common problems, discuss whether or how these problems might be solved.

COLLECTING

With a possible subject and audience in mind, write out answers for each of the following topics. Remember that not all of these approaches will apply to your subject; some topics will suggest very little, while others may prompt you to generate ideas or specific examples appropriate to your problem and solution. A hypothetical problem—large classes that hinder learning—illustrates how these topics may help you focus on your subject and collect relevant ideas and information.

IDENTIFY AND FOCUS ON THE SPECIFIC PROBLEM   Answer the first four "Wh" questions:

Who: A Psychology I professor; the Psychology Department

What: Psychology I class

When: Spring semester (the structure of this class may be slightly different from previous semesters)

Where: University of Illinois (large lecture classes at one school may be different from those at another)

You may want to generalize about large lecture classes everywhere, but begin by identifying the specific problem at hand.

DEMONSTRATE THAT THE PROBLEM NEEDS A SOLUTION   Map out the *effects* of a problem. (See the diagram.)

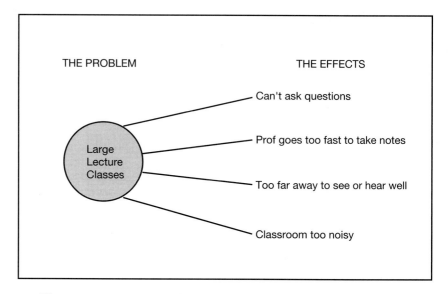

You may want to map out both *short-term effects* and *long-term effects*. Over the short term, large lecture classes prevent you from asking questions; over the long term, you may do poorly on examinations, get a lower grade in the class, lose interest in the subject, be unable to cope with your own and others' psychological problems, or end up in a different career or job.

DISCOVER POSSIBLE SOLUTIONS   One strategy is to map out the history or the causes of the problem. If you can discover what caused the problem in the first place, you may have a possible solution. (See the diagram.)

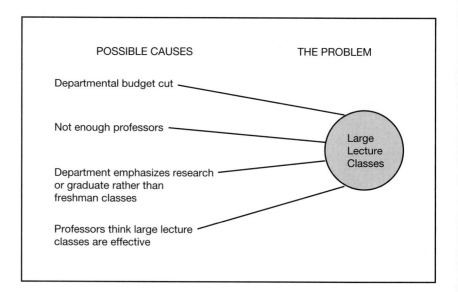

A second strategy takes the imaginative approach. Brainstorm hypothetical cases by asking, "What if . . . "

"What if students petitioned the president of the university to abolish all lecture classes with enrollments over 100 students?" Would that work?

"What if students invited the professor to answer questions at a weekly study session?" Would the professor attend? Would students attend?

"What if students taught each other in a psychology class?" How would that work?

EVALUATE POSSIBLE SOLUTIONS Apply the "If . . . then . . . " test on each possible solution: Consider whether each proposal would:

A. actually solve the problem;
B. meet certain criteria, such as cost-effectiveness, practicality, ethicality, legality;
C. not create new problems.

"*If* classes were smaller, *then* students would learn more":

If classes were smaller, students might learn more, but a small class size does not necessarily guarantee greater learning.

Although students might learn more, do smaller classes meet other criteria? While they are legal and ethical, are they practical and cost-effective?

Would smaller classes create new problems? Smaller classes might mean fewer upper-level course offerings. Is that a serious new problem?

CONVINCE YOUR READERS Support your proposed solutions by stating *reasons* and finding supporting *evidence*:

Reason: Smaller classes are worth the additional expense because students actually engage the material rather than just memorizing for exams.

Evidence: Data from studies comparing large and small classes; personal testimony by students, interviews, or questionnaires; testimony or evidence from authorities on teaching.

ANSWER POSSIBLE OBJECTIONS TO YOUR PROPOSAL Every solution has a down side or possible drawbacks. You need to respond to the most important objections.

LIST DRAWBACKS
Small classes cost more.

Small classes might reduce course offerings.

Small classes might mean less money for research.

RESEARCH TIP

As you begin researching your problem, *don't* rush off to the library and start collecting articles. *Do* start by interviewing people who may know about your problem. Use your investigating skills to locate authorities and interview them. (See Chapter 6.) Find out what other people have already done to solve the problem—or why current solutions are not working. Interview a teacher who knows about the problem, a student who has firsthand experience with the problem, an owner of a local business, or the coordinator of a community service. Save your library research until you know what the problem really is and what is currently being done to correct it.

LIST YOUR RESPONSES

Good education does cost more. The University of Illinois has a reputation as an excellent undergraduate institution, and small classes would help it maintain quality education.

Perhaps some classes with low demand could be cut, but the necessary funds should not be taken out of upper-division classes for psychology majors or research projects.

LIST POSSIBLE STEPS FOR IMPLEMENTATION   If appropriate, indicate the key steps or chronological sequence of your proposal:

1.   Poll students and teachers in large lecture classes to confirm that the problem warrants attention.
2.   Gather evidence from other colleges or universities to show how they reduced class sizes.
3.   Present results of polls and other evidence to the state legislature to request more funds.

OBSERVING   As you gather evidence and examples, use your observation skills. If the problem is large lecture classes, attend classes and *observe* the behavior of students and professors. Are students distracted by noise? Can they ask questions? Does the professor talk too softly to be heard in the back row? Remember that *repeated* observation is essential. If necessary, observe your subject over a period of several days or weeks.

REMEMBERING   Use *freewriting*, *looping*, or *clustering* to help you remember examples from your experience of the problem or of possible solutions. Brainstorm or freewrite about previous class sessions in Psychology I. Do looping or mapping on other small-enrollment classes: What made these classes effective or ineffective? What teaching strategies, projects, or small-group activities were possible in these classes that would not be possible in a class of 250 students?

READING AND INVESTIGATING *Use the library* to find books or articles about the particular problem. Other writers have no doubt offered solutions to your problem that you could consider. Articles may even suggest objections to your proposed solution that you need to answer.

Interview participants or authorities on the problem. The professor who is teaching your Psychology I class may have some ideas about a solution. Administration—department chairs, deans, even the president—may agree to answer your questions and react to your possible solutions; schedule interviews.

Design a questionnaire that addresses aspects of your problem. Responses to questionnaires provide evidence that a problem is serious, immediate, and in need of a solution. If the results of a questionnaire show that 175 of the 200 people in Psychology I who returned it favor smaller sections, you can include those data in your letter to the head of the department and the dean of the college.

SHAPING

Writers of proposals often do the following:

- Identify and demonstrate problems
- Evaluate alternative solutions
- Make proposals
- Give reasons and evidence to support their proposals; answer objections, discuss feasibility and costs
- Indicate implementation or call for action

Of course not all problem-solving essays have all five elements. Some do not discuss feasibility or do not evaluate alternative solutions. Estrich's proposal, for example, suggests only one important way to solve the problem—without considering alternative solutions.

OUTLINES FOR PROBLEM SOLVING   The following patterns indicate four possible ways to organize a problem-solving essay. One of these patterns may help you organize your proposal:

Problem-Solving Pattern
- I.   Introduction
- II.   The problem: Identify and demonstrate

  III. The solution(s)

  IV. Answering possible objections, costs, drawbacks

  V. Conclusion: Implementation plan; call to action

Point-by-Point Pattern

  I. Introduction

  II. The overall problem: Identify and demonstrate

  III. One part of the problem, solution, evidence, answers to possible objections, feasibility

  IV. Second part of the problem, solution, evidence, answers to possible objections, feasibility

  V. Third part of the problem, solution, evidence, and so on

  VI. Conclusion: Implementation; call to action

Alternative Pattern

  I. Introduction

  II. The problem: Identify and demonstrate

  III. Alternative Solution 1; why it's not satisfactory

  IV. Alternative Solution 2; why it's not satisfactory

  V. Alternative Solution 3; why it works best: Evidence, objections, feasibility

  VI. Conclusion: Implementation; call to action

Step-by-Step Pattern

  I. Introduction

  II. The problem: Identify and demonstrate

  III. Plan for implementing the solution or how solution has worked in the past:

    A. Step 1: Reasons and evidence showing why this step is necessary and feasible

    B. Step 2: Reasons and evidence showing why this step is necessary and feasible

    C. Step 3: Reasons and evidence showing why this step is necessary and feasible

  IV. Conclusion

CAUSAL ANALYSIS   Causal analysis can be used to organize some paragraphs of a proposal. In arguing the benefits or advantages of a proposed solution, you are actually explaining the *effects* of your solution.

- The effects or advantages of smaller class sections in Psychology I would be greater student participation, fewer distractions, more discussion during lectures, and more individual or small-group learning.
- Shortening the work week to thirty-two hours would increase the number of jobs, reduce tensions for working parents, and give employees time to learn new skills.
- Eliminating steroid use among NFL athletes would reduce the impact of collisions and enable players to recover from injuries faster. Long-term effects of eliminating steroids would be to reduce incidence of cancers and urinary-tract problems.

In each of these cases, each effect or advantage can become a separate point and, sometimes, a separate body paragraph.

CRITERIA ANALYSIS   In some cases, the *criteria* for a good solution are quite clear. For example, cost-effectiveness, feasibility, and worker morale might be important criteria for a business-related proposal. If you work in a fast-food restaurant and are concerned about the increasing number of crimes, for example, you might propose that your manager add a video surveillance system. In order to overcome the manager's resistance to spending the needed funds, you could defend your proposal (and answer possible objections) by discussing relevant criteria:

Proposal: To reduce theft and protect the employees of the restaurant by installing a video surveillance system.

- *Cost-effectiveness*. Citing evidence from other stores that have video cameras, you could prove that the equipment would pay for itself in less than a year. In addition, you could argue that if the life of just one employee—or possibly one manager—were saved, the cost would be worth it.
- *Feasibility*. Installing a security system would not require any extensive remodeling or any significant training time for employees to learn how to operate the system.
- *Employee morale*. The benefits to employee morale would be significant: Workers would feel more secure, they would feel that the management cares about them, and they would work more productively.

CHRONOLOGICAL ORDER   If your proposal stresses the means of implementing your solution to a problem, you may organize several paragraphs or even an entire essay using a chronological order or step-by-step pattern.

A proposal to improve the reading skills of children might be justified by a series of coordinated steps, beginning by organizing seminars for teachers and PTA meetings to discuss possible solutions; establishing minimal reading requirements in Grades K–6 that teachers and parents agree on; offering reading prizes; and organizing media coverage of students who participate in reading programs.

DRAFTING

Vigorous writing is concise.

—WILLIAM STRUNK, JR.,

AUTHOR AND TEACHER

Using your examples, recorded observations, reading, interviews, results from questionnaires, or your own experience, make a sketch outline and begin writing. As you write, let your own proposal and your intended audience guide you. In your first draft, get as much as possible on paper. Don't worry about spelling or awkward sentences. If you hit a snag, stop and read what you have written so far or reread your collecting and shaping notes.

REVISING

When you have a completed draft and are ready to start revising your essay, get another member of your class to read and respond to your essay. Use the peer response guidelines that follow to get—and give—constructive advice on your draft.

Use the following revising guidelines to identify areas for improving your draft. Even at this point, don't hesitate to collect additional information, if necessary, or reorganize your material. If a reader makes suggestions, reread your draft to see if those changes will improve your essay.

Guidelines for Revision

- **Have a classmate or someone who might understand your audience read your draft and play devil's advocate.** Have your reader pretend to be hostile to your solution and ask questions about alternative solutions or weaknesses in your own solution. Revise your proposal so that it answers any important objections.
- **Review your proposal for key elements.** If you are missing one of the following, would adding it make your proposal more effective for your audience? *Remember:* Proposals do not necessarily have to have all of these elements.
- Develop the items that are most applicable to your proposal.
- Show that a problem exists and needs attention.
- Evaluate alternative solutions.
- Propose your solution.

PEER RESPONSE

Writer: Provide the following information about your essay before you exchange drafts with a peer reader.

1. a. Audience
   b. Statement of problem
   c. Possible or alternative solutions
   d. Your recommended solution(s)

2. Write out one or two questions about your draft that you want your reader to answer.

Reader: Read the writer's entire draft. As you *reread* the draft, do the following:

1. Without looking at the writer's responses, describe (a) the essay's intended audience, (b) the main problem that the essay identifies, (c) the possible or alternative solutions, and (d) the writer's recommended solution. What feasibility problems or additional solutions should the writer consider? Why?

2. Indicate one paragraph in which the writer's evidence is strong. Then find one paragraph in which the writer needs more evidence. What additional *kinds* of evidence (personal experience, testimony from authorities, statistics, specific examples, etc.) might the writer use in this paragraph? Explain.

3. Number the paragraphs in the writer's essay and then describe, briefly, the purpose or main idea of each paragraph: paragraph 1 introduces the problem, paragraph 2 gives the writer's personal experience with the problem, etc. When you finish, explain how the writer might improve the organization of the essay.

4. List the three most important things that the writer should focus on during revision.

5. Respond to the writer's questions in Number 2.

Writer: When your essay is returned, read the comments by your peer reader(s) and do the following:

1. Compare your description of the audience, the problem, and the solutions with your reader's description. Where there are differences, try to clarify your essay.

2. Reconsider and revise your recommended solution(s).

3. What additional kinds of evidence will make your recommendations stronger?

4. Make a revision plan. List, in order, the three most important things that you need to do as you revise your essay.

- Show that your solution meets certain criteria: feasibility, cost-effectiveness, legality.
- Answer possible objections.
- Suggest implementation or call for action.
- **Be sure that you *show* what you mean, using specific examples, facts, details, statistics, quotations from interviews or articles.** Don't rely on general assertions.
- **Signal the major parts of your proposal with key words and transitions.**
- **Avoid the following errors in logic and generalization.**
- *Don't commit an "either-or" fallacy.* For example, don't say that "*either* we reduce class sizes *or* students will drop out of the university." There are more than two possible alternatives.
- *Don't commit an "ad hominem" fallacy* by arguing "to the man" or "to the woman" rather than to the issue. Don't say, for example, that Deborah Tannen is wrong about argument because she is just another pushy woman who should stick to teaching linguistics.
- *Test your proposal for "If . . . then . . ." statements.* Does it really follow that "if we reduce class size, teaching will be more effective"?
- *Avoid overgeneralizing your solution.* If all your research applies to solving problems in large lecture classes in psychology, don't assume that your solution will apply to, say, classes in physics or physical education.
- **If you are citing data or quoting sources, check to be sure that your material is accurately cited.**
- **Read your proposal aloud for flabby, wordy, or awkward sentences.** Revise your sentences for clarity, precision, and forcefulness.
- **Edit your proposal for spelling, appropriate word choice, punctuation, usage, mechanics, and grammar.** Remember that, in part, your form and audience help determine what are appropriate usage and mechanics.

■ POSTSCRIPT ON THE WRITING PROCESS   Before you turn in your essay, answer the following questions in your journal.

1. List the skills you used in writing this paper: observing people, places, or events; remembering personal experience; using questionnaires and interviews; reading written material; explaining ideas; evaluating solutions. Which of these skills was most useful to you in writing this essay?
2. What was your most difficult problem to solve while writing this paper? Were you able to solve it yourself, or did your readers suggest a solution?
3. In one sentence, describe the most important thing you learned about writing while working on this essay.
4. What were the most successful parts of your essay?

No Parking

Kristy Busch, Steve Krause, and Keith Wright

Kristy Busch, Steve Krause, and Keith Wright worked together on a proposal to solve the parking problem at their university. They met several times to discuss the topic, select questions for the survey and interview, divide the research responsibilities, and determine who was going to draft each section. They agreed that Keith Wright would interview the director of parking management, and that Kristy Busch and Steve Krause would survey students about the parking problem. After they collected their information, Wright drafted a first version of the section on the multilevel garage, Busch worked on the shuttle bus proposal, and Krause wrote out the introduction and the rezoning proposal. Then they worked together to combine and revise their drafts, adding new information, reorganizing the paragraphs, and editing the final draft. Shown below are the questions for the interview, the results of the survey, the first draft of the introduction and rezoning proposal, and the revised draft of the entire proposal.

Interview

Interview Questions for Wes Westfall, Director of Parking Management

1. Do you perceive a serious parking problem at CSU?

2. Do you think that students' arguments about lack of "X" parking spaces along the dorms on the north side of the campus are valid?

3. How many stickers for each zone are issued each year? Do these numbers fluctuate?

4. Are you in favor of building a multilevel parking facility?
   Where would you build such a structure?
   What would it cost? Is it feasible?
   How long would it take to build?

5. Have you considered a shuttle bus system between Moby Gym and the central campus?
   What would it cost? Is it feasible?

6. Is rezoning possible? Is it currently under consideration? Would it solve the problem? Is it feasible? What would it cost?

Parking Survey Results

1. Do you drive to CSU?
   Yes: 36
   Occasionally: 53
   No: 11

2. Does CSU need more parking for students?
   Yes: 62
   No: 38

3. Would rezoning close-in lots to eliminate dorm parking help?
   Yes: 78
   No: 22

4. Class (Fr., Soph., Jr., Sr., Other)
   Fr: 33
   Soph: 20
   Jr: 22
   Sr: 13
   Other: 12

First Draft

If you drive to CSU, you may already know how hard it can be to find a parking place. If not, then now would be a good time to make the changes necessary to accommodate more cars (before you start driving). Not only is the parking inadequate for the number of cars, but it is also poorly organized and poorly distributed among the groups who use it. A very common occurrence is being forced to park very far from the building where you need to go. Not only students are affected; faculty, staff, and visitors also have problems finding somewhere to park. For a visitor, this is very distressing and certainly doesn't present an attractive first impression of CSU. It is clear that something will have to be done; what is unclear is exactly what would be the most practical and cost-effective solution. First, and probably the most effective for the immediate future, would be to rezone the existing parking to better accommodate the users. A shuttle bus system could also be used; however, this could be costly and would have to be used a lot to make it a practical investment. The ominous "multilevel parking facility" is a drastic last measure that we would have a lot of trouble paying for. [add closing sentence]

The most cost-effective and probably the most immediately effective would be a partial rezoning of existing parking. This year, the office of parking management sold 7,641 parking stickers for an available 6,238 spaces, a difference of 1,703. This means that there are a lot more stickers than places to park. Granted, all these people do not drive at the same time, but enough do to cause a problem. In a poll taken this March, 78 percent of the people said that they would like to see the parking rezoned. In rezoning, we should first look at the parking areas which are not full and determine why and then shift the zones in a way in which they will help. For example, the western sections of the "Z" lot at Moby Gym could be changed to "X" for those dorm dwellers. Then the close-in lots could be changed to "Z" for the commuting students. Or we could eliminate the metered parking and put "Z" parking in its place. Rezoning the lots would seem to be the easiest solution to the problem, but it cannot be permanent, since if this school survives it will inevitably grow.

Revised Version
No Parking

On Monday morning, Jennifer Martin left her apartment at 8:30 to   *1*
drive to the Colorado State University campus, hoping to arrive on time for a test in her 9 A.M. sociology class. When she arrived at the student parking lot west of Aylesworth Hall, there were no parking spots. So she began cruising up and down the lot, hoping that someone would soon pull out. As she drove slowly up and down the lanes, she muttered to herself and clenched her hands on the steering wheel. She did have a permit to park in the lot, but there were obviously more permits than spaces. About five minutes before class, a car pulled out of a place at the far end of the lot. She accelerated down the next lane, driving as fast as she could without running over other students, but just as she arrived, a green Ford Focus cut in front of her and darted into the vacant space. She honked her horn and waved her fist, but the person quickly got out of the car and walked away. At this point, she realized that she had no choice. She wheeled into the area marked for motorcycles, parked her car, and raced for class. She was angry because she knew she was going to get a ticket even though she had a legal permit.

If you drive to the CSU campus for classes, you have probably had   *2*
a similar experience. But students are not the only ones who have parking problems on campus: Faculty, staff, and visitors also have problems finding places to park. Especially for visitors, the overcrowded conditions don't present an attractive first impression of the campus. Clearly, something has to be done to improve parking facilities. After studying the problem, interviewing the director of parking management, and polling 100 students, we believe that there are three alternatives that the CSU administration should consider: building a multilevel parking facility, starting a shuttle bus from remote lots, and rezoning the existing parking lots to better serve the users.

A first possible solution to CSU's parking problem would be to   *3*
build a multilevel parking facility. This sounds like a promising idea because it would allow more students, faculty, and staff to park over the same amount of ground space. CSU could build this facility at any of several locations. One place is on the west side of the Morgan Library, where the "A" parking zone—for faculty—is now. This location would provide parking convenient to classes, faculty offices, and the library. A second site would be the open parking lot west of Moby Gym.

Although this location is farther from classes, it would also be used during basketball games and concerts. A third location might be the large parking lot north of the Student Center. This, too, like the library lot, would be close to classrooms and faculty offices.

While these sites are all promising, we discovered that a multilevel parking facility has some serious drawbacks. Wes Westfall, manager of CSU parking, explained that there are several problems with these garages that most people don't consider. A first drawback to the parking garage is the expense. Westfall said that a multilevel garage would cost a minimum of $6,000 per parking space, raising the price of a parking permit from $30 to over $300. And that would be for a sticky piece of paper that still wouldn't guarantee a parking space for every car. Perhaps the president of the university could pay $300 a year, but most students can barely afford $30.

A second drawback to a parking garage is that it doesn't last forever, and the maintenance costs can be considerable. Mr. Westfall has some frightening photographs of sections of strong, stable-looking concrete that has collapsed for no visible reason at all. One picture shows a whole garage leveled as though a good-sized bomb had hit it—nothing was left standing except for a pillar here and there. Unless garages are carefully maintained, Westfall stated, they may not last over twenty years. The problem, he explained, lies in the rebarb (steel rods inside the concrete) that reinforces the concrete. Gas, oil, and antifreeze from cars are gradually absorbed into the concrete, a condition causing the rebarb to deteriorate and weaken the whole structure. The only way to check for this kind of damage, Westfall noted, is to use an expensive concrete X-ray machine. So even the maintenance of a garage can be an expensive proposition.

The third and most serious problem, Westfall claims, is security. Parking garages can become just another place for sexual assault, drug trafficking, vandalism, and theft. Westfall commented that most garages have a monitor system and guards, but those precautions are not totally effective. By the time the guard detects a theft over the security system and arrives at the location, the thief has usually fled. In addition, any security system adds to the already high costs of a parking facility. Clearly, the problems connected with a multilevel garage make it a last resort for solving the parking problems on campus.

A second alternative for solving the parking problems on the CSU campus is to use a bus shuttle service from the outlying "Z" lot at Moby Gym to the central campus. Many of the students who responded to our survey said that the lots on the perimeter of the campus were nearly empty, but they were too far away from the library and the classrooms. The shuttle would solve this problem by taking the following route: Beginning at the Lory Student Center, the bus would head west down North Drive (along the residence halls) to the Moby Gym lot and then stop and pick up drivers at both the north and the south ends of the lot. It would then turn south onto Shields at the stoplight and turn east on South Drive, returning to central campus. This system would allow easier access to the core of the campus and, in return, put to full use the 539 parking spaces available in the Moby Gym parking lot. Of course, the shuttle, driver, and maintenance would cost money, so this solution would require a commitment from the university administration.

8   The most cost-effective solution would be a partial rezoning of the parking lots. This past year, the office of parking management sold 7,461 parking stickers for an available 6,238 spaces, a difference of 1,403. This means that they sold 1,403 more stickers than there are places to park. Not all people need to park at the same time, but enough do to cause a problem. Of the 100 students that we polled, 78 percent said that they would like to see the central campus lots rezoned. In this scheme, students parking their cars for long periods of time would use the outlying lots, and commuting students, faculty, and staff would use the closer lots. For example, if we changed the western section of the outlying "Z" lot to "X" for those students living in the dorms, the parking spaces near the dorms along South Drive could be made available to those who have to drive every day to campus to attend classes. Such rezoning seems to be the easiest and least expensive solution.

9   One main obstacle to overcoming CSU's parking problem is money. A multilevel parking facility would accommodate more cars per acre of ground space, yet it is the most expensive solution. The shuttle bus system—which could still be implemented—is more economical, but it would require raising additional revenue, most likely by raising the price of parking stickers. We certainly recommend that the university try a shuttle system on an experimental basis to determine the exact costs and to see whether the number of riders justifies the expense. Rezoning the lots, however, is clearly the least complicated and most economical solution. Signs could be changed during the summer months, and new maps and brochures printed in time for the beginning of fall semester. Our group proposes that the university rezone the lots at the end of this academic year and start planning for a shuttle bus and a garage to meet the need in future years. With more careful management of the close-in lots, the new parking stickers might be more than just a hunting license. A person with a permit might actually be able to arrive at a lot at 8:45 and still make that nine o'clock class.

1. After reading the revised version, look again at the questions for the interview and the survey. How would you advise the authors to modify either set of questions? What questions would you add? What questions would you change or delete? Explain.

2. Compare the introduction in the first draft with the introduction in the revised version. Which is more effective? Jot down an idea for a third introduction that the authors might consider.

3. Reread the revised version and *outline* the major parts of the proposal. Then compare that outline with the authors' initial outline, given here:

   I.   Introduction

   II.   Rezoning proposal

   III.   Shuttle bus proposal

   IV.   Multilevel garage proposal

   V.   Conclusion

   Do you think that their revised plan for organizing the paper was an improvement? Explain.

4. Who is the intended audience for this proposal? What revisions would make this proposal appeal even more strongly to that audience? (During the planning stages of this essay, the authors decided to send this proposal to Wes Westfall, director of parking management. How do you think Westfall would react to this proposal as it stands?)

S T U D E N T   W R I T I N G

WHO SHOULD TAKE CHARGE?

Eui Young Hwang

Eui Young Hwang, a student at the University of Illinois, wrote his problem-solving paper on the issue of black–Asian conflicts. After reading a conversation published in Ms. magazine between Vicki Alexander, an African-American civil and medical rights activist, and Grace Lyu-Volckhausen, the Asian-American founder of the Korean YWCA, Hwang decided to enter their conversation by offering his own solutions to the racial tensions between the two communities. Hwang's solutions are to use the Korean-American media to help educate the community about cul-

tural differences, to ask Korean-American churches to create religious and
social opportunities for interaction, and to ask Korean-American business-
es to return some profits to the African-American communities. Reprinted
here is an excerpt from the Ms. *conversation, followed by Hwang's own essay.*

BLACK/ASIAN CONFLICT: WHERE DO WE BEGIN?

Vicki Alexander and Grace Lyu-Volckhausen

Grace Lyu-Volckhausen: For me, being a feminist is in my genes. My grandmother was one of the earliest Korean feminists; my mom was one of the founders of the Korean Women's Association, and my father was one of the few Korean legislators who sponsored a women's rights bill. So when I came here in 1960 and women were fighting for their rights, I asked, "What is this? We have always been fighting."

I got involved with the women's movement here as a student in the 1960s. At that time, there were about 80 Koreans in New York, mostly students. Within five years, Koreans started to come in. I realized that Korean women were getting jobs in all kinds of labor markets and were getting taken advantage of. So we started the Korean YWCA; I worked with women's groups like Asian Women United. Now I spend most of my time and energy with immigrant women.

Vicki Alexander: I grew up in Los Angeles. My father was U.S. black, Blackfoot Indian, and Irish. Indians often allowed blacks or people escaping disasters like the Irish potato famine to stay on the reservation. We were welcomed there. My mother was a Polish-Russian Jew. My father was a union organizer, and from a very early age I was involved in progressive activities. In the early 1960s I married a college classmate— he was from Korea, a mathematician; he died in 1974 from a brain tumor.

I first was in the movement to free South Africa in the early 1960s, and then the movement for civil rights in this country. I had always wanted to be a doctor, but when I graduated from college I was not accepted by any medical school; after the civil rights movement, I reapplied and was accepted everywhere, with scholarships, and with no change in my record. So the civil rights movement was very important in my becoming a doctor. I decided to become an ob-gyn because the ones I saw didn't help women. . . .

Grace: The yearlong boycott of two Korean grocery stores by people in the African American community [on Church Avenue in the Flatbush section of Brooklyn] really soured a lot of things. I think it has soured New York as a whole. During the crisis I was behind the scenes trying to work things out. It was very frustrating.

Vicki: Well, everybody was talking about it. In the group I was in at the time, we were trying to analyze it and ask ourselves, "What's going on here? Should we take a side? Is there a side to take? Is there a middle road?" We tried to understand Korean immigration, because none of the people in the group were Korean.

Grace: So they just studied the situation.

Vicki: Right. We didn't engage in it. It was so nasty; it was terrible. All these guys, the black leaders, who have become discredited—the Sharptons and the Carsons—really discredited us.

Grace: I think Koreans wondered, why didn't David Dinkins [New York City's African-American mayor] come down to the store? It took him eight months. When the crisis started, we asked him to come out right away—but he vacillated.

Our children remember these things. When they see their parents getting hurt, they remember it. And they have long memories.

Vicki: I think that among U.S. blacks there is a real hatred of people coming into our community and ripping us off. Once again getting ripped off by people who aren't us. Nationalism in the black community is very high, so blacks can come in and rip us off really badly, and they don't get chastised. The feeling gets fueled by racial incidents. And it's certainly been fueled on a national level by Reagan and Bush.

I feel that there is a long-standing kind of negativism that stems from nationalism; it says if it isn't black, it isn't good. No matter what. I think that's where a lot of the community is coming from. When you look historically at where black people have lived, we have not owned the stores. And on the whole, the money generated through the stores does not get reinvested in the community. So historically, you have a level of oppression not only based on class, but in the eyes of those blacks and in reality, based on race.

Then come Koreans. Koreans—and Arabs—own stores. But still, they are not black. There is that resentment, but what is clear about Arabs is that they are coming from a poor section of the world. So that's not as antagonistic as the white Jewish store owner. But then, in come Koreans, and nobody knows nothing about Koreans or the struggle in Korea—that's that world over there, Korea, China. The U.S. population is so ignorant, purposely so. But in the eyes of U.S. blacks, that is another body of folks coming over, taking over, and we don't know where they are from. So we must assume there is some money behind them. Maybe they don't have money, but we are assuming that they must have some money to come into our community and build whatever.

When it was just white-black, it wasn't as hard to understand. But when it is black-Asian-Arab, it starts to get very confusing, the class and race stuff starts to overlap. Because of the lack of education in the U.S., it's really a problem. What people need to start is a major education campaign.

Grace: From the Korean point of view, it doesn't matter what community we come into—black or white. The Koreans come in with a small amount of capital that they borrowed from their friends. They have trouble getting jobs because of discrimination, so they try to make a living by starting businesses that use the least amount of capital; they expend whatever amount of labor is necessary. Where do they go? The places with lowest rents, where there are not that many stores. So they end up going to black neighborhoods, where rent is cheap, where, if you work long hours, you can make profits—they all end up going there. But they don't know who these people are in the communities they go into.

Let me tell you an interesting story, an incredible misunderstanding between blacks and Koreans. Once a former black coworker of mine was furious. He said, "You see that Korean woman there. I am so angry. She is insulting us." I asked, "What did she do?" He said, "Whenever I go there, the woman never puts the change in my hand, she always puts it on the counter." And I said, "Richard, this is because in Korea, a woman does not touch a man's hand. Except her own husband's—in private." He didn't know. It's just a little thing that becomes a big problem. I hear such comments all the time: "That Korean woman never smiles. They are so unfriendly." But in Korea, if you smile that much, they think you are stupid.

Vicki: Also, if you smile at men, it has a prostitution connotation.

Grace: Absolutely. This cultural gap is so great. Of course, Koreans will say, "These black people, they are always dancing, they are always loud."

Vicki: Or, "They're lazy. They don't work very hard."

Grace: My only regret in the Church Avenue crisis was that women were not able to get together. Korean women couldn't get together with African American women because we were just so engrossed in our own problems. We were all wringing our hands, "What do we do? What do we do?" And then all these politicians were running away from us. I felt like a pariah when I went to community meetings. People would see me and would not see me. They didn't want to deal with the Koreans because we were a time bomb.

I agonized that we could not pull our women together. Maybe next time there is a crisis we should bring our women together and tell these guys to shut up.

If I called you because of a black-Korean crisis, would you come out with your friends?

Vicki: Sure. You have to start building toward it now, at a time of no crisis. You have to establish a relationship with people. And one of the best places to do that is the Medgar Evers College women's center, a black women's center. I think it would be good if the overture came from Korean women, as people who come from an oppressed state. You were born in South Korea, an oppressed state, and I was born in the U.S., an oppressed state. We're both women oppressed within the oppressed state. There is a real commonality. We are struggling and fighting for our people, but to bridge some of those gaps, we have to start educating now.

WHO SHOULD TAKE CHARGE?

Eui Young Hwang

A boycott by blacks of a Korean grocery store in New York and lootings primarily of Korean-owned stores during the L.A. riots have focused Americans' attentions on racial conflicts between blacks and Koreans. Most Koreans are immigrants, not familiar with the American culture yet, and do business in poor black communities in the inner city. Vicki Alexander and Grace Lyu-Volckhausen, in "Black/Asian Conflict: Where Do We Begin?" assert that education on cultural differences and interactions is needed to reduce tension between blacks and Koreans. However, the authors fail to specify how to implement their solutions. Intervention by Korean-American media, churches, and business organizations is needed in order to reduce racial conflict between blacks and Koreans caused by a lack of knowledge, few interactions, and Koreans' dominant business in black inner-city communities.

Korean-American media can help to avoid misunderstandings between Koreans and blacks by educating Koreans about cultural differences. Korean merchants are often accused of insulting customers by not smiling and not putting change into a customer's hand. Lyu-Volckhausen explains that in Korean culture, a person smiling too often is considered stupid, and a woman does not touch a man's hand. Koreans, unaware of the cultural differences in America, often behave "rudely" to their black customers. Such little misunderstandings due to cultural differences often create an unfriendly relationship between blacks and Koreans. Korean-American media can readily educate Koreans about cultural differences. An organization might try to hold a program to educate Koreans on cultural sensitivities. Many Koreans are, however, too busy to attend any educational programs. The easiest way to get the attention of Koreans would be to use media in

Korean communities. In big cities like New York, Los Angeles, and Chicago, where most Koreans live, there are a number of Korean-American television stations, radio channels, and newspapers. Korean-American media have large Korean audiences. With such a big influence on Koreans, Korean-American media can easily get Koreans' attention in order to teach them about the cultural differences between Koreans and blacks. When compared to other organizations, Korean media provide the easiest method to reach and educate Koreans on cultural sensitivities.

Korean-American churches can also increase cultural sensitivity *3* and generate interactions between blacks and Koreans. Many Koreans think that blacks are lazy, untrustworthy, and violent. Blacks may perceive that Koreans feel racism against blacks. On the other hand, Koreans may build bad images about blacks, since they often hear about blacks having no jobs, stealing, and murdering. To make matters worse, Koreans have too few contacts with blacks to overcome their stereotypical images about blacks. Therefore, frequent interactions between Koreans and blacks are necessary. Korean-American churches have the most potential in terms of promoting interactions between Koreans and blacks. One may argue that churches are too limited because they appeal only to Christians. On the contrary, churches include more Koreans than any other Korean-American organization, since many Koreans go to churches. Lyu-Volckhausen talks about blacks and Koreans singing together in church choirs and the opportunity it gives the two groups to get to know each other. Korean churches could cooperate with churches in black communities to hold religious activities and thus give both Koreans and blacks chances to establish friendly relationships. Korean-American churches can help Koreans to overcome stereotypical images of blacks by promoting interactions between blacks and Koreans and by holding religious activities with black churches.

Finally, Korean-American business organizations need to reduce *4* blacks' anger toward Korean businesses in black communities. They could begin by contributing some of their profits to black communities and helping blacks economically. Alexander points out that historically, blacks have not owned stores in their own communities, and the profit generated through stores does not get reinvested in black communities. Blacks often assume that Koreans take over black communities with money and that Koreans have an advantage over black businesses because they get money from secret financial sources or were wealthy in Korea. Lyu-Volckhausen explains that Koreans with a small amount of capital often go to the poor black community because the rent is cheap, and then make profits by working hard. There are several Korean-American business organizations which lead many

Korean businesses. Those Korean-American business organizations can reduce hatred among blacks toward Koreans by contributing some of the profits of Korean businesses to black communities and helping blacks economically. In fact, some business organizations in Chicago have been trying to reduce tension between blacks and Koreans by donating scholarships to local black students, helping the homeless in black communities, encouraging Koreans to hire black employees, and helping local blacks' businesses by using their products. Some Koreans may say they should use their money however they want to. However, it may be more logical to contribute some of the profit to the community where they made the profit. By contributing a part of the profit to the black community, Korean business organizations can reduce not only the hatred among blacks toward Koreans but also the racial incidents like boycotts and lootings that have greatly hurt Koreans' businesses.

Korean-American media, churches, and business organizations *5* can greatly help to clear up misunderstandings and reduce tension between blacks and Koreans. Black organizations also need to cooperate with Korean-American organizations in order to establish friendly relationships between blacks and Koreans. Korean and black communities are too involved with each other to ignore the conflicts between them. That is, they need each other. First, Koreans and blacks need to show their willingness to listen to each other. Then, both Koreans and blacks should volunteer their efforts to reduce tension. Koreans and blacks cannot wait for the government to intervene to solve the conflicts between two communities. Conflicts between them hurt both Koreans and blacks too much to wait, and Koreans and blacks themselves are the only ones who can solve the problems.

QUESTIONS FOR WRITING AND DISCUSSION

1. Before you read Hwang's essay, read the *Ms.* conversation and write your own response. Explain which of the ideas might work and which might not work. Then brainstorm a list of other actions that might reduce the racial tensions that Alexander and Lyu-Volckhausen describe.

2. Read Hwang's essay. In which paragraphs does he refer to ideas that Alexander and Lyu-Volckhausen discuss? Explain how his solutions further develop the ideas in their conversation.

3. Describe Hwang's three solutions. Which has the greatest promise for solving the problem? Which solutions might not work or might

cause other problems? What other solutions from your list might Hwang consider? Explain your responses.

4. In "Solving for Pattern," Wendell Berry argues that good solutions must consider the harmony, health, and quality of the overall system. How well does Hwang meet Berry's criteria for a good solution? Explain.

5. In which paragraphs does Hwang anticipate possible objections, analyze feasibility problems, or provide effective supporting evidence for his solutions? In which paragraphs should Hwang provide more analysis or more specific examples? Citing specific passages, point out strengths and suggest possible revisions for Hwang.

6. Use the excerpts from the *Ms.* conversation and Hwang's essay as starting points for your own essay on solving some aspect of interracial or intercultural tension. You may focus on conflicts between or among any racial or cultural groups. Draw on your own experience. Describe the problems and offer your solution(s).

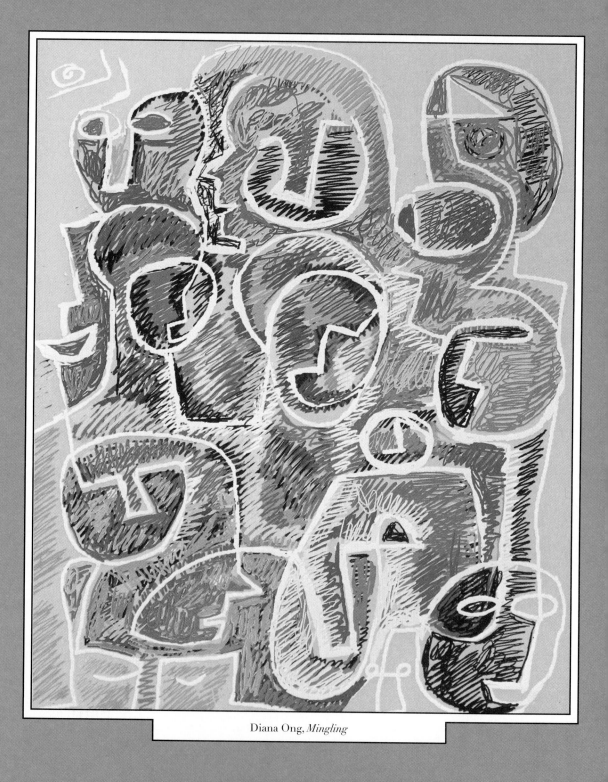

Diana Ong, *Mingling*

Chapter 10 Arguing

After being cited for not wearing a seat belt while operating a motor vehicle, you decide that your rights have been violated. In order to write a convincing argument to your representative that seat belt laws are unfair, you research current articles about the law and interview a law professor on the issue. You decide to claim that the seat belt laws should be repealed because they are a fundamental violation of individual liberty. You believe that the opposing argument—that seat belts save lives and reduce insurance rates for everyone—is not relevant to the issue of individual liberty. Because your representative has supported seat belt laws, you present both sides of the issue but stress the arguments supporting your viewpoint.

As a recent high school graduate, you decide to write about the increasing number of standardized tests currently required of primary and secondary school students. The question you want to investigate is whether schools are teaching students important skills and making them better members of society or whether schools are just teaching them how to do well on tests. After reading current articles on standardized tests and interviewing your classmates, you decide to write to politicians who are in favor of standardized tests and argue that, while the tests should not be thrown out, they should be changed in order to solve several serious problems they have created for students, teachers, and parents.

Give me liberty to know, to utter, and to argue freely according to conscience, above all liberties.

—JOHN MILTON,
POET

Freedom of speech is established to achieve its essential purpose only when different opinions are expounded in the same hall to the same audience. . . . The opposition is indispensable.

—WALTER LIPPMANN,
JOURNALIST

HEN PEOPLE ARGUE WITH EACH OTHER, THEY OFTEN BECOME HIGHLY EMOTIONAL OR CONFRONTATIONAL. REMEMBER THE LAST HEATED ARGUMENT YOU HAD WITH A FRIEND OR FAMILY member: At the end of the argument, one person stomped out of the room, slammed the door, and didn't speak to the other for days. In the aftermath of such a scene, you felt angry at the other person and angry at yourself. Nothing was accomplished. Neither of you came close to achieving what you wanted when you began the argument. Rather than understanding each other's point of view and working out your differences, you effectively closed the lines of communication.

When writers construct arguments, however, they try, through reason and use of evidence, to avoid the emotional outbursts that often turn verbal arguments into displays of temper. Strong feelings may energize an argument—few of us make the effort to argue without emotional investment in the subject—but written argument stresses a fair weighing of pros and cons. While you advocate one position, you keep the lines of communication open by acknowledging and evaluating opposing arguments. Because written arguments are public, they take on a civilized manner. They implicitly say, "Let's be reasonable about this. Let's look at the evidence on all sides. Let's not shout or fight; let's be as constructive as we can."

As writers construct written arguments, they carefully consider their audiences. Does the audience know about this controversy, or does it need background information? Do the readers hold an opposing viewpoint, or are they likely to listen to both sides and decide what to believe? What arguments will they find most persuasive? A written argument creates an atmosphere of reason, which encourages readers to examine their own views clearly and dispassionately. When successful, such argument convinces rather than alienates an audience. It changes people's minds or persuades them to adopt a recommended course of action.

All writing . . . is propaganda for something.

—ELIZABETH DREW,

WRITER AND CRITIC

Techniques for Writing: Argument

A written argument is similar to a public debate—between attorneys in a court of law or members of Congress who represent different political parties. It begins with a *debatable* issue: Is this a good bill? Should we vote for it? In such debates, one person argues for a position or proposal, while the other argues against it. The onlookers (the members of Congress, the jury, or the public) then decide what to believe or what to do. *Written argument imitates this situation by examining the opinions both for and against a position and then advocating one of the positions or proposing a solution.* Written argument evaluates the conflicting positions and then uses reasons and evidence to support the writer's claim. The writer represents the opposing arguments, responds to them, and advocates his or her own position. A sound written argument uses the following techniques:

- **Focusing on a *debatable* proposition or claim.** This claim becomes your thesis.
- *Analyzing the audience.* Knowing what your audience believe will help you convince them of your position or persuade them to act on your thesis.
- **Representing and evaluating the *opposing points of view* on the issue fairly and accurately.** The key to a successful arguing paper is anticipating and responding to the most important opposing positions.
- **Arguing reasonably *against opposing arguments* and *for your claim.*** State and refute opposing arguments. Present the best arguments supporting your claim. Argue reasonably and fairly.
- **Supporting your claims with *sufficient* evidence.** Use firsthand observations; examples from personal experience; statistics, facts, and quotations from your reading; and results of surveys and interviews.

In an article entitled "Active and Passive Euthanasia," James Rachels claims that active euthanasia may be defensible for patients with incurable and painful diseases. The following paragraphs from that article illustrate the key features of argument:

The distinction between active and passive euthanasia is thought to be crucial for medical ethics. The idea is that it is permissible, at least in some cases, to withhold treatment and allow a patient to die, but it is never permissible to take any direct action designed to kill the patient. This doctrine seems to be accepted by most doctors. . . .

Opposing position

However, a strong case can be made against this doctrine. In what follows I will set out some of the relevant arguments, and urge doctors to reconsider their views on this matter.

Claim
Audience

To begin with a familiar type of situation, a patient who is dying of incurable cancer of the throat is in terrible pain, which can no longer be satisfactorily alleviated. He is certain to die within a few days, even if present treatment is continued, but he does not want to go on living for those days, since the pain is unbearable. So he asks the doctor for an end to it, and his family joins in the request.

Argument for claim
Example

Example

Argument against opposition

Suppose the doctor agrees to withhold treatment, as the conventional doctrine says he may. The justification for his doing so is that the patient is in terrible agony, and since he is going to die anyway, it would be wrong to prolong his suffering needlessly. But now notice this. If one simply withholds treatment, it may take the patient longer to die, and so he may suffer more than he would if more direct action were taken and a lethal injection given. This fact provides strong reason for thinking that, once the initial decision not to prolong his agony has been made, active euthanasia is actually preferable to passive euthanasia, rather than the reverse. To say otherwise is to endorse the option that leads to more suffering rather than less, and is contrary to the humanitarian impulse that prompts the decision not to prolong his life in the first place.

CLAIMS FOR WRITTEN ARGUMENT

The thesis of your argument is a *debatable claim*. Opinions on both sides of the issue must have some merit. Claims for a written argument usually fall into one of four categories: claims of fact, claims about cause and effect, claims about value, and claims about solutions and policies. A claim may occasionally fall into several categories or may even overlap categories.

Claims of Fact

- Grades do not measure intelligence or achievement.
- Polygraph tests do not accurately detect lies.
- Women face serious discrimination in the job market.

These claims are about matters of "fact" that are not easily measured or agreed upon. If I claim that a Lhasa apso was an ancient Chinese ruler, you can check a dictionary and find out that I am wrong. A Lhasa apso is, in fact, a small Tibetan dog. There is no argument. But people do disagree about some *supposed* "facts": Do grades measure achievement? Are polygraph tests accurate? They also disagree about matters of "degree": Sexual discrimination exists in the marketplace, but is it "serious"? How prevalent and extreme are the economic inequities? What is "discrimination," anyway? *Definition* is a key to claims of fact: What do we mean by "detect lies"? Does "accurate" mean one hundred percent of the time? Ninety percent? Eighty percent? What does "serious discrimination" mean? Does the fact that female workers currently earn only seventy-three cents for every dollar that male workers earn qualify as "serious discrimination"?

In an excerpt from a *Newsweek* column entitled "A Case of Severe Bias," Patricia Raybon makes a claim of fact when she argues that the news media's portrayal of black America is inaccurate, biased, and stereotyped:

This is who I am not. I am not a crack addict. I am not a welfare mother. I am not illiterate. I am not a prostitute. I have never been in jail. My children are not in gangs. My husband doesn't beat me. My home is not a tenement. None of these things defines who I am, nor do they describe the other black people I've known and worked with and loved and befriended over these 40 years of my life.

Nor does it describe most of black America, period.

Yet in the eyes of the American news media, this is what black America is: poor, criminal, addicted and dysfunctional. Indeed, media coverage of black America is so one-sided, so imbalanced that the most victimized and hurting segment of the black community—a small segment, at best—is presented not as the exception but as the norm. It is an insidious practice, all the uglier for its blatancy.

In recent months, oftentimes in this very magazine, I have observed a steady offering of media reports on crack babies, gang warfare, violent youth, poverty and homelessness—and in most cases, the people featured in the photos and stories were black. At the same time, articles that discuss other aspects of American life—from home buying to medicine to technology to nutrition—rarely, if ever, show blacks playing a positive role, or for that matter, any role at all.

Day after day, week after week, this message—that black America is dysfunctional and unwhole—gets transmitted across the American landscape. Sadly, as a result, America never learns the truth about what is actually a wonderful, vibrant, creative community of people.

Claims About Cause and Effect

- Cigarettes cause lung cancer.
- Capital punishment does not deter violent crime.
- Rock music weakens the moral fiber of America's youth.

Unlike the claim "Grades affect admission to college," these claims about cause and effect are debatable. The claim that cigarettes cause lung cancer is, of course, less debatable than it was twenty years ago, before the evidence demonstrating the link became overwhelming. The deterring effect of capital punishment is still an arguable proposition with reasonable arguments on both sides. The argument that rock music weakens the moral fiber of youth is certainly debatable; the writer would have to counter the argument that rock music sometimes raises social consciousness and fights world hunger.

In a selection from her book *The Plug-In Drug: Television, Children, and the Family*, Marie Winn argues that television has a negative effect on family life. In her opening paragraphs, she sets forth both sides of the controversy and then argues that the overall effect is negative:

> Television's contribution to family life has been an equivocal one. For while it has, indeed, kept the members of the family from dispersing, it has not served to bring them *together*. By its domination of the time families spend together, it destroys the special quality that depends to a great extent on what a family does, what special rituals, games, recurrent jokes, familiar songs, and shared activities it accumulates.

> "Like the sorcerer of old," writes Urie Bronfenbrenner, "the television set casts its magic spell, freezing speech and action, turning the living into silent statues so long as the enchantment lasts. The primary danger of the television screen lies not so much in the behavior it produces—although there is danger there—as in the behavior it prevents: the talks, the games, the family festivities and arguments through which much of the child's learning takes place and through which his character is formed. Turning on the television set can turn off the process that transforms children into people."

> Yet parents have accepted a television-dominated family life so completely that they cannot see how the medium is involved in whatever problems they might be having.

Claims About Value

- Boxing is a dehumanizing sport.
- The Ford Edsel is the ugliest automobile ever built in America.
- Toni Morrison is a great American novelist.

Claims about value lead to evaluative essays. All the strategies discussed in Chapter 8 apply here, with the additional requirement that you must anticipate and respond to alternate or opposing arguments. The argumentative essay that attempts to prove that boxing is dehumanizing must respond to the argument that boxing is merely another form of competition that promotes athletic excellence. Arguing that Morrison is a great American novelist requires setting criteria for great American novels and then responding to critics who argue that Morrison's work does not reach those standards.

In "College Is a Waste of Time and Money," teacher and journalist Caroline Bird argues that many students go to college simply because it is the "thing to do." For those students, Bird claims, college is not a good idea:

> Nowadays, says one sociologist, you don't have to have a reason for going to college; it's an institution. His definition of an institution is an arrangement everyone accepts without question; the burden of proof is not on why you go, but why anyone thinks there might be a reason for not going. The implication is that an 18-year-old . . . should listen to those who know best and go to college.

> I don't agree. I believe that college has to be judged not on what other people think is good for students, but on how good it feels to the students themselves.

> I believe that people have an inside view of what's good for them. If a child doesn't want to go to school some morning, better let him stay at home, at least until you find out why. Maybe he knows something you don't. It's the same with college. If high-school graduates don't want to go, or if they don't want to go right away, they may perceive more clearly than their elders that college is not for them. It is no longer obvious that adolescents are best off studying a core curriculum that was constructed when all educated men could agree on what made them educated, or that professors, advisors, or parents can be of any particular help to young people in choosing a major or a career. High-school graduates see college graduates driving cabs and decide it's not worth going. College students find no intellectual stimulation in their studies and drop out.

Claims About Solutions or Policies

- Pornography on the Internet should be censored.
- The penalty for drunk driving should be a mandatory jail sentence and loss of driver's license.
- To reduce exploitation and sensationalism, the news media should not be allowed to interview victims of crime or disaster.

Claims about solutions or policies sometimes occur *along with* claims of fact, cause and effect, or value. Because grades do not measure achievement (argue that this is a fact), they should be abolished (argue for this policy). Boxing is a dehumanizing sport (argue this claim of value); therefore, boxing should be banned (argue for this solution). Claims about solutions or policies involve all the strategies used for problem solving (see Chapter 9), but with special emphasis on countering opposing arguments: "Although advocates of freedom of speech suggest that we cannot suppress pornography on the Internet, in fact, we already have self-monitoring devices in other media that could help reduce pornography on the Internet."

In *When Society Becomes an Addict*, psychotherapist Anne Wilson Schaef argues that our society has become an "Addictive System" that has many characteristics in common with alcoholism and other addictions. Advertising becomes addictive, causing us to behave dishonestly; the social pressure to be "nice" can become addictive, causing us to lie to ourselves. Schaef argues that the solution for our social addictions begins when we face the reality of our dependency:

> We cannot recover from an addiction unless we first admit that we have it. Naming our reality is essential to recovery. Unless we admit that we are indeed functioning in an addictive process in an Addictive System, we shall never have the option of recovery. Once we name something, we own it. . . . Remember, to name the system as addict is not to condemn it: it is to offer it the possibility of recovery.

> Paradoxically, the only way to reclaim our personal power is by admitting our powerlessness. The first part of Step One of the AA [Alcoholics Anonymous] Twelve-Step Program reads, "We admitted we were powerless over alcohol." It is important to recognize that admitting to powerlessness over an addiction is not the same as admitting powerlessness as a person. In fact, it can be very powerful to recognize the futility of the illusion of control.

Mere knowledge of the truth will not give you the art of persuasion.
—PLATO,
PHAEDRUS

APPEALS FOR WRITTEN ARGUMENT

To support claims and respond to opposing arguments, writers use *appeals* to the audience. Argument uses three important types of appeals: to *reason* (logic and evidence support the claim), to *character* (the writer's good character itself supports the claim), and to *emotion* (the writer's expression of feelings about the issue may support the claim). Effective arguments emphasize the appeal to reason but may also appeal to character or emotion.

APPEAL TO REASON   An appeal to reason depends most frequently on *inductive logic*, which is sometimes called the *scientific method*. Inductive logic draws a general conclusion from personal observation or experience, specific facts, reports, statistics, testimony of authorities, and other bits of data.

Experience is the best teacher, we always say, and experience teaches inductively. Suppose, using biologist Thomas Huxley's famous example, you pick a green apple from a tree and take a bite. Halfway through the bite you discover that the apple is sour and quickly spit it out. But, you think, perhaps the next green apple will be ripe and will taste better. You pick a second green apple, take a bite, and realize that it is just as sour as the first. However, you know that some apples—like the Granny Smith—look green even when they're ripe, so you take a bite out of a third apple. It is also sour. You're beginning to draw a conclusion. In fact, if you taste a fourth or fifth apple, other people may begin to question your intelligence. How many green apples from this tree must you taste before you get the idea that all of these green apples are sour?

Experience, however, may lead to wrong conclusions. You've tasted enough of these apples to convince *you* that all these apples are sour, but will others think that these apples are sour? Perhaps you have funny taste buds. You may need to ask several friends to taste the apples. Or perhaps you are dealing with a slightly weird tree—in fact, some apple trees are hybrids, with several different kinds of apples grafted onto one tree. Before you draw a conclusion, you may need to consult an expert in order to be certain that your tree is a standard, single-variety apple tree. If your friends and the expert also agree that all of these green apples are sour, you may use your experience *and* their testimony to reach a conclusion—and to provide evidence to make your argument more convincing to others.

In inductive logic, a reasonable conclusion is based on a *sufficient* quantity of accurate and reliable evidence that is selected in a *random* manner to reduce human bias or to take into account variation in the sample. The definition of *sufficient* varies, but generally the number must be large enough to convince your audience that your sample fairly represents the whole subject.

Let's take an example to illustrate inductive reasoning. Suppose you ask a student, one of fifty in a Psychology I class, a question of value: "Is Professor X a good teacher?" If this student says, "Professor X is the worst teacher I've ever had!" what conclusion can you draw? If you avoid taking the class based on a sample of one, you may miss an excellent class. So you decide to gather a *sufficient sample* by polling twenty of the fifty students in the class. But which twenty do you interview? If you ask the first student for a list of students, you may receive the names of twenty other students who also hate the professor. To reduce human or accidental bias, then, you choose a random method for collecting your evidence: As the students leave the class, you give a questionnaire to two out of every five students. If they all fill out the questionnaires, you probably have a *sufficient* and *random* sample.

Finally, if the responses to your questionnaire show that fifteen out of twenty students rate Professor X as an excellent teacher, what *valid conclusion* should you draw? You should not say, categorically, "X is an excellent teacher." Your conclusion must be restricted by your evidence and the method of gathering it: "Seventy-five percent of the students polled in Psychology I believe that Professor X is an excellent teacher."

Most arguments use a shorthand version of the inductive method of reasoning. A writer makes a claim and then supports it with *reasons* and representative *examples* or *data*:

Claim: Professor X is an excellent psychology teacher.

Reason #1:   Professor X is an excellent teacher because she gives stimulating lectures that students rarely miss.

           Evidence: Sixty percent of the students polled said that they rarely missed a lecture. Three students cited Professor X's lecture on "assertiveness" as the best lecture they'd ever heard.

Reason #2:   Professor X is an excellent teacher because she gives tests that encourage learning rather than sheer memorization.

           Evidence: Seventy percent of the students polled said that Professor X's essay tests required thinking and learning rather than memorization. One student said that Professor X's tests always made her think about what she'd read. Another student said he always liked to discuss Professor X's test questions with his classmates and friends.

APPEAL TO CHARACTER   An appeal based on your good character as a writer can also be important in argument. (The appeal to character is frequently called the *ethical appeal* because readers make a value judgment about the writer's character.) In a written argument, you show your audience—through your reasonable persona, voice, and tone—that you are a person who abides by moral standards that your audience shares: You have a good reputation, you are honest and trustworthy, and you argue "fairly."

A person's reputation often affects how we react to a claim, but *the argument itself* should also establish the writer's trustworthiness. You don't have to be a Mahatma Gandhi or a Mother Teresa to generate a strong ethical appeal for your claim. Even if your readers have never heard your name before, they will feel confident about your character if you are knowledgeable about your subject, present the pros and cons fairly, and support your own claim with sufficient, reliable evidence.

If your readers have reason to suspect your motives or think that you may have something personal to gain from your argument, you may need to bend over backward to be fair. If you do have something to gain, lay your cards on the table. Declare your vested interest but explain, for example, how your solution would benefit everyone equally. Similarly, don't try to cover up or distort the opponents' arguments; acknowledge the opposition's strong arguments and refute the weak ones.

APPEAL TO EMOTION   Appeals to emotion can be tricky because, as we have seen, when emotions come in through the door, reasonableness may fly out the window. Argument emphasizes reason, not emotion. We know, for example, how advertising plays on emotions, by means of loaded or exaggerated language or through images of famous or sexy people. Emotional appeals designed to *deceive* or *frighten* people or to *misrepresent* the virtues of a person, place, or object have no place in rational argument. But emotional appeals that illustrate a truth or movingly depict a reality are legitimate and effective means of convincing readers.

COMBINED APPEALS   Appeals may be used in combination. Writers may appeal to reason and, at the same time, establish trustworthy characters and use legitimate emotional appeals. The following excerpt from Martin Luther King, Jr.'s "Letter from Birmingham Jail" illustrates all three appeals. He appeals to reason, arguing that, historically, civil rights reforms are rarely made without political pressure. He establishes his integrity and good character by treating the opposition (in this case, the Birmingham clergy) with respect and by showing moderation and restraint. Finally, he uses emotional appeals, describing his six-year-old daughter in tears and recalling his own humiliation at being refused a place to sleep. King uses these emotional appeals legitimately; he is not misrepresenting reality or trying to deceive his readers.

One of the basic points in [the statement by the Birmingham clergy] is that the action that I and my associates have taken in Birmingham is untimely. Some have asked: "Why didn't you give the new city administration time to act?" The only answer that I can give to this query is that the new Birmingham administration must be prodded about as much as the outgoing one, before it will act. We are sadly mistaken if we feel that the election of Albert Boutwell as mayor will bring the millennium to Birmingham. While Mr. Boutwell is a much more gentle person than Mr. Connor, they are both segregationists, dedicated to the maintenance of the status quo. I have hoped that Mr. Boutwell will be reasonable enough to see the futility of massive resistance to desegregation. But he will not see this without pressure from devotees of civil rights. My friends, I must say to you that we have not made a single gain in civil rights without determined legal and nonviolent pressure. Lamentably, it is an historical fact that privileged groups seldom give up their privileges voluntarily. Individuals may see the moral light and voluntarily give up their unjust posture; but, as Reinhold Niebuhr has reminded us, groups tend to be more immoral than individuals.

Appeal to character and appeal to reason

Appeal to reason

Evidence

We know through painful experience that freedom is never voluntarily given by the oppressor; it must be demanded by the oppressed. Frankly, I have yet to engage in a direct-action campaign that was "well timed" in the view of those who have not suffered unduly from the disease of segregation. For years now I have heard the word "Wait!" It rings in the ear of every Negro with piercing familiarity. This "Wait"

Appeal to character and reason

has almost always meant "Never." We must come to see, with one of our distinguished jurists, that "justice too long delayed is justice denied."

Appeal to emotion
Evidence

Appeal to emotion

Evidence

Appeal to emotion

Evidence

Appeal to character

We have waited for more than 340 years for our constitutional and God-given rights. . . . Perhaps it is easy for those who have never felt the stinging darts of segregation to say, "Wait." But when you have seen vicious mobs lynch your mothers and fathers at will and drown your sisters and brothers at whim; when you have seen hate-filled policemen curse, kick, and even kill your black brothers and sisters; when you see the vast majority of your twenty million Negro brothers smothering in an airtight cage of poverty in the midst of an affluent society; when you suddenly find your tongue twisted and your speech stammering as you seek to explain to your six-year-old daughter why she can't go to the public amusement park that has just been advertised on television, and see tears welling up in her eyes when she is told that Funtown is closed to colored children . . . when you take a cross-country drive and find it necessary to sleep night after night in the uncomfortable corners of your automobile because no motel will accept you; when you are humiliated day in and day out by nagging signs reading "white" and "colored"; when your first name becomes "nigger," your middle name becomes "boy" (however old you are) and your last name becomes "John" . . . —then you will understand why we find it difficult to wait. There comes a time when the cup of endurance runs over, and men are no longer willing to be plunged into the abyss of despair. I hope, sirs, you can understand our legitimate and unavoidable impatience.

ROGERIAN ARGUMENT

Traditional argument assumes that people are most readily convinced or persuaded by a confrontational "debate" on the issue. In a traditional argument, the writer argues reasonably and fairly, but the argument becomes a kind of struggle or "war" as the writer attempts to "defeat" the arguments of the opposition. The purpose of a traditional argument is thus to convince an undecided audience that the writer has "won a fight" and emerged "victorious" over the opposition.

In fact, however, there are many situations in which a less confrontational and less adversarial approach to argument is more effective. Particularly when the issues are highly charged or when the audience that we are trying to persuade is the opposition, writers may more effectively use negotiation rather than confrontation. *Rogerian argument*—named after psychologist Carl Rogers—is a kind of negotiated argument where understanding and compromise replace the traditional, adversarial approach. Rogerian, or *nonthreatening*, argument opens the lines of communication by reducing conflict. When people's beliefs are attacked, they instinctively become defensive and strike back. As a result, the argument becomes polarized: The writer argues for a claim, the reader digs in to defend his or her position, and no one budges.

Crucial to Rogerian argument is the fact that convictions and beliefs are not abstract but reside in people. If people are to agree, they must be sensitive to each other's beliefs. Rogerian argument, therefore, contains a clear appeal to character. While Rogerian argument uses reason and logic, its primary goal is not to "win" the argument but to open the lines of communication. To do that, the writer must be sympathetic to different points of view and willing to modify his or her claims in response to people who hold different viewpoints. Once the reader sees that the writer is open to change, the reader may become more flexible.

Once both sides are more flexible, a compromise position or solution becomes possible. As Rogers says, "This procedure gradually achieves a mutual communication. Mutual communication tends to be pointed toward solving a problem rather than toward attacking a person or group." Rogerian argument, then, imitates not a courtroom debate but the mutual communication that may take place between two people. Whereas traditional argument intends to change the actions or the beliefs of the opposition, Rogerian argument works toward changes *in both sides* as a means of establishing common ground and reaching a solution.

If you choose Rogerian argument, remember that you must actually be willing to change your beliefs. Often, in fact, when you need to use Rogerian argument most, you may be least inclined to use it—simply because you are inflexible on an issue. If you are unwilling to modify your own position, your reader will probably sense your basic insincerity and realize that you are just playing a trick of rhetoric.

Rogerian argument is appropriate in a variety of sensitive or highly controversial situations. You may want to choose Rogerian argument if you are an employer requesting union members to accept a pay cut in order to help the company avoid bankruptcy. Similarly, if you argue to husbands that they should assume responsibility for half the housework, or if you argue to Anglo-Americans that Spanish language and culture should play a larger role in public education, you may want to use a Rogerian strategy. By showing that you empathize with the opposition's position and are willing to compromise, you create a climate for mutual communication.

Rogerian argument makes a claim, considers the opposition, and presents evidence to support your claim, but in addition, it avoids threatening or adversarial language and promotes mutual communication and learning. A Rogerian argument uses the following strategies:

- **Avoiding** a *confrontational stance*. Confrontation threatens your audience and increases their defensiveness. Threat hinders communication.
- **Presenting** your *character* as someone who understands and can empathize with the opposition. Show that you understand by restating the opposing position accurately.

- **Establishing** *common ground* with the opposition. Indicate the beliefs and values that you share.
- **Being willing** *to change your views.* Show where your position is not reasonable and could be modified.
- **Directing your argument** toward *a compromise or workable solution.*

Note: An argument does not have to be either entirely adversarial or entirely Rogerian. You may use Rogerian techniques for the most sensitive points in an argument that is otherwise traditional or confrontational.

In his essay "Animal Rights Versus Human Health," biology professor Albert Rosenfeld illustrates several features of Rogerian argument. Rosenfeld argues that animals should be used for medical experiments, but he is aware that the issues are emotional and that his audience is likely to be antagonistic. In these paragraphs, Rosenfeld avoids threatening language, represents the opposition fairly, grants that he is guilty of *speciesism*, and says that he sympathizes with the demand to look for alternatives. He indicates that his position is flexible: Most researchers, he says, are delighted when they can use alternatives. He grants that there is some room for compromise, but he is firm in his position that some animal experimentation is necessary for advancements in medicine.

States opposing position fairly and sympathetically

It is fair to say that millions of animals—probably more rats and mice than any other species—are subjected to experiments that cause them pain, discomfort, and distress, sometimes lots of it over long periods of time. . . . All new forms of medication or surgery are tried out on animals first. Every new substance that is released into the environment, or put on the market, is tested on animals. . . .

States opposing position fairly

In 1975, Australian philosopher Peter Singer wrote his influential book called *Animal Liberation*, in which he accuses us all of "speciesism"—as reprehensible, to him, as racism or sexism. He freely describes the "pain and suffering" inflicted in the "tyranny of human over nonhuman animals" and sharply challenges our biblical license to exercise "dominion over the fish of the sea, and over the fowl of the air, and over every living thing that moveth upon the Earth."

Acknowledges common ground

Sympathetic to opposing position

Well, certainly we are guilty of speciesism. We do act as if we had dominion over other living creatures. But domination also entails some custodial responsibility. And the questions continue to be raised: Do we have the right to abuse animals? To eat them? To hunt them for sport? To keep them imprisoned in zoos—or, for that matter, in our households? Especially to do experiments on these creatures who can't fight back?

Hardly any advance in either human or veterinary medicine—cure, vaccine, operation, drug, therapy—has come about without experiments on animals. . . . I certainly sympathize with the demand that we look for ways to get the information we want without using animals. Most investigators are delighted when they can get their data by means of tissue cultures or computer simulations. But as we look for alternative ways to get information, do we meanwhile just do without?

Suggests compromise position

■ WARMING UP: JOURNAL EXERCISES   The following exercises will help you practice arguing. Read all of the following exercises and then write on the three that interest you most. If another idea occurs to you, write about it.

1. From the following list of "should" statements, choose one that relates to your experience and freewrite for ten minutes. When you finish your freewriting, state a claim and list arguments on both sides of the issue.

- Tuition should be free at state universities.
- Bicyclists should be subject to regular traffic laws, including DWI.
- The sale of all handguns should be illegal.
- Unions should be abolished.
- NCAA football should have playoffs.
- High-quality child care should be available to all working parents at public expense.
- Computer literacy courses should be required at the college level.
- Police should live in the neighborhoods they serve.
- Fraternities and sororities should be forbidden to serve alcoholic beverages.
- Students should work for one year between high school and college.
- Businesses should be required to provide free health insurance for all employees.
- Unsportsmanlike behavior in tennis should result in a match forfeit.
- Nonmajor courses should be graded pass/fail.
- After committing three felonies, criminals should receive mandatory life sentences.

2. Controversial subjects depend as much on the audience as they do on the issue itself. Make a quick list of things you do every day: the kind of clothes you wear, the food you eat, the books you read, the friends you have, the ideas you discuss. For one of these activities, imagine people who might find what you do immoral, illogical, unjust, or unhealthy.

A society which is clamoring for choice [is] filled with many articulate groups, each arguing its own brand of salvation.

—MARGARET MEAD,

ANTHROPOLOGIST

What claim might they make about your activity? What reasons or evidence might they use to argue that your activity should be abolished, outlawed, or changed? Write for five minutes arguing *their* point of view.

3. Television and television advertising are often the subject of much criticism, such as in Marie Winn's excerpt from "The Plug-In Drug." Write a letter to Marie Winn, to your local or college newspaper, or to members of the PTA in your city defending the *positive* effects or value of television. Cite one particular program or commercial as an example.

4. Grades are important, but in some courses, they get in the way of learning. Choose an actual course that you have taken and write an open letter to the school administration, arguing for credit/no-credit grading in that particular course. Assume that you intend to submit your letter to the campus newspaper.

5. News items often contain incidents that spark arguments about morality or justice. Choose a recent controversial news story and write out the arguments for or against the action taken in the case.

6. The following essay by columnist Mike Royko appeared in the *Chicago Tribune*. Read Royko's essay. Next, write out your definition for an effective written argument. Finally, write your own response to the essay, arguing that Royko's column does or does not meet your definition of an effective argumentative essay.

PROFESSIONAL   WRITING

THE ETHICS OF ENDORSING A PRODUCT

Mike Royko

The man from an advertising agency had an unusual proposition. His agency does the TV commercials for a well-known chain of Mexican restaurants in Chicago.

"You may have seen our commercials," he said. "They include a cameo appearance by Lee Smith and Leon Durham of the Cubs. It shows them crunching into a tortilla."

No, I somehow missed seeing that.

"Well, anyway, we'd like to have you in a commercial."

Doing what?

"Crunching into a tortilla."

I thought tortillas were soft. I may be wrong, but I don't think you can crunch into a tortilla. Maybe you mean a taco.

"Well, you'd be biting into some kind of Mexican food."

What else would I have to do?

"That's it. It would be a cameo appearance. You'd be seen for about four seconds. You wouldn't have to say anything."

I'd just bite into a piece of Mexican food?

"Right. For a fee, of course."

How big a fee?

He named a figure. It was not a king's ransom, but it was more than walking-around money.

"It would take about 45 minutes to film," he said.

Amazing. In my first newspaper job almost 30 years ago, I had to work 12 weeks to earn the figure he had mentioned.

It was a small, twice-a-week paper, and I was the only police reporter, the only sports reporter, the only investigative reporter, the assistant political writer, and on Saturday I would edit the stories going into the entertainment page. The publisher believed in a day's work for an hour's pay.

Now I could make the same amount just for spending 45 minutes biting into a taco in front of a TV camera.

"Well, what do you think?" he asked.

I told him that I would think about it and get back to him.

So I asked Slats Grobnik, who has sound judgment, what he thought of the deal.

"That's a lot of money just to bite a taco on TV. For that kind of scratch, I'd bite a dog. Grab the deal."

But there is a question of ethics.

"Ethics? What's the ethics in biting a taco? Millions of people bite tacos every day. Mexicans have been biting them for hundreds of years. Are you saying that Mexicans are unethical? Careful, some of my best friends are Mexicans."

No, I'm not saying that at all. I like Mexicans, too, although I'm opposed to bullfighting.

"Then what's unethical?"

The truth is, I can't stand tacos.

"What has that got to do with it? I can't stand work, but I do it for the money."

It has everything to do with it. If I go on TV and bite into a taco, won't I be endorsing that taco?

"So what? You've endorsed politicians and I've never met a politician that I liked better than a taco."

But endorsing a taco I didn't like would be dishonest.

"Hey, that's the American way. Turn on your TV and look at all the people who endorse junk. Do you think they really believe what they're saying?"

Then it's wrong. Nobody should endorse a taco if they don't like a taco.

"Then tell them you'll bite something else. A tortilla or an enchilada."

But I don't like them, either. The truth is, I can't stand most Mexican food. The only thing I really like is the salt on the edge of a margarita glass.

"Can't you just bite the taco and spit it out when the camera is turned off?"

That would be a sham. Besides, even if I liked tacos or tortillas, what does it matter? Why should somebody eat in a restaurant because they see me biting into that restaurant's taco? Am I a taco expert? What are my credentials to tell millions of people what taco they should eat? I'm not even a Mexican.

"You're as Mexican as Jane Byrne, and she's doing it."

To get the Hispanic vote, she would go on TV and eat a cactus.

"Well, you're a sucker to turn it down. Why, it's almost un-American. Do you think that in Russia any newsman would ever have an opportunity to make that much money by biting into a pirogi?"

That may be so.

But maybe someday a food product will come along that I can lend my name to, something I can truly believe in.

"I doubt it. Not unless they start letting taverns advertise shots and beers on TV."

PROFESSIONAL WRITING

THE INTERNET: A CLEAR AND PRESENT DANGER?

Cathleen A. Cleaver

Cathleen Cleaver is a former director of legal studies at the Family Research Council, an organization based in Washington, D.C. She has published extensively on issues relating to children and the Internet, in newspapers and magazines such as USA Today, Newsday, *and the* Congressional Quarterly Researcher. *The following essay was originally a speech given at Boston University as part of a College of Communication Great Debate. In this speech, she argues that some industry and government regulation of the Internet is necessary.*

- Someone breaks through your firewall and steals proprietary   1
  information from your computer systems. You find out and

contact a lawyer who says, "Man, you shouldn't have had your stuff online." The thief becomes a millionaire using your ideas, and you go broke, if laws against copyright violation don't protect material on the Internet.

- You visit the Antiques Anonymous Web site and decide to pay their hefty subscription fee for a year's worth of exclusive estate sale previews in their private online monthly magazine. They never deliver and, in fact, never intended to—they don't even have a magazine. You have no recourse, if laws against fraud don't apply to online transactions. *2*

- Bob Guccione decides to branch out into the lucrative child porn market and creates a Teen Hustler Web site featuring nude adolescents and preteens. You find out and complain, but nothing can be done, if child pornography distribution laws don't apply to computer transmissions. *3*

- A major computer software vendor who dominates the market develops his popular office software so that it works only with his browser. You're a small browser manufacturer who is completely squeezed out of the market, but you have to find a new line of work, if antitrust laws don't apply online. *4*

- Finally, a pedophile e-mails your son, misrepresenting himself as a twelve-year-old named Jenny. They develop an online relationship and one day arrange to meet after school, where he intends to rape your son. Thankfully, you learn in advance about the meeting and go there yourself, where you find a forty-year-old man instead of Jenny. You flee to the police, who'll tell you there's nothing they can do, if child-stalking laws don't apply to the Internet. *5*

The awesome advances in interactive telecommunication that we've witnessed in just the last few years have changed the way in which many Americans communicate and interact. No one can doubt that the Internet is a technological revolution of enormous proportion, with outstanding possibilities for human advancement. *6*

As lead speaker for the affirmative, I'm asked to argue that the Internet poses a "clear and present danger," but the Internet, as a whole, isn't dangerous. In fact, it continues to be a positive and highly beneficial tool, which will undoubtedly improve education, information exchange, and commerce in years to come. In other words, the Internet will enrich many aspects of our daily life. Thus, instead of defending this rather apocalyptic view of the Internet, I'll attempt to explain why some industry and government regulation of certain aspects of the Internet is necessary—or, stated another way, why people who use the Internet should not be exempt from many of the laws and regulations *7* that govern their conduct elsewhere. My opening illustrations were meant to give examples of some illegal conduct which should not become legal simply because someone uses the Internet. In looking at whether Internet regulation is a good idea, I believe we should consider whether regulation is in the public interest. In order to do that, we have to ask the question: Who is the public? More specifically, does the "public" whose interests we care about tonight include children?

Children and the Internet

Dave Barry describes the Internet as a "worldwide network of university, government, business, and private computer systems, run by a thirteen-year-old named Jason." This description draws a smile precisely because we acknowledge the highly advanced computer literacy of our children. Most children demonstrate computer proficiency that far surpasses that of their parents, and many parents know only what their children have taught them about the Internet, which gives new relevance to Wordsworth's insight: "The child is father of the man." In fact, one could go so far as to say that the Internet is as accessible to many children as it is inaccessible to many adults. This technological evolution is new in many ways, not the least of which is its accessibility to children, wholly independent of their parents.

8

When considering what's in the public interest, we must consider the whole public, including children, as individual participants in this new medium.

9

Pornography and the Internet

This new medium is unique in another way. It provides, through a single avenue, the full spectrum of pornographic depictions, from the more familiar convenience store fare to pornography of such violence and depravity that it surpasses the worst excesses of the normal human imagination. Sites displaying this material are easily accessible, making pornography far more freely available via the Internet than from any other communications medium in the United States. Pornography is the third largest sector of sales on the Internet, generating $1 billion annually. There are an estimated seventy-two thousand pornographic sites on the World Wide Web alone, with approximately thirty-nine new explicit sex sites every day. Indeed, the *Washington Post* has called the Internet the largest pornography store in the history of mankind.

10

There is little restriction of pornography-related activity in cyberspace. While there are some porn-related laws, the specter of those laws does not loom large in cyberspace. There's an implicit license there

11

that exists nowhere else with regard to pornography—an environment where people are free to exploit others for profit and be virtually untroubled by legal deterrent. Indeed, if we consider cyberspace to be a little world of its own, it's the type of world for which groups like the ACLU have long fought but, so far, fought in vain.

I believe it will not remain this way, but until it changes, we should *12* take the opportunity to see what this world looks like, if for no other reason than to reassure ourselves that our decades-old decisions to control pornography were good ones.

With a few clicks of the mouse, anyone, any child, can get graph- *13* ic and often violent sexual images—the kind of stuff it used to be difficult to find without exceptional effort and some significant personal risk. Anyone with a computer and a modem can set up public sites featuring the perversion of their choice, whether it's mutilation of female genitals, eroticized urination and defecation, bestiality, or sites featuring depictions of incest. These pictures can be sold for profit, they can be sent to harass others, or posted to shock people. Anyone can describe the fantasy rape and murder of a specific person and display it for all to read. Anyone can meet children in chat rooms or via e-mail and send them pornography and find out where they live. An adult who signs onto an AOL chat room as a thirteen-year-old girl is hit on thirty times within the first half hour.

All this can be done from the seclusion of the home, with the feel- *14* ing of near anonymity and with the comfort of knowing that there's little risk of legal sanction.

The phenomenon of this kind of pornography finding such a wel- *15* come home in this new medium presents abundant opportunities for social commentary. What does Internet pornography tell us about human sexuality? Photographs, videos, and virtual games that depict rape and the dehumanization of women in sexual scenes send powerful messages about human dignity and equality. Much of the pornography freely available without restriction on the Internet celebrates unhealthy and antisocial kinds of sexual activity, such as sadomasochism, abuse, and degradation. Of course, by its very nature, pornography encourages voyeurism.

Beyond the troubling social aspects of unrestricted porn, we face *16* the reality that children are accessing it and that predators are accessing children. We have got to start considering what kind of society we'll have when the next generation learns about human sexuality from what the Internet teaches. What does unrestricted Internet pornography teach children about relationships, about the equality of women? What does it teach little girls about themselves and their worth?

Opponents of restrictions are fond of saying that it's up to the   *17*
parents to deal with the issue of children's exposure. Well, of course
it is, but placing the burden solely on parents is illogical and ineffective. It's far easier for a distributor of pornography to control his material than it is for parents, who must, with the help of software,
search for and find the pornographic sites, which change daily, and
then attempt to block them. Any pornographer who wants to can
easily subvert these efforts, and a recent Internet posting from a
teenager wanting to know how to disable the filtering software on
his computer received several effective answers. Moreover, it goes
without saying that the most sophisticated software can only be effective where it's installed, and children will have access to many computers that don't have filtering software, such as those in libraries,
schools, and at neighbors' houses.

Internet Transactions Should Not be Exempt

Opponents of legal restrictions often argue simply that the laws   *18*
just cannot apply in this new medium, but the argument that old laws
can't apply to changing technology just doesn't hold. We saw this argument last in the early '80s with the advent of the videotape. Then,
certain groups tried to argue that, since you can't view videotapes without a VCR, you can't make the sale of child porn videos illegal, because, after all, they're just plastic boxes with magnetic tape inside.
Technological change mandates legal change only insofar as it affects
the justification for a law. It just doesn't make sense that the government may take steps to restrict illegal material in *every* medium—video,
television, radio, the private telephone, *and* print—but that it may do
nothing where people distribute the material by the Internet. While old
laws might need redefinition, the old principles generally stand firm.

The question of enforcement usually is raised here, and it often   *19*
comes in the form of: "How are you going to stop people from doing
it?" Well, no law stops people from doing things—a red light at an intersection doesn't force you to stop but tells you that you should stop
and that there could be legal consequences if you don't. Not everyone
who runs a red light is caught, but that doesn't mean the law is futile.
The same concept holds true for Internet laws. Government efforts to
temper harmful conduct online will never be perfect, but that doesn't
mean they shouldn't undertake the effort at all.

There's clearly a role for industry to play here. Search engines don't   *20*
have to run ads for porn sites or prioritize search results to highlight
porn. One new search engine even has sex as the default search term.
Internet service providers can do something about unsolicited e-mail

with hotlinks to porn, and they can and should carefully monitor any chat rooms designed for kids.

Some charge that industry standards or regulations that restrict *21* explicit pornography will hinder the development of Internet technology. But that is to say that its advancement depends upon unrestricted exhibition of this material, and this cannot be true. The Internet does not belong to pornographers, and it's clearly in the public interest to see that they don't usurp this great new technology. We don't live in a perfect society, and the Internet is merely a reflection of the larger social community. Without some mitigating influences, the strong will exploit the weak, whether a Bill Gates or a child predator.

Conclusion: Technology Must Serve Man

To argue that the strength of the Internet is chaos or that our lib- *22* erty depends upon chaos is to misunderstand not only the Internet but also the fundamental nature of our liberty. It's an illusion to claim social or moral neutrality in the application of technology, even if its development may be neutral. It can be a valuable resource only when placed at the service of humanity and when it promotes our integral development for the benefit of all.

Guiding principles simply cannot be inferred from mere techni- *23* cal efficiency or from the usefulness accruing to some at the expense of others. Technology by its very nature requires unconditional respect for the fundamental interests of society.

Internet technology must be at the service of humanity and of our *24* inalienable rights. It must respect the prerogatives of a civil society, among which is the protection of children.

VOCABULARY

In your journal, write the meanings of the following words:

- steals *proprietary* information **(1)**
- rather *apocalyptic* view **(7)**
- legal *deterrent* **(11)**
- don't have *filtering* software **(17)**
- the law is *futile* **(19)**
- cannot be *inferred* **(23)**
- usefulness *accruing* to some **(23)**
- respect the *prerogatives* **(24)**

QUESTIONS FOR WRITING AND DISCUSSION

1. Before you read or reread Cleaver's essay, write down your own thoughts and experiences about pornography on the Internet. Have you run into sites that you find offensive? Should access to such sites be made more difficult? Do you think children should be protected from accessing such sites—either by accident or on purpose? What do you think are the best method(s) for such regulation: Internet software programs, parental regulation, governmental regulation? Explain.

2. Cleaver begins her essay with several scenarios describing potential abuses and crimes that occur on-line. Did you find these scenarios effective as a lead-in to her argument? Did they help you focus on her thesis? Should she use fewer scenarios? Why do you think she used all of these examples when only two dealt with child pornography on the Internet?

3. Cleaver states her case for government regulation of pornography on the Internet, but who is against regulation, and what are their arguments? What arguments opposing Internet regulation does Cleaver cite? (Are there other opposing arguments that Cleaver does not consider?) How well does Cleaver answer these opposing arguments?

4. Arguing essays make appeals to reason, to character, and to emotion. Find examples of each type of appeal in Cleaver's essay. Which type of appeal does she use most frequently? Which appeals are most or least effective? Does she rely too much on her emotional appeals (see paragraph 13, for example)? For her audience and her context (a debate), should she bolster her rational appeals with more evidence and statistics? Why or why not?

5. Imagine that you are at this debate on the Internet and that your side believes that there should be no or very little regulation of the Internet. What arguments might you make in response to Cleaver? Make a list of the possible pro-con arguments on this topic and explain which ones you will focus on as you respond to Cleaver.

P R O F E S S I O N A L   W R I T I N G

THE DAMNATION OF A CANYON
Edward Abbey

"In wildness is the preservation of the world." Henry David Thoreau's words serve to introduce Edward Abbey's own nature ethic. Beginning with the

classic Desert Solitaire *(1968) and including* The Monkey Wrench Gang *(1975),* Abbey's Road *(1979), and* Down the River *(1982), Abbey's writings celebrate the American West, its deserts, canyons, mountains, and rivers. But always in full view are Abbey's villains in the black hats: Industrialists, Bureaucrats, and Developers. And Dammers. In this selection, taken from* Beyond the Wall *(1984), Abbey contrasts the Eden that was Glen Canyon with the stagnant, lifeless waters of Lake Powell. Abbey's argument is shaped by a clear outline—his claim, his refutation of the opposing view, his analysis of consequences, and his solution—and also by Abbey's insistent, cranky, and passionate voice, which echoes throughout the essay.*

There was a time when, in my search for essences, I concluded that *1* the canyonland country has no heart. I was wrong. The canyonlands did have a heart, a living heart, and that heart was Glen Canyon and the golden, flowing Colorado River.

In the summer of 1959 a friend and I made a float trip in little *2* rubber rafts down through the length of Glen Canyon, starting at Hite and getting off the river near Gunsight Butte—The Crossing of the Fathers. In this voyage of some 150 miles and ten days our only motive power, and all that we needed, was the current of the Colorado River.

In the summer and fall of 1967 I worked as a seasonal park ranger *3* at the new Glen Canyon National Recreation Area. During my five-month tour of duty I worked at the main marina and headquarters area called Wahweap, at Bullfrog Basin toward the upper end of the reservoir, and finally at Lee's Ferry downriver from Glen Canyon Dam. In a number of powerboat tours I was privileged to see almost all of our nation's newest, biggest and most impressive "recreational facility."

Having thus seen Glen Canyon both before and after what we *4* may fairly call its damnation, I feel that I am in a position to evaluate the transformation of the region caused by construction of the dam. I have had the unique opportunity to observe firsthand some of the differences between the environment of a free river and a power plant reservoir.

One should admit at the outset to a certain bias. Indeed I am a *5* "butterfly chaser, googly eyed bleeding heart and wild conservative." I take a dim view of dams; I find it hard to learn to love cement; I am poorly impressed by concrete aggregates and statistics in the cubic tons. But in this weakness I am not alone, for I belong to that ever-growing number of Americans, probably a good majority now, who have become aware that a fully industrialized, thoroughly urbanized, elegantly computerized social system is not suitable for human habitation. Great for machines, yes: but unfit for people.

Lake Powell, formed by Glen Canyon Dam, is not a lake. It is a   6
reservoir, with a constantly fluctuating water level—more like a bathtub that is never drained than a true lake. As at Hoover (or Boulder)
Dam, the sole practical function of this impounded water is to drive the
turbines that generate electricity in the powerhouse at the base of the
dam. Recreational benefits were of secondary importance in the minds
of those who conceived and built this dam. As a result the volume of
water in the reservoir is continually being increased or decreased according to the requirements of the Basin States Compact and the
power-grid system of which Glen Canyon Dam is a component.

The rising and falling water level entails various consequences.   7
One of the most obvious, well known to all who have seen Lake Mead,
is the "bathtub ring" left on the canyon walls after each drawdown of
water, or what rangers at Glen Canyon call the Bathtub Foundation.
This phenomenon is perhaps of no more than aesthetic importance; yet
it is sufficient to dispel any illusion one might have, in contemplating
the scene, that you are looking upon a natural lake.

The utter barrenness of the reservoir shoreline recalls by contrast   8
the aspect of things before the dam, when Glen Canyon formed the
course of the untamed Colorado. Then we had a wild and flowing river
lined by boulder-strewn shores, sandy beaches, thickets of tamarisk
and willow, and glades of cottonwoods.

The thickets teemed with songbirds: vireos, warblers, mockingbirds   9
and thrushes. On the open beaches were killdeer, sandpipers, herons,
ibises, egrets. Living in grottoes in the canyon walls were swallows, swifts,
hawks, wrens and owls. Beaver were common if not abundant: not an
evening would pass, in drifting down the river, that we did not see them
or at least hear the whack of their flat tails on the water. Above the river
shores were the great recessed alcoves where water seeped from the sandstone, nourishing the semitropical hanging gardens of orchid, ivy and
columbine, with their associated swarms of insects and birdlife.

Up most of the side canyon, before damnation, there were springs,   10
sometimes flowing streams, waterfalls and plunge pools—the kind of
marvels you can now find only in such small scale remnants of Glen
Canyon as the Escalante area. In the rich flora of these laterals the
larger mammals—mule deer, coyote, bobcat, ring-tailed cat, gray fox,
kit fox, skunk, badger and others—found a home. When the river was
dammed almost all of these things were lost. Crowded out—or
drowned and buried under mud.

The difference between the present reservoir, with its silent ster-   11
ile shores and debris choked side canyons, and the original Glen
Canyon, is the difference between death and life. Glen Canyon was
alive. Lake Powell is a graveyard.

For those who may think I exaggerate the contrast between the *12* former river canyon and the present man-made impoundment, I suggest a trip on Lake Powell followed immediately by another boat trip on the river below the dam. Take a boat from Lee's Ferry up the river to within sight of the dam, then shut off the motor and allow yourself the rare delight of a quiet, effortless drifting down the stream. In that twelve-mile stretch of living green, singing birds, flowing water and untarnished canyon walls—sights and sounds a million years older and infinitely lovelier than the roar of motorboats—you will rediscover a small and imperfect sampling of the kind of experience that was taken away from everybody when the oligarchs and politicians condemned our river for purposes of their own.

Lake Powell, though not a lake, may well be as its defenders as- *13* sert the most beautiful reservoir in the world. Certainly it has a photogenic backdrop of buttes and mesas projecting above the expansive surface of stagnant waters where the speedboats, houseboats and cabin cruisers play. But it is no longer a wilderness. It is no longer a place of natural life. It is no longer Glen Canyon.

The defenders of the dam argue that the recreational benefits avail- *14* able on the surface of the reservoir outweigh the loss of Indian ruins, historical sites, wildlife and wilderness adventure. Relying on the familiar quantitative logic of business and bureaucracy, they assert that whereas only a few thousand citizens ever ventured down the river through Glen Canyon, now millions can—or will—enjoy the motorized boating and hatchery fishing available on the reservoir. They will also argue that the rising waters behind the dam have made such places as Rainbow Bridge accessible by powerboat. Formerly you could get there only by walking (six miles).

This argument appeals to the wheelchair ethos of the wealthy, *15* upper-middle-class American slob. If Rainbow Bridge is worth seeing at all, then by God it should be easily, readily, immediately available to everybody with the money to buy a big powerboat. Why should a trip to such a place be the privilege only of those who are willing to walk six miles? Or if Pikes Peak is worth getting to, then why not build a highway to the top of it so that anyone can get there? Anytime? Without effort? Or as my old man would say, "By Christ, one man's just as good as another—if not a damn sight better."

It is quite true that the flooding of Glen Canyon has opened up *16* to the motorboat explorer parts of side canyons that formerly could be reached only by people able to walk. But the sum total of terrain visible to the eye and touchable by hand and foot has been greatly diminished, not increased. Because of the dam the river is gone, the inner canyon is gone, the best parts of the numerous side canyons are gone—

all hidden beneath hundreds of feet of polluted water, accumulating silt, and mounting tons of trash. This portion of Glen Canyon—and who can estimate how many cubic miles were lost?—*is no longer accessible to anybody.* (Except scuba divers.) And this, do not forget, was the most valuable part of Glen Canyon, richest in scenery, archaeology, history, flora and fauna.

Not only has the heart of Glen Canyon been buried, but many of   17
the side canyons above the fluctuating waterline are now rendered more difficult, not easier, to get into. This because the debris brought down into them by desert storms, no longer carried away by the river, must unavoidably build up in the area where flood meets reservoir. Narrow Canyon, for example, at the head of the impounded waters, is already beginning to silt up and to amass huge quantities of driftwood, some of it floating on the surface, some of it half afloat beneath the surface. Anyone who has tried to pilot a motorboat through a raft of half-sunken logs and bloated dead cows will have his own thoughts on the accessibility of these waters.

Second, the question of costs. It is often stated that the dam and   18
its reservoir have opened up to the many what was formerly restricted to the few, implying in this case that what was once expensive has now been made cheap. Exactly the opposite is true.

Before the dam, a float trip down the river through Glen Canyon   19
would cost you a minimum of seven days' time, well within anyone's vacation allotment, and a capital outlay of about forty dollars—the prevailing price of a two-man rubber boat with oars, available at any army-navy surplus store. A life jacket might be useful but not required, for there were no dangerous rapids in the 150 miles of Glen Canyon. As the name implies, this stretch of the river was in fact so easy and gentle that the trip could be and was made by all sorts of amateurs: by Boy Scouts, Camp Fire Girls, stenographers, schoolteachers, students, little old ladies in inner tubes. Guides, professional boatmen, giant pontoons, outboard motors, radios, rescue equipment were not needed. The Glen Canyon float trip was an adventure anyone could enjoy, on his own, for a cost less than that of spending two days and nights in a Page motel. Even food was there, in the water: the channel catfish were easier to catch and a lot better eating than the striped bass and rainbow trout dumped by the ton into the reservoir these days. And one other thing: at the end of the float trip you still owned your boat, usable for many more such casual and carefree expeditions.

What is the situation now? Float trips are no longer possible. The   20
only way left for the exploration of the reservoir and what remains of Glen Canyon demands the use of a powerboat. Here you have three options: (1) buy your own boat and engine, the necessary auxiliary equip-

ment, the fuel to keep it moving, the parts and repairs to keep it running, the permits and licenses required for legal operation, the trailer to transport it; (2) rent a boat; or (3) go on a commercial excursion boat, packed in with other sightseers, following a preplanned itinerary. This kind of play is only for the affluent.

The inescapable conclusion is that no matter how one attempts to 21 calculate the cost in dollars and cents, a float trip down Glen Canyon was much cheaper than a powerboat tour of the reservoir. Being less expensive, as well as safer and easier, the float trip was an adventure open to far more people than will ever be able to afford motorboat excursions in the area now.

All of the foregoing would be nothing but a futile exercise in nos- 22 talgia (so much water over the dam) if I had nothing constructive and concrete to offer. But I do. As alternate methods of power generation are developed, such as solar, and as the nation establishes a way of life adapted to actual resources and basic needs, so that the demand for electrical power begins to diminish, we can shut down the Glen Canyon power plant, open the diversion tunnels, and drain the reservoir.

This will no doubt expose a drear and hideous scene: immense 23 mud flats and whole plateaus of sodden garbage strewn with dead trees, sunken boats, the skeletons of long-forgotten, decomposing water-skiers. But to those who find the prospect too appalling, I say give nature a little time. In five years, at most in ten, the sun and wind and storms will cleanse and sterilize the repellent mess. The inevitable floods will soon remove all that does not belong within the canyons. Fresh green willow, box elder and redbud will reappear; and the ancient drowned cottonwoods (noble monuments to themselves) will be replaced by young of their own kind. With the renewal of plant life will come the insects, the birds, the lizards and snakes, the mammals. Within a generation—thirty years—I predict the river and canyons will bear a decent resemblance to their former selves. Within the lifetime of our children Glen Canyon and the living river, heart of the canyonlands, will be restored to us. The wilderness will again belong to God, the people and the wild things that call it home.

VOCABULARY

In your journal, write the meanings of the following words:

- concrete *aggregates* **(5)**
- *aesthetic* importance **(7)**
- recessed *alcoves* **(9)**

- *oligarchs* and politicians **(12)**
- the wheelchair *ethos* **(15)**
- richest in . . . *archaeology* **(16)**
- preplanned *itinerary* **(20)**
- a *drear* and hideous scene **(23)**

QUESTIONS FOR WRITING AND DISCUSSION

1. Do you consider yourself an "environmentalist"—someone who is in favor of preserving wild rivers, designating wilderness areas, and forbidding mining, grazing, or the use of motorized vehicles in national parks? Or do you believe that federal lands, parks, and rivers should serve multiple uses? Explain, using a state or national park you have visited to give specific examples.

2. Which of Abbey's arguments did you find most persuasive? Which were least persuasive? Are there opposing arguments that Abbey does not answer? Explain, *referring to your own beliefs* outlined above.

3. An argument contains a *claim*, *reasons* that support the claim or refute the opposition, and *evidence*.

   - What sentence or sentences best illustrate Abbey's overall claim or thesis for this essay? Does he make a claim of fact, value, cause, or solution—or some combination of these? Explain.

   - List the *reasons* Abbey gives to support his claim and refute the opposing arguments.

   - For *one* of his reasons, list the evidence, facts, examples, or testimony that Abbey gives.

4. Note passages in which Abbey's *appeal to character* is evident. Where is he most reasonable? Where is he most cantankerous or even misanthropic? Are these facets of his character consistent with the persona portrayed in paragraph 5? In your judgment, does his appeal to character help or hurt his argument? Explain.

5. Cite one sentence in which Abbey uses an *emotional appeal*. Does this sentence make his argument more effective?

6. Assume you are the controller of the Glen Canyon dam. Write a short response to Abbey explaining why his solution—to "open the diversion tunnels, and drain the reservoir"—is absurd. Choose either an adversarial or a Rogerian strategy, whichever would work best for Abbey.

7. On the Internet, visit several Glen Canyon websites, such as the site for draining the dam at http://www.drainit.org/doa2001.htm, a report on the "Decommissioning of Glen Canyon Dam" at http://www. glencanyon.org, or a tourism site such as http://www.gorp.com. What do each of these sites recommend about Glen Canyon dam? Who sponsors each site? What biases do each of these sites have? Do they support, refute, or revise Abbey's analysis and recommendations?

PROFESSIONAL WRITING

THREE PERSPECTIVES ON THE DEATH PENALTY

The three essays that follow, by Edward Koch, Robert Badinter, and John O'-Sullivan, address the controversy surrounding the death penalty in the United States. In order to read these essays actively and critically, begin by writing down your *ideas on the death penalty. List your own reasons why the death penalty should or should not be used. Should it be used only under certain circumstances? Are there circumstances under which it should not be used?*

After you have written out your ideas, read all three essays. As you read—and reread—these essays, consider the following questions: Can there be three perspectives about an issue such as capital punishment? Are there other perspectives not described in these essays? Which of these writers makes the best argument to support his position? Which of these positions most closely agrees with yours? How exactly is your position different?

As you reread, also consider the different contexts within which each essay was written. "Death and Justice," by Edward I. Koch, was written during one of his terms as mayor of New York City and appeared in The New Republic *in 1985 during a period of high crime rates. The second essay, "Death Be Not Proud," was written by Robert Badinter, a Senator and former Justice Minister of France. Badinter was the prime mover behind France's decision to abolish the death penalty in 1981. Badinter's essay appeared in* Time International *in 2001 in response to the controversy surrounding the death penalty in Texas and Illinois at that time. The third essay, also titled "Death and Justice," appeared originally in the* Chicago Sun-Times *in 2001 and was reprinted in the* National Review Online. *The author, John O'Sullivan, is an editor-at-large for the* National Review *and writes a regular column on national and international political issues. The occasion of O'Sullivan's essay was the execution of Timothy McVeigh, the convicted bomber of the Murrah Federal Building in Oklahoma*

City. As you read, consider how each of these different contexts helps deter-
mine each writer's argument.

DEATH AND JUSTICE
Edward I. Koch

Last December a man named Robert Lee Willie, who had been con-   *1*
victed of raping and murdering an 18-year-old woman, was executed
in the Louisiana state prison. In a statement issued several minutes
before his death, Mr. Willie said: "Killing people is wrong. . . . It makes
no difference whether it's citizens, countries, or governments. Killing
is wrong." Two weeks later in South Carolina, an admitted killer named
Joseph Carl Shaw was put to death for murdering two teenagers. In an
appeal to the governor for clemency, Mr. Shaw wrote: "Killing is wrong
when I did it. Killing is wrong when you do it. I hope you have the
courage and moral strength to stop the killing."

It is a curiosity of modern life that we find ourselves being lectured   *2*
on morality by cold-blooded killers. Mr. Willie previously had been
convicted of aggravated rape, aggravated kidnapping, and the murders
of a Louisiana deputy and a man from Missouri. Mr. Shaw committed
another murder a week before the two for which he was executed, and
admitted mutilating the body of the 14-year-old girl he killed. I can't help
wondering what prompted these murderers to speak out against killing
as they entered the death-house door. Did their newfound reverence
for life stem from the realization that they were about to lose their own?

Life is indeed precious, and I believe the death penalty helps to af-   *3*
firm this fact. Had the death penalty been a real possibility in the minds
of these murderers, they might well have stayed their hand. They might
have shown moral awareness before their victims died, and not after.
Consider the tragic death of Rosa Velez, who happened to be home
when a man named Luis Vera burglarized her apartment in Brooklyn.
"Yeah, I shot her," Vera admitted. "She knew me, and I knew I wouldn't
go to the chair."

During my 22 years in public service, I have heard the pros and   *4*
cons of capital punishment expressed with special intensity. As a district leader, councilman, congressman, and mayor, I have represented
constituencies generally thought of as liberal. Because I support the
death penalty for heinous crimes of murder, I have sometimes been
the subject of emotional and outraged attacks by voters who find my
position reprehensible or worse. I have listened to their ideas. I have
weighed their objections carefully. I still support the death penalty. The
reasons I maintained my position can be best understood by examining the arguments most frequently heard in opposition.

1. *The death penalty is "barbaric."* Sometimes opponents of capital punishment horrify with tales of lingering death on the gallows, of faulty electric chairs, or of agony in the gas chamber. Partly in response to such protests, several states such as North Carolina and Texas switched to execution by lethal injection. The condemned person is put to death painlessly, without ropes, voltage, bullets, or gas. Did this answer the objections of death penalty opponents? Of course not. On June 22, 1984, *The New York Times* published an editorial that sarcastically attacked the new "hygienic" method of death by injection, and stated that "execution can never be made humane through science." So it's not the method that really troubles opponents. It's the death itself they consider barbaric.

Admittedly capital punishment is not a pleasant topic. However, one does not have to like the death penalty in order to support it any more than one must like radical surgery, radiation, or chemotherapy in order to find necessary these attempts at curing cancer. Ultimately we may learn how to cure cancer with a simple pill. Unfortunately, that day has not yet arrived. Today we are faced with the choice of letting the cancer spread or trying to cure it with the methods available, methods that one day will almost certainly be considered barbaric and would certainly delay the discovery of an eventual cure. The analogy between cancer and murder is imperfect, because murder is not the "disease" we are trying to cure. The disease is injustice. We may not like the death penalty, but it must be available to punish crimes of cold-blooded murder, cases in which any other form of punishment would be inadequate and, therefore, unjust. If we create a society in which injustice is not tolerated, incidents of murder—the most flagrant form of injustice—will diminish.

2. *No other major democracy uses the death penalty.* No other major democracy—in fact, few other countries of any description—are plagued by a murder rate such as that in the United States. Fewer and fewer Americans can remember the days when unlocked doors were the norm and murder was a rare and terrible offense. In America the murder rate climbed 122 percent between 1963 and 1980. During that same period, the murder rate in New York City increased by almost 400 percent, and the statistics are even worse in many other cities. A study at M.I.T. showed that based on 1970 homicide rates a person who lived in a large American city ran a greater risk of being murdered than an American soldier in World War II ran of being killed in combat. It is not surprising that the laws of each country differ according to differing conditions and traditions. If other countries had our murder problem, the cry for capital punishment would be just as

loud as it is here. And I daresay that any other major democracy where 75 percent of the people supported the death penalty would soon enact it into law.

3. *An innocent person might be executed by mistake.* Consider the work of Adam Bedau, one of the most implacable foes of capital punishment in this country. According to Mr. Bedau, it is "false sentimentality to argue that the death penalty should be abolished because of the abstract possibility that an innocent person might be executed." He cites a study of the 7,000 executions in this country from 1893 to 1971, and concludes that the record fails to show that such cases occur. The main point, however, is this. If government functioned only when the possibility of error didn't exist, government wouldn't function at all. Human life deserves special protection, and one of the best ways to guarantee that protection is to assure that convicted murderers do not kill again. Only the death penalty can accomplish this end. In a recent case in New Jersey, a man named Richard Biegenwald was freed from prison after serving 18 years for murder; since his release he has been convicted of committing four murders. A prisoner named Lemuel Smith, who, while serving four life sentences for murder (plus two life sentences for kidnapping and robbery) in New York's Green Haven Prison, lured a woman corrections officer into the chaplain's office and strangled her. He then mutilated and dismembered her body. An additional life sentence for Smith is meaningless. Because New York has no death penalty statute, Smith has effectively been given a license to kill.

But the problem of multiple murder is not confined to the nation's penitentiaries. In 1981, 91 police officers were killed in the line of duty in this country. Seven percent of those arrested in the cases that have been solved had a previous arrest for murder. In New York City in 1976 and 1977, 85 persons arrested for homicide had a previous arrest for murder. Six of these individuals had two previous arrests for murder, and one had four previous murder arrests. During those two years the New York police were arresting for murder persons with a previous arrest for murder on the average of one every 8.5 days. This is not surprising when we learn that in 1975, for example, the median time served in Massachusetts for homicide was less than two-and-a-half years. In 1976 a study sponsored by the Twentieth Century Fund found that the average time served in the United States for first-degree murder is ten years. The median time served may be considerably lower.

4. *Capital punishment cheapens the value of human life.* On the contrary, it can be easily demonstrated that the death penalty strengthens

8

9

10

the value of human life. If the penalty for rape were lowered, clearly it would signal a lessened regard for the victims' suffering, humiliation, and personal integrity. It would cheapen their horrible experience, and expose them to an increased danger of recurrence. When we lower the penalty for murder, it signals a lessened regard for the value of the victim's life. Some critics of capital punishment, such as columnist Jimmy Breslin, have suggested that a life sentence is actually a harsher penalty for murder than death. This is sophistic nonsense. A few killers may decide not to appeal a death sentence, but the overwhelming majority make every effort to stay alive. It is by exacting the highest penalty for the taking of human life that we affirm the highest value of human life.

5. *The death penalty is applied in a discriminatory manner.* This fac- 11 tor no longer seems to be the problem it once was. The appeals process for a condemned prisoner is lengthy and painstaking. Every effort is made to see that the verdict and sentence were fairly arrived at. However, assertions of discrimination are not an argument for ending the death penalty but for extending it. It is not justice to exclude everyone from the penalty of the law if a few are found to be so favored. Justice requires that the law be applied equally to all.

6. *Thou shalt not kill.* The Bible is our greatest source of moral in- 12 spiration. Opponents of the death penalty frequently cite the sixth of the Ten Commandments in an attempt to prove that capital punishment is divinely proscribed. In the original Hebrew, however, the Sixth Commandment reads, "Thou Shalt Not Commit Murder," and the Torah specifies capital punishment for a variety of offenses. The biblical viewpoint has been upheld by philosophers throughout history. The greatest thinkers of the 19th century—Kant, Locke, Hobbes, Rousseau, Montesquieu, and Mill—agreed that natural law properly authorizes the sovereign to take life in order to vindicate justice. Only Jeremy Bentham was ambivalent. Washington, Jefferson, and Franklin endorsed it. Abraham Lincoln authorized executions for deserters in wartime. Alexis de Tocqueville, who expressed profound respect for American institutions, believed that the death penalty was indispensable to the support of social order. The United States Constitution, widely admired as one of the seminal achievements in the history of humanity, condemns cruel and inhuman punishment, but does not condemn capital punishment.

7. *The death penalty is state-sanctioned murder.* This is the defense 13 with which Messrs. Willie and Shaw hoped to soften the resolve of

those who sentenced them to death. By saying in effect, "You're no better than I am," the murderer seeks to bring his accusers down to his own level. It is also a popular argument among opponents of capital punishment, but a transparently false one. Simply put, the state has rights that the private individual does not. In a democracy, those rights are given to the state by the electorate. The execution of a lawfully condemned killer is no more an act of murder than is legal imprisonment an act of kidnapping. If an individual forces a neighbor to pay him money under threat of punishment, it's called extortion. If the state does it, it's called taxation. Rights and responsibilities surrendered by the individual are what give the state its power to govern. This contract is the foundation of civilization itself.

Everyone wants his or her rights, and will defend them jealously.   *14*
Not everyone, however, wants responsibilities, especially the painful responsibilities that come with law enforcement. Twenty-one years ago a woman named Kitty Genovese was assaulted and murdered on a street in New York. Dozens of neighbors heard her cries for help but did nothing to assist her. They didn't even call the police. In such a climate the criminal understandably grows bolder. In the presence of moral cowardice, he lectures us on our supposed failings and tries to equate his crimes with our quest for justice.

The death of anyone—even a convicted killer—diminishes us all.   *15*
But we are diminished even more by a justice system that fails to function. It is an illusion to let ourselves believe that doing away with capital punishment removes the murderer's deed from our conscience. The rights of society are paramount. When we protect guilty lives, we give up innocent lives in exchange. When opponents of capital punishment say to the state: "I will not let you kill in my name," they are also saying to murderers: "You can kill in your *own* name as long as I have an excuse for not getting involved."

It is hard to imagine anything worse than being murdered while   *16*
neighbors do nothing. But something worse exists. When those same neighbors shrink back from justly punishing the murderer, the victim dies twice.

VOCABULARY

In your journal, write the meanings of the following words:

- I have represented *constituencies* (**4**)
- find my position *reprehensible* (**4**)

- the most *flagrant* form of injustice **(6)**
- the most *implacable* foes **(8)**
- this is *sophistic* nonsense **(10)**
- capital punishment is divinely *proscribed* **(12)**
- one of the *seminal* achievements **(12)**

PROFESSIONAL WRITING

DEATH BE NOT PROUD
Robert Badinter

I belong to a generation of Europeans for whom the United States *1* embodies democracy, progress and liberty. I went there as a student after the war. I have never forgotten the warmth and friendship that the American people showed me. In a word, I belong to that vanishing species: the Americanophile.

That is why I am writing this article. I don't believe that Ameri- *2* cans fully understand how their use of the death penalty has profoundly degraded the country's image in the eyes of other democratic nations. Today, all the Western democracies have abolished the death penalty. Almost all of Europe has banished it. Can one seriously believe that, if it constituted an effective instrument for fighting murderous crimes, the leaders of Europe's great states would not have reinstated it long ago? Every study done in the abolitionist countries has reached the same conclusion: the death penalty has never been a deterrent to crime. In the U.S. itself, the murder rate is higher in Texas than it is in the 12 states that have dropped the death penalty.

Today, 88% of all known executions in the world are carried out *3* by four countries: China, Iran, Saudi Arabia and the U.S. What, apart from the death penalty, does the U.S. have in common with those countries? Useless as an instrument to fight crime, capital punishment brings with it all the evils of Western society: racism, social injustice, economic and cultural inequality. These traits are not unique to America, but they take on a particular intensity when viewed in light of the death penalty.

Capital punishment is infected by racism. African-Americans and *4* Hispanics are the most at risk. Are they condemned to death more often than whites because their crimes are more atrocious or because they are black or Hispanic? This question alone should suffice in a democratic society to rule out the death penalty, as it has in South Africa.

The death penalty is not only racist but inegalitarian. Most prisoners on death row come from the poorest classes, those excluded from American society. They're criminals, we are told. Without a doubt. But has the society that puts them to death really given them the same chance as those more fortunate? Moreover, capital punishment strikes mainly those who don't have the money to hire competent, motivated and well-paid lawyers. Financial inequality before the law can lead to the worst possible consequences. Do Americans know that during a period of almost 20 years after the U.S. reinstated the death penalty, the overall rate of prejudicial error in the capital punishment system was 68%? Worse still, many innocent people have been condemned to death. Some have been saved in extremis, but how many others have been executed without anyone asking for a reconsideration of the trial? If a crime that goes unpunished is a challenge to society, the execution of an innocent person is the worst act that any community of free men can commit. It is the complete negation of justice. What kind of justice is it that, in order to avenge victims, becomes criminal itself by executing innocent people?

What about the barbaric practice, in the 21st century, of executing the feeble-minded and mentally defective, or the men and women whose crimes were committed when they were minors? What kind of society is it that treats adolescents as adults when it comes to sentencing them to death? Is this society ignorant of the fact that every adolescent is a human being in progress; that for every young murderer, part of the responsibility lies with the parents, the associates, the brief life he has lived so far—all of which means he cannot be considered guilty in the same way as an adult?

It is true that the suffering of the victims calls for both justice and punishment. But to make the execution of the criminal a bloody retribution for the victim's pain is a return to the darkest practices of the past. Other forms of punishment exist. The criminal's death does not bring the victim back. It merely adds one death to another, and adds society's injustices to the horror of the crime.

When France abolished the death penalty in 1981 and I gave the guillotine to a museum, there were 35 abolitionist nations in the world. Today, there are 108, *de facto* and *de jure*, among the 189 that belong to the U.N. Therefore, I ask my American friends: Where is your place in the world, you who aspire to assume its leadership, not just militarily and technologically, but also morally and culturally? Among the democrats who have banned the death penalty? Or alongside totalitarian China and fanatical Iran?

VOCABULARY

In your journal, write the meanings of the following words:

- the *Americanophile* (**1**)
- in the *abolitionist* countries (**2**)
- crimes are more *atrocious* (**4**)
- should *suffice* in a democratic society (**4**)
- not only racist but *inegalitarian* (**5**)
- the rate of *prejudicial* error (**5**)
- some have been saved *in extremis* (**5**)
- I gave the *guillotine* to a museum (**8**)
- *de facto* and *de jure* (**8**)

PROFESSIONAL   WRITING

DEATH AND JUSTICE

John O'Sullivan

Of the many controversies swirling around the death penalty, whether *1* or not Tim McVeigh's execution should be observed by the relatives of his victims is the most misleading. For it subtly discredits capital punishment by implying that it is a form of private revenge for the benefit of the victims' families.

Admittedly there is a link between justice and revenge. Bacon expressed it well when he described revenge as "a kind of wild justice." *2* When we move; from a state of nature to a civilized society, however, we give up our rights of self-protection and revenge in return for the state's promise of justice and retribution. And McVeigh's execution is the expression of that public retribution rather than of private revenge.

The eighteenth century took this view even further, holding that *3* public retribution required a public execution. As Dr. Johnson pointed out, this gave a certain dignity to the condemned man who was visibly paying for his crimes. He would sometimes make a speech of repentance and admonition from the gallows: "Friends, be warned by my fate. Here is the dreadful consequence of a life of crime. I go now to seek mercy from the God who will judge us all. Pray for my wretched soul. Etc."

We no longer hold public executions because we think ourselves *4* more civilized. In fact, we may merely be more squeamish. Restricting the seats at an execution to a victim's family is arguably less justifiable than a public gallows. For it treats a man's death not as an awesome punishment for a terrible crime but as a means of emotional compensation for those he has injured. Retributive justice is thus replaced by therapeutic revenge—a step toward our sentimental modernity but away from a civilized rule of law.

Of course, some argue that the death penalty is uncivilized by its very nature. But the death penalty, like all formal legal punishments, is a sign of civilization. It is to civilization what lynching, vendettas, and vigilantism are to barbarism and anarchy. Those who describe capital punishment as "barbaric" are generally defining "civilization" and "barbarism" quite arbitrarily to mean whatever they like or dislike. Thus when they say, "The death penalty is uncivilized," their words should be translated as "We don't like the death penalty." That is not a statement about reality, nor a logical argument, but a pure expression of preference.   5

To be sure, some undoubtedly civilized European nations have abandoned the death penalty in favor of other punishments in the last few decades. But the political elites in those countries usually did so over majority public opposition. What that demonstrates is not that Europe is more civilized than the U.S. but that it is less democratic.   6

So we come finally to the argument that the death penalty is a cruel and unnecessary punishment offensive to religious (and specifically Christian) morality. In recent years something like this view has been adopted by no less a figure than Pope John Paul II. This has raised difficult questions for Catholics (and indeed other Christians) who have thus far supported capital punishment.   7

They will be helped through the theological thickets by a fine article in the April issue of the religious magazine, *First Things*, by the newly created Cardinal Avery Dulles (the son of John Foster Dulles.) Cardinal Dulles agrees with the Pope. But because the death penalty is a question that mixes both moral and secular prudential judgments, he also makes room for conscientious disagreement by Catholics after prayerful consideration of the Church's teaching.   8

The Cardinal's strongest points, as it seems to me, are that the death penalty should not be imposed, first, if there is a serious risk of wrongful execution and, second, if the legitimate purposes of punishment can be equally well achieved by imprisonment. He feels that these considerations override the traditional Christian endorsement of capital punishment. But do they?   9

Take miscarriages of justice first. The number of known wrongful executions is tiny and the legal safeguards against them are so strict that very few murderers ever reach the electric chair. The last federal   10 execution, for instance, took place 38 years ago. Above all, the arrival of DNA—which has both exonerated some people on Death Row and increased public nervousness about capital punishment—ensures that the already low risk of wrongful execution will now be reduced still further. Since there was a risk of wrongful execution down the centuries when the Church supported capital punishment, our recent progress to a lesser risk strengthens the case for it.

Nor can imprisonment effectively mimic the death penalty for the *11* very clear reason that it is less final. Some murderers are imprisoned, released, and able to murder again. As Professor Paul G. Cassell pointed out in his testimony to the House Judiciary Committee in 1993: "Of the roughly 52,000 state prison inmates serving time for murder in 1984, an estimated 810 had previously been convicted of murder and had killed 821 persons following those convictions. Executing each of these inmates following their initial murder conviction would have saved 821 innocent lives."

Nor does life without parole entirely solve this problem: Five of the *12* murders were committed in prison. Again, we have no reason to think that in the modern world imprisonment safeguards us as effectively as capital punishment.

Where Cardinal Dulles does persuade me is in rejecting public *13* executions on the grounds that, in our debased *Survivor* and MTV culture, they would quickly be transformed from an awesome deterrent into bloodthirsty Roman spectacles—unless, final irony, the death penalty is abolished even as our society spirals downwards into a new sort of barbarism which mingles casual cruelty with sentimentality and moral self-congratulation.

VOCABULARY

In your journal, write down the meanings of the following words:

- public *retribution* (**2**)
- a speech of repentance and *admonition* (**3**)
- *retributive* justice (**4**)
- barbarism and *anarchy* (**5**)
- secular *prudential* judgments (**8**)
- *exonerated* some people on Death Row (**10**)

QUESTIONS FOR WRITING AND DISCUSSION

1. What exactly is Edward Koch's thesis or overall claim? Find one or two sentences from his essay that clearly express his thesis. In paragraph 13, Koch says, "the state has rights that the private individual does not." Why is this statement important for Koch's thesis? Explain.

2. Where does Robert Badinter state his thesis most clearly? How is his thesis related to the fact that he is French and is responsible for abolishing the death penalty in France?

3. Is John O' Sullivan for or against the death penalty? What conditions would capital punishment have to meet in order for him to support it? Where does he state his conditional position most clearly?

4. Edward Koch's essay follows a classical argumentative organization. Look at the six-part classical structure in the "Shaping" section of this chapter. Does Koch's essay follow the classical sequence outlined there (Introduction, Narration, Partition, Argument, Refutation, and Conclusion)? How does he revise or adapt this structure?

5. Compare the organization of Badinter's and O'Sullivan's essays. Which of the elements of a classical organization does each essay use? Where does each essay consider opposing positions and counter them with reasons and evidence?

6. Argumentative essays use appeals to reason, character, and emotion. Review all three essays, looking for examples of each of these appeals by all three writers. Which writer is most logical? Which writer uses appeals to character most frequently? Are these appeals effective? Finally, find examples of appeals to emotion by all three writers. Which appeals are most effective and which are too emotional?

7. Evaluate all three essays based on their use of supporting evidence. Find examples, if you can, of statistics, specific references to crimes or criminals, and comparisons or analogies used by each writer. Which writer's evidence most effectively supports his argument?

8. In the preface to these essays, you were asked to consider how the *context* for the writing of each essay helped determine each writer's argument. Explain the influence that the writing context—the events occurring during the time of the writing of the essay, the writer's own occupation and experiences, and the place of publication—had on the argument of each writer.

9. On the Internet, use your browser or a database such as Electric Library to find more recent articles on capital punishment. Print

out three or four of the most interesting articles and bring them to class. Be prepared to summarize the argument in each essay and to discuss how the new essays add to the conversation created in the three essays by Koch, Badinter, and O'Sullivan. What arguments are still being debated? What new perspectives do these articles bring to the discussion?

10. Consider the arguing essay that you are currently writing. Keeping your own particular context, purpose, and audience in mind, should you use Edward Koch's classical organization? How do you intend to respond to opposing or alternative viewpoints? Should you use all three kinds of appeals (to reason, to character, and to emotion)? What personal experiences, specific examples, statistics, quotations from authorities, and comparisons could you use?

Arguing: The Writing Process ●●●

■ ASSIGNMENT FOR ARGUING   For this assignment, choose a subject that interests you or relates to your own experience. You may even choose a subject that you have already written about for this class. Then examine the subject for a debatable claim of fact, value, cause and effect, or policy that you could make about it. If the claim is arguable, you have a focus for your arguing paper. Analyze your probable audience to guide your argumentative strategy. (Avoid ready-made pro-con subjects such as abortion, drinking age, drugs, and euthanasia *unless* you have clear beliefs based on your own experience.)

Arguments can appear in a wide range of genres, depending on your purpose and audience. Letters to the editor, essays for a college class, postings to an Internet forum, scripts for a debate, and political documents use the strategies of argument. Sometimes, as in the Mike Royko essay in this chapter, a dialogue can form the basis of an argument. As you select your topic, consider what audience and genre would most effectively meet the assignment, purpose, and audience.

CHOOSING A SUBJECT

If a journal entry suggested a possible subject, do the collecting and shaping strategies. Otherwise, consider the following ideas:

- Review your journal entries from previous chapters and the papers that you have already written for this class. Test these subjects for an arguable

You can write about anything, and if you write well enough, even the reader with no intrinsic interest in the subject will become involved.

—TRACY KIDDER,
NOVELIST

claim that you could make, opposing arguments you could consider, and an appropriate audience for an argumentative piece of writing.

- Brainstorm possible ideas for argumentative subjects from the other courses you are currently taking or have taken. What controversial issues in psychology, art, philosophy, journalism, biology, nutrition, engineering, physical education, or literature have you discussed in your classes? Ask current or past instructors for possible controversial topics relating to their courses.
- Newspapers and magazines are full of controversial subjects in sports, medicine, law, business, and family. Browse through current issues or on-line magazines looking for possible subjects. Check news items, editorials, and cartoons. Look for subjects related to your own interests, your job, your leisure activities, or your experiences.
- Interview your friends, family, or classmates. What controversial issues are affecting their lives most directly? What would they most like to change about their lives? What has irritated or angered them most in the recent past?

COLLECTING

NARROWING AND FOCUSING YOUR CLAIM   Narrow your subject to a specific topic, and sharpen your focus by applying the "Wh" questions. If your subject is "grades," your responses might be as follows.

Subject: Grades
- *Who:* College students
- *What:* Letter grades
- *When:* In freshman and sophomore years
- *Where:* Especially in nonmajor courses
- *Why:* What purpose do grades serve in nonmajor courses?

Determine what claim or claims you want to make. Make sure that your claim is *arguable*. (Remember that claims can overlap; an argument may combine several related claims.)

Claim of Fact
- Letter grades exist. (not arguable)
- Employers consider grades when hiring. (slightly more arguable, but not very controversial)
- Grades do not measure learning. (very arguable)

Claim About Cause or Effect
- Grades create anxiety for students. (not very arguable)
- Grades actually prevent discovery and learning. (arguable)

Claim About Value

- Grades are not fair. (not very arguable: "fairness" can usually be determined)
- Grades are bad because they discourage individual initiative. (arguable)
- Grades are good because they give students an incentive to learn. (arguable)

Claim About a Solution or Policy

- Grades should be eliminated altogether. (arguable—but difficult)
- Grades should be eliminated in humanities courses. (arguable)
- Grades should change to pass/fail in nonmajor courses. (arguable—and more practical)

Focusing and narrowing your *claim* helps determine what evidence you need to collect. Use your observing, remembering, reading, and investigative skills to gather the evidence. *Note:* An argumentative essay should not be a mathematical equation that uses only abstract and impersonal evidence. *Your experience* can be crucial to a successful argumentative essay. Start by doing the *remembering* exercises. Your audience wants to know not only why you are writing on this particular *topic*, but also why the subject is of interest to *you*.

REMEMBERING   Use *freewriting, looping, branching*, or *clustering* to recall experiences, ideas, events, and people who are relevant to your claim. If you are writing about grades, brainstorm about how *your* teachers used grades, how you reacted to specific grades in one specific class, how your friends or parents reacted, and what you felt or thought. These prewriting exercises will help you understand your claim and give you specific examples that you can use for evidence.

OBSERVING   If possible for your topic, collect data and evidence by observing, firsthand, the facts, values, effects, or possible solutions related to your claim. *Repeated* observation will give you good inductive evidence to support your argument.

INVESTIGATING   For most argumentative essays, some research or investigation is essential. Because it is difficult to imagine all the valid counterarguments, interview friends, classmates, family, coworkers, and authorities on your topic. From the library, gather books and articles that contain arguments in support of your claim. ***Note:*** As you do research in the library, make photocopies of key passages from relevant sources to hand in with your essay. If you cite sources from your research, list them on a "Works Cited" page following your essay. (See Chapter 12 for the proper format.)

As you begin your shaping activities, reconsider your audience. Imagine one real person who might be among your readers. Is this person open-minded and likely to be convinced by your evidence? Does this person represent the opposing position? Would a Rogerian strategy be effective in this case? Reread your collecting notes and *underline* the reasons and evidence that would be most effective for this reader. After reconsidering your audience and rereading your collecting notes, try the shaping strategies that follow.

No one can write decently who is distrustful of the reader's intelligence, or whose attitude is patronizing.
—E. B. WHITE,
ESSAYIST

LIST OF "PRO" AND "CON" ARGUMENTS   Either on paper or in a computer file, write out your *claim*, and then list the arguments for your position (pro) and the arguments for the opposing positions (con). After you have made the list, match up arguments by drawing lines, as indicated. (On the computer file, move "Con" column arguments so they appear directly opposite the corresponding "Pro" column arguments.)

Claim: Grades should be changed to pass/fail in nonmajor courses.

PRO	CON
Grades inhibit learning by putting too much emphasis on competition	Grades actually promote learning by setting students to study as hard as possible.
Pass/fail grading encourages students to explore nonmajor fields.	Students should be encouraged to compete with majors. They may want to change majors and need to know if they can compete.
Grade competition with majors in the field can be discouraging.	
Some students do better without the pressure of grades; they need to find out if they can motivate themselves without grades, but they shouldn't have to risk grades in their major field to discover that.	If students don't have traditional grading, they won't take nonmajor courses seriously.

If some pro and con arguments "match," you will be able to argue against the con and for your claim at the same time. If some arguments do not "match," you will need to consider them separately. The outlines below suggest ways of organizing your arguments.

OUTLINES FOR ARGUMENTS   For more than two thousand years, writers and speakers have been trying to determine the most effective means to persuade audiences. One of the oldest outlines for a successful argument comes from classical rhetoric. The following six-part outline is intended as a guideline rather than a rigid list. Test this outline; see if it will work for *your* argument.

Introduction:	Announces subject; *gets audience's interest and attention*; establishes a trustworthy character for the writer
Narration:	Gives *background*, context, statement of problem, or definition
Partition:	States thesis or *claim*, outlines or *maps* arguments
Argument:	Makes *arguments* and gives *evidence* for the claim or thesis
Refutation:	Shows why *opposing arguments* are not true or valid
Conclusion:	Summarizes arguments, suggests solution, *ties into the introduction or background*

Most arguments have these features, but not necessarily in this order. Some writers prefer to respond to or refute opposing arguments before giving the arguments in support of their claims. When con and pro arguments match, refuting an argument followed by the argument for your claim may work best. As you organize your own arguments, put your strongest argument last and your weakest argument either first or in the middle.

Because most short argumentative essays contain the introduction, narration, and partition all in a few introductory paragraphs, you may use the following abbreviated outlines for argument:

Outline 1	Introduction (attention getter, background, claim or thesis, map)
	Your arguments
	Refutation of opposing arguments
	Conclusion
Outline 2	Introduction
	Refutation of opposing arguments
	Your arguments
	Conclusion
Outline 3	Introduction
	Refutation of first opposing argument that matches your first argument
	Refutation of second opposing argument that matches your second argument, and so on
	Additional arguments
	Conclusion

For Rogerian arguments, you can follow one of the above outlines, but the emphasis, tone, and attitude are different:

Introduction:	Attention getter, background
	Claim (often downplayed to reduce threat)
	Map (often omitted)
	Appeal to character (crucial to Rogerian argument)
Opposing arguments:	State opposing arguments fairly
	Show where, how, or when those arguments may be valid; establish common ground
Your arguments:	State your position fairly
	Show where, how, or when your arguments are valid
Resolution:	Present compromise position
	State your solution to the problem, and show its advantages to both sides

DEVELOPING ARGUMENTS   Think of your argument as a series of *because* statements, each supported by evidence, statistics, testimony, expert opinion, data, specific examples from your experience, or a combination of these.

Thesis or Claim: Grades should be abolished in nonmajor courses

Reason 1	Because they may keep a student from attempting a difficult nonmajor course
	Statistics, testimony, data, and examples
Reason 2	Because competition with majors in the field can be discouraging
	Statistics, testimony, data, and examples
Reason 3	Because grades inhibit students' learning in nonmajor fields
	Statistics, testimony, data, and examples

You can develop each reason using a variety of strategies. The following strategies may help you generate additional reasons and examples:

Definition:	Define the crucial terms or ideas. (What do you mean by *learning?*)
Comparison:	Compare the background, situation, and context with another similar context. (What other schools have tried pass/fail grading for nonmajor courses? How has it worked?)
Process:	How does or should a change occur? (How do nonmajors become discouraged? How should a school implement pass/fail in grading?)

These strategies may help you develop an argument coherently and effectively. If several strategies are possible, consider which would be most effective for your *audience*.

RESEARCH TIP

When you draft your arguing essay, don't let your citations or direct quotations overpower your own argument. Two tactics will keep you in control of your argument:

First, always avoid "unidentified flying quotations" by *sandwiching* your quotations. *Introduce* quotations by referring to the author, the source, and/or the author's study. *Follow* quotations with a sentence explaining how the author's evidence supports your argument. For examples, see paragraphs 4 and 5 in the essay by student writer Crystal Sabatke at the end of this chapter.

Second, keep your direct quotations *short*. If possible, reduce a long passage to one sentence and incorporate the quoted material in the flow of your own language. For example, in her essay at the end of this chapter, Sabatke writes,

> According to Ruth Conniff, author of "Big Bad Welfare: Welfare Reform Politics and Children," the welfare reform discussion "indicates that what happens to children doesn't matter to Americans, so long as mothers are forced to work" (8).

DRAFTING

You will never really know "enough" about your subject or have "enough" evidence. At some point, however, you must stop collecting and start your draft. The most frequent problem in drafting an argumentative essay is delaying the actual writing too long, until the deadline is too close.

For argumentative essays, start with a working order or sequence and sketch an outline on paper or in your head. Additional examples and appeals to reason, character, or emotion may occur to you as you develop your argument or refute opposing arguments. In addition, if you have done some research, have your notes, photocopies of key data, statistics, quotations, and citations of authorities close at hand. As you write, you will discover that some information or arguments simply don't fit into the flow of your essay. Don't force arguments into your draft if they no longer seem to belong.

REVISING

Argumentation is the most public of the purposes for writing. It requires that you become aware of many different points of view. You must counter the arguments of others and recognize the flaws in your own logic. Test your argument by having friends or classmates read it. Explain your claim, your focus, and your intended audience. Ask your readers to look for possible opposing arguments that you need to counter or weaknesses in your own argument or evidence. Were your appeals effective? Ask your readers if your argument should be more adversarial or more Rogerian.

Guidelines for Revision

- **When you finish your draft, reconsider your *audience*.** Persuading your audience requires that you tailor your reasons and evidence to your audience and situation. Do an audience analysis, and then reread your draft and make appropriate changes.
- **Ask a class member or friend to read your draft to determine the intended audience for your argument.** See which arguments your reader thinks would not be effective for your audience.
- **Ask your reader to tell you what kind of *claim* you are making, whether your arguments or counterarguments are logical, and whether your ethical or emotional appeals are effective for your audience.**
- **Which of your *because* arguments are most effective?** Least effective? Should you change the outline or structure that you initially chose?
- **Revise your draft to avoid fallacies or errors in reasoning.** Errors in logic create two problems: They can destroy your rational appeal and open your argument to a logical rebuttal, and they lessen your credibility—and thus reduce your appeal to your character. (Review the list of fallacies below.)
- **Support your reasons with evidence: *data, facts, statistics, quotations, observations, testimony, statistics,* or *specific examples from your experience*.** Check your collecting notes once again for additional evidence to add to your weakest argument. Is there a weak or unsupported argument that you should simply omit?
- **Signal the major arguments and counterarguments in your partition or map.** Between paragraphs, use clear transitions and paragraph hooks.
- **If you cite sources in your essay, check the *accuracy* of your statistics, quotations, and source references.** (See Chapter 12 for the proper format of in-text documentation and the "Works Cited" page.)
- **Revise sentences to improve conciseness and clarity.**
- **Edit sentences for grammar, punctuation, and spelling.**

PEER RESPONSE

Writer: Before you exchange drafts with a peer reader, provide the following information about your essay:

1.
   a. Intended audience
   b. Primary claim or thesis
   c. Opposing arguments that you refute
   d. Arguments supporting your claim

2. Write out one or two questions about your draft that you want your reader to answer.

Reader: Read the writer's entire draft. As you reread, answer the following questions:

1. *Arguments.* Without looking at the writer's responses above, describe the essay's (a) target audience, (b) primary claim, (c) opposing arguments that are refuted, (d) arguments supporting the claim. Which of these did you have trouble identifying? What additional pro or con arguments should the writer consider?

2. *Organization.* Identify the following parts of the writer's draft: introduction, narration, partition, argument, refutation, and conclusion. Does the writer need all of these for his or her particular subject and audience? Why or why not? Where could the writer clarify transitions between sections? Explain.

3. *Appeals.* Identify places where the writer appeals to reason, to character, and to emotion. Where could these appeals be stronger? Identify sentences where the writer is overly emotional or illogical (see the section "Revising Fallacies in Logic").

4. *Evidence.* Identify at least one paragraph in which the supporting evidence is strong. Then identify at least one paragraph in which the writer makes assertions without sufficient supporting evidence. What kind of evidence might the writer use—firsthand observation, personal examples, testimony from experts, interviews, statistics, or other? Explain.

5. *Revision plan.* List three key changes that the writer should make during the revision.

6. Answer the writer's questions.

(continued on next page)

(continued from previous page)

Writer: When your essay is returned, read the comments by your peer reader(s) and do the following:

1. Compare your descriptions of the audience, claim, and pro and con arguments with your reader's descriptions. Where there are differences, clarify your essay.

2. Read all of your peer reader's responses. List revisions that you intend to make in each of the following areas: *arguments, organization, appeals,* and *supporting evidence.*

Revising Fallacies in Logic

Listed below are common fallacies in logic. Reread your draft or your peer's draft and revise as appropriate to eliminate these logical errors.

- *Hasty generalization:* Conclusion not logically justified by sufficient or unbiased evidence. If your friend Mary tells you that Professor Paramecium is a hard grader because he gave her a 36 percent on the first biology test, she is making a hasty generalization. It may be *true*— Prof P. may *be* a difficult grader—but Mary's logic is not valid. She cannot logically draw that conclusion from a sample of one; the rest of the class may have received grades of between 80 and 100.

- *Post hoc ergo propter hoc:* Literally, "after this, therefore because of this." Just because Event B *occurred after* Event A does not mean that A *necessarily caused* B. You washed your car in the morning, and it rained in the afternoon. Though we joke about how it always rains after we wash the car, there is, of course, no causal relationship between the two events. "I forgot to leave the porch light on when I went out last night, and someone robbed my house": Without further evidence, we cannot assume that the lack of light contributed to the robbery. A more obvious cause might be the back door left unlocked.

- *Genetic fallacy:* Arguing that the origins of a person, object, or institution determine its character, nature, or worth. Like the post hoc fallacy, the genetic fallacy is an error in causal relationships.

    This automobile was made in Detroit. It'll probably fall apart after 10,000 miles.

    He speaks with a funny German accent. He's really stupid, you know.

    He started Celestial Seasonings Herb Teas just to make a quick buck; it's just another phony yuppie product.

The second half of each statement *may* or *may not* be true; the logical error is in assuming that the origin of something will necessarily determine its worth or quality. Stereotyping is frequently caused by a genetic fallacy.

- *Begging the question:* Loading the conclusion in the claim. Arguing that "pornography should be banned because it corrupts our youth" is a logical claim. However, saying that "filthy and corrupting pornography should be banned" is begging the question: The conclusion that the writer should *prove* (that pornography corrupts) is assumed in the claim. Other examples: "Those useless psychology classes should be dropped from the curriculum"; "Senator Swingle's sexist behavior should be censured by Congress"; "Everyone knows that our ineffective drug control program is a miserable failure." The writers must *prove* that the psychology classes are useless, that Senator Swingle is sexist, and that the drug program is a failure.

- *Circular argument:* A sentence or argument that restates rather than proves. Thus, it goes in a circle: "President Reagan was a great communicator because he had that knack of talking effectively to the people." The terms in the beginning of the sentence (*great communicator*) and the end of the sentence (*talking effectively*) are interchangeable. The sentence ends where it started.

- *Either/or:* An oversimplification that reduces alternatives to only two choices, thereby creating a false dilemma. Statements such as "Love it or leave it" attempt to reduce the alternatives to two. If you don't love your school, your town, or your country, you don't have to leave: A third choice is to change it and make it better. Proposed solutions frequently have an either/or fallacy: "Either we ban boxing or hundreds of young men will be senselessly killed." A third alternative is to change boxing's rules or equipment. "If we don't provide farmers with low-interest loans, they will go bankrupt." Increasing prices for farm products might be a better alternative.

- *Faulty comparison or analogy:* Basing an argument on a comparison of two things, ideas, events, or situations that are similar but not identical. Although comparisons or analogies are often effective in argument, they can hide logical problems. "We can solve the cocaine problem the same way we reduced the DWI problem: Attack it with increased enforcement and mandatory jail sentences." Although the situations are similar, they are not identical. The DWI solution will not necessarily work for drugs. An analogy is an extended comparison that uses something simple or familiar to explain something complex or less familiar. "Solving a mathematics problem is like baking a cake: You have to take it one step at a time. First, you assemble your ingredients or your known data. . . . " Like baking, solving a problem does involve a process; unlike baking, however, mathematics is more exact. Changing the amount of flour in a recipe by 1 percent will not make the cake fall; changing a numeric value by 1 percent, however, may ruin the whole problem. The point, however, is not to avoid comparisons or analogies. Simply make sure that your conclusions are qualified; acknowledge the *differences* between the two things compared as well as the similarities.

- *Ad hominem (literally, "to the man"):* An attack on the character of the individual or the opponent rather than his or her actual opinions, arguments, or qualifications: "Susan Davidson, the prosecuting attorney, drinks heavily. There's no way she can present an effective case." This is an attack on Ms. Davidson's character rather than an analysis of her legal talents. Her record in court may be excellent.

- *Ad populum (literally, "to the people"):* An emotional appeal to positive concepts (God, mother, country, liberty, democracy, apple pie) or negative concepts (fascism, atheism) rather than a direct discussion of the real issue: "Those senators voting to increase the defense budget are really warmongers at heart." "If you are a true American, you should be for tariffs to protect the garment industry."

- *Red herring and straw man:* Diversionary tactics designed to avoid confronting the key issue. *Red herring* refers to the practice of dragging a smelly fish across the trail to divert tracking dogs away from the real quarry. A red herring occurs when writers avoid countering an opposing argument directly: "Of course equal pay for women is an important issue, but I wonder whether women really want to take the responsibility that comes with higher-paying jobs. Do they really want the additional stress?" This writer diverts attention away from the argument about equal pay to another issue, stress—thus, a red herring. In the *straw man* diversion, the writer sets up an artificially easy argument to refute in place of the real issue. Former President Richard Nixon's famous "Checkers" speech is a good example. Accused of spending $18,000 in campaign gifts for personal use, Nixon described how he received Checkers, a little black-and-white spotted cocker spaniel dog. Because his daughter Tricia loved this dog, Nixon decided to keep it. Surely, there's nothing wrong with that, is there? The "Checkers" argument is a "straw man" diversion: Justifying his personal use of this gift was much easier than explaining how and why he spent the $18,000. Avoid red herring and straw man tactics by either refuting an argument directly or acknowledging that it has some merit. Don't just change the subject.

■ POSTSCRIPT ON THE WRITING PROCESS   In your journal, answer the following questions:

1. Describe how your beliefs about your subject changed from the time you decided on your claim to when you revised your essay. What caused the change in your views?

2. What opposing argument was most difficult to counter? Explain how you handled it.

3. Which was your strongest argument? Did you use logical appeals and evidence, or did you rely more on appeals to character or emotion? Explain.
4. How did your writing process for the argumentative essay change from the process for your previous essays? What steps or stages took longer? What stages did you have to go back and rework?

WELFARE IS STILL NECESSARY FOR WOMEN AND CHILDREN IN THE U.S.

Crystal Sabatke

Crystal Sabatke decided to write her arguing essay about changes in the welfare system that require women to work in order to receive certain welfare payments. She decided to focus particularly on readers who believe that welfare mothers will simply become lazy if they don't have to work for the money to support their families. She hopes that "by showing examples of positive welfare stories, I can show that mothers and their children are more important than saving a few cents per dollar." Reproduced below are Sabatke's notes for her audience analysis, her rough draft, the responses to her peer review workshop, and her final, revised draft.

Audience Analysis: Readers' Beliefs

My readers will assume that women on welfare who have children can go out and get jobs. That they should get jobs for the betterment of themselves and their children. That when they do get a job, their financial problems will be solved and that welfare will be a thing of the past. In order to shake these assumptions, I believe that emotional appeals should be used. Examples of factual women on welfare in negative situations that prevent them from getting jobs—children, low-income wage jobs, etc.

My readers also believe in the principle of a strong work ethic, the idea that if you work hard, you can achieve the "American Dream." I do feel that I should show how this principle is not applicable in certain situations—ones that my readers probably do not take into strong consideration.

Finally, I feel that my readers blindly value getting jobs more than taking care of children (even though these are the same people who hypocritically focus on family values). I think that family values should be focused on because this is something that is held in high regard by nearly every human being.

WELFARE IN THE UNITED STATES—A NECESSITY WITHOUT PROGRAMMING

First Draft

What defines an American woman? Women in the United States play numerous roles; many are successful executives, mothers, wives, and scholars. Women have broken many barriers throughout U.S. history and have become, in general, a very successful group in society. But what about the women who haven't broken the barriers? What about the women who had children at a young age with a boyfriend or husband who left them alone soon after? What about the women who can't find a job because their education level hinders their prosperity? What about the women who can't seem to find their way above the poverty level and have to seek help from the government?

Throughout the United States, poverty is not abnormal—especially for women and children. With "44.6 percent of the children who lived in [female-headed households] poor in 1994, and almost half of all children who are poor living in female-headed households," (A) doesn't it seem ironic that the government is cutting welfare expenditures for women and children? Many government officials believe that "the welfare system and its recipients are the cause of the problem." (B) What the lawmakers aren't considering, however, is that poverty is essentially the catalyst in a circle of controversy, and that the only way out of the problems is to provide adequate educational opportunities for welfare recipients, along with ample child care programs and options and a sufficient minimum wage for all citizens. The answer is not ending welfare, but dealing with the problems of poverty in a realistic manner.

In contrast to opposing arguments, most women aren't poor and having children because they want more welfare money or because they are lazy, but because they don't have a sufficient education. As Nicholas Zill, a writer for *Public Health Reports*, states, "Girls and boys who become parents while they are still of school age are . . . predominantly those with low test scores and grades, who are disengaged from school or in active conflict with parents, teachers, or school authorities." (C) The government needs to provide for all Americans an education system that works not only for the successful student, but also for the students that are not doing well. Female students, especially, should be educated about birth control and negative outcomes of having children at younger ages. We should not be punishing and impeding children for the mistakes of their parents and the deficiencies of our education system. Welfare is indispensable for uneducated women and their children until a system of education and support can be initiated and proven successful.

For people opposing government assistance of the poor, another popular argument is that welfare needs to be ended in all forms, and women with children need to get jobs. According to Charles Murray, a strong oppressor of the welfare system in America and an advocate of family values, a "strict job program" needs to be established that will force women to "drop out of a welfare program altogether." (D) Essentially, to the opposition, "the welfare-reform discussion indicates that what happens to children doesn't matter to Americans, so long as mothers are forced to work." (E) Unfortunately, however, for women with children who either decide to go into or are forced into the job market, there isn't a child care system that works with mothers to make a "strict job program" successful. The truth is, there is a scarcity of child care options in this country, and the ones that are available are generally out of the price range of a welfare mother. Shouldn't children be put foremost in this debate? If our country is really focused on family values, shouldn't women have the option to stay home and give their children good care even if it means keeping them on welfare? Welfare is essential in providing a means for women to provide not only adequate care for their children, but positive values for their future.

Another category of women on welfare who are quite often overlooked are those mothers who have minimum-wage jobs and who still need government assistance. The current method of getting women into the workplace is the Job Training Partnership Act, or "the Government's biggest training program." (E) According to *The Wall Street Journal*, however, this program, which offers low-wage jobs such as fast food "is a sham" (E) and "actually led to lower wages for poor young women compared with a control group." (E) Once a woman is in the workplace, it is easy to assume that she will be removed from welfare and become an effective member of society. What is not taken into consideration, however, is that a minimum wage can hardly keep up with the needs of a single mother. "The average [welfare] recipient who gets a full-time job . . . makes $6.74 an hour—about $14,000 a year. Daycare for two children can easily cost $12,000." (E) It is obvious that after subtracting child care, this equation leaves a mother with virtually nothing left to provide herself and her children with necessities such as food, clothing, and shelter. The answer is clearly not to simply put women in low-wage-earning jobs. Until Washington can come up with a solution that involves education and child care assistance and has raised the minimum wage enough to support a mother with children, a welfare system still needs to be provided.

The answer is not ending welfare, but providing supplemental programs that can realistically assist a single mother. With the minimum wage being too low, child care costs being impractical, and education programs virtually nonexistent, it is not fair to assume that welfare can be abolished. Of course, there are problems with the current welfare system, but supplemental programming is the only way to effectively change these glitches.

Arguing Essay: Peer-Response Worksheet

To the Writer: Briefly describe the audience for this paper. (Be sure to include your audience's position on the issue you're writing about.) Also note what you want your readers to focus on as they read.

My audience is white, conservative males who are against any welfare. Please comment on my development—and I kind of gave up on my conclusion. How can I make it better?

To the Reader: Answer the following questions:

1. Underline the *claim/thesis*. Is it clear? Make suggestions for improvement.

    Bev: Good thesis. It is clear and placed in a good spot, just after enough background and before the bulk of the paper. However, I would elaborate more on the "realistic manner" either in your thesis sentence or a separate sentence.

    Amy: *The thesis is very clear—however, the sentence after it confused me.*

2. Is the claim adequately *focused*—narrow within manageable/defensible limits? Why or why not? Explain.

    Bev: The claim is well focused and clear.

    Amy: *Possibly even too focused. Reads more like an essay map than a thesis.*

3. Do you feel the writer needs to add any *qualifiers* or exceptions in order to avoid overgeneralizing? If yes, explain.

    Bev: You sort of overgeneralize about women on welfare, but not too noticeably. Maybe some statistics concerning these women would help.

    Amy: *Possibly qualify for 2 parent and singles—see paragraph #5.*

4. Does the paper deal with *opposing arguments*? How successful do you feel the paper is in conceding and/or refuting opposing arguments? Explain.

    Bev: Good job of laying out the opposing sides of the argument.

Amy: *Opposition clearly stated each time and then refuted. No work needed on the ones you have stated. Does not take into consideration two-parent welfare families or singles. Will some of your claims work for them as well?*

5. Does the *evidence* support the reasons? Where is more evidence needed? What kind of evidence is needed?

   Bev: Your use of evidence is effective. However, I would suggest more evidence in the first body paragraph. You only have one quotation—maybe throw another one in there.

   Amy: *More statistics would be helpful, for example, test scores as related to teen pregnancy.*

6. What are *one* or *two* areas that you feel the writer should address *first* in revising this paper? What suggestions can you make for conducting those revisions?

   Bev: Good organization of the paper. You follow a clear layout and it is easy to follow. I would develop your quotations more in paragraph 2. You use good evidence. Just develop it more. In your conclusion, maybe if you tied it into the intro, it would help you out. Restate arguments that you made in the introduction.

   Amy: *The lead paragraph seems to give an essay map but doesn't. Possibly phrase some of the questions to relate to the paragraphs? Conclusion: Instead of summing up what you said, try an analysis of the problem and its solutions.*

7. Return the paper to the writer and discuss your comments.

Final Draft

WELFARE IS STILL NECESSARY FOR WOMEN AND CHILDREN IN THE U.S.

What defines an American woman? Women in the United States play 1 numerous roles; many are successful executives, mothers, wives, and scholars. Women have broken many barriers throughout U.S. history and have become, in general, a very successful group in society. But what about the women who haven't broken the barriers? What about the women who had children at a young age with a boyfriend or husband who left them soon after? What about the women who can't find a job because their education level hinders their prosperity? What about the women who can't seem to find their way above the poverty level and have to seek help from the government?

   In the United States, poverty is not abnormal—especially for 2 women and children. With "44.6 percent of the children who lived in [female-headed households] in 1994, and almost half of all children who are poor living in female-headed households," doesn't it seem ironic that the government continues to cut welfare expenditures for women and children? (Wellstone 1). Many government officials believe that "the welfare system and its recipients are the cause of the problem" (Rank 1). What these lawmakers aren't considering, however, is that poverty is essentially the catalyst in a circle of controversy, and that the only way out of the problem is to provide adequate educational opportunities for welfare recipients, ample child care programs and options, and a sufficient minimum wage for all citizens. Until methods such as these are instituted, it is necessary for the government to maintain a supportive welfare system for the women and children of our country.

In refutation of opposing arguments, most women aren't poor and having children because they want more welfare money or because they are lazy, but because they don't have a sufficient education. As Nicholas Zill, a writer for *Public Health Reports*, states, "Girls and boys who become parents while they are still of school age are . . . predominantly those with low test scores and grades, who are disengaged from school or in active conflict with parents, teachers, or school authorities" (6). Recent studies by the National Center for Health Statistics show that "nearly one in every four children in the U.S. is born to a mother who has not finished high school" (Zill 2). The government needs to provide an educational system that focuses not only on the successful student, but also on the student who is performing poorly. Because "parent education is linked to children's economic well-being," positive programs need to be created that provide support and alternatives to mainstream education for students who are "high risk" or are not college-bound (Zill 3). Female students, specifically, should be educated about birth control and the negative consequences of having children at younger ages. Until our nation takes active measures to improve the educational system, welfare is necessary to support the children who are born because of the inadequacies of our schools. America should not be punishing and impeding children for the mistakes of their parents and the deficiencies of our school system. Welfare is indispensable for uneducated women and their children until a better system of education and support can be initiated and proven successful.

Another popular argument given by people who oppose welfare is that single women with children should be working, not accepting welfare. According to Charles Murray, a strong critic of the welfare system, we need to institute a "strict job program" that will force women to "drop out of welfare altogether" (285). According to Ruth Conniff, author of "Big Bad Welfare: Welfare Reform Politics and Children,"

3

4

the welfare reform discussion "indicates that what happens to children doesn't matter to Americans, so long as mothers are forced to work" (8). Unfortunately, however, for single women with children who either decide to work or are forced into the job market, there isn't a child care system that could make a "strict job program" successful (Murray 285). With child care costing "about $116 a week for a toddler and $122 for an infant," not only is American day care economically insensitive, but day care options are limited as well (Conniff 8). According to Mark Robert Rank, author of "Winners and Losers in the Welfare Game," the "scarcity of affordable child care for low-income families" makes the current welfare system in this country a "losing game" (1). How can women be expected to get jobs when there aren't sufficient means to care for their children? Ruth Conniff wonders that if our country "is so concerned about family values, wouldn't it make sense to let mothers stay home with their young children?" (8). Welfare is essential to provide means for women to supply not only adequate care for their children but also positive values for their children's future.

Another category of women on welfare who are quite often over- 5
looked are those mothers who have minimum-wage jobs and who still need government assistance. The current method of getting women into the work place is the Job Training Partnership Act, or "the Government's biggest training program" (Conniff 5). According to *The Wall Street Journal*, however, this program—which offers low-wage jobs such as fast-food work—has "actually led to lower wages for poor young women compared with a control group" (Conniff 5). Once a woman is in the workplace, many people assume that she will be removed from welfare and become an independent member of society. What is not considered, however, is that the minimum wage can scarcely keep up with the needs of a single mother. According to a survey done of welfare recipients in Dane County, Wisconsin, "the average [welfare] recipient who gets a full-time job . . . makes $6.74 an hour—about $14,000 a year. Day care for two children can easily cost $12,000" (Conniff 7). It is obvious that after subtracting child care costs, this equation leaves a mother with virtually nothing left to provide herself and her children with necessities such as food, clothing, and shelter—making it necessary to stay on government assistance. Until the minimum wage has been raised to keep up with these strenuous living situations, Washington needs to continue providing welfare to help single mothers and their children survive.

One of the many roles that American women assume is often that 6
of a poverty-stricken single mother. With current education programs that are not effective for "high-risk" women students, with child care costs that are overwhelming, and with a minimum wage so low that it

can't keep up with the needs of single mothers, it is not fair to assume that welfare can be abolished. As Michelle Tingling Clement of National Public Radio states, "What [women] truly need is . . . education, skills development . . . and not just any job but jobs that pay living wages with family health benefits and child care" (2). Until programs that can realistically assist women and children are created, welfare is still a definite necessity.

Works Cited

Clement, Michelle T. "Republicans Finalize Welfare Reform Package." *All Things Considered*. National Public Radio. 15 Nov. 1998. Transcript.

Conniff, Ruth. "Big Bad Welfare: Welfare Reform Politics and Children." *The Progressive* 84 (1994): 1–10.

Murray, Charles. "Keeping Priorities Straight on Welfare Reform." *The Aims of Argument*. Ed. Timothy W. Crucius and Carolyn E. Channell. Mountain View, CA: Mayfield, 1998. 285–88.

Rank, Mark Robert. "Winners and Losers in the Welfare Game." Editorial. *St. Louis Post-Dispatch* 15 Sept. 1994: 1–2.

Wellstone, Paul. "If Poverty Is the Question." *The Nation Digital Edition* 4 Apr. 1997. 10 Oct. 1998 <http://www.thenation.com>.

Zill, Nicholas. "Parental Schooling and Children's Health." *Public Health Reports* 111 (1996): 1–10.

QUESTIONS FOR WRITING AND DISCUSSION

1. Sabatke says that her audience consists of white, conservative males who believe that everyone should have a job and no one should be on welfare. Where in her essay does she address this audience? Could she revise her essay to focus on this audience even more specifically? Explain.

2. Read Sabatke's first draft and then the responses by Bev and Amy on the peer-response sheet. Which of Bev's and/or Amy's suggestions do you agree with? What other suggestions might you give Sabatke? Which of the peer-response suggestions does Sabatke take or ignore in her final draft? How might Sabatke have improved her final version even more? Explain.

3. What opposing arguments does Sabatke consider? Choose one of her responses, and explain why you think the counterargument is or is not effective. Think of one additional counterargument that she might consider. Should she address that argument? Why or why not?

4. At what points in her essay should Sabatke give additional evidence? Should she use more statistics about welfare mothers? Should she give a more specific description of the current welfare system? Should she give evidence from case studies of welfare recipients? Explain your choices.

Standardized Tests: Shouldn't We Be Helping Our Students

Eric Boese

As standardized testing has increased in the nation's high schools in recent years, so have the attacks against these tests. Several universities have followed the University of California's lead and deemphasized the SAT test. High school tests, such as the Texas TAAS, California's Stanford 9, Minnesota's MJCA, or Colorado's CSAP, have come under fire because they seem to punish the poorer school districts mainly for having insufficient funds to compete with the wealthy suburban schools. Eric Boese, a student at Colorado State University, decided to write about the problems created by these standardized tests. His purpose, he explains, is to persuade his readers—primarily politicians who set testing policies—that "the use of standardized tests in the education system has to be changed."

Over the past few decades our nation's school systems have progressed 1 with leaps and bounds. We have seen improvements in textbooks, technology, teacher resources, and so much more. The opportunities for children to excel going through primary education are enormous, greater now than they have ever been. Still we see so many children being held back. Funds are being used inefficiently, and our priorities have become a little mixed up. I'm talking about what it is that we actually teach in primary schools. Are we teaching students skills and giving them knowledge that will make them better members of society or have we decided that it is more important to teach kids how to do well on tests? The answer to this question you may not like, but it is an answer that we can do something about.

To begin working on a solution, we should first locate the source 2 of the problem. As I have said, everything in the world of education is changing, and I have seen that there is one change in particular can go a long way towards explaining, and solving, our problem. This change is in the use of standardized tests. They have become a more important and more destructive component of our schools. Of course I'm not suggesting that we throw the tests out, for they can be a vital part of education. I hope to show how the current use of these tests is harming the educational process and show how we can use them in a more productive manner in the future.

Over the last ten years in Texas some interesting things have happened. The first was that, in 1990, an exam called the Texas Assessment of Academic Skills (TAAS) was administered for the first time in a number of schools (Weisman). The test was given in grades three through eight and was used as an exit exam early in school. A lot of stress was placed on this test because it was used to determine the longevity of the careers of teachers and administrators. Their jobs depended on the success of their students in taking the exam. In 1994 George W. Bush, the test's biggest supporter, mandated that it be administered statewide. Over six years, the pass rate of the test increased in all student populations (Weisman). The test appeared to be a huge success.

George W. Bush credited the better scores to the test challenging students to do better. I, however, credit it to how the test changed the way the schools function. An alarming article by Jonathan Weisman reviews just this case. He shows how improvements on the TAAS are not correlated to improvements on other standardized tests that were given to the same students. While the TAAS scores went up, the other scores did nothing. The biggest revelation in his article is when he explains why students raised their test scores on that exam and not on others. What he found was that teachers were teaching them how to take the exam. Student learning was compromised because too much stress was put on teachers to make sure their students scored well. Jonathan Weisman knows this to be true:

> In a study published by the Harvard Civil Rights Project in January, Professors Linda McNeil of Rice University and Angela Valenzuela of the University of Texas delivered a scathing assessment of the TAAS's impact on Texas classrooms, asserting that "behind the rhetoric of the test scores are a growing set of classroom practices in which test-prep activities are usurping a substantive curriculum."

Of course it didn't really take experts to figure this out anyone involved in the classrooms of these schools knew that was going on:

Teachers protested that they were spending eight to ten hours a week in test-preparation drills and that their principals were pressuring them to spend even more. Only 27 percent said they believed the rising TAAS scores reflected increased learning and higher-quality teaching; half said the scores indicated nothing of the sort. (Weisman)

This is a situation that is simply unacceptable. Endorsing tests that have these kinds of side effects is pumping out graduating classes of test takers. It's causing students to become less capable of meeting challenges that will face them in college and in the future. Texas isn't the only place this is taking place, but it is a great example of the way our nation's schools will turn out if we allow the use of these tests to continue to spread.

In Texas there are still other factors that cause the test scores to be   5 misleading. There was legislation that allowed schools to exempt special-ed students from taking the test. The number of exemptions increased during the years that the test was administered (Weisman). From this we see that the students aren't even improving as much on the tests as the figures show.

The fact that students score better on this kind of exam reveals   6 nothing about their personal improvements. If used differently, however, the exams could be much more effective in meeting students' needs and less destructive of their education. We could eliminate undue stress on teachers and create better evaluations of students' abilities.

In other places than Texas, standardized tests are being used in   7 counterproductive ways. The biggest problem seems to be that the tests have too much riding on them. In her article "Test Case: Now the Principal's Cheating," Carolyn Kleiner gives some examples of how the stakes of standardized tests have been raised:

Twenty-eight states now use standard exams to determine graduation and 19 to govern student promotion; a growing number also dole out performance-based bonuses for schools that show progress and threaten intervention, even closure, for those that don't.

Kleiner links the growing importance of the tests to an inevitable side effect, cheating. Of course there are more ways that tests have grown in importance, and yes, more downfalls. The results of standardized tests can have impacts on the jobs of teachers and principals, the money they will make, the reputation of a school or district, and the high school graduation rates. The scores can also affect school funding and various different community issues. People would rather send their children to school somewhere that has a reputation for scoring well on exams and that doesn't have funding problems. In extreme cases, test results can have effects on the property values of residents in a district. George Madaus notes that the test results "don't provide a full picture of a child's—or a school's—accomplishments" and says that "You can't use these tests by themselves to make any decisions" (Kantrowitz et al.). The tests have, however, been used to determine a number of the things above, and as a result, some drawbacks of the tests are that they affect student learning in the classroom, and they cause great stress to students and teachers.

In "Schools for Scandal," Thomas Toch and Betsy Wagner discuss   8
how standardized tests have ultimately led to a problem of educators cheating. The problem of cheating has been one that, until recently, involved students breaking the rules. The new problem we are seeing is that teachers and even principals have started to help their students cheat on some tests. Why would they do this, you ask? It's similar to the situation in Texas—high stakes tests put pressure on them. They are pressured by administrators, principals, and parents alike, all of whom want to see the students get good scores for their own benefit. For parents, good scores are expected, and they see them as being equivalent to their students' doing well in school. In other words, if they see that a school has scored poorly on any given test, they see it as a failure on the part of the school, a further incentive for schools to improve their scores.

It's not something may of us want to hear, but the need for high   9
scores has caused many school officials to encourage cheating as well as raise their school's score by any means possible. "In a national survey of educators in 1990, 1 in 11 teachers reported pressure from administrators to cheat on standardized tests" (Toch and Wagner). On top of the pressures of cheating, there is almost nothing stopping teachers from giving out answers. In most common standardized tests, security monitoring is minimal, answers are available to test givers (who are usually the teachers), and tests are used multiple times. This makes it easy for teachers not only to cheat, but to teach the material that they know will be covered on any given test. Researchers in Colorado found that tests scores dropped dramatically from a first test that teachers had the time to prepare their students for and a very similar test given only a few weeks later. University of Colorado testing expert Lorrie Shepard said, "Teachers are not teaching students skills and concepts. . . . They are teaching specific examples by rote memorization" (Toch and Wagner).

Due to cheating and various other issues, standardized tests reveal   10
less accurate scores each year. In other words, tests are getting worse at

what they were designed to do: measure skill levels of students. The reason, Toch and Wagner mention, is that people want high scores. Many tests that challenge students are not being used by schools simply because they yield low scores. The basic skills covered by these tests are inflating scores and forcing teachers to focus on teaching remedial skills and not on the needs of the individual students. In "Education: Is that Your Final Answer?," Jodie Morse gives an example in which the problem is even worse:

> Educators say they have had to dumb down their lessons to teach the often picayune factoids covered by the exams. A study released last month by the University of Virginia found that while some schools had boosted their performance on Virginia's exam, teachers had to curtail field trips, elective courses and even student visits to the bathroom—all in an effort to cram more test prep into the school day. Says the study's author, education professor Daniel Duke: "These schools have become battlefield units."

Causing practices like these to occur in our nation's schools is unjustifiable. The inflation of scores doesn't stop there; tests are being reused to a point where most schools can manage to do very well on them. This creates a false impression of students' skills. The U.S. Department of Education agreed that "with respect to national averages, [school] districts and states are presenting inflated results and misleading the public." How can somebody defend a policy that diminishes the education of students for tests that don't accurately reflect student achievement or, in some cases, even challenge them to think on their own?

So far we have considered some of the many effects of our current testing system. It is equally important to review exactly what materials the tests cover and whether or not they are testing the right things. First of all, 80 percent of standardized tests used in America are produced by corporations (Toch and Wagner). Who says corporations know what should be on these tests in the first place? The relevancy and difficulty of tests are determined by people who have little or no concern for their effects on schools. They are not held accountable for the material covered on their exams and do not feel that security is their concern. Often-times, the corporations will make the materials on their tests easier because more schools will buy tests that make themselves look good. In other cases, the corporations simply don't know what to include in their tests for different grade levels. A side effect of corporations writing tests is that they usually recycle their tests and so they rarely "allow schools to return copies of their graded exams to students so they, and their teachers, might learn from their mistakes" (Toch and Wagner). Of the students I surveyed, none claimed that they had ever even learned their own scores on school-mandated standardized tests, and none claimed that they learned anything substantial from the exams that they had taken. On many exams, questions relating to students' advanced-thinking skills are almost nonexistent. Corporations are just not giving tests that are beneficial to students. This is the first change we need to make: either make the corporations answer to a selected group of educational officials or have somebody make tests that have the student in mind.

Along the same lines as above, we need to throw out the tests that are too difficult for students of any particular age group. Only a few people actually oppose this argument. New York State Education Commissioner Richard Mills said that "subjecting 9-year-olds to tests they can't pass is one of the strategies to change things for the better" (Ohanian). I wish somebody would explain this to me. Is this supposed to make students want to work harder because they failed miserably or is it going to discourage them? This may not be an opinion that is held by too many people, but it sure seems to be in some cases. In some states, like Massachusetts for example, students are required to take tests that can last up to 18 hours in order to graduate from high school. We can't expect this much of students who are only 18 years old; not many of them would be able to pass such a test if their classes weren't so focused on preparing them for it, and as we have seen, test preparation often adversely affects student learning.

A level of testing has to be found such that students will be challenged and yet they will not be overwhelmed. Standardized tests should include materials relevant to a student's grade level, some materials that would require the student to explore new ideas, and some questions designed to test a student's advanced-thinking skills. This test would cover materials that would be included in a normal school curriculum and therefore would take up less class time. A teacher could concentrate on students' needs again, and classes could cover more material, explore subjects more deeply and give students the education they deserve. There would be time to do more of what one student claims to love most about school, "getting into great conversations and developing ideas" (Selzer). A test that fits these criteria would give a more accurate evaluation of the student's skills and of the student's potential to succeed in higher-level and college courses. Such a test may not be easy to make, but it would definitely be worth the effort.

It's getting harder and harder to see the positive side of using *14* today's standardized tests. Not only are the tests giving inaccurate evaluations of students' skills, but they are causing corruption in our schools and diminishing the opportunities for educational excellence of our students. I've discussed ideas for new tests that could be used, but that is not enough to make up for the disturbances involved with the importance of the tests. It is my opinion that we cannot allow these tests to undermine the current system. First of all, funding should not be determined by scores; it should be determined by need. Taxpayers in any given region would also be able to vote to increase funding for the schools that they support. I mentioned that, in Texas, for teachers and administrators the tests held an additional, personal importance. Determining who holds these positions needs a more personal evaluation than looking at test scores. We need to look at how their students are really improving and the effort they put into their students' education.

I'm sure that the public will still have the bias that their students *15* should be getting the best scores, but this is an issue that will have to be faced. They need to be shown that the test scores are a sign for teachers to read to determine the extra attention that some students may require, and this is what the test should be used for. There is no greater purpose for having these tests than for improving education. Many of the problems of the current system will prove to be very difficult to resolve, but any steps towards a new system are ones for the better.

It may all sound difficult now, but the state of our schools is in *16* desperate need of change. Pushing for more tests as so many people are doing is not the answer. I urge you to consider how bright children are being discouraged by an unproductive testing system and to be the person who puts the needs of the children first.

Works Cited

Kantrowitz, Barbara, Daniel McGinn, Ellise Pierce, and Erika Check. "When Teachers Are Cheaters." *Newsweek* 19 June 2000. 15 Apr. 2001 <http://www.elibrary.com>.

Kleiner, Carolyn. "Test Case: Now the Principal's Cheating." *U.S. News and World Report* 12 June 2000. 10 Apr. 2001 <http://www.elibrary.com>.

Morse, Jodie. "Education: Is That Your Final Answer?" *Time* 19 June 2000. 15 Apr. 2001 <http://www.elibrary.com>.

Ohanian, Susan. "Editorials: Standardized Schools." *The Nation* 18 Sep. 1999. 10 Apr. 2001 <http://www.elibrary.com>.

Selzer, Adam. "High-Stakes Testing: It's Backlash Time." *U.S. News & World Report* 3 Apr. 2000. 15 Apr. 2001 <http://www. usnews.com/usnews/issue/000403/education.htm>.

Toch, Thomas, and Betsy Wagner. "Schools for Scandal." *U.S. News & World* Report 27 Apr. 1992. 10 Apr. 2001 <http://www. elibrary.com>.

Weisman, Jonathan. "Only a Test." *The New Republic* 10 Apr. 2000. 15 Apr. 2001 <http://www.thenewrepublic.com/041000/ weisman041000.html>.

VOCABULARY

In your journal, write down the meanings of the following words:

- determine the *longevity* of the careers of teachers **(3)**
- test-prep activities are *usurping* a *substantive* curriculum **(4)**
- a further *incentive* **(8)**
- teach the often *picayune factoids* **(10)**
- preparation often *adversely* affects student learning **(12)**

QUESTIONS FOR WRITING AND DISCUSSION

1. In your journal, write three short paragraphs explaining your own experience with standardized tests. First, which tests have you taken, and when did you take them? Next, what was the purpose of the tests—to evaluate you or your school? Finally, describe the effect of these tests on your own education. Did they detract from the regular curriculum? Did they give you motivation and incentive to learn? Did they help you get into college?

2. Eric Boese uses a problem-solving format for his arguing essay. Which paragraphs describe the problems with standardized tests? List these problems. Which paragraphs indicate his solutions? What are his solutions? Is his essay clear or would you give him suggestions for improving his organization? Explain.

3. Boese writes that the intended audience for his essay is politicians who are in favor of increased use of standardized tests. Where does Boese address this audience? Where and how could he make his

appeal to this audience even stronger? Write out actual sentences Boese could add to his essay.

4. On the Internet, read more recent articles on standardized testing. Has testing in high schools changed since Boese wrote his essay in 2001? Do more or fewer high schools give mandated tests? Has the quality of the tests improved? Do students and teachers like or dislike these tests? Explain.

Berthe Morisot, French, 1841–1895. *La Lecture (Reading)*, *1888*. Oil on canvas, 1888, 29.25 × 36.5. Museum of Fine Arts, St. Petersburg, Florida. Given in memory of Margaret Acheson Stuart by family and friends.

Chapter 11 Responding to Literature

In a film class, you watch Roman Polanski's *Tess*, an adaptation of Thomas Hardy's novel *Tess of the D'Urbervilles*. You decide to compare the film with the novel, focusing on four key episodes: the "strawberry scene," in which Tess meets Alec; the rape scene at night; the harvesting scene; and the final scene at Stonehenge. On the basis of your comparison, you argue that Polanski's interpretation (and the acting of Nastassia Kinski) retains Hardy's view of Tess as a victim of social and sexist repression.

In an Introduction to Literature class, you and a friend are assigned to work collaboratively on an essay about Eudora Welty's "A Worn Path." You are both interested in how Phoenix Jackson's journey contains images of the phoenix: a mythological bird said to live for five hundred years, after which it burns itself to death and then rises from its ashes to become youthful and beautiful again. You draft your essays separately and then read each other's drafts. At that point, you collaborate on a single essay, combining the best ideas and evidence from your separate drafts. Your collaborative essay shows how Phoenix Jackson is characterized by birdlike images, how she calmly faces images of fire and death on her journey, and how her grandson represents her rebirth.

I hungered for new books, new ways of looking and seeing. It was not a matter of believing or disbelieving what I read, but of feeling something new, of being affected by something that made the look of the world different.

—RICHARD WRIGHT,

AUTHOR OF BLACK BOY

No one else can read a literary work for us. The benefits of literature can emerge only from creative activity on the part of the reader.

—LOUISE ROSENBLATT,

AUTHOR OF LITERATURE AS EXPLORATION

ESPONDING TO LITERATURE REQUIRES THAT READERS PARTICI-
PATE IMAGINATIVELY WHILE THEY READ A LITERARY WORK,
REREAD TO SEE HOW THE PARTS OF THE WORK RELATE TO THE
whole, and share their interpretations of a piece of literature with
other readers.

First, readers must *imagine* and recreate that special world described by the writer. The first sentences of a short story, for example, throw open a door to a world that—attractive or repulsive—tempts our curiosity and imagination. Like Alice in *Alice in Wonderland*, we cannot resist following a white rabbit with pink eyes who mutters to himself, checks his watch, and then zips down a rabbit hole and into an imaginary world.

Here are three opening sentences of three very different short stories:

> Young Goodman Brown came forth at sunset into the street at Salem village; but put his head back, after crossing the threshold, to exchange a parting kiss with his young wife.
>
> —Nathaniel Hawthorne, "Young Goodman Brown"

> As Gregor Samsa awoke one morning from uneasy dreams he found himself transformed in his bed into a gigantic insect.
>
> —Franz Kafka, "The Metamorphosis"

> The morning of June 27th was clear and sunny, with the fresh warmth of a full-summer day; the flowers were blossoming profusely and the grass was green.
>
> —Shirley Jackson, "The Lottery"

Whether our imaginations construct the disturbing image of a "gigantic insect" or the seemingly peaceful picture of a perfect summer day, we actively recreate each story. Responding to literature does not mean passively reacting to the writer's story. As readers, we should anticipate, imagine, feel, worry, and question. A story is like an empty balloon that we must inflate with the warm breath of our imagination and experience. Our participation makes us partners with the author in the artistic creation.

Responding to literature also requires that readers *reread*. If we read a story or a poem only once, we have misunderstood the whole point of literature. Great literature is worthy of study because the more we reread, the more we learn and discover. If we assume that the purpose of a story is merely to entertain us or to provide a moment's diversion, then we should stick to television sitcoms written for an audience of couch potatoes who want only predictable, unimaginative plots and canned studio laughter.

Rereading requires two distinct but related operations. First, you should *reread for yourself*, that is, reread to write down your ideas, questions, feelings, and reactions. To heighten your role in creating a story, you should note, in the margins, your questions and responses to important events, main characters, bits of description, and images that catch your attention: "What about the names Hawthorne uses? Is Young Goodman Brown really good? Is his wife, Faith, really faithful?" "I don't understand why Kafka's narrator thinks he is a gigantic insect. Is this happening, or is he dreaming?" "Why does Shirley Jackson's lottery happen on such a beautiful summer day?" Don't just underline or highlight passages. Actually *write* your responses in the margin.

Second, you should *reread with a writer's eye*. In fiction, identify the main and minor characters. Look for and note the conflicts between characters. Mark passages that contain *foreshadowing*—that urge you to think ahead imaginatively. Pinpoint sentences that reveal the narrative point of view. Use the appropriate critical terms (*character, plot, conflict, point of view, setting, style,* and *theme*) to help you reread with a writer's eye and to see how the parts of a story relate to the whole. Each critical term is a tool—a magnifying glass that helps you understand and interpret the story more clearly.

In addition to rereading, responding to literature requires that readers *share* ideas, reactions, and interpretations. Sharing usually begins in small-group or class discussions, but it continues as you explain your interpretation in writing. A work of literature is not a mathematical equation with a single answer. Great literature is worth interpreting precisely because each reader responds differently. The purpose of literature is to encourage you to reflect on your life and the lives of others—to look for new ways of seeing and understanding your world—and ultimately to expand your world. Sharing is crucial to appreciating literature.

> Hawthorne doesn't come right out and say that people become disillusioned by experiencing evil. He shows how it actually happens in the life of young Goodman Brown.

> Shirley Jackson's "The Lottery" helps me see that the notion of human sacrifice and the idea of the human scapegoat still exist in our culture today.

Writing about your responses and sharing them with other readers helps you "reread" your own ideas in order to explain them fully and clearly to other readers.

■ RESPONDING TO A SHORT STORY   Read and respond to Kate Chopin's "The Story of an Hour." Use your imagination to help create the story as you read. Then *reread* the story, noting in the margin your questions and responses. When you finish rereading and annotating your reactions, write your interpretation of the last line of the story.

PROFESSIONAL   WRITING

THE STORY OF AN HOUR
Kate Chopin

Kate O'Flaherty Chopin (1851–1904) was an American writer whose mother was French and Creole and whose father was Irish. In 1870, she moved from St. Louis to New Orleans with her husband, Oscar Chopin, and over the next ten years she gave birth to five sons. After her husband died in 1882, Chopin returned to St. Louis to begin a new life as a writer. Many of her best stories are about Louisiana people and places, and her most famous novel, The Awakening, *tells the story of Edna, a woman who leaves her marriage and her children to fulfill herself through an artistic career.*

Knowing that Mrs. Mallard was afflicted with a heart trouble, great care was taken to break to her as gently as possible the news of her husband's death. 1

It was her sister Josephine who told her, in broken sentences, veiled hints that revealed in half concealing. Her husband's friend Richards was there, too, near her. It was he who had been in the newspaper office when intelligence of the railroad disaster was received, with Brently Mallard's name leading the list of "killed." He had only taken the time to assure himself of its truth by a second telegram, and had hastened to forestall any less careful, less tender friend in bearing the sad message. 2

She did not hear the story as many women have heard the same, with a paralyzed inability to accept its significance. She wept at once, with sudden, wild abandonment, in her sister's arms. When the storm of grief had spent itself she went away to her room alone. She would have no one follow her. 3

There stood, facing the open window, a comfortable, roomy armchair. Into this she sank, pressed down by a physical exhaustion that haunted her body and seemed to reach into her soul. 4

She could see in the open square before her house the tops of trees that were all aquiver with the new spring life. The delicious breath of rain was in the air. In the street below a peddler was crying his wares. The notes of a distant song which someone was singing reached her faintly, and countless sparrows were twittering in the eaves. 5

There were patches of blue sky showing here and there through the clouds that had met and piled one above the other in the west facing her window. 6

She sat with her head thrown back upon the cushion of the chair   *7*
quite motionless, except when a sob came up into her throat and shook
her, as a child who has cried itself to sleep continues to sob in its dreams.

She was young, with a fair, calm face, whose lines bespoke re-   *8*
pression and even a certain strength. But now there was a dull stare in
her eyes, whose gaze was fixed away off yonder on one of those patches of blue sky. It was not a glance of reflection, but rather indicated a
suspension of intelligent thought.

There was something coming to her and she was waiting for it,   *9*
fearfully. What was it? She did not know; it was too subtle and elusive
to name. But she felt it, creeping out of the sky, reaching toward her
through the sounds, the scents, the color that filled the air.

Now her bosom rose and fell tumultuously. She was beginning to   *10*
recognize this thing that was approaching to possess her, and she was
striving to beat it back with her will—as powerless as her two white
slender hands would have been.

When she abandoned herself a little whispered word escaped her   *11*
slightly parted lips. She said it over and over under her breath: "Free,
free, free!" The vacant stare and the look of terror that had followed it
went from her eyes. They stayed keen and bright. Her pulses beat fast,
and the coursing blood warmed and relaxed every inch of her body.

She did not stop to ask if it were not a monstrous joy that held her.   *12*
A clear and exalted perception enabled her to dismiss the suggestion
as trivial.

She knew that she would weep again when she saw the kind, ten-   *13*
der hands folded in death; the face that had never looked save with love
upon her, fixed and gray and dead. But she saw beyond that bitter moment a long procession of years to come that would belong to her absolutely. And she opened and spread her arms out to them in welcome.

There would be no one to live for during those coming years; she   *14*
would live for herself. There would be no powerful will bending her in
that blind persistence with which men and women believe they have
a right to impose a private will upon a fellow creature. A kind intention or a cruel intention made the act seem no less a crime as she looked
upon it in that brief moment of illumination.

And yet she had loved him—sometimes. Often she had not. What   *15*
did it matter! What could love, the unsolved mystery, count for in face
of this possession of self-assertion which she suddenly recognized as
the strongest impulse of her being.

"Free! Body and soul free!" she kept whispering.   *16*

Josephine was kneeling before the closed door with her lips to the   *17*
keyhole, imploring for admission. "Louise, open the door! I beg; open

the door—you will make yourself ill. What are you doing, Louise? For heaven's sake open the door."

"Go away. I am not making myself ill." No; she was drinking in a very elixir of life through that open window.   *18*

Her fancy was running riot along those days ahead of her. Spring days, and summer days, and all sorts of days that would be her own. She breathed a quick prayer that life might be long. It was only yesterday she had thought with a shudder that life might be long.   *19*

She arose at length and opened the door to her sister's importunities. There was a feverish triumph in her eyes, and she carried herself unwittingly like a goddess of Victory. She clasped her sister's waist, and together they descended the stairs. Richards stood waiting for them at the bottom.   *20*

Someone was opening the front door with a latchkey. It was Brently Mallard who entered, a little travel-stained, composedly carrying his grip-sack and umbrella. He had been far from the scene of accident, and did not even know there had been one. He stood amazed at Josephine's piercing cry; at Richards's quick motion to screen him from the view of his wife.   *21*

But Richards was too late.   *22*

When the doctors came they said she had died of heart disease— of joy that kills.   *23*

Techniques for Responding to Literature

As you read and respond to a work of literature, keep the following techniques in mind.

- **Understanding the assignment and selecting a possible purpose and audience.** Unless stated otherwise in your assignment, your purpose is to *interpret* a work of literature. Your audience will be other members of your class, including the teacher.
- **Actively reading, annotating, and discussing the literary work.** Remember that literature often contains *highly condensed experiences*. In order to give imaginative life to literature, you need to reread patiently both the major events and the seemingly insignificant passages. In discussions, look for the differences between your responses and other readers' ideas.
- **Focusing your essay on a single, clearly defined interpretation.** In your essay, clearly state your main idea or thesis, focusing on a *single* idea or aspect of the piece of literature. Your thesis should *not be a*

statement of fact. Whether you are explaining, evaluating, or arguing, your interpretation must be clearly stated.

- **Supporting your interpretation with evidence.** Because your readers will probably have different interpretations, you must show which specific characters, events, conflicts, images, or themes prompted your response, and you must support your interpretation. *Do not merely retell the major events of the story—your readers have already read it.*

■ WARMING UP: JOURNAL EXERCISES   Read all of the following questions and then write for five minutes on two or three. These questions should clarify your perceptions about literature and develop your specific responses to "The Story of an Hour."

1. Describe a work of literature (a poem, short story, novel, or play) that you have read recently. Why did you read it? What did you like best about it? What did you not like about it?

2. On your bookshelves or in the library, find a short story or poem that you read at least six months ago. Before you reread it, write down the name of the author and the title of the work. Note when you read it last and describe what you remember about it. Then reread the story or poem. When you finish, write for five minutes, describing what you noticed that you did not notice the last time you read it.

3. Find a popular song whose lyrics describe a character and tell a story about that person. Listen to the recording and copy down the words. Compare it to Kate Chopin's "The Story of an Hour." Do the lyrics have the basic ingredients of short fiction (character, plot, point of view, setting, style, and theme)? Is it a miniature story? What elements does it lack?

4. Write out the *question* that "The Story of an Hour" seems to ask. What is your answer to this question? What might have been Kate Chopin's answer?

5. Read the "Responding to Short Fiction" section in this chapter. Review the descriptions of character, plot, point of view, setting, and style. Explain which of these terms and definitions best helps you find *evidence* in "The Story of an Hour" to answer the question that you identified in Question 4.

6. The words *heart, joy, free, life,* and *death* appear several times in "The Story of an Hour." Underline these words (or synonyms) each time they appear. Explain how the meaning of each of these words seems to *change* during the story. Is each word used ironically?

7. Write out a dictionary definition of the word *feminism*. Then write out your own definition. Is Mrs. Mallard a feminist? Is Kate Chopin a feminist? What evidence in the story supports your answers?

8. Kate Chopin's biographer, Per Seyersted, says that Chopin saw that "truth is manifold" and thus preferred not to "take sides or point a moral." Explain how "The Story of an Hour" does or does not illustrate Seyersted's observations.

9. Literature often expresses common themes or tensions, such as the individual versus society, appearance versus reality, self-knowledge versus self-deception, or civilization versus nature. Which of these themes are most apparent in "The Story of an Hour"? Explain your choices.

Purposes for Responding to Literature

In responding to literature, you should be guided by the purposes that you have already practiced in previous chapters. As you read a piece of literature and respond in the margin, begin by writing *for yourself.* Your purposes are to observe, feel, remember, understand, and relate the work of literature to your own life: What is happening? What memories does it trigger? How does it make you feel? Why is this passage confusing? Why do you like or dislike this character? Literature has special, personal value. You should write about literature initially in order to discover and understand its importance in your life.

When you write an interpretive essay, however, you are writing *for* others. You are sharing your experience in working with the author as imaginative partners in recreating the work. Your purposes will often be mixed, but an interpretive essay often contains elements of *explaining, evaluating, problem solving,* and *arguing.*

- **Explaining.** Interpretive essays about literature explain the *what, why,* and *how* of a piece of literature. What is the key subject? What is the most important event or character? What are the major conflicts or the key images? What motivates a character? How does a character's world build or unravel? How does a story meet or fail to meet our expectations? How did our interpretations develop? Each of these questions might lead to an interpretive essay that explains the *what, why,* and *how* of your response.
- **Evaluating.** Readers and writers often talk about "appreciating" a work of literature. *Appreciating* means establishing its value or worth. It may mean praising the work's literary virtues; it may mean finding faults or weaknesses. Usually, evaluating essays measure *both strengths and weaknesses,* according to specific criteria. What important standards for literature do you wish to apply? How does the work in question measure up? What kinds of readers might find this story worth reading? An evaluative essay cites evidence to show why a story is exciting, boring, dramatic, puzzling, vivid, relevant, or memorable.
- **Problem solving.** Writers of interpretive essays occasionally take a problem-solving approach, focusing on how the reader overcomes obstacles in understanding the story or how the author of a story solved problems in writing key scenes, creating characters, setting a plot in motion, and creating and resolving conflicts. Particularly if you like to

write fiction yourself, you may wish to take the writer's point of view: How did the writer solve (or fail to solve) problems of setting, character, plot, or theme?

- **Arguing.** As readers share responses, they may discover that their interpretations diverge sharply from the ideas of other readers. Does "The Story of an Hour" have a "feminist" theme? Is it about women or about human nature in general? Is the main character admirable, or is she selfish? In interpretive essays, writers sometimes argue for their beliefs. They present evidence that refutes an opposing interpretation and supports their own reading.

Most interpretive essays about literature will be focused by these purposes, whether used singly or in combination. Writers should *select* the purpose(s) that are most appropriate for the work of literature and their own responses.

Responding to Short Fiction ● ● ●

RESPONDING AS A READER

Begin by noting in the margins your reactions at key points. *Summarize* in your own words what is happening in the story. Write down your *observations* or *reactions* to striking or surprising passages. Ask yourself *questions* about ambiguous or confusing passages. Following are examples written by students that illustrate all three kinds of responses.

Summary Comments

Mrs. Mallard is initially paralyzed by the news.

Mrs. Mallard feels her sister will protect her. She weeps in her sister's arms.

From the security of her chair, she stares at life outside her window.

Mrs. Mallard is young, but the lines on her face reveal repression.

Mrs. Mallard now feels "free, free, free" of the bonds of marriage.

News of her husband's death does not kill her, but news of his life does.

Observations and Reactions

Mrs. Mallard has "heart trouble"—possible double meaning.

Although Mrs. Mallard is experiencing shock and grief, outside her window the world is full of life.

The mistaken belief that men and women have a right to impose their will on others—this may be the point of the story.

Joy that kills = monstrous joy.

She does not die of the joy that kills—she dies of killed joy.

Questions

Why does the "storm" of grief come so quickly and then disappear?

She would live for herself: Is this selfishness or just a desire to be free?

Why does Chopin make Mrs. Mallard seem powerless, as though she is overcome by a fever?

Should we admire Mrs. Mallard for wanting her freedom?

Is this the story of an hour or the story of her life?

READING WITH A WRITER'S EYE

After you respond initially and make your marginal annotations, use the following basic elements of fiction to help you *analyze how the parts of a short story relate to the whole.* Pay attention to how setting or plot affects the character, or how style and setting affect the theme. Because analysis artificially separates plot, character, and theme, look for ways to *synthesize* the parts: Seeing how these parts relate to each other should suggest an idea, focus, or angle to use in your interpretation.

CHARACTER   A short story usually focuses on a *major character*—particularly on how that character faces conflicts, undergoes changes, or reveals himself or herself. *Minor characters* may be flat (one-dimensional), static (unchanging), or stereotyped. To get a start on analyzing character, diagram the *conflicts* between or among characters. Examine characters for motivation: What causes them to behave as they do? Is their behavior affected by *internal* or *external* forces? Do the major characters reveal themselves *directly* (through their thoughts, dialogue, and actions) or *indirectly* (through what other people say, think, or do)?

PLOT   *Plot* is the sequence of events in a story, but it is also the cause-and-effect relationship of one event to another. As you study a story's plot, pay attention to *exposition, foreshadowing, conflict, climax,* and *denouement.* To clarify elements of the plot, draw a time line for the story, listing in chronological order every event—including events that occur before the story opens. *Exposition* describes the initial circumstances and reveals what has happened before the story opens. *Foreshadowing* is an author's hint of what will occur before it happens. *Conflicts* within characters, between characters, and between characters and their environment may explain why one event leads to the next. The *climax* is the high point, the point of no return, or the most dramatic moment in a story. At the climax of a story, readers discover something important about the main character. *Denouement* literally means the "unraveling" of the complications and conflicts at the end of the story. In "The Story of an Hour," climax and denouement occur almost at the same time, in the last lines of the story.

NARRATIVE POINT OF VIEW   Fiction is usually narrated from either the first-person or the third-person point of view.

A *first-person narrator* is a character who tells the story from his or her point of view. A first-person narrator may be a minor or a major character. This character may be relatively *reliable* (trustworthy) or *unreliable* (naive or misleading). Although reliable first-person narrators may invite the reader to identify with their perspectives or predicaments, unreliable narrators may cause readers to be wary of their naive judgments or unbalanced states of mind.

A *third-person omniscient narrator* is not a character or participant in the story. Omniscient narrators are assumed to know everything about the characters and events. They move through space and time, giving readers necessary information at any point in the story. A *selective omniscient narrator* usually limits his or her focus to a single character's experiences and thoughts, as Kate Chopin focuses on Mrs. Mallard in "The Story of an Hour." One kind of selective omniscient point of view is *stream-of-consciousness narration*, in which the author presents the thoughts, memories, and associations of one character in the story. Omniscient narrators may be *intrusive*, jumping into the story to give their editorial judgments, or they may be *objective*, removing themselves from the action and the minds of the characters. An objective point of view creates the impression that events are being recorded by a camera or acted on a stage.

Reminder: As you reread a story, do not stop with analysis. Do not quit, for example, after you have identified and labeled the point of view. Determine how the point of view affects your reaction to the central character or to your understanding of the theme. How would a different narrative point of view change the story? If a different character told the story, how would that affect the theme?

SETTING   *Setting* is the physical place, scene, and time of the story. It also includes the social or historical context of the story. The setting in "The Story of an Hour" is the house and the room in which Mrs. Mallard waits, but it is also the social and historical time frame. *Setting is usually important for what it reveals about the characters, the plot, or the theme of the story.* Does the setting reflect a character's state of mind? Is the environment a source of tension or conflict in the story? Do changes in setting reflect changes in key characters? Do sensory details of sight, touch, smell, hearing, or taste affect or reflect the characters or events? Does the author's portrait of the setting contain images and symbols that help you interpret the story?

STYLE   *Style* is a general term that may refer to sentence structure and to figurative language and symbols, as well as to the author's tone or use of irony. *Sentence structure* may be long and complicated or relatively short and simple. Authors may use *figurative language* (Mrs. Mallard is described in "The Story of an Hour" as sobbing, "as a child who has cried itself to sleep continues to sob in its dreams"). A *symbol* is a person, place, thing, or event that suggests or signifies something beyond itself. In "The Story of an Hour," the open window and the new spring life suggest or represent Mrs. Mallard's new freedom. *Tone* is the author's attitude toward the characters, setting, or plot. Tone may be sympathetic, humorous, serious, detached, or critical. *Irony* suggests a double meaning. It occurs when the author or a character says or does one thing but means the opposite or something altogether different. The ending of "The Story of an Hour" is ironic: The doctors say Mrs. Mallard has died "of joy that kills." In fact, she has died of killed joy.

THEME   The focus of an interpretive essay is often on the *theme* of a story. In arriving at a theme, ask how the characters, plot, point of view, setting, and style *contribute* to the main ideas or point of the story. The theme of a story depends, within limits, on your reactions as a reader. "The Story of an Hour" is *not* about relationships between sisters, nor is it about medical malpractice. It is an ironic story about love, personal freedom, and death, but what precisely is the *theme*? Does "The Story of an Hour" carry a feminist message, or is it more universally about the repressive power of love? Is Mrs. Mallard to be admired or criticized for her impulse to free herself? Do not trivialize the theme of a story by looking for some simple "moral." In describing the theme, deal with the complexity of life recreated in the story.

PROFESSIONAL   WRITING

A WORN PATH
Eudora Welty

Eudora Welty was born in Jackson, Mississippi, in 1909 and earned degrees from Mississippi State College, the University of Wisconsin, and Columbia University. While she was writing short stories during the early 1930s, Welty held jobs with the Works Progress Administration, a Jackson radio station, and local newspapers. Like Flannery O'Connor and William

Faulkner, Eudora Welty wrote stories and novels set in the American South. Her first major publication, A Curtain of Green and Other Stories, *appeared in 1941 and was followed by three more collections of short stories. Her novels include* Delta Wedding *(1946) and* The Optimist's Daughter *(1972), which won a Pulitzer Prize. Welty's collection of reviews and essays,* The Eye of the Story *(1978), and her brief autobiography,* One Writer's Beginnings *(1984), provide insight into her fiction and her life.*

It was December—a bright frozen day in the early morning. Far out *1* in the country there was an old Negro woman with her head tied in a red rag, coming along a path through the pinewoods. Her name was Phoenix Jackson. She was very old and small and she walked slowly in the dark pine shadows, moving a little from side to side in her steps, with the balanced heaviness and lightness of a pendulum in a grandfather clock. She carried a thin, small cane made from an umbrella, and with this she kept tapping the frozen earth in front of her. This made a grave and persistent noise in the still air, that seemed meditative like the chirping of a solitary little bird.

She wore a dark striped dress reaching down to her shoe tops, and *2* an equally long apron of bleached sugar sacks, with a full pocket: all neat and tidy, but every time she took a step she might have fallen over her shoe-laces, which dragged from her unlaced shoes. She looked straight ahead. Her eyes were blue with age. Her skin had a pattern all its own of numberless branching wrinkles and as though a whole little tree stood in the middle of her forehead, but a golden color ran underneath, and the two knobs of her cheeks were illuminated by a yellow burning under the dark. Under the red rag her hair came down on her neck in the frailest of ringlets, still black, and with an odor like copper.

Now and then there was a quivering in the thicket. Old Phoenix *3* said, "Out of my way, all you foxes, owls, beetles, jack rabbits, coons, and wild animals! . . . Keep out from under these feet, little bob-whites. . . . Keep the big wild hogs out of my path. Don't let none of those come running my direction. I got a long way." Under her small black-freckled hand her cane, limber as a buggy whip, would switch at the brush as if to rouse up any hiding things.

On she went. The woods were deep and still. The sun made the *4* pine needles almost too bright to look at, up where the wind rocked. The cones dropped as light as feathers. Down in the hollow was the mourning dove—it was not too late for him.

The path ran up a hill. "Seem like there is chains about my feet, *5* time I get this far," she said, in the voice of argument old people keep to use with themselves. "Something always take a hold of me on this hill—pleads I should stay."

After she got to the top she turned and gave a full, severe look be-   6
hind her where she had come. "Up through pines," she said at length.
"Now down through oaks."

Her eyes opened their widest, and she started down gently. But be-   7
fore she got to the bottom of the hill a bush caught her dress.

Her fingers were busy and intent, but her skirts were full and   8
long, so that before she could pull them free in one place they were
caught in another. It was not possible to allow the dress to tear. "I in
the thorny bush," she said. "Thorns, you doing your appointed work.
Never want to let folks pass—no sir. Old eyes thought you was a pretty little green bush."

Finally, trembling all over, she stood free, and after a moment   9
dared to stoop for her cane.

"Sun so high!" she cried, leaning back and looking, while the thick   10
tears went over her eyes. "The time getting all gone here."

At the foot of this hill was a place where a log was laid across the   11
creek.

"Now comes the trial," said Phoenix.   12

Putting her right foot out, she mounted the log and shut her eyes.   13
Lifting her skirt, leveling her cane fiercely before her, like a festival
figure in some parade, she began to march across. Then she opened
her eyes and she was safe on the other side.

"I wasn't as old as I thought," she said.   14

But she sat down to rest. She spread her skirts on the bank around   15
her and folded her hands over her knees. Up above her was a tree in a
pearly cloud of mistletoe. She did not dare to close her eyes, and when
a little boy brought her a little plate with a slice of marblecake on it she
spoke to him. "That would be acceptable," she said. But when she went
to take it there was just her own hand in the air.

So she left that tree, and had to go through a barbed-wire fence.   16
There she had to creep and crawl, spreading her knees and stretching
her fingers like a baby trying to climb the steps. But she talked loudly to herself: she could not let her dress be torn now, so late in the day,
and she could not pay for having her arm or her leg sawed off if she got
caught fast where she was.

At last she was safe through the fence and risen up out in the   17
clearing. Big dead trees, like black men with one arm, were standing
in the purple stalks of the withered cotton field. There sat a buzzard.

"Who you watching?"   18

In the furrow she made her way along.   19

"Glad this not the season for bulls," she said, looking sideways,   20
"and the good Lord made his snakes to curl up and sleep in the

winter. A pleasure I don't see no two-headed snake coming around that tree, where it come once. It took a while to get by him, back in the summer."

She passed through the old cotton and went into a field of dead 21 corn. It whispered and shook and was taller than her head. "Through the maze now," she said, for there was no path.

Then there was something tall, black, and skinny there, moving 22 before her.

At first she took it for a man. It could have been a man dancing 23 in the field. But she stood still and listened, and it did not make a sound. It was as silent as a ghost.

"Ghost," she said sharply, "who be you the ghost of? For I have 24 heard of nary death close by."

But there was no answer—only the ragged dancing in the wind. 25

She shut her eyes, reached out her hand, and touched a sleeve. 26 She found a coat and inside that an emptiness, cold as ice.

"You scarecrow," she said. Her face lighted. "I ought to be shut 27 up for good," she said with laughter. "My senses is gone, I too old. I the oldest people I ever know. Dance, old scarecrow," she said, "while I dancing with you." She kicked her foot over the furrow, and with mouth drawn down, shook her head once or twice in a little strutting way. Some husks blew down and whirled in stream-ers about her skirts.

Then she went on, parting her way from side to side with the cane, 28 through the whispering field. At last she came to the end, to a wagon track where the silver grass blew between the red ruts. The quail were walking around like pullets, seeming all dainty and unseen.

"Walk pretty," she said. "This the easy place. This the easy going." 29

She followed the track, swaying through the quiet bare fields, 30 through the little strings of trees silver in their dead leaves, past cab-ins silver from weather, with the doors and windows boarded shut, all like old women under a spell sitting there. "I walking in their sleep," she said, nodding her head vigorously.

In a ravine she went where a spring was silently flowing through 31 a hollow log. Old Phoenix bent and drank. "Sweet-gum makes the water sweet," she said, and drank more. "Nobody know who made this well, for it was here when I was born."

The track crossed a swampy part where the moss hung as white 32 as lace from every limb. "Sleep on, alligators, and blow your bubbles." Then the track went into the road.

Deep, deep the road went down between the high green-colored 33 banks. Overhead the live-oaks met, and it was as dark as a cave.

A black dog with a lolling tongue came up out of the weeds by the   *34*
ditch. She was meditating, and not ready, and when he came at her
she only hit him a little with her cane. Over she went in the ditch, like
a little puff of milkweed.

Down there, her senses drifted away. A dream visited her, and she   *35*
reached her hand up, but nothing reached down and gave her a pull.
So she lay there and presently went to talking. "Old woman," she said
to herself, "that black dog come up out of the weeds to stall you off, and
now there he sitting on his fine tail, smiling at you."

A white man finally came along and found her—a hunter, a young   *36*
man, with his dog on a chain.

"Well, Granny!" he laughed, "what are you doing there?"   *37*

"Lying on my back like a June-bug waiting to be turned over,   *38*
mister," she said, reaching up her hand.

He lifted her up, gave her a swing in the air, and set her down.   *39*
"Anything broken, Granny?"

"No sir, them old dead weeds is springy enough," said Phoenix,   *40*
when she had got her breath. "I thank you for your trouble."

"Where do you live, Granny?" he asked, while the two dogs were   *41*
growling at each other.

"Away back yonder, sir, behind the ridge. You can't even see it   *42*
from here."

"On your way home?"   *43*

"No, sir, I going to town."   *44*

"Why, that's too far! That's as far as I walk when I come out my-   *45*
self, and I get something for my trouble." He patted the stuffed bag he
carried, and there hung down a little closed claw. It was one of the
bob-whites, with its beak hooked bitterly to show it was dead. "Now
you go on home, Granny!"

"I bound to go to town, mister," said Phoenix. "The time come   *46*
around."

He gave another laugh, filling the whole landscape. "I know you   *47*
old colored people! Wouldn't miss going to town to see Santa Claus!"

But something held Old Phoenix very still. The deep lines in her   *48*
face went into a fierce and different radiation. Without warning, she
had seen with her own eyes a flashing nickel fall out of the man's pocket onto the ground.

"How old are you, Granny?" he was saying.   *49*

"There is no telling, mister," she said, "no telling."   *50*

Then she gave a little cry and clapped her hands and said, "Git on   *51*
away from here, dog! Look! Look at that dog!" She laughed as if in
admiration. "He ain't scared of nobody. He a big black dog." She whispered, "Sic him!"

"Watch me get rid of that cur," said the man. "Sic him, Pete! Sic *52* him!"

Phoenix heard the dogs fighting, and heard the man running and *53* throwing sticks. She even heard a gunshot. But she was slowly bending forward by that time, further and further forward, the lids stretched down over her eyes, as if she were doing this in her sleep. Her chin was lowered almost to her knees. The yellow palm of her hand came out from the fold of her apron. Her fingers slid down and along the ground under the piece of money with the grace and care they would have in lifting an egg from under a sitting hen. Then she slowly straightened up, she stood erect, and the nickel was in her apron pocket. A bird flew by. Her lips moved. "God watching me the whole time, I come to stealing."

The man came back, and his own dog panted about them. "Well, *54* I scared him off that time," he said, and then he laughed and lifted his gun and pointed it at Phoenix.

She stood straight and faced him. *55*

"Doesn't the gun scare you?" he said, still pointing it. *56*

"No, sir, I seen plenty go off closer by, in my day, and for less than *57* what I done," she said, holding utterly still.

He smiled, and shouldered the gun. "Well, Granny," he said, "You *58* must be a hundred years old, and scared of nothing. I'd give you a dime if I had any money with me. But you take my advice and stay home, and nothing will happen to you."

"I bound to go on my way, mister," said Phoenix. She inclined *59* her head in the red rag. Then they went in different directions, but she could hear the gun shooting again and again over the hill.

She walked on. The shadows hung from the oak trees to the road *60* like curtains. Then she smelled wood-smoke, and smelled the river, and she saw a steeple and the cabins on their steep steps. Dozens of little black children whirled around her. There ahead was Natchez shining. Bells were ringing. She walked on.

In the paved city it was Christmas time. There were red and green *61* electric lights strung and crisscrossed everywhere, and all turned on in the daytime. Old Phoenix would have been lost if she had not distrusted her eyesight and depended on her feet to know where to take her.

She paused quietly on the sidewalk where people were passing by. *62* A lady came along in the crowd, carrying an armful of red-, green-, and silver-wrapped presents; she gave off perfume like the red roses in hot summer, and Phoenix stopped her.

"Please, missy, will you lace up my shoe?" She held up her foot. *63*

"What do you want, Grandma?" *64*

"See my shoe," said Phoenix. "Do all right for out in the country, but wouldn't look right to go in a big building." *65*

"Stand still then, Grandma," said the lady. She put her packages down on the sidewalk beside her and laced and tied both shoes tightly. *66*

"Can't lace 'em with a cane," said Phoenix. "Thank you, missy. I doesn't mind asking a nice lady to tie up my shoe, when I gets out on the street." *67*

Moving slowly and from side to side, she went into the big building and into a tower of steps, where she walked up and around and around until her feet knew to stop. *68*

She entered a door, and there she saw nailed up on the wall the document that had been stamped with the gold seal and framed in the gold frame, which matched the dream that was hung up in her head. *69*

"Here I be," she said. There was a fixed and ceremonial stiffness over her body. *70*

"A charity case, I suppose," said an attendant who sat at the desk before her. *71*

But Phoenix only looked above her head. There was sweat on her face, the wrinkles in her skin shone like a bright net. *72*

"Speak up, Grandma," the woman said: "What's your name? We must have your history, you know. Have you been here before? What seems to be the trouble with you?" *73*

Old Phoenix only gave a twitch to her face as if a fly were bothering her. *74*

"Are you deaf?" cried the attendant. *75*

But then the nurse came in. *76*

"Oh, that's just old Aunt Phoenix," she said. "She doesn't come for herself—she has a little grandson. She makes these trips just as regular as clockwork. She lives away back off the old Natchez Trace." She bent down. "Well, Aunt Phoenix, why don't you just take a seat? We won't keep you standing after your long trip." She pointed. *77*

The old woman sat down, bolt upright in the chair. *78*

"Now, how is the boy?" asked the nurse. *79*

Old Phoenix did not speak. *80*

"I said, how is the boy?" *81*

But Phoenix only waited and stared straight ahead, her face very solemn and withdrawn into rigidity. *82*

"Is his throat any better?" asked the nurse. "Aunt Phoenix, don't you hear me? Is your grandson's throat any better since the last time you came for the medicine?" *83*

With her hands on her knees, the old woman waited, silent, erect and motionless, just as if she were in armor. *84*

"You mustn't take up our time this way, Aunt Phoenix," the nurse *85* said. "Tell us quickly about your grandson, and get it over. He isn't dead, is he?"

At last there came a flicker and then a flame of comprehension *86* across her face, and she spoke.

"My grandson. It was my memory had left me. There I sat and *87* forgot why I made my long trip."

"Forgot?" The nurse frowned. "After you came so far?" *88*

Then Phoenix was like an old woman begging a dignified for- *89* giveness for waking up frightened in the night. "I never did go to school, I was too old at the Surrender," she said in a soft voice. "I'm an old woman without an education. It was my memory fail me. My little grandson, he is just the same, and I forgot it in the coming."

"Throat never heals, does it?" said the nurse, speaking in a loud, *90* sure voice to Old Phoenix. By now she had a card with something written on it, a little list. "Yes. Swallowed lye. When was it—January—two-three years ago—"

Phoenix spoke unasked now. "No, missy, he not dead, he just the *91* same. Every little while his throat begin to close up again, and he not able to swallow. He not get his breath. He not able to help himself. So the time come around, and I go on another trip for the soothing medicine."

"All right. The doctor said as long as you came to get it, you could *92* have it," said the nurse. "But it's an obstinate case."

"My little grandson, he sit up there in the house all wrapped up, *93* waiting by himself," Phoenix went on. "We is the only two left in the world. He suffer and it don't seem to put him back at all. He got a sweet look. He going to last. He wear a little patch quilt and peep out holding his mouth open like a little bird. I remembers so plain now. I not going to forget him again, no, the whole enduring time. I could tell him from all the others in creation."

"All right." The nurse was trying to hush her now. She brought her *94* a bottle of medicine. "Charity," she said, making a check mark in a book.

Old Phoenix held the bottle close to her eyes and then carefully *95* put it into her pocket.

"I thank you," she said. *96*

"It's Christmas time, Grandma," said the attendant. "Could I give *97* you a few pennies out of my purse?"

"Five pennies is a nickel," said Phoenix stiffly. *98*

"Here's a nickel," said the attendant. *99*

Phoenix rose carefully and held out her hand. She received the nick- *100* el and then fished the other nickel out of her pocket and laid it beside the new one. She stared at her palm closely, with her head on one side.

Then she gave a tap with her cane on the floor. *101*

"This is what come to me to do," she said. "I going to the store and *102* buy my child a little windmill they sells, made out of paper. He going to find it hard to believe there such a thing in the world. I'll march myself back where he waiting, holding it straight up in this hand."

She lifted her free hand, gave a little nod, turned round, and walked *103* out of the doctor's office. Then her slow step began on the stairs, going down.

QUESTIONS FOR WRITING AND DISCUSSION

1. Which of the following approximates your response(s) to the character of Phoenix Jackson: Surprise that she should be the subject of a story? Anger that no one helps her on her journey? Boredom that you just read a story in which nothing seems to happen? Puzzlement at her apparently senile behavior? Amazement at her determination and courage? Describe any other responses you may have.

2. According to legend, the Phoenix is a mythological bird that lives for five hundred years, burns itself to death, and then rises from its ashes in the freshness of youth to live through another life cycle. What *events*, *references*, and *images* in the story suggest that Welty's Phoenix Jackson is like the mythological bird?

3. One reader has suggested that during her journey, Phoenix encounters twelve obstacles (internal and external) that represent tests, or trials, of her faith and courage. How many of these tests can you find? Does she "pass" each test? What do these tests reveal about her character?

4. In an essay entitled "Is Phoenix Jackson's Grandson Really Dead?" Eudora Welty says, "The story is told through Phoenix's mind as she undertakes her errand. As the author is at one with the character as I tell it, I must assume that the boy is alive. As the reader, you are free to think as you like, of course: the story invites you to believe that no matter what happens, Phoenix for as long as she is able to walk and can hold to her purpose will make her journey." Explain how the boy's actual condition might affect your interpretation of the story.

5. Kate Chopin's "The Story of an Hour" and Eudora Welty's "A Worn Path" are both stories about love. By way of contrast, what do the character and behavior of Mrs. Mallard tell you about Phoenix? What do the character and behavior of Phoenix reveal about Mrs. Mallard?

PROFESSIONAL WRITING

THE LESSON
Toni Cade Bambara

Toni Cade Bambara is an activist for the African-American community on many fronts: political, cultural, and literary. She has worked for political and social causes in urban communities, taught African-American studies at half a dozen different colleges and universities, and is the author of several collections of short stories and novels, including Gorilla, My Love *(1972),* The Sea Birds Are Still Alive *(1977),* The Salt Eaters *(1980), and* If Blessing Comes *(1987). "The Lesson," which appears in* Gorilla, My Love, *dramatizes the gradual awakening of several children to the political and economic realities of contemporary urban life. As you read the story, pay attention to the narrator, Sylvia. What is the lesson, and what does Sylvia learn?*

Back in the days when everyone was old and stupid or young and foolish and me and Sugar were the only ones just right, this lady moved on our block with nappy hair and proper speech and no makeup. And quite naturally we laughed at her, laughed the way we did at the junk man who went about his business like he was some big-time president and his sorry-ass horse his secretary. And we kinda hated her too, hated the way we did the winos who cluttered up our parks and pissed on our handball walls and stank up our hallways and stairs so you couldn't halfway play hide-and-seek without a goddamn gas mask. Miss Moore was her name. The only woman on the block with no first name. And she was black as hell, cept for her feet, which were fish-white and spooky. And she was always planning these boring-ass things for us to do, us being my cousins, mostly, who lived on the block cause we all moved North the same time and to the same apartment then spread out gradual to breathe. And our parents would yank our heads into some kinda shape and crisp up our clothes so we'd be presentable for travel with Miss Moore, who always looked like she was going to church, though she never did. Which is just one of the things the grownups talked about when they talked behind her back like a dog. But when she came calling with some sachet she'd sewed up or some gingerbread she'd made or some book, why then they'd all be too embarrassed to turn her down and we'd get handed over all spruced up. She'd been to college and said it was only right that she should take responsibility for the young ones' education, and she not even related by marriage or blood. So they'd go for it. Specially Aunt Gretchen. She was the main gofer in the family. You got some ole dumb shit foolishness you want somebody to go for, you send for Aunt Gretchen. She been screwed into the go-along for so long, it's a blood-deep natural thing with her. Which is how she got saddled with me and Sugar and Junior in the first place while our mothers were in a la-de-da apartment up the block having a good ole time.

So this one day Miss Moore rounds us all up at the mailbox and   2
it's puredee hot and she's knockin herself out about arithmetic. And school suppose to let up in summer I heard, but she don't never let up. And the starch in my pinafore scratching the shit outta me and I'm really hating this nappy-head bitch and her goddamn college degree. I'd much rather go to the pool or to the show where it's cool. So me and Sugar leaning on the mailbox being surly, which is a Miss Moore word. And Flyboy checking out what everybody brought for lunch. And Fat Butt already wasting his peanut-butter-and-jelly sandwich like the pig he is. And Junebug punchin on Q.T.'s arm for potato chips. And Rosie Giraffe shifting from one hip to the other waiting for somebody to step on her foot or ask her if she from Georgia so she can kick ass, preferably Mercedes's. And Miss Moore asking us do we know what money is, like we a bunch of retards. I mean real money, she say, like it's only poker chips or monopoly papers we lay on the grocer. So right away I'm tired of this and say so. And would much rather snatch Sugar and go to the Sunset and terrorize the West Indian kids and take their hair ribbons and their money too. And Miss Moore files that remark away for next week's lesson on brotherhood, I can tell. And finally I say we oughta get to the subway cause it's cooler and besides we might meet some cute boys. Sugar done swiped her mama's lipstick, so we ready.

So we heading down the street and she's boring us silly about what   3
things cost and what our parents make and how much goes for rent and how money ain't divided up right in this country. And then she gets to the part about we all poor and live in the slums, which I don't feature. And I'm ready to speak on that, but she steps out in the street and hails two cabs just like that. Then she hustles half the crew in with her and hands me a five-dollar bill and tells me to calculate 10 percent tip for the driver. And we're off. Me and Sugar and Junebug and Flyboy hangin out the window and hollering to everybody, putting lipstick on each other cause Flyboy a faggot anyway, and making farts with our sweaty armpits. But I'm mostly trying to figure how to spend this money. But they all fascinated with the meter ticking and Junebug starts laying bets as to how much it'll read when Flyboy can't hold his breath no more. Then Sugar lays bets as to how much it'll be when we get there. So I'm stuck. Don't nobody want to go for my plan, which is to jump out at the next light and run off to the first bar-b-que we can find. Then the driver tells us to get the hell out cause we there already.

And the meter reads eighty-five cents. And I'm stalling to figure out the tip and Sugar say give him a dime. And I decide he don't need it bad as I do, so later for him. But then he tries to take off with Junebug foot still in the door so we talk about his mama something ferocious. Then we check out that we on Fifth Avenue and everybody dressed up in stockings. One lady in a fur coat, hot as it is. White folks crazy.

"This is the place," Miss Moore say, presenting it to us in the voice 4 she uses at the museum. "Let's look in the windows before we go in."

"Can we steal?" Sugar asks very serious like she's getting the 5 ground rules squared away before she plays. "I beg your pardon," say Miss Moore, and we fall out. So she leads us around the windows of the toy store and me and Sugar screamin, "This is mine, that's mine, I gotta have that, that was made for me, I was born for that," till Big Butt drowns us out.

"Hey, I'm goin to buy that there." 6

"That there? You don't even know what it is, stupid." 7

"I do so," he say punchin on Rosie Giraffe. "It's a microscope." 8

"Whatcha gonna do with a microscope, fool?" 9

"Look at things." 10

"Like what, Ronald?" ask Miss Moore. And Big Butt ain't got the 11 first notion. So here go Miss Moore gabbing about the thousands of bacteria in a drop of water and the somethinorother in a speck of blood and the million and one living things in the air around us is invisible to the naked eye. And what she say that for? Junebug go to town on that "naked" and we rolling. Then Miss Moore ask what it cost. So we all jam into the window smudgin it up and the price tag say $300. So then she ask how long'd take for Big Butt and Junebug to save up their allowances. "Too long," I say. "Yeh," adds Sugar, "outgrown it by that time." And Miss Moore say no, you never outgrow learning instruments. "Why, even medical students and interns and," blah, blah, blah. And we ready to choke Big Butt for bringing it up in the first damn place.

"This here costs four hundred eighty dollars," say Rosie Giraffe. 12 So we pile up all over her to see what she pointin out. My eyes tell me it's a chunk of glass cracked with something heavy, and different-color inks dripped into the splits, then the whole thing put into a oven or something. But for $480 it don't make sense.

"That's a paperweight made of semi-precious stones fused to- 13 gether under tremendous pressure," she explains slowly, with her hands doing the mining and all the factory work.

"So what's a paperweight?" asks Rosie Giraffe. 14

"To weigh paper with, dumbbell," say Flyboy, the wise man 15 from the East.

"Not exactly," say Miss Moore, which is what she say when you   *16*
warm or way off too. "It's to weigh paper down so it won't scatter and
make your desk untidy." So right away me and Sugar curtsy to each
other and then to Mercedes who is more the tidy type.

"We don't keep paper on top of the desk in my class," say June-   *17*
bug, figuring Miss Moore crazy or lyin one.

"At home, then," she say. "Don't you have a calendar and a pencil   *18*
case and a blotter and a letter-opener on your desk at home where you
do your homework?" And she know damn well what our homes look
like cause she nosys around in them every chance she gets.

"I don't even have a desk," say Junebug. "Do we?"   *19*

"No. And I don't get no homework neither," says Big Butt.   *20*

"And I don't even have a home," say Flyboy like he do at school   *21*
to keep the white folks off his back and sorry for him. Send this poor
kid to camp posters, is his specialty.

"I do," says Mercedes. "I have a box of stationery on my desk and   *22*
a picture of my cat. My godmother bought the stationery and the desk.
There's a big rose on each sheet and the envelopes smell like roses."

"Who wants to know about your smelly-ass stationery," say Rosie   *23*
Giraffe fore I can get my two cents in.

"It's important to have a work area all your own so that. . . ."   *24*

"Will you look at this sailboat, please," say Flyboy, cuttin her off   *25*
and pointin to the thing like it was his. So once again we tumble all over
each other to gaze at this magnificent thing in the toy store which is
just big enough to maybe sail two kittens across the pond if you strap
them to the posts tight. We all start reciting the price tag like we in assembly. "Handcrafted sailboat of fiberglass at one thousand one hundred ninety-five dollars."

"Unbelievable," I hear myself say and am really stunned. I read it   *26*
again for myself just in case the group recitation put me in a trance.
Same thing. For some reason this pisses me off. We look at Miss Moore
and she lookin at us, waiting for I dunno what.

"Who'd pay all that when you can buy a sailboat set for a quarter   *27*
at Pop's, a tube of glue for a dime, and a ball of string for eight cents?
It must have a motor and a whole lot else besides," I say. "My sailboat
cost me about fifty cents."

"But will it take water?" say Mercedes with her smart ass.   *28*

"Took mine to Alley Pond Park once," say Flyboy. "String broke.   *29*
Lost it. Pity."

"Sailed mine in Central Park and it keeled over and sank. Had to   *30*
ask my father for another dollar."

"And you got the strap," laugh Big Butt. "The jerk didn't even have   *31*
a string on it. My old man wailed on his behind."

Little Q.T. was staring hard at the sailboat and you could see he *32* wanted it bad. But he too little and somebody'd just take it from him. So what the hell. "This boat for kids, Miss Moore?"

"Parents silly to buy something like that just to get all broke up," *33* say Rosie Giraffe.

"That much money it should last forever," I figure. *34*

"My father'd buy it for me if I wanted it." *35*

"Your father, my ass," say Rosie Giraffe getting a chance to final- *36* ly push Mercedes.

"Must be rich people shop here," say Q.T. *37*

"You are a very bright boy," say Flyboy. "What was your first clue?" *38* And he rap him on the head with the back of his knuckles, since Q.T. the only one he could get away with. Though Q.T. liable to come up behind you years later and get his licks in when you half expect it.

"What I want to know is," I says to Miss Moore though I never *39* talk to her, I wouldn't give the bitch that satisfaction, "is how much a real boat costs? I figure a thousand'd get you a yacht any day."

"Why don't you check that out," she says, "and report back to the *40* group?" Which really pains my ass. If you gonna mess up a perfectly good swim day least you could do is have some answers. "Let's go in," she say like she got something up her sleeve. Only she don't lead the way. So me and Sugar turn the corner to where the entrance is, but when we get there I kinda hang back. Not that I'm scared, what's there to be afraid of, just a toy store. But I feel funny, shame. But what I got to be shamed about? Got as much right to go in as anybody. But somehow I can't seem to get hold of the door, so I step away for Sugar to lead. But she hangs back too. And I look at her and she looks at me and this is ridiculous. I mean, damn, I have never ever been shy about doing nothing or going nowhere. But then Mercedes steps up and then Rosie Giraffe and Big Butt crowd in behind and shove, and next thing we all stuffed into the doorway with only Mercedes squeezing past us, smoothing out her jumper and walking right down the aisle. Then the rest of us tumble in like a glued-together jigsaw done all wrong. And people lookin at us. And it's like the time me and Sugar crashed into the Catholic church on a dare. But once we got in there and every- thing so hushed and holy and the candles and the bowin and the hand- kerchiefs on all the drooping heads, I just couldn't go through with the plan. Which was for me to run up to the altar and do a tap dance while Sugar played the nose flute and messed around in the holy water. And Sugar kept givin me the elbow. Then later teased me so bad I tied her up in the shower and turned it on and locked her in. And she'd be there till this day if Aunt Gretchen hadn't finally figured I was lyin about the boarder takin a shower.

Same thing in the store. We all walkin on tiptoe and hardly touch-   *41*
in the games and puzzles and things. And I watched Miss Moore who
is steady watchin us like she waitin for a sign. Like Mama Drewery
watches the sky and sniffs the air and takes note of just how much
slant is in the bird formation. Then me and Sugar bump smack into
each other, so busy gazing at the toys, 'specially the sailboat. But we
don't laugh and go into our fat-lady bump-stomach routine. We just
stare at that price tag. Then Sugar run a finger over the whole boat. And
I'm jealous and want to hit her. Maybe not her, but I sure want to
punch somebody in the mouth.

"Watcha bring us here for, Miss Moore?"   *42*

"You sound angry, Sylvia. Are you mad about something?" Givin   *43*
me one of them grins like she tellin a grown-up joke that never turns
out to be funny. And she's lookin very closely at me like maybe she
plannin to do my portrait from memory. I'm mad, but I won't give her
that satisfaction. So I slouch around the store bein very bored and say,
"Let's go."

Me and Sugar at the back of the train watchin the tracks whizzin   *44*
by large then small then gettin gobbled up in the dark. I'm thinkin
about this tricky toy I saw in the store. A clown that somersaults on a
bar then does chin-ups just cause you yank lightly at his leg. Cost $35.
I could see me askin my mother for a $35 birthday clown. "You wanna
who that costs what?" she'd say, cocking her head to the side to get a
better view of the hole in my head. Thirty-five dollars could buy new
bunk beds for Junior and Gretchen's boy. Thirty-five dollars and the
whole household could go visit Granddaddy Nelson in the country.
Thirty-five dollars would pay for the rent and the piano bill too. Who
are these people that spend that much for performing clowns and
$1,000 for toy sailboats? What kinda work they do and how they live
and how come we ain't in on it? Where we are is who we are, Miss
Moore always pointin out. But it don't necessarily have to be that way,
she always adds then waits for somebody to say that poor people have
to wake up and demand their share of the pie and don't none of us
know what kind of pie she talkin about in the first damn place. But she
ain't so smart cause I still got her four dollars from the taxi and she
sure ain't gettin it. Messin up my day with this shit. Sugar nudges me
in my pocket and winks.

Miss Moore lines us up in front of the mailbox where we started   *45*
from, seem like years ago, and I got a headache for thinkin so hard. And
we lean all over each other so we can hold up under the draggy-ass
lecture she always finishes us off with at the end before we thank her
for borin us to tears. But she just looks at us like she readin tea leaves.
Finally she say, "Well, what did you think of F. A. O. Schwarz?"

Rosie Giraffe mumbles, "White folks crazy." 46

"I'd like to go there again when I get my birthday money," says 47
Mercedes, and we shove her out the pack so she has to lean on the
mailbox by herself.

"I'd like a shower. Tiring day," say Flyboy. 48

Then Sugar surprises me by sayin, "You know, Miss Moore, I don't 49
think all of us here put together eat in a year what that sailboat costs."
And Miss Moore lights up like somebody goosed her. "And?" she say,
urging Sugar on. Only I'm standin on her foot so she don't continue.

"Imagine for a minute what kind of society it is in which some 50
people can spend on a toy what it would cost to feed a family of six or
seven. What do you think?"

"I think," say Sugar pushing me off her feet like she never done be- 51
fore, cause I whip her ass in a minute, "that this is not much of a democracy if you ask me. Equal chance to pursue happiness means an equal
crack at the dough, don't it?" Miss Moore is besides herself and I am dis-
gusted with Sugar's treachery. So I stand on her foot one more time to see
if she'll shove me. She shuts up, and Miss Moore looks at me, sorrowful-
ly I'm thinkin. And somethin weird is goin on, I can feel it in my chest.

"Anybody else learn anything today?" lookin dead at me. I walk 52
away and Sugar has to run to catch up and don't even seem to notice
when I shrug her arm off my shoulder.

"Well, we got four dollars anyway," she says. 53

"Uh hunh." 54

"We could go to Hascombs and get half a chocolate layer and then 55
go to the Sunset and still have plenty money for potato chips and ice
cream sodas."

"Uh hunh." 56

"Race you to Hascombs," she say. 57

We start down the block and she gets ahead which is O.K. by me 58
cause I'm going to the West End and then over to the Drive to think
this day through. She can run if she want to and even run faster. But
ain't nobody gonna beat me at nuthin. ●─◄─■─►─

QUESTIONS FOR WRITING AND DISCUSSION

1. Describe one incident when a parent, friend, or family member
   tried to get you to do something that you didn't want to do. How
   did you react? How was your behavior similar to or different from
   the reaction of Sylvia, the narrator in "The Lesson"?

2. Reread the opening sentence of the story. What does the first half
   of that sentence reveal about the character of the narrator? Does
   the rest of the story confirm that initial impression? Explain.

3. Locate at least one sentence or passage describing the reactions of each of the following children to the merchandise at F. A. O. Schwarz: Sylvia (the narrator), Sugar, Flyboy, Mercedes, Big Butt, Junebug, Rosie Giraffe, and Q.T. How do their reactions to the toys and their prices affect the narrator? Why does Bambara include all of these children in the story rather than tell it using just Miss Moore, Sylvia, and Sugar?

4. Miss Moore is the "teacher" for this "lesson," but what kind of teacher is she and how do her students react to her? What strategies does she use to help the children learn? Are her methods effective? How do the children react to each other's learning? Does Miss Moore make some mistakes?

5. What evidence (cite specific sentences) suggests that Sylvia is learning more from this lesson than she wants to? What exactly is she learning? Describe what she might do in the future as a result of what she learns.

6. Explain how each of the following quotations from Sylvia's thoughts relates to the theme or main idea of "The Lesson":

White folks crazy.

I mean, damn, I have never ever been shy about doing nothing or going nowhere.

If you gonna mess up a perfectly good swim day least you could do is have some answers.

But ain't nobody gonna beat me at nuthin.

7. Write two paragraphs comparing and contrasting the "awakenings" of Mrs. Mallard in "The Story of an Hour" and Sylvia in "The Lesson." What—and how—does each character learn? How do they react to what they learn? What do we, as readers, learn?

Responding to Literature: The Writing Process

■ ASSIGNMENT FOR RESPONDING TO LITERATURE

Choose one of the short stories from this chapter (or a work of literature assigned in your class), and read it actively, reread and annotate the work, and share your responses with others in the class. Then write an interpretative essay. Assume that you are writing for other members of your class (including your instructor) who have read the work but who may not understand or agree with your interpretation.

COLLECTING

In addition to reading, rereading, annotating, and sharing your responses, try the following collecting strategies:

- **Collaborative annotation.** In small groups, choose a work of literature or select a passage that you have already annotated. In the group, read each other's annotations. Then discuss each annotation. Which annotations does your group agree are the best? Have a group recorder record the best annotations.
- **Elements of fiction analysis.** Reread the paragraphs defining character, plot, point of view, setting, and style. Choose three of these elements that seem most important in the story that you are reading. Reread the story, annotating for these three elements. Then freewrite a paragraph explaining *how these three elements are interrelated or how they explain the theme.*
- **Time line.** In your journal, draw a time line for the story. List above the line everything that happens in the story. Below the line, indicate where the story opens, when the major conflicts occur, and where the climax and the denouement occur. For "The Story of an Hour," student writer Karen Ehrhardt drew the following time line:

TIME LINE FOR "THE STORY OF AN HOUR"

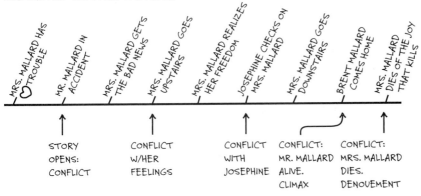

- **Feature list.** Choose a character trait, repeated image, or idea that you wish to investigate in the story. List, in order of appearance, every word, image, or reference that you find in the story.
- **Scene vision or revision.** Write a scene for this story in which you change some part of it. You may *add* a scene to the beginning, middle, or end of the story. You may *change* a scene in the story. You may write a scene in the story from a different character's point of view. You may change the style of the story for your scene. How, for example, might Eudora Welty have described the opening scene of "The Story of an Hour"?

- **Story picture.** Draw a picture of the story, based on the time line and conflict mapping, that represents the entire story. Use the information from your character analysis, time line, and character conflicts to help you draw a single picture of the complete story. Student writer Lori Van Skike drew a picture for "The Story of an Hour" that shows how the rising and falling action of the plot parallels Mrs. Mallard's ascent and descent of the stairs:

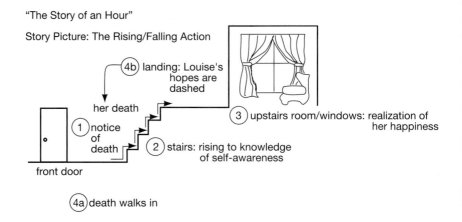

"The Story of an Hour"

Story Picture: The Rising/Falling Action

4b) landing: Louise's hopes are dashed

her death

1) notice of death

front door

2) stairs: rising to knowledge of self-awareness

3) upstairs room/windows: realization of her happiness

4a) death walks in

- **Character conflict map.** Start with a full page of paper. Draw a main character in the center of the page. Locate the other major characters, internal forces, and external forces (including social, economic, and environmental pressures) in a circle around the main character. Draw a line between each of these peripheral characters or forces and the main character. For his character conflict map for "The Story of an Hour," student writer Darren Marshall used images from his computer program to surround his picture of Mrs. Mallard (see p. 543).
- **Background investigation.** Investigate the biographical, social, historical, or geographical context for the story. Locate a biography of the author. How are the major events of the author's life relevant to the story? Read about the historical or economic background of the story. Look at maps or descriptions of the setting for the story. How do these background sources increase your appreciation or widen your understanding of the story?
- **Reconsideration of purposes.** What idea, theme, or approach most interests you? Will you be explaining, evaluating, problem solving, or arguing? Are you combining purposes? Do these purposes suggest what kinds of information you might collect?

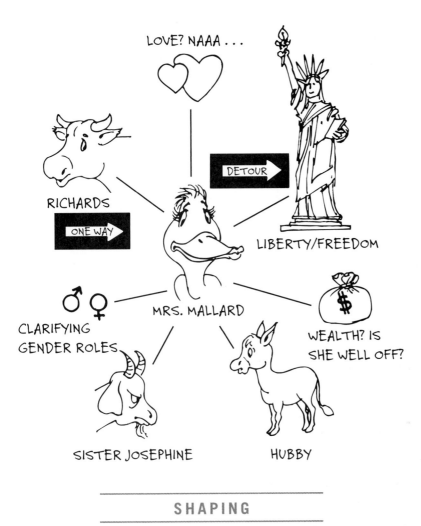

SHAPING

Test each of the following possible shapes against your ideas for your essay. Use or adapt the shape or shapes that are most appropriate for your own interpretation.

EXPLAINING RELATIONSHIPS   Often interpretive essays analyze how the parts of a story relate to the whole. As you explain these relationships, you should show how key lines or scenes contribute to the portrait of the major character or to the overall theme of the story. Your focus might be on how *plot* or *character conflicts* affect your understanding of the major character, on how the *setting* reflects the theme, or on how *images* reveal character and/or contribute to the theme.

Introduction and thesis:	The images in story X reveal that the theme is Y.
First scene or part:	How key images contribute to theme.

Second scene or part: How key images contribute to theme.
Third scene or part: How key images contribute to theme.
Conclusion:

EVALUATING   If your response suggests an evaluating purpose, you may wish to set up *criteria* for an effective short story and then provide evidence that shows how the particular story does or does not measure up to your standards. Your thesis might be "Story X is highly dramatic because the main character undergoes emotional changes, the character conflicts heighten the tension, and the theme is controversial." A similar shaping strategy might be to set a *definition* of a "hero" or "heroine" and then analyze how the main character fits your definition.

Introduction and thesis: Story X is highly dramatic.
Criterion 1:   A dramatic short story should focus on a character who changes his or her behavior or beliefs.
    Judgment and evidence for Criterion 1:
Criterion 2:   A dramatic story must have striking conflicts that lead to a crisis or a predicament.
    Judgment and evidence for Criterion 2:
Criterion 3:   A dramatic story should have a theme that makes a controversial point.
    Judgment and evidence for Criterion 3:
Conclusion:

ARGUING   During class discussion, you may disagree with another person's response. Your thesis may then take the form, "Although some readers believe this story is about X, the story is really about Y." In an argumentative structure, you counter opposing interpretations by first pointing to evidence in the story and then supporting your interpretation with evidence.

Introduction and thesis: Although some readers suggest that the story is about X, it is really about Y.
Body paragraphs: State the opposing interpretation and give evidence that this interpretation cites:
    State your interpretation and give evidence (description, dialogue, images, points of conflict, incidents from the plot):
Conclusion:

INVESTIGATING CHANGES IN INTERPRETATION   Often, readers *change* interpretations during the course of responding to a piece of literature.

Thus, your main point might be "Although I initially thought X about the story, I gradually realized the theme of the story is Y." If that sentence expresses your main idea, you may wish to organize your essay following the *chronology* or the *steps* in the changes in your interpretation:

Introduction and thesis: Although I initially thought X, I now believe Y.

Body paragraphs: First step (your original interpretation of the story and supporting evidence):

Second step (additional or contradictory ideas and evidence that forced you to reconsider your interpretation):

Third step (your final interpretation and supporting evidence):

Conclusion:

Note: One strategy you should *not* use is simply to retell the main events of the story. A review of the plot is not an acceptable interpretation. Your audience has already read the story. They want you to state your interpretation and then use details from the story to show how and why your interpretation is credible. *Although you will cite events from the plot, you must explain how or why these events support your interpretation.*

DRAFTING

To prepare to draft your essay, read through your annotations and gather your collecting and shaping notes. Some writers prefer to write one-sentence statements of their main ideas at the top of the page to keep them focused as they write. Other writers prefer to make rough outlines to follow, based on their adaptations of one of the preceding shaping strategies. When you begin drafting, you may wish to skip your introduction and start with the body of your essay. You can fill in the introduction after you have written a draft.

Once you start writing, keep your momentum going. If you draw a blank, reread what you have already written or look at your notes. If you cannot think of a particular word or are unsure about a spelling, draw a line _____ and keep on writing.

REVISING

Use the following guidelines as you read your classmates' drafts and revise your own essay. Be prepared to make changes in your ideas, organization, and evidence, as well as to fix problems in sentences and word choice.

Guidelines for Revisions

- **Clarify your main idea or interpretation.** Ask your readers to write, in one sentence, the main point of your interpretation. If their statements do not exactly match your main point, clarify your thesis. Your interpretation (not a statement of fact) should be clearly stated early in your essay.

- **Do not give a plot summary.** Your readers have read the story, so do not simply retell the plot. Do, however, give ample evidence. You must also explain how that evidence supports your main point.

- **Support each part of your interpretation with references to specific passages from the text.** Do not be satisfied with one piece of evidence. Find as many bits of evidence as possible. The case for your interpretation grows stronger with each additional piece of evidence.

- **Explain how each piece of evidence supports your interpretation.** Do not just cite several pieces of evidence and go on to your next point. Explain for your readers *how* the evidence supports your interpretation.

- **Define key terms in your essay.** If you are writing about the hero in a story, define what you mean by *hero* or *heroine*. If you are arguing that "The Story of an Hour" has a *feminist* theme, define *feminism*.

- **Signal the major parts of your interpretation.** Let your readers know when you shift to a new point. Use transitions and paragraph hooks at the beginning of body paragraphs.

- **Use the present tense as you describe the events in the story.** If you are describing the end of "The Story of an Hour," write, for example, "Mrs. Mallard descends the stairs and learns the 'good news' about her husband."

- **Quote accurately and cite page numbers for each reference.** Double-check your quotations to make sure they are accurate, word-for-word transcriptions. Following each direct quotation, cite page references as follows:

  > In the first sentence, Kate Chopin says, "Mrs. Mallard was afflicted with a heart trouble" (479).

  Note: The period goes outside the parentheses. See Chapter 12 for correct documentation style.

- **Revise your essay for sentence clarity and conciseness.** Read your essay aloud or have a classmate read it. Reduce unnecessary repetition. Use active verbs. Rework awkward or confusing sentences.

- **Edit your essay.** Check your essay for correct spelling, word choice, punctuation, and grammar.

■ POSTSCRIPT ON THE WRITING PROCESS   Before you turn in your essay, answer the following questions in your journal:

1. Explain what part of this essay (collecting ideas and evidence, focusing on your interpretation, shaping your essay, drafting, or revising) was most difficult for you. How did you work around the problems?
2. What do you like best about your essay? Refer to specific places in the essay (lead-in, thesis, pieces of evidence, ideas, conclusion). Which specific paragraphs do you like best? Why?
3. What did you learn about the story by writing your interpretation? What do you realize now that you did not understand when you first read the story?
4. If you had two more hours to work on this essay, what would you change? Why?

A WORN PATH

Julia MacMillan and Brett MacFadden

Julia MacMillan and Brett MacFadden collaboratively wrote their essay on the Phoenix imagery in Eudora Welty's "A Worn Path." They drafted their own essays separately and then collaborated on a revision that shared their interpretations and their best textual evidence. The following are their original separate notes and drafts, their plans for their collaborative revision, and their final revised interpretation. Read their separate versions first, and then see how they collaborated to produce their revised essay.

Rough Drafts

Julia MacMillan

The journey that Phoenix Jackson makes in Eudora Welty's "A Worn Path" is very similar to that made by the mythological phoenix on its way to rebirth. Much of the symbolism and figurative language throughout the story shows the succession of events that parallel a Phoenix-like ending to the old woman.

We can feel, almost from the beginning, that Phoenix's long life is coming to an end. She is described with "the two knots of her cheeks illuminated by a yellow burning under the dark" (289). In only a few more sentences, however, we hear the mourning dove, apparently mourning for Phoenix. The yellow burning under the dark is almost a desperate, final fiery burst in the face of oncoming death.

Her death is also foreshadowed in the mention of a buzzard, watching her from the tall, dead trees. She asks of him, "Who you watching?" as if she knows it is herself. Further in her journey, upon meeting the white hunter, her impending death as well as her expectation of it are shown. The little bob-white, "its beak hooked bitterly to show it was dead" (262), that the hunter is carrying on his bag quite forcefully shows us her death. The fact that she does not fear but expects this death is shown when the hunter points his gun at Phoenix, and she "stood straight and faced him" quite fearlessly (263). In not fearing this death and seeming to understand its nearness, Phoenix Jackson becomes more like the bird she is named for.

It is most clearly seen that the author intended her reader to see the Phoenix imagery when the grandson is introduced near the end of the story. On page 264, she "entered a door, and there she saw the document that had been stamped with the gold seal and framed in the gold frame, which matched the dream that was hung up in her head." The gold in this passage seems to represent flame—the flame of her funeral pyre and the dream in her head of perpetuation and reincarnation through her grandson's life. It is even more clearly stated when, once in the doctor's office, she goes into a strange trance, becoming unable to answer the agitated nurse's questions. When finally asked, "He isn't dead, is he?" "a flicker and then a flame of comprehension" come across her face" (265). These flames are symbolic of her death, yet they are caused by her remembering the importance of her grandson's life to her. This life is most precious to her, because it is through her grandson that Phoenix, like the mythological bird, will live again.

Brett MacFadden

In many ways Phoenix Jackson is like the mythical bird she is named after; her physical characteristics, her purpose in life, and her extreme age and nearness to death all support her likeness to the mythological phoenix.

The phoenix is a bird of myth that lives for five hundred years and then burns itself to death, rising from its ashes renewed and beautiful. Phoenix Jackson in the story "A Worn Path" by Eudora Welty is a very old black woman near the end of her life cycle who takes a long walk through the woods to town in order to get medicine for her ailing grandson. The core story is very simple, and it is because of this simplicity that the reader is forced to look beyond the core for a more complex tale. One of the first clues to the inner story is the name of the main character, Phoenix. With the knowledge of what a Phoenix is, we can find many clues supporting the idea of the old woman living her life as a Phoenix.

Throughout the short story, words and phrases that describe the old woman might also describe the mythological bird. Her skin is black with a "golden color underneath" (259) and the "two knobs of her cheeks were illuminated by a yellow burning under the dark" (259). Both the golden color and especially the yellow burning are colors of fire, symbolizing the bird's fiery death. A red rag that she wears on top of her head is also another color of flame. Her black, wrinkled skin can be thought of as looking quite like ashes, and assuming that her grandson is a blood relative, his skin should also be the color of charred ash. She is like a fire that is almost out. It is mostly black, but there is the small flicker of flame to show you it is not yet extinguished.

Assuming the reader chooses to believe that Phoenix does in fact have a grandson and he is in fact sick, then the main purpose of her trip is to get the boy his medicine. This idea goes along nicely with the phoenix theme because she is giving everything she has left for the benefit of her grandson. She is essentially burning herself up so that the new person can exist. We can assume from the physical appearance and actions of Phoenix that she is pretty nearly burnt out. Phoenix knows her grandson is the one with the potential now, and so she gives all the effort she has to get him his medicine. Her only wish is to see him rise from his sick bed.

There are many hints of Phoenix's extreme age. At one time she tells herself, "I is the oldest person I ever know" (261), indicating that she has lived longer than most. Another time the hunter that she comes across estimates that she is "a hundred years old" (263). Much of the imagery in the story symbolizes her oncoming death. The fact that it is winter can be seen as the winter of her life. Other death images include the big dead trees, the buzzard, the scarecrow she mistakes for a ghost, and the black dog that knocks her into the ditch.

Revised Draft

A SINGULAR PERPETUATION

Brett MacFadden and Julia MacMillan

Phoenix Jackson, in the story "A Worn Path," by Eudora Welty, is in many ways like the mythological bird she is named after. Her purpose in life, birdlike characteristics, and nearness to death all support a clear parallel between the character and her namesake. The story is very *1* simple, and because of this simplicity the reader is forced to search for a more meaningful tale. One of the first clues to the inner story is the name of the main character, Phoenix. With the knowledge of what a phoenix is, it is possible to find many clues supporting the idea of the old woman living her life as a phoenix, burning herself out for the benefit of the new bird, her grandson.

The phoenix is a mythological bird who, after living for five *2* hundred years, burns itself to ashes on a pyre and rises renewed to live another cycle. Phoenix Jackson journeys through the woods to town to get medicine for her ailing grandson. This idea parallels the phoenix theme, because she is making what appears to be her final journey, in order that her grandson may rise from his sickbed. The legend of the phoenix is one of singular perpetuation; only one exists in the world. This is shown when she tells the nurses that "We is the only two left in the world" (255). Phoenix is concerned because if both of them were to die, then it would result in the extinction of the species. As much as she worries about him surviving, she is confident that he, like the immortal bird, will survive. Speaking to the nurses again, she says, "He suffer and it don't seem to put him back at all. . . . He going to last" (265–66). As well as his immortality, his birdlike characteristics and dependence on Phoenix for his perseverance are shown when he peeps out of his quilt "holding his mouth open like a little bird" (266). He is her reincarnation, and she is devoted to his successful ascension.

Throughout the story many words and phrases that describe *3* the old woman might also describe the mythological bird. Her skin is described as black with "a golden color underneath," and the "two knobs of her cheeks were illuminated by a yellow burning under the dark" (259). She wears on top of her head a red rag. Both the "golden color" and the "yellow burning," as well as the red of her rag, are colors of fire, symbolizing her approaching death. As she walks, the tapping of her umbrella sounds like "the chirping of a solitary little bird" (259). Her likeness to a bird is evidenced when, in passing a scarecrow in a field, she is frightened, as a bird would be. When startled by a dog, she falls into a ditch "like a little puff of milkweed" (262). This gives the appearance that she is a light creature, mostly flame and feather. These birdlike characteristics of Phoenix seem to imply that the author intended her to represent the mythical bird.

The myth of the phoenix holds that when "its eyes begin to grow *4* dim, it knows that the time of death has come" (Oswalt 239). When we are first introduced to the main character, as well as being old, she is described as having "eyes . . . blue with age" (259). Many images of death, some quite vivid, link Phoenix Jackson's impending death to that of the phoenix of myth. At one point in her journey she stoops and looks upward, exclaiming, "Sun so high! Time getting all gone here" (260). This clearly indicates her knowledge of her approaching death. Her death is also foreshadowed by the mention of several images that bombard us from the dawn of the story. Early on she reflects on the call of a mourning dove—mourning being something done in the wake of death. Later she comes upon a buzzard sitting in a dead tree. She asks of him, "Who you watching?" (261), as if she knows it is herself. Her death is foreshadowed further when walking through a cornfield she happens upon what she perceives to be a ghost. Upon closer inspection, the ghost turns out to be a scarecrow. However, she shows no fear approaching what she thinks is a ghost, which demonstrates that she is comfortable with dying. The black dog that knocks her into a ditch is another vivid image of death. Further in her journey, upon meeting a white hunter, her impending death as well as her expectation of it are shown. The little bob-white, "its beak hooked bitterly to show that it was dead" (262), that the hunter is carrying in his bag quite forcefully shows us her anticipated death. The fact that she does not fear but expects this death is shown when the hunter points his gun at Phoenix, and she "stood straight and faced him" quite fearlessly (263). In not fearing this death and seeming to understand its nearness, Phoenix Jackson becomes more like the bird she is named for.

A carefully wrought story, "A Worn Path" is more than a tale of an 5 old woman's formidable journey. It is the rebirth of an age-old myth wrapped in the cloak of conventionality. In examining some of the symbols, allusions, and the underlying legend, we find a well-hidden but evident parallel between the lives of the main character and her namesake, the phoenix.

Works Cited

Oswalt, Sabine G. *Concise Encyclopedia of Greek and Roman Mythology.* Chicago: Follett, 1969.

■ POSTSCRIPT ON THE COLLABORATIVE REVISION

We began this collaboration by reading each other's papers and rereading our own in order to find the strengths and weaknesses of each paper. Then together we combed through each paper, pulling out what we both agreed were our strongest points, and compiled these into a thesis. For our thesis, we used the second sentence in the first paragraph: "Her [Phoenix's] purpose in life, bird-like characteristics, and nearness to death all support a clear parallel between the character and her namesake."

Having decided on a thesis and a rough plan of action, we then went to the computer lab and began writing. At this point, the paper became more difficult because we had to narrow two papers into one and decide what we should omit. For example, Julia's paper discussed the emblem on the doctor's office wall as another symbol of Phoenix's fiery death. After discussing this scene, we decided that the symbolism was not strong enough and should be left out. We knew each other before deciding to write the collaborative essay, so we were both comfortable around each other and were able to say what we really thought about each other's writing. We knew also that our basic writing styles are opposing. Brett's is concise, and Julia's is more flowing. Our different writing styles had to be combined into one smooth style. We did this by having one person dictate and the other type, which caused an intertwining of our styles by the time the words hit the screen. We had fun working on this paper and learned quite a bit about collaboration in the process. For example, we found it challenging because we had to work on one sentence at a time, making sure each sentence was right before we went on to the next one. This process made the revision take far longer to complete than if it had been done by one person.

QUESTIONS FOR WRITING AND DISCUSSION

1. What are the best ideas or evidence in this essay? Explain the points at which you might disagree with the writers' interpretation.

2. Compare MacMillan's and MacFadden's drafts with the final version of their essay. Explain how their interpretation changed as they worked collaboratively on the final version. What did they add to their final version? What did they omit from the earlier drafts?

3. In the final version, MacMillan and MacFadden do not cite evidence from the final part of the story. Explain why the events in town support or do not support the Phoenix parallels.

4. Review the "Guidelines for Revisions." In the authors' essay, underline sentences that contain the *main idea*, that *define key terms*, that contain *evidence* or support, that *explain* how the evidence supports the thesis, that *signal* major parts of the interpretation, and that contain *accurate quotations*. Based on your annotations, what suggestions for further revision do you have for the authors?

DEATH: THE FINAL FREEDOM
Pat Russell

Following a class discussion of the feminist theme in Kate Chopin's "The Story of an Hour," Pat Russell wrote in his journal, "Is the story a feminist one? No. It is not just about feminism but about how people stifle their own needs and desires to accommodate those of their mate." In his essay, Russell argues that the traditional feminist reading limits the universal theme of the story. As you read his essay, see if you are persuaded by his argument.

The poor treatment of women and their struggle for an individual 1 identity make up a major underlying theme of Kate Chopin's stories. Although many regard Chopin's "The Story of an Hour" as a feminist story, today a more universal interpretation is appropriate. This story is not about the oppression of a woman, but about how people strive to maintain the normality and security of their relationships by suppressing their own individual wants and needs.

Evidence in favor of the feminist argument begins with the peri- 2 od the story was written in, sometime around the turn of the century. Society prevented women from coming out of the household. Most women weren't allowed to run a business, and for that matter, they couldn't even vote. Their most important jobs were wife and mother. This background sets the tone for the main character's life. In the beginning we are told Mrs. Mallard has a "fair, calm face whose lines bespoke repression" (414). There is also evidence that suggests her husband is ignorant of her ideas and forceful with his own. Chopin writes: "There would be no powerful will bending her in that blind persistence with which men and women believe they have a right to impose a private will upon a fellow creature" (415). In addition, Mrs. Mallard is described early as fearful and powerless, and later as a triumphant "goddess of Victory," indicating her rebirth. These citations suggest that this is a feminist story, but this label limits the meaning behind the story.

Many people who are unhappy with their marriages either fail to 3 recognize their unhappiness or refuse to accept responsibility for it. I feel sorry for those who don't recognize their unhappiness. However, it is pathetic to see someone such as Mrs. Mallard hold onto a relationship simply because she doesn't know how to let go. "And yet she had loved him—sometimes. Often she had not" (415). She continuously fell in and out of love with her husband until he "died," at which point she told herself that love didn't matter compared to the self-assertion "which she suddenly recognized as the strongest impulse of her being" (415). It is as if she has waited for all of her life for this moment; she prays for a long life, when only the day before she dreaded it. She weeps for him but at the same time compares her husband to a criminal, a man whom she has lived her life for, never once thinking of herself. But now "there would be no one to live for during those coming years; she would live for herself" (415). She is lucky in that she feels "free." Her emotional suppression is over, and she will no longer have anyone to blame for her unhappiness.

It is important not only to try to interpret the author's intended meaning of the story, but also to think about what message "The Story of an Hour" has for us today. As a feminist story, the lesson "The Story of an Hour" teaches is one-dimensional. Interpreting it as a story about the struggle of all people opens up the possibility of teaching others that selfishness and selflessness are both good, when used in moderation. In Mrs. Mallard's case, correcting this balance becomes a matter of life and death. In the face of her suppressor, her desperation for freedom forces her to choose death.

4

QUESTIONS FOR WRITING AND DISCUSSION

1. With what parts of Russell's interpretation do you agree? What additional evidence from the story might Russell cite in support of his interpretation? What ideas or sentences might you challenge? What evidence from the story might refute those statements?

2. Write out your definition of *feminism*. Where does or should Russell explain his definition? How should Russell clarify his definition?

3. Write out Russell's main idea or thesis. Explain why his thesis is an interpretation and not just a statement of fact.

4. What shaping strategy does Russell use to organize his essay?

5. Write out two other possible titles for Russell's essay. Explain why your alternate titles are (or are not) better than Russell's title.

Jacob Lawrence (b.1917). *The Library*. 1960.
Tempera on Fiberboard.

Chapter 12 Writing a Research Paper

While reading Toni Morrison's *Song of Solomon* and talking with relatives about your own family tree, you decide to learn more about your ancestors—where they came from, what jobs they held, which ones were famous and which were not, and why these people lived the lives they did. In the process, you hope to learn more about yourself and your immediate family. During your research, you read family records and letters, interview your parents and grandparents, check county records, and research genealogies in the library. You intend to write an investigative paper documenting not only what you find but the process of your search and the discoveries that you make along the way.

After spending two months in France living with a family and trying to understand their dinner conversation, you wonder why you—and other Americans—know so little about foreign languages. After reflecting on your inadequate background in French language and culture, you decide to investigate the current state of foreign-language studies in the United States. During your research, you discover that Americans know very little about foreign languages and cultures simply because foreign languages are rarely required of students either in high school or in college. You decide to write a research paper that documents the current state of foreign-language studies and demonstrates a need for a mandatory foreign-language requirement for secondary schools. You hope that it will persuade more students to study foreign languages and encourage some schools to revise their requirements.

Research is formalized curiosity. It is poking and prying with a purpose.
—ZORA NEALE HURSTON,
NOVELIST AND FOLKLORE RESEARCHER

You know when you think about writing a book, you think it is overwhelming. But, actually, you break it down into tiny little tasks any moron could do.
—ANNIE DILLARD,
NATURALIST, AUTHOR OF PILGRIM AT TINKER CREEK

LTHOUGH THE WORDS *RESEARCH PAPER* SOUND IMPOSING TO MOST PEOPLE, RESEARCH IS REALLY A NATURAL AND ENJOYABLE PART OF OUR EVERYDAY EXPERIENCE, BOTH OUTSIDE AND inside college classrooms. We pride ourselves on being good detectives—whether it's window-shopping for a good bargain, finding the hottest used sports car, asking coworkers for tips on the best Mexican food in town, or just browsing in bookstores for something that's fun to read. Even in college classes, curiosity leads us to discover new ideas. Whenever we wonder about what causes ozone holes, what makes the Internet work, how artists turn clay into beautiful pottery, or what the national debt means, the seed for a research idea drops into our minds. At some point, the idea becomes a question, takes root, and begins to grow. When that happens, we want to learn about something, to find out what others already know or don't know. Curiosity blooms into research when we'd rather discover the answers for ourselves than be handed an answer—an "answer" that may have the manufactured feel of a plastic flower.

Whether or not you called it by that name, the essays that you have already written in this course have involved research. The verb *research* literally means "seek out" or "search again." All writing requires research. Your observing essay, for example, required you to "look again" at your subject in order to describe it well. For your remembering essay, you recalled special events from the past, researching your mind for memories. You have also investigated topics by searching in written documents and by doing surveys and interviews. You have explained, evaluated, argued, and even explored subjects using research. In short, you are already a researcher with considerable experience in presenting the results of your research to a chosen audience. A research paper—sometimes called a *term paper*—is simply a more thorough and systematic extension of skills that you have already practiced.

This chapter will show you how to write a research paper—preparing, locating sources, taking notes, collecting and shaping information, revising, and documenting your sources. As in other writing assignments, the process is recursive. Often, you will need to back up, collect new information, redraft parts of your paper, or refocus your subject during the writing process. At the end of this chapter, student writer Kate McNerny's paper, "Foreign Language Study: An American Necessity," illustrates the important features of a research paper. Throughout the chapter, however, samples from her research log, bibliography, notes, drafts, and documentation illustrate various stages in one writer's process of writing a research paper.

Techniques for Writing a Research Paper

Criticism [is] a disinterested endeavor to learn and propagate the best that is known and thought in the world.
—**MATTHEW ARNOLD**,
POET AND ESSAYIST

Like other kinds of writing, a research paper requires that you focus on a particular subject, develop a claim or thesis, and support your position with convincing evidence: background information, facts, statistics, descriptions, and other people's evaluations and judgments. The evidence that you present in a research paper, however, is more detailed than that in an essay, and the sources must be cited in the text and documented at the end of the paper.

In a sense, a research paper is like a scientific experiment. **Your readers should be able to trace your whole experiment—to see what ideas and evidence you worked with, where you found them, and how you used them in your paper.** If readers have any questions about the information you've presented or the conclusions you've reached, they can start with your sources and recreate or check the "experiment" for themselves. If they want to investigate your subject further, your sources will guide their reading. As you write your research paper, keep the following techniques in mind:

- **Using** *purpose, audience,* **and** *form* **as your guides for writing.** Research is just a method of collecting and documenting ideas and evidence. Purpose, audience, and form should still direct your writing.
- **Finding the** *best that has been written or said* **about your subject.** Instead of trying to reinvent the wheel, discover what other people or writers already know (or don't know), and then build on what they have learned. Learn to evaluate your sources—be especially critical of Internet or Web sources.
- **Using sources to make** *your* **point.** As you gather information, you may revise your thesis in light of what you learn, but don't let the tail wag the dog. Don't allow your sources to control you or your paper.
- *Documenting* **your sources, both in the text and at the end of the paper.** Using ideas, information, or actual language from your sources without proper documentation is *plagiarism.*

USING PURPOSE, AUDIENCE, AND FORM AS GUIDES

Like any other kind of writing, research papers have a *purpose.* Reporting, explaining, evaluating, problem solving, and arguing are all purposes for research papers. Purposes may appear in combinations, as in a paper that summarizes current research and then proposes a solution to a problem. Research papers, however, are not just reports of other people's ideas or evidence. What you, the researcher, observe and remember and learn is important, too. Most subjects are not interesting until writers make them so. Your curiosity, your interest in the subject, your reason and intuition establish why the subject is worth researching in the first place—and why a reader would want to read the paper once it is finished.

Research papers have a defined *audience*, too. The subject you choose, the kind of research you do, the documentation format, the vocabulary and style you use—all should be appropriate for your selected audience. If you write a senior research paper in your major, you will write for a professor and for a community of people knowledgeable about your field. If you are a legal assistant or a junior attorney in a law firm, a superior may ask you to research a specific legal precedent. If you work for a manufacturer, a manager may assign you a research report on the sales and strategies of a competitor. Although your classmates and teacher will probably read the research paper that you write for this class, you will ask them to role-play your audience. They will try to read your paper from the point of view of a defined audience—an employer, a politician, a nutritionist, an artist, an astronomer, or a senior law partner. In fact, your instructor may ask you to send your paper to some person or persons who actually are part of your audience.

Finally, your research paper will follow a *form* that fits your purpose and meets the expectations and needs of your audience. First, form is controlled by purpose. If you are writing a research paper evaluating some product or performance, it may look like an evaluating paper, organized around your claims, criteria, judgments, and evidence. If you are writing a problem-solving paper, you will demonstrate the problem, propose a solution, and convince your readers that your proposal is necessary or will work. If you are arguing for a position or claim, you will present research showing both sides of the controversy and then try to convince your reader to believe or act on your claim. In each case, however, you will cite your sources in the body or text of your paper and include a list of your sources (a *bibliography*) at the end.

The *form* for your research paper is also affected by your intended audience. If you are researching new advances in sports medicine for an audience of experts, you may choose an elaborate form, with an abstract or summary of your ideas at the beginning, a section reviewing and evaluating current research, subsections for each of your main points with diagrams and charts, and an appendix with supplementary materials. If, however, you are writing primarily for jogging enthusiasts, your research paper may look more like an informal essay. Magazines and journals in the field illustrate a variety of appropriate forms for research papers. The student essay by Kate McNerny at the end of this chapter illustrates one form.

FINDING THE BEST SOURCES

Accessing information from both published and unpublished sources is central to all research. To find good sources, you need to hone your detective skills. Unfortunately, Hollywood has promoted the myth that good detectives follow their suspects in high-speed car chases or through glamorous affairs. Of course, that's just fantasy. Detectives must do actual research—paperwork and legwork—to track down leads. Writers are, in a real sense, also detectives, constantly researching their own experiences and the experiences of others. Journalists, lawyers, psychologists, doctors, businesspeople, coaches, scientists, novelists—all sorts of people practice their skills in locating key bits of information and tracking down good leads.

Research combines careful planning with good luck, mindless drudgery and moments of inspiration, many dead ends and a few rare discoveries. As coaches sometimes say, those who prepare and work hard make their own luck. The following excerpt from the introduction to Pauli Murray's *Proud Shoes: The Story of an American Family* recounts her research into her family genealogy, which included slaves, free blacks, some racially mixed family members, and other relatives who were white and socially prominent. Although her detective work took several years and involved both library and field research, her account reflects the problems and successes that all researchers experience.

My field research had the thrill of detection when the clues panned out. Rigorous discipline was needed for the drudgery of sifting through masses of documentary material in search of one relevant fact or one confirmation of a family legend. The trail of the Fitzgerald family led me into nearly a dozen localities in several states. It took me into musty basements of old courthouses to pore over dust-silted and sometimes indecipherable handwritten entries in old volumes. I found that each locality had its own captivating legends preserved in family papers; its traditions recorded in pamphlets and privately published little books; its stories printed in almanacs, newspapers, business directories. Almost every place had "the oldest living inhabitants" and their recollections. Most important, almost every locality had its own regional-history enthusiasts, who welcomed me into a fellowship of digging into the past. Some of them gave me expert guidance which improved the efficiency of my research and shortened my labors.

USING SOURCES TO MAKE YOUR POINT

When your hard work does yield a source that has good information and ideas on your exact subject, don't be tempted to let that source take over your paper. If you start stringing together passages from only one or two key sources, you'll be summarizing rather than doing research. You'll be letting the sources tell you what to think, what information is important, or what conclusions to reach. Use your sources, then, to support *your* point. Write your own paper; don't let your sources write it for you.

DOCUMENTING YOUR SOURCES

Documenting your sources is an important part of writing a research paper. Documentation takes place in two stages: First, in the body or text of your paper, you give credit for any material that you have taken from your sources. Then, at the end of the paper, you include a list of "Works Cited" or "Works Consulted" that gives fuller information about these sources for your readers. If your readers doubt a fact or statistic, they can check your sources for themselves. If your readers want more information, your documentation enables them to track down the sources. *Note:* Decide on the documentation format (usually MLA or APA style) before you begin your research. You need to know what relevant bibliographical information you need to record in your notes.

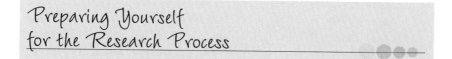

Preparing Yourself for the Research Process

Writing a research paper involves the same process that you used in writing essays. The major difference is that each stage or dimension of the process takes longer. You may spend two weeks just collecting sources, reading articles and books, jotting down ideas, testing your ideas on classmates and friends, and narrowing and focusing your subject. And because you gather so much material, the shaping and organizing processes are also more demanding. Sometimes you may feel as if you're trying to put forty frogs in a dishpan: By the time you arrange ten, the first four have already jumped out. The revising also takes longer, partly because you have to include your documentation, but partly because the sections of the paper may not fit together as smoothly as you had hoped. There is really no way to rush research. If writing an ordinary paper is like fixing your lunch, then writing a research paper is like preparing Thanksgiving dinner. You can't microwave a research paper. Good things take time.

The first step in writing a research paper is to *readjust your inner clock*. Initially, you'll think that you're not making much progress. You'll think that you're in a slow-motion movie or that you're trying to jog through butter. However, once you readjust your inner clock, set more modest goals, and content yourself with a slower but more persistent pace, you've won half the battle. By reducing the pressure on yourself, you'll feel less frustrated when you reach a dead end and also readier to appreciate valuable information when you discover it.

To help you adjust mentally and physically to a new pace and an extended writing process, begin your preparation by making a research notebook, outlining a realistic timetable for the paper, and selecting a documentation format.

■ WARMING UP: JOURNAL EXERCISES   Do at least one of the following journal exercises to help get yourself into a research frame of mind or to discover a possible research subject:

1. In the library, find an issue of a magazine or newspaper published on or near the date and year of your birth. The issue may be on microfilm. Record the date and title of the newspaper or magazine. Browse through the issue, looking at headlines, articles, advertisements, editorials, comics, weather, sports, local news, and so forth. As you look through the issue, record any items, facts, or historical incidents that interest you. Photocopy one page that you find especially interesting. Explain why that page captured your attention.

2. Sit down with a family member, friend, or classmate. On a sheet of paper, write down the subject of the most interesting course that you are currently taking. Hand the sheet of paper to that person and ask him or her to write down questions for an interview designed to find out *why* you like this course and *what* you like best about it. Then have that person interview you and record your responses. At the end of the interview, discuss your responses. What ideas could you research in order to explain to your interviewer what is interesting about this subject?

3. If you are *not* in the library, try this exercise. Reread your authority list from the journal entries in Chapter 6, "Investigating." Choose one subject from that list. Assume that you are on a scavenger hunt, trying to track down bits of information about that subject without leaving the building that you are currently in. Anything is fair game: a dictionary, a textbook, a telephone directory, a telephone, a computer terminal, a friend or roommate, this textbook, your journal, or anything you can observe or remember. You have twenty-five minutes to complete the hunt. Write down all the sources you use and the information you discover from each source.

4. In the library, wander down the stacks, looking at titles of books that might interest you. Choose one volume from the shelf. In your journal, record the basic information about that book: author, title, place of publication, publisher, date. In that book, find *three* specific sources that the author refers to or used to write the book. (If the book does not cite sources, choose another volume.) Does your library have these sources? If so, determine where these sources are located. Ask the reference librarian for help if you need it.

RESEARCH NOTEBOOK

Although some researchers still recommend using index cards for recording bibliographical entries and notes, for most shorter research projects (up to twenty pages), a notebook computer, a loose-leaf notebook, or a spiral notebook with pockets for additional papers and photocopies may be more functional. Divide your notebook into four sections: research log, bibliography, notes from sources (including photocopies), and drafts and ideas.

The *research log* section of your notebook serves as a scratch pad and log of your research progress. In it, you will record what you accomplish during each research session, potential references you need to check, reminders to yourself, questions to ask a librarian or your instructor, and notes about your problems, progress, and intended next steps. As you work, jot down what you did and what you still need to do. These notes about your problems, progress, questions, and next steps will help you maintain momentum on your research project. Each time you return to the library or to your research, you can check your notes to see what you need to do next.

Below is an excerpt from student writer Kate McNerny's research log:

4/26

4:30–6:00 p.m.

Still working on finding articles. Found the Delbert and Roberta Long article. It has some good stuff. <u>Education</u> is on microfilm, so I learned how to photocopy from microfilm. Of course, just when I had the machine turned to exactly the right page, I discovered I didn't have a dime for the copy machine, so I had to leave the room (some guy waiting in line looked irritated as I explained I'd be back in a minute). I ran to the change machine, got my nickels and copied the article!

April issue of <u>Parents</u> magazine missing from the shelves. UGH – I hate that.

Question: Do I want to survey students to find out about typical attitudes toward taking foreign languages? What questions could I ask?

Another question: Is this going to be an arguing paper? Is there a controversy? Are there two sides??

Try to find tomorrow: three <u>Education Digest</u> articles on microfilm (L11/E3): Oct. 94, p. 32
Dec. 95, p. 89
Mar. 96, p. 52

Check <u>Education Index</u>.

Remember that 5-6 p.m. is a good time to work in the library. Everyone clears out, so I don't have to fight over the Internet computers, the photocopiers, and the microfilm machines.

In the *bibliography* section of your notebook, keep a list of every source that you consult, with complete information about each source. If your library's on-line catalog system shows the status of every source, be sure to print out every source you want to check. If you cannot print the source, you'll need to copy it in your notebook. Leave space between entries for additional information, such as call numbers. This list becomes *your working bibliography*. McNerny's bibliography included the following entries:

Honan, William H. "Language Study Shifts Again: Chinese is up, Russian down." <u>The New York Times</u> 9 Oct. 1996: B9

AN 1. N4   Current issues in basement east wing; Older issues in microtext

Lambert, Richard D. "Some Issues in Language Policy for Higher Education" <u>The Annals of the American Academy of Political and Social Science</u> 532(1994): 123-37.

H 1 .A4   Current issues in Current Periodicals Room; Older issues in Stacks

In the *source notes* section, leave plenty of pages to record direct quotations, paraphrases of key ideas, and facts from the sources in your bibliography list. Introduce each section with a reference to the author and a short version of the title. After each note, indicate the page number or numbers. One page of McNerny's notes contained the following entries:

Lambert, "Some Issues in Language Policy."

Lambert explains how the lack of coordination between secondary schools and higher education causes problems. As Lambert notes, "The result of this strong tradition of university autonomy is that in the United States, foreign language planning for higher education must take place one institution at a time and implementation of change must occur in house-to-house, hand-to-hand combat" (125).

Ranwez and Rogers, Status of Foreign Languages

91% of the 536 Colorado secondary schools responding to the questionnaire offered foreign languages, but 91% of schools responding didn't require any foreign language credits for graduation. pp. 99-100

For your source notes section, make *photocopies* of any valuable source materials. Write author, title, and page numbers on each photocopied source.

In the *drafts and ideas* section of the notebook, jot down brainstorms, looping or clustering exercises, sketch outlines, trial drafts, and examples from your own experience. During a research project, ideas can come to you at any time. When they do, take time to write them down. This section of your notebook serves as a journal devoted solely to your research paper. One example from McNerny's drafts and ideas section records her personal experience with foreign languages:

4/29

I can remember my mom always telling me, "Take French classes, learn how to speak French so that you can go visit your cousins in France some day." At the time (junior high school) though, learning a foreign language was low on my priority list. I did take French classes for two years – but dropped out after my sophomore year and immediately lost any basic competency I might have acquired.

In college, I'd like to take a language again, but it never seems to fit with my schedule. But last year, as my mom had promised, I got the opportunity to visit my cousins in France. For some reason, the fact that I couldn't speak French didn't seem to me like it would be a big problem. That was until I stepped off the train at Gare du Nord in Paris and couldn't find the relative who was supposed to meet me. After frantically searching the entire station several times, I had to break down and ask for help. At the information desk a few completely butchered French phrases escaped my lips – only to be received by an unimpressed, unresponsive station attendant. He muttered something about dumb Americans and then pointed me off toward some unknown destination. Well I survived that ordeal – but at the same time swore to myself that I would never make another trip to France until I could speak the language.

RESEARCH TIMETABLE

Before you begin your research, write out a tentative schedule. Your instructor may assign due dates for specific parts of the paper (invention exercises, topic selection, working bibliography, rough draft), but you should make a schedule that fits your work habits and your weekly schedule.

The following schedule assumes that you have at least a month to work on your research paper. The amount of time required by each part depends on the amount of time you can work each day. On some days, you may have only thirty minutes. On other days, you may have several hours. The key is to do a little bit every day to keep your momentum going.

Prepare for research. Buy and organize a research notebook; set up a timetable; select a documentation format.	1–2 days
Choose a subject. Begin the narrowing and focusing process.	2–3 days
Collect sources. Find library sources; identify and find unpublished sources; do interviews or surveys; record personal experiences; browse sites on the Internet.	
Evaluate source materials; take *notes* on selected sources; *photocopy* sources.	12–14 days
Shape and outline ideas; *reread* notes and photocopies; *draft* sections of essay. Continue to *focus* thesis while rereading, planning, and drafting.	6–10 days
Revise draft. Get peer response, collect additional information, sharpen thesis, reshape or revise outline, cite sources in the text and in the bibliographical list, and edit and proofread the paper.	6–8 days

Tailor your schedule to your own temperament and work habits. If you like to work exactly to a schedule or even finish early, design your schedule so you can finish a day or two before the due date. If you are like most writers—you love to procrastinate or you are often up all night just before an assignment is due—then use your schedule to set early target dates, to get your momentum going. When you finish drafting your schedule, put a copy in the *research log* section of your notebook, so that you can check your progress as you work.

DOCUMENTATION FORMAT: MLA AND APA STYLES

A final step in preparing for the research paper is to select a documentation style. This chapter illustrates both the MLA and APA styles. If you are writing a paper for the humanities, follow the Modern Language Association (MLA) style set forth in the *MLA Handbook for Writers of Research Papers* (5th ed., 1999). If you are writing a paper in the behavioral sciences, use the American Psychological Association (APA) style as described in the *Publication Manual of the American Psychological Association* (5th ed., 2001).

Leading academic and professional journals also illustrate the documentation styles customary in specialized fields. You may want to consult issues of those journals to determine the exact format for footnotes or in-text citation of sources. *Before you begin doing research, however, select a documentation style* that is appropriate for your subject, purpose, and audience. Then practice that style as you compile your working bibliography.

Research Paper: The Writing Process

■ ASSIGNMENT FOR THE RESEARCH PAPER   Choose a subject that strongly interests you and about which you would like to learn more. It may be a subject that you have already written about in this course. Research this subject in a library and, as appropriate, supplement your library research with questionnaires, interviews, Internet research, or other unpublished sources of information. Check with your instructor for suggested length, appropriate number or kinds of sources, and additional format requirements. Use a documentation style appropriate for your subject, purpose, and audience.

CHOOSING A SUBJECT

For this research paper, choose a subject in which you already have personal interest or experience. Start by rereading your journal entries for possible research subjects. Even a personal entry may suggest an idea. If you wrote about how you fainted in the gym during aerobics or weight training, you might research the potential dangers of exercising in high heat and humidity or sitting in a sauna after hard exercise. If you wrote a journal entry about a friend's drinking problem, you might like to read more about the causes and treatments of alcoholism.

In addition, reread the essays that you have written to see whether one of them refers to a possible research subject. If your observing essay, for example, was about a tattoo parlor that you visited, use that essay as the starting point for further investigation and research. Whom could you interview to find out more about tattooing? What is the history of tattooing? Why is it becoming more popular? What controversies surround its use? What resources does your library have? What sites can you find on the Internet? You might also use a topic from your remembering, reading, or investigating essays as starting places for additional reading and research. *Build on what you already know and what already interests you rather than launch into an entirely unknown subject.*

NARROWING AND FOCUSING YOUR SUBJECT   Once you have a tentative idea, remember that you'll need to narrow it, focus it, or otherwise limit the subject to make it appropriate for your audience and context. The topic of alcoholism is too general. Focus on a particular research question: "Do beer commercials on television contribute to alcoholism?" "Are there really positive effects of drinking moderate amounts of alcohol?" "What methods does Alcoholics Anonymous use to help people?" "Have DWI laws actually reduced the number of fatal automobile accidents?" Your research question may lead to a **thesis statement** that you will demonstrate in your research essay: "Although some studies show a definite link between consuming moderate amounts of red wine and reduced incidence of heart disease, the negative effects of alcohol consumption far outweigh the potential benefits."

Only after you've started your research, however, will you know whether your research question is still too broad (you can't begin to read everything about it in just two weeks) or too narrow (in two weeks, you can't find enough information about that question).

Two techniques may help narrow and focus your subject. You may wish to try these now, wait until you have done some initial reading, or do them several times during your collecting and shaping.

The first strategy is simply to think about your *purpose* and *audience*. The best way to focus your paper is to reflect on your purpose: What kinds of claims do you want to make about your topic? (If necessary, review the claims of fact, cause and effect, value, and policy outlined in Chapter 10, "Arguing.") As you collect articles, think about the kinds of claims you might want to make about your topic.

Claims of Fact: Are makers of hard liquor being discriminated against by not being allowed to advertise on TV? Is alcoholism a disease or just an addiction?

Claims of Cause and Effect: Does TV advertising increase alcohol consumption or just affect the brands that are consumed? Can students who are "recreational" drinkers become alcoholics? Do recovery programs like Alcoholics Anonymous really work?

Claims of Value: Does beer have any nutritional value? Are microbrews really made better or fresher than beers from larger breweries?

Claims of Policy: Do age-based drinking laws really work? Should liquor consumption be banned at campus sporting events? At dorms, fraternities, and sororities? At any campus function? Should makers of hard liquor be allowed to advertise on television?

Asking questions about your potential audience may also help you find a focus for your essay. If you are writing for a local audience, consider what they believe and what they might be interested in. Is the topic of alcohol regulation controversial? Who are your readers? What are they likely to believe on this issue? Profile your audience and brainstorm how you can connect your research question to those particular readers.

Question analysis is a second narrowing and focusing strategy. The who, what, when, where, and why questions that you use to focus your topic are the same questions that reference librarians use to help you focus your research in the library.

Who:	What group of people is interested or affected?
What:	How are key terms defined? What academic discipline is involved?
When:	What is the period or time span?
Where:	What continent, country, state, or town is involved?
Why:	What are possible effects or implications?

Answering these questions—by yourself, in a group, or with a reference librarian—may suggest new angles, new avenues for research, or subtopics that could lead to a focus for your research paper. As you narrow your topic, you are narrowing and focusing the range of your research in the library. Student writer Kate McNerny, brainstorming with another class member, applied these questions to her subject about foreign-language study and came up with the following possibilities:

Foreign Language Study

Who?   Ans: I am interested in Americans. Specifically, I want to focus on why Americans should begin learning a foreign language early in school, in grade school, secondary school, and college. Learning a foreign language would affect how foreigners see us.

What?   Ans: Key terms defined – perhaps what
         "learning" means. Does it mean just basic
         speaking competency? Probably. If I could
         have asked a few simple questions in the Gare du
         Nord, I wouldn't have felt so stupid. Academic
         discipline – learning the foreign language is
         important, but culture is part of it, too. History
         should teach us about foreign cultures. So
         should psychology – do the Japanese think
         differently from the Spanish? Why did the
         French seem rude and Italians friendly?
         Do I want to research the psychology of
         languages? I don't think so.

When?   Ans: I really want to know why foreign
         language studies are currently not emphasized.
         But what about trends – is it getting better or
         worse? Are more people learning foreign
         languages than a few years ago? I don't know.

Where?   Ans: In the United States. In my home town.
         Why is it that in the French schools, children
         as a matter of course learn several languages
         while we aren't required to learn any?

         Supposedly, we are the "melting pot" for
         many different languages and cultures, but
         we don't know each other's languages.

Why?   Ans. I can make a long list of the effects
         – We can't communicate when we're tourists.
         – We can't read anything printed in their
           language.
         – We don't understand their culture.
         – We don't even understand the cultures of
           the millions of Americans from other
           cultures.
         – We isolate ourselves in business, too.

         To avoid these effects, I want to argue
         for stronger foreign language requirements
         in secondary schools and colleges.

As a result of her question analysis, McNerny decided to discuss both language and culture, to focus on the current conditions, and to recommend that secondary schools require foreign languages. *In any research, however, what you look for and what you find are always different. You will need to modify your focus as you read and learn.*

COLLECTING

With ideas for a tentative subject, a possible purpose, and an audience, you can focus on collecting information. Collecting data for your research paper will require identifying and locating published and unpublished sources, evaluating your sources and choosing those that are the most appropriate for your needs, and then taking notes on your selected sources. *Remember, however, that finding sources—like writing itself—is an ongoing and recursive process.* You often identify new sources after you have taken notes on others. Although you may begin your search in the on-line catalog, in the reference section, or on the Internet, as you narrow and focus your topic or draft sections of your paper, you may come back and recheck the on-line catalog, basic references, periodical indexes, or bibliographies.

Use *informal contacts* with friends or acquaintances as an integral part of your collecting process. Friends, family members, business associates, or teachers may be able to suggest key questions or give you some sources: relevant books and magazine articles, television programs that are available in transcript, or local experts on your subject.

UNPUBLISHED SOURCES   Although the library may be your main source of information, other sources can be important, too. You may *interview* authorities on your subject or design a *questionnaire* to measure people's responses. (Interviews and questionnaires are discussed in Chapter 6.) *Phone calls* and *letters* to experts, government agencies, or businesses may yield background information, statistics, or quotations. *Notes from classes, public lectures,* or *television programs* are useful sources. Use a tape recorder to ensure that you transcribe your information accurately. A *scientific experiment* may even be appropriate. *Unpublished public documents,* such as deeds, wills, surveyors' maps, and environmental impact statements, may contain gold mines of information. Finally, don't ignore the most obvious sources: Your room, the attic in your home, or your relatives may have repositories of valuable unpublished data—private letters, diaries, old bills, or check stubs.

For her research paper, Kate McNerny decided to conduct an informal survey of attitudes toward foreign languages. She recorded the responses in the *drafts and ideas* section of her research notebook. When she drafted her paper, she used some of these responses in the introduction to her paper:

Q: Should foreign languages be required in Junior and Senior High?

A: (Mindy, 21, student) Yes, I think its a good idea – It would have been more valuable to me than some of the other required classes I took – like P.E.

A: (Jodi, 22, student) No, I had a hard enough time with English. Besides, I don't think I'd ever need to use it.

A: (Roger, 23, carpenter) Yes, I was in Europe last year and missed out on a lot because I couldn't speak any other language. Europeans don't speak English as much as we hear they do, but most of the people I Met there spoke at least two languages.

A: (Jim, 49, contractor) No, I've never gone to Europe and never needed to speak another language for any other reason. I had enough trouble getting through other classes.

A: (Carolyn, 59, teacher) Yes, when I was teaching there were few language classes available. But as a reading teacher I can see many ways in which language studies would have enhanced our program.

PRIMARY AND SECONDARY SOURCES   Some sources—accounts of scientific experiments, transcripts of speeches or lectures, questionnaires, interviews, private documents—are known as *primary sources*. They are original, firsthand information, "straight from the horse's mouth." Secondhand reports, analyses, and descriptions based on primary sources are known as *secondary sources*. Secondary sources may contain the same information, but they are once-removed. For example, a lecture or experiment by an expert in food irradiation is a primary source; the newspaper report of that lecture or experiment is a secondary source.

The distinction between primary and secondary sources is important for two related reasons. First, secondary sources may contain errors. The newspaper account, for example, may misquote the expert or misrepresent the experiment. If possible, therefore, find the primary source—a copy of the actual lecture or a published article about the experiment. Second, finding the primary sources may make your research document more persuasive through an appeal to character (see Chapter 10, "Arguing"). If you can cite the original source—or even show how some secondary accounts distorted the original experiment—you will gain your readers' trust and faith. Not only does uncovering the primary data make your research more accurate, but your additional effort makes all your data and arguments appear more credible.

LIBRARY SOURCES   Before you begin collecting information, acquaint yourself with the library itself. If you have not already done so, inquire at the information desk about library tours, or walk through the library with a friend or classmate. Locate the *reference section;* the *on-line catalog* for books and articles; the *indexes* for newspapers, journals, and magazines; the *microfilm room;* the *stacks;* and the *government documents* section. Don't assume that because you've used one library, you can immediately start your research in a new library. Remember: *Librarians* themselves are valuable sources of information. Use their expertise early in your research.

BACKGROUND INFORMATION AND GENERAL REFERENCE   Before you consult the on-line catalog, you may need a *general overview* of your subject. Start with an encyclopedia, dictionary, almanac, or biography for background information. Many people associate encyclopedias with their grade-school "research"—when they copied passages out of *The World Book* or *Collier's Encyclopedia.* But encyclopedias are an excellent source of basic information and terminology that may help you focus, narrow, and define your subject. *Use them as background reading, however, not as major sources.*

In addition to the general encyclopedias, there are hundreds of references—one or two might just save you hours of research in the library and lead you directly to key facts or important information on your topic. (You may wish to begin your collecting in the reference room or check there only after you have collected information from other books and articles. Often these references are more valuable *after* you have done some reading on your subject.) Beyond the standard college dictionary or thesaurus, the *Oxford English Dictionary,* known as the *OED*, or *Webster's Third New International Dictionary of the English Language* may help you find key ideas or definitions.

There are also many specialized dictionaries for scientific terms, slang words, symbols, and a host of other specialized vocabularies. If you need facts, figures, or statistics, consult the *World Almanac*, the *Book of Facts*, or the *Statistical Abstracts of the United States*. If your subject is a person, look at *Who's Who in America*, or check one of the references that indexes collections of biographies. *Biography and Genealogy Master Index* and *Biographical Dictionaries* reference more than three million biographical sketches.

The *librarian* is still the most valuable resource for your research. At some point during your research in the library, probably after you have a focused topic and have collected some sources, talk to a reference librarian. For many writers, asking for help can be really intimidating. To make the process of asking for help as painless—and productive—as possible, try saying something like the following: "Hi, I'm Kate McNerny. I'm doing a research project for my college writing course. My topic is foreign-language study in the United States. I'm trying to find information about the current state of foreign-language study in the United States and collect some arguments for increasing requirements in secondary schools and colleges. Here's what I've found so far [explain what you've done]. What additional reference books, websites, indexes, dictionaries, or bibliographies might help me in my research?" The resulting conversation may be the most productive five minutes of your entire library research. After you've talked to the librarian once, it will be easier to return and ask a question when you hit a snag.

Knowledge is of two kinds. We know a subject ourselves, or we know where we can find information upon it.

—SAMUEL JOHNSON,

FROM JAMES BOSWELL'S LIFE OF JOHNSON

THE ON-LINE CATALOG   The good news for researchers in the twenty-first century is that computerized databases have revolutionized the whole process of library research. In most university libraries, a computer terminal can, in a few seconds, give you information that used to require hours of searching card catalogs or printed indexes. You can easily locate books, articles, and government documents relevant to your topic. You can find the library call numbers and locations of sources. You can determine if a source is available or checked out and get an abstract or a short description of a source. For some systems, you can print out the bibliographical information so that you don't have to take notes. Often, you can print out whole articles right there.

The only bad news is that nearly every on-line catalog system is different. Some colleges have OPACs (on-line public access catalogs) that allow you to access the library's holdings. Your college may use OCLC (On Line Computer Library System), which is the largest of the public access catalogs, or you may use systems such as NOTIS, RLIN, MELVYL, CARL, or SAGE. But whatever system your library uses, you need to spend time learning the tricks of that particular database. Don't try to learn the system by yourself. Take a library orientation tour. Collect the library's handouts about its computerized databases. Ask the librarians for help. And don't wait until your research paper is assigned to walk into the library. If you have to learn a new computer system *and* write your paper at the same time, you will be inviting massive frustration.

When McNerny started her search in her library's on-line database, she found the following sample entry on her topic. Notice that the information she received on her printout contained the following information: (1) the database she was searching; (2) the location of the periodical; (3) the author, title, and source; and (4) a short abstract. (For some of the references she found, she was able to print out the entire article.)

DATABASE:	Expanded Academic ASAP
KEY WORDS:	Language and languages study and teaching
LIBRARY:	Colorado State University
HOLDINGS:	Current issues in Current Periodicals Room. Older issues in Microtext, 1st floor, north wing. LB 2300 .C4
SOURCE:	*The Chronicle of Higher Education*, Nov 22, 1996 v43 n13 pA35(2).
TITLE:	A new program ends the stress of tackling a foreign language: NYU uses an informal approach to whet students' appetites for formal classes later. (New York University)
AUTHOR:	Amy Magaro Rubin
ABSTRACT:	New York University offers an experimental foreign language program called Speaking Freely, designed to encourage students to study foreign languages and travel abroad. The program incorporates music, food, and other cultural aspects of the country and language being studied. Classes in French, Italian, Chinese, German, Japanese, Korean, Spanish, and Swahili have been well received by students and provide them a unique perspective on a culture as well as a refreshing approach to language study.

SEARCH STRATEGY   As you practice with your library's on-line or compact disk (CD-ROM) systems, you'll discover that the *search strategy* you use and the *key words* you enter become very critical. Should you use a *word* or a *subject* search? Should you use *browse* or *express* to search your database? You need to *practice with your library's system* to see *how it works*. Next, you need to pay careful attention to the key words you enter. If you are writing an essay about teenagers' psychological problems, entering the word *teen* may get you nowhere, while entering the word *adolescent* or even *teenage* may hit the jackpot. To help with your key-word search, try the following. First, make a list in your research notebook of all the possible terms that may relate to your subject. When you do a search, note the other possible terms or headings given on the computer terminal.

If you are having trouble gathering information on your topic, be sure to consult a librarian and discuss your search strategy and the list of key words you are using for your search. *A brief discussion with a reference librarian will probably be the most productive ten minutes you will spend in the library!*

INTERNET SOURCES   Where should you start your search for relevant sources—in the library databases or on the Internet? The answer to that question depends on your topic, your purpose, and your audience. But the explosion of websites at the end of the 1990s indicates that, for many writers and topics, the Internet may well be the place to start. The immense variety of sources makes the Internet a great place to do your browsing—especially if you're not quite sure exactly what your topic will be or what angle you wish to investigate. Other writers—especially those who are already sure of their focus—may wish to begin with an on-line search in their library, and to save their Internet research for later, when they want to find sources they cannot locate in the library. Whatever choice you make, you will probably want to browse the Internet at some point during your research.

Especially if you are not an expert at Internet research, you should think about the strengths and weaknesses of Internet research. The strengths of Internet research are many:

- The Internet has a mind-boggling number of sources, Usenet groups, and Web pages.
- The Internet can have an amazing retrieval speed for sources from around the world.
- The Internet gives you the ability to chat with other people who share similar interests.
- The Internet gives you personal access—from your library or your home—to key information from libraries, businesses, organizations, and governments.

Unfortunately, doing research on the Internet does have drawbacks that are often related to its strengths. Internet enthusiasts often praise the Web for creating a democratic space where every person and site is equal. On the downside, however, librarians often shudder at doing research on the Internet simply because everything is so decentralized and disorganized. And there are other problems as well:

- The sheer number of possible sources on the Internet may make finding the exact source you need very difficult.
- Browsing on the Web may be fun, but you may spend hours going from one site to the next without making any real progress.
- The increasing commercialization of websites may interfere with locating relevant information.
- Waiting for a source to download from a busy site can be tedious and frustrating.
- Sources on the Internet may not be accurate or reliable—and thus not appropriate for your paper.

altavista
THE SEARCH COMPANY

| **Web** Image Audio Video Directory News | Family Filter: off   Help |

| | Any language ◆ | Search |

Advanced

Breaking news: Sharon Says Prisoners Implicate Arafat in Financing of... [New York Times]

Tools
Translate
Maps
Yellow Pages
People Finder
Shopping
Real Searches
Search Settings
  More >>

Web Directory
Computing
Gaming
Home
Movies
Music
People & Chat
Work & Money
  Entire Directory >>

Web Resources
Shopping
Electronics,Video Games,More

Autos
New,Used,Research

Personals & Dating
Pictures & Profiles,Dating Tips

Travel
Flights,Cars,Hotels

Careers
Find Jobs,Post Jobs,Resumes

Auctions
Electronics,Collectibles

Marketplace
Try Free Personals
Gambling Online
Web Site Hosting
Car Warranty Special
Dedicated Servers

Auto Insurance
Attend IT Training
Quality Personals
Free Loan Quotes
Free Credit Report

Online Sportsbook
Online Career Test
Merchant Accounts
$8.95 Domain Names
Online Casino

AltaVista Worldwide: Australia Brazil Canada France Germany Italy Spain UK More>>
Business Solutions: Submit a Site Express Inclusion Advertise with Us AltaVista Software

Help About AltaVista Terms Of Use Submit a Site Advertise with Us
© 2002 AltaVista Company. AltaVista® is a registered trademark of AltaVista Company.

With realistic estimations about the Internet's virtues and faults, however, you should be able to find relevant and even exciting sources that will help you learn about your topic and communicate your findings to your audience.

Note: As you continue to read in this section of the chapter, you may want to open a connection to the Internet so you can check out several of the sites. Also, remember to start making bookmarks for any sites you want to revisit later.

Internet Browsers and Search Engines

Once you have an idea for a possible topic, you can begin searching sites on the Internet for relevant information. If you need to review the basics of Internet research and terminology, refer to the Internet glossary on pages 581–582. If you are sitting at a computer with a browser, such as Netscape or Internet Explorer, you can begin working on your topic right now by accessing one of the popular search engines described below. Of course, there are actually hundreds of such searching tools available on the Web, but the ones described here can get you started.

AltaVista <http://www.altavista.com> AltaVista is still one of the most powerful search engines on the Web. It is especially effective after doing a search on Yahoo to help narrow your topic. Researchers rely on AltaVista for its comprehensive coverage. It also has supplementary features such as news search, multimedia searches, and human-powered results from LookSmart's directory.

Ask Jeeves <http://www.askjeeves.com> Ask Jeeves gives you the human touch. Instead of entering key words, you type a question in plain English. Ask Jeeves records millions of questions and then gives websites that answer each question.

Dogpile <http://www.dogpile.com> Dogpile is a meta search engine—which means that it searches other engines or services. Other meta search engines include Inference Find and MetaCrawler. What these engines gain in terms of breadth of search they may lose in accuracy because they use the "lowest common denominator" search terms.

Excite <http://www.excite.com> Excite is a popular, medium-sized crawler-based Web page index that offers human-powered results from LookSmart. Since Excite now owns WebCrawler, the search results of those sites are similar.

Google <http://www.google.com> Google has quickly become very popular with researchers because of its huge index on the Web and the high relevancy of responses. Google's responses are based on the number of links to that site created by other Web users—so Web users have in essence "voted" for the usefulness of each site.

HotBot <http://hotbot.lycos.com> HotBot is a standard search engine that takes results first from Direct Hit and then from Inktomi, which is widely used by other services. HotBot is run by Lycos as a separate search engine.

Lycos <http://www.lycos.com> Lycos has shifted to a directory service similar to Yahoo. It combines results from FAST and Direct Hit.

Northern Light <http://www.northernlight.com> Northern Light is a favorite search engine of many researchers because it features a large index and groups its results by topic and subtopics.

Yahoo! <http://www.yahoo.com> Yahoo! is the web's most popular search service—because it searches hierarchically and retrieves highly relevant sources. The key to its success is the team of 150 editors who search, categorize, and compile its websites. Yahoo!'s results are supplemented from Google listings.

Electric Library <http://www.elibrary.com> Electric Library is an article retrieval service, not a search engine as such. The Electric Library, however, searches over 150 full-text newspapers, 800 magazines and journals, and 2,000 reference works and also prints out entire articles on your printer. The main drawback to Electric Library is that its sources are valuable primarily for current, popular topics where work with secondary sources is appropriate.

Of course, websites and search engines are constantly changing. But the good news is that you can find comparative reviews and data about the various research tools and search engines on the Internet. Access **Search Engine Watch** at <http://searchenginewatch.com> for reviews and comparisons of popular and specialized search engines.

BASIC INTERNET GLOSSARY

The URL (uniform resource locator) is the address that identifies each Internet site. In the address that follows, for example, **http** stands for "hypertext transfer protocol," **www** stands for World Wide Web, **Yahoo!** is the manager of the website, and **.com** indicates a commercial site:

URL: http://www.yahoo.com

In addition to commercial **(.com),** you can access a variety of locations, including educational **(.edu),** governmental **(.gov),** noncommercial **(.org),** military **(.mil),** and networking **(.net).** Other URLs can access gopher sites **(gopher://),** ftp **(ftp://),** newsgroups **(news://),** and so forth. For further explanation, see Gene Cowan's essay "How the Web Works" in Chapter 6, "Investigating."

Note: URLs have no spaces between any letters, periods, or slashes. URLs must be typed with complete accuracy—one missed slash or period or letter and your computer will not be able to find the correct address.

As you get started doing research on the Internet, acquaint yourself with the following key terms and definitions. If you know the basic language for navigating the Internet, you won't remain a newbie very long.

bookmark Your computer's browser (see below) will enable you to record each URL that you want to remember, so that the next time you want to visit that site, you merely have to click on the right line in your bookmark rather than type out a complete URL string. Remember to bookmark sites that look promising as you do your research!

browser Your computer needs a browser such as Netscape or Internet Explorer to help you access Telnet, gopher, or websites on the Internet. (A browser is not the same as a search engine such as Yahoo!, Excite, or AltaVista.)

cyberspace The on-line world created in electronic space or on the Internet.

FTP The file transfer protocol is the set of commands that enables you to transfer files between two sites on the Internet.

gopher A program that "goes for" or finds items in a long list or menu is a gopher. Gopher addresses begin with "gopher://" rather than with " http://." Gopher was an early search program prior to the hypertext searches supported on the Web.

home page The home page is usually the first page of any website, and it identifies the author of the page, the location or sponsor of the site, and the basic information about the site.

html Hypertext markup language is the computer code used to write pages on the Web.

hyperlink Often just called *links*, these are highlighted words, icons, or bits of graphic that you can click on to move to a related site. A hypertext is simply a collection of documents or graphics connected by these links.

listserv A listserv is a mail list that enables users to conduct an ongoing e-mail conversation about a particular topic.

MOO A multiuser domain, object-oriented, provides a space in which people can meet, at a given time, to discuss a particular topic.

MUD A multiuser domain (or dungeon) enables simultaneous communication, often by role-playing a certain character or persona.

newsgroup Any group of people who post messages on Usenet. Usenet is a network that gives access to an electronic discussion group.

search engine A program that enables Internet users to find relevant sites on the Internet. Popular search engines or search tools include Yahoo!, AltaVista, Excite, and Google.

Telnet An electronic program that enables you to communicate with another computer with a user name and a password. If you access the Internet or the Web from your home, you probably need to "telnet" into America Online or an educational or commercial source in order to access the Internet.

This short list is just the tip of the iceberg of Internet terminology. If you want to know about **ASCII, baud rates, bytes, cookies, flame wars, MIMEs, POPs, spam, Veronica, WYSIWYG,** or literally hundreds of other terms, visit one of the dozens of Internet glossaries available on-line, such as the Internet Literacy Consultants' Glossary of Internet Terms at **http://www.matisse.net/files/ glossary.html**. Check out this site and make a bookmark so you can return whenever you have a question.

Tips for Doing Research on the Internet

If you are still learning to use the Internet, here are some tips that may save you quite a bit of time during your research.

The Library *of* Congress

SEARCH THE CATALOG | SEARCH OUR WEB SITE | ABOUT OUR SITE
SHOP | SITE MAP | JOBS | TODAY IN HISTORY

COLLECTIONS & SERVICES
For Researchers, Libraries & the Public

THOMAS
Legislative Information

AMERICAN MEMORY
American History in Words, Sound & Pictures

AMERICA'S LIBRARY
Fun Site for Kids & Families

COPYRIGHT OFFICE
Forms & Information

EXHIBITIONS
An Online Gallery

THE LIBRARY TODAY
News, Events, & More

POETRY 180

HELP & FAQs
General Information

101 INDEPENDENCE AVENUE, S.E.
WASHINGTON, D.C. 20540
(202) 707-5000
Library of Congress Help Desk
Please Read Our Legal Notices

COLLECTIONS & SERVICES | AMERICAN MEMORY | THOMAS | THE LIBRARY TODAY
COPYRIGHT OFFICE | AMERICA'S LIBRARY | EXHIBITIONS | HELP & FAQs

- The time of day you access the Internet may be crucial. Obviously, 3 A.M. is a good time for minimal Net traffic, but you do need your sleep. Log on at different times of the day to find out when is best for your location.
- If you have the option on your browser or search engine, choose "text only" format for Web displays—downloading graphics adds significant time.
- If it takes more than a couple of minutes to get files from your site, click on the "Stop" button and try another source.
- Use the "bookmark" or "favorites list" to record your best sites. You may even want to organize your favorites or bookmarks into a folder designated specifically for the topic of this paper.
- Make sure your browser is set so that the location (URL), title, date, and page are recorded on the copies you print. If they do not appear, ask your laboratory monitor or teacher for assistance.

- Make sure you have enough information from your source (author, title, title of work, full URL address, and date of visit) so that you can write an in-text citation and a references citation in either MLA or APA format. (See the sections on MLA and APA citation of on-line sources later in this chapter.)

Useful Research Addresses

In some cases, instead of browsing through a search engine such as AltaVista or Yahoo! you may wish to go directly to a reliable and relevant site. Here are a few you may wish to visit as you research your topic. Each of these sites offers links to other relevant sites.

- **ERIC <http://www.cal.org/ericll>** Your library will probably have an ERIC (Educational Resources Information Center) database on CD-ROM that you can conveniently search, but if you are not at a library, you can access the ERIC site at this URL. You may even order ready-made searches on popular topics such as "English Only/English Plus," "Teaching ESL Abroad," or "Peace Corps Language Teaching Materials."
- **The Library of Congress <http://lcweb.loc.gov>** The Library of Congress site can give you direct access to an immense range of government and library resources.
- **News Index <http://www.newsindex>** News Index is one of many news and newspaper indexes. News Index searches the current issue and archives of over three hundred newspapers and news sources. Also use Google and Yahoo! to find specific newspapers with searchable indexes.
- *The New York Times* **<http://www.nytimes.com>** You will need to register with *The New York Times*, but then you can access the current paper or do a key-word search of the archives for relevant articles, editorials, and feature stories.
- **On-Line Writing Centers** Check out the on-line writing centers at the following addresses for help with writing as well as with finding relevant research strategies and sites: Colorado State University Online Writing Center at **<http://writing.colostate.edu>** or the Purdue University On-Line Writing Lab at **<http://www.owl.trc.purdue.edu>**.
- **Popular Magazines** Many magazines, such as *Mother Jones* and *Utne* have home pages that allow you to access articles and participate in on-line listservs or "salon" conversations on current issues. Use your search engine to find their URLs.
- **Uncover <http://www.ingenta.com>** Uncover has changed to Ingenta, but it still accesses over 11 million articles and 26,000 publications. If you access Uncover from a library, the service is free of charge.
- **U.S. Government Printing Office <http://www.access.gpo/gov/su_docs/index.html>** The Government Printing Office (GPO) is the largest publisher in the world, and the GPO Access site allows you to find government publications on almost every topic imaginable.

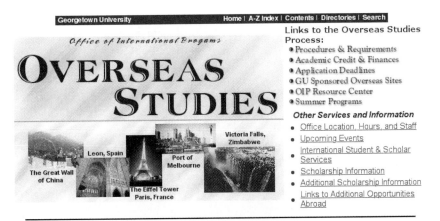

The mission of Overseas Studies at Georgetown University is to promote, support, and develop international and intercultural educational opportunities for students, and in so doing, help to define the international character of Georgetown. These programs are developed and evaluated in collaboration with the wider Georgetown community to ensure that they are academically rigorous, linguistically appropriate, and complementary to the Georgetown curriculum. In keeping with the Jesuit philosophy of education, these overseas studies opportunities serve to invite participants to reflect on the values that form their own identities, and to encourage them to assume their roles as responsible world citizens.

EVALUATING INTERNET SOURCES

Evaluating sources on the Internet requires much more care and attention than judging print sources. Printed sources in the library have often been screened and filtered for accuracy and reliability, whereas often Web sources may represent simply one person's opinion, reaction, or point of view. Even more problematic is our inability to judge the context of the information. When we read an article in *The New York Times*, for example, we can expect a certain level of accuracy and reliability; conversely, when we read an article in a supermarket tabloid, we know we should expect very little accuracy. We know not to quote a tabloid article about diet supplements when we are writing an academic paper about health and nutrition. Even in the television media, we know when we're watching *CNN News* and when we're seeing an infomercial. On the Internet, however, we may have very few context cues to help us judge what we're reading.

Internet sources must be evaluated with a critical eye. Unless you critically appraise your sources, you don't know whether the site you are using was written by a sixth-grader doing research for a class assignment, a grandmother doing her first Web page, a wild-eyed radical, or a neighborhood dog. When we find a source, we need to ask some key questions: Who is the author? Is the

"On the Internet, nobody knows you're a dog."

author an expert, a salesperson, or a person with a reason to be biased? What organization is publishing this information? Where did the author find his or her sources? Can we verify the information in other reliable sources? How current is this information? As you read and download texts from the Internet, pay particular attention to the six criteria below. (These criteria are adapted from guidelines designed by Elizabeth E. Kirk, the Library Instruction Coordinator for the Milton S. Eisenhower Library at Johns Hopkins University and are available at http://milton.mse.jhu.edu:8001/research/education/net.html.)

- **Authorship.** Who is the author? Is the author well known? Are the author's credentials or biographical information available on the Internet or elsewhere? Does the author have a reason to be biased? The less you know about the author, the more cautious you need to be about using the source. *If you decide to use a document by a questionable authority, indicate exactly what you know or don't know about the author's credentials.*
- **Publishing organization.** Does the site indicate the organization responsible for the text? Is there information in the header or footer indicating the organization, webmaster, or designer of the home page? Is this organization recognized in its field? Is the organization selling

something? *If you know the source is not authoritative or has a commercial basis, indicate the organization's identity if you quote from the site.*

- **Point of view or bias.** Every document or text has a point of view or bias—but some biases may mean that the site's information is not reliable or accurate. Does the author or the organization have a commercial, political, philosophical, religious, environmental, or even "scientific" agenda? *When you use a source with highly selective or biased information or perspectives, indicate the author's probable bias or agenda when you cite the text.*

- **Knowledge of the literature.** Reliable sources refer to other texts available or published in that discipline or field. Look for documents that have in-text citation or reference to other sources, a fair and reasonable appraisal of alternative points of view, and a bibliography. *Any source that has no references to other key works may simply be one writer's opinion and/or may contain erroneous information.*

- **Accuracy and reliability.** Can the information in the text be verified for accuracy? Are the methods of gathering information indicated? Has this study been replicated elsewhere? *If you have reason to believe the source is not reliable or accurate, find other sources.*

- **Currency.** Depending on your purpose and audience, currency may or may not be important. If you are writing about the reception of Shakespeare's plays, information from texts written in the seventeenth century may be more relevant than current ones. If you are writing about stem cell research or about censorship on the Internet, however, you need the most current available information. Can you determine the date the text was written? Can you find the date the information was posted on the site? Are cited statistics based on recent data? *You may use information from an older study, but acknowledge that it is dated and supplement it with more recent studies.*

As you gather sources from the Internet, be skeptical! Question the authority of the texts you find. If you think the source is not reliable, trust your judgment and don't use it. If the text seems accurate and reliable, but you cannot verify all of these criteria, indicate the problems in the source when you introduce your citation:

> Certainly Mind Extension University is in the business of selling on-line education, but they may be right when they claim that distance learning is the wave of the future.

> Karen Levine is a Spanish teacher at Thousand Oaks High School and has sponsored school-to-school exchange programs, but her testimonial for the International Education Forum's program—an exchange program for which she has worked—should be balanced against recommendations of other foreign-language exchange programs.

If you have a question about the reliability, relevance, or accuracy of any source, check with your instructor or a librarian. *If you decide to use any questionable or biased sources, you need to qualify their findings and data when you introduce the source.* Otherwise, your reader may believe that your argument is based on biased, inaccurate, or unreliable data.

PERIODICAL INDEXES   Magazines, journals, and newspapers are called *periodicals* because most are published on a daily, weekly, or monthly basis. An index is just a list of citations or articles, organized for easy reference. An index may be in print or in computerized form, such as CD-ROM or computer database. Just as the index of a textbook refers to topics, ideas, or names in that book, a periodical index refers to articles published in a selected group of magazines, journals, or newspapers.

Although some periodical indexes, such as the *Readers' Guide to Periodical Literature*, still exist in print format, many general and specialized indexes are on computerized databases. Periodical indexes can list abstracts of articles, can contain both abstracts and full-text articles, or can contain almost entirely full-text citations. Below is a list of frequently used indexes. Ask your instructor or reference librarian which would be most helpful for your audience, purpose, and topic.

- **Academic Universe** is a full-text database that indexes thousands of periodicals and accesses articles on a wide range of news, business, legal, and reference information. It uses Lexis-Nexis services to retrieve full-text documents.
- **Electric Library** is not an index so much as a full-text article retrieval service. It is especially useful for popular magazines and nonacademic articles.
- **FirstSearch** is a full-text database which searches 15 databases including ArticleFirst (for articles), NetFirst (web resources), WorldCat (books), Medline (medical journals), ERIC (language and education journals), GPO (Government Printing Office publications), and *World Almanac.*
- **Ingenta** (formerly called Uncover) is a full-text database and article retrieval service. It features a searchable database of more than 11 million citations from more than 25,000 journals, covering a wide range of subjects from agriculture and biology to medicine and philosophy.
- **Newspaper Abstracts** covers twenty-five national and regional newspapers. Index references newspapers such as the *Wall Street Journal*, the *Los Angeles Times*, the *Chicago Tribune* and provides only abstracts of articles.
- **Readers' Guide Abstracts** provides abstracts of articles on current events and news, fine arts, education, business, sports, consumer affairs, and so forth.

EVALUATING LIBRARY SOURCES   Even with published library sources, you should appraise your sources with a critical eye, just as you do for Internet and Web sources. Just because something is published or printed does not mean that it is relevant, current, accurate, or reliable. Some sources will not relate specifically to your topic; others will be too superficial or too technical. Some will be out of date; others will be biased or simply inaccurate. Evaluate your printed sources based on the following criteria:

- **Sources should be relevant.** The sources you select should be relevant to your subject, your purpose, and your intended audience. If your narrowed topic is still too general, all your sources will look relevant. In that case, narrow your subject even more. Sources must also be relevant to your purpose. If you are writing an argumentative research paper, for example, you need sources representing both sides of the issue. If you are proposing a solution to a problem, look for sources describing the problem or the solution. Finally, sources should be appropriate for your intended audience. The articles that Kate McNerny found in *Foreign Language Annals* were more appropriate for her academic audience than was a brief and superficial article she found in *Parents* magazine.

- **Sources should be current.** As a rule of thumb, look for the most current sources—especially those on scientific or technical subjects. Research and data on AIDS are more accurate and complete now than they were in 1990. Sometimes, however, older books and articles are important. If you are doing historical research about the Great Depression in the United States, you may want to read key documents from the 1930s. In every academic discipline, some sources remain authoritative for decades. When you find that many writers refer to a single source, it may be valuable regardless of its date of publication.

- **Sources should be reliable.** Check for possible biases in articles and books. Don't expect the National Rifle Association to give an unbiased report on gun-control legislation. Don't assume that representatives of right-to-life or prochoice groups will objectively represent the full range of facts about abortion. Because at least some bias is inevitable in any source, locate and use a variety of sources representing several points of view. If you are in doubt about an author's point of view or credibility, consult experts in the field or check book reviews. *Book Review Digest,* for example, contains references to reviews that may indicate the author's reputation or reliability.

TAKING NOTES   Taking careful notes from both published and unpublished sources is, of course, fundamental to accurate documentation. When a source appears relevant and useful, do the following:

1.   *Record complete bibliographical information in the bibliography section of your research notebook (or in your computer notebook).* For many on-line library systems, you will be able to print out the bibliographical information you need right from your computer terminal. For *books,* you need authors, editors, titles, volumes, publishers, places of publication, and years of publication.

For *articles*, you need authors; article titles; magazine or journal titles; volume numbers or dates, months, and years of publication; and beginning and ending page numbers. As Kate McNerny did in her log, leave a space between each entry to record call numbers or locations of documents:

(Book): Freed, Barbara F., ed. <u>Second Language Acquisition in a Study Abroad Context.</u> Philadelphia: John Benjamins, 1995.
　　HF5549.A2P38　　Current Periodical Room
(Article): Brady, Robert I. "English-Only Rules Draw Controversy." <u>HR Focus</u> June 1996: 20.
　　P118.2.S433　　1995　　First Floor East

If the source is unpublished—such as a telephone conversation, a letter, or a public document in the county courthouse—record all the information about it that your readers will need to identify and consult the source themselves. (See the "Documenting Sources" section in this chapter.)

2. *Record notes in the source notes section of your research notebook.* Identify each entry with the author's name and the title. If your notes fill two or more pages, put the author and title at the top of each page. Write on only one side of each page. Briefly *summarize* the main points made in the source, note specific information useful to you, paraphrase key ideas, transcribe interesting quotations, and jot down your own brief comments, questions, and memories. Place page numbers immediately following each paraphrase or quotation. Use direct quotation rather than paraphrase when the actual words in the source are more concise, authoritative, or persuasive than your paraphrase might be. *Be sure that direct quotations are accurate, word-for-word transcriptions from the original.*

3. *Photocopy important sources for later rereading and reference.* Make sure all photocopies clearly show authors, titles, and page numbers. (For some research projects, your instructor may request photocopies of every source you paraphrase or quote.) *Tip:* If you photocopy several pages, *copy title pages or the magazines' covers,* and staple the copies together. Then, you will have all the necessary bibliographical information, and you can underline key passages or make notes on the photocopies themselves.

Photocopying has distinct advantages. You can copy the relevant pages of a source so you don't have to lug thirty books home. (Leaving the sources in the library also helps other researchers.) Photocopies are good insurance against losing key information—in case the book or journal is checked out the next time you need it. Photocopies also allow you to reread sources *after* you have read other books or articles; often, on the first reading of a source, you're not certain what is important and what is not. Finally, photocopies allow you to recheck the final draft of your research paper against sources, to make sure that paraphrases, direct quotations, and page citations are accurate. You may save yourself an extra trip to the library to check a page number, a date, or a journal title.

4.   *As you read sources and take notes, record your own reactions and ideas in the drafts-and-ideas section of your research or computer notebook.* Be an active reader of your sources. When you agree or disagree with what you are reading, stop for a minute and jot down your ideas. When you think of a comparison, a process, a way to analyze or evaluate something, possible causes and effects, or examples from your own experience, *write out your ideas as completely as you can, right then, while they're fresh in your mind.* Don't get so absorbed in taking notes that you forget to record your own ideas. You don't have to collect twenty sources and *then* do a draft; instead, draft ideas *as* you collect information.

SHAPING

Once you've collected information for your research paper, you may feel overwhelmed by the task of shaping it into a coherent form. You can assert control over your data, however, and shape them into coherent form by reconsidering your purpose and thesis. *Reread your own notes and especially your draft sections from your research notebook.* Then, in the draft section of your notebook, answer the following questions:

Subject:	What is your general subject?
Narrowed topic or question:	What aspect of your subject is most interesting to you now? What question will you answer or explain?
Purpose:	Is your purpose primarily to inform, explain, evaluate, describe a problem and propose a solution, or argue a claim?
Working thesis:	What thesis, claim, or proposal do you want to impress upon your readers?
Audience:	Analyze your audience. How can you interest them in your subject? What aspects of your collected data are most appropriate for your audience?

As you shape, draft, and revise your research paper, you may continue to refocus your topic and question, refine your thesis, or revise your sense of audience.

SHAPING STRATEGIES

Your goal now is to design some order, sequence, plan, or outline for your research paper. Forcing yourself to write an outline, however, simply may not work. You should have an idea from your previous papers about how your

Writing is the hardest work in the world not involving heavy lifting.
—PETE HAMILL,
JOURNALIST

Writing a book is not as tough as it is to haul 35 people around the country and sweat like a horse five nights a week.
—BETTE MIDLER,
SINGER, ACTOR, AUTHOR

writing process works best, but if you're stuck, feeling frustrated, or overwhelmed, try several of the following strategies:

- *Review strategies for shaping* that are appropriate for your particular purpose. If you are arguing for a certain claim, reread the shaping strategies discussed in Chapter 10. If you are evaluating something or analyzing a problem and proposing a solution, review the strategies discussed in Chapter 8 or 9.
- *Explain to a friend or classmate your purpose, audience, and working thesis.* Then try to explain how you might proceed.
- *Try freewriting, looping, or clustering* to develop a plan.
- *Reread your notes and drafts* from your research notebook.
- *Take a break.* Let your ideas simmer for a while. Go for a walk. Work on assignments for another course. Go jogging or swimming. Let your mind run on automatic pilot for a while—the information and ideas in your mind may begin organizing themselves into an initial "sketch outline" without your conscious effort.
- *Try branching or treeing your main ideas.* On paper or at the chalkboard, begin with your topic and draw the trunk and main branches of your topics. Try to explain your sketch or chalkboard drawing to someone.

Think of these activities as a circle: Begin at any point, work in either direction, and repeat them as necessary. When something starts to work, stay with it for a while. If you start to block or become frustrated, go on to the next activity.

WORKING OUTLINE   If the shaping activities helped you discover a basic design or plan, translate it into a working outline. If not, you may need to begin drafting in order to discover an outline. Kate McNerny decided to follow a pattern for writing an argument. Although she modified it considerably to change her purpose to problem solving, the sketch outline helped her organize her ideas and source material so she could begin drafting.

Introduction:		Comments—quotations from informal survey—why people feel they don't need to know a foreign language. Mention study on misconceptions of school-aged children about Russian children.
I.	**Narration:**	Foreign-language studies' position in other countries as opposed to U.S. Mention "Official English" here? Include example of European requirements? Statistics on how many Americans are actually competent in another language. Mention bills to require a state language? U.S. position in world as far as power, trade.
II.	**Partition:**	American students should be required to study a foreign language throughout the six years of junior and senior

high school. To increase number of students studying foreign language, we need changes in administrators and teachers, changes in students, and changes in state and national policies.

III. Arguments: An increase in number of students studying foreign languages would:
Help to improve diplomatic relations with other countries—peace cannot be achieved without this.
Change Americans' attitudes toward foreigners and change foreigners' attitudes toward Americans.
Facilitate international trade and other business.
Increase jobs for students abroad and at home.
Without requirement, no incentive for many students.

IV. Refutation: Not necessary because other countries can speak English. (This is more an argument against learning a language, not against a requirement.)
Not essential for quality education.
As requirement, would detract from other important subjects.
Not enough federal, state, or local money to change number of foreign-language courses offered.

Conclusion: Call for action on part of federal government.
Contrary to popular belief, we are not an isolated country.
A required study of languages will bring us one step closer to global understanding and peace.

ORGANIZING YOUR NOTES   With a rough outline as a guide, reread your draft ideas, notes, and photocopies, and label them according to headings and subheadings in your working outline (for instance, I: Intro; II: Background and History; III: Required Changes; IV: Advantages of Changes; and V: Conclusion). Before you remove pages from the source notes section of your notebook or unstaple photocopied articles or sections of books, *make sure each entry or photocopy contains the author, title, and page numbers*. Now you are ready to arrange your notes and copies for use during drafting. Organize your notes into groups according to each section of your working outline. Reread each group, deciding which information should come first, in the middle, or last.

DRAFTING

At this point, some of the most difficult work is behind you. Congratulate yourself—there aren't many people who know as much as you do right now about your subject. You are an authority: You have information, statistics, statements, ideas from other writers and researchers, and your own experiences and observations at your fingertips. As you write, remember your purpose and audience. What is your purpose—to inform, explain, evaluate, offer a solution, or argue? Who exactly is your audience? What arguments and evidence will convince them? Your sources will become the evidence and support for *your ideas*. Remember that your voice and point of view should unify the information for your reader.

Many writers prefer to start a draft with the first main idea, leaving the introduction until later. As you write, you may discover a quotation, example, or narrative that doesn't fit anywhere else but that would be a perfect lead-in. Or you may already know how you want to start, using an idea that will help organize and direct your thoughts. As you draft, be guided by your working outline and your notes. Avoid copying passages verbatim from your own notebook ideas; instead, reread your notes and express those ideas in language that fits the idea you're working on.

If you get stuck, go back and reread what you have drafted so far or reread the source notes and ideas that you have assembled from your notebook and photocopies. Try to maintain your momentum by writing as quickly as possible. Don't be upset if the natural flow of your writing suggests a slightly different order or deviates from your working outline. Consider the new possibility. You may have discovered a better way to shape your material. If you are missing some fact or quotation, just leave a long line and keep writing. Later you can find the source and add the material you need.

USING SOURCES   Proper use of sources requires both creativity and scrupulous honesty. On the one hand, you want to use other people's information and ideas when and where they serve *your* purpose and *your* ideas. A research paper is not simply a long string of quotations connected by a few transitions. On the other hand, the sources you cite or quote must be used *fairly* and *honestly*. You must give credit for other writers' ideas and information. You must quote accurately, cite your sources in your text, and document those sources accurately.

WHAT SOURCES TO CITE   You must cite a source for any fact or bit of information that is not *general knowledge*. Obviously, what is "general knowledge" varies from one writer and audience to another. **As a rule, however, document any information or fact that you did not know before you began your research.** You may know, for example, that America spends more money on defense than it does on education. However, if you state that the defense budget for the previous year is greater than the total amount spent on education for the past forty years, then cite the source for that fact.

Knowing when you must cite a source for an idea, however, can be tricky. You do not need to indicate a source for *your* ideas, of course. But if you find a source that agrees with your idea, or if you suspect that your idea may be related to ideas from a particular source, cite that source. A citation will give your idea additional credibility: You show your reader that another authority shares your perception.

How to Cite Sources   In the text of your research paper, you will need to cite your sources according to either the Modern Language Association (MLA) style or the American Psychological Association (APA) style. Remember: Choose either the MLA style or the APA style and stick with it. Don't mix styles.

According to the MLA style, the in-text citation contains the author and page number of your source (Torres 50). No comma appears between author and page number. (If the author is unknown, identify the title and page number of your source. Underline book titles; place quotation marks around article titles.)

According to the APA style, the in-text citation contains author and date (Torres, 1996). Use a comma between author and date. If you refer to a page number, it should appear after the author and date (Torres, 1996, p. 50). Use a *p.* (or *pp.* for more than one page) before the page number(s).

The in-text citation (either MLA or APA) refers readers to the end of your paper, where you give complete information about each source in a "Works Cited" (MLA) or "References" (APA) list. For illustration purposes, the following examples use MLA style. See the "Documenting Sources" section (pp. 599–615) for examples of both APA and MLA styles.

Identify Cited References (**MLA** Style)   Once you have decided that a fact, a paraphrase, or a direct quotation contributes to your thesis and will make a strong impression on your reader, use the following guidelines for in-text citation.

- *Identify in the text the persons or source for the fact, paraphrased idea, or quotation:*

As two foreign-language teachers noted, "Like it or not, we are members of a world community consisting of hundreds of nations, and our fates are closely intertwined" (Long and Long 366).

Note: The parentheses and the period *follow* the final quotation marks.

- *If you cite the author in your sentence, the parentheses will contain only the page reference:*

According to Paul Simon, former member of the President's Commission on Foreign Language, the United States should erect a sign at each port of entry that reads, "WELCOME TO THE UNITED STATES—WE CANNOT SPEAK YOUR LANGUAGE" (1).

- *Use block format (separated from the text by a blank line, indented ten spaces, and double-spaced) for quotations of five lines or more:*

Educator Gerald Unks points out two instances in which a lack of language proficiency caused companies to initiate fatal marketing programs.

> When Pepsi-Cola went after the Chinese market, "Come Alive with Pepsi" was translated into Chinese in Taiwan as "Pepsi Brings Your Ancestors Back from the Dead." No Sale! General Motors sought to sell its Nova in South America, oblivious to the fact that "No va" in Spanish means "It doesn't go." (24)

Note: In block quotations, the final period comes *before* the parentheses containing the citation of your source.

- *Vary your introductions to quotations:*

Educator Gerald Unks claims that "only 15 percent of American high school students study a foreign language. Only 8 percent of our colleges require credit in a foreign language for admission (down from 34 percent in 1966)" (24).

The problem is that high school students are not taking foreign languages, and most colleges no longer require a foreign language for admission: "Only 15 percent of American high school students study a foreign language. Only 8 percent of our colleges require credit in a foreign language for admission (down from 34 percent in 1966)" (Unks 24).

- *Edit quotations when necessary to condense or clarify.* Use three ellipsis points or spaced periods (. . .) if you omit words from the middle of a quoted sentence:

As two foreign language teachers noted, "We are members of a world community . . . and our fates are closely intertwined" (Long and Long 366).

If you omit words from the end of a quoted sentence or omit sentences from a long quoted passage, place a period after the last word quoted before the omission; follow it with three ellipsis points—for a total of four periods. (Be sure that you have a complete sentence both before and after the four periods.)

Paul Simon advises us that our nation's lack of language proficiency may have been a partial cause of our disastrous policies in Vietnam:

> Vietnam and the Middle East have taught us that our security position is not solely a matter of dealing with the Warsaw Pact countries or the giants among the nations. Before our heavy intervention in Vietnam, fewer than five American-born experts on Vietnam, Cambodia, or Laos . . . could speak with ease one of the languages of that area. . . . What if—a big if—we had had . . . a mere twenty Americans who spoke Vietnamese fluently, who

> understood their culture, aspirations, and political history?
> Maybe, just maybe, we would have avoided that conflict. (9)

Note: The first line is indented five spaces because in the source the quotation begins a new paragraph.

In some cases you may want to change the wording of a quotation or add explanatory words of your own to clarify your quotation. If you do so, clearly indicate your changes or additions by placing them within square brackets:

> As Simon suggests, if only a few Americans knew Vietnamese, then "maybe, just maybe, we would have avoided [the Vietnam War]" (9).

HOW TO AVOID PLAGIARISM   Plagiarism is the act of passing off another researcher's or writer's *information, ideas, or language* as one's own. Whether intentional or not, plagiarism is a serious offense. In this class, the result may be a failing grade in both the research project and the course. In the working world, people have lost jobs and presidential candidates have been forced to end campaigns because they have been caught plagiarizing.

To avoid such consequences, be honest and give credit for the work of others by carefully documenting *all* facts, ideas, charts, diagrams, and actual phrases or sentences borrowed from your sources. Assume, for example, that an accurate quotation from your source would read as follows:

> "Most Americans take it for granted that English is the language of the United States and even imagine that every American speaks it fluently. According to the 1980 U.S. Census, however, 11 percent of Americans come from non-English-speaking homes, and over 1 percent of the U.S. population speaks English not well or not at all. No indicators suggest that these percentages will soon decrease" (Conklin and Lourie 3).

The most blatant form of plagiarism involves using *both* your source's information and your source's language (shown below in italics) without giving credit:

> It is ironic that *11 percent of Americans come from non-English-speaking homes,* and yet most Americans say they will never need to speak a foreign language.

A second form of plagiarism, equally serious, involves giving credit to a source for facts or ideas, but *failing to use quotation marks to indicate that you have borrowed the exact language from the source.* In essence, you are saying that these ideas and facts come from Conklin and Lourie, page 3, but that the language is your own. That, of course, is untrue:

It is ironic that most Americans take it for granted that English is the language of the United States and even imagine that every American speaks it fluently (Conklin and Lourie 3).

Avoid plagiarism by documenting the passage as follows:

It is ironic, as two researchers recently pointed out, that "most Americans take it for granted that English is the language of the United States and even imagine that every American speaks it fluently" (Conklin and Lourie 3).

To avoid plagiarism, don't randomly copy out interesting passages. Take accurate notes and transcribe quotations *exactly* as they appear in sources. Either put quotation marks around the exact words of the source or paraphrase the main ideas in your own words.

REVISING

What makes me happy is rewriting. . . . It's like cleaning house, getting rid of all the junk, getting things in the right order, tightening things up.

—ELLEN GOODMAN,

JOURNALIST

You have been revising your research essay since the first day of the project. You thought about several subjects, for example, but you chose only one. You started with a focus but revised it as you thought, read, and wrote more. You initially tested your ideas in the draft section of your research notebook, but you revised those ideas as you drafted. At this point, you are just continuing your revising; now, however, you have a complete draft to revise.

Start the revision of your complete draft by taking a break. Fix your schedule so that you can do something else for a couple of days. When you return and reread your draft, be prepared to be flexible. If there is something missing in your data, prepare yourself to track down the information. If a favorite source or quotation no longer seems relevant, have the courage to delete it. If an example on page 4 would work better as a lead-in for the whole paper, reorder your material accordingly. If the evidence for one side of an argument appears stronger than you initially thought, change your position and your thesis. *Being willing to make such changes is not a sign of poor research and writing. Often, in fact, it demonstrates that you have become more knowledgeable and sophisticated about your subject.*

After you have finished your rough draft, ask friends or classmates to give you their responses. Accept their criticism gracefully, but ask them to explain *why* they think certain changes would help. Would they help to make your purposes clearer? Would they be more appropriate for your audience? Don't be intimidated and feel that you must make every change that readers suggest. You must make the final decisions.

DOCUMENTING SOURCES

Both the MLA and APA documentation styles require citation of sources in the text of your paper, followed by a "Works Cited" (MLA style) or "References" list (APA style) at the end of your paper. Use footnotes only for content or supplementary notes that explain a point covered in the text or offer additional information. *Note:* MLA in-text documentation and "Works Cited" documentation are explained here. See pages 608–615 for APA in-text documentation and "References" format.

IN-TEXT DOCUMENTATION: MLA STYLE   In the MLA style, give the author's name and the page numbers in parentheses following your use of a fact, paraphrase, or direct quotation from a source. These in-text citations then refer your readers to the complete documentation of the source in a "Works Cited" or "Works Consulted" list at the end of the paper.

As you cite your sources in the text, use the following guidelines:

If you cite the author in the text, indicate only the page number in parentheses:

According to Vicki Galloway, Project Director for the American Council on the Teaching of Foreign Languages, a student's horizons will not be broadened by "grammar lectures and manipulative classroom exercises" (33).

If the author is unknown, use a short version of the title in the parentheses:

Most students in the United States would be surprised to learn that the Communist Party in Russia actually sponsors rock concerts (A Day in the Life 68).

If the source is unpublished, cite the name or title used in your bibliography:

In an informal interview, one university administrator noted that funding of foreign-language study has steadily decreased over the past ten years (Meyers).

If the source is from the Internet or the Web, use the author, or if there is no author, use the title:

Many websites now provide detailed information about how to plan a study-abroad semester or year (Foreign Language).

If your bibliography contains more than one work by an author, cite the author, a short title, and page numbers. The following examples show various ways of citing a reference to Paul Simon, *The Tongue-Tied American:*

In The Tongue-Tied American, Simon explains that students can earn a doctorate degree in the United States without ever studying a foreign language (2).

> As Simon notes, "It is even possible to earn a doctorate here without study-
> ing any foreign language" (Tongue-Tied 2).

> In the United States, one can earn a doctorate degree without studying a
> single foreign language (Simon, Tongue-Tied 2).

Note: Use a comma between author and title but not between title and page number.

If a source has two authors, cite both authors' names in the text or in the parentheses:

> A recent study sampling 536 secondary schools revealed that 91 percent
> did not require foreign-language credits for graduation (Ranwez and
> Rodgers 98).

If a source has three or more authors, give the name of the author listed first in your bibliography followed by the abbreviation *et al.*, meaning "and others":

> Teachers should integrate the study of history, culture, politics, literature,
> and religion of a particular region with the study of language (Berryman
> et al. 96).

If a source has several volumes, precede the page number with the volume number and a colon, as indicated:

> Language and grammar can be taught with real-life contexts or scenarios
> (Valdman 3:82).

If you are citing a quotation or information from a source that itself cites another source, use the abbreviation *qtd. in* for "quoted in" to indicate that you have used an indirect source for your information or quotation. (If possible, however, check the original source.)

> As Sue Berryman et al. explain, "The course is developed as a world tour
> during which time the students take a vicarious trip . . . to become satu-
> rated in every aspect of a particular area of the globe" (qtd. in Simon 96).

If you cite two or more authors as sources for a fact, idea, or plan, separate the citations with a semicolon, as follows:

> Most recently, two prominent foreign language educators have published
> plans to coordinate foreign-language studies (Lambert 9–19; Lange 70–96).

CONTENT OR SUPPLEMENTARY NOTES You may use footnote numbers in the text of your paper to refer to a "Notes" section at the end of the paper. If you have an important idea, a comment on your text, or additional informa-tion or sources *that would interrupt the flow of your ideas in the text,* you may use that idea or comment in your supplementary "Notes" section. During her research, for example, McNerny read about the movement to make English the "official language" of the United States. She didn't want to digress in her paper, so she described the controversy in a supplementary note at the end of the paper. Here is a first draft of that note:

> [1]Several states currently have bills before their legislatures to make English the "official language." Proponents of these bills argue that immigrants need incentives to learn English. Many opponents from ethnic and civil rights groups believe these bills are racist (McBee 64). If Americans were all educated in foreign languages, these bills would be unnecessary. Americans' ignorance and fear of foreign languages are probably a reason that these bills are so popular.

"WORKS CITED" LIST: MLA STYLE   After you have revised your essay and are certain that you will not change any in-text documentation, you are ready to write your list of sources. Depending on what you include, it will be one of the following:

- A "Works Cited" list (only those works actually cited in your essay)
- A "Works Consulted" list (works cited and works you read)
- A "Selected Bibliography" (works cited and the most important other works)
- An "Annotated List of Works Cited" (works cited, followed by a short description and evaluation of each source)

A "Works Cited" list alphabetically orders, by author's last name, all published and unpublished sources cited in your research paper. If the author is unknown, alphabetize by the first word (excluding *A*, *An*, or *The*) of the title. As a general rule, underline or italicize titles of books, periodicals, and newspapers, but use quotation marks to enclose titles of newspaper and magazine articles. Use the following abbreviations for missing information (other than an unknown author): n.p. (no place of publication given), n.p. (no publisher given), n.d. (no date of publication given), or n. pag. (no pagination in source). The first line of each citation begins at the left margin, and succeeding lines are indented five spaces. Double-space the entire "Works Cited" list.

Following are examples of MLA-style entries in a "Works Cited" list, organized by kind of source: books, articles, and unpublished sources. Use these as models for your own "Works Cited" list. For additional information and examples, see *MLA Handbook for Writers of Research Papers* (5th ed., 1999).

BOOKS: MLA STYLE

Order the information as follows, omitting information that does not apply:

Author's last name, first name. "Title of Article or Part of Book." Title of Book. Ed. or Trans. Name. Edition. Number of volumes. Place of publication: Name of publisher, Date of publication.

A Book by One Author

Krakauer, Jon. Into Thin Air: A Personal Account of the Mt. Everest Disaster. New York: Villard, 1997.

Additional Books by Same Author

Morrison, Toni. Song of Solomon. New York: Knopf, 1977.

---. Jazz. New York: Knopf, 1992.

A Book with Two or Three Authors

Conklin, Nancy F., and Margaret A. Lourie. A Host of Tongues: Language Communities in the United States. New York: Free Press, 1983.

Padilla, Amando M., Halford H. Fairchild, and Concepcion M. Valadez. Foreign Language Education. Newbury Park, CA: Sage, 1990.

A Book with More Than Three Authors

Comley, Nancy R., et al. Fields of Writing. New York: St. Martin's, 1997.

An Unknown or Anonymous Author

New York Public Library Student's Desk Reference. New York: Prentice, 1993.

A Book with an Author and an Editor

Austen, Jane. Pride and Prejudice. Ed. Mark Schorer. Boston: Houghton, 1956.

[The names of well-known publishers are often shortened to the first key word. Thus, "Houghton Mifflin Co." becomes "Houghton," and "Harcourt Brace Jovanovich, Inc." becomes simply "Harcourt."]

An Edited Book

Myers, Linda, ed. Approaches to Computer Writing Classrooms. Albany: State U of New York P, 1993.

A Translation

Allende, Isabel. Paula. Trans. Margaret Sayers Peden. New York: HarperCollins, 1996.

An Article or Chapter in an Edited Book

Sophocles. Electra. Trans. David Grene. Greek Tragedies. Ed. David Grene and Richmond Lattimore. Vol 2. Chicago: U of Chicago P, 1960. 2 vols. 45–109.

A Work in More Than One Volume

Morrison, Samuel Eliot, and Henry Steele Commager. The Growth of the American Republic. 2 vols. New York: Oxford UP, 1941.

A Work in an Anthology

Chopin, Kate. "The Awakening." The Harper Single Volume American Literature. Ed. Donald McQuade et al. 3rd ed. New York: Longman, 1999.

An Encyclopedia or Dictionary Entry

"Don Giovanni." The Encyclopedia Americana. 2001 ed.

A Government Document: Known Author

Juhnke, Gerald A. Addressing School Violence: Practical Strategies & Interventions. ERIC Counseling and Student Services Clearinghouse. Greensboro, NC: GPO, 2001.

[*GPO* stands for "Government Printing Office."]

A Government Document: Unknown Author

United States. Maternal and Child Health Bureau. Babies Sleep Safest on Their Backs: Reduce the Risk of Sudden Infant Death Syndrome (SIDS). Bethesda, MD: GPO, 2001.

An Unpublished Dissertation

Burnham, William A. "Peregrine Falcon Egg Variation, Incubation, and Population Recovery Strategy." Diss. Colorado State U, 1984.

A Pamphlet

Guide to Raptors. Denver: Center for Raptor Research, 2001.

PERIODICALS: MLA STYLE

For all articles published in periodicals, give the author's name, the title of the article, and the name of the publication. For newspapers and magazines, add complete dates and inclusive page numbers. Use the first page number and a plus sign if an article is not printed on consecutive pages. For most professional journals, add volume numbers, issue numbers if appropriate, years of publication, and inclusive page numbers.

An Article in a Weekly or Biweekly Magazine

McCarthy, Terry. "L. A. Gangs Are Back." Time 3 Sept. 2001: 46–49.

An Article in a Monthly or Bimonthly Magazine

Edwards, Mike. "Sons of Genghis Khan." National Geographic Feb. 1997: 2–35.

Morrison, Ann M., Randall P. White, and Ellen Van Velsor. "Executive Women: Substance Plus Style." Psychology Today Aug. 1987: 18+.

An Unsigned Article in a Magazine

"Catching a Cold: It's Up in the Air." Science 86 July–Aug. 1986: 8.

An Article in a Professional Journal

Many professional journals have continuous page numbers throughout the year. The first issue of the year begins with page 1, but every issue after that begins with the number following the last page number of the previous issue. For such journals, give volume followed by the year.

> Swope, Christopher. "Panel OKs Bill to Make English Official Government
> Language." Congressional Quarterly Weekly Report 54 (1996):
> 2128–29.

[For page numbers over 100, use only two digits for the final page citation: 2128–29.] If each issue of a professional journal begins with page 1, cite the volume number followed by a period, then the issue number and year. In the following example, the article is in Volume 9, Issue 1, published in January 1987.

> Brodkey, Linda. "Writing Ethnographic Narratives." Written Communication
> 9.1 (1987): 25–50.

An Article in a Newspaper

Omit the introductory article (*Wall Street Journal* instead of *The Wall Street Journal*). If the masthead includes an edition, include it in your entry.

> Mundy, Alicia. "Attorney General of Social Work." Wall Street Journal 5 Jan.
> 1994: A14.

An Unsigned Article in a Newspaper

> "A Jet Crash That Defies Resolution" Los Angeles Times 5 Sept. 2001: A1.

An Editorial

> Fish, Stanley. "When Principles Get in the Way." Editorial. New York Times 26
> Dec. 1996, late ed.: A27.

ELECTRONIC AND INTERNET SOURCES: MLA STYLE

The World Wide Web and the Internet are still changing, so even the latest MLA guidelines, available in the fifth edition of the *MLA Handbook for Writers of Research Papers* (1999), will continue to change. The current abbreviated basic features of an electronic or Internet citation, given below, appear in complete form on the MLA home page at http://www.mla.org. Use the specific citations following this list as models for your own citations. For additional examples, consult the MLA home page or the most recent edition of the *MLA Handbook for Writers of Research Papers.*

1. Name of author (if known)
2. Title of article, short story, poem, or short work within a book, periodical, or database
3. Title of book (underlined)
4. Name of the editor or translator (if relevant), preceded by appropriate abbreviation, such as *Ed.* or *Trans.*
5. Publication information for any print version of the source
6. Title of periodical, database, scholarly project, or site (underlined), or for a site with no title, a description such as *home page*
7. Name of the editor of the project or database (if available)
8. The volume number, issue number, or other version number of the source
9. Data of electronic publication, update, or posting
10. Name of the subscription service and—if the library is a subscriber—the name and city (and state abbreviation, if necessary) of the library
11. For a posting to a discussion list or forum, the name of the list or forum
12. The number of pages, paragraphs, or sections, if they are numbered
13. The name of any organization sponsoring the website
14. Data when researcher accessed the source or site
15. Electronic address or URL of the source in angle brackets. *Note:* If a URL must be divided between two lines, break it only after a slash. Do not use a hyphen.

A Book

Austin, Jane. Pride and Prejudice. Ed. Henry Churchyard. 1996. 7 Sept. 2001
    <http://www.pemberley.com/janeinfo/pridprej.html>.

A Poem

Carrol, Lewis. "Jabberwocky." 1872. 6 Mar. 1998
    <http://www.jabberwocky.com/carroll/jabber/jabberwocky.html>.

A Scholarly Project

The History Channel Online. 2001. History Channel. 17 Sept. 2001
    <http://historychannel.com/>.

A Document Within an Online Scholarly Project

"Monet, Claude." Britannica Online. September 2001. Encyclopaedia
    Britannica. 7 Sept. 2001 <http://members.eb.com>.

An Article in a Scholarly Journal

Mossman, Mark. "Acts of Becoming: Autobiography, Frankenstein, and the
    Postmodern Body." Postmodern Culture 11.3 (2001). 10 Sept. 2001
    <http://jefferson.village.virginia.edu/pmc/current.issue/
    11.3mossman.html>.

An Article in a Magazine

Goleman, Daniel. "What's Your Emotional Intelligence Quotient?" Utne
　　Reader Online 5 Sept. 2001. 7 Sept. 2001 <http://www.utne.com/
　　azEQ.tmpl>.

An Anonymous Article in a Magazine

"The War Crimes Trial of Slobodan Milosevic." US News Online 30 Aug. 2001.
　　8 Sept. 2001 <http://www.usnews.com/usnews/briefings/
　　warcrimes0801.htm>.

A Work from an Online Database

[To cite online material from a database to which a library subscribes, complete
the citation by giving the name of the database (underlined), the name of the
service (if available), the name of the library, and the date of access, followed by
the URL of the service's home page, in angle brackets.]

Greene, Jay P. "The Surprising Consensus on School Choice." Public Interest
　　144 (Summer 2001). ABI/INFORM. OCLC FirstSearch. Colorado State U
　　Lib. 7 Sept. 2001 <http://newfirstsearch.oclc.org>.

Vogel, Gretchen. "Stem Cell Policy: An Embryonic Alternative." Science 6
　　Aug. 2001. Electric Library. Colorado State U Lib. 5 Sept. 2001
　　<http://www.elibrary.com>.

An Article in a Newspaper

Schwartz, John. "Government Is Wary of Tackling Online Privacy." New York
　　Times on the Web 6 Sept. 2001. 10 Sept. 2001
　　<http://www.nytimes.com/2001/09/06/technology/06COOK.html>.

An Editorial

Regan, Tom. "The New Political Correctness and the GOP." Editorial.
　　Christian Science Monitor 2 Feb. 1999. 3 Feb. 1999
　　<http://www.csmonitor.com/atcmonitor/commop/regan/>.

A Letter to the Editor

Fuld, Leonard. Letter. New York Times on the Web 4 Sept. 2001. 6 Sept. 2001
　　<http://www.nytimes.com/2001/09/05/opinion/L0CELL.html>.

Posting to a Discussion List

Etter, Beth. "Composition Philosophies and Rhetoric." On-line posting.
　　Syllabase Discussion Group. 24 Aug. 2001. 10 Sept. 2001
　　<http://writing.colostate.edu/SyllaBase/classroom/communication/
　　discussion/display_message.asp?MessageID=16232>.

A Professional Site

The Official Website of the Nobel Foundation. The Nobel Foundation. Aug.

2001. 11 Sept. 2001 <http://www.nobel.se/>.

A Personal Web Page

Palmquist, Michael. Home page. Jan. 2001. 10 Sept. 2001

<http://lamar.ColoState.EDU/~mp/>.

Synchronous Communications (MOOs, MUDs)

Grigar, Dene. Online defense of dissertation "Penelopeia: The Making of

Penelope in Homer's Story and Beyond." 25 July 1995. LinguaMOO. 25

July 1995 <telnet://lingua.utdallas.edu:8888>.

A Publication on CD-ROM, Diskette, or Magnetic Tape

"World War II." Encarta. CD-ROM. Seattle: Microsoft, 1999.

Godwin, M. E. "An Obituary to Affirmative Action and a Call for Self-

Reliance." ERIC. CD-ROM. SilverPlatter. Oct. 1992.

An E-Mail Communication.

Palmquist, Michael. "Re: Computer Classroom Tutorial." E-mail to Kate Kiefer.

15 July 2001.

An Unsigned Editorial in a Newspaper

"A Primary Choice: Mark Green." New York Times 2 Sept. 2001, sec. 5:8.

A Review

Ansen, David. "Final Score: O, What a Pity." Rev. of O, dir. Tim Blake Nelson.

Newsweek 10 Sept. 2001: 67.

Molotoch, Harvey. Rev. of A Cycle of Outrage, by James Gilbert. Science 15

Aug. 1996: 794–95.

A Published Interview

Lamm, Richard D. "Governments Face Tough Times." With Robert Baun.

Coloradoan [Ft. Collins, CO] 30 Nov. 1995: B9.

OTHER SOURCES: MLA STYLE

For unpublished sources, give relevant information that may help your reader
identify or locate the source.

Computer Software

Microsoft Word. Computer Software. Microsoft, 1999.

A Film

<u>Star Trek IV: The Voyage Home</u>. Dir. Leonard Nimoy. Perf. William Shatner
and Leonard Nimoy. Paramount, 1986.

A Recording

Carey, Mariah. "Hero." <u>Music Box</u>. Sony Songs, Inc, Columbia Records, 1993.

A Television or Radio Program

"Not Quite Dead." Narr. Mike Wallace. <u>Sixty Minutes</u>. CBS. WCBS, New York.
13 Apr. 1997.

A Letter

Ehrlich, Gretel. Letter to the author. 15 May 2001.

A Lecture or Speech

Gridley, Rita. Lecture on Texas Folklore. U of Kansas, Lawrence. 10 Aug. 2001.

If title is unknown, list type of oral presentation such as *Reading*, *Speech*, or *Lecture*.

A Personal Interview

Miller, J. Philip. Personal interview. 15 Sept. 2001.

A Personal Survey

Morgan Library Interlibrary Loan Questionnaire. Personal survey. 15 March 2000.

A Cartoon

Roberts, Victoria. Cartoon. <u>New Yorker</u> 13 Jan. 1997: 47.

An Advertisement

Toshiba. Advertisement. <u>Time</u> 20 Jan. 1997: 35.

IN-TEXT DOCUMENTATION: APA STYLE   In the APA style, give the
author's name and date in parentheses following your use of a summary or
paraphrase. If you quote material directly, give author's name, date, and page
number. (Use *p.* for one page and *pp.* for more than one page.) These
citations will direct your reader to your "References list," where you give complete bibliographical information. As you cite your sources, use the following
guidelines:

If you do not cite the author in the text, give author, date, and page in
parentheses at the end of the citation. If you are specifically citing a quotation
or a part of a source, indicate the page with *p.* or the chapter with *chap:*

> In a recent survey, New Jersey secondary school administrators "rated so-
> cial studies objectives as contributing most to the attainment of high priority
> goals, and foreign language as contributing least" (Koppel, 1982, p. 437).

If you cite the author in the text, indicate the date in parentheses immediately following the author's name, and cite the page number in parentheses following the quotation:

> According to Vicki Galloway (1984), a student's horizons will not be broadened by "grammar lectures and manipulative classroom exercises" (p. 33).

If you cite a long direct quotation (more than forty words), indent the passage five spaces from the left margin. Omit the enclosing direct quotation marks. Place the period at the end of the passage, not after the parentheses that include the page reference:

> Educator Gerald Unks (1985) points out two instances in which a lack of language proficiency caused companies to initiate fatal marketing programs:
>
>> When Pepsi-Cola went after the Chinese market, "Come Alive with Pepsi" was translated into Chinese in Taiwan as "Pepsi Brings Your Ancestors Back from the Dead." No Sale! General Motors sought to sell its Nova in South America oblivious to the fact that "no va" in Spanish means "It doesn't go." (p. 24)

If you are paraphrasing or summarizing material (no direct quotations), you may omit the page number:

> According to Coxe (1984), many top American businesspeople agree that students who combine some business or economics training with fluency in Japanese have unlimited job possibilities.

Note: Although the APA style manual says that writers may omit page citation for summaries and paraphrases, check with your instructor before you omit page references. If you have previously cited the author and date of a study, you may omit the date:

> In addition, Coxe points out that many top American businesspeople agree that students who combine some business or economics training with fluency in Japanese have unlimited job possibilities.

If the work has between two and five authors, cite all authors in your text or in parentheses in the first reference. *Note:* In your text, write "Long and Long"; in parenthetical citation, use an ampersand "(Long & Long)":

> Long and Long (1985) refer to two foreign-language teachers who noted, "We are members of a world community . . . and our fates are closely intertwined" (p. 366).

> As two foreign-language teachers noted, "We are members of a world community . . . and our fates are closely intertwined" (Long & Long, 1985, p. 366).

For subsequent citations, cite both names each time if a work has two authors. If a work has three to five authors, give the last name of the first author followed by *et al.* Include the year for the first citation within a paragraph:

> Taylor et al. (1997) found . . .

If a work has six or more authors, use only the last name of the first author and the abbreviation *et al.* followed by the date for the first and subsequent in-text and parenthetical citations:

> Teachers should integrate the study of history, culture, politics, literature, and religion of a particular region with the study of language (Berryman et al., 1988).

If a work has no author, give the first few words of the title and the year:

> Most students in the United States would be surprised to learn that the Russian government has sponsored rock concerts (A Day in the Life, 1988).

If the source is from the Internet or the Web, use the author, or if there is no author, use the title:

> Many Web sites now provide detailed information about how to plan a study-abroad semester or year (Foreign Language, 1997).

If the author is a corporation, cite the full name of the company in the first reference:

> Foreign-language study must be accompanied by in-depth understanding and experience of culture (University of Maryland, 1990).

If the source is a personal communication (letter, memo, interview, phone conversation), cite in text but do not include in your "References" list (personal communications are not recoverable data):

> As Professor Devlin (personal interview, September 21, 1996) explained, "Foreign-language study encourages students to see their own language and culture from a fresh perspective."

If you are citing a government document, give the originating agency, its abbreviation (if any), the year of publication, and (if you include a direct quotation) the page number:

> Newcomers to a foreign culture should "pay attention to their health as well as their grammar. What the natives regularly eat may be dangerous to a foreigner's constitution" (Department of Health and Human Services [DHHS], 1989, p. 64).

If your citation refers to several sources, list the authors and dates in alphabetical order:

> Several studies (Lambert, 1996; Lange, 1987; Long & Long, 1985) have documented severe deficiencies in Americans' foreign-language preparation.

"REFERENCES" LIST: APA STYLE   If you are using the APA style, you should make a separate list, titled "References" (no underlining or quotation marks), that appears after your text but before any appendixes. Include only sources actually used in preparing your essay. List the sources cited in your text *alphabetically*, by author's last name. Use only *initials* for authors' first and middle names. If the author is unknown, alphabetize by the first word in the title (but not *A*, *An*, or *The*). In titles, capitalize only the first word, proper names, and the first word following a colon. As in MLA reference style, begin first line of each reference flush left and indent subsequent lines five spaces. Double-space the entire "References" list. *Note*: APA now recommends using italics—not underlining—for titles of books, journals, and other documents.

Following are samples of APA-style reference list entries. For additional information and examples, consult the *Publication Manual of the American Psychological Association* (5th ed., 2001).

BOOKS: APA STYLE

A Book by One Author

Krakauer, J. (1997). Into thin air: A personal account of the Mt. Everest disaster. New York: Villard.

A Book by Several Authors

Corbett, P. J., Myers, N., & Tate, G. (2000). *The writing teacher's sourcebook* *(4th ed.).* New York: McGraw-Hill.

Additional Books by Same Author

Morrison, T. (1977). *Song of Solomon.* New York: Knopf.

Morrison, T. (1992). *Jazz.* New York: Knopf.

A Book with Two or More Authors

Conklin, N. F., & Lourie, M. A. (1983). *A host of tongues: Language communities in the United States.* New York: Free Press.

An Unknown or Anonymous Author

New York Public Library student's desk reference (1993). New York: Prentice Hall.

Note: In titles of books and journals, capitalize the first word, the first word after a colon, and any proper names. (New York Public Library is a proper name.)

A Book with an Author and an Editor

Austen, J. (1956). *Pride and prejudice* (M. Schorer, Ed.). Boston: Houghton Mifflin.

Note: The APA style usually uses the full name of publishing companies.

A Work in an Anthology

Chopin, K. (1989). The story of an hour. In E. V. Roberts & H. E. Jacobs (Eds.), *Literature: An introduction to reading and writing* (pp. 304–306). Englewood Cliffs, NJ: Prentice Hall.

Note: Titles of poems, short stories, essays, or articles in a book are not underlined or italicized or put in quotation marks. Only the title of the anthology is underlined or italicized.

A Translation

Lefranc, J. R. (1976). *A treatise on probability* (R. W. Mateau & D. Trilling, Trans.). New York: Macmillan. (Original work published 1952).

An Article or Chapter in an Edited Book

Sophocles. (1960). *Electra* (D. Grene, Trans.). In D. Grene & R. Lattimore (Eds.), *Greek tragedies* (Vol. 2, pp. 45–109). Chicago: University of Chicago Press.

A Government Document: Known Author

Machenthun, K. M. (1973). *Toward a cleaner aquatic environment.* Environmental Protection Agency. Office of Air and Water Programs. Washington, DC: U.S. Government Printing Office.

A Government Document: Unknown Author

Maternal and Child Health Bureau. (2001). *Babies sleep safest on their backs: Reduce the risk of sudden infant death syndrome (SIDS).* Bethesda, MD: U.S. Government Printing Office.

PERIODICALS: APA STYLE

The following examples illustrate how to list articles in magazines and periodicals according to APA style. ***Note***: Do *not* underline or italicize or put quotation marks around titles of articles. Do italicize titles of magazines or periodicals. Cite the volume number for magazines and omit the *p.* or *pp.* before any page numbers. If an article is not printed on continuous pages, give all page numbers, separated by commas.

An Article in a Weekly or Biweekly Magazine

McCarthy, T. (2001, September 3). L. A. gangs are back. *Time* 158, 46–49.

An Article in a Monthly or Bimonthly Magazine

Dunbar, D. (1997, February). White noise. *Travel and Leisure, 27,* 106–110,
150–158.

An Unsigned Article in a Magazine

Catching a cold: It's up in the air. (1986, July–August). *Science, 86,* 8.

An Article in a Journal with Continuous Pagination

Italicize the volume number and do not include *pp*. Also, APA style requires repeating all number digits: Write 2552–2555.

Sady, S. P. (1986). Prolonged exercise augments plasma triglyceride clearance.
Journal of the American Medical Association, 256, 2552–2555.

An Article in a Journal That Paginates Each Issue Separately

Italicize the volume number followed by the issue number in parentheses.

Brodkey, L. (1987). Writing ethnographic narratives. *Written Communication,*
9 (1), 25–50.

An Article in a Newspaper

Use *p*. or *pp*. before newspaper section and page numbers.

Mundy, A. (1994, January 5). Attorney general of social work. *The Wall Street*
Journal, p. A14.

An Unsigned Article in a Newspaper

A jet crash that defies resolution. (2001, September 5). *Los Angeles Times,* p. A1.

An Editorial

Fish, S. (1996, December 26). When principles get in the way. [Editorial.] *The*
New York Times, p. A27.

An Unsigned Editorial

European summit of uncertainty. (1994, January 7). [Editorial.] *Los Angeles*
Times, p. B6.

ELECTRONIC AND INTERNET SOURCES: APA STYLE

The World Wide Web and the Internet are still changing, so even the latest APA guidelines, available in the fifth edition of the *Publication Manual of the American Psychological Association* (2001), will continue to change. The basic features of an electronic or Internet citation, given in abbreviated form below, are available for downloading from the APA home page at http://www.apa.org/journals/webref.html. Use the specific citations following this list as models for your own citations.

1. Name of author (if given)
2. Title of article (with APA capitalization rules)
3. Title of periodical or electronic text (italicized)
4. Volume number and/or pages (if any)
5. If information is retrieved from an electronic database (e.g., ABI/FORM, PsychINFO, Electric Library, Academic Universe), give the name of the database. (No library address or URL needed.)
6. Use the words "Retrieved" (include date here) "from" (give the URL here). (Use the words "Available from" to indicate that the URL leads to information on how to obtain the cited material rather than the complete address of the material itself.)
7. Do not use angle brackets around URL.
8. If citation ends with the URL, do not end URL with a period.

Note: APA style does not cite personal communications such as e-mail in a reference list. Cite such references in the text only.

An Article in a Journal

Mossman, M. (2001, May). Acts of becoming: Autobiography, Frankenstein, and the postmodern body. *Postmodern Culture 11*, 68–89. Retrieved September 10, 2001, from http://jefferson.village.virginia.edu/pmc/current.issue/11.3mossman.html

An Article in an Internet-Only Journal

Fredrickson, B. L. (2000, March 7). Cultivating positive emotions to optimize health and well-being. *Prevention & Treatment, 3,* Article 0001a. Retrieved November 20, 2000, from http://journals.apa.org/prevention/volume3/pre0030001a.html

An Article in a Newspaper

Schwartz, J. (2001, September 6). Government is wary of tackling online privacy. *New York Times on the Web.* Retrieved September 10, 2001, from http://www.nytimes.com

Message Posted to an On-Line Forum

Etter, B. (2001, August 24). Composition philosophies and rhetoric. Message posted to http://writing.colostate.edu/SyllaBase/classroom/communication/discussion/display_message.asp?MessageID=16232

A Work from an On-Line Database

Greene, J. P. (2001, Summer). The surprising consensus on school choice. *Public Interest 144.* Retrieved September 7, 2001, from ABI/INFORM database.

OTHER SOURCES: APA STYLE

In the APA system, unpublished letters and interviews are personal communications and do not represent recoverable data. Therefore, they should not appear in a "References" list. Do, however, cite personal letters or interviews in your text. (See "In-Text Documentation: APA Style.")

A Review

Molotch, H. (1986, August 15). A cycle of outrage. [Review of the book *A cycle of outrage*]. Science, 794–795.

A Published Interview

Lamm, R. (1995, November 30). Governments face tough times. [Interview with Baun, R.] *Coloradoan,* p. B9.

Computer Software

Microsoft word. Vers. 5.0 [Computer software]. (1992). Microsoft.

A Film

Nimoy, L. (Director). (1986). *Star trek IV: The voyage home* [Film]. Paramount.

A Recording

Carey, M. (1993). Hero. On *Music box* [CD]. New York: Columbia Records.

A Television or Radio Program

Bogdonich, R. (Producer). (1997, April 13). *Sixty Minutes.* New York: WCBS.

EDITING AND PROOFREADING   Edit your paper for conciseness, clarity, and accuracy of grammar, spelling, and punctuation. See your handbook for assistance in revising errors and improving usage. Check your direct quotations to make sure they are *accurate, word-for-word transcriptions* of the originals. Make sure that your in-text citation of sources is accurate. Proofread both the text *and* the "Works Cited" or "References" section. Finally, have someone else proofread your research paper for typos, spelling errors, missing words, or confusing sentences.

■ **POSTSCRIPT ON THE WRITING PROCESS**   As your final entry in your research notebook, answer the following questions:

1. Reread your research log section. Compare your initial schedule with your actual progress. What parts of the research paper took longer than you anticipated? What took less time?
2. What was the most difficult problem you encountered while writing the research paper? How did you try to solve that problem?
3. What do you like best about the final version of your research paper? Why? What do you like least? Why?

STUDENT   WRITING

FOREIGN LANGUAGE STUDY: AN AMERICAN NECESSITY

Kate McNerny

Kate McNerny's purpose was to persuade students, administrators, and ordinary citizens that learning the language and culture of a foreign country is important, both to people as individuals and to America as a nation. In this paper, she uses interviews, library research, research on the Internet, and her own experience to alert her readers to the seriousness of the problem and to recommend a solution. She argues that American schools should require students to study at least one foreign language during junior and senior high school. McNerny follows the MLA style for in-text documentation, supplementary notes, and "Works Cited" list. The marginal annotations highlight key features of her research paper.

↕ **1"**

↓ **½"**
McNerny 1

Kate McNerny

Professor Thomas

English 101

18 November 1999

/double space

/double space

Foreign-Language Study:

An American Necessity

/double space

"Why should I learn a foreign language—everyone speaks English!" "I would never use another language—I never plan to leave the United States." "I had a hard enough time learning English!" These are only a few of the excuses people have given for opposing foreign-language studies, and unfortunately they represent the ideas of more than a few American citizens. In possibly the most multicultural nation in the world, it is ironic that so many people— who themselves have come from foreign cultures and foreign languages—should want to remain isolated from international languages and cultures. A recent indication of the backlash against foreign languages came when the House of Representatives passed legislation recommending that English should be the official language of the U.S. Government.[1] In addition, twenty-three states already have Official English laws on the books (Swope 2128; Torres 51). Because these attitudes are so widespread, we need a national policy supporting foreign-language study in elementary and secondary schools. If we are to continue to develop as a people and a nation, we must be able to communicate with and understand the cultures of people from countries around the globe.

Historically, Americans' attitudes toward foreign languages have swayed from positive to negative, depending on current

←→ **1"**   ←→ **1"**

↕ **1"**

For her lead-in, McNerny uses quotations she collected in her informal survey.

*McNerny gives first version of her **thesis** for her problem-solving essay: "We need a national policy supporting foreign-language study." McNerny presents historical background on the problem.*

events around the world. Theodore Huebener's study Why Johnny Should Learn Foreign Languages shows how attitudes reflect the times. In 1940, in an isolationist period before World War II, a committee of the American Youth Commission issued a report labeling foreign-language studies as "useless and time-consuming" (Huebener 13). An even more appalling statement came from a group of Harvard scholars. They suggested that "foreign language study is useful primarily in strengthening the student's English. . . . For the average student, there is no real need at all to learn a foreign language" (Huebener 14). With such attitudes, it is no wonder that students and administrators ignored foreign language programs during the 1940s and 1950s.[2] With the advent of Sputnik, however, interest in Russian increased, and with the growing trade with Pacific Rim countries in recent years, the United States has experienced short bursts of interest in Japanese and Chinese foreign-language study.

Despite some occasional surges of interest, however, foreign-language study still holds the weakest position of any major subject in American secondary schools. A recent study of foreign-language programs reports that "only 15 percent of American high school students study a foreign language. Only 8 percent of [American] colleges require credit in a foreign language for admission (down from 34 percent in 1966)" (Unks 24). Because available programs at the junior and senior high school level are generally limited in variety and scope, only a small percentage of those students who take a foreign language ever become fluent in it. A 1984

Ellipsis points indicate material omitted from the source.

The superscript number refers the reader to the "Notes" page for McNerny's comment on the history of the problem.

Square brackets in quoted material indicate a word added by McNerny to clarify the sentence.

1"   ½"
1"   1"   1"
1"

McNerny 3

study that sampled 536 secondary schools revealed that most offered a foreign language, but 91 percent did not require foreign-language credits for graduation (Ranwez and Rodgers 98). In contrast, most European countries require all students to learn at least one and often two foreign languages. Norway, Spain, France, Sweden, Italy, England, Germany, and Finland all require at least one foreign language. According to Rune Bergentoft, currently a Mellon Fellow at the National Foreign Language Center, "Several [European] countries require knowledge of two foreign languages for entry to the upper secondary school; in the Netherlands, the requirement is three foreign languages" (18).

The United States cannot continue to lag behind other countries in language capability. As two foreign-language researchers noted, "We are members of a world community consisting of hundreds of nations, and our fates are closely intertwined" (Long and Long 366). It is time to change attitudes and to recognize that in order to successfully interact with its "world community," the United States must drastically change its foreign-language practices and policies. American students should be encouraged to start their language studies in elementary school and required to study at least one foreign language during their six years of junior and senior high school.

How do we encourage more students to study a foreign language in our elementary and secondary schools? The solution requires changes on the part of administrators and teachers, changes in the attitudes and experiences of students

In-text citation for a source with two authors.

McNerny restates her thesis, using more specific language: "American students should be . . . required to study at least one foreign language during . . . junior and senior high school."

*McNerny's **essay map:** The solution requires changes by administrators, by students, and by national policymakers.*

themselves, and changes in our state and national foreign language policies.

School administrators across the country often oppose the idea of requiring foreign languages because they cannot see the contribution these studies make to the overall goals of the schools' curriculum. In a recent survey, New Jersey secondary school administrators "rated social studies objectives as contributing most to the attainment of high priority goals, and foreign language as contributing least" (Koppel 437). These administrators fail to realize that language studies can add a valuable dimension to a social studies program. Educators can use a combined program to emphasize a global perspective in language and cultural studies. "The world looks and sounds different when one is 'standing in the shoes' of another, speaking another language, or recognizing another's point of view based on an alternative set of values" (Bragaw 37). This global awareness is crucial in our increasingly interdependent world.

Likewise, teachers need to continue to make changes in their foreign-language courses to attract more students. More and more primary and secondary language courses already focus on cultural issues more than grammar, but now they need to use all the computer, on-line, and Internet resources currently available to attract and motivate their students. Linguist Mark Warschauer, in a preface to papers collected at a conference on Global Networking in Foreign Language Learning, asserts that "foreign language learners can communicate rapidly and inexpensively with other learners or speakers of the target language around the world. With the World Wide Web, learners can access a broad array of authentic foreign

*Notice **punctuation** for in-text citation: Source appears in parentheses after the quotation marks but **before** the period.*

McNerny 5

language materials . . . or they can develop and publish their own materials to share with others across the classroom or across the globe" (ix). Teachers need to make use of the Internet communication possibilities to help motivate and interest their students.

Of course, students themselves need motivation in order to enroll in foreign-language classes. Many students simply fail to see why they will ever need to use a foreign language. I used to belong to that group. I remember my mom always telling me, "Take French classes. Learn how to speak French so you can visit your cousins in France someday." At the time, during junior high, I did take French classes for a while, but then dropped them when my schedule became "too busy." Then, as my mom had promised, I got the opportunity to visit my cousins in France. For some reason, the fact that I couldn't speak French didn't really hit me—until I stepped off the train at Gare du Nord in Paris and couldn't find the relative who was supposed to meet me. After frantically searching the entire station several times, I had to break down and ask for help. At the information desk, a few completely butchered French phrases escaped my lips—only to be received by an unimpressed, unresponsive station attendant. He muttered something about dumb Americans. Then, with a wave of his hand, he gestured toward some unknown destination. I did survive that painful ordeal, but I vowed I wouldn't embarrass myself—and other Americans— again.

Another way to change students' attitudes is to encourage them to participate in exchange programs or study-abroad

*McNerny uses **personal experience** in her research paper. Her experience provides a great example of why students can benefit from studying a foreign language.*

McNerny introduces the author, the title of the book, and the author's credentials to lend authority to the quoted passage.

McNerny 6

programs.[3] Again, the Internet and the World Wide Web offer students and their teachers immediate access to a variety of exchange and study-abroad programs. The World Wide Web has hundreds of sites related to foreign-language study that can help both teachers and students. The International House World Organization, at http://www. international-house.org, is "a worldwide network of language schools sharing a common commitment to the highest standards of teaching and training" (International). Students wishing to find out about exchange and study-abroad programs should browse the Web, perhaps beginning at a site such as Foreign Language Study Abroad Service at http://www.netpoint.net/~flsas. The Foreign Language Study Abroad Service was started in 1971 and is, according to its home page, "the oldest study abroad service in the U.S." (Foreign).

Study-abroad programs and exchange programs help students learn the language, but just as important, they enable students to learn about different cultures. In his resource book, Teaching Culture, H. Ned Seelye, Director of Bilingual-Bicultural Education for the State of Illinois, cites just one of many cultural lessons that American students—and tourists—need to learn:

> At a New Year's Eve celebration in an exclusive Guatemalan hotel, one American was overheard telling another, "You see all these people? They're all my wife's relatives. And every damn one of them has kissed me tonight. If another Guatemalan man hugs and kisses me I'll punch him right in the face!" The

McNerny 7

irritated American was disturbed by two things: the

extended kinship patterns of the group and the *abrazo*

de ano neuvo as executed by the men (he did not

complain of the female *abrazos*). Both customs—close

family ties that extend to distant relatives and the *abrazo*

given as a greeting or sign of affection devoid of sexual

overtures—elicited hostility in the American who was

bored by unintelligible language and depressed by

nostalgia and alcohol. (85)

In order to prevent such linguistic and cultural misunderstandings,
more and more Americans should take advantage of study-abroad
and exchange programs that will acquaint them with a variety of
cultures and languages.

　　Finally, in order to coordinate our schools' foreign-language
studies, America needs changes in our state and national foreign-
language policies to ensure that every child will receive some basic
instruction in foreign languages and culture. Changes in our
foreign-language requirements would not only promote cultural
understanding but also would strengthen U. S. international
relations in business and diplomacy. International trade is
continually increasing in the United States and has created a
demand for businesspeople competent in foreign languages. Many
top American businesspeople agree that students who combine
some business or economics training with fluency in Japanese have
unlimited job possibilities (Coxe 194). Company executives simply
cannot expect to make efficient, sound decisions in their
international markets without understanding and speaking

*At the end of the
quotation, McNerny cites
only the page number,
since she has already
introduced the author.
The page number follows
the period in indented
block quotations.*

*McNerny does not end
her paragraph with a
quotation; instead, she
shows how this evidence
supports her point.*

the language of the country they are dealing with (Huebener 45). Educator Gerald Unks points out two instances in which a lack of language proficiency caused companies to initiate fatal marketing programs:

> When Pepsi-Cola went after the Chinese market, "Come Alive With Pepsi" was translated into Chinese in Taiwan as "Pepsi Brings Your Ancestors Back from the Dead." No Sale! General Motors sought to sell its Nova in South America oblivious to the fact that "No va" in Spanish means "It doesn't go." (24)

These examples illustrate that businesspeople need thorough competence in, not just a rudimentary knowledge of, foreign languages.

Finally, proficiency in foreign languages and cultures is important not only for business and trade overseas, but also for jobs in America. Required foreign-language study would help our future citizens understand and appreciate our multicultural heritage—and help them become employable. Verada Bluford, writing in Occupational Outlook Quarterly, argues that as our country "becomes more involved in foreign trade, tourism, and international cooperative ventures, the number of jobs open to fluent speakers of a foreign language increases" (25). Bluford explains that there are "language-centered jobs" such as teaching, translating, and interpreting, but there are also "language-related jobs," such as jobs in marketing and finance, engineering, airlines, banking, and government, where language skills are necessary. These "language-related jobs" will go to students who have language skills *in addition*

Before quoting from Bluford, McNerny names the author and the journal from which the article is taken.

McNerny 9

to some other skill (Bluford 26). A foreign-language requirement, whether mandated by each state or by Congress, would make all Americans better citizens of the world and their own country.

The need for required language study in the United States is urgent. Some states already require schools to introduce children to some foreign language during their grade school years (Kuo 2). For example, North Carolina, Arkansas, Louisiana, Arizona, and Oklahoma already have laws, and Oregon has a proposed law that will require all tenth-graders to know a language other than English (Kuo 2). Since some individual schools and states realize the benefits of foreign-language requirements, Congress should guide all the states and formulate a national foreign-language policy that would make all our schools more like the European model.

Although the ideas and the plans for a national policy exist, often the funds do not. Some funds can be diverted from within school districts, but the federal government must take some initiative. The current administration spends endless time and money subsidizing business interests and propping up weak foreign economies. Since foreign-language knowledge contributes strongly to success in both these areas, however, it would be practical for the administration also to support expansion of language studies. Instead, it continues to reduce funding for special programs, including language studies centers and international teaching facilities (Unks 25). Realistically, a foreign-language requirement in junior and senior high school cannot be initiated without the support of both local school districts and the federal government. Americans must acknowledge the fact

McNerny begins her conclusion, citing precedents and calling for state and federal administrators to support a foreign-language requirement.

that they are not isolated from the rest of the world. Successful interaction in the "world community" depends on our ability, as a nation, to effectively communicate with and understand people from other countries. Understanding, communication, and world peace cannot be achieved without cultural awareness and foreign-language proficiency.

1"

½"
McNerny 11

Notes

[1]Americans not only hesitate to take a foreign language but also seem bent on keeping foreign languages officially "out of sight." The debate over "official English" has spilled over into the workplace, in the form of "English-only" rules in business. Robert Brady, writing in HR Focus, reviews the two sides of the English-only debate: "Advocates of English-only rules argue that a single language promotes good organizational communications, ensures workplace safety, improves service to the English-speaking customer base, and avoids discrimination" (20). On the other side, Brady says, opponents believe that requiring employees to speak English goes against the melting-pot heritage of our country—and may violate Title VII of the Civil Rights Act (20). Many opponents from ethnic and civil rights groups believe these bills and rules are racist (McBee 64). Americans' ignorance of foreign languages (and the fear that ignorance breeds) is an important cause of the popularity of both the "official English" laws and the "English-only" rules.

[2]One of the most disturbing facts is that although Huebener's study was done in 1961, very little has changed in almost forty years. Except for slight changes in statistics, dates, and names of wars, Americans have remained strikingly insular in their attitudes toward foreign languages and foreigners.

[3]Recent figures on study-abroad programs illustrate the huge gap between the number of foreign students who study in the United States and U.S. students who study abroad. In an article on language learning and study abroad, Barbara Freed gives the following figures: "Close to half a million international students

1"

1"

1"

Content notes are placed on a separate page and double-spaced. Use raised footnote numbers and indent the first line five spaces.

In her notes, McNerny includes her ideas about "English-only" and "official English," which would have been digressive in the text of her paper.

In this footnote, McNerny puts statistics that didn't seem to fit in the flow of her paragraph but are relevant to study-abroad programs.

1"

came to the United States to study in 1993–94 [while] approximately 71,000 American undergraduates participated in study abroad programs" (3). That means that nearly ten times more foreign students study English in the United States than American students study foreign languages abroad.

1"

1"

1"

McNerny 13

Works Cited

Bergentoft, Rune. "Foreign Language Instruction: A Comparative Perspective." The Annals of the American Academy of Political and Social Science 532 (1994): 8–34.

Bluford, Verada. "Working with Foreign Languages." Occupational Outlook Quarterly 38.4 (1994): 25–28.

Brady, Robert I. "English-Only Rules Draw Controversy." HR Focus June 1996: 20.

Bragaw, Donald H., and Helene Zimmer-Loew. "Social Studies and Foreign Language: A Partnership." Education Digest Dec. 1985: 36–39.

Coxe, Donald. "The Back Page." Canadian Business Feb. 1984: 194.

Foreign Language Study Abroad Service. 21 Feb. 1997 <http://www.netpoint.net/flas>.

Freed, Barbara F. "Language Learning and Study Abroad." Second Language Acquisition in a Study Abroad Context. Ed. Barbara F. Freed. Philadelphia: John Benjamins, 1995, 3–33.

Huebener, Theodore. Why Johnny Should Learn Foreign Languages. New York: Chilton, 1961.

International House: The Worldwide Language Teaching Organization. Jan. 1997. 2 Mar. 1997 <http://www.international-house.org>.

Koppel, Irene E. "The Perceived Contribution of Foreign Language to High Priority Education Goals." Foreign Language Annals 15 (1982): 435–37.

Kuo, Fidelius. "Foreign Language Proposal in Washington State Worthy." Northwest Asian Weekly 9 Dec. 1994: 4.

The "Works Cited" list begins a new page. List the entries alphabetically by the author's last name. If no author is given, list by the first word in the title. Double-space all lines.

Indent five spaces after first line of each entry.

Book

Internet Web page

Article from a journal with contiguous pagination

McNerny 14

Long, Delbert H., and Roberta A. Long. "Toward the Promotion of
    Foreign Language Study and Global Understanding."
    Education 105 (1985): 366–68.

McBee Susanna. "A War over Words." U.S. News and World Report 6
    Oct. 1986: 64.

Ranwez, Alain D., and Judy Rodgers. "The Status of Foreign
    Languages and International Studies: An Assessment in
    Colorado." Foreign Language Annals 17 (1984): 97–102.

Seelye, H. Ned. Teaching Culture: Strategies for Foreign Language
    Educators. Skokie, IL: National Textbook, 1974.

Swope, Christopher. "Panel OKs Bill to Make English Official
    Government Language." Congressional Quarterly Weekly
    Report 54 (1996): 2128–29.

Torres, Joseph. "The Language Crusade." Hispanic 9.6 (1996): 50–54.

Unks, Gerald. "The Perils of Our Single-Language Policy." Education
    Digest Mar. 1985: 24–27.

Warschauer, Mark. Preface. Telecollaboration in Foreign Language
    Learning. By Warschauer. Ed. Mark Warschauer. Honolulu:
    Second Language Teaching & Curriculum Center, 1996.

1"

1"   1"

1"

For inclusive page numbers over 100, use only the last two digits in the second number (366–68).

Article from a monthly magazine

Appendix: Writing Under Pressure

The main chapters of this text describe purposes for writing and strategies for collecting, shaping, drafting, and revising an essay. These chapters assume that you have several days or even weeks to write your paper. They work on the premise that you have time to read model essays, time to think about ideas for your topic, and time to prewrite, write several drafts, and receive feedback from other members of your class. Much college writing, however, occurs on midterm or final examinations, when you may have only fifteen to twenty minutes to complete the whole process of writing. When you must produce a "final" draft in a few short minutes, your writing process may need drastic modification.

A typical examination has some objective questions (true/false, multiple-choice, definition, short-answer) followed by an essay question or two. For example, with just twenty-five minutes left in your Western Civilization midterm, you might finish the last multiple-choice question, turn the page, and read the following essay question:

> Erich Maria Remarque's *All Quiet on the Western Front* has been hailed by critics the world over as the "twentieth century's definitive novel on war." What does Remarque's novel tell us about the historical, ideological, national, social, and human significance of twentieth-century warfare? Draw on specific illustrations from the novel, but base your observations on your wider perspective on Western civilization. Good luck!

Overwhelmed by panic, you find the blood drains from your face and your fingers feel icy. You now have twenty-two minutes to write on the "historical, ideological, national, social, and human significance of twentieth-century warfare." Do you have to explain everything about modern warfare? Must you use specific examples from the novel? Good luck, indeed! Everything you remembered about the novel has now vanished. Bravely, you pick up your pen and start recounting the main events of the novel, hoping to show the instructor at least that you read it.

You can survive such an essay examination, but you need to prepare yourself emotionally and intellectually. Following is some advice from senior English majors who have taken dozens of essay examinations in their four years of college. These seniors answer the question, "What advice would you give to students who are preparing to take an essay examination?"

> Even though I'm an English major, I'm perfectly petrified of writing impromptu essays. My advice is to calm yourself. Read the question. Study key words and concepts. Before beginning an essay question, write a brief, informal outline. This will organize your ideas and help you remember them as well. Take a deep breath and write. I would

also recommend *rereading* the question while you are writing, to keep you on track.

The first step is to know the material. Then, before you begin, read the instructions. Know what the teacher expects. Then try to organize your thoughts into a small list—preferably a list that will become your main paragraphs. Don't babble to fill space. Teachers hate reading nonsense. Reread what you've written often. This will ensure that you won't repeat yourself. Proofread at the end.

Organization is important but difficult in a pressure situation. Well-organized essays do have a tendency to impress the professor, sometimes more than information-packed essays. Organize your notes and thoughts about those notes as you study (not necessarily in a chronological order, but rather in a comprehensible order). Good luck.

Read the question carefully.

Get your thoughts in order.

Write what the question asks, not what you wish it asked.

Don't ramble.

Give textual facts or specific examples.

Summarize with a clear, understandable closing.

Proofread.

Keep calm. Your life doesn't depend on one test.

My advice would be first to learn how to consciously relax and practice writing frequently. *Practice!!!* It's important to practice writing as much as possible in any place possible, because the more writing you do, the better and easier it becomes. Also, your belief that it *can* be done is critical!

Know the information that you will be tested on well enough so that you can ask yourself tough and well-formed questions in preparation. You should be able to predict what essay questions your professor will ask, at least generally. I always go to the test file or ask friends for sample essay questions that I can practice on. Then I practice writing on different areas of the material.

The common threads in these excerpts of advice are to know your audience, analyze key terms in the question, make a sketch outline, know the material, practice writing before the test, and proofread when you finish writing. Knowing how to read the question and practicing your writing before the test will help you relax and do your best.

KNOW YOUR AUDIENCE

Teachers expect you to answer a question exactly as it is asked, not just to give the information that you know. Because teachers must read dozens of essays, they are impressed by clear organization and specific detail. As one senior says, teachers hate babble because they cannot follow the thread of your argument. Although they demand specific examples and facts from the text, they want you to explain how these examples *relate* to the overall question. In a pile of two hundred history exams graded by one professor, margins featured comments like "Reread the question. This doesn't answer the question." "What is your main point? State your main point clearly." "Give more specific illustrations and examples." Keep this teacher in mind as you write your next essay response.

ANALYZE KEY TERMS

Understanding the key terms in the question is crucial to writing an essay under pressure. Teachers expect you to respond to *their* specific question, not just to write down information. They want you to use your writing to *think* about the topic—to analyze and synthesize the information. In short, they want you to make sense of the information. Following are key terms that indicate teachers' expectations and suggest how to organize your answer.

Discuss: A general instruction that means "write about." If the question says *discuss,* look for other key words to focus your response.

Describe: Give sensory details or particulars about a topic. Often, however, this general instruction simply means "discuss."

Analyze: Divide a topic into its parts, and show how the parts are related to each other and to the topic as a whole.

Synthesize: Show how the parts relate to the whole or how the parts make sense together.

Explain: Show relationships between specific examples and general principles. Explain what (define), explain why (causes/effects), and/or explain how (analyze process).

Define: Explain what something is. As appropriate, give a formal definition, describe it, analyze its parts or function, describe what it is not, and/or compare and contrast it with similar events or ideas.

Compare: Explain similarities and (often) differences. Draw conclusions from the observed similarities and differences.

Contrast: Explain key differences. Draw conclusions from the observed differences.

Illustrate: Provide specific examples of an idea or process.

Trace: Give the sequence or chronological order of key events or ideas.

Evaluate: Determine the value or worth of an idea, thing, process, person, or event. Set up criteria and provide evidence to support your judgments.

Solve: Explain your solution; show how it fixes the problem, why it is better than other alternatives, and why it is feasible.

Argue: Present both sides of a controversial issue, showing why the opposing position should not be believed or accepted and why your position should be accepted. Give evidence to support your position.

Interpret: Offer your understanding of the meaning and significance of an idea, event, person, process, or work of art. Support your understanding with specific examples or details.

MAKE A SKETCH OUTLINE

The key terms in a question should not only focus your thinking but also suggest how to organize your response. Use the key terms to make a sketch outline of your response. You may not regularly use an outline when you have more time to write an essay, but the time pressure requires that you revise your normal writing process.

Assume that you have twenty-five minutes to read and respond to the following question from a history examination. Read the instructions carefully, note the key terms, and make a brief outline to guide your writing.

- Answer *one* of the following. Draw on the reading for your answer. (25 pts)

1. Explain the arguments that the balance of power does and does not work in the nuclear age (discuss and illustrate both sides of the argument). Then take a stand—citing the evidence for your position.

2. Explain the arguments that the United Nations does and does not play a positive role in international relations (discuss and illustrate both sides of the argument). Then take a stand—citing the evidence for your position.

Let's assume that because you know more about the United Nations, you choose the second question. First, you should identify and underline key words in the question. The subject for your essay is the *United Nations* and its role in *international relations*. You need to *explain* the reasons why the UN does or does not have a positive effect on international relations. You will need to *discuss* and *illustrate* (give specific examples of) both sides of the controversy. Finally, you need to *take a stand* (argue) for your belief, citing *evidence* (specific examples from recent history) of how the UN has or has not helped to resolve international tensions.

Based on your rereading and annotation of the key words of the question, make a quick outline or list, perhaps as follows:

I. Reasons (with examples) why some believe the UN is effective
  A. Reason 1 + example
  B. Reason 2 + example

II. Reasons (with examples) why some believe the UN is not effective
  A. Reason 1 + example
  B. Reason 2 + example

III. Reasons why you believe the UN is effective

  Refer to reasons and examples cited in I, above, but explain why these reasons and examples outweigh the reasons cited in II, above.

With this sketch outline as your guide, jot down reasons and examples that you intend to use, and then start writing. Your outline will make sure that you cover all the main points of the question, and it will keep your essay organized as you concentrate on remembering specific reasons and examples.

■ JOURNAL EXERCISE For practice, analyze at least one question from two of the following subject areas. First, underline key terms. Then, in your journal explain what these terms ask you to do. Finally, sketch an outline to help organize your response. If you are not familiar with the topics, check a dictionary or encyclopedia. (Do not write the essay.)

Biology
- Describe the process by which artificial insulin was first produced.
- What is reverse transcriptase and how was it used in genetic engineering?

- Humans—at least most of us—walk on two legs as opposed to four. How might you account for this using a Darwinian, Lamarckian, and Theistic model?

History

- Discuss the significant political developments in the English colonies in the first half of the eighteenth century.
- Account for the end of the Salem witchcraft delusion, and discuss the consequences of the outbreak for Salem Village.

Human Development

- Discuss evidence for nature versus nurture effects in human development.
- Contrast Piaget's, Vygotsky's, and Whorf's ideas on connections between language and thought.

Humanities

- How and why did early Christian culture dominate the Roman Empire? In terms of art and architecture, discuss specific ways in which the early Christians transformed or abolished the Greco-Roman legacy.

Literature

- Aristotle wrote that a tragedy must contain certain elements, such as a protagonist of high estate, recognition, and reversal, and should also evoke pity and fear in the audience. Which of the following best fits Aristotle's definition: *Hamlet*, *Death of a Salesman*, or *The Old Man and the Sea?* Explain your choice.

Philosophy

- On the basis of what we have studied in this class, define "philosophy." Taking your major subject of study (for example, biology, history, literature), discuss three philosophical problems that arise in this field.
- Write an essay explaining the following statement. Be clear in your explanation and use specific examples. "Egoism allows for prudent altruism."

Political Science

- Evaluate the achievements of the current administration's policy in Africa.
- Analyze the role of force in the contemporary international system.

Psychology

- Contrast Freud's and Erikson's stage theories of personality.
- What is meant by triangulation of measurement (multiple methodology)?

KNOW THE MATERIAL

It goes without saying that you must know the material in order to explain the concepts and give specific examples or facts from the text. But what is the best way to review the material so that you can recall examples under pressure? The following three study tactics will improve your recall.

First, read your text actively. Do not just mark key passages in yellow highlighter. Write marginal notes to yourself. Write key concepts in the margin. Ask questions. Make connections between an idea in one paragraph and something you read earlier. Make connections between what you read in the text and what you heard in class.

Second, do not depend only on your reading and class discussion. Join or form a study group that meets regularly to review course material. Each person in the group should prepare some question for review. Explaining key ideas to a friend is an excellent way to learn the material yourself.

Finally, use your writing to help you remember. Do not just read the book and your notes and head off for the test. Instead, review your notes, *close* your notebook, and write down as much as you can remember. Review the assigned chapters in the text, close the book, and write out what you remember. If you can write answers to questions with the book closed, you know you're ready for an essay examination.

■ JOURNAL EXERCISE   Get out the class notes and textbook for a course that you are currently taking. Annotate your notes with summary comments and questions. In the margins, write out the key ideas that the lecture covered. Then write out questions that you still have about the material. Open your textbook for that class. Annotate the margins of the chapter that you are currently reading. Write summary comments about important material. Write questions in the margins about material that you do not understand. Note places in the text that the instructor also covered in class.

PRACTICE WRITING

As several of the senior English majors suggested, practicing short essays *before* an examination will make you feel comfortable with the material and reduce your panic. A coach once noted that while every athlete wants to win, only the true winners are willing to *prepare* to win. The same is true of writing an examination. Successful writers have already completed 80 percent of the writing process *before* they walk into an examination. They have written notes in the margins of their notebooks and textbooks. They have discussed the subject with other students. They have closed the book and written out key definitions. They have prepared questions and practiced answering them. Once they read a question, they are prepared to write out their "final" drafts.

■ JOURNAL EXERCISE   For an upcoming examination in one of your other courses, write out three possible essay questions that your instructor might ask. For each question, underline the key words, and make a sketch outline of your response. Set your watch or timer for fifteen minutes, and actually write out your response to *one* of your questions.

PROOFREAD AND EDIT

In your normal writing process, you can put aside your draft for several days and proofread and edit it later. When you are writing under pressure, however, you need to save three or four minutes at the end to review what you have written. Often, you may be out of time before you have finished writing what you wanted to say about the question. At this point, one effective strategy is to draw a line at the end of what you have written, write "Out of Time," and then write one or two quick sentences explaining what you planned to say: "If I had more time, I would explain how the UN's image has become more positive following the crises in Israel and Iraq." Then use your remaining two or three minutes to reread what you have written, making sure that your ideas are clear and that you have written in complete sentences and used correct spelling and punctuation. If you don't know how to spell a word, at least write "sp?" next to a word to show that you think it is spelled incorrectly.

SAMPLE ESSAY QUESTIONS AND RESPONSES

The following are sample essay questions, students' responses, and instructors' comments and grades.

HISTORY 100: WESTERN CIVILIZATION
Examination II over Chapter 12, class lectures, and Victor Hugo's *The Hunchback of Notre Dame*

Essay I (25 Points)

What was the fifteenth-century view of "science" as described in *The Hunchback?* How did this view tend to inhibit Claud Frollo in his experiments in his closet in the cathedral?

ANSWER 1

The fifteenth-century view of "science" was characterized by superstition and heresy. In *The Hunchback of Notre Dame,* for example, we see superstition operating when the king's physician states that a gunshot wound can be cured by the application of a roasted mouse. Claud Frollo, a high-ranking church official, has a thirst for knowledge, but unfortunately it pushes beyond the limits of knowledge permitted by the church. When he works in his closet on the art of alchemy and searches for the "Philosopher's Stone" (gold), he is guilty of heresy. Frollo has read and mastered the arts and sciences of the university and of the church, and he wants to know more. He knows that if he presses into the "Black Arts," the Devil will take his soul. And indeed, the "Devil" of passion does. Frollo feels inhibited because many of the experiments he has performed have made him guilty of heresy and witchcraft in the eyes of the church. And this seems to be the case in almost anything "new" or out of the ordinary. La Esmeralda, for instance, is declared "guilty" of witchcraft for the training of her goat. Her goat appears to have been possessed by the Devil himself, when, in fact, all the girl is guilty of is training the goat to do a few simple tricks. All in all, the fifteenth-century view of "science" was one not of favor, but of oppression and fear. Thankfully, the Renaissance came along!

An excellent response. Your focus on superstition and heresy along with the specific examples of the roasted mouse, the "Philosopher's Stone," and La Esmeralda's goat illustrate the fifteenth-century view of science and its inhibiting effect. Grade: A

ANSWER 2

The fifteenth-century view of science was that according to the Bible, God was the creator of all, and as to scientific theory, the subject was moot. No one was a believer in the scientific method—however, we do find some science going on in Claud Frollo's closet, alchemy. At that time he was trying to create gold by mixing different elements together. Though alchemy seems to be the only science of that time period, people who practiced it kept it to themselves. We even find King Louis IX coming to Frollo, disguised, to dabble in a little of the science himself. At this time people were rejecting the theory of the Earth revolving around the sun because, as a religious ordeal, God created the Earth and man, and they are the center of all things, so there were no questions to be answered by science, because the answer was God.

Give more examples from the novel and show how the fifteenth-century view actually inhibited Frollo. Otherwise, generally good response. (Why was creating the Earth such a religious "ordeal"?) Grade: B

ANSWER 3

According to *The Hunchback of Notre Dame,* the view of "science" in the fifteenth century was basically alchemy, that is, being able to turn base metals into gold. Everything else that we would regard as scientific today was regarded as sorcery or magic in the fifteenth century. What inhibited Claud Frollo in his experiments of turning base metals into gold was that, according to the laws of alchemy, one needed "The Philosopher's Stone" to complete the experiment, and Claud Frollo was unable to find this particular stone.

Needs more specific illustrations from the novel. Frollo is inhibited by his lack of scientific method and the censure of the church. Underline title of novel: The Hunchback of Notre Dame. Grade: C

ANSWER 4

During the period that the *Hunchback* took place, the attitude toward science was one of fear. Because the setting was in the medieval world, the people were afraid to admit to doing some things that were not being done by a majority of people. The overall view during that period was to keep one's own self out of trouble. The fright may be the result of the public executions which were perhaps Claud Frollo's deterrent in admitting to performing acts of science which others are uneducated in. Claud Frollo was outnumbered in the area of wanting to be "educated" and he kept to himself because he feared the people. He was in a position that didn't give him the power to try and overcome people's attitude of fear toward science. If he tried, he risked his life.

State your ideas more clearly. Your response doesn't answer the question. Very limited in your examples of science. Grade: D

BIOLOGY 220: ECOLOGY
FINAL EXAMINATION

Essay II (20 Points)

Water running down a mountainside erodes its channel and carries with it considerable material. What is the basic source of the energy used by the water to do this work? How is the energy used by water to do this work related to the energy used by life in the stream ecosystem?

ANSWER 1

The process begins with the hydrologic cycle. The sun radiates down and forces evaporation. This H_2O gas condenses and forms rain or snow, which precipitates back to earth. If the precipitation falls on a mountain, it will eventually run down the hillside and erode its channel. (Some water will evaporate without running down the hill.) The energy used by water to do its work relates directly to the energy used by life in the stream system. The sun is an energy input. It is the source of energy for stream life just as it is the source of energy for the water. Through photosynthesis, the energy absorbed by the stream is used by

Good response. Clear focus on the hydrolic cycle, photosynthesis, and solar energy and the source of energy for both the stream and its ecosystems. Grade: A

higher and higher trophic levels. So the sun is the energy source for both running water and the life in the stream. It all starts with solar energy.

ANSWER 2

Ultimately, the sun is the basic source of energy that allows water to do the work it does. Solar power runs the hydrologic cycle, which is where water gets its energy. Heat evaporates water and allows molecules to rise in the atmosphere, where it condenses in clouds. Above the ground, but still under the effects of gravity, water has potential energy at this point. When enough condensation occurs, water drops back to the ground, changing potential energy to kinetic energy, which is how water works on mountainsides to move materials. As water moves materials, it brings into streams a great deal of organic matter, which is utilized by a number of heterotrophic organisms. That is the original source of energy for the ecosystems and also how energy used by water is related to the energy that is used by life in streams.

Very clear explanation of the hydrolic cycle, but response doesn't explain how source of energy for the stream ecosystem is related, through photosynthesis, to solar energy. Grade: B

ANSWER 3

The actual energy to move the water down the mountains is gravitational pull from the center of the earth. The stream's "growth" from the beginning of the mountaintop to the base starts out with being a heterotrophic system. This is because usually there is not enough light to bring about photosynthesis for the plants and in turn help other organisms' survival, so the streams use outside resources for energy. Once the stream gets bigger (by meeting up with another stream), it is autotrophic. It can produce its own energy sources. When the water reaches the base and becomes very large, it falls back to a heterotrophic system because the water has become too deep for light to penetrate and help with photosynthesis.

Reread the question. The basic source of energy is solar power. You almost discover the answer when you discuss photosynthesis, but after that, you get off track again. Grade: C−

A piece of writing is never finished. It is delivered to a deadline, torn out of a typewriter on demand, and sent off with a sense of accomplishment and shame and pride and frustration. If only there were a couple more days, time for just another run at it, perhaps then . . .

—DONALD
MURRAY,

TEACHER AND WRITER

SECTION 1

REVIEW OF BASIC SENTENCE ELEMENTS

If you are unfamiliar with grammatical terms, parts of speech, or basic sentence elements, check the definitions and examples in this section.

1a Sentence Structure
1b Nouns and Pronouns
1c Adjectives and Adverbs
1d Verbs
1e Phrases and Clauses
1f Articles, Prepositions, Interjections

SECTION 2

SENTENCE STRUCTURE AND GRAMMAR

This section shows you how to revise such common problems as sentence fragments, faulty parallelism, unnecessary use of passive voice, and lack of subject-verb agreement.

2a Fragments
2b Mixed Constructions and Faulty Predication
2c Dangling Modifiers and Misplaced Modifiers
2d Faulty Parallelism
2e Active and Passive Voice
2f Nominals and *Be* Verbs
2g Subject-Verb Agreement
2h Verb Tense
2i Pronoun Agreement
2j Pronoun Reference

SECTION 3

DICTION AND STYLE

This section contains tips on making your writing more precise, concise, and effective. You will learn to recognize and eliminate vague words, needless words, clichés, and jargon. At the end of this section, the Usage Glossary explains distinctions between confusing pairs of words such as *affect/effect, advise/advice,* and *amount/number.*

SECTION 4

....

PUNCTUATION AND MECHANICS

If you have problems using commas, semicolons, colons, or dashes, this section will help you pinpoint errors and fix them. The examples show you how to revise comma splices and fused sentences, how to punctuate dialogue, and how to use numbers, apostrophes, italics, and capitals.

The information in this Handbook will help you with the final stages of the revising process: editing and proofreading. Most writers and researchers agree that editing and proofreading should wait until the end of the writing process, when you are least likely to interrupt the flow of your ideas. During this final stage, you should clarify your sentences and correct any errors in grammar, usage, diction, spelling, and mechanics. As you edit, concentrate on polishing the surface blemishes in your writing, but don't get so locked in on punctuation or grammar that you ignore the meaning, organization, or development of your essay. Even when you are proofreading, you may find an occasional spot to add another bit of detail, take out a repetitious phrase, or sharpen a transition.

To be a good editor, you need to understand the *conventions* of language and the *expectations* of the reader instead of memorizing rules. In fact, the "rules" of grammar, punctuation, and usage may vary from one occasion to the next. A sentence fragment or a substandard usage such as "ain't" may be appropriate in one situation but not in another. Moreover, the notion of "rules" tends to suggest that language is static or unchanging. In fact, the opposite is true: Vocabulary, acceptable usage, even grammatical choices depend on current conventions and expectations. What is acceptable for one occasion or audience may be totally inappropriate for another. If you are not aware of these conventions, all your hard work in collecting, shaping, drafting, and revising may be wasted. A sloppy job of editing can ruin the best of essays.

This chapter describes standard conventions of editing in formal American English usage. As you edit your writing, however, remember that your purpose and audience should be your final guide.

WHY EDIT AND PROOFREAD?

Easy writing's curst hard reading.
—RICHARD BRINSLEY SHERIDAN, DRAMATIST

Most writers and readers agree that grammar, usage, spelling, and mechanics are less important than content and ideas. But writers should realize that readers react not only to the ideas in an essay but also to the clarity, accuracy, and even the surface appearance of the writing. Often, writers will say, rather defensively, "Of course, there are a few typos and grammar problems in my essay, but readers can still get the message. After all, it's my *ideas* that count." Unfortunately, ideas count only if the reader *gets* them. If the reader becomes irritated by unclear sentences and errors in spelling or usage, your good ideas may never reach their destination.

Writers who say that surface errors are unimportant are either rationalizing or living in a fantasy world. In the real world, most readers react negatively if writing is not neat, accurate, and readable. If your friend or roommate leaves a scrawled note that says, "I borried your shert for too day—hope you do'nt mind!" you may worry about the "shert"—and look for a new roommate. If your bank statement has misspellings, crossed-out numbers, or penciled-in debits, you may change banks in a hurry. If your doctor writes a note saying, "In my opinnion you should have bone serjury immediately!" you may rush to get another "opinnion" before agreeing to "serjury." The medium may communicate the real message: If the medium—your language—is flawed by surface errors, readers often suspect that the message is flawed, too.

The man snoozing in his chair with an unfinished magazine open on his lap is a man who was being given too much unnecessary trouble by the writer.
—WILLIAM ZINSSER, WRITER AND TEACHER

Some readers believe that writers who do not edit or proofread are just lazy. Although you need time to polish your writing, effective editing and proofreading are not just matters of effort or willpower. Rereading your essay ten times will not necessarily resolve all the problems. Editing is often difficult because many of your errors really don't look like mistakes—primarily because *you already know what you are trying to say*. When you reread what you have written, you tend to recall the idea already in your mind instead of reading the words exactly as they are written on the page.

If you live with a friend or roommate, try this experiment. Sit in a neutral corner of the room and look at your desk. It looks relatively clean, right? A few books, papers, and pencils are scattered here and there, but you know where everything is. It has an order. It makes sense. The math book is on the corner of the desk—under the notebook, the sock, and the coffee—just where you left it last night. The psychology book is open to Chapter 4, right underneath the sweatshirt and the lecture notes that you're going to study after dinner. Stuff is kind of stacked up, but not really messy. Now look at your friend's desk. Everything looks disorganized, as if it were dumped upside down from a backpack. You count four books, two spiral notebooks, four dog-eared sheets of paper, one cup of stale coffee, a broken ballpoint pen, and a T-shirt. It's a mess, right? And sometimes it really irritates you. *How can your roommate stand to live in such chaos?* But wait. Your roommate's desk has some order to it, too, just as yours does. You just can't see the order for the mess.

Unfortunately, the same is true of writing: In your *own* writing, all you see is the meaning—the order that is in your mind. In other people's writing, you see the errors first and then, only after careful reading, the meaning. The bedrock truth is that readers will more easily see your mess than your meaning. Your writing will be more effective if your readers aren't irritated about the mess that they have had to read through. Errors or surface distractions may even undermine your credibility as a writer. For some kinds of writing—letters of application or essays for classes—the result of a few errors may be more than irritation; you simply may not be admitted, get the job, or get a passing grade.

How to Edit and Proofread

The purpose of editing is, of course, to keep language problems from interfering with the ideas or message—to make language work for your purpose rather than against it. Editing usually requires that you read over your work several times, checking for errors and anticipating problems that your readers might have. However, because you literally may not see many "obvious" errors, have friends or classmates look over your draft for problems or mistakes. When you use other readers, however, explain your purpose and audience. Then ask them to use conventional proofreading and editing marks to indicate their suggestions. *Remember: Your editors' marks are suggestions.* If they mark errors you've simply overlooked, make the correction. But if they mark something that you don't understand, check the appropriate section in this Handbook. If you disagree with their marks or suggestions, ask them to explain why they are suggesting the change. *You are responsible for deciding whether and how to make the change.*

Begin your editing and proofreading process for each essay by *reviewing your previous essays*. What problems and errors did your peer readers notice or your teacher mark? If you are keeping a log in your journal of your problems in grammar, usage, punctuation, or mechanics, review your entries. If you typically have punctuation problems and wordy sentences, reread those sections in this Handbook and focus on those specific items as you edit.

To improve your editing and proofreading skills, learn the following proofreading marks and correction symbols.

PROOFREADING MARKS

⋏	Insert comma
embar̆assing	Insert letter or word
hot tub.ⱽ	Insert quotation marks
south‿bound	Close up
¶	Begin a new paragraph
NO ¶	Do not begin a new paragraph
down his face⊙	Add period
hop#back	Add space
pe͡ice of pie	Transpose letters
left⁄will⁄that⁄	Transpose words
in a ~~large~~ sweat	Delete words
encounter⸛is	Delete punctuation
Los Angelͤøs	Replace a letter
deep ~~inhilations~~ breaths	Replace a word
Ⱥanure	Use lowercase
friday̲̲	Capitalize

The following paragraph by student writer Kenneth Clause illustrates how to use these proofreading marks.

MY HOME TOWN, LA STYLE

It is 11:00 p.m. on a chilly friday̲̲ night. We are traveling S̸outh on the 405 freeway and have just entered Los Angeles city limits. A thick, damp fog rolls in from the ocean to blanket the city. Visibility is low. The vehicle dͤiscends through a sharp, banked turn⋏and the headlights reveal the first glimpse of "it" looming in the distance. What my weary traveling companion from New York is about to encounter⸛is the most embarrassing and horrifying beast known to residents of Los Angeles. I break out in a ~~large~~ sweat, realizing there are no exits left will that detour this formation. In a moment of desperation, I step on the accelerator. Perhaps I can speed by this ~~depraved~~ ugly monument so my friend will not notice. Unfortunately, I'm too late. In that instant, he begins howling with laughter. We are suddenly upon it. The head-lights reveal a heaping pile of Manure ~~appears~~ with a sign posted on the pinnacle that says, "Welcome to Los Angeles! A town where the grass is greener . . . on the other side of the hot tub." Well, no use in trying to hide any longer. I hit the brakes and pull the car over to the side of the road. Immediately, my jovial friend from New York opens the door and falls to the pavement with tears of laughter streaming down his face. The last thing he expected to see among the palm trees of California was a huge dungheap. The laughter of my merry schoolmate quickly ceases after a few deep ~~inhilations.~~ breaths The foul stench of this revolting glob of dung is enough to make even his pollution-hardened lungs feel weak. Upon my request, we hop back in the car and head for home. After recieving such a shock to his senses, his only hope for revival is a long shower and a peice of my dad's hot apple pie.

EDITING SYMBOLS

As you edit someone else's draft, use the following symbols to refer the writer to problems discussed in this Handbook. Your instructor may also use these correction marks to guide your own editing. Listed here are some of the most common symbols, with an explanation and reference to the section number in this Handbook.

adj	use adjective, 1C
adv	use adverb, 1C
cs	comma splice, 4B
d	revise diction (word choice)
dm	dangling modifier, 2C
frag	sentence fragment, 2A
fs	fused sentence, 4B
mm	misplaced modifier, 2C
//	revise faulty parallelism, 2D
p	punctuation needed, 4A–J
pn agr	make pronoun agree with antecedent, 2I
ref	pronoun referent problem, 2J
sp	spelling error

sv agr	subject-verb agreement error, 2G
sxt	sexist language, 3E
t	verb tense error, 1D, 2H
trans	needs transition
v	verb form problem, 1D
wdy	wordy—omit needless words, 2F, 3A, 3B
wc	revise word choice

TIPS FOR EDITING AND PROOFREADING

1. Review sections of this chapter just before you begin editing. If you need to review basic grammatical terms, begin with Section 1. Otherwise, review appropriate parts of Sections 2, 3, or 4.

2. Practice your editing and proofreading skills first on others' essays. You will see others' problems much more readily than you will see your own. Becoming a good editor of their writing will, in turn, help you recognize your own problems more easily.

3. As you edit, look for one problem at a time. Concentrate, for example, just on punctuation, or just on subject-verb agreement, or just on diction or word choice.

4. Have a friend or classmate read your essay aloud. Listen as the person reads. If you notice something that is not clear, stop and revise the sentence. If the reader does not understand what he or she is reading, stop and revise.

5. If you are writing on a computer, reformat and print out your essay, double-spaced, in narrow columns, forty to forty-five spaces wide. Many obvious errors will jump out at you as you reread your writing in a new format.

6. For proofreading, place a ruler or a blank piece of paper underneath the line you are checking. If you are proofreading for typos, try reading backward, one word at a time, from the bottom of the page to the top.

SECTION 1

REVIEW OF BASIC SENTENCE ELEMENTS

This section reviews the names and definitions of basic sentence elements. Other sections in this Handbook use the terms defined and illustrated in this section.

1A SENTENCE STRUCTURE

A sentence is a group of words beginning with a capital letter and ending with a period or other end mark; it has a subject and a predicate and expresses a complete thought. The *subject* is the word or group of words that is the topic or focus of the sentence. It acts, is acted upon, or is described. The *predicate* gives information about the subject: what the subject is, what it is doing, or what is done to it.

SUBJECT	PREDICATE
Piranhas	bite!
The McNeils	dig clams at the seashore.
Bubble gum	can cause cancer in rats.

Sentences may contain the following elements: subject (S), verb (V), direct object (DO), indirect object (IO), subject complement (SC), object complement (OC), modifier (M), and conjunction (+).

    S   V

Piranhas bite.

    S   V   DO + DO   M

Piranhas attack fish or animals in their waters.

    S   V   IO   M   DO

Andrea gave Carlos two piranhas.

    S   V   DO   OC

Carlos considers Andrea a prankster.

    S   V   SC

Andrea is a prankster.

Subjects may be nouns, pronouns, noun phrases, or noun clauses.

Verbs may be single words (*bite*) or verb phrases (*will have bitten*). Verbs may be transitive or intransitive; verbs have tense, voice, and mood.

Direct objects can be nouns, pronouns, noun phrases, or noun clauses. A direct object receives the action of a transitive verb. Direct objects usually answer the question "What?" or "Whom?" about the subject and verb:

Piranhas bit [whom?] people.

Indirect objects can be nouns, pronouns, noun phrases, or noun clauses. The indirect object answers the question "To whom?" or "For whom?" about the subject and verb:

Andrea gave [to whom?] Carlos two piranhas.

Complements occur in the predicate of the sentence following a *to be* or other linking verb. Subject complements rename or describe the subject. Object complements rename or describe the object:

SC

Carlos is *upset*.

OC

Carlos named one piranha *Bucktooth*.

Modifiers describe or limit a subject, verb, object, or complement. They may be single words, groups of words, or entire clauses:

M

Piranhas have a nasty disposition.

Conjunctions are words that link words, phrases, clauses, or sentences. The word *conjunction* means "a joining together." (See Section 4a for additional examples of conjunctions.)

- *Coordinating conjunctions (and, but, or, yet, for, nor, so)* join equal sentence elements:
  Carlos is angry, *but* Andrea is laughing.

- *Correlative conjunctions (both . . . and, either . . . or)* also join equal sentence elements:
  Neither Carlos *nor* his aquarium fish are particularly happy about the piranhas.

- *Subordinating conjunctions (because, since, although, if, until, while,* and others) begin many dependent clauses:
  If Andrea plays another joke on Carlos, she may lose a good friend.

1B **n/pr**

1B NOUNS AND PRONOUNS

A *noun* names a person, place, object, or idea. Nouns may be grouped in several classes:

- *Proper nouns* name specific people, places, or things:
  Abraham Lincoln, Cape Hatteras, Buick

- *Common nouns* name all nouns that are not proper nouns:
  cat, ocean, helicopter

- *Concrete nouns* name things that can be sensed:
  table, waves, coat

- *Abstract nouns* name things not knowable by the senses:
  justice, pity, freedom

- *Collective nouns* name groups:

  family, committee, team

- *Compound nouns* are several words joined by hyphens to form a noun:

  brother-in-law, commander-in-chief

A *pronoun* takes the place of a noun. Pronouns must meet three requirements:

- *Reference:* A pronoun must refer to a specific, identifiable word, phrase, or clause. This referent or antecedent occurs within the sentence or in a preceding sentence. (See Section 2J for examples of how to solve problems in pronoun reference.)

  Evelyn has the flu. *She* has missed two classes. [*Evelyn* is the referent for *she.*]

- *Agreement:* A pronoun must agree with or correspond to the noun that it replaces. A pronoun must agree in *person* (first, second, or third person), *number* (singular or plural), and *gender* (he, she, it). (See Section 2I for examples of how to solve problems in pronoun agreement.)

  Each girl should check on *her friend.* [*Her* agrees in person (third person), in number (singular), and gender (feminine) with the referent, *girl.*]

- *Case:* Pronouns must take the appropriate case (subjective, objective, possessive):

  Subjective pronouns (I, you, he, she, it, we, they, who) should be the subject or the complement in a sentence:

  They have the flu. [Subject]
  Who is sleeping there? It is she. [Complement]

  Objective pronouns *(me, you, her, him, whom, us, you, them)* should act as objects in a sentence:

  Evelyn gave *me* the flu. [Indirect object]

  Possessive pronouns *(my, mine, your, yours, his, her, hers, its, our, ours, their, theirs, whose)* show possession:

  I am sick as a dog with *her* flu virus.

Pronouns may be grouped in several classes:

- *Personal pronouns (I, me, mine, we, us, our, ours, you, yours, she, her, hers, he, him, his, it, its, they, them, theirs)* refer to people or things:

  She bought a cat for *him.*

- *Relative pronouns (that, who, whom, which, what, whose, whoever)* introduce clauses:

  Whoever fed the cat made a mistake.

- *Interrogative pronouns (who, whose, what, which, whom)* introduce a question:

  Which cat is the mother?

- *Reflexive* and *intensive pronouns (myself, yourself, herself, ourselves,* and so on) refer back to a pronoun or antecedent or intensify the antecedent:

  She says she paid for the cat *herself.* I *myself* suspect she just found it.

- *Indefinite pronouns (all, anyone, another, anybody, both, each, few, most, some, several, none, someone, something, such,* and so on) refer to nonspecific persons or things:

  Someone will turn up and claim the cat.

- *Demonstrative pronouns (this, that, these, those)* refer to an antecedent:

  On Tuesday morning, I must pay my bill. *That* will be a painful moment.

1C ADJECTIVES AND ADVERBS

Adjectives are modifiers that limit, describe, or add information about nouns and pronouns:

> Secretariat was my *favorite* horse. [modifies noun, *horse*]
> Even standing still, he looked *dynamic.* [modifies pronoun, *he*]

Adverbs limit, describe, or add information about verbs, adjectives, or other adverbs, and they complete sentences:

> He won *overwhelmingly.* [modifies verb, *won*]
> The Kentucky Derby was a *very* important victory. [modifies adjective, *important*]
> On that day, he ran *extremely* fast. [modifies adverb, *fast*]
> *Fortunately,* he won the Triple Crown. [modifies whole sentence]

1D VERBS

The *verb* is the heart of most sentences. Verbs can set up equations or definitions ("A flotilla *is* a small fleet of ships"). They can describe states of being ("Fear and confusion *exist* in Lebanon"). They can explain occurrences ("The players *became* angry at the referee's call") or describe actions ("The candidate *defeated* her opponent"). When sentences communicate clearly, verbs often deserve the credit.

The great variety of verb forms creates a richness in the language. This richness, however, can create confusion. Some verbs are regular; others, irregular. In some cases, combinations of verb tense, voice, and mood may entangle sentences. The following explanations and examples will help you resolve problems in verb forms so that you can communicate precisely and vividly.

PRINCIPAL PARTS OF VERBS

Verbs have three principal parts: simple form, past tense, and past participle:

SIMPLE FORM (INFINITIVE)	PAST TENSE	PAST PARTICIPLE
live (to live)	lived	lived
go (to go)	went	gone

REGULAR AND IRREGULAR VERBS   *Regular verbs* form the past tense and past participle by adding *-ed* or *-d* to the simple form:

SIMPLE FORM	PAST TENSE	PAST PARTICIPLE
count	counted	counted
dance	danced	danced
create	created	created

Irregular verbs can cause problems because they form the past tense and past participle by changing letters, sounds, or entire words. Check your dictionary to determine if a verb is irregular. If the dictionary gives only two forms *(catch, caught)*, the past participle is the same as the past tense *(caught)*. Following are some examples of the nearly two hundred irregular English verbs:

SIMPLE FORM	PAST TENSE	PAST PARTICIPLE
sing	sang	sung
begin	began	begun
break	broke	broken
drive	drove	driven
sink	sank, sunk	sunk
sleep	slept	slept
read	read	read
eat	ate	eaten
see	saw	seen
slide	slid	slid

LINKING VERBS   *Linking verbs* (*is, becomes, seems, looks,* and so on) equate subjects with predicates, so that the word or words in the predicate rename or describe the subject. A linking verb creates a subject complement (SC)—a word or words that complete the equation:

    S   V   SC   M

Lillian was president of the company. [Lillian = president]

    s   v   sc

The storm seemed threatening. [Storm = threatening]

AUXILIARY VERBS   *Auxiliary verbs*, also called *helping verbs*, combine with main verbs to show tense, voice, or mood. The verbs *be, do,* and *have* are common auxiliary verbs:

> She is running a marathon. [auxiliary verb = *is*]
> They did enjoy the dinner. [auxiliary verb = *did*]
> He had left before she arrived. [auxiliary verb = *had*]

TENSE   *Tense* tells *when* a verb's action, occurrence, or state of being takes place. The six verb tenses in English are illustrated here with the regular verb *create*. The parentheses contain the *progressive* form (*-ing*) to show continual or ongoing action, occurrence, or state of being:

1D verbs

Present	I create (I am creating)
Past	I created (I was creating)
Future	I will create (I will be creating)
Present Perfect	I have created (I have been creating)

The present perfect tense describes actions occurring or conditions existing at an unspecified time in the past and continuing into the present: *I have created several award-winning recipes for chili.*

Past Perfect   I had created (I had been creating)

The past perfect tense describes actions occurring or conditions existing before a specific time in the past: *I had created three different recipes for extra-hot chili before I won my first award.*

Future Perfect   I will have created (I will have been creating)

The future perfect tense describes actions that have already occurred or conditions that will exist by a specific future time: *I will have created a new salsa recipe before the county fair begins.*

TRANSITIVE AND INTRANSITIVE   Many verbs in English can be either transitive or intransitive, depending on the sentence. *Transitive* verbs take objects. As the prefix *trans-* suggests, they carry the action across to the object:

S   V   DO

Myrna developed the film.

S   V   DO

Michael sees the oncoming car.

Intransitive verbs do not take objects:

S   V   M

Myrna developed early. [*Early* is not a direct object; it describes when Myrna developed]

S   V   M

Michael sees in the dark. [*in the dark* is not a direct object]

VOICE Verbs have *active* and *passive* voice. *Active voice* means that the subject of the sentence performs the action. *Passive voice* means that the subject is acted upon. A passive-voice sentence uses a form of *be* plus a past participle. (For additional discussion of active and passive voice, see Section 2e.)

Active Voice	Inuits *build* stone and peat houses.
Passive Voice	Stone and peat houses *are built* by Inuits. [Contains a form of *be* + past participle: *are* + *built*]

MOOD Verbs have three moods that indicate a writer's attitude toward a statement. *Indicative mood* expresses a statement of fact or asks a question. *Imperative mood* expresses commands or directives. *Subjunctive mood* expresses a wish or condition contrary to fact:

Indicative	She has perfect pitch. [fact]
	Why does she sing opera? [question]
Imperative	Pay attention to the music. [command]
	Turn and face the spotlight. [directive]
Subjunctive	I wish that I were more talented. [wish]
	If she were to catch a cold, she would not sing on opening night. [condition contrary to fact]

1E PHRASES AND CLAUSES

PHRASES

A *phrase* is a group of related words that does not contain a subject or a predicate:

Prepositional Phrase	He wrote *on the computer.*
Noun Phrase	A *notebook computer* is handy.
Appositive Phrase	The Apple II, *the first popular school computer,* is the Model T of home computers. [An appositive phrase identifies or provides more information about the preceding noun or pronoun.]

A *verbal phrase* is a group of related words that contains a verbal: an infinitive *(to talk)*, a present participle *(talking)*, or a past participle *(talked)*. There are three kinds of verbals:

- *Infinitives* usually use *to + simple verb*; they function as nouns, adjectives, or adverbs:

Infinitive	*To talk*
Infinitive Phrase	He planned *to talk for three minutes.* [infinitive phrase = direct object] *To listen carefully* was his first objective. [infinitive phrase = subject]

- *Gerunds* are nouns made from the *-ing* or present participle form of the verb:

Gerund	*Talking* got her into trouble. [*Talking* is a gerund; gerund = subject]
Gerund Phrase	*Talking during the lecture* got her into trouble. [gerund phrase = subject]

- *Participles* are adjectives made from verb forms. As adjectives, they modify nouns or pronouns. They can use either the *-ing* (present participle) or the *-ed* (past participle) verb form:

Participle	*Coughing* students may bother the teacher. [Participle modifies *students.*] *Whispered* conversations may distract students. [Participle modifies *conversations.*]
Participial Phrases	*Rustling their papers and snapping their notebooks closed,* they prepare to leave the lecture hall. [Participial phrase modifies *they.*] Several students, *entranced by the final scene in the film,* write quietly for a few moments. [Participial phrase modifies *students.*]

CLAUSES

A *clause* is a group of words containing a subject and a verb. It need not be an entire sentence or a complete thought. Clauses can be independent (main) or dependent (subordinate):

- *Independent* or *main clause:* A group of words containing a subject and a verb that can stand by itself as a complete thought:

  We drank decaffeinated coffee.

- *Dependent clause:* A group of words that contains a subject and verb but cannot stand by itself as a complete thought:

  Because we drank decaffeinated coffee

- *Subordinate clauses* (sometimes called *adverb clauses*): Dependent clauses that begin with a subordinating conjunction, such as *because, if, although, unless, when, while, since, as, until, before,* and *after*:

  Although I drank coffee, everyone else drank tea.

- *Relative clauses* (also called *adjective clauses*): Dependent clauses that begin with *when, where,* or *why,* or with relative pronouns (*who, that, which, whom, whoever, whomever, whatever*):

  Driving *when you are under the influence of alcohol* may result in a mandatory jail sentence. [Adjective clause modifies *driving*.]

  Free coffee, *which the bar serves after midnight*, is part of a campaign for responsible drinking. [Adjective clause modifies *coffee*.]

  The police officer gave a ticket to the woman *who was driving the red pickup truck*. [Adjective clause modifies *woman*.]

1F ARTICLES, PREPOSITIONS, INTERJECTIONS

ARTICLES

Articles (a, an, the) often appear before nouns. They are modifiers that limit a noun. *A* and *an* are less limiting than *the*:

  I have a plan to solve our problems.
  I have the plan to solve our problems. [*The* suggests that the plan is more definitive.]

The article *a* appears before words that begin with a *consonant sound* (not necessarily a consonant): *a* kite, *a* hammer, *a* university, *a* one-sided victory.

The article *an* appears before words that begin with a *vowel sound* (not necessarily a vowel): *an* opening, *an* egg, *an* old shirt, *an* honor, *an* E.

PREPOSITIONS

Prepositions (in, on, up, to, after, by, for, across, within, and others) usually occur in prepositional phrases with a noun or pronoun that is the object of the preposition:

> *In* the hot sun *by* the edge *of* the water, a small turtle lay perfectly still.

Note that some words can function as either prepositions or conjunctions:

> We will row home *after* lunch. [preposition]
> *After* you finish your sandwich, we will row home. [conjunction]

INTERJECTIONS

Interjections (oh, alas, yea, damn, hooray, ouch, and others) are words conveying strong feeling or surprise. Interjections occasionally appear in informal writing or in a dialogue:

> The Cardinals won the pennant (yea!) but lost the World Series (boo, hiss).
> Alas, their hitting was anemic.
> "Oh, she moped about it for days."

SECTION 2

SENTENCE STRUCTURE AND GRAMMAR

When sentences don't follow standard American English conventions, readers may become aggravated, confused, or simply lost. While some deviations from established conventions barely distract the reader, others totally scramble meaning. If "sickening grammar" detracts from your meaning, your readers may react uncharitably. If you write a confusing sentence fragment, some readers will think, "This writer doesn't know what a sentence is." If you have a problem in subject-verb agreement, readers may think, "This writer didn't reread the sentence or doesn't know what the subject of the sentence is." If you write a sentence with a dangling modifier, the reader may think, "The writer doesn't know how comical this sounds." This section will help you avoid those embarrassing problems that confuse readers or invite them to think about your grammar rather than your meaning.

I've noticed a good deal, and there's no bird, or cow, or anything that uses as good grammar as a bluejay. You may say a cat uses good grammar. Well, a cat does—but you let a cat get excited once; you let a cat get to pulling fur with another cat on a shed, nights, and you'll hear grammar that will give you the lockjaw. Ignorant people think it's the noise which fighting cats make that is so aggravating, but it ain't so; it's the sickening grammar they use.

—MARK TWAIN,

FROM "BAKER'S BLUEJAY YARN"

1F art

2A FRAGMENTS

Use sentence fragments only for special emphasis. A *fragment* is an incomplete sentence. A fragment may lack a subject or verb, or it may be only a dependent clause. *Test* for sentence fragments by taking the group of words out of context. If the group of words cannot stand by itself as a complete thought, it is a fragment.

Revise sentence fragments by adding a subject or verb or by combining the fragment with the preceding sentence:

Fragment: I still remember the championship basketball game when I scored forty points. *Breaking the existing conference record.* ["Breaking the existing conference record" is not a complete sentence. It cannot stand by itself as a complete thought. Combine with previous sentence.]

Revision: I still remember the championship basketball game when I broke the existing conference record by scoring forty points.

Fragment: At home I enjoy many water sports. *Waterskiing and sailing, which are my two favorites.* ["Waterskiing and sailing, which are my two favorites" cannot stand by itself as a complete thought. Revise to make one complete sentence.]

Revision: At home, I enjoy my two favorite water sports: waterskiing and sailing.

Fragment: She stood in line for four hours in the freezing rain. *To get tickets for the rock concert.* ["To get tickets for the rock concert" cannot stand by itself as a complete thought. Combine with previous sentence.]

Revision: To get tickets for the rock concert, she stood in line for four hours in the freezing ain.

Fragment: After a tough class, I took a long shower, dried my hair, and put on my underwear. Then I walked into the living room. *Because I thought no one was home.* Was I surprised to discover my mother talking to Reverend Jones! ["Because I thought no one was home" cannot stand by itself as a complete thought. It is a dependent clause or fragment.]

Revision: After a tough class, I took a long shower, dried my hair, and put on my underwear. Because I thought no one was home,

I walked into the living room. Was I surprised to discover my mother talking to Reverend Jones!

Fragment: At the end of the game, the frustrated fans began to throw snowballs on the field. *The score being 42–0.*
["The score being 42–0" is not a complete sentence. Change *being* to *is* or *was*.]

Revision: At the end of the game, the frustrated fans began to throw snowballs on the field because the score was 42–0.

For special emphasis, however, sparingly used sentence fragments can be effective. In context, the following are examples of effective sentence fragments:

When the river was dammed almost all of these things were lost. Crowded out—or drowned and buried under mud.

—Edward Abbey

Head off? Decapitation cases are rather routinely handled.

—Jessica Mitford

When I finally did fall asleep, I had that same hideous nightmare in which a woodchuck is trying to claim my prize at a raffle. Despair.

—Woody Allen

EXERCISE

In the following passage, identify all sentence fragments. Then revise the passage to eliminate inappropriate fragments.

(1) Most people think that a library is as quiet as growing grass, but often it is the noisiest place on campus to study. (2) The worst time being finals week. (3) Some of the chatter is from people who come to the library just to visit: "How did you like the party Saturday night?" (4) "Did you get the notes from chemistry?" (5) The chatter goes on continually, punctuated by coughs, gasps, and giggles. (6) Just when I start to panic about my calculus examination. (7) Someone across the table tells a joke, and they all start laughing. (8) They try to cover their laughter with their hands, but the sound explodes out anyway. (9) Irritating ten other students who are trying to study. (10) Sometimes I wish the library had its own police force. (11) To arrest those gabby, discourteous "party people." (12) I would sit there smiling as they handcuffed these party people and dragged them out of the library. (13) Ah, the sweet revenge of daydreams.

2B MIXED CONSTRUCTIONS AND FAULTY PREDICATION

MIXED CONSTRUCTIONS

Occasionally, writers begin sentences with one structure and then switch, right in the middle, to another. Revise sentences with mixed constructions by choosing one structure and sticking to it:

Mixed: Because the repairs were so expensive is why I ended up selling the car.

Revised: Because the repairs were so expensive, I sold the car.

Mixed: By getting behind in math classes is a quick way to flunk out.

Revised: Getting behind in math classes is a quick way to flunk out.

FAULTY PREDICATION

Sometimes the predicate does not *logically* fit with the subject. Remember that the verb *to be* is an *equals* sign. Revise faulty predication by changing either the subject or the predicate:

Faulty: Freestyle ski jumping is where skiers take crazy chances in midair.
Note: "Ski jumping" is an activity, not a place. It is illogical to say, "Ski jumping is where . . ."

Revised: Freestyle ski jumping is a sport that encourages skiers to take crazy chances in midair.

Faulty: My dog Noodles is the reason I'm feeling depressed.
Note: "My dog Noodles" is a specific animal, not a "reason." Missing Noodles, however, could be a cause for depression.

Revised: I'm feeling depressed because I miss my dog Noodles.

Faulty: Real intelligence is when you can say no to that third piece of chocolate cream pie.
Note: "Intelligence" is or equals a mental condition, not a "when."

Revised: Saying no to that third piece of chocolate cream pie requires real intelligence.

EXERCISE

In the following passage, identify sentences with mixed constructions, faulty predication, or both, and then revise them.

2B
mix con

(1) After my sophomore year, I intend to transfer to Boston College. (2) Basically, I want to attend a school that has a city environment and a diverse population of students. (3) I suppose my sister Nadine is a big reason I want to transfer. (4) She wants me to move closer to home. (5) Also, by attending a city school will enable me to see plays, to visit museums occasionally, and to eat out at good restaurants. (6) Finally, I'd like to meet all sorts of students. (7) A good university is when a student can meet people from all walks of life. (8) Because Boston College has diversity is really why I intend to transfer.

2C DANGLING MODIFIERS AND MISPLACED MODIFIERS

DANGLING MODIFIERS

Modifying phrases must clearly describe, qualify, or limit some word in the sentence. When the modifying phrase occurs at the beginning of a sentence, the word that is modified must appear *immediately* following the phrase. Otherwise, the modifying phrase "dangles" or is logically "unattached" to the sentence. Such sentences are confusing and often comical:

2C
dm/mm

Faulty:	Rushing to get to class on time, my shoelace broke. [*Who* was rushing to get to class? The shoelace? Revise by indicating the person immediately after the comma.]
Revised:	Rushing to get to class, I broke a shoelace.
Faulty:	Flying at five thousand feet, the cars looked like tiny toys. [*Who* is flying at five thousand feet? The cars? Revise by indicating that person immediately after the comma.]
Revised:	Flying at five thousand feet, I saw cars that looked like tiny toys.
Faulty:	From birth until the first grade, one parent should be home with the children. [Does the opening phrase, "From birth until the first grade," modify *parent* or *children*? Revise by placing the appropriate word immediately after the introductory phrase.]
Revised:	From birth until the first grade, children should have one parent at home.
Faulty:	Sue practiced her freestyle stroke until she knew she could swim faster than Flipper, being a fanatical swimmer. [Who is the fanatical swimmer—*Sue* or *Flipper*? When modifying phrases "dangle" from the *end* of a sentence, revise by placing the phrase next to the word it modifies.]

Revised: Being a fanatical swimmer, Sue practiced her freestyle stroke until she knew she could swim faster than Flipper.

MISPLACED MODIFIERS

Place a modifying word, phrase, or clause immediately before or after the word it modifies. In the following sentences, notice how changing the placement of the word *only* changes the meaning of the sentence:

Only I tasted grandfather's pumpkin pie. [I was the only one who tasted it.]

I only tasted grandfather's pumpkin pie. [I only tasted it; Pete actually ate it.]

I tasted only grandfather's pumpkin pie. [I didn't taste anything else; I didn't even taste Aunt Margaret's pecan pie.]

I tasted grandfather's only pumpkin pie. [Grandfather made only one pumpkin pie, and I tasted it.]

Confusing: He borrowed a computer from his professor with a faulty memory.

[*Who* or *what* has the faulty memory? Place the phrase "with a faulty memory" next to the word it modifies (*computer*).]

Revised: He borrowed a computer with a faulty memory from his professor.

Confusing: The hamburgers have been horrible in the fast-food restaurants that I've eaten.

[Did the writer eat restaurants or hamburgers? Revise by placing the clause "that I've eaten" next to the word it should modify (*hamburgers*).]

Revised: The hamburgers that I've eaten in fast-food restaurants have been horrible.

EXERCISE

In the following passage, identify sentences with dangling modifiers and misplaced modifiers, and then revise each faulty sentence.

(1) SP302, History of Film, is a worthwhile class to take. (2) Occurring on Tuesday night from 7:00 P.M. to 9:45 P.M., Professor Hancock teaches the class so that it coincides with dollar movie night at the campus theater. (3) Normally, a long class would be boring because of the Nod Factor. (4) However, Professor Hancock keeps everyone awake and entertains the students, being very energetic. (5) Her lecture on *Citizen Kane* was a particularly good example. (6) Unfortunately, the film began before she finished her lecture. (7) Rushing across the stage just as the film was beginning,

an electrical cord tripped her up, causing her to lose her balance and fall. (8) She regained her composure in time to remind us that Orson Welles also wrote and performed the famous broadcast about the invasion of the Martians on the radio. (9) We certainly were relieved to get that important information!

2D FAULTY PARALLELISM

Repeated elements in a sentence that are similar in meaning or function should be *parallel* in grammatical form. The parallel form should, in turn, help to emphasize the meaning. Any repeated sentence elements, from subjects and verbs to prepositional phrases, may occur in parallel form:

Parallel Clauses	*I came, I saw, I conquered.*
Parallel Adverbs	He read *slowly* and *thoroughly.*
Parallel Prepositional Phrases	She walked *through the archway,* *across the quadrangle,* and *into the library.*

Identifying and numbering the repeated elements may help you see the parallel elements in a sentence:

2D

//

She walked   (1) through the archway,
                (2) across the quadrangle,
                    and
                (3) into the library.

Faulty: Walking, biking, and automobiles are the three most popular modes of transportation.
                [Identify and number elements that should be parallel. "(1) *Walking,* (2) *biking,* and (3) *automobiles* are the three most popular modes of transportation." Revise, choosing one pattern for all three elements.]

Revised: Walking, biking, and driving are the three most popular modes of transportation.

Faulty: Traveling abroad last summer, John increased his social awareness, his cultural knowledge, and overall sophistication.
                [Identify and number elements that should be parallel. "Traveling abroad last summer, John increased (1) *his social awareness,* (2) *his cultural knowledge,* and (3) _____ *overall sophistication.*" Then revise, choosing one grammatical pattern for all three elements.]

Revised:	Traveling abroad last summer, John increased his social awareness, his cultural knowledge, and his overall sophistication.
	[or]
Revised:	Traveling abroad last summer, John increased his social awareness, cultural knowledge, and overall sophistication.
Faulty:	There are three commandments for college students: Thou shalt go to class; thou shalt read the text; and be sure to borrow your neighbor's notes.
	[Identify and number elements that should be parallel. Since the first and second "commandments" set the grammatical pattern, the reader expects the third commandment to take the same "thou shalt" form.]
Revised:	There are three commandments for college students: Thou shalt go to class; thou shalt read the text; and thou shalt borrow thy neighbor's notes.
Faulty:	She was angry not only because he was late but also he forgot the tickets.
	Note: Compared or contrasted sentence elements introduced by "either . . . or," "both . . . and," or "not only . . . but also" must be parallel.
	[Identify and number elements that should be parallel. "She was angry not only (1) because he was late but also (2) _____ he forgot the tickets." Revise to make (1) and (2) parallel.]
Revised:	She was angry not only because he was late but also because he forgot the tickets.

EXERCISE

In the following passage, identify and revise any sentences with faulty parallelism.

(1) Alcohol abuse is a primary cause of spectator violence at college football games. (2) On average, the police department makes between five and ten arrests at each home football game. (3) These arrests are for property destruction, public intoxication, and occasionally when students conduct themselves in a disorderly manner. (4) When spectators consume too much alcohol not only do they hurt themselves but also act obnoxiously toward others. (5) Following a recent fight, ambulance attendants said that some drunken spectators or "animals" actually pelted them with sod while they tried to assist an injured man. (6) The attendants tried pleading, reason, and shouting, but to no avail. (7) To reduce these ugly incidents and restoring the

enjoyment of the game, alcohol should not be sold at football games after the beginning of the second half.

2E ACTIVE AND PASSIVE VOICE

Verbs that can have direct objects (transitive verbs) are in the *active voice* when the subject of the sentence *acts upon the object*:

The wolfhound bit Perry.

Wolfhound, the subject of the sentence, *acts upon the object, Perry*. The arrow shows that in the active voice, the action of the verb *bit* goes forward, toward the object, *Perry*.

Verbs that can have objects (transitive verbs) are in the *passive voice* when the *subject is acted upon*. The passive voice uses a form of *be (is, am, are, was, were, been, being)* followed by the past participle of the main verb (in this case, *bitten*):

Perry was bitten by the wolfhound.

The verb *was bitten* is transitive, but *Perry*, now the subject of the sentence, is acted upon. The arrow shows that the action of the verb goes backward, so that *Perry* receives the action.

Notice the following *differences* between active and passive voice:

The active-voice sentence, "The wolfhound bit Perry," uses two fewer words than the passive version, its action moves in a normal forward direction, and it clearly identifies the actor.

The passive-voice sentence, "Perry was bitten by the wolfhound," uses two more words, and it inverts the direction of the action in the sentence. In some cases, the passive voice may omit the actor altogether: "Perry was bitten on Friday." In that case, the reader does not know who or what bit Perry.

ACTIVE VOICE

Usually, *active voice* is preferable because it is more direct, vivid, and concise than passive voice. Remember, however, that sentences must be judged *in the context* of the writer's purpose, audience, and focus.

Following are examples of passive-voice constructions that, in context, may be more effective in the active voice. To change from passive to active, move the actor (often identified in the *by* phrase) to become the subject of the sentence:

Passive: Children's unruly behavior cannot be accepted by their parents.

Note: The actor in the *by* phrase is *parents*. Change to active voice by making *parents* the subject of the sentence.

Active: Parents cannot accept their children's unruly behavior. [The active-voice version makes the actor the subject of the sentence and has two fewer words.]

Passive: It is argued by the members of our class that the teacher grades too hard.
Note: The *actor* in the *by* phrase is *members*. Change to the active voice by making *members* the subject of the sentence.

Active: Members of our class argue that the teacher grades too hard. [This active-voice version is more direct and has four fewer words.]

Passive: Under the current proposal, property taxes will be raised $1,000 dollars over the next two years.
Note: The *actor* is not identified in a *by* phrase; however, the *governor* actually proposed the tax increase. Change to active voice by making *governor* the subject of the sentence.

Active: The governor currently proposes to raise property taxes by $1,000 over the next two years. [The active-voice version reveals who, in fact, is responsible. It adds information without increasing the length of the sentence.]

PASSIVE VOICE

The *passive voice* is appropriate when the actor is unknown or is less important than the action or the receiver of the action. Use the passive voice in the following situations:

When the actor is unknown:

When her sports car swerved off the road and into the river, Carolyn was killed. [We don't know who or what actually killed her.]

When you want to emphasize that some person or thing is helpless or is a victim:

The small Kansas town was leveled by the tornado.
Our football team was mauled by the Bears, 42–0.
The bag lady was mugged in broad daylight.

When the scientific experiment and the results should be the focus of the sentence or the passage (scientific writing typically uses the passive voice to lend objectivity to the findings):

The first recordings of humpback whales were obtained in 1952 from a U.S. Navy hydrophone installation.
The titration experiment was performed under careful laboratory conditions.

One typical *abuse of the passive voice* occurs when writers omit the actor in order to conceal responsibility:

> The tuition for nonresident students was increased by $500 for the upcoming academic year.

This sentence, which was written by university officials, omits the actor or the agency responsible for the change. Because tuition increases are unpopular with students, university officials may have deliberately omitted the responsible actor or agency to avoid confrontation or blame. Careful readers should recognize such deceptive uses of the passive voice.

Caution: Don't assume that all verbs that follow the pattern, *be* verb form = past participle ["was _____ ed"], are necessarily in the passive voice. In the sentence "I was scared," for example, the verb *scared* can be either transitive or intransitive, depending on the context. Only *transitive verbs* can be in either the active or the passive voice:

Transitive Active	A horrible Halloween mask scared me.
Transitive Passive	I was scared by a horrible Halloween mask.
Intransitive	At the Cave of Horrors, I was upset and scared.

Transitive Active	The boss fired me.
Transitive Passive	I was fired.
Intransitive	I was tired.

Test: To distinguish between intransitive and transitive passive, try adding the word *very*. If *very* cannot logically be used, the construction is passive voice:

> I was [very] tired. [*Very* works; *tired* is intransitive.]
> I was [very] fired. [*Very* doesn't work; *fired* is transitive passive.]

In addition, a good dictionary will indicate whether a verb is transitive, intransitive, or both.

EXERCISES

Identify sentences containing the passive voice. Change passive-voice sentences into the active voice:

1. People communicate using body movements.
2. A nod, a gesture, or a glance can be interpreted by people in several ways.
3. A wave and a smile mean one thing, but a wave and a tear can be interpreted to mean something else.
4. In addition, some people may be irritated by a continual or intense stare.

2E
act

5. We may also be intimidated by a person who talks to us at very close range.

Read the following passage and identify sentences that are in the active or passive voice. Then determine which sentences should be in the active voice and which should be in the passive voice. Revise the passage, leaving sentences as they are, changing active-voice sentences to passive, or changing passive-voice sentences to active—as appropriate for the context.

(1) Writing on a word processor can transform the act of writing, but only if the writer has some rudimentary typing skills. (2) Unfortunately, many men have a sexist hang-up about typing, so that their writing on a computer is inhibited. (3) Traditionally, it has been felt by most men that only females (i.e., secretaries) should type. (4) Only the macho Hemingways and Mailers of the world actually type their own novels and stories. (5) Now, however, many male business executives are caught by conflicting role images. (6) It is socially acceptable for them to be computer-literate, but it is still somehow demeaning to sit at a keyboard and practice the "female" skill of typing. (7) One more example of how notions about sexist roles can hurt men as well as women is thus provided by word processing.

2F Nominals and *Be* Verbs

Nominals

Nominals (also called *nominalizations*) are *nouns* created from verbs. Nominals often make sentences less dynamic because they disguise or eliminate the action in a sentence. Frequently, nominals are nouns ending in *-ment, -ance, -ence, -ion,* and *-ing*. Each of the following nominals "contains" a verb: *expectation (expect), description (describe), solution (solve), resistance (resist), government (govern), preference (prefer), meeting (meet)*. For many purposes and audiences, you can make your writing more vigorous, dynamic, and readable by changing nominals into verbs:

Nominal:	Bill's *expectation* was to win the marathon.
Revised:	Bill *expected* to win the marathon.
Nominal:	The owner's manual contains a *description* of how to adjust the timing.
Revised:	The owner's manual *describes* how to adjust the timing.
Nominal:	On this campus, there exists some *resistance* among students to tuition increases.
Revised:	On this campus, students *resist* tuition increases.

Nominal: *Dissatisfaction* with drinking-policy *decisions* is likely to be a major *contribution* to student *objections*.
Note: When repeated nominals obscure the meaning, rewrite the whole sentence, making the primary *actor* the subject of the sentence.

Revised: Students object to the drinking policy.

Be Verbs

Be verbs *(is, am, are, was, were, been, being)* are effective in stating conditions, definitions, or concepts:

> Edgar Allan Poe's "The Raven" is a literary classic.
> An iconoclast is one who destroys sacred images or seeks to overthrow popular ideas or institutions.

Often, however, *be* verbs create static, flat, or lifeless sentences. Where appropriate, make your writing more dynamic by replacing *be* verbs with action verbs.

Eliminate *be* verbs by changing passive voice to active voice, by changing nominals or adjectives into verbs, by selecting a more vigorous verb, or by combining sentences:

2F nom

_Be_ Verb: The classical mythology course that *is* offered by the English department *is* fascinating.

Revised: The English department *offers* a fascinating course in classical mythology.

_Be_ Verb: The driving force for many workaholics *is* their fear of failure.
Revised: Fear of failure *drives* many workaholics.

_Be_ Verb: AIDS *is* a simple but sometimes lethal malfunction of the immune system. AIDS *is* a disease that can lead to the physical and mental destruction of its victim.

Revised: AIDS, a simple but sometimes lethal malfunction of the immune system, can *destroy* its victim physically and mentally.

EXERCISE

In the following passage, identify *nominals* and *be* verbs. Then revise the passage to make it more vivid, energetic, and concise by eliminating inappropriate nominals and be verbs.

(1) As parents, we know that many young people love to ride motorcycles, motorbikes, and motorscooters. (2) Today, however, our ten-year-old kids have some attraction to those off-road three-wheelers. (3)

Although kids get enjoyment from riding three-wheelers in the hills, these vehicles can be the cause of serious injury. (4) Unfortunately, these young drivers—and their parents—do not receive sufficient education from salespeople about the potential dangers. (5) As a result, some activist groups are in opposition to the sales of all three-wheelers. (6) These groups want regulations for the industry in order to make riding safer for children and adults. (7) The efforts of these groups to reform the industry are commendable to every responsible parent.

2G SUBJECT-VERB AGREEMENT

A verb must agree *in number* with its subject. Remember: *-s* or *-es* added to a noun makes it plural: *whale, whales*. Adding *-s* to a present-tense verb makes it singular: *whales sing; whale sings*.

1. Many agreement problems occur when plural words come between a singular subject and its verb. To correct a subject-verb error, first identify the actual subject, and then use the correct verb ending for that subject:

   Faulty: A list of campaign promises often hurt the candidate.
   [Put brackets around any prepositional phrases. The subject of the sentence is never in a prepositional phrase. "A list [of campaign promises] often hurt the candidate." *List* is the subject and *hurt* is the verb. Read without the words inside the brackets and revise the verb.]

   Revised: A *list* of campaign promises often *hurts* the candidate.

   Faulty: This company, with few skilled mechanics and electricians, do not guarantee any repairs.
   [Put brackets around the prepositional phrase. "This company [with few skilled mechanics and electricians], do not guarantee any repairs." Read the sentence without the words in brackets and revise the verb.]

   Revised: This company, with few skilled mechanics and electricians, *does* not guarantee any repairs.

2. Two subjects connected by *and* take a plural verb. "The sergeant and his recruits march double-time across the grounds." When two subjects are connected by *or* or *nor*, however, the verb agrees with the closer subject:

   Faulty: Neither the recruits nor the sergeant know how to march.

Revised:	Neither the recruits nor the sergeant *knows* how to march.
	[or]
Revised:	Neither the sergeant nor the recruits *know* how to march.

3. Indefinite pronouns *(each, one, either, everyone, neither, everybody, nobody, no one, none, somebody, someone)* usually take a singular verb:

Faulty:	Each of the books cost twenty dollars.
	[Remove the prepositional phrase: "Each [of the books] cost twenty dollars." *Each* is singular, so the verb should be *costs*.]
Revised:	Each of the books *costs* twenty dollars.
Faulty:	Everybody in all three classes are going to see the film.
	[Remove the prepositional phrase: "Everybody [in all three classes] are going to see the film." *Everybody* is singular, so the verb should be *is*.]
Revised:	Everybody in all three classes *is* going to see the film.

4. A collective noun as a subject usually takes a singular verb. Collective nouns *(family, committee, audience, class, crowd,* and *army)* usually refer to a single *unit* or *group* of several individuals or elements, and thus they take a singular verb:

Faulty:	The audience at the concert whistle its approval.
Revised:	The audience at the concert *whistles* its approval.
	Note: When referring to the action or condition of *several individuals* within a group, use the phrase *the members of* or the phrase *a number of* followed by the plural verb: The members of the committee *argue* about the policy.

5. Even when the normal subject-verb order is reversed, the verb should agree in number with the subject:

Faulty:	For such a small dormitory, there is far too many students.
	[Put the subject and verb in their normal order: Too many students are in the small dormitory. (*Students* is the subject, so the verb is plural: *are*.)]
Revised:	For such a small dormitory, there *are* far too many students.

EXERCISE

In the following passage, revise all errors in subject-verb agreement.

2G
sv agr

(1) If you have friends or a family member who smoke, I have some suggestions to help this person quit. (2) First, if the family are supportive, try talking openly about the facts. (3) There is a few public service agencies that will provide evidence demonstrating the link between smoking and cancer. (4) Next, investigate this person's behavior: What does this person do just before he or she smokes? (5) To quit smoking, the smoker must disrupt the patterns of behavior that leads to smoking. (6) An inventory of the activities and places that cause a person to smoke provide key information. (7) For example, if the person always smokes after dinner, suggest eating snacks over a two-hour period instead of having a sit-down meal. (8) If he or she always smoke in a certain chair in the living room, change the furniture. (9) Breaking any habit is always easier if you break the entire behavior pattern. (10) Of course, each of these smokers need to want to stop smoking.

2H VERB TENSE

Avoid unnecessary shifts in verb tense:

Shift:	After they *ate* ice cream and cake for dessert, they *are* ready to relax.
Revised:	After they *ate* ice cream and cake for dessert, they *were* ready to relax.
Shift:	Peter *ate* dinner before you *had offered* to cook tacos.
Revised:	Peter *ate* dinner before you *offered* to cook tacos.
Shift:	At one point in this film, Gandhi *gathered* his followers together to discuss strategy. Suddenly, a British general *gave* an order to fire upon them. People then *scurry* around and *try* to protect themselves and their children from the hail of bullets. *Note:* For summaries or accounts of artistic works, films, literary works, or historical documents, use the present tense.
Revised:	At one point in this film, Gandhi *gathers* his followers together to discuss strategy. Suddenly, a British general *gives* an order to fire upon them. People then *scurry* around and *try* to protect themselves and their children from the hail of bullets.

EXERCISE

In the following passage, revise any unnecessary shifts in tense.

(1) In Sophocles' play, *Antigone*, two characters are tragic figures: Antigone and Creon. (2) In the play, Antigone faced a choice of conscience. (3) Should she be loyal to her family and bury her brother, or should she have been loyal to the state and obeyed the edict of Creon,

the king of Thebes? (4) She assumes that she knew the best way to handle the situation and willfully chooses her own death. (5) Creon also faced a choice of conscience. (6) Should he punish someone who has betrayed the state, even if that person is a member of his family? (7) Like Napoleon and General Custer, Creon thought primarily about himself and his public image. (8) In Creon's case, ego or "hubris" leads to tragic results for the people around him.

21 PRONOUN AGREEMENT

A pronoun must agree in number and person with the noun to which it refers:

Faulty: One of the scientists signed their name to the report. [Because the subject is never in the prepositional phrase, put parentheses around the prepositional phrase ("of the scientists"). Now look for another noun that could be the subject of the sentence. *One* is the subject of the sentence, and it is a singular noun. Change *their* to the singular form, *his* or *her*.]

Revised: One of the scientists signed her name to the report.

Faulty: Each of the students felt cheated on their test. *Note: Each* is singular: *their* is plural.

Revised: The *students* felt cheated on *their* tests.

Faulty: Everyone brought their gift to the party.

Revised: Everyone brought *his* or *her* gift to the party. *Note:* Avoiding sexist language by using "his or her" can be wordy or awkward in some contexts. Rewrite the sentence with a plural subject and a plural pronoun.

Revised: The *guests* brought *their* gifts to the party.

Avoid shifts in person. Avoid shifting between third person *(people, one, they, he, she)* and second person *(you):*

Faulty: When you come to the party, everyone should bring a friend. *Note: You* is second person; *everyone* is third person. Revise the sentence, using either second or third person throughout.

Revised: When *you* come to the party, bring a friend.

Faulty: A good party should make *people* feel at ease, so *you* can make new friends.

Revised: A good party should make *people* feel at ease, so *they* can make new friends.

Revised: A good party should make *you* feel at ease, so *you* can make new friends.

2J PRONOUN REFERENCE

A pronoun should refer clearly and unambiguously to its antecedent:

Unclear: Joan told Bev that her bank account was overdrawn.
[Whose bank account was overdrawn?]

Revised: When Joan discovered that her bank account was overdrawn, she told Bev.

Unclear: If people do not take care of their cats, we should turn them in to the humane society.
[Who should be turned in—the cats or their owners?]

Revised: If people do not take care of their cats, we should report the owners to the humane society.

EXERCISE

In the following passage, correct problems in pronoun agreement and reference.

(1) People use the term *best friend* to describe a person who has a special warmth and friendliness. (2) I still remember when Michelle Martin, one of my best friends, said that they really like me, too. (3) I called her my best friend; we stood by each other. (4) One time at a party, I saw her talking angrily to another woman. (5) It turned out that she had dated Tom, the guy she was going with at the time. (6) Each of them felt cheated by their boyfriend. (7) Before I knew what was happening, they were screaming at each other. (8) When I tried to stick up for her, she took a swing at me, and so I swung back with my best left hook, popping her in the right eye. (9) As a result, I was suspended from school for a week. (10) It just goes to show that when you have a best friend, everyone expects that you'll help them if you can.

SECTION 3

....

DICTION AND STYLE

Effective writing hides a curious paradox. On the one hand, good writing contains vivid detail. Good writing does not merely assert that thus-and-so is true; it supports a claim or assertion with evidence. It recreates an experience, shows exactly how the writer feels, or communicates precisely what the writer thinks. To accomplish this, writers *add* specific details, examples, facts, or other data. On the other hand, good writing is also concise. Good writers *take out* vague words, weak verbs, and empty language. Their writing is as lean and sinewy as a long-distance runner. As you edit your writing for diction (choice of words) and clarity of style, you should *add* specific examples but *remove* vague, imprecise language. Your details should be ample; your diction and style, spare.

Vigorous writing is concise. A sentence should contain no unnecessary words, a paragraph no unnecessary sentences, for the same reason that a drawing should have no unnecessary lines and a machine no unnecessary parts. This requires not that the writer make all his sentences short, or that he avoid all detail . . . . but that every word tell.

—WILL STRUNK, JR.,

COAUTHOR OF
ELEMENTS OF STYLE

2J
ref

3A VAGUE WORDS

Replace vague words with more specific or concrete language.

1. The following *nouns* are vague or unspecific. Vague nouns encourage writers to *tell* rather than to *show* with specific details or examples. Vague nouns may also lead to wordy and imprecise sentences. In most cases, *replace* the following nouns with more specific words, details, or examples:

thing	situation	difficulty
something	type	feeling
anything	way	beauty
someone	fun	people
some	trouble	deal
area	problem	place
case	field	character
manner	nature	appearance
factor	aspect	

Vague: During their freshman year, students worry about all sorts of *things*. [Be specific: What things?]

Revised: During their freshman year, students worry about leaving their families, making new friends, and passing their courses.

Vague: I have taken courses in the *field* of statistics for two years, and it has changed my *feeling* toward studying in the *area* of mathematics.

Revised: After taking statistics courses for two years, I no longer hate studying mathematics.

Vague: Meteorologists occasionally have a *great deal of trouble* in forecasting a *situation* where an upper-level disturbance becomes a *factor* in local weather. [Be specific: What kind of trouble? Be concise: Omit unnecessary, vague words.]

Revised: When an upper-level disturbance affects local weather, meteorologists occasionally miss a forecast.

2. The following *modifiers* are weak, vague, or unspecific. Replace them with stronger modifiers or add specific details:

very	a lot	pretty
really	good	bad
a few	certain	happy
many	nice	much
regular	similar	soon

Vague:	I *really* liked *certain* classes in high school very much, but I just couldn't stand *a lot* of the *really boring* courses. [Be specific: What *certain classes?* Be specific: How or why were they *really boring?*]
Revised:	I really looked forward to learning about the turtles, snakes, and birds in the biology lab, but I couldn't stand just sitting still and practicing grammar hour after hour in French class.
Vague:	Overall, *The Cosby Show* is *pretty good*, but sometimes it gets somewhat *unreal*. [Be specific: What makes it pretty good? What makes it unreal?]
Revised:	*The Cosby Show* has entertaining stories about family problems—I still remember the episode when Theo decides he just has to join the Blue Angels—but in many episodes, the family seems to resolve the conflict too easily and simply.

3. The following *verbs* are weak, vague, or unspecific. Where appropriate, replace them with more active, energetic, or vivid verbs. When these verbs occur with nominals or the passive voice, change to active verbs or the active voice. Always test your revision: In your context, is the change more effective, concise, or vivid?

deals with	take	get
gets involved with	relate to	go
has to do with	make	give

Vague:	He *gets* some enjoyment from sky diving.
Revised:	He *enjoys* sky diving.
Vague:	Her job *deals with* collecting rare species of lizards.
Revised:	She *collects* rare species of lizards.
Vague:	Jogging along the path, she *got involved with* a rattlesnake in a serious way. [How exactly was she "involved" with this rattlesnake?]
Revised:	Jogging along the path, she was seriously bitten by a rattlesnake.

EXERCISE

In the following passage, substitute specific and vivid words or phrases for all vague nouns, verbs, and modifiers.

(1) When I was separated from my girlfriend, I missed her a lot. (2) Being alone sometimes gave me a pretty empty-type feeling. (3) When I called her on the phone, we talked about all the nice times we spent together, not about all the very big fights we used to

have. (4) Since there was no stress to deal with, we had a fun-filled, long-distance relationship. (5) I know that one aspect of this relationship will improve the way we get along, now that we're back together. (6) We always had difficulty talking in a serious manner about our future. (7) Now we are more involved with each other and can really talk about all sorts of things. (8) For anyone who is having troubles, I recommend this kind of separate situation because, in the long run, the relationship will be much happier.

3B WORDINESS

1. The following wordy phrases can be made more concise:

WORDY	CONCISE
due to the fact that	because
despite the fact that	though
regardless of the fact that	although
at this point in time	now
at the present time	now
until such time as	until
in the event that	if, when
at all times	always
there is no doubt that	doubtless
in a deliberate manner	deliberately
by means of	by
the reason is that	[omit]

2. The following phrases are redundant; they say the same thing twice or repeat unnecessarily:

REDUNDANT	CONCISE
new innovation	innovation
disappear from view	disappear
repeat again	repeat
reflected back	reflected
circle around	circle
few in number	few
cheaper in cost	cheaper
oblong in shape	oblong
blue in color	blue
consensus of opinion	consensus
important essentials	essentials
resulting effect	effect
cooperate together	cooperate

3. Where appropriate, make your writing more concise by omitting *there is*, *there are*, *it is*, and *this is* constructions:

Wordy:	There are seven people living in that apartment.
Revised:	Seven people live in that apartment.
Wordy:	This is the step that is crucial for getting a job.
Revised:	This step is crucial for getting a job.

4. Some *who*, *which*, and *that* clauses can be changed into modifying words or phrases:

Wordy:	Cheryl Stickfinger, who is the mayor, is accused of embezzling city funds.
Revised:	Mayor Cheryl Stickfinger is accused of embezzling city funds.
Wordy:	Then they each wolfed down a banana split that contained five-hundred calories.
Revised:	Then they each wolfed down a five-hundred-calorie banana split.
Wordy:	The police officer, who was frustrated about missing his promotion, started taking kickbacks.
Revised:	The police officer, frustrated about missing his promotion, started taking kickbacks.

EXERCISE

Revise the following passage to reduce wordiness.

(1) One of the most recent new discoveries in medicine is the so-called diving reflex. (2) When people fall into water that is icy, their circulation slows down due to the fact that the water is so cold. (3) In addition, the metabolism of every cell that is in the body slows down, conserving oxygen. (4) In a recent case, Alvaro Garza, who is eleven years old, disappeared from view underneath the ice for forty-five minutes. (5) When rescuers finally pulled him at long last from beneath the ice, he was unconscious, his body temperature was cold and below normal, and his skin was grayish-blue in color. (6) Regardless of the fact that rescuers could find no pulse or heartbeat, they began CPR (cardiopulmonary resuscitation) immediately. (7) Within a few days, Alvaro began to recover in a steady manner, and soon he was asking for a hamburger and french fries. (8) Although he may have some lingering effects from his ordeal that do not go away in a short period of time, the unexplainable miracle is that he survived.

3C COLLOQUIAL LANGUAGE AND SLANG

Your audience and purpose should determine whether conversational language is appropriate. In informal or expressive writing, colloquial language (spoken language), slang, or trendy expressions may be vivid and effective.

3C
wdy

In conversation or informal writing, we may say that something is *cool*, *hip*, *gross*, *weak*, *sweet*, or *too much*. We may call a friend *dude*, a skateboarder a *thrasher*, or someone we don't like a *wimp* or *geek*.

In formal writing, however, you should avoid colloquial expressions and slang. Your readers may not know the expressions, they may find some slang offensive, or they may think *gross* is simply too vague to describe what really happened. Slang, in fact, tends to become a shorthand for a whole experience and thus invites *telling* ("This guy was a real geek") rather than *showing* ("Rudolph had messy hair, wore adhesive tape on his glasses, and always had one green and one orange sock sticking out of his polyester pants. He lived out of a forty-pound bookpack, watched *Dr. Who* on TV every day, and spoke like William F. Buckley").

3D Clichés and Jargon

Clichés

Some expressions are so commonly used that they have become automatic, predictable, trite, or hackneyed. The phrases in the left-hand column, for example, may have been fresh and original once, but now they are as stale as dirty dishwater and about as exciting as a secondhand sock. The expressions in the right-hand column, for example, are so predictable that we can easily guess the missing word:

tried and true	strong as an _____
needle in a haystack	dark as _____
easier said than done	heavy as _____
burning the midnight oil	cold as _____
didn't sleep a wink	busy as a _____
crack of dawn	happy as a _____
dead of night	white as _____
last but not least	quick as a _____
birds of a feather	blind as a _____
hit the nail on the head	sober as a _____
face the music	tough as _____
straw that broke the camel's back	gentle as a _____

Jargon

Jargon is the technical vocabulary of any specialized occupation, field, or profession. In technical or specialized writing, writers should use the vocabulary of their field. In the following passage, the specialized vocabulary *(homeotic, mutant, rudimentary,* and *thoracic)* is entirely appropriate:

> In the cockroach *Bletella germanica*, a homeotic mutant produces rudimentary wings on the first thoracic segment. No modern insect normally

bears wings on its first thoracic segment, but the earliest winged fossil insects did!

—Stephen J. Gould, *Hen's Teeth and Horse's Toes*

Jargon, however, is also a generic label for impressive words used for their own sake. Any specialized vocabulary is inappropriate when used not to *inform* but to *impress* an audience with the writer's intelligence. When writers use jargon inappropriately, they are not communicating—they're showing off.

Below is a jargon-filled parody, in legalese, of the simple, clear sentence, "Have an orange." This passage, by the editors of *Labor Magazine*, appears in Stuart Chase's essay "Gobbledygook":

I hereby give and convey to you, all singular, my estate and right, title, claim and advantages of and in said orange, together with all rind, juice, pulp and pits, and all rights and advantages therein . . . anything hereinbefore or hereinafter or in any other deed or deeds, instrument or instruments of whatever nature or kind whatsoever, to the contrary, in any wise, notwithstanding.

Sometimes writers use jargon not to make themselves sound impressive but to promote the *subject* they're writing about. We commonly call the result *advertising*. Here is a sample of a Nike advertisement for a walking shoe:

Walking. To you, it's a simple matter of putting one foot in front of another. To Nike, it's an entire science.

In fact, we have studied walking in one of the world's leading biomechanical labs. Our own. And as a result, we've designed a technically advanced shoe specifically for the walking motion. The EXW. We built it close to the ground for stability. With a tri-density midsole that supports and centers your foot. A vented toe area for cool comfort. Flex grooves that bend with your foot. And a Nike-Air cushioning system that makes you feel, literally, like you're walking on air.

Now, all this technology may seem a bit much. But try on a pair. You'll see that the EXW doesn't make walking more complicated. It just takes it one step further.

Nike hopes the inflated language and technical jargon in this passage will make you feel better about spending eighty dollars for a walking shoe. "World's leading biomechanical labs," "advanced shoe specifically for the walking motion," "tri-density midsole," "vented toe area," and "flex grooves"—all this jargon does seem a bit much. We may ridicule such language, but remember that if the advertisement causes us to buy the shoe, the language is appropriate for the audience.

E X E R C I S E

In the following passage, replace clichés with fresh, figurative language, and eliminate or replace inappropriate jargon.

(1) The television news media in America need to be reformed. (2) The bottom line is that serious news has been lost as stations rush to entertain the viewer. (3) Trying to find an informative story on the evening news is like looking for a needle in a haystack. (4) The station executives who finalize the programmatic output for the evening news believe that the average American is dumber than an ox. (5) As a result, viewers see in-depth stories about a sex scandal involving a local politician, but only a few seconds explaining why the stock market is scraping the bottom of the barrel. (6) Newscasters attempt to maximize their humor by telling jokes that go over like a lead balloon rather than informing the viewer about the latest decision-making process on armament restrictions. (7) If station programmers actually interfaced with the public occasionally, they would recognize the error of their ways.

3E Sexist Language

Do not use language that unfairly stereotypes people or discriminates against either women or men. Just as you would avoid racist terms, you should avoid language that stereotypes people's roles, occupations, or behavior by gender. Sentences such as "A doctor always cares for his patient" or "A secretary should always help her boss" imply that all doctors are men and all secretaries are women. Phrases such as *female logic, male ego, emotional woman,* or *typical male brutality* imply that all women are excessively emotional and all men are egotistical brutes. In fact, those stereotypes are not true. If you use sexist language, you will offend your readers. Even more important, your language should not encourage you or your reader to see the world in sexist stereotypes.

1. Avoid words that suggest sexist roles:

SEXIST	REVISED
man	people, person
chairman	chair, head
businessman	businessperson
policeman	police officer
mankind	humanity
congressman	representative
statesman	politician, diplomat
lady lawyer	lawyer
career girl	professional woman

SEXIST	REVISED
coed	student
mailman	letter carrier
old wives' tale	superstition

Note, however, that some words that link occupation with gender are still appropriate. Most writers still use *actor* and *waiter* for men and *actress* and waitress for women. Other words, however, such as *stewardess* or *seamstress*, are often replaced with *flight attendant* or *garment worker*.

2. Be consistent in your use of people's names. If you write *Ernest Heming-way*, then write *Emily Dickinson*, not *Miss Dickinson*. If you write Lennon instead of *John Lennon*, then write *Parton*, not *Dolly Parton* or *Dolly*.

3. Avoid using the pronouns *he*, *his*, or *him* when you are referring to activities, roles, or behavior that could describe either sex:

Sexist:	A doctor should listen carefully to his patient.
	Note: Use a plural if it does not alter your meaning.
Revised:	Doctors should listen carefully to their patients.
Sexist:	An effective teacher knows each of her students.
	Note: You may use *his or her* sparingly, but avoid using the construction *s/he*.
Revised:	An effective teacher knows each of his or her students.
Sexist:	Everyone hopes that he will survive the first year of college.
	Note: Often, you can revise the sentence by using first or second person or by omitting the pronoun.
Revised:	I hope to survive the first year of college.
Revised:	All of us hope to survive the first year of college.
Revised:	You hope to survive the first year of college.
Revised:	Everyone hopes to survive the first year of college.
	Note: Do *not* mix singular and plural by saying, "Everyone hopes *they* will survive the first year of college."

EXERCISE

Revise the following passage to eliminate sexist language.

(1) Everyone in college now is looking for that special job that will match his talents and yet bring him sufficient income. (2) Teaching is a low-paying but good career if you don't mind being a professor who spends his life reading papers, getting grants, and serving on committees. (3) A secretary or stewardess can begin her career with minimal

training, but a nurse must dedicate herself to rigorous medical schooling. (4) In business and entertainment, girls can work right alongside the men. (5) In the entertainment field, many people dream of being a Bruce Springsteen or a Tina Turner, although most singers don't have Springsteen's talent or Tina's perseverance. (6) A businessman often works his way up the ladder and becomes chairman of the company. (7) Even staying at home and raising a family is a respectable career for either a man or his wife, though most men simply don't have the temperament to raise children. (8) Whatever your chosen career, from mailman to congressman, hard work and dedication are the keys to landing and keeping that important job.

3F DENOTATION AND CONNOTATION

The *denotation* of a word is its literal or dictionary definition. Both *house* and *home* refer, denotatively, to a structure in which people live. Many words have, in addition, a *connotation* or emotional association that can be negative, neutral, or positive. *House* has, for most people, a *neutral* or sterile connotation, whereas *home*, for most people, has a *positive* connotation, suggesting warmth, comfort, security, and family.

Choose words appropriately for their connotative value:

Inappropriate:	Dr. Aileen Brown, a *notorious* scientist, just received the Nobel Prize for her work with superconductors. [*Notorious* people are usually famous for their *misconduct*.]
Revised:	Dr. Aileen Brown, a *famous* scientist, just received the Nobel Prize for her work with superconductors.
Inappropriate:	Beverly looked at her friend Steve and said, "Why don't you finish your dinner? You need the food—you're already a bit *scrawny* looking." [Steve prefers to think of himself as *thin* or *slim* rather than scrawny.]
Revised:	Beverly looked at her friend Steve and said, "Why don't you finish your dinner? You need the food—you're already a bit *thin*."
Inappropriate:	Lynn's father told Paul that the apartment was decorated cheaply but tastefully. [Paul's feelings may be hurt. He does have good taste in furnishings, and he did the best he could on his tight budget.]
Revised:	Lynn's father told Paul that the apartment was decorated tastefully but inexpensively.

Exercise

The following groups of words have similar denotative meanings but vary widely in their emotional associations or connotative meanings. Rank the words in each group from most negative, to neutral, to most positive.

- social drinker, wino, lush, reveler, alcoholic, sot, party animal, elbow bender, inebriate, problem drinker, booze hound, bar hopper
- scholar, intellectual, four-eyes, walking encyclopedia, geek, savant, bookworm, genius, pedant, bibliophile
- thrifty, penny-pinching, frugal, miserly, tight-fisted, cheap, economical, prudent, stingy
- steady, loyal, stubborn, firm, unyielding, dedicated, obstinate, devoted

3G Usage Glossary

This glossary lists alphabetically words and phrases that frequently cause problems for writers. In many cases, writers disagree about the preferred usage in formal writing. If you are in doubt, check a dictionary, such as *The American Heritage Dictionary*, *The Random House Dictionary*, or a guide, such as Margaret Bryant's *Current American Usage*.

Because this glossary references only the most obvious usage errors, refer to a standard or unabridged dictionary for items not included.

a, an: Use *a* when the following word begins with a *consonant sound:* a book, a clever saying, a hat. Use *an* when the following word begins with a *vowel sound:* an apple, an old building, an honor.

accept, except: *Accept* is a verb meaning "to receive": "I accept the gift." *Except* is a preposition meaning "other than" or "excluding": "Everyone received a gift except John." Rarely, *except* is a verb meaning "to exclude": "The editor excepted the footnote from the article."

advise, advice: *Advise* is a verb: "I advise you to exercise regularly." *Advice* is a noun: "Please take this advice."

affect, effect: *Affect* is a verb: "The flying beer cups did not affect the outfielder's concentration." *Effect* is a noun: "His obvious poise had a calming effect on the crowd." ***Remember:*** If you can say, "The effect," then you are correctly using the noun form. Less often, *effect* is also a verb: "His behavior effected a change in the crowd's attitude."

all right, alright: *All right*, two words, is the accepted spelling. *Alright* is nonstandard, in the opinion of most experts.

a lot: *A lot* is always two words that mean "many." Wherever possible, however, *avoid* using *a lot*. Replace with a more specific description. See Section 3A.

already, all ready: *Already* means "by now" or "previously": "The essay was already completed." *All ready* means "completely prepared": "The paragraphs were all ready to be printed."

among, between: Use *among* for *three or more* people or things: "We should distribute the winnings among all the players." **Note:** *Between* is used for three or more items when location or a reciprocal relationship is indicated: "They found the treasure at a point equidistant between the three trees." "Through careful negotiations, a nonaggression treaty was reached between the four nations."

amount, number: *Amount* refers to quantity: "He saved a large amount of food for the winter months." *Number* refers to countable items: "She owned a large number of expensive sports cars."

anyone, any one: *Anyone* is a pronoun: "Anyone who likes Mayan art should hear the lecture." *Any one* is an adjective phrase modifying a noun: "He owns more Mayan art than any one person could possibly appreciate."

bad, badly: *Bad* is an adjective used in the predicate ("After a week of the flu, she looked bad") or before a noun ("She caught my cold at a bad time"): "She felt bad because she had a bad cold." *Badly* is an adverb: "He wrote badly because he had a high fever."

being, being that: *Being* cannot be used as a complete verb. "The seat being taken" is not a complete sentence. *Being that* is nonstandard: "Being that the bus was late, we missed the show." Use *because* or *since*: "Because the bus was late, we missed the show."

beside, besides: *Beside* is a preposition meaning "next to" or "by the side of": "Peggi sat beside the senator." *Besides* is a preposition meaning "moreover" or "in addition to": "Besides, the senator likes several people besides George."

can, may: In formal writing, use *can* for ability: "I can take out the garbage." Use *may* for permission: "May I have the honor of taking out the garbage?" Also use *may* for possibility: "If I have time, I may take out the garbage."

center around: Illogical: One can "circle around" but not "center around." Replace with "center on" or "focus on": "The controversy focused on the right of the worker to a safe, smoke-free environment."

cite, site: *Cite* is a verb meaning "to quote as an authority" or "to mention": "She cited Newcastle's blue law, which forbade card playing on Sunday." *Site* is a noun meaning a "place" or "location": "The church basement was, in fact, the site of Newcastle's first bingo game."

continual, continuous: *Continual* means "frequently repeated": "Most soap operas have continual interruptions for commercials." *Continuous* means "unceasing": "Throughout the broadcast, we heard a continuous buzzing sound."

3G
gls

could of, should of: Nonstandard. Use *could have* or *should have*.

data, media, criteria: The singular forms are *datum*, *medium*, and *criterion*. In formal writing, use plural verbs and pronouns with the plural noun. "Our data reveal a sharp increase in rapes and assaults since last year." "The media use their own criteria for sex and violence."

different from, different than: For prepositional phrases, use *different from*: "His chili recipe is different from yours." Although *different from* is preferred, sometimes *different than* results in a more concise sentence. "She is a different player than she used to be" is less wordy than "She is a different player from the player she used to be."

disinterested, uninterested: *Disinterested* means "objective or impartial": "As a disinterested third party, Marji resolved our dispute." *Uninterested* means "not interested": "We were uninterested in the outcome of the fall elections."

farther, further: *Farther* usually refers to distance: "How much farther are we going to jog?" *Further* refers to additional time, amount, or degree: "Furthermore, if you cannot hire me, I will go further into debt."

fewer, less: *Fewer* refers to numbers or countable items: "Fewer teenagers smoke than a decade ago." *Less* refers to amount ("less sugar") or degree ("less important"): "Teenagers spend less money on cigarettes than they did a decade ago."

hopefully: *Hopefully* means "with hope," or "in a hopeful manner": "Charlene waited hopefully for a letter from home." Most good writers still object to the colloquial usage of *hopefully* (meaning, "I hope," or "it is to be hoped"): "Hopefully, Charlene will get her letter from home." Change to: "I hope Charlene gets her letter from home."

imply, infer: *Imply* means to suggest without directly stating: "The news report implied that the president was seriously ill." *Infer* means to draw a conclusion: "I inferred from the news report that the president was seriously ill." Writers and speakers *imply;* readers and listeners *infer*.

its, it's: *Its*, like *his* or *her*, is a possessive pronoun: "The tree is losing its leaves." *It's* is a contraction of *it is*: "It's your turn to rake the leaves."

lay, lie: *Lay* is the transitive verb *(lay, laid)*, *laid* meaning "put" or "place": "Please lay the book on the table." *Lie* is an intransitive verb *(lie, lay, lain)* meaning "recline" or "occupy a place": "The books lie on the table."

like, as, as if: *Like* is a preposition: "A great race driver is like an opera singer—vain and arrogant." *As* can be a preposition ("His mission as a driver was to demonstrate his grace and courage"), but it can also introduce a clause: "Even at the end of the race, he looked as if he had just stepped off the cover of a magazine."

**3G
gls**

lose, loose: *Lose* is a verb meaning "misplace" or "be deprived of": "Good detectives never lose their nerve." *Loose* is an adjective meaning "free" or "not tight": "The psychopath got loose by climbing through the ventilating system."

principal, principle: *Principal* as an adjective means "major" or "main"; as a noun, *principal* refers either to a "chief official" or to a "capital sum of money": "The principal of the high school listed as his principal debt the $50,000 he owed on the principal of his house mortgage." *Principle* is a noun meaning "basic truth," "rule," or "moral standard": "He learned the principles of accounting and finance."

quote, quotation: *Quote* is a verb: "I quoted the passage from Thoreau's *Walden*." Do not use *quote* as a noun ("The following quote from *Walden*"); instead, use *quotation, remark,* or *passage*: "The following passage from *Walden* illustrates Thoreau's politics."

that, which: *That* always introduces restrictive clauses; *which* introduces either restrictive or nonrestrictive clauses. Some writers prefer, however, to use *that* only for restrictive clauses and *which* only for nonrestrictive. "The hat that has the pheasant feather was a birthday present." The clause "that has the pheasant feather" restricts, limits, and identifies which hat was the present. "The hat, which is nearly ten years old, was a birthday present." The clause "which is nearly ten years old" is only incidental information; it does not specify which hat was the present.

their, they're, there: *Their* is a pronoun: "She is playing with their tennis balls." *They're* is a contraction: "They're really upset that she didn't even ask." *There* is an adverb or an expletive: "She's practicing over there. There are the tennis balls."

to, too, two: *To* is a preposition: "I am writing to Bev." *Too* is an adverb meaning "in addition" or "also": "You too can write her a letter." *Too* also is an intensifier meaning "very": "Dad expects me to write too often." *Two* is a number: "I have written two times this month."

used to, supposed to: Use the past tense ("used to") not ("use to"): "I used to go there every weekend." "I was supposed to be at swimming practice at 3:30 P.M."

SECTION 4

PUNCTUATION AND MECHANICS

The purpose of punctuation is to clarify meaning and promote communication. Commas, periods, semicolons, dashes, and other punctuation marks guide readers to meanings, just as traffic signals, double yellow lines, turning lanes, and one-way signs guide motorists to destinations. The conventions of punctuation create *expectations* in the reader. Just as you are surprised when a car runs a red light and nearly hits you, readers are surprised when writers fail to follow the conventions of punctuation.

Punctuation—or the lack of it—can change the entire meaning of a sentence. In actual conversation, pauses, inflections, intonation, gestures, and facial expressions do the work of punctuation. In writing, however, punctuation must provide these clues.

Read the following sentences. How many different ways can you find to punctuate each sentence? How does each version alter the meaning?

> Give the peanuts to my daughter Ella
>
> She said walk quietly
>
> Let's go see the lions eat Marcia.

Sometimes writers unintentionally create confusion by omitting important punctuation. Notice how the appropriate use of commas in the following sentences prevents a possible surprise and clarifies the meaning:

Confusing:	To keep the pipes from freezing the plumber advised us to run the water all night. [How exactly did the pipes freeze the plumber?]
Revised:	To keep the pipes from freezing, the plumber advised us to run the water all night.
Confusing:	On the menu for lunch was ham and Sam was doing the cooking. [Is Sam on the menu?]
Revised:	On the menu for lunch was ham, and Sam was doing the cooking.

The guidelines for punctuation and mechanics in this section will help you to avoid unintentional problems and to clarify your writing. Review these guidelines as you edit your own and other people's writing.

4A SENTENCE PUNCTUATION

Much of the confusion about punctuation occurs because connecting words often have similar meanings but signal different punctuation conventions. A stop sign, a red light, and a blinking red light, for example, all mean that motorists must stop, but each signals a slightly different procedure. In English, *but*, *although*, and *however* mean that a contrast is coming, but each requires different punctuation:

> We won the volleyball game, *but* our best hitter broke her wrist.
>
> *Although* we won the game, our best hitter broke her wrist.
>
> We won the game; *however*, our best hitter broke her wrist.

4A
P

"Sorry, but I'm going to have to issue you a summons for reckless grammar and driving without an apostrophe."

4A

p

Using commas and semicolons to punctuate sentences and clauses requires knowing the three basic types of connecting or *conjunctive* words.

Coordinate conjunctions: Conjunction means "a joining together"; "coordinates" are "equals." A coordinate conjunction (coord. conj.) joins equals together. The acronym BOYFANS will help you remember the coordinate conjunctions:

B	O	Y	F	A	N	S
but	or	yet	for	and	nor	so

Subordinating conjunctions: A subordinate conjunction (sub. conj.) joins a dependent or subordinate clause to an independent or main clause. The following are the most common subordinating conjunctions:

after	before	since	until
although	even if	so that	when
as	even though	than	whenever
as if	if	that	where
as though	in order that	though	wherever
because	rather than	unless	while

Adding a subordinating conjunction changes an independent clause (IC) to a dependent clause (DC):

IC

Independent Clause   He buys a newspaper.

SUB
CONJ   DC

Dependent Clause   *If* he buys a newspaper

DC   IC

Complete Sentence   If he buys a newspaper, he will see the story.

Conjunctive adverbs: A conjunctive adverb (conj. adv.) acts as a transitional phrase. Following are the most common conjunctive adverbs:

accordingly	however	meanwhile	still
also	incidentally	moreover	thereafter
consequently	indeed	nevertheless	therefore
furthermore	instead	otherwise	thus
hence	likewise	similarly	

If you are uncertain whether a connecting word is a conjunctive adverb, *test* by moving the connecting word to another place in the clause. Conjunctive adverbs can be moved; subordinating conjunctions (such as *if* or *because*) and coordinating conjunctions *(but, or, yet, for, and, nor, so)* cannot.

Conjunctive adverbs can be moved:

We won the game; *however*, our best hitter broke her wrist.
We won the game; our best hitter, *however*, broke her wrist.
We won the game; our best hitter broke her wrist, *however*.

Subordinating conjunctions cannot be moved:

Although our best hitter broke her wrist, we won the game.
Our best hitter, *although*, broke her wrist, we won the game.
[Obviously, *although* cannot be moved to another position in the clause.]

Coordinating conjunctions cannot be moved:

We won the game, *but* our best hitter broke her wrist.
We won the game, our best hitter, *but*, broke her wrist.
[Moving a coordinating conjunction scrambles the sentence.]

Follow these rules for joining independent clauses (IC) and dependent clauses (DC):

1. Join two independent clauses with a *comma* and a *coordinating conjunction*:

COORD
IC,   CONJ   IC
The pizza is good, *but* the mystery meat is disgusting.

2. Join two independent clauses with a *semicolon* and a *conjunctive adverb*:

CONJ

IC;   ADV   IC.

The pizza is good; *however*, the mystery meat is disgusting.

3. Join two independent clauses with a *semicolon*:

IC;   IC.

The pizza is good; the mystery meat is disgusting.

4. Join a dependent clause to an independent clause with a *comma:*

DC,   IC.

Although mystery meat tastes all right, it looks disgusting.

4B COMMA SPLICES AND FUSED SENTENCES

Two common errors in joining independent clauses are the *comma splice* and the *fused sentence* (also called a *run-on sentence*). Revise by following one of the patterns in 1–3 in the rules just cited:

Comma Splice:	[IC, IC.] I know that airplanes are safer than cars, I still have a fear of flying.
Revised:	I know that airplanes are safer than cars, *but* I still have a fear of flying.
Comma Splice:	[IC, Conj. Adv., IC.] I know that airplanes are safer than cars, however, I still have a fear of flying.
Revised:	I know that airplanes are safer than cars; *however*, I still have a fear of flying.
Fused Sentence:	[IC IC.] I know that airplanes are safer than cars I still have a fear of flying.
Revised:	*Although* I know that airplanes are safer than cars, I still have a fear of flying.

EXERCISE

In the following passage, correct all comma splices and fused sentences.

(1) For years, scientists have attempted to teach animals to communicate for the most part, their efforts have failed. (2) In the 1950s, psychologists failed to teach a chimpanzee to speak, the ape was able to grunt only a few words. (3) In the 1960s, however, a chimp named Washoe learned the sign language of the deaf. (4) Washoe came to understand hundreds of words, he used them to communicate and express original ideas. (5) As it turns out, the great apes have the capacity to learn language, but they cannot speak. (6) This research proved that

humans are not the only animals capable of using language they are, however, the most sophisticated users of language.

4C COMMAS

COMMAS FOR INTRODUCTORY ELEMENTS

Use commas to set off most introductory elements:

> Because I broke three flasks, I'm going to have a large bill for chemistry lab. [introductory dependent clause]
>
> In the middle of finals week last semester, I became seriously depressed. [long introductory prepositional phrase]
>
> Jogging home after classes, I see children playing in the schoolyard. [introductory participial phrase]
>
> To save money, I often take the bus.[introductory infinitive phrase]
>
> Incidentally, I hope my roommate will be here this weekend. [introductory adverb]

ITEMS IN A SERIES

Use *commas* to separate items in a series (a, b, and c). Generally, use a comma before the *and*. In some cases, omitting the comma before the final item in the series may cause confusion:

Confusing: She rented an apartment with a convection oven, a microwave, a refrigerator with an icemaker and a garbage disposal. [Does the refrigerator have a built-in icemaker and garbage disposal?]

Revised: She rented an apartment with a convection oven, a microwave, a refrigerator with an icemaker, and a garbage disposal.

EXERCISE

Revise the punctuation in the following passage.

(1) Everyone can have fun outside in the wintertime by following some commonsense rules. (2) If you are going to be outside for several hours be sure to eat a nutritious meal before leaving. (3) On cold damp or windy days wear clothes that are warm and dry. (4) To stay warm protect yourself against moisture that builds up from the inside. (5) Most experts recommend dressing in layers. (6) The inner layer wicks moisture away from your body the middle layer provides thermal protection and the outer layer protects against rain or wind. (7) Curiously enough most people tend to put on too many

clothes, underestimating their body's ability to exercise comfortably naturally and safely in cold weather.

NONRESTRICTIVE ELEMENTS

Nonrestrictive modifiers should be separated from the sentence by commas. Always *test* the phrase or clause. If it can be removed from the sentence without a change in the meaning, use commas:

Nonrestrictive:	Coach Hall, who was invited to the party, celebrated the victory. [The clause "who was invited to the party" is incidental information. It does not restrict or specify which coach was celebrating. The two commas indicate that removing the clause from the sentence will not change the meaning: "Coach Hall celebrated the victory."]
Nonrestrictive:	Seattle, which has a reputation as a rainy city, is actually drier than New Orleans. [Remove the clause, and the meaning of the sentence is not altered: "Seattle is actually drier than New Orleans."]
Nonrestrictive:	Charles, the man in the gray suit, eats fried grasshoppers when no one is looking. [The appositive "the man in the gray suit" can be removed from the sentence without an alteration in the meaning.]
Restrictive:	Demonstrators who hurled bricks were arrested by the police. [The meaning is that *only those* demonstrators *who hurled bricks* were arrested by the police. The phrase *who hurled bricks* cannot be removed from the sentence without a change in meaning. Do *not* use commas to separate restrictive elements.]
Nonrestrictive:	The class, which was taught by Anne Perkins, met at eight o'clock in the morning. *Note:* This sentence says that the class met at eight o'clock, and Anne Perkins was, incidentally, the teacher. (Usually use *which* for nonrestrictive clauses.)
Restrictive:	The class that was taught by Anne Perkins met at eight o'clock in the morning. *Note:* This sentence says that the particular class taught by Professor Perkins met at eight o'clock. Other classes met at some other time. (Use *that* for restrictive clauses. Do not use commas.)

4C
,

Unnecessary Commas

Do not use a comma to separate a subject and a verb:

Faulty: My toughest class of the day, met at eight o'clock.
Revised: My toughest class of the day met at eight o'clock.

Do not use a comma to separate compound subjects or predicates:

Faulty: The dean of students, and the chancellor decided to cancel
                  classes. [compound subject]
Revised: The dean of students and the chancellor decided to cancel
                  classes.
Faulty: Because of the heavy snowfall, I stayed inside all afternoon,
                  and popped popcorn. [compound predicate]
                  Note: When coordinate conjunctions do not join indepen-
                  dent clauses or items in a series, a comma is usually not nec-
                  essary (see Section 4A for appropriate use of commas with
                  coordinate conjunctions).
Revised: Because of the heavy snowfall, I stayed inside all afternoon
                  and popped popcorn.

Coordinate Adjectives

Use a comma to separate coordinate (equal) adjectives. Test for coordinate adjectives: (1) Insert an *and* between the adjectives and (2) reverse the order of the
adjectives. If the meaning of the sentence remains unchanged, the adjectives
are equal or coordinate:

Example: It was a dull dark day.
                  [Insert *and*; reverse adjectives: *It was a dull and dark day. It
                  was a dark and dull day.* Since the meaning of the sentence
                  has not changed, these are coordinate or equal adjectives.
                  Remove the *and* and add a comma.]
Revised: It was a dull, dark day.

Example: The car had studded snow tires.
                  [Insert *and*; reverse adjectives: *The car had studded and snow
                  tires. The car had snow and studded tires.* The meaning of the
                  original sentence is changed; therefore, the adjectives
                  are not coordinate. Do *not* separate with comma.]
Revised: The car had studded snow tires.

DIALOGUE

Use commas to set off a direct quotation or dialogue.

Direct quotation:

> The author points out, "One of the effects of embalming by chemical injection, however, has been to dispel fears of live burial."
>
> —Jessica Mitford

Dialogue:

> "We'll try it," the professor said to me, grimly, "with every adjustment of the microscope known to man."
>
> —James Thurber

In fiction or nonfiction, indent (begin a new paragraph) when the dialogue shifts from one person to the next:

> A white man finally came along and found her—a hunter, a young man, with his dog on a chain.
>
> "Well, Granny!" he laughed, "what are you doing there?"
>
> "Lying on my back like a June-bug waiting to be turned over, mister," she said, reaching up her hand.
>
> He lifted her up, gave her a swing in the air, and set her down. "Anything broken, Granny?"
>
> "No sir, them old dead weeds is springy enough," said Phoenix, when she had got her breath. "I thank you for your trouble."
>
> —Eudora Welty, "A Worn Path"

ADDRESSES, DATES, DEGREES

Use commas to set off addresses, dates, and degrees/titles:

Addresses: What Cheer, Iowa, is his hometown.
Dates: On December 7, 1941, the Japanese bombed Pearl Harbor.
Degrees: Randall Beaver, D.D.S., is my orthodontist.

EXERCISE

Revise the punctuation in the following passage.

(1) Dinosaurs which have been extinct for millions of years are making news again. (2) At a meeting of the Geological Society of America in November 1987 scientists announced a startling discovery. (3) Dinosaurs, that lived 80 million years ago, benefited from an atmosphere that contained nearly 50 percent more oxygen than it does now. (4) Gary Landis geochemist for the U.S. Geological Service and Robert

Berner professor at Yale University reached that conclusion after analyzing, air bubbles trapped in bits of amber. (5) They found that the tiny, air bubbles contained 32 percent oxygen, compared with 21 percent in the modern atmosphere. (6) When asked whether a decreasing oxygen supply, could have caused the extinction of the dinosaurs, Berner explained "It was a very gradual change, and most organisms easily adapt." (7) "The large slow-moving dinosaurs probably became extinct" he said "following some cataclysmic, geological, event."

4D PERIODS AND SEMICOLONS

PERIODS

Use periods at the end of sentences, indirect questions, and commands:

Sentence:	The Statue of Liberty was officially rededicated.
Indirect Question:	I asked my friend when he was going to stop taking pictures.
Command:	Wait until the ship moves into the picture.

SEMICOLONS

Use a semicolon to join related independent clauses. Remember to test for independent clauses by using a period. If you can use a period at the end of each independent clause, and if the sentences are related, you may wish to use a semicolon. Remember, however, that semicolons are usually more appropriate in formal writing:

> Nowadays, says one sociologist, you don't have to have a reason for going to college; it's an institution. His definition of an institution is an arrangement everyone accepts without question; the burden of proof is not on why you go, but why anyone thinks there might be a reason for not going.
>
> —Caroline Bird

> I take a dim view of dams; I find it hard to learn to love cement.
>
> —Edward Abbey

Use a semicolon to separate items in a series that already have internal punctuation:

> We quickly meet the "good guys" of *Star Wars*: Luke Skywalker, played by Mark Hamill; Ben "Obi-Wan" Kenobi, played by Alec Guinness; and Han Solo, played by Harrison Ford.
>
> —Judith Crist

4D
./;

Do *not* use a semicolon to join dependent with independent clauses:

> Harrison Ford played the leading role in *Raiders of the Lost Ark;* which made him an instant star.

4E COLONS AND DASHES

COLONS

Use a colon to introduce a list or an explanation. Colons often create formal, structured sentences:

> When you go to the grocery store, please get the following items: two boxes of frozen peas, five pounds of baking potatoes, and a package of stuffing for the turkey.

> There is only one guaranteed method to lose weight: Eat less and exercise more.

Usually, a colon following a verb is unnecessary:

Unnecessary:	The best way to lose weight is: eat less and exercise more.
Revised:	The best way to lose weight is to eat less and exercise more.
Unnecessary:	I need: peas, baking potatoes, and stuffing.
Revised:	I need peas, baking potatoes, and stuffing.

DASHES

Use a single dash for an abrupt shift. Use a pair of dashes for an interrupting or parenthetical comment. Use a dash instead of a comma, colon, or parentheses when you want a sentence to have a more informal, colloquial flavor:

> At last a happy thought struck me—I would draw the fish.
>
> —Samuel Scudder

> Indeed, there are moments today—amid outlaw litter, tax cheating, illicit noise, and motorized anarchy—when it seems as though the scofflaw represents the wave of the future.
>
> —Frank Trippett

EXERCISE

In the following passage, insert semicolons, colons, or dashes at the appropriate places. In some cases, there are several ways to punctuate the sentence correctly, so be prepared to explain your choice.

4E
: / —

(1) Yo-yo dieting the process of repeatedly losing and gaining weight is common today. (2) Instead of changing eating habits and exercise patterns, the yo-yo dieter uses three common strategies to lose weight taking diet pills, drinking diet liquids, and fasting outright. (3) The yo-yo dieter, however, needs to know the truth about dieting diet cycles decrease the muscle-to-fat ratio in the body and decrease the body's ability to lose weight during the next dieting cycle. (4) Quick-fix diets, in other words, will lead to rapid weight losses however, they will be followed by an even faster weight gain. (5) Ultimately, crash diets do more harm than good the body just wasn't designed to be a yo-yo.

4F EXCLAMATION POINTS AND QUESTION MARKS

EXCLAMATION POINTS

Use exclamation points sparingly, for stylistic emphasis:

> I saw the sleek gray-haired manager standing near the dance floor, snapping his fingers and smiling. . . . I bet myself that he owned one of the few blow-dryers in Moscow. . . . He was watching the growing success of the only Western-style club in town and thinking: These kids! Right on! Crazy, but I love 'em!
>
> —Andrea Lee

> Bicyclists often ride as though two-wheeled vehicles are exempt from all traffic laws. Litterbugs convert their communities into trash dumps. . . . And then there are (hello, Everybody!) the jaywalkers.
>
> —Frank Trippett

QUESTION MARKS

Use a question mark after a direct question:

> What is your first childhood memory?

Do not combine question marks with commas or periods:

> "What is your earliest memory?" she asked me. [Do not use a comma and a question mark: "What is your earliest memory?," she asked me.]

4G QUOTATION AND ELLIPSIS MARKS

QUOTATION MARKS

Use quotation marks to indicate a writer's or speaker's exact words:

> Marya Mannes says, "Woman, in short, is consumer first and human being fourth."

Use quotation marks for titles of *essays, articles, short stories, poems, chapters,* and *songs*—any title that is part of a larger collection:

> "Television: The Splitting Image" is the title of an essay by Marya Mannes.

Use single quotation marks for quotations within a quotation:

> James said, "I know I heard her say, 'Meet me outside the east door.'"

ELLIPSIS MARKS

Use ellipsis marks (three *spaced* periods) to indicate material omitted from a direct quotation:

> Marya Mannes said, "Woman . . . is consumer first and human being fourth." [The ellipses indicate that words are omitted from the middle of the sentence.]

Use a period *plus* three spaced periods to signal either omitted words at the end of a sentence or omitted intervening sentence(s):

> Marya Mannes said, "Woman, in short, is consumer first and human being fourth. . . . The conditioning starts very early. . . . "

PUNCTUATION WITH QUOTATION MARKS

The following guidelines will help you to punctuate sentences with quotation marks. Periods and commas go *inside* quotation marks:

> According to biologist Julie Earwig, "Penguins are more densely covered with feathers than any other bird—nearly 180 feathers per square inch."

Colons and semicolons go *outside* quotation marks:

> Recent data about the eagle's feathers may revise the old saying "light as a feather": The vaned feathers on a bald eagle weigh more than its entire skeleton.

Exclamation points and question marks go *inside* or *outside* quotation marks. They go *inside* if they are a part of the quoted material:

> The award for the highest number of feathers, according to Earwig, "goes to the whistling swan with a staggering 25,000 feathers!" [The original sentence ends with an exclamation point.]

They go *outside* if they are not a part of the quoted material:

> Is it true that, as Earwig claims, "the tiny ruby-throated hummingbird has 940 feathers"? [The original sentence ends with a period.]

4H ITALICS

Most word-processing programs allow you to *italicize* certain words for emphasis. When using a typewriter or writing by hand, use underlining to indicate words that should be set in italics.

Titles:
"Down the River" is the most interesting chapter in Edward Abbey's *Desert Solitaire*.
[Underline (or italicize) titles of books, magazines, films, paintings, newspapers—any work published separately. Use quotation marks for titles of chapters, articles, or poems—any title that is part of some collection in a book or magazine.]
Exceptions: Do not underline the Bible or titles of legal documents, such as the Deed of Trust or the U.S. Constitution.

Names:
The most famous travel ships used to be the *Santa Maria*, the *Titanic*, and the *Queen Mary*. Now the great ones are the *Apollo* and the Challenger.
[Underline (or italicize) names of ships, trains, aircraft, or spacecraft.]

Foreign Words:
He graduated *cum laude*, while his friend, who barely passed freshman mathematics, graduated *magna cum laude*. "*C'est la vie*," he thought.
[Note, however, that many foreign words (burrito, bourgeois, genre, cliché, junta, and many others) have been incorporated into the language and do not need italics. Consult your dictionary if you are in doubt.]

Words or Letters:
Suppose to should have a *d: supposed to*.
[Quotation marks are also used to indicate italics in handwritten or typed manuscripts.]
Note: Do not underline or put quotation marks around the title of your essay when it appears on a title page or the first page of your manuscript.

4H italic

EXERCISE

Revise the following passage, underlining appropriate words and titles.

(1) Tom Wolfe, author of The Right Stuff, wrote a novel about a Wall Street broker, The Bonfire of the Vanities. (2) This novel first appeared in twenty-seven installments in Rolling Stone magazine. (3) Wolfe's style has always been au courant, and Bonfire is no exception. (4) This

novel features New York characters who run the gamut from drug pushers to the cunning and ambitious young lions of the investment world. (5) It is not a cliché to say that this book is difficult to put down.

4I PARENTHESES AND BRACKETS

PARENTHESES

Use parentheses ( ) to set off additional information, examples, or comments:

> Outside our lifeboat, let us imagine another 210 million people (say the combined populations of Colombia, Ecuador, Venezuela, Morocco, Pakistan, Thailand, and the Philippines), increasing at a rate of 3.3 percent per year.
>
> —Garrett Hardin

> Writing a film review requires that you carefully examine the criteria for your judgment (see Chapter 7).

BRACKETS

Use brackets [ ] to set off editorial remarks in quoted material. Brackets indicate that you, as an editor, are adding comments to the original material:

Original: After you hear my arguement, you will reelect Eastwood.

Edited: After you hear my arguement [sic], you will reelect [Mayor Clint] Eastwood. [As editor, you add information about Eastwood and indicate by using *sic* ("thus it is") that the misspelling, grammatical mistake, or inappropriate usage occurs in the original source and is not your error.]

4J APOSTROPHES AND HYPHENS

APOSTROPHES

Use apostrophes for contractions, possession, and some plurals:

Contractions: It's too bad you don't agree.

Possession: The wind blew the student's notes across the front lawn. [The notes belonging to one student blew across the lawn.]
The wind blew the students' notes across the front lawn. [The notes belonging to several students blew across the lawn.]
Your sister-in-law's accident was someone else's fault. [In compounds, make the last word possessive.]

Plurals:	The 1980's [or 1980s] were the Yuppie years.
	Eliminate unnecessary *which's* in your sentences.

HYPHENS

Use hyphens for compound words, compound adjectives before nouns, some prefixes, and some numbers. When in doubt, always check a good dictionary.

Compounds:	cross-reference; president-elect
Adjectives:	a twentieth-century writer; the slate-blue sea; the three-year-old child
	Note: When the compound adjectives follow a noun, omit the hyphen: He is a writer well known only in Vermont.
Prefixes:	ex-President Reagan; self-motivation
Numbers:	twenty-six; one hundred sixty-five; one-fifth

4K CAPITALS AND NUMBERS

CAPITALS

Capitalize proper nouns and adjectives, professional titles, principal words in titles of books or articles, and regional locations:

Proper Names:	Judson Smith, Atlanta, Los Angeles, Missouri River, English, Swahili, American, Labor Day, Christmas, Hanukkah, Wednesday, October [Do not capitalize seasons or terms: autumn, spring, summer, fall semester, freshman year.]
Titles:	Senator Kennedy, President Lincoln, Professor Findlay, Associate Dean Natalie Renner, Uncle Don, Father [Do not capitalize family titles preceded by a pronoun: my mother, my uncle, our grandfather.]
Titles:	*Gone with the Wind*, "The Short Happy Life of Francis Macomber," "The Triumph of the Wheel," *Star Wars* [Some style manuals suggest capitalizing only the first word in a title. If you are citing titles in a bibliography or list of works cited, check your style manual.]
Regions:	the South, the Northwest, the Middle East [Do not capitalize directions: traveling east, walking due north.]

NUMBERS

Conventions regarding numbers vary. Generally, except in scientific or technical writing, spell out numbers of one hundred or less or numbers that require two words or less. If a passage requires many numbers, be consistent in your usage:

> This stadium seats fifty thousand people, but adding the end-zone bleachers increases the seating to fifty-seven thousand. [Hyphenated words count as one word.]

> Our chemistry lecture hall seats 425 students, but only 310 are enrolled this semester in Chemistry 201. [However, at the beginning of sentences, spell out numbers ("Three hundred and ten students are enrolled this semester") or rewrite the sentence ("In Chemistry 201, 310 students are enrolled").]

EXERCISE

Revise the following passage for proper use of apostrophes, hyphens, capitals, italics, and numbers. Use your dictionary to help you edit this passage.

(1) The advertisement shows a sky-diver floating down to earth, and the pictures caption says, "I take vitamin supplements every day, just to be on the safe side." (2) Self styled experts, from your local pharmacist to physicians from the mount Sinai school of Medicine in New York city, encourage the public to believe that vitamins are a cure all. (3) There are only thirteen known vitamin deficiencies (such as scurvy, which is a Vitamin C deficiency), but nearly sixty percent of the two hundred fifty two american's responding to our questionnaire believed in taking vitamin supplements. (4) These days, its almost patriotic to take vitamins—even your Mother says, "Don't forget to take your vitamins!" (5) During the 1980's, vitamins popularity rose an astonishing twenty nine percent, and revenue from vitamin sale's jumped to nearly three billion. (6) Although sales are generally higher in the west, some Eastern cities such as boston and Philadelphia have also shown dramatic increase's in sales. (7) If you want to learn more about vitamins, read The Vitamin-Pushers in a recent issue of Consumer Reports.

4K
cap

Index

ALPHABETICAL REFERENCE TO THE HANDBOOK